CUSTOM EDITION FOR VANIER COLLEGE

ANTHROPOLOGY

THE HUMAN EXPERIENCE
An Introduction to Anthropology

(381-100-VA)

Taken from:
Anthropology, Eleventh Edition
by Carol R. Ember, Melvin Ember, and Peter N. Peregrine

Taken from:

Anthropology, Eleventh Edition
by Carol R. Ember, Melvin Ember, and Peter N. Peregrine
Copyright © 2005, 2002, 1999, 1996, 1993, 1990, 1988, 1985, 1981, 1977, 1973 by Pearson Education, Inc.
Published by Prentice Hall, Inc.
Upper Saddle River, New Jersey 07458

This special edition published in cooperation with Pearson Custom Publishing.

Printed in Canada

10 9 8 7 6 5 4 3 2 1

ISBN 0-536-94263-3

2005420249

AG

Please visit our web site at *www.pearsoncustom.com*

PEARSON CUSTOM PUBLISHING
75 Arlington Street, Suite 300, Boston, MA 02116
A Pearson Education Company

BRIEF CONTENTS

WHAT IS ANTHROPOLOGY?

CHAPTER OUTLINE

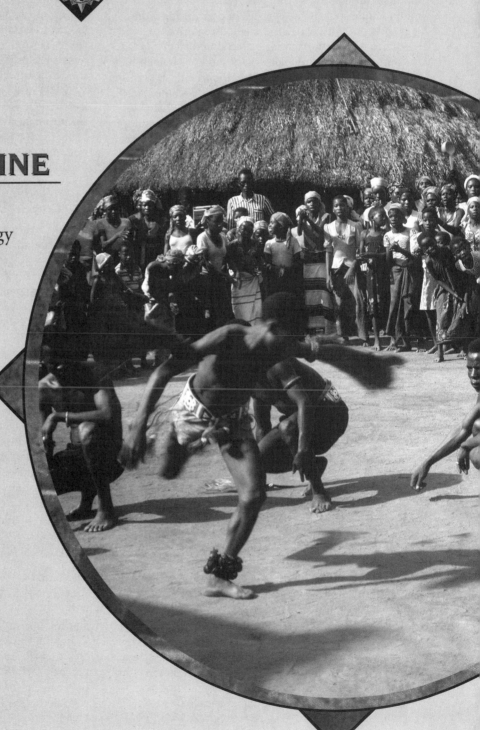

Anthropology, by definition, is a discipline of infinite curiosity about human beings. The term comes from the Greek *anthropos* for "man, human" and *logos* for "study." Anthropologists seek answers to an enormous variety of questions about humans. They are interested in discovering when, where, and why humans appeared on the earth, how and why they have changed since then, and how and why modern human populations vary in certain physical features. Anthropologists are also interested in how and why societies in the past and present have varied in their customary ideas and practices. There is a practical side to anthropology too. Applied and practicing anthropologists put anthropological methods, information, and results to use, in efforts to solve practical problems.

But defining anthropology as the study of human beings is not complete, for such a definition would appear to incorporate a whole catalog of disciplines: sociology, psychology, political science, economics, history, human biology, and perhaps even the humanistic disciplines of philosophy and literature. Needless to say, practitioners of the many other disciplines concerned with humans would not be happy to be regarded as being in subbranches of anthropology. After all, most of those disciplines have existed longer than anthropology, and each is somewhat distinctive. There must, then, be something unique about anthropology—a reason for its having developed as a separate discipline and for its having retained a separate identity over the last 100 years.

The Scope of Anthropology

Anthropologists are generally thought of as individuals who travel to little-known corners of the world to study exotic peoples or who dig deep into the earth to uncover the fossil remains or the tools and pots of people who lived long ago. These views, though clearly stereotyped, do indicate how anthropology differs from other disciplines concerned with humans. Anthropology is broader in scope, both geographically and historically. Anthropology is concerned explicitly and directly with all varieties of people throughout the world, not just those close at hand or within a limited area. It is also interested in people of all periods. Beginning with the immediate ancestors of humans, who lived a few million years ago, anthropology traces the development of humans until the present. Every part of the world that has ever contained a human population is of interest to anthropologists.

Anthropologists have not always been as global and comprehensive in their concerns as they are today. Traditionally, they concentrated on non-Western cultures and left the study of Western civilization and similarly complex societies, with their recorded histories, to other disciplines. In recent years, however, this division of labor among the disciplines has begun to disappear. Now anthropologists work in their own and other complex societies.

What induces anthropologists to choose so broad a subject for study? In part, they are motivated by the belief that any suggested generalization about human beings, any possible explanation of some characteristic of human culture or biology, should be shown to apply to many times and places of human existence. If a generalization or explanation does not prove to apply widely, we are entitled or even obliged to be skeptical about it. The skeptical attitude, in the absence of persuasive evidence, is our best protection against accepting invalid ideas about humans.

For example, when American educators discovered in the 1960s that African American schoolchildren rarely drank milk, they assumed that lack of money or education was the cause. But evidence from anthropology suggested a different explanation. Anthropologists had known for years that in many parts of the world where milking animals are kept, people do not drink fresh milk; rather, they sour it before they drink it, or they make it into cheese. Why they do so is now clear. Many people lack an enzyme, lactase, that is necessary for breaking down lactose, the sugar in milk. When such people drink regular milk, it actually interferes with digestion. Not only is the lactose in milk not digested but other nutrients are less likely to be digested as well; in many cases, drinking milk will cause cramps, stomach gas, diarrhea, and nausea. Studies indicate that milk intolerance is found in many parts of the world.[1] The condition is common in adulthood among Asians, southern Europeans, Arabs and Jews, West Africans, Inuit (Eskimos), and North and South American Indians, as well as African Americans. Because anthropologists are acquainted with human life in an enormous variety of geographic and historical settings, they are often able to correct mistaken beliefs about different groups of people.

The Holistic Approach

In addition to the worldwide as well as historical scope of anthropology, another distinguishing feature of the discipline is its **holistic,** or multifaceted, approach to the study of human beings. Anthropologists study not only all varieties of people but many aspects of human experience as well. For example, when describing a group of people, an anthropologist might discuss the history of the area in which the people live, the physical environment, the organization of family life, the general features of their language, the group's settlement patterns, political and economic systems, religion, and styles of art and dress.

In the past, individual anthropologists tried to be holistic and cover many subjects. Today, as in many other disciplines, so much information has been accumulated that anthropologists tend to specialize in one topic or area. Thus, one anthropologist may investigate the physical characteristics of some of our prehistoric ancestors. Another may study the biological effect of the environment on a human population over time. Still another will concentrate on the customs of a particular group of people. Despite this specialization, however, the discipline of anthropology retains its holistic orientation in that its many different specialties, taken together, describe many aspects of human existence, both past and present.

The Anthropological Curiosity

Thus far we have described anthropology as being broader in scope, both historically and geographically, and more holistic in approach than other disciplines concerned with human beings. But this statement again implies that anthropology is the all-inclusive human science. How, then, is anthropology really different from those other disciplines? We suggest that anthropology's distinctiveness lies principally in the kind of curiosity it arouses.

Anthropologists are concerned with many types of questions: Where, when, and why did people first begin living in cities? Why do some peoples have darker skin than others? Why do some languages contain more terms for color than other languages? Why do women have more of a voice in politics in some societies than in others? Why do populations differ in their acceptance of birth control? Although these questions deal with very different aspects of human existence, they have at least one thing in common: They all deal with *typical characteristics* (traits, customs) of particular populations. The typical characteristic of a people might be relatively dark skin, a language with many color terms, female participation in politics, or acceptance of birth control. This concern with typical characteristics of populations is perhaps the most distinguishing feature

of anthropology. For example, whereas economists take a monetary system for granted and study how it operates, anthropologists ask why only some societies during the last few thousand years used money. In short, anthropologists are curious about the typical characteristics of human populations—how and why such populations and their characteristics have varied throughout the ages.

Fields of Anthropology

Different anthropologists concentrate on different typical characteristics of societies. Some are concerned primarily with *biological*, or *physical characteristics* of human populations; others are interested principally in what we call *cultural characteristics*. Hence, there are two broad classifications of subject matter in anthropology: **biological (physical) anthropology** and **cultural anthropology**. Biological anthropology is one major field of anthropology. Cultural anthropology is divided into three major subfields—archaeology, linguistics, and ethnology. Ethnology, the study of recent cultures, is now usually referred to by the parent name, cultural anthropology (see Figure 1–1). Cross-cutting these four fields is a fifth, **applied** or **practicing anthropology**.

CD-ROM Activity I

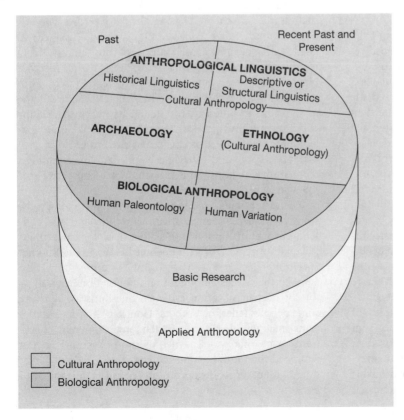

Figure 1–1 *The Subdivisions of Anthropology*

The four major subdivisions of anthropology (in bold letters) may be classified according to subject matter (biological or cultural) and according to the period with which each is concerned (distant past versus recent past and present). There are applications of anthropology in all four subdisciplines.

Nadine Peacock, a biological anthropologist, studying reproduction and health among the Efe of Zaire.

BIOLOGICAL ANTHROPOLOGY

Biological (physical) anthropology seeks to answer two distinct sets of questions. The first set includes questions about the emergence of humans and their later evolution (this focus is called **human paleontology** or **paleoanthropology**). The second set includes questions about how and why contemporary human populations vary biologically (this focus is called **human variation**).

In order to reconstruct human evolution, human paleontologists search for and study the buried, hardened remains or impressions—known as **fossils**—of humans, prehumans, and related animals. Paleoanthropologists working in East Africa, for instance, have excavated the fossil remains of humanlike beings who lived more than 4 million years ago. These findings have suggested the approximate dates when our ancestors began to develop two-legged walking, very flexible hands, and a larger brain.

In attempting to clarify evolutionary relationships, human paleontologists may use not only the fossil record but also geological information on the succession of climates, environments, and plant and animal populations. Moreover, when reconstructing the past of humans, paleoanthropologists are also interested in the behavior and evolution of our closest relatives among the mammals—the prosimians, monkeys, and apes, which, like ourselves, are members of the order of **Primates.** Anthropologists, psychologists, and biologists who specialize in the study of primates are called **primatologists.** The various species of primates are observed in the wild and in the laboratory. One especially popular subject of study is the chimpanzee, which bears a close resemblance to humans in behavior and physical appearance, has a similar blood chemistry,

and is susceptible to many of the same diseases. It now appears that chimpanzees share 99 percent of their genes with humans.[2]

From primate studies, biological anthropologists try to discover characteristics that are distinctly human, as opposed to those that might be part of the primate heritage. With this information, they may be able to infer what our prehistoric ancestors were like. The inferences from primate studies are checked against the fossil record. The evidence from the earth, collected in bits and pieces, is correlated with scientific observations of our closest living relatives. In short, biological anthropologists piece together bits of information obtained from different sources. They construct theories that explain the changes observed in the fossil record and then attempt to evaluate their theories by checking one kind of evidence against another. Human paleontology thus overlaps disciplines such as geology, general vertebrate (and particularly primate) paleontology, comparative anatomy, and the study of comparative primate behavior.

The second major focus of biological anthropology, the study of human variation, investigates how and why contemporary human populations differ in biological or physical characteristics. All living people belong to one species, *Homo sapiens,* for all can successfully interbreed. Yet there is much that varies among human populations. Investigators of human variation ask such questions as: Why are some peoples taller than others? How have human populations adapted physically to their environmental conditions? Are some peoples, such as Inuit (Eskimos), better equipped than other peoples to endure cold? Does darker skin pigmentation offer special protection against the tropical sun?

To understand better the biological variations observable among contemporary human populations, biological anthropologists use the principles, concepts, and techniques of at least three other disciplines: human genetics (the study of human traits that are inherited), population biology (the study of environmental effects on, and interaction with, population characteristics), and epidemiology (the study of how and why diseases affect different populations in different ways). Research on human variation, therefore, overlaps research in other fields. Biological anthropologists, however, are concerned most with human populations and how they vary biologically.

CULTURAL ANTHROPOLOGY

Cultural anthropologists are interested in how populations or societies vary in their cultural features. But what is culture? Because the concept of culture is so central to anthropology, we devote a whole chapter to it. To an anthropologist, the term **culture** refers to the customary ways of thinking and behaving of a particular population or society. The culture of a social group includes many things—its language, religious beliefs, food preferences, music, work habits, gender roles, how they rear their children, how they construct their houses, and many other learned behaviors and ideas that have come to be widely shared or customary among the group. The three main branches of cultural anthropology are **archaeology** (the study of past cultures, primarily through their material remains), **anthropological linguistics** (the anthropological study of languages), and **ethnology** (the study of existing and recent cultures), now usually referred to by the parent name, cultural anthropology.

ARCHAEOLOGY The archaeologist seeks not only to reconstruct the daily life and customs of peoples who lived in the past but to trace cultural changes and to offer possible explanations for those changes. This concern is similar to that of the historian, but the archaeologist reaches much farther back in time. The historian deals only with societies that left written records and is therefore limited to the last 5,000 years of human history. Human societies, however, have existed for more than a million years, and only a small proportion in the last 5,000 years had writing. For all those past societies lacking a written record, the archaeologist serves as historian. Lacking written records for study, archaeologists must try to reconstruct history from the remains of human cultures. Some of these remains are as grand as the Mayan temples discovered at Chichén Itzá in Yucatán, Mexico. More often they are as ordinary as bits of broken pottery, stone tools, and garbage heaps.

Most archaeologists deal with **prehistory,** the time before written records. But there is a specialty within archaeology, called **historical archaeology,** that studies the remains of recent peoples who left written records. This specialty, as its name implies, employs the methods of both archaeologists and historians to study recent societies for which there is both archaeological and historical information.

In trying to understand how and why ways of life have changed through time in different parts of the world, archaeologists collect materials from sites of human occupation. Usually, these sites must be unearthed. On the basis of materials they have excavated and otherwise collected, they then ask various questions: Where, when, and why did the distinctive human characteristic of toolmaking first emerge? Where, when, and why did agriculture first develop? Where, when, and why did people first begin to live in cities?

To collect the data they need in order to suggest answers to these and other questions, archaeologists use techniques and findings borrowed from other disciplines, as well as what they can infer from anthropological studies of recent and contemporary cultures. For example, to guess where to dig for evidence of early toolmaking, archaeologists rely on geology to tell them where sites of early human occupation are likely to be found, because of erosion and uplifting, near the surface of the earth. To infer when agriculture first developed, archaeologists date the relevant excavated materials by a process originally developed by chemists. And to try to understand why cities first emerged, archaeologists may use information from historians, geographers, and others about how recent and contemporary cities are related economically and politically to their hinterlands. If we can discover what recent and contemporary cities have in common, we can speculate on why cities developed originally. Thus, archaeologists use information from the present and recent past in trying to understand the distant past.

ANTHROPOLOGICAL LINGUISTICS Anthropological linguistics is another branch of cultural anthropology. Linguistics, or the study of languages, is a somewhat older discipline than anthropology, but the early linguists concentrated on the study of languages that had been written for a long time—languages such as English that had been written for nearly a thousand years. Anthropological linguists began to do fieldwork in places where the language was not yet written. This meant that anthropologists could not consult a dictionary or grammar to help them learn the language. Instead, they first had to construct a dictionary and grammar. Then they could study the structure and history of the language.

Like biological anthropologists, linguists study changes that have taken place over time, as well as contemporary variation. Some anthropological linguists are concerned with the emergence of language and also with the divergence of languages over thousands of years. The study of how languages change over time and how they may be related is known as **historical linguistics.** Anthropological linguists are also interested in how contemporary languages differ, especially in their construction. This focus of linguistics is generally called **descriptive** or **structural linguistics.** The study of how language is used in social contexts is called **sociolinguistics.**

NEW PERSPECTIVES ON GENDER
Researcher at Work: **Elizabeth M. Brumfiel**

Now a professor of anthropology at Albion College, Elizabeth Brumfiel became interested in the origins of social inequality when she was an undergraduate. Archaeologists had known for some time that substantial wealth differences between families developed only recently (archaeologically speaking), that is, only after about 6,000 years ago. The archaeological indicators of inequality are fairly clear—elaborate burials with valuable goods for some families and large differences in houses and possessions. But why the transformation occurred was not so clear. When she was in graduate school at the University of Michigan, Brumfiel says, she didn't accept the then-current explanation, that inequality provided benefits to the society (for example, the standard of living of most people improved as the leaders got richer). Consequently, for her Ph.D. research in central Mexico, she began to test the "benefit" explanation in an area that had been independent politically at first and then became part of the Aztec Empire. She studied the surface material remains in the area and historical documents written by Europeans and Aztec nobility. Her findings contradicted the benefit

Elizabeth Brumfiel.

explanation of social inequality; she found little improvement in the standard of living of the local people after the Aztec Empire had absorbed them.

Another important part of her research agenda was understanding the lives of women. How were they affected by the expansion of the Aztec Empire? Did their work change? How were women portrayed in art? In the Aztec capital of Tenochtitlán, images of militarism and masculinity became increasingly important with the growth of

the empire, and sculptures showed women in subordinate positions (for example, kneeling). But the images of women in the area of Brumfiel's fieldwork did not change. For example, most of the sculptures after the Aztecs had taken over still showed women standing, not kneeling.

Like many anthropologists, Brumfiel asked herself how she could contribute to the community in which she did her fieldwork. She decided to design an exhibit to display the successes of the people who had lived in the area for 1,200 years. The exhibit tells the people of Xaltocan what she found out from her studies.

As she continues to explore issues about the origins of inequality and the position of women, Brumfiel is quite comfortable with knowing that someone will think that she has "gotten it wrong, and will set out on a lifetime of archaeological research to find her own answers."

Source: Elizabeth M. Brumfiel, "Origins of Social Inequality," in Carol R. Ember, Melvin Ember, and Peter N. Peregrine, eds., *Archaeology: Original Readings in Method and Practice* (Upper Saddle River, NJ: Prentice Hall, 2002); also in Carol R. Ember and Melvin Ember, eds., *New Directions in Anthropology* (Upper Saddle River, NJ: Prentice Hall, CD-ROM, 2003).

In contrast with the human paleontologist and archaeologist, who have physical remains to help them reconstruct change over time, the historical linguist deals only with languages—and usually unwritten ones at that. (Remember that writing is only about 5,000 years old, and most languages since then have not been written.) Because an unwritten language must be heard in order to be studied, it does not leave any trace once its speakers have died. Linguists interested in reconstructing the history of unwritten languages must begin in the present, with comparisons of contemporary languages. On the basis of these comparisons, they draw inferences about the kinds of

change in language that may have occurred in the past and that may account for similarities and differences observed in the present. The historical linguist typically asks such questions as these: Did two or more contemporary languages diverge from a common ancestral language? If they are related, how far back in time did they begin to differ?

Unlike the historical linguist, the descriptive (or structural) linguist is typically concerned with discovering and recording the principles that determine how sounds and words are put together in speech. For example, a structural description of a particular language might tell us that the sounds *t* and *k* are interchangeable in a word without causing a difference in meaning. In American Samoa, one could say *Tutuila* or *Kukuila* as the name of the largest island, and everyone, except perhaps the newly arrived anthropologist, would understand that the same island was being mentioned.

The sociolinguist is interested in the social aspects of language, including what people speak about and how they interact conversationally, their attitudes toward speakers of other dialects or languages, and how people speak differently in different social contexts. In English, for example, we do not address everyone we meet in the same way. "Hi, Sandy" may be the customary way a person greets a friend. But we would probably feel uncomfortable addressing a doctor by first name; instead, we would probably say, "Good morning, Dr. Brown." Such variations in language use, which are determined by the social status of the persons being addressed, are significant for the sociolinguist.

ETHNOLOGY (CULTURAL ANTHROPOLOGY) Ethnologists seek to understand how and why peoples today and in the recent past differ in their customary ways of thinking and acting. Ethnology—now usually called *cultural anthropology*—is concerned with patterns of thought and behavior, such as marriage customs, kinship organization, political and economic systems, religion, folk art, and music, and with the ways in which these patterns differ in contemporary societies. Ethnologists also study the dynamics of culture—that is, how various cultures develop and change. In addition, they are interested in the relationship between beliefs and practices within a culture. Thus, the aim of ethnologists is largely the same as that of archaeologists. Ethnologists, however, generally use data collected through observation and interviewing of living peoples. Archaeologists, on the other hand, must work with fragmentary remains of past cultures, on the basis of which they can only make inferences about the customs of prehistoric peoples.

One type of ethnologist, the **ethnographer,** usually spends a year or so living with, talking to, and observing the people whose customs he or she is studying. This fieldwork provides the data for a detailed description (an **ethnography**) of customary behavior and thought. Ethnographers vary in the degree to which they strive for completeness in their coverage of cultural and social life. Earlier ethnographers tended to strive for holistic coverage; more recent ethnographers have tended to specialize or focus on narrower realms such as ritual healing or curing, interaction with the environment, effects of modernization or globalization, or gender issues. Ethnographies often go beyond description; they may address current anthropological issues or try to explain some aspect of culture.

Because so many cultures have undergone extensive change in the recent past, it is fortunate that another type of ethnologist, the **ethnohistorian,** is prepared to study how the ways of life of a particular group of people have changed over time. Ethnohistorians investigate written documents (which may or may not have been produced by anthropologists). They may spend many years going through documents, such as missionary accounts, reports by traders and explorers, and government records, to try to establish the cultural changes that have occurred. Unlike ethnographers, who rely mostly on their own observations, ethnohistorians rely on the reports of others. Often, they must attempt to piece together and make sense of widely scattered, and even apparently contradictory, information. Thus, the ethnohistorian's research is very much like that of the historian, except that the ethnohistorian is usually concerned with the history of a people who did not themselves leave written records. The ethnohistorian tries to reconstruct the recent history of a people and may also suggest why certain changes in their way of life took place.

With the data collected and analyzed by the ethnographer and ethnohistorian, the work of a third type of ethnologist, the **cross-cultural researcher,** can be done. The cross-cultural researcher is interested in discovering general patterns about cultural traits—what is universal, what is variable, why traits vary, and what the consequences of the variability might be. Why, for example, is there more gender inequality in some societies than in others? Is family violence related to aggression in other areas of life? What are the effects of living in a very unpredictable environment? In testing possible answers to such questions, cross-cultural researchers use data from samples of cultures to try to arrive at explanations or relationships that are generally observable across cultures. Archaeologists may find the results of cross-cultural research useful for making inferences about the past, particularly if they can discover material indicators of cultural variation.

Because ethnologists may be interested in many aspects of customary behavior and thought—from economic behavior to political behavior to styles of art, music, and religion—ethnology overlaps with disciplines that concentrate on some particular aspect of human existence, such as sociology, psychology, economics, political science, art, music, and comparative religion. But the distinctive feature of cultural anthropology is its interest in how all these aspects of human existence vary from society to society, in all historical periods, and in all parts of the world.

◆ Applied Anthropology

All knowledge may turn out to be useful. In the physical and biological sciences it is well understood that technological breakthroughs like DNA splicing, spacecraft docking in outer space, and the development of miniscule computer chips could not have taken place without an enormous amount of basic research to uncover the laws of nature in the physical and biological worlds. If we did not understand fundamental principles, the technological achievements we are so proud of would not be possible. Researchers are often simply driven by curiosity, with no thought to where the research might lead, which is why such research is sometimes called basic research. The same is true of the social sciences. If a researcher finds out that societies with combative sports tend to have more wars, it may lead to other inquiries about the relationships

CURRENT RESEARCH AND ISSUES
Researcher at Work: Terence E. Hays

Books and articles often report research in a straightforward manner: Here's the problem; here's the answer—that kind of thing. But many researchers know from experience that knowledge does not always come in a straightforward manner. Now a professor at Rhode Island College, Terence Hays has reflected on the twists and turns in his fieldwork among the Ndumba in the Eastern Highlands Province of Papua New Guinea. He first started out studying whether different types of people (for example, women and men) had different types of plant knowledge and whether they classified plants differently. (The interest in plant and animal classification, ethnobiology, is closely connected with linguistic research.) In the course of his first fieldwork, in 1972, he witnessed an initiation ceremony for 10- to 12-year-old males—a dramatic and traumatic rite of passage ceremony that included the physical trauma of nose-bleeding as well as the social traumas of "attacks" by women and seclusion in the forest. The ceremony was full of symbolism of why the sexes needed to avoid each other. And while he collected stories and myths about plants for his research on ethnobiology, he kept uncovering themes in the stories about the danger of men's associating with women.

Hays's curiosity was aroused about these ceremonies and myths.

Terence Hays.

How important are myths in perpetuating cultural themes? Do other societies that have separate men's houses have similar myths? He realized when he returned home from the field that many societies have similar stories. Are these stories generally linked to initiation rites and to physical segregation of the sexes? Answering these questions required comparison, so he embarked on collecting myths and folktales from colleagues who worked in other New Guinea Highland societies. In the course of collecting these comparative materials, he realized he didn't have all the ethnographic information he needed, so he went back

to the field to get it. As Hays remarked, "As an ethnographer I was continually faced with the question, How do you know it's true? But even when I could reach a (hard-won) conviction that something was true for the Ndumba, the second question awaited: How do you know it's generally true, which you can't know without comparison?"

___

Source: Terence E. Hays, "From Ethnographer to Comparativist and Back Again," in Carol R. Ember, Melvin Ember, and Peter N. Peregrine, eds., *Research Frontiers in Anthropology,* in Carol R. Ember and Melvin Ember, eds., *New Directions in Anthropology* (Upper Saddle River, NJ: Prentice Hall, CD-ROM, 2003).

between one kind of aggression and another. The knowledge acquired may ultimately lead to discovering ways to correct social problems, such as family violence and war.

Whereas basic research may ultimately help to solve practical problems, applied research is more explicit in its practical goals. Today about half of all professional anthropologists are applied, or practicing, anthropologists.

Applied or **practicing anthropology** is explicit in its concern with making anthropological knowledge useful.[3] Applied anthropologists may be trained in any or all of the subfields of anthropology. In contrast to basic researchers, who are almost always employed in colleges, universities, and museums, applied anthropologists are usually employed in settings outside of traditional academia, includ-

APPLIED ANTHROPOLOGY
Getting Development Programs to Notice Women's Contributions to Agriculture

When Anita Spring first did fieldwork in Zambia in the 1970s, she was not particularly interested in agriculture. Rather, medical anthropology was her interest. Her work focused on customary healing practices, particularly involving women and children. She was surprised at the end of the year when a delegation of women came to tell her that she didn't understand what it meant to be a woman. "To be a woman is to be a farmer," they said. She admits that it took her a while to pay attention to women as farmers, but then she began to participate in efforts to provide technical assistance to them. Like many others interested in women in development, Spring realized that all too often development agents downplay women's contributions to agriculture.

How does one bring about change in male-centered attitudes and practices? One way is to document how much women actually contribute to agriculture. Beginning with the influential writing of Ester Boserup in *Woman's Role in Economic Development* (1970), scholars began to report that in Africa south of the Sahara, in the Caribbean, and in parts of Southeast Asia, women were the principal farmers or agricultural laborers. Moreover, as agriculture became more complex, it required more work time in the fields, so the women's contribution to agriculture increased. In addition, men increasingly went away to work, so women had to do much of what used to be men's work on the farms.

In the 1980s, Spring designed and directed the Women in Agricultural Development Project in Malawi, funded by the Office of Women in the U.S. Agency for International Development. Rather than focusing just on women, the project aimed to collect data on both women and men agriculturalists and how they were treated by development agents. The project did more than collect information; mini-projects were set up and evaluated so that successful training techniques could be passed on to development agents in other regions. Spring points out that the success of the program was due not just to the design of the project. Much of the success depended on the interest and willingness of Malawi itself to change. And it didn't hurt that the United Nations and other donor organizations increasingly focused attention on women. It takes the efforts of many to bring about change. Increasingly, applied anthropologists like Anita Spring are involved in these efforts from beginning to end, from the design stage to implementation and evaluation.

Source: Anita Spring, *Agricultural Development and Gender Issues in Malawi* (Lanham, MD: University Press of America, 1995).

---

ing government agencies, international development agencies, private consulting firms, businesses, public health organizations, medical schools, law offices, community development agencies, and charitable foundations.

Biological anthropologists may be called upon to give forensic evidence in court, or they may work in public health, or design clothes and equipment to fit human anatomy. Archaeologists may be involved in preserving and exhibiting artifacts for museums and in doing contract work to find and preserve cultural sites that might be damaged by construction or excavation. Linguists may work in bilingual educational training programs or may work on ways to improve communication. Ethnologists may work in a wide variety of applied projects ranging from community development, urban planning, health care, and agricultural improvement to personnel and organizational management and assessment of the impact of change programs on people's lives.[4] We discuss applied anthropology more fully in the section of the book devoted to "Using Anthropology."

SPECIALIZATION

As disciplines grow, they tend to develop more and more specialties. This trend is probably inevitable because, as knowledge accumulates and methods become more advanced, there is a limit to what any one person can reasonably keep track of. So, in addition to the general divisions we have outlined already, particular anthropologists tend to identify themselves with a variety of specializations. It is common for anthropologists to have a geographic specialty, which may be as broad as Old World or New World or as narrow as the southwestern United States. And those who study the past (archaeologists or human paleontologists) may also specialize in different time periods. Ethnologists often specialize in more specific subject matters in addition to one or two cultural areas. Just as most of the chapters in this book refer to broad subject specialties, so some ethnologists identify themselves as economic anthropologists, or political anthropologists, or psychological anthropologists. Others may identify themselves by theoretical orientations, such as cultural ecologists, who are concerned with the relationship between culture and the physical and social environments. These specialties are not mutually exclusive, however. A cultural ecologist, for example, might be interested in the effects of the environment on economic behavior, or political behavior, or how people bring up their children.

Does specialization isolate an anthropologist from other kinds of research? Not necessarily. Some specialties have to draw on information from several fields, inside and outside anthropology. For example, medical anthropologists study the cultural and biological contexts of human health and illness. Thus, they need to understand the economy, diet, and patterns of social interaction, as well as attitudes and beliefs regarding illness and health. In addition, they may need to draw on research in human genetics, public health, and medicine.

◆ The Relevance of Anthropology

Anthropology is a comparatively young discipline. It was only in the late 1800s that anthropologists began to go to live with people in faraway places. Compared to our knowledge of the physical laws of nature, we know much less about people, about how and why they behave as they do. That anthropology and other sciences dealing with humans began to develop only relatively recently is not in itself a sufficient reason for our knowing less than in the physical sciences. Why, in our quest for knowledge of all kinds, did we wait so long to study ourselves? Leslie White suggests that those phenomena most remote from us and least significant as determinants of human behavior were the first to be studied. The reason, he surmises, is that humans like to think of themselves as citadels of free will, subject to no laws of nature. Hence, there is no need to see ourselves as objects to be explained.[5]

The idea that it is impossible to account for human behavior scientifically, either because our actions and beliefs are too individualistic and complex or because human beings are understandable only in otherworldly terms, is a self-fulfilling notion. We cannot discover principles explaining human behavior if we neither believe such principles exist nor bother to look for them. The result is assured from the beginning. Persons who do not believe in principles of human behavior will be reinforced by their finding none. If we are to increase our understanding of human beings, we first have to believe it is possible to do so.

If we aim to understand humans, it is essential that we study humans in all times and places. We must study ancient humans and modern humans. We must study their cultures and their biology. How else can we understand what is true of humans generally or how they are capable of varying? If we study just our own society, we may come up only with explanations that are culture-bound, not general or applicable to most or all humans. Anthropology is useful, then, to the degree that it contributes to our understanding of human beings everywhere.

In addition, anthropology is relevant because it helps us avoid misunderstandings between peoples. If we can understand why other groups are different from ourselves, we might have less reason to condemn them for behavior that appears strange to us. We may then come to realize that many differences between peoples are products of physical and cultural adaptations to different environments. For example, someone who first finds out about the !Kung as they lived in the Kalahari Desert of southern Africa in the 1950s might think that the !Kung were savages.[6] The !Kung wore little clothing, had few possessions, lived in meager shelters, and enjoyed none of our technological niceties. But let us reflect on how a typical North American community might react if it awoke to find itself in an environment similar to that in which the !Kung lived. The people would find that the arid land makes both agriculture and animal husbandry impossible, and they might have to think about adopting a nomadic existence. They might

Archaeologists working at a historical site in New York City. Two people are sifting soil to find small objects.

Even before the emergence of high-tech medical science, people all over the world had discovered how plants could be used as effective medicine. Here are some medicinal plants used by Native Americans in Arizona.

then discard many of their material possessions so that they could travel easily, in order to take advantage of changing water and food supplies. Because of the extreme heat and the lack of extra water for laundry, they might find it more practical to be almost naked than to wear clothes. They would undoubtedly find it impossible to build elaborate homes. For social security, they might start to share the food brought into the group. Thus, if they survived at all, they might end up looking and acting far more like the !Kung looked than like typical North Americans.

Physical differences, too, may be seen as results of adaptations to the environment. For example, in our society we admire people who are tall and slim. If these same individuals were forced to live above the Arctic Circle, however, they might wish they could trade their tall, slim bodies for short, compact ones, because stocky physiques conserve body heat more effectively and may therefore be more adaptive in cold climates.

Exposure to anthropology might help to alleviate some of the misunderstandings that arise between people of different cultural groups from subtle causes operating below the level of consciousness. For example, different cultures have different conceptions of the gestures and interpersonal distances that are appropriate under various circumstances. Arabs consider it proper to stand close enough to other people to smell them.[7] On the basis of the popularity of deodorants in our culture, we can deduce that Americans prefer to keep the olfactory dimension out of interpersonal relations. We may feel that a person who comes too close is being too intimate. We should remember, however, that this person may only be acting according to a culturally conditioned conception of what is proper in a given situation. If our intolerance for others results in part from a lack of understanding of why peoples vary, then the knowledge accumulated by anthropologists may help lessen that intolerance.

Knowledge of our past may also bring both a feeling of humility and a sense of accomplishment. If we are to attempt to deal with the problems of our world, we must be aware of our vulnerability so that we do not think that our problems will solve themselves. But we also have to think enough of our accomplishments to believe that we can find solutions to our problems. Much of the trouble we get into may be a result of feelings of self-importance and

ANTHROPOLOGICAL ORIGINALS

Each chapter from now on includes a box with an extract from an article specially commissioned by the authors of this text. The article appears in an original series designed to convey how individual anthropologists think about their work. The articles together reflect the varieties of research in anthropology—see the sample articles on the CD-ROM included with this book. In the chapters dealing with physical anthropology and archaeology, the invited author discusses issues on the frontier of the subdiscipline. In the chapters dealing with cultural anthropology the various extracts reflect the varieties of human culture; these portraits show how customs and beliefs can be so different, and yet sometimes be so similar, from culture to culture. Many of the portraits describe the personal experiences of the ethnographers in the field. We deliberately intended this. We want students to appreciate not only how anthropological research varies, but also how anthropologists vary. Thus, the boxes titled "Anthropological Originals" that you will encounter in the following chapters convey the scope and richness of contemporary anthropological thinking and writing.

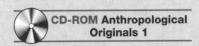 **CD-ROM Anthropological Originals 1**

Source: Carol R. Ember and Melvin Ember, eds., *New Directions in Anthropology* (Upper Saddle River, NJ: Prentice Hall, CD-ROM, 2003). This CD-ROM contains three specially commissioned sections: Carol R. Ember, Melvin Ember, and Peter N. Peregrine, eds., *Research Frontiers in Anthropology;* Melvin Ember and Carol R. Ember, eds., *Portraits of Culture: Ethnographic Originals;* and Carol R. Ember and Melvin Ember, eds., *Cross-Cultural Research for Social Science.*

invulnerability—in short, our lack of humility. Knowing something about our evolutionary past may help us to understand and accept our place in the biological world. Just as for any other form of life, there is no guarantee that any particular human population, or even the entire human species, will perpetuate itself indefinitely. The earth changes, the environment changes, and humanity itself changes. What survives and flourishes in the present might not do so in the future.

Yet our vulnerability should not make us feel powerless. There are many reasons to feel confident about the future. Consider what we have accomplished so far. By means of tools and weapons fashioned from sticks and stones, we were able to hunt animals larger and more powerful than ourselves. We discovered how to make fire, and we learned to use it to keep ourselves warm and to cook our food. As we domesticated plants and animals, we gained greater control over our food supply and were able to establish more permanent settlements. We mined and smelted ores to fashion more durable tools. We built cities and irrigation systems, monuments and ships. We made it possible to travel from one continent to another in a single day. We conquered some illnesses and prolonged human life.

In short, human beings and their cultures have changed considerably over the course of history. Human populations have often been able to adapt to changing circumstances. Let us hope that humans continue to adapt to the challenges of the present and future.

 CD-ROM Flashcards Chapter 1

 # Summary

1. Anthropology is literally the study of human beings. It differs from other disciplines concerned with people in that it is broader in scope. It is concerned with humans in all places of the world (not simply those places close to us), and it traces human evolution and cultural development from millions of years ago to the present day.

2. Another distinguishing feature of anthropology is its holistic approach to the study of human beings. Anthropologists study not only all varieties of people but also all aspects of those peoples' experience.

3. Anthropologists are concerned with identifying and explaining typical characteristics (traits, customs) of particular human populations.

4. Biological or physical anthropology is one of the major fields of the discipline. Biological anthropology studies the emergence of humans and their later physical evolution (the focus called human paleontology). It also studies how and why contemporary human popula-

tions vary biologically (the focus called human variation).

5. Another broad area of concern to anthropology is cultural anthropology. Its three subfields—archaeology, anthropological linguistics, and ethnology (now usually referred to by the parent name, cultural anthropology)—all deal with aspects of human culture, that is, with the customary ways of thinking and behaving of particular societies.

6. Archaeologists seek not only to reconstruct the daily life and customs of prehistoric peoples but also to trace cultural changes and offer possible explanations for those changes. Therefore, archaeologists try to reconstruct history from the remains of human cultures.

7. Anthropological linguists are concerned with the emergence of language and with the divergence of languages over time (a subject known as historical linguistics). They also study how contemporary languages differ, both in construction (descriptive or structural linguistics) and in actual speech (sociolinguistics).

8. The ethnologist (now often called simply a cultural anthropologist) seeks to understand how and why peoples of today and the recent past differ in their customary ways of thinking and acting. One type of ethnologist, the ethnographer, usually spends a year or so living with and talking to a particular population and observing their customs. Later, she or he may prepare a detailed description (an ethnography) of many or some aspects of cultural and social life. Another type of ethnologist, the ethnohistorian, investigates written documents to determine how the ways of life of a particular group of people have changed over time. A third type of ethnologist, the cross-cultural researcher, studies data collected by ethnographers and ethnohistorians for a sample of cultures and attempts to discover which explanations of particular customs may be generally applicable.

9. In all four major subdisciplines of anthropology, there are applied anthropologists, people who apply anthropological knowledge to achieve more practical goals, usually in the service of an agency outside the traditional academic setting.

10. Anthropology may help people to be more tolerant. Anthropological studies can show us why other people are the way they are, both culturally and physically. Customs or actions that appear improper or offensive to us may be other people's adaptations to particular environmental and social conditions.

11. Anthropology is also valuable in that knowledge of our past may bring us both a feeling of humility and a sense of accomplishment. Like any other form of life, we have no guarantee that any particular human population will perpetuate itself indefinitely. Yet knowledge of our achievements in the past may give us confidence in our ability to solve the problems of the future.

Glossary Terms

anthropological linguistics

anthropology

applied (practicing)
   anthropology

archaeology

biological (physical)
   anthropology

cross-cultural researcher

cultural anthropology

culture

descriptive (or structural)
   linguistics

ethnographer

ethnography

ethnohistorian

ethnology

fossils

historical archaeology

historical linguistics

holistic

Homo sapiens

human paleontology

human variation

paleoanthropology

prehistory

Primates

primatologists

sociolinguistics

Critical Questions

1. Why study anthropology?

2. How does anthropology differ from other fields of
   study you've encountered?

3. What do you think about the suggestion that anthropology is the fundamental discipline concerned with
   humans?

Internet Exercises

1. Many of you may keep up with the news and weather
   on the Internet. But have you ever tried to keep up with
   the latest news in anthropology? Check out the latest
   on what is happening in anthropology at http://
   www.tamu.edu/anthropology/news.html. Read and
   comment on two recent news items.

2. Have you ever gone to a virtual museum? Check out
   one of these virtual museums. In a visit to the
   Canadian Museum of Civilization (http://www
   .civilization.ca/), click on First Peoples and explore
   the main features presented. For a virtual museum experience whose content is created by students, visit
   Minnesota State University, Mankato's Emuseum at

http://www.anthro.Mankato.msus. Explore the various floors in the museum.

3. Anthropology is an interdisciplinary subject with
   many specializations. Check out the various sections
   and interest groups of the American Anthropological
   Association (http://aaanet.org). Look at three or four
   sections that seem interesting to you.

Suggested Reading

BOAZ, N. T., AND ALMQUIST, A. J. *Biological Anthropology: A
   Synthetic Approach to Human Evolution.* 2nd ed. Upper
   Saddle River, NJ: Prentice Hall, 2001. After briefly reviewing the principles and sequences of biological evolution,
   the authors review human evolution from earliest times to
   the present. The book also includes chapters on human
   variation, human growth and adaptability, and applied biological anthropology.

EMBER, C. R. AND EMBER, M., EDS. *New Directions in Anthropology,* Upper Saddle River, NJ: Prentice Hall, CD-ROM,
   2003. Particularly appropriate to this chapter are pieces
   written by 10 researchers from different subfields of anthropology about their careers and personal research experiences ("Researchers at Work"). They are biological anthropologists Timothy Bromage and Katharine Milton,
   archaeologists Richard Blanton and Elizabeth Brumfiel,
   linguists Benjamin Blount and Susan Philips, ethnologists
   Carol Ember and Terence Hays, and applied anthropologists Andrew Miracle and Susan Weller.

FOLEY, W. A. *Anthropological Linguistics: An Introduction.*
   Malden, MA: Blackwell, 1997. An overview of anthropological linguistics, including the evolution of language, linguistic universals, linguistic relativism, and the ethnography of speaking.

HOWELLS, W. *Getting Here: The Story of Human Evolution,* 2nd
   ed. Washington, DC: Compass Press, 1997. An accessible
   introduction to the study of human evolution.

PEREGRINE, P. N. *World Prehistory: Two Million Years of Human
   Life.* Upper Saddle River, NJ: Prentice Hall. 2002. A survey
   of world prehistory, describing what we know from archaeology about hunters and gatherers, farmers, and cities
   and civilizations in all areas of the world.

SELIG, R. O., AND LONDON, M. R., EDS. *Anthropology Explored:
   The Best of Smithsonian AnthroNotes.* Washington, DC:
   Smithsonian Institution Press, 1998. Also in E-book format. 2000. A collection of nontechnical articles on the
   work of anthropologists in different subfields.

VAN WILLIGEN, J. *Applied Anthropology: An Introduction,* 3rd
   ed. Westport, CT: Bergin and Garvey, 2002. A survey of applied anthropology that includes a history of the discipline,
   research techniques, examples of applied anthropology,
   and a discussion of ethics.

HOW WE DISCOVER THE PAST

CHAPTER OUTLINE

How can archaeologists and **paleoanthropologists** (anthropologists who study human evolution) know about what may have happened thousands or even millions of years ago? There are no written records from those periods from which to draw inferences. But we do have other kinds of evidence from the past, and we have ways of "reading" this evidence that allow us to know quite a lot about how our human ancestors evolved and how they lived long ago.

◆ The Evidence of the Past

Archaeologists and paleoanthropologists rely on four kinds of evidence to learn about the past: *artifacts, ecofacts, fossils,* and *features.* As we will see, each provides unique information about the past. Together, artifacts, ecofacts, fossils, and features provide a detailed story about human life long ago. However, we need to be trained to "read" this story.

ARTIFACTS

Anything made or modified by humans is an **artifact.** The book you are reading now, the chair you are sitting in, the pen you are taking notes with are all artifacts. In fact, we are surrounded by artifacts, most of which we will lose or throw away. And that is exactly how things enter the archaeological record. Think about it: How much garbage do you produce in a day? What kinds of things do you throw away? Mostly paper, probably, but also wood (from the ice cream bar you had at lunch), plastic (like the pen that ran out of ink last night), and even metal (the dull blade on your razor). Into the garbage they go and out to the dump or landfill. Under the right conditions many of those items will survive for future archaeologists to find. Most of the artifacts that make up the archaeological record are just this kind of mundane waste—the accumulated garbage of daily life that archaeologists may recover and examine to reconstruct daily life long ago.

By far the most common artifacts from the past are stone tools, which archaeologists call **lithics.** Indeed, lithics are the only artifact available for 99 percent of human history. Humans first started using stone tools more than two and a half million years ago, and some tools of stone (grinding and polishing stones, for example) are still used today. Stone has been used for almost any purpose you can think of, from cutting tools to oil lamps, although their most common use has probably been as hunting, butchering, and hide-processing tools. Another common kind of artifact is **ceramics** (pots and other items made from baked clay). Humans first started making ceramics about 10,000 years ago, and ceramic objects such as storage and cooking vessels quickly came to be widely used. Because they are both fragile and relatively easy to make, ceramics show up frequently in the garbage that makes up the archaeological record. Wood and bone artifacts are common too, and were used to make hide-working, cooking, hunting, and even butchering tools. Wood and bone tools have been used by humans at least as long as stone tools, but unlike stone tools, they tend not to survive well in the archaeological record. In some places metals and glass are common artifacts. These survive well in the archaeological record, and hence they are often found where they were used.

ECOFACTS

Ecofacts are natural objects that have been used or affected by humans. A good example are the bones of animals that people have eaten. These bones are somewhat like artifacts, but they haven't been made or modified by humans, just used and discarded by them. Another example is pollen found at archaeological sites. Because humans bring plants back to their houses to use, pollens from many plants are commonly found. These pollens may not have come from the same location. The only reason they are together is that they have been brought together by human use. Yet another example are the remains of insect and animal pests that associate with humans, such as cockroaches and mice. Their remains are found in sites because they associate with humans and survive by taking advantage of the conditions that humans create. Their presence is in part caused by the human presence, and thus they are considered ecofacts too.

FOSSILS

And then there are fossils, which are rare but particularly informative about human biological evolution. A **fossil** may be an impression of an insect or leaf on a muddy surface that now is stone. Or it may consist of the actual hardened remains of an animal's skeletal structure. When an

A ceramic pot from China, dating to the period when agriculture first developed there—some 6,000 years ago.

animal dies, the organic matter that made up its body begins to deteriorate. The teeth and skeletal structure are composed largely of inorganic mineral salts, and soon they are all that remains. Under most conditions, these parts eventually deteriorate too. But once in a great while conditions are favorable for preservation—for instance, when volcanic ash, limestone, or highly mineralized groundwater is present to form a high-mineral environment. If the remains are buried under such circumstances, the minerals in the ground may become bound into the structure of the teeth or bone, hardening the remains and thus making them less likely to deteriorate.

But we don't have fossil remains of everything that lived in the past, and sometimes we only have fragments from one or a few individuals. So the fossil record is very incomplete. For example, Robert Martin estimates that the earth has probably seen 6,000 primate species; remains of only 3 percent of those species have been found. It is hardly surprising that primate paleontologists cannot identify most of the evolutionary connections between early and later forms. The task is particularly difficult with small mammals, such as the early primates, which are less likely than large animals to be preserved in the fossil record.[1]

FEATURES

Features are a kind of artifact, but archaeologists distinguish them from other artifacts because they cannot be easily removed from an archaeological site. Hearths are a good example. When humans build a fire on bare ground the soil becomes heated and is changed—all the water is driven out of it and its crystalline structure is broken down and re-formed. It becomes hard, redder, and even slightly magnetic (as we discuss later). When an archaeologist finds a hearth, what exactly is found? An area of hard, reddish soil, often surrounded by charcoal and ash. Here, then, is an artifact—an object of human manufacture. But it would be very hard, if not impossible, for the archaeologist to pick the hearth up and take it back to the lab for study like a lithic or ceramic. A hearth is really an intrinsic feature of a site—hence the name *feature.*

The fossil of a trilobite from the Cambrian period, 500 million years ago.

Hearths are common features, but by far the most common features are called *pits.* Pits are simply holes dug by humans that are later filled with garbage or eroded soil. They are usually fairly easy to distinguish because the garbage or soil they are filled with is often different in color and texture from the soil the pit was dug into. *Living floors* are another common type of feature. These are the places where humans lived and worked. The soils in these locations are often compacted through human activity and are full of minute pieces of garbage—seeds, small stone flakes, beads, and the like—that became embedded in the floor. A large or very deep area of such debris is called a *midden.* Middens are often the remains of garbage dumps or areas repeatedly used over long periods of time, such as caves. Finally, *buildings* are a common feature on archaeological sites. These can range from the remains of stone rings that once held down the sides of tents to palaces built of stones that had been shaped and fitted together. Even the remains of wooden houses (or parts of them) have been preserved under some conditions. Features are a diverse array of things that can provide lots of information about the past.

 ## Finding the Evidence

Evidence of the past is all around us, but finding it is not always easy or productive. Archaeologists and paleoanthropologists usually restrict their search to what are called *sites.* **Sites** are known or suspected locations of human activity in the past that contain a record of that activity. Sites can range from places where humans camped for perhaps only one night to entire ancient cities. Regardless of their size or complexity, sites can reveal many things about life in the past.

HOW ARE SITES CREATED?

Sites are created when the remnants of human activity are covered or buried by some natural process. The most dramatic one is volcanic activity; the record of human behavior (and even the humans themselves) can be totally buried within seconds. The most impressive example of this must be Pompeii, an entire city that was buried in the eruption of Mount Vesuvius in A.D. 79. Today archaeologists are digging out the city and finding the remains of ancient life just as it was left in the moments before the eruption.[2] Less dramatic means of burying the record of human behavior are the natural processes of dirt accumulation and erosion. Wind- or water-borne soil and debris can cover a site either quickly (as in a flood) or over a long period of time, preserving intact the artifacts, ecofacts, fossils, and features left by humans. Finally, the processes through which soils are built up can also bury artifacts, ecofacts, fossils, and features in a way that allows archaeologists to uncover them later. In forests, for example, falling leaves cover the locations where humans camped. Over time the leaves decay and build up soil, covering the remains of the human encampment slowly but completely over many years.

A site is a location where archaeological materials are found in context. Even a site as large as the ancient city of Pompeii, shown here, can be buried and preserved.

Since good locations to live and work in are often reused by humans, many sites contain the remains of numerous human occupations. The most valuable sites to archaeologists and paleoanthropologists are those in which the burial processes worked quickly enough that each use of the site is clearly separated from the previous one. Such sites are called **stratified;** each layer, or *stratum,* of human occupation is separate like a layer in a layer cake. Not only do stratified sites allow the archaeologist or paleoanthropologist to distinguish easily the sequence of site occupations, but the strata themselves provide a way to know the relative ages of the occupations—earlier occupations will always be below later ones.

TAPHONOMY

It is important to note that the very processes that create sites can often damage or destroy them. The study of the processes of site disturbance and destruction is called **taphonomy.** Some archaeologists and paleoanthropologists argue that natural processes such as wind and water erosion not only bury the materials left by humans but may affect them so significantly that we need to be very cautious when interpreting what is found in an archaeological site. For example, Harold Dibble and his colleagues have argued

that the Lower Paleolithic site of Cagny-L'Epinette in France does not actually contain locations where Lower Paleolithic peoples lived and worked, as previous excavators suggested. Rather, Dibble and his colleagues argue that what looks like locations of human activity were created by water running across the site and accumulating artifacts in low-lying places.[3] This doesn't mean that nothing can be learned from such a site, even one that has been subjected to considerable disturbance, but rather that archaeologists and paleoanthropologists must use caution when interpreting them. An understanding of site taphonomy can help an archaeologist make an informed and cautious interpretation of the past.[4]

HOW ARE SITES FOUND?

There is no single method of finding sites, and indeed many sites are found by happenstance—someone digs into the ground and discovers a lot of artifacts or perhaps a feature. But when archaeologists and paleoanthropologists want to go out and find sites, they typically employ one of two basic methods: pedestrian survey and remote sensing.

Pedestrian survey is what the name suggests—walking around and looking for sites. But there are a number of techniques that archaeologists and paleoanthropologists use to enhance the effectiveness of pedestrian survey beyond simply walking around. These include the use of sampling and systematic surveying methods to reduce the area to be covered on foot. Another way archaeologists reduce the area to be examined is by focusing their search on places humans are likely to have occupied. Paleoanthropologists, for example, typically focus only on those locations where there are exposed fossil beds dating to the time period of the early humans or apes they are interested in finding. Pedestrian survey, while very low tech, can be an extremely effective way of finding sites.

Remote sensing is a much more high-tech way of finding sites. With remote sensing techniques, archaeologists and paleoanthropologists find archaeological deposits by sensing their presence from a remote location, usually the current surface of the ground beneath which the archaeological deposits are buried. Most remote sensing techniques are borrowed from exploration geology, and are the same ones geologists use to find mineral or oil deposits. They typically involve the measurement of minute variations in phenomena like the earth's magnetic or gravitational field, or changes in an electric current or pulse of energy directed into the ground. When these subtle changes, called *anomalies,* are located, more detailed exploration can be done to map the extent and depth of the buried archaeological deposits.

One of the most common remote sensing techniques used in archaeology is *geomagnetics.* Geomagnetic sensing is based on the fact that the earth has a strong magnetic field that varies locally depending on what is beneath the ground. Features such as hearths, stone walls, and pits filled with organic material can alter the earth's magnetic field, as can metal and ceramic artifacts. By carefully measuring the earth's magnetic field, an archaeologist can often locate these features and artifacts. The archaeologist uses a highly sensitive instrument called a magnetometer to map the earth's magnetic field over a large area. When the map is complete, areas with anomalously high or low readings point to locations where buried features or artifacts may be present. In many cases, these anomalies form patterns that can be easily interpreted.

Geomagnetic sensing is called a "passive" technique because the archaeologist simply measures the existing magnetic field. There are also "active" remote sensing techniques by which the archaeologist sends a pulse of energy into the ground and records how it is affected by whatever is buried. One of the most commonly used active techniques is *soil interface radar* (SIR), sometimes also called *ground penetrating radar* (GPR). This technique is based on the fact that different soils reflect radar energy differently. By sending a radar pulse into the ground and recording how the soils reflect it, the archaeologist can map the various soils below the ground. More importantly, if there are features such as walls and pits below the ground, those can be mapped as well. To conduct a radar survey, the archaeologist pulls an antenna along the ground, the size of which depends on the depth of penetration the archaeologist wants and the features expected. The antenna both sends and receives the radar pulses, and the received radar reflections are recorded on a paper strip or in a computer file. These recordings give the archaeologist a picture of what is below the ground.

HOW ARE ARTIFACTS, ECOFACTS, AND FEATURES RECOVERED FROM SITES?

Whether they are identified by pedestrian survey or remote sensing, once archaeological deposits are found there is only one way to recover them—by excavation. Excavation itself is a complex process with two goals: (1) to find every scrap of evidence (or a statistically representative sample) about the past that a given site holds, and (2) to record the horizontal and vertical location of that evidence with precision. Archaeologists and paleoanthropologists have developed many excavation strategies and techniques to accomplish these goals, but all of them involve the careful removal of the archaeological deposits, the recovery of artifacts, ecofacts, fossils, and features from the soil in which those deposits have been buried, and the detailed recording of where each artifact, ecofact, fossil, and feature was located on the site.

Excavation does not mean simply digging holes, not even neat square ones. Because few sites can ever be fully excavated (the cost involved would be tremendous, and most archaeologists feel it is important to leave some archaeological deposits undisturbed in case new techniques are developed that might be employed on the site), archaeological excavations must be carefully planned, usually using some method of sampling. Sampling allows archaeologists to recover a full range of artifacts, ecofacts, fossils, and features while excavating only a small portion of a site. Sampling, however, requires that the archaeologist carefully plan where excavations will be conducted so that all areas of the site have an equal likelihood of being examined.

To date, no one has figured out a way to recover artifacts, ecofacts, fossils, and features from a site without destroying the site in the process, and this is one of the strange ironies of archaeological research. As we discuss shortly, it is the relationships between and among artifacts, ecofacts, fossils, and features that are of most interest to archaeologists, and it is precisely these relationships that are destroyed when archaeologists remove them from a site. For this reason most excavation by professional archaeologists today is done only when a site is threatened with destruction, and then only by highly trained personnel using rigorous techniques.

Archaeologists and paleoanthropologists collect data in basically the same ways, with one important difference. Archaeologists tend to be most concerned with recovering

Paleoanthropologists excavating an early human site in northwestern Kenya. The exposed fossils are those of an elephant that may have been butchered by humans.

intact features, whereas paleoanthropologists tend to be most concerned with recovering intact fossils. This leads to some differences in approaches to collecting data, particularly where to look.

Archaeologists tend to seek out undisturbed sites where intact features can be found. Paleoanthropologists, on the other hand, seek sites dating to the time period when the species of interest lived and might have been fossilized. In many cases, disturbances are a plus for paleoanthropologists, because disturbed sites may make finding fossils easier—they may be eroding out of the surface of the ground and be easily visible without digging. This doesn't mean archaeologists never excavate disturbed sites, because they do. And paleoanthropologists have sometimes made important discoveries by excavating undisturbed sites.[5]

Analyzing the Evidence

Once archaeologists and paleoanthropologists have found a site and recovered artifacts and other materials from it, they are ready to begin "reading" what they've found to learn the story of the past. This "reading" of the archaeological record is called *analysis*. Like excavation, archaeological analysis is a varied and sophisticated process that we will touch on only briefly here.

It should be obvious from our discussion of the archaeological record that much of what is lost or discarded by humans never survives. It is also the case that much of what does survive comes to us in fragments and in a fragile, deteriorated state. Before doing analysis, then, archaeologists and paleoanthropologists must first conserve and reconstruct the materials they have found.

CONSERVATION AND RECONSTRUCTION

Conservation is the process of treating artifacts, ecofacts, and in some cases even features, to stop decay and, if possible, even reverse the deterioration process. Some conservation is very simple, involving only cleaning and drying the item. Some conservation is highly complex, involving long-term chemical treatments and, in some cases, long-term storage under controlled conditions. The so-called

ANTHROPOLOGICAL ORIGINALS
Ancestor Veneration in Lowland Maya Society

Among the most difficult aspects of culture for archaeologists to investigate are religious beliefs. While subsistence practices and even social organization may have clear correlates in the archaeological record, beliefs rarely do, and archaeologists must struggle to find ways to identify and comprehend the belief systems of prehistoric peoples. Patricia McAnany found that in order to understand how the ancient Maya used land, she had to first understand the connections between people, ancestors, and land use. But how can one do that when one is dealing with a culture more than 1000 years old? McAnany argues that the religious beliefs of prehistoric peoples can be discovered if a researcher has clear expectations based on sound ethnographic or historical models.

Archaeologists do not collect evidence of ancient behavior but the material residue or "fall out" of behavior; in fact, one of the great challenges within archaeology stems from the fact that archaeologists study physical materials (broken pottery, building ruins, and so forth) in order to evaluate abstract ideas about the past, such as why and how a social institution such as ancestor veneration developed. I find it easier to pose research questions about human behavior and to imagine the different types of archaeological patterns that might result by first reading ethnographic works. Contemporary Maya of the Yucatán Peninsula and the highlands of Chiapas, México, and Guatemala have been studied extensively, particularly their cosmology and ritual—two topics that are highly pertinent to an ar-

chaeological investigation of ancestor veneration. In Maya studies there is another rich source of ideas about the past that comes from the past itself—Maya hieroglyphic writing and elite iconography [images communicating things about rulers].

 CD-ROM Anthropological Originals 2

Source: Patricia McAnany, "Ancestor Veneration in Lowland Maya Society: A Case Study from K'axob, Belize," in Peter N. Peregrine, Carol R. Ember, and Melvin Ember, eds., *Archaeology: Original Readings in Method and Practice* (Upper Saddle River, NJ: Prentice Hall, 2002), pp. 360–377. Also in Carol R. Ember and Melvin Ember, eds., *New Directions in Anthropology* (Upper Saddle River, NJ: Prentice Hall, CD-ROM, 2003).

"Ice Man," for example, the 5,000-year-old individual found in 1993 in the Italian Alps, is kept in permanently glacial-like conditions after investigators found to their dismay that warming the remains for study induced the growth of mold. The archaeologists removed the mold, but decided that his remains would have to be kept under the same conditions that preserved them in the first place, and so a complex storage facility had to be built to recreate the glacial environment in which he was originally found.[6]

Reconstruction is like building a puzzle—but a three-dimensional puzzle where you're not sure which pieces belong and you know not all of the pieces are there. First, materials have to be sorted into similar types. For example, to reconstruct ceramics from a site, all the ceramics have to be sorted into types with similar color, decoration, and shapes. Then the similar pieces are compared to see if any seem to come from the same vessel. Once all the pieces thought to be from the same vessel are located, they can be assembled. Reconstruction is clearly a long, difficult process—in some cases taking years.

WHAT CAN WE LEARN FROM ARTIFACTS?

Once conservation and reconstruction are complete, the archaeologist or paleoanthropologist can begin to analyze the artifacts they've found. Archaeologists have developed

A conservator applying preservative to a decaying Alaskan totem pole.

specific and often unique ways to analyze the many different types of artifacts. Stone tools are examined in different ways from ceramics, and both are examined differently from bone. But there are some commonalities in the way artifacts are analyzed, regardless of what they are made of.

First, archaeologists typically examine the *form* of an artifact—how it is shaped. For most common artifacts, such as lithics and ceramics, forms are known well enough to be grouped into typologies. Placing artifacts into a **typology** is often the primary purpose of *formal analysis,* because typologies allow archaeologists to place a particular artifact into context with other artifacts found at the site or even at other sites. Typologies often provide a lot of information about an artifact, including its age, the species or culture with which it is affiliated, and in some cases even how it was made, used, or exchanged in the past. Figure 2–1 shows a projectile point typology for a site in Tennessee and the time period between about 7300 and 5000 B.C. Over time the forms of the projectile points changed. The bases of points (*f*) and (*g*) are very different in their form from those of (*c*), (*d*), and (*e*), and all of them are different from (*a*). With this sort of typology, an archaeologist can estimate the age of a projectile point just by looking at the form of its base.

Second, archaeologists often measure artifacts, recording their size in various, often strictly defined, dimensions. Such *metric analysis,* as this activity is called, is used much like formal analysis to group artifacts into a typology. Figure 2–2 shows the standard measurements taken from projectile points. With these measurements one can create a typology similar to that in Figure 2–1. Instead of looking at the form of the projectile points, one looks at their sizes. Clearly, the base widths of points (*a*), (*d*), and (*f*) in Figure

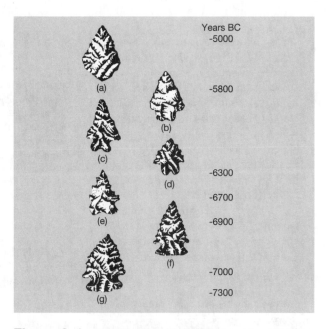

Figure 2–1 *A Projectile Point Chronology from the Icehouse Bottom Site in Tennessee*

Source: Jefferson Chapman, *Tellico Archaeology* (Knoxville: Tennessee Valley Authority, 1985), Fig. 1.15.

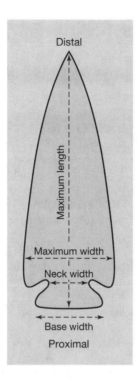

Figure 2–2 *Standard Metrical Measurements of Chipped Stone Tools*

2–1 are going to differ in a manner similar to the way their base forms differ. The value of metric analysis, however, is that the typology created is less subjective than a typology using forms. In addition, many measurements can be taken from broken or partial artifacts that might not be classifiable by formal analysis.

Third, archaeologists often attempt to understand how an artifact was made. By examining the material the artifact is made from and how that material was manipulated, archaeologists can learn about the technology, economy, and exchange systems of the peoples who made the artifact. For example, if the material is not locally available, that means the people traded for it. Archaeologists can also study present-day peoples and how they make similar artifacts in order to understand how ancient artifacts were made. Anne Underhill was interested in understanding how ceramics were produced during the Longshan period in China—a time known for its elegant, thin-walled pottery. In addition to studying the Longshan ceramics and the sites they came from, Underhill also visited living potters who make similar vessels today. She found that both full-time and part-time potters produce ceramics today, but was this the case in the past? Underhill measured ceramics being produced by these potters and performed a metric analysis. She found, to her surprise, that both full-time and part-time potters produce high-quality and highly uniform ceramics, difficult to distinguish from one another.[7]

Finally, archaeologists attempt to understand how an artifact was used. Knowing how an artifact was used allows the archaeologist a direct window onto ancient life. Because this information is so important, a number of so-

phisticated techniques have been developed to determine how artifacts were used. For stone, bone, and wood tools, a technique called *use-wear analysis* has been developed, which can determine how a tool was used through the careful examination of the wear on its edges. We discuss use-wear analysis in more detail in later chapters. For ceramic vessels, techniques have been developed to extract residues trapped in the clay and determine what the vessel held. Archaeologist Patrick McGovern and chemist Rudolf Michel, for example, took samples of a pale yellow residue found in grooves inside ceramic vessels from Grodin Tepe in Turkey. Their analysis determined that the residue was from barley beer, providing the earliest evidence of brewing in the world (the ceramics date from 3500 to 3100 B.C.).[8]

But what can archaeologists really learn by placing artifacts in typologies through formal and metric analysis, or by learning how an artifact was manufactured and used? A lot. Typologies allow archaeologists to use relative dating (which we discuss below) to determine the age of an artifact or site by locating it in a sequence involving other artifacts and sites with known ages. Typologies thus allow archaeologists to determine which groups were related to one another in the distant past, how information was shared among those groups, and in some cases even what social behavior was like (how labor was organized, who traded with whom).

For example, Carla Sinopoli examined the ceramics from the Iron Age site of Vijayanagara, in southern India. Previous excavations had identified distinct residential areas of the site, including a "Noblemen's Quarter," composed of elite residences of high-caste Hindus, the "East Valley," which was thought to contain residences of lower-caste Hindus, and the "Islamic Quarter," which was thought to house Muslim mercenaries. When Sinopoli compared ceramics across the three areas, she found distinct differences: The "Islamic Quarter" had significantly more eating vessels than either of the two other areas, a difference which Sinopoli interpreted as being related to Hindu restrictions on the use of ceramics for holding food (some Hindus will not reuse food containers, so they are often made of disposable materials, such as leaves). Ceramics not only can inform the archaeologist about the social organization of a site, they can also reveal religious beliefs![9] Even gender roles can be revealed archaeologically (see the box "Women in the Shell Mound Archaic").

Knowing how an artifact was made allows the archaeologist to understand the technology and technical abilities of peoples in the past. For example, Thomas Wynn analyzed both the final forms and the methods used by early humans—*Homo erectus*—to make stone tools roughly 300,000 years ago. He found that manufacturing these tools was a multistage process, involving several distinct steps and several distinct stone-working techniques to arrive at the finished product. He then took this information and evaluated it in terms of a measure of human cognitive ability developed by Jean Piaget, and concluded that the people who made these tools probably had organizational abilities similar to those of modern humans.[10]

NEW PERSPECTIVES ON GENDER
Women in the Shell Mound Archaic

One of the main issues addressed by archaeologists interested in gender is how we can learn about and understand gender roles in prehistoric cultures. Gender roles might seem impossible to study in archaeological contexts. How is gender preserved in the archaeological record? How can knowledge about gender roles be recovered? Information about gender roles can be recovered if one maintains an awareness of how material culture that is associated ethnographically with particular gender roles changes over time. Archaeologists argue that such an awareness leads not only to a better understanding of gender in prehistory but can also lead to a fuller understanding of prehistoric cultures overall.

An example is Cheryl Claassen's work on the Shell Mound Archaic culture of the Tennessee River valley. The Shell Mound Archaic represents the remains of people who lived in Tennessee and Kentucky between about 5,500 and 3,000 years ago. They were hunters and gatherers who lived in small villages, and probably moved seasonally between summer and winter communities. The most distinctive feature of the Shell Mound Archaic is the large mounds of mollusk shells they constructed for burying their dead. Tens of thousands of shells were piled together to create these mounds. Yet, around 3,000 years ago, shellfishing and thus the creation of shell burial mounds stopped abruptly. Claassen wondered why.

Suggested explanations include climate change, overexploitation of shellfish themselves, and emigration of shellfishing peoples from the area. None has proven wholly satisfactory. In contemporary cultures shellfishing is typically done by women and children, and Claassen wondered whether an approach that considered gender roles might be more productive. She decided to approach the problem through the perspective of women's workloads, since it would have been women who would have most likely been the ones shellfishing. The end of shellfishing would have meant that women would have had a lot of free time—free time that could have been put to use in some other way. What might have changed to lead women to stop shellfishing? Would something else have perhaps become more important, so that women's labor was needed more for those other tasks?

Women's labor might have been redirected toward domesticated crops. There is archaeological evidence that about 3,000 years ago several productive but highly labor-intensive crops became widely used. For example, *chenopodium*, one of the more plentiful and nutritious of these new crops, has tiny seeds that require considerable labor to harvest, clean, and process. Women were likely the ones burdened with such work. They not only would have harvested these crops but also would have been the ones to process and prepare meals from them. Thus the emergence of agricultural economies would have required women to undertake new labor in food production and processing that may well have forced them to stop other tasks, like shellfishing.

The development of agricultural activities might also have brought about changes in ritual and ceremonialism. The shell burial mounds were clearly central to Shell Mound Archaic death ceremonies. Considerable labor, mostly by women, would have been required to collect the shells and to build these mounds. Later societies in the region buried their dead in earthen mounds. Could this be a reflection of the new importance earth had in an emerging agricultural economy? If so, what role did women play in ceremonies of death and burial? If they were no longer the providers of the raw materials needed for burial, does that mean their status in society as a whole changed?

We may never know exactly why the Shell Mound Archaic disappeared, or how women's work and women's roles in society changed. But as Claassen points out, taking a gender perspective provides new avenues along which to pursue answers to these questions, and interesting new questions to pursue.

Sources: Cheryl Claassen, "Gender and Archaeology," in P. N. Peregrine, C. R. Ember, and M. Ember, eds., *Archaeology: Original Readings in Method and Practice* (Upper Saddle River, NJ: Prentice Hall, 2002), pp. 210–224, also in Carol R. Ember and Melvin Ember, eds., *New Directions in Anthropology* (Upper Saddle River, NJ: Prentice Hall, CD-ROM, 2003); Cheryl Claassen, "Gender, Shellfishing, and the Shell Mound Archaic," in J. Gero and M. Conkey, eds., *Engendering Archaeology: Women and Prehistory* (Oxford: Blackwell, 1991), 276–300.

Finally, knowing how an artifact was used allows the archaeologist to know something of people's behavior and activities. Lawrence Keeley conducted detailed use-wear analyses on Acheulian hand axes made by *Homo erectus* peoples and found that they had a variety of uses. Some were apparently used to cut meat, others to cut wood, and others to dig in the ground (probably for edible roots). On some hand axes, one edge was apparently used for one activity and the other for a different activity. Thus hand axes appear to have been multipurpose tools for our *Homo erectus* ancestors—something like a Swiss Army knife that they carried along with them. This knowledge gives us an interesting picture of these people: They used a fairly sophisticated manufacturing technique to make multipurpose tools that they carried with them and used for whatever job was at hand. This is a picture of the behavior of our ancient ancestors that is unavailable from any other source.[11]

WHAT CAN WE LEARN FROM ECOFACTS AND FOSSILS?

Ecofacts are diverse, and what archaeologists and paleoanthropologists can learn from them is highly diverse as well. Here we'll focus on fossils, but in a later chapter on the Upper Paleolithic world we'll discuss how archaeologists use ecofacts to reconstruct ancient environments; and in a still later chapter on the origins of domesticated plants and animals we'll learn how archaeologists use ecofacts to distinguish wild from domestic plants and animals and to reconstruct how these plants and animals were domesticated.

Paleontologists (studying humans or other species) can tell a great deal about an extinct animal from its fossilized bones or teeth, but that knowledge is based on much more than just the fossil record itself. Paleontologists rely on comparative anatomy to help reconstruct missing skeletal pieces, as well as the soft tissues attached to bone. New techniques, such as electron microscopy, CAT scans, and computer-assisted biomechanical modeling, provide much information about how the organism may have moved about, the microstructure of bone and teeth, and how the organism developed. Chemical analysis of fossilized bone can suggest what the animal typically ate. Paleontologists

are also interested in the surroundings of the fossil finds. With methods developed in geology, chemistry, and physics, paleontologists use the surrounding rocks to identify the time period in which the organism died. In addition, the study of associated fauna and flora can suggest what the ancient climate and habitat were like.[12]

Much of the evidence for primate evolution comes from teeth, which are the most common animal parts (along with jaws) to be preserved as fossils. Animals vary in *dentition*—the number and kinds of teeth they have, their size, and their arrangement in the mouth. Dentition provides clues to evolutionary relationships because animals with similar evolutionary histories often have similar teeth. For example, no primate, living or extinct, has more than two incisors in each quarter of the jaw. That feature, along with others, distinguishes the primates from earlier mammals, which had three incisors in each quarter. Dentition also suggests the relative size of an animal and often offers clues about its diet. For example, comparisons of living primates suggest that fruit-eaters have flattened, rounded tooth cusps, unlike leaf- and insect-eaters, which have more pointed cusps.[13] CAT scan methodology has helped paleontologists image the internal parts of teeth, such as the thickness of enamel, which can also suggest the diet (seed- and nut-eaters have thicker enamel). Electron microscopy has revealed different patterns of growth in bones and teeth; different species have different patterns.[14]

Paleontologists can tell much about an animal's posture and locomotion from fragments of its skeleton. Arboreal quadrupeds have front and back limbs of about the same length; because their limbs tend to be short, their center of gravity is close to the branches on which they move. They also tend to have long grasping fingers and toes. Terrestrial quadrupeds are more adapted for speed, so they have longer limbs and shorter fingers and toes. Disproportionate limbs are more characteristic of vertical clingers and leapers and *brachiators* (species that swing through the branches). Vertical clingers and leapers have longer, more powerful hind limbs; brachiators have longer forelimbs.[15] Even though soft tissues are not preserved, much can be inferred from the fossils themselves. For example, the form and size of muscles can be estimated by marks found on the bones to which the muscles were attached. And the underside of the cranium may provide information about the proportions of the brain devoted to vision, smell, or memory. The skull also reveals information about characteristics of smell and vision. For example, animals that rely more on smell than on vision tend to have large snouts. Nocturnal animals tend to have large eye sockets.

WHAT CAN WE LEARN FROM FEATURES?

The analysis of features is a little bit different from the analysis of artifacts, ecofacts, and fossils. Because features cannot be removed to the lab (see our earlier discussion of hearths), they cannot be subjected to the same range of analyses as artifacts, ecofacts, and fossils. However, archaeologists have developed a number of powerful tools to

An Acheulian hand axe. Lawrence Keeley examined the edge wear on hand axes to determine how they were used.

analyze features in the field. The primary one is detailed mapping, usually using a surveyor's transit. Extensive records are made about each feature, explaining not only what the feature is but also what archaeological materials were found associated with it. This information can be brought together using a *geographic information system* (GIS). A GIS allows the archaeologist to produce a map of the features on a site and combine that map with information about the archaeological materials that were also found. Combining these kinds of information can reveal patterns in the archaeological record that tell us about human behaviors in the past.

A good example of how patterns of features can reveal past human behavior comes from the Range Site in west-central Illinois. Humans lived on the Range Site for over a thousand years, and during that time the ways they organized their settlement changed. About 2,300 years ago the people at the Range Site lived in small houses arranged around a circular courtyard. This pattern continued and was elaborated upon for almost 700 years; the courtyard area was a focus of activity and perhaps ritual. About 1,000 years ago the pattern changed. Houses became more substantial and were arranged linearly, in rows. This change suggests a radical alteration in social organization. From cross-cultural research (comparative studies using ethnographic data), we know that where circular communities are found, the communities commonly function as a single political and economic unit, whereas communities arranged linearly often do not function as one political and economic unit. What the changes in the Range Site seem to show is an attenuation or reduction of the basic social and economic unit, from the community to the individual household. This change seems to be related to the evolution of a large, centralized polity located at Cahokia, only 15 kilometers from the Range Site, whose impact on surrounding communities like the one at the Range Site may have been dramatic, transforming a socioeconomic structure that had persisted for almost a millennium.[16]

PUTTING IT ALL IN CONTEXT

You might have gained the impression from our discussion that archaeologists and paleoanthropologists analyze artifacts, ecofacts, fossils, and features as individual objects, separate from one another. Nothing could be further from the truth. In fact, the analysis of the Range Site just described is much more like a typical archaeological analysis. It combined information about features across time to come to a generalization about how the social and economic organization of the people living there changed. We call this putting the material in context. **Context** is the relationship between and among artifacts and other materials. The analysis of context is really what archaeology and paleoanthropology are all about. Artifacts, ecofacts, fossils, and features in isolation may be beautiful or interesting by themselves, but it is only when they are placed in context with the other materials found on a site that we are able to "read" and tell the story of the past.

To illustrate this point, let's consider a set of letters that were found separately: A E G I M N N. They are arranged here in alphabetical order, the way a set of beautiful artifacts might be arranged in a display case in order of size. But do these arrangements tell us anything? No. What if we knew something about the relationships between and among these letters—their context? What if, for example, we knew that the *M* was the first letter found, and that the *A* and *E* were found next to the *M,* but in reverse order, that one *N* was found between the *E* and *I,* and that the other *N* was found between the *I* and the *G?* Knowing in what context the letters were found would tell us that the letters should be arranged like this: *M E A N I N G.* And meaning is exactly what context gives to artifacts, ecofacts, fossils, and features.

◆ Dating the Evidence

An important, indeed vital, part of putting artifacts and other materials into context is putting them in chronological order. To reconstruct the evolutionary history of the primates, for example, one must know how old primate fossils are. For some time, relative dating methods were the only methods available. The last 45 years have seen important advances in absolute dating, including techniques that allow the dating of the earliest phases of primate evolution.[17] **Relative dating** is used to determine the age of a specimen or deposit relative to another specimen or deposit. **Absolute dating,** or chronometric dating, is used to measure how old a specimen or deposit is in years.

RELATIVE DATING METHODS

The earliest, and still the most commonly used method of relative dating, is based on **stratigraphy,** the study of how different rock or soil formations are laid down in successive layers or strata (see Figure 2–3). Older layers are generally deeper or lower than more recent layers. Indicator artifacts or ecofacts are used to establish a stratigraphic sequence for the relative dating of new finds. These **indicator artifacts or ecofacts** are items of human manufacture or remains from animals and plants that spread widely over short periods of time, or that disappeared fairly rapidly, or that changed rapidly. Different artifacts and ecofacts are used as indicators of relative age in different areas of the world. In Africa, elephants, pigs, and horses have been particularly important in establishing stratigraphic sequences. Figure 2–3 shows the stratigraphy of Olduvai Gorge, an important site where early human fossils have been found. The stratigraphy here was established in part on the basis of fossil pigs.[18] The species of pig in each successive strata are different, allowing the archaeologist or paleoanthropologist to differentiate the strata based on the species found within them. Once the stratigraphy of an area is established, the relative ages of two different fossils, or features, in the same or different sites are indicated by the associated indicator artifacts or ecofacts.[19] Major transitions in indicator artifacts or ecofacts define the epochs and larger units of geologic time.

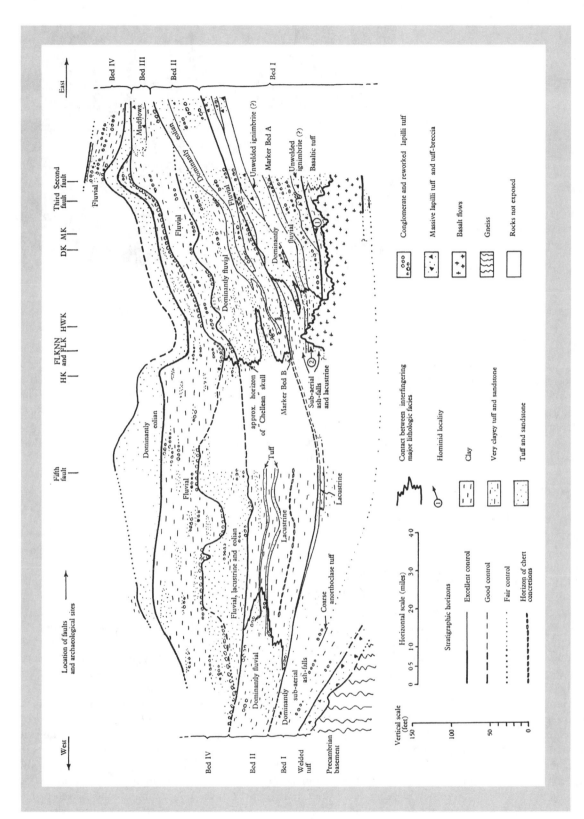

Figure 2-3 *Stratigraphy of Beds I-IV along Olduvai Main Gorge.*

Notice how complex the four stratigraphic layers are—each has numerous layers of soil and rock within them. Index fossils, particularly pigs, along with a series of potassium-argon dates, allowed the researchers to identify the four major strata of the site, which correspond to four major periods of human occupation.

Source: Olduvai Gorge, 1951–61, Volume I, by L.S.B. Leakey. Copyright © 1965. Reprinted with the permission of Cambridge University Press.

Archaeologists examining the wall of an excavation at Nippur, Iraq. The thick white line in the wall is the plastered floor of a building. Items found on the floor can all be assumed to date from the same time, while items found below it can be assumed to date from an earlier time. This is a simple example of using stratigraphy for relative dating.

The dates of the boundaries between such units are estimated by absolute dating, described in the next section.

If a site has been disturbed, stratigraphy will not be a satisfactory way to determine relative age. As noted earlier, remains from different periods may be washed or blown together by water or wind. Or a landslide may superimpose an earlier on a later layer. Still, it may be possible using chemical methods to estimate the relative age of the different fossils found together in a disturbed site.

Three of the chemical methods used to date fossil bones relatively are the fluorine, uranium, and nitrogen tests, sometimes known as the **F-U-N trio.**[20] All are based on the same general principle: Bones and teeth undergo a slow transformation in chemical composition when they remain buried for long periods, and this transformation reflects the mineral content of the groundwater in the area in which they are buried. Fluorine is one mineral present in groundwater; therefore, the older a fossil is, the higher its fluorine content will be. Uranium, like fluorine, is also present in groundwater, so the longer bones or teeth remain in the ground, the greater their uranium content. The proportions are reversed for nitrogen: The older the fossil is, the smaller the amount of nitrogen present in it. Thus, older bones have relatively higher concentrations of fluorine and uranium and less nitrogen than do recent bones.

But a problem can arise with the F-U-N tests because the mineral content of bones reflects the mineral content of the groundwater in the area. A 30-million-year-old fossil from a high-mineral area may have the same fluorine content as a 50-million-year-old fossil from a low-mineral site. So these chemical relative dating methods cannot be used to find the relative ages of specimens from widely separated sites. The F-U-N tests are restricted, then, to specimens from the same site or from neighboring sites.

Each of the chemical relative dating methods, used alone, can give only tentative evidence. But when the three methods are combined and confirm—that is, corroborate—one another, they are very effective. Of the three

methods, the uranium test is by far the most reliable when used alone. It is not strictly a relative dating method. There seems to be some consistency in the increase in radioactivity with age, even in bones from different deposits. The uranium test has another distinct advantage over the other tests. Because uranium is radioactive, measuring the radioactivity does not require the destruction of any part of the sample in testing.

ABSOLUTE, OR CHRONOMETRIC, DATING METHODS

Many of the absolute dating methods are based on the decay of a radioactive isotope. Because the rate of decay is known, the age of the specimen can be estimated, within a range of possible error.

RADIOCARBON DATING   Radiocarbon, or **carbon-14** (^{14}C), dating is perhaps the most popularly known method of determining the absolute age of a specimen. It is based on the principle that all living matter possesses a certain amount of a radioactive form of carbon (carbon-14, or ^{14}C). Radioactive carbon, produced when nitrogen-14 is bombarded by cosmic rays, is absorbed from the air by plants and then ingested by animals that eat the plants (see Figure 2–4). After an organism dies, it no longer takes in any of the radioactive carbon. Carbon-14 decays at a slow but steady pace and reverts to nitrogen-14. (By *decays,* we mean that the ^{14}C gives off a certain number of beta radiations per minute.) The rate at which the carbon decays—its **half-life**—is known: ^{14}C has a half-life of 5,730 years. In other words, half of the original amount of ^{14}C in organic matter will have disintegrated 5,730 years after the organism's death; half of the remaining ^{14}C will have disintegrated after another 5,730 years; and so on. After about 50,000 years, the amount of ^{14}C remaining in the organic matter is too small to permit reliable dating.

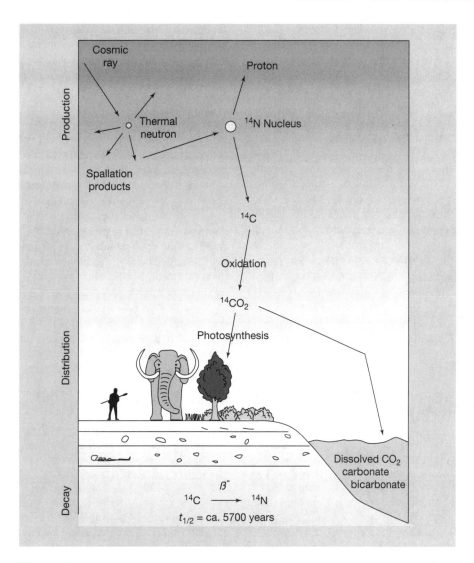

Figure 2–4 *The Carbon-14 Cycle*

Source: "The Carbon-14 Cycle" from "Radiocarbon Dating" by R. E. Taylor, from *Chronometric Dating in Archaeology* by R. E. Taylor and M. J. Aitken, eds. Copyright © 1997 by Plenum Publishers. Reprinted by permission of Plenum Publishers.

To discover how long an organism has been dead—that is, to determine how much ^{14}C is left in the organism and therefore how old it is—we either count the number of beta radiations given off per minute per gram of material, or use a particle accelerator to measure the actual amount of ^{14}C in a sample. Modern ^{14}C emits about 15 beta radiations per minute per gram of material, but ^{14}C that is 5,730 years old emits only half that amount (the half-life of ^{14}C) per minute per gram. So if a sample of some organism gives off 7.5 radiations a minute per gram, which is only half the amount given off by modern ^{14}C, the organism must be 5,730 years old.[21] Similarly, because the amount of ^{14}C in a sample slowly declines over time, the atoms in a sample can be sent through a particle accelerator to separate them by weight (the lighter ^{12}C accelerates faster than the heavier ^{14}C) and measure the actual amount of each. This method, called AMS (accelerator mass spectrometry),

is more accurate than the beta radiation method, requires only a very small sample of material, and provides a way to date specimens that are up to 80,000 years old.[22]

The accuracy of radiocarbon dating was tested by using it to judge the age of parts of the Dead Sea Scrolls and some wood from an Egyptian tomb, the dates of which were already known from historical records. The results based on ^{14}C analysis agreed very well with the historical information.

THERMOLUMINESCENCE DATING Many minerals emit light when they are heated (*thermoluminescence*), even before they become red hot. This cold light comes from the release, under heat, of "outside" electrons trapped in the crystal structure. **Thermoluminescence dating** makes use of the principle that if an object is heated at some point to a high temperature, as when clay is baked to form a pot, it will release all the trapped electrons it held previously.[23] Over time, the object will continue to trap electrons from radioactive elements (potassium, thorium, uranium) around it. The amount of thermoluminescence emitted when the object is heated during testing allows researchers to calculate the age of the object, if it is known what kind of radiation the object has been exposed to in its surroundings (for example, the surrounding soil in which a clay pot is found).

Thermoluminescence dating is well suited to samples of ancient pottery, brick, tile, terra cotta, and other objects that are made at high temperatures. This method can also be applied to burnt flint tools, hearth stones, lava or lava-covered objects, meteorites, and meteor craters.[24]

ELECTRON SPIN RESONANCE DATING Electron **spin resonance dating** is a technique that, like thermoluminescence dating, measures trapped electrons from surrounding radioactive material. But the method in this case is different. The material to be dated is exposed to varying magnetic fields, and a spectrum of the microwaves absorbed by the tested material is obtained. Because no heating is required for this technique, electron spin resonance is especially useful for dating organic material such as bone and shell, which decompose if heated.[25]

PALEOMAGNETIC DATING When rock of any kind forms, it records the ancient magnetic field of the earth. When this knowledge is put together with the fact that the earth's magnetic field has reversed itself many times, the geomagnetic patterns in rocks can be used to date the fossils within those rocks. **Paleomagnetic dating** dates rocks in terms of the sequence of geomagnetic patterns in them. Strictly speaking, paleomagnetic dating is not an absolute dating method, but geomagnetic time periods have been dated absolutely in conjunction with potassium-argon dating (described below). Paleomagnetic dating has dated primate finds from the Eocene through the Miocene, from 55 million to 5 million years ago.[26]

Not only does the earth's magnetic field reverse itself, but the locations of its poles move constantly (albeit very slowly) over time. The wanderings of the North Pole have

CURRENT RESEARCH AND ISSUES
Are There Unilinear Trends in Cultural Evolution?

Late in the 1800s, in the early days of anthropology, the prevailing view of theorists like Edward Tylor and Lewis Henry Morgan was that culture generally develops or evolves in a uniform or progressive manner. It was thought that most societies pass through similar stages, to arrive ultimately at a common end. The early evolutionists believed that European and European-derived cultures were at the highest stages of evolution. Other cultures were still in the lower stages. The school of historical particularism associated with Franz Boas rejected the idea that there were universal laws governing all human cultures. Instead, the historical particularists proposed that culture traits had to be studied in the context of the society in which they appeared. Boas stressed the need to collect data on as many societies as possible, an activity that became a central part of the anthropological enterprise.

Evolutionism did not die with the early evolutionists, however. For example, in the 1960s, Marshall Sahlins and Elman Service discussed two kinds of evolutionary processes—specific evolution, which refers to the particular changes of a particular society, and general evolution. General evolution refers to the general tendency of "higher" forms to surpass "lower" forms, but it does not insist that every society goes through exactly the same stages or progresses toward the "higher" stages. Nonetheless, anthropologists are not particularly keen on the idea of unilinear (one-directional) evolution, perhaps because the idea is still associated with the assumption of European superiority by the early evolutionists. But looking at the long stretch of human history, we see that some things seem to have changed in a fairly consistent way. For example, human populations have grown, technology has

become more sophisticated, and most people on earth have come to live in state societies. Surely there are some unilinear trends in cultural evolution—or are there? How can we tell?

The third author of this textbook (Peter Peregrine) approached the question through cross-cultural research. He decided to test whether overall cultural complexity has increased over time. To do so he needed a measure of cultural complexity, and he needed a group of cultures to measure that represented all the cultures on earth over a long period of time. Happily, both exist. The measure of cultural complexity he used was developed by anthropologist George Peter Murdock to examine variation in cultural complexity among ethnographically known cultures. The measure looks at 10 different features of the culture, including its technology, economy, political system, and population density. Pere-

been determined for the recent past, and this knowledge allows archaeologists to date some archaeological features. When soil, rock, or metal is heated to a high temperature, it liquifies and its constituent molecules align themselves to the earth's magnetic field. When cooled, the molecules retain their alignment, and thus create something of an arrow pointing to the earth's magnetic poles. When an archaeologist finds a hearth, pottery kiln, metal workshop, or something else in which earth, rock, or metal was heated to its melting point and cooled in place, the archaeologist can take a sample of that material, carefully recording its location in terms of the earth's present-day magnetic field, and then measure the material's magnetic field in the laboratory. The difference between the direction of the earth's current magnetic field and that recorded in the material can be used to date when the material was melted and cooled.

POTASSIUM-ARGON DATING AND ARGON-ARGON DATING Potassium-40 (^{40}K), a radioactive form of potassium, decays at an established rate and forms argon-40 (^{40}Ar). The half-life of ^{40}K is a known quantity, so

the age of a material containing potassium can be measured by the amount of ^{40}K compared with the amount of ^{40}Ar it contains.[27] Radioactive potassium's (^{40}K's) half-life is very long—1,330 million years. This means that **potassium-argon (K-Ar) dating** may be used to date samples from 5,000 years up to 3 billion years old.

The K-Ar method is used to date potassium-rich minerals in rock, not the fossils that may be found in the rock. A very high temperature, such as occurs in a volcanic event, drives off any original argon in the material. Therefore, the amount of argon that accumulates afterward from the decay of radioactive potassium is directly related to the amount of time since the volcanic event. This type of dating has been extremely useful in East Africa, where volcanic events have occurred frequently since the Miocene, which began 24 million years ago.[28] If the material to be dated is not rich in potassium, or the area did not experience any high-temperature events, other methods of absolute dating are required.

One problem with the K-Ar method is that the amounts of potassium and argon must be measured on different rock samples; researchers must assume that the potassium and

---

(continued)

grine simplified this measure to make it easier to use with archaeologically known cultures, and he limited himself to Old World cultures dating to the last 15,000 years listed in the *Outline of Archaeological Traditions*. He measured cultural complexity for these cultures using the information about them given in the *Encyclopedia of Prehistory*.

Peregrine found strong evidence that cultural complexity has increased in a fairly regular manner over the last 15,000 years. The figure in this box displays this trend graphically. The horizontal scale is the date of the culture, starting with today at the left and going back into the past as you move to the right. The vertical scale is the culture's cultural complexity score. It's clear from the figure that cultural complexity scores have tended to increase over time. Indeed the increase is statistically significant (unlikely to be due to chance). However, it is also clear that the increase is not universal: Some cultures scored low

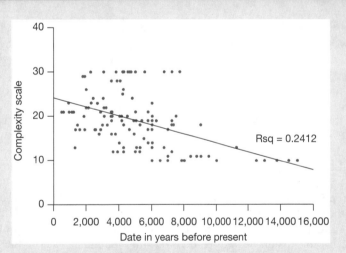

The Relationship between Cultural Complexity and Time

In general, cultural complexity has increased over time.

in the past while others scored higher, and some score low today while others score higher. Thus not all cultures have undergone change in the same way. But the figure suggests that human cultures generally have tended to become more complex over time. Why? We offer no answer, but we suggest it is an excellent question

to ponder as you read through this book.

Sources: Peter N. Peregrine, *Outline of Archaeological Traditions* (New Haven, CT: HRAF, 2001); Peter N. Peregrine and Melvin Ember, eds., *Encyclopedia of Prehistory* (New York: Kluwer Academic/Plenum, 2001); Peter N. Peregrine, "Cross-Cultural Approaches in Archaeology," *Annual Review of Anthropology*, 30 (2001).

argon are evenly distributed in all the rock samples from a particular stratum. Researchers got around this problem by developing the ^{40}**Ar-**^{39}**Ar dating method.** After measuring the amount of ^{40}Ar, a nuclear reactor is used to convert another kind of argon, ^{39}Ar, to potassium so that the potassium-argon ratio can be measured from the same sample.[29]

URANIUM-SERIES DATING   The decay of two kinds of uranium, ^{235}U and ^{238}U, into other isotopes (such as ^{230}Th, thorium) has also proved useful for dating sites with remains of *Homo sapiens* (modern-looking humans), particularly in caves where stalagmites and other calcite formations form. Because water that seeps into caves usually contains uranium but not thorium, the calcite formations trap uranium. Uranium starts decaying at a known rate into other isotopes (such as thorium-230, or ^{230}Th), and the ratio of those isotopes to uranium isotopes can be used to estimate the time elasped. The thorium-uranium ratio is useful for dating cave sites less than 300,000 years old where there are no volcanic rocks suitable for the potassium-argon method. Early *Homo sapiens* from European cave sites in Germany, Hungary, and Wales were dated this way.[30] There are different varieties of **uranium-series dating,** depending on the specific isotope ratios used.

FISSION-TRACK DATING   **Fission-track dating** is another way to determine the absolute age of fossil deposits.[31] Like the K-Ar method, it dates minerals contemporaneous with the deposit in which fossils are found and it also requires the prior occurrence of a high-temperature event, such as a volcanic eruption. But the kinds of samples it can be used to date, such as crystal, glass, and many uranium-rich minerals, include a much wider variety than those that can be dated by the K-Ar method. The age range of fission-track dating, like that of K-Ar dating, is extensive—20 years to 5 billion years.[32]

How does fission-track dating work? This method is basically the simplest of all the methods discussed here. It entails counting the number of paths or tracks etched in the sample by the fission—explosive division—of uranium atoms as they disintegrate. Scientists know that ^{238}U, the most common uranium isotope, decays at a slow, steady rate. This decay takes the form of spontaneous fission, and each separate fission leaves a scar or track on the sample which can be seen, when chemically treated, through a microscope. To find out how old a sample is, one counts the tracks, then measures their ratio to the uranium content of the sample.

The fission-track method was used to date Bed I at Olduvai Gorge in Tanzania, East Africa, where some early human ancestors were found.[33] It was able to corroborate earlier K-Ar estimates that the site dated back close to 2 million years. That the K-Ar and fission-track methods use different techniques and have different sources of error makes them effective as checks on each other. When the two methods support each other, they provide very reliable evidence.

OTHER TECHNIQUES   The dating techniques outlined above are the most commonly used in archaeology and paleoanthropology, but there are many others, and new techniques are being developed all the time. For example, stone tools made from obsidian can be dated in some cases because a thin layer of stone, called an hydration layer, builds up on the obsidian over time when it is exposed to air. Similarly, rock art is sometimes dated by measuring the build-up of a patina over the art after it has been painted or carved on a piece of stone. Bones can sometimes be dated by measuring the breakdown of DNA, which occurs in a regular manner (similar to radioisotope decay) when heat and humidity are stable. These and many other techniques add a wide range of choices to the tool-kit that archaeologists and paleoanthropologists can use to date their finds.

The Results of Archaeological Research

When archaeologists and paleoanthropologists finish a research project, what is the result? What are the goals of archaeological research? There are several distinct answers.

One goal of archaeological research is the description or reconstruction of what happened in the past. Much of what archaeologists do, and much of what we do in this book, fall under this goal. Archaeologists attempt to determine how people lived in a particular place at a particular time, and when and how their life-styles changed. Also of interest, of course, is whether new cultures arrived or established cultures moved out of a given area. Creating histories of cultures and their changes over time is called, simply enough, **culture history.** Doing culture history was the primary goal of archaeology until the 1950s.[34]

A second major goal of archaeological research, and one that has become the primary goal since the 1950s, is testing specific theories and hypotheses about human evolution and behavior. In part this change in focus is due to the growth in our knowledge about the past—the culture history of many areas is today well known. But this change is also due to changes going on in anthropology as a whole. Until the 1950s a school of thought called *historical particularism* was dominant in American anthropology. It suggested that variation in human cultures was best explained by considering the specific historical developments of particular cultures. Like the purpose of historical particularism, the purpose of culture history was to trace historical developments.

After the 1950s a variety of new approaches became prominent in anthropology, most of them sharing the idea that the environment and how humans use it actively shapes cultures and mostly explains cultural variability. Archaeology became a key tool for anthropologists attempting to understand how changes in the ways humans used the environment explained variation in human cultures. One of the outgrowths of this focus on hypothesis testing and human use of the environment was research on agricultural origins, which we discuss in the chapter on the origins of food production and settled life. Another was a concern with the rise of cities and states, which radically transformed human use of the environment. We devote a separate chapter to that subject.

In addition to testing hypotheses, archaeology has a primary role within anthropology in its attempt to identify and understand general trends and patterns in human biological and cultural evolution. As we discussed in the last chapter, cross-cultural research has this as a goal as well. But only archaeology is able to look through time and directly examine evolutionary trends. In the box "Are There Unilinear Trends in Cultural Evolution?" we consider one way archaeology is able to elucidate long-term trends. In later chapters in this book we trace the evolution of humans and human cultures from their beginnings. As we shall see, a major emphasis in paleoanthropology is demonstrating long-term trends and patterns that help us understand how and why we have come to be the way we are. In this pursuit, archaeology and paleoanthropology come together to help answer what may be the fundamental question of anthropology: What does it mean to be human?

 CD-ROM Flashcards Chapter 2

 # Summary

1. Archaeologists and paleoanthropologists have four basic sources of evidence about the past: artifacts, ecofacts, fossils, and features.

2. Sites are locations where the evidence of the past has been buried and preserved. Sites are found through pedestrian survey or remote sensing, and artifacts, ecofacts, fossils, and features are recovered from sites through excavation.

3. Information about the past is obtained by analyzing the evidence recovered from sites. Much information can be gained through the analysis of the forms, sizes, and composition of archaeological materials, but the materials themselves are not the primary focus of analysis. Rather it is the context between and among artifacts, ecofacts, fossils, and features that allows the archaeologist or paleoanthropologist to gain insights about the past.

4. A key aspect of putting archaeological material into context is being able to date material accurately. A wide variety of dating techniques are used. Relative dating techniques determine the age of archaeological materials relative to other materials of known ages. Absolute dating techniques determine the age of the archaeological deposits or materials themselves.

5. Archaeology allows for cultural histories to be developed and hypotheses about cultural change to be tested. Its primary goal is to provide insights into human physical and cultural evolution—the central concern of this book.

 # Glossary Terms

absolute dating
^{40}Ar-^{39}Ar dating
artifact
ceramics
conservation
context
culture history
ecofacts
electron spin resonance dating
features
fission-track dating
fossils
F-U-N trio
half-life
indicator artifacts and ecofacts

lithics
paleoanthropologists
paleomagnetic dating
potassium-argon (K-Ar) dating
radiocarbon, or carbon-14 (^{14}C), dating
relative dating
sites
stratified
stratigraphy
taphonomy
thermoluminescence dating
typology
uranium-series dating

 # Critical Questions

1. Why is context so important in archaeological research?

2. What kinds of information can be learned from a stone projectile point?

3. What factors have to be considered when choosing a dating technique?

 # Internet Exercises

1. Visit http://archnet.asu.edu and explore one or more of the subject areas concerning archaeological methods. Write a brief essay describing a new method or technique you learned about.

2. Learn about archaeological sampling at http://archnet.asu.edu/archnet/uconn_extras/theory/sampling/sampling.html Try the various techniques and determine which gives the best results.

3. Visit the carbon-14 dating Web site at http://www.c14dating.com/. Read about the method's history, and how carbon-14 samples are collected, prepared, and analyzed. Summarize what you learned.

4. Take the seriation test at http://emuseum.mankato.msus.edu/archaeology/dating/seriate.html and determine your potential as an archaeologist.

Suggested Reading

BAHN, P. *Archaeology: A Very Short Introduction.* New York: Oxford University Press, 1996. Just what the name says—a short, well-written introduction to archaeology.

CONROY, G. C. *Reconstructing Human Origins: A Modern Synthesis.* New York: W.W. Norton, 1997. A thorough and well-written overview of paleoanthropological research.

FAGAN, B. *In the Beginning: An Introduction to Archaeology,* 10th ed. Upper Saddle River, NJ: Prentice Hall, 2000. A classic introduction to archaeological research.

KLEIN, R. G. *The Human Career: Human Biological and Cultural Origins.* Chicago: University of Chicago Press, 1999. A comprehensive introduction to paleoanthropology.

PEREGRINE, P. *Archaeological Research: A Brief Introduction.* Upper Saddle River, NJ: Prentice Hall, 2001. An overview of the purposes, practices, and results of archaeological research, written for a general audience.

PURDY, B. *How to Do Archaeology the Right Way.* Gainesville: University Press of Florida, 1996. An introduction to archaeological excavation and field methods.

RENFREW, C., AND BAHN, P. *Archaeology: Theories, Methods, and Practice,* 3rd ed. New York: Thames and Hudson, 2000. A comprehensive and detailed overview of archaeology.

THE EMERGENCE OF HOMO SAPIENS

CHAPTER OUTLINE

- ◆ The Transition from *Homo erectus* to *Homo sapiens*

- ◆ Middle Paleolithic Cultures

- ◆ The Emergence of Modern Humans

- ◆ What Happened to the Neandertals?

Until about 20 years ago, paleoanthropologists thought that our species *Homo sapiens* evolved in the last 50,000 years. Now we know that our species appeared earlier (see Figure 8–1). The date of about 50,000 years ago is for Europe, but recent finds in southern Africa and elsewhere indicate the presence of *Homo sapiens* perhaps 100,000 years ago. Completely modern-looking humans, **Homo sapiens sapiens,** did appear by 50,000 years ago. One paleoanthropologist, Christopher Stringer, characterizes the modern human, *Homo sapiens sapiens,* as having "a domed skull, a chin, small eyebrows, brow ridges, and a rather puny skeleton."[1] Some of us might not like to be called puny, but except for our larger brain, most modern humans definitely are puny compared with *Homo erectus* and even with earlier forms of our own species, *H. sapiens.* We are relatively puny in several respects, including our thinner and lighter bones, as well as our smaller teeth and jaws.

In this chapter we discuss the fossil evidence, as well as the controversies, about the transition from *H. erectus* to modern humans, which may have begun 500,000 years ago. We also discuss what we know archaeologically about the Middle Paleolithic cultures between about 300,000 and 40,000 years ago.

◆ The Transition from *Homo erectus* to *Homo sapiens*

Most paleoanthropologists agree that *H. erectus* evolved into *H. sapiens,* but they disagree about how and where the transition occurred. There is also disagreement about how

Figure 8–1 *Timeline for the Emergence of Modern Humans*[*]

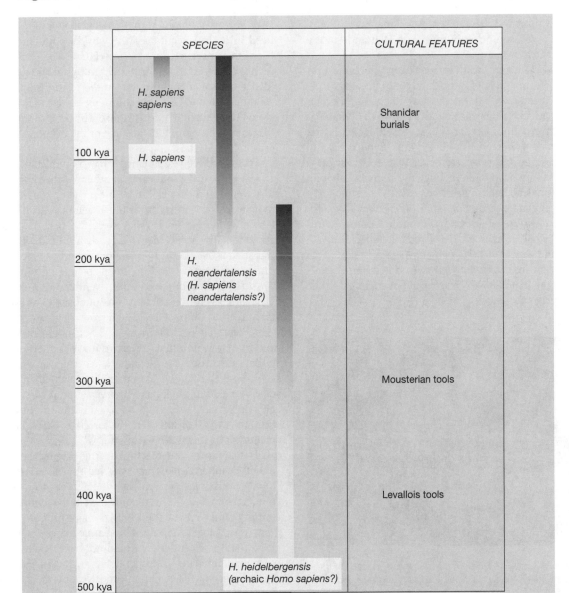

*Alternative classifications are in parentheses.

to classify some fossils from about 500,000 to 200,000 years ago that have a mix of *H. erectus* and *H. sapiens* traits.[2] A particular fossil might be called *H. erectus* by some anthropologists and "archaic" *Homo sapiens* by others. And, as we shall see, still other anthropologists see so much continuity between *H. erectus* and *H. sapiens* that they think it is completely arbitrary to call them different species. According to these anthropologists, *H. erectus* and *H. sapiens* may just be earlier and later varieties of the same species and therefore all should be called *H. sapiens*. (*H. erectus* would then be *H. sapiens erectus*.)

HOMO HEIDELBERGENSIS

In recent years some scholars have suggested that the "transitional" fossils share common traits and may actually represent a separate species—***Homo heidelbergensis,*** named after a jaw found in 1907 in the village of Mauer near Heidelberg, Germany.[3] Other specimens that have been suggested as members of this species have been found in many parts of the world: Bodo, Hopefield, Ndutu, Elandsfontein, and Rabat in Africa; Bilzingsleben, Petralona, Arago, Steinheim, and Swanscombe in Europe; and Dali and Solo in Asia.

Homo heidelbergensis differs from *Homo erectus* in having smaller teeth and jaws, a much larger brain (on the order of 1,300 cc), a skull that lacks a sagittal keel and occipital torus, a brow ridge that divides into separate arches above each eye, and a more robust skeleton (see Figure 8–2). *Homo heidelbergensis* differs from *Homo sapiens* in retaining a large and prognathic face with relatively large teeth and jaws, a brow ridge, a long, low cranial vault with a sloping forehead, and in its more robust skeleton.[4]

Many scholars question whether *Homo heidelbergensis* represents one or several species of Middle Pleistocene hominid, or whether it is indeed a separate species at all. Many would argue that *Homo heidelbergensis* should be considered an archaic *Homo sapiens*. As noted, some scholars also argue that *Homo erectus* should be included in the *Homo sapiens* species.

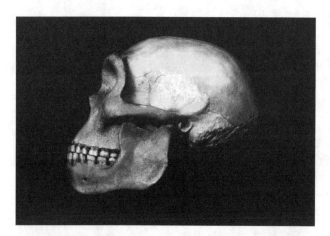

A reconstructed skull of *Homo heidelbergensis*, based on the mandible found at Mauer, Germany. While resembling *Homo erectus*, *Homo heidelbergensis* has smaller teeth and jaws and a larger brain.

NEANDERTALS: *HOMO SAPIENS* OR *HOMO NEANDERTALENSIS*?

There may be disagreement about how to classify the mixed-trait fossils from 500,000 to 200,000 years ago, but recently an outright battle has emerged about many of the fossils that are less than 200,000 years old. Some anthro-

CD-ROM Activity III-c

pologists argue that they were definitely *Homo sapiens* and classify them as *Homo sapiens neandertalensis*. Others, that they were part of a distinct species, **Homo neandertalensis,** more commonly referred to as the **Neandertals.** The Neandertals have been a confusing hominid fossil group since the first specimen was found in 1856. Somehow through the years, the Neandertals have become the victims of their cartoon image, which usually misrepresents them as burly and more ape than human. Actually, they might go unnoticed in a cross section of the world's population today. Were they part of our species? For a while the answer seemed to be yes. But recent archaeological and genetic evidence has led many to question the relationship between Neandertals and modern humans, and today the tide seems to be turning against those who would group them together. Let's take a look at some of the history of research on the Neandertals.

In 1856, three years before Darwin's publication of *The Origin of Species,* a skullcap and other fossilized bones were discovered in a cave in the Neander Valley (*tal* is the German word for "valley"), near Düsseldorf, Germany. The fossils in the Neander Valley were the first that scholars could tentatively consider as an early hominid. (The fossils classified as *Homo erectus* were not found until later in the nineteenth century, and the fossils belonging to the genus *Australopithecus* not until the twentieth century.) After Darwin's revolutionary work was published, the Neandertal find aroused considerable controversy. A few evolutionist scholars, such as Thomas Huxley, thought that the Neandertal was not that different from modern humans. Others dismissed the Neandertal as irrelevant to human evolution; they saw it as a pathological freak, a peculiar, disease-ridden individual. However, similar fossils turned up later in Belgium, Yugoslavia, France, and elsewhere in Europe, which meant that the original Neandertal find could not be dismissed as an oddity.[5]

The predominant reaction to the original and subsequent Neandertal-like finds was that the Neandertals were too "brutish" and "primitive" to have been ancestral to modern humans. This view prevailed in the scholarly community until well into the 1950s. A major proponent of this view was Marcellin Boule, who claimed between 1908 and 1913 that the Neandertals would not have been capable of complete bipedalism. Boule, however, misinterpreted the bowed legs and bent spine in the Neandertal skeleton he examined—these were not normal in Neandertals, but were the result of disease in this particular individual. It is

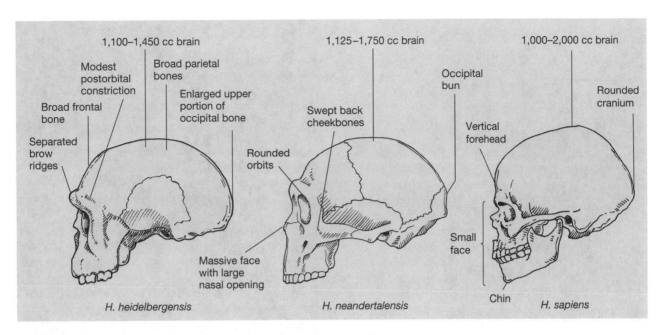

Figure 8–2 *Comparison of the crania of* Homo heidelbergensis, Homo neandertalensis, *and* Homo sapiens, *showing important differences.*

now universally agreed that the skeletal traits of the Neandertals are completely consistent with bipedalism.

Perhaps more important, when the much more ancient australopithecine and *H. erectus* fossils were accepted as hominids in the 1940s and 1950s, anthropologists realized that the Neandertals did not look that different from modern humans—despite their sloping foreheads, large brow ridges, flattened braincases, large jaws, and nearly absent chins (see Figure 8–2).[6] After all, they did have larger brains (averaging more than 1,450 cc) than modern humans (slightly more than 1,300 cc).[7] Some scholars believe that the large brain capacity of Neandertals suggests that they were capable of the full range of behaviors characteristic of modern humans. Their skeletons did, however, attest to one behavioral trait markedly different from behaviors of most modern humans: Neandertals apparently made very strenuous use of their bodies.[8]

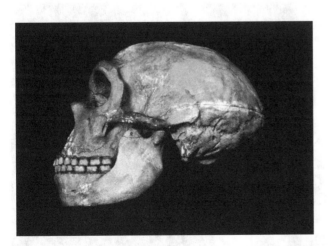

The reconstructed skull of a *Homo neandertalensis* man found at La Chapelle-aux-Saints, France.

It took almost 100 years for scholars to accept the idea that Neandertals were not that different from modern humans and perhaps should be classified as *Homo sapiens neandertalensis.* But in the last few years there has been a growing debate over whether the Neandertals in western Europe were ancestral to modern-looking people who lived later in western Europe, after about 40,000 years ago. Neandertals lived in other places besides western Europe. A large number of fossils from central Europe strongly resemble those from western Europe, although some features, such as a projecting midface, are less pronounced.[9] Neandertals have also been found in southwestern Asia (Israel, Iraq) and Central Asia (Uzbekistan). One of the largest collections of Neandertal fossils comes from Shanidar cave in the mountains of northeastern Iraq, where Ralph Solecki unearthed the skeletons of nine individuals (see site 31 in Figure 8–3).[10]

What has changed scholars' opinions of the Neandertals so that they are now most commonly seen as not belonging to the *Homo sapiens* group?

In 1997, a group of researchers from the United States and Germany published findings that forced a reconsideration of the Neandertals and their relationship to modern humans. These scholars reported that they had been able to extract DNA from the original Neandertal specimen found in 1856.[11] The DNA they extracted was not nuclear DNA—the material that makes up the human genome. Rather, it came from a tiny structure found in all eukaryotic cells (that is, cells with a membrane-bound nucleus and DNA in the chromosomes) called *mitochondria.* Mitochondria produce enzymes needed for energy production, and they have their own DNA, which replicates when a cell replicates but is not thought to be under any pressure from natural selection.[12]

The only source of change in mitochondrial DNA (usually referred to as *mt*DNA) is random mutation.

Boule's reconstruction of Neandertal (left) as displayed at Chicago's Field Museum in 1929, and a more recent reconstruction (right). The recent reconstruction makes Neandertal seem more like modern humans.

Mitochondrial DNA is inherited only from mothers in animals; it is not carried into an egg cell by sperm, but is left with the sperm's tail on the outside of the egg. These unique characteristics make it possible to use mtDNA to measure the degree of relatedness between two species, and even to say how long ago those species diverged.[13] The longer two species have been separated, the more differences there will be in their mtDNA, which is thought to

mutate at a fairly constant rate of about 2 percent per million years. Thus, the number of differences between the mtDNA of two organisms can be converted into an estimated date in the past when those organisms stopped being part of the same breeding population. While controversy remains over many of the details of how and why mtDNA mutates and about its accuracy for determining absolute dates of divergence, most scholars agree that it is a

The Neandertal on the left has bigger brow ridges and a more sloping forehead than the Cro-Magnon on the right. The Neandertal brain was larger on average than the Cro-Magnon brain.

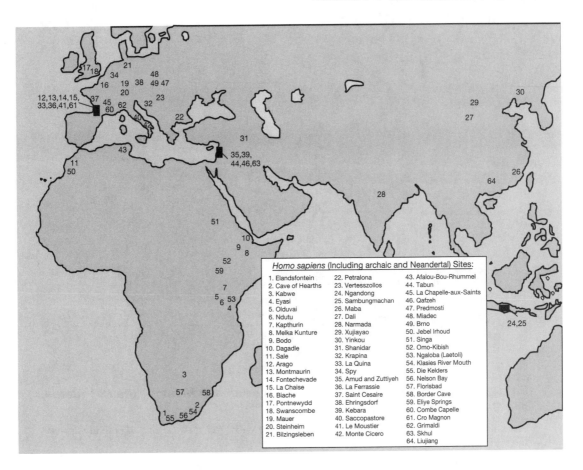

Figure 8–3 Homo sapiens *Sites*

Source: From Russell L. Ciochon and John G. Fleagle, eds., *The Human Evolution Source Book.* Copyright © 1993. Reprinted by permission of Pearson Education, Inc., Upper Saddle River, NJ 07458.

powerful tool for examining relative degrees of relatedness between species.[14]

How similar is Neandertal mtDNA to modern human DNA? Not as similar as many scholars would have expected. Among individual modern humans, there are usually five to ten differences in the sequence of mtDNA examined by the U.S. and German researchers. Between modern humans and the Neandertal specimen, there tend to be about 25 differences—more than three times that among modern humans (see Figure 8–4). This suggested to the researchers that the ancestors of modern humans and the Neandertal must have diverged about 600,000 years ago.[15] If the last common ancestor of ours and the Neandertal lived that long ago, the Neandertal would be a much more distant relative than previously thought. This research has since been replicated with mtDNA from other Neandertal fossils.[16]

Recent archaeological findings from Europe and the Near East may also indicate that Neandertals and the modern human were different species. It has been known for decades that both modern human and Neandertal fossils are found in the same locations in parts of the Levant, but recent improvements in dating technology and newly discovered fossils have even more clearly demonstrated that

the two kinds of hominid coexisted. In fact, several caves in the Mount Carmel region of Israel contain both modern human and Neandertal occupations. The fact that these two groups of hominids co-inhabited the Near East for perhaps as much as 30,000 years and did not interbreed or share much in the way of tool technology strongly suggests that the two are different species.[17] And finds in Europe seem to corroborate that assessment. As early modern humans began moving into Europe they appear to have displaced populations of Neandertals already living there. Sites with tools thought to be associated with Neandertals disappear throughout Europe as sites with tools thought to be associated with modern humans expand their range.[18] Significantly, the area of Europe (Iberia) last colonized by modern humans contains the very latest Neandertal fossils yet found, dating to some 30,000 years ago.[19]

With all this evidence pointing to Neandertals not being part of the modern human species, why is there an ongoing debate? In part this is because none of the evidence is conclusive, and much of it can be interpreted in alternate ways. There is also evidence suggesting that Neandertals were not all that different physically from modern humans (see the box "Neandertal Growth and Development"). Perhaps more important, however, Neandertal culture,

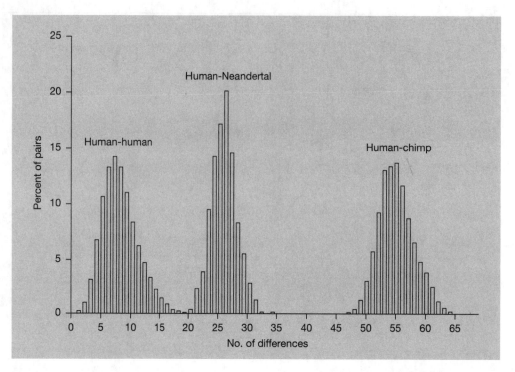

Figure 8–4 *Differences in mtDNA Sequences among Humans, the Neandertal, and Chimpanzees*

The x-axis shows the number of sequence differences; the y-axis shows the percent of individuals that share that number of sequence differences.

Source: Reprinted from *Cell*, 90 (1997): 25 with permission from Elsevier Science.

typically referred to as Middle Paleolithic after the predominant tool technology, has some features that make it seem similar to the culture of early modern humans.

Middle Paleolithic Cultures

The period of cultural history associated with the Neandertals is traditionally called the **Middle Paleolithic** in Europe and the Near East and dates from about 300,000 years to about 40,000 years ago.[20] For Africa, the term *Middle Stone Age* is used instead of Middle Paleolithic. The tool assemblages from this period are generally referred to as Mousterian in Europe and the Near East and as *post-Acheulian* in Africa.

 CD-ROM Activity III-d

TOOL ASSEMBLAGES

THE MOUSTERIAN The Mousterian type of tool complex is named after the tool assemblage found in a rock shelter at Le Moustier in the Dordogne region of southwestern France. Compared with an Acheulian assemblage, a **Mousterian tool assemblage** has a smaller proportion of large core tools such as hand axes and cleavers and a bigger proportion of small flake tools such as scrapers.[21] Although

many flakes struck off from a core were used "as is," the Mousterian is also characterized by flakes that were often altered or "retouched" by striking small flakes or chips from one or more edges (see Figure 8–5).[22] Studies of the wear on scrapers suggest that many were used for scraping hides or working wood. The fact that some of the tools, particularly points, were thinned or shaped on one side suggests that they were hafted or attached to a shaft or handle.[23]

Toward the end of the Acheulian period, a technique developed that enabled the toolmaker to produce flake tools of a predetermined size instead of simply chipping flakes away from the core at random. In this **Levalloisian method,** the toolmaker first shaped the core and prepared a "striking platform" at one end. Flakes of predetermined and standard sizes could then be knocked off. Although some Levallois flakes date as far back as 400,000 years ago, they are found more frequently in Mousterian tool kits.[24]

The tool assemblages in particular sites may be characterized as Mousterian, but one site may have more or fewer scrapers, points, and so forth, than another site. A number of archaeologists have suggested possible reasons for this variation. For example, Sally Binford and Lewis Binford suggested that different activities may have occurred in different sites. Some sites may have been used for butchering and other sites may have been base camps; hence the kinds of tools found in different sites should vary.[25] And Paul Fish has suggested that some sites may have more tools

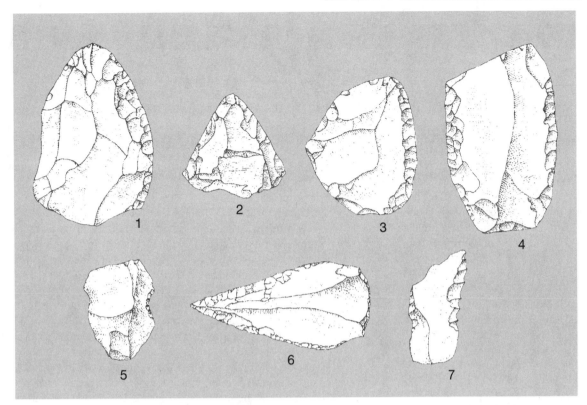

Figure 8–5 *A Typical Mousterian Tool Kit*

A Mousterian tool kit emphasized sidescrapers (1–4), notches (5), points (6), and saw-toothed denticulates (7). How these stone artifacts were actually used is not known, but the points may have been joined to wood shafts, and denticulates could have been used to work wood. The tools illustrated here are from Mousterian sites in western Europe.

Source: From Richard G. Klein, "Ice-Age Hunters of the Ukraine." Reprinted with permission of Nelson H. Prentiss.

produced by the Levalloisian technique because larger pieces of flint were available.[26]

THE POST-ACHEULIAN IN AFRICA   Like Mousterian tools, many of the post-Acheulian tools in Africa during the Middle Stone Age were struck off prepared cores in the Levalloisian way. The assemblages consist mostly of various types of flake tools. A well-described sequence of such tools comes from the area around the mouth of the Klasies River on the southern coast of South Africa. This area contains rock shelters and small caves in which early and later *Homo sapiens* lived. The oldest cultural remains in one of the caves may date back 120,000 years.[27] These earliest tools include parallel-sided flake blades (probably used as knives), pointed flakes (possibly spearpoints), burins or gravers (chisel-like tools), and scrapers. Similar tools discovered at Border cave, South Africa, may have been used almost 200,000 years ago.[28]

HOMESITES

Most of the excavated Middle Paleolithic homesites in Europe and the Near East are located in caves and rock shelters. The same is true for the excavated Middle Stone Age homesites in sub-Saharan Africa. We might conclude, therefore, that Neandertals (as well as many early modern humans) lived mostly in caves or rock shelters. But that

conclusion could be incorrect. Caves and rock shelters may be overrepresented in the archaeological record because they are more likely to be found than are sites that originally were in the open but now are hidden by thousands of years, and many feet, of sediment. Sediment is the dust, debris, and decay that accumulate over time; when we dust the furniture and vacuum the floor, we are removing sediment.

Still, we know that many Neandertals lived at least part of the year in caves. This was true, for example, along the Dordogne River in France. The river gouged deep valleys in the limestone of that area. Below the cliffs are rock shelters with overhanging roofs and deep caves, many of which were occupied during the Middle Paleolithic. Even if the inhabitants did not stay all year, the sites do seem to have been occupied year after year.[29] Although there is evidence of some use of fire in earlier cultures, Middle Paleolithic humans seem to have relied more on fire. There are thick layers of ash in many rock shelters and caves and evidence that hearths were used to increase the efficiency of the fires.[30]

Quite a few Neandertal homesites were in the open. In Africa, open-air sites were located on floodplains, at the edges of lakes, and near springs.[31] Many open-air sites have been found in Europe, particularly eastern Europe. The occupants of the well-known site at Moldova in western Rus-

CURRENT RESEARCH AND ISSUES
Neandertal Growth and Development

One of the reasons many scholars think the Neandertals did not belong to the *Homo sapiens* species is that their material culture was less sophisticated than that of early modern humans who lived at the same time. Since much of contemporary human behavior is dependent on learning that takes place during our long period of infant dependency, could it be that Neandertals matured more rapidly than modern humans and thus had a shorter period of time in which to learn cultural behaviors?

Paleoanthropologist Nancy Minugh-Purvis decided to test this idea by examining growth and development of the skull and face in Neandertals. Minugh-Purvis's study of Neandertal growth and development was feasible largely because Neandertals may have buried their dead. Juvenile and infant skeletons are rare in the archaeological record and often do not preserve well. In juveniles and infants, many of the bones are still growing and thus are relatively delicate. They are also smaller than adult bones, and a wider variety of scavengers can consume them. But because Neandertals may have buried their dead, a number of well-preserved juvenile and infant skeletons are available for study. Indeed, Minugh-Purvis was able to locate more than 100 Neandertal skeletons, ranging in age from newborn to young adult.

To chart the way the skull and face of Neandertals grew from infancy to adulthood, Minugh-Purvis measured the available fossils on a set of standard anthropometric indices—indices that are widely used in physical anthropology to compare the size and shape of bones. She found that newborn Neandertals and modern humans do not differ very much, but that Neandertal infants tend to have thicker cranial bones than modern humans and perhaps heavier musculature. Many of the more striking features of adult Neandertals—a large face with a protruding nose, brow ridges, and a long skull—are not present in infants. These typical Neandertal characteristics begin to appear in children. For example, a 4-year-old Neandertal from the site of Engis, Belgium, already has brow ridges. A 7-year-old from the site of La Quinta in France not only has brow ridges but also a large, protruding nose and face and a long skull. Finally, a 10-year-old from the site of Teshik-Tash in Uzbekistan has all of the typical Neandertal features, and is basically identical to an adult Neandertal except in size.

In short, Neandertals are born similar to modern humans, but by the age of about 10 have developed all of the striking physical features that differentiate Neandertals from modern humans. What does this tell us about Neandertal growth and development? Minugh-Purvis suggests that it was much like our own. Indeed, she argues that many of the physical differences between the Neandertal face and skull and those of modern humans might not be due to genetic differences but rather to behavioral ones. Neandertal teeth show wear patterns that suggest they were used as tools, particularly to hold objects while working on them with the hands. The teeth and jaws were apparently placed under tremendous stress from these uses. Minugh-Purvis suggests that the prognathic face and heavy musculature may be a result of the teeth and jaws being used as tools from a young age, rather than from developmental differences between modern humans and Neandertals.

However, there are other differences between Neandertals and modern humans that cannot be explained by behavior. The overall picture that appears from Minugh-Purvis's study is that Neandertals did indeed mature slightly faster than modern humans. But was their maturation fast enough to account for the lack of cultural elaboration among the Neandertals? Did Neandertals grow so fast they had no time to learn? Minugh-Purvis suggests the differences are not that significant, and that other factors must be sought to explain the differences in cultural elaboration between Neandertals and modern humans.

Sources: Nancy Minugh-Purvis, "Neandertal Growth: Examining Developmental Adaptations in Earlier *Homo sapiens*," in Peter N. Peregrine, Carol R. Ember, and Melvin Ember, eds., *Physical Anthropology: Original Readings in Method and Practice* (Upper Saddle River, NJ: Prentice Hall, 2002), also in Carol R. Ember and Melvin Ember, eds., *New Directions in Anthropology* (Upper Saddle River, NJ: Prentice Hall, CD-ROM, 2003); Erik Trinkaus, "The Neandertal Face: Evolutionary and Functional Perspectives on a Recent Hominid Face," *Journal of Human Evolution*, 16 (1987): 429–43; Christopher Stringer and Clive Gamble, *In Search of the Neanderthals* (New York: Thames and Hudson, 1993).

sia lived in river-valley houses framed with wood and covered with animal skins. Bones of mammoths, huge elephants now extinct, surround the remains of hearths and were apparently used to help hold the animal skins in place. Even though the winter climate near the edge of the glacier nearby was cold at that time, there still would have been animals to hunt because the plant food for the game was not buried under deep snow.

The hunters probably moved away in the summer to higher land between the river valleys. In all likelihood, the higher ground was grazing land for the large herds of animals the Moldova hunters depended on for meat. In the winter river-valley sites, archaeologists have found skeletons of wolf, arctic fox, and hare with their paws missing. These animals probably were skinned for pelts that were made into clothing.[32]

GETTING FOOD

How Neandertals and early modern humans got their food probably varied with their environment. In Africa, they lived in savanna and semiarid desert. In western and eastern Europe, they had to adapt to cold; during periods of increased glaciation, much of the environment was steppe grassland and tundra.

The European environment during this time was much richer in animal resources than the tundra of northern countries is today. Indeed, the European environment inhabited by Neandertals abounded in game, both big and small. The tundra and alpine animals included reindeer, bison, wild oxen, horses, mammoths, rhinoceroses, and deer, as well as bears, wolves, and foxes.[33] Some European sites have also yielded bird and fish remains. For example, people in a summer camp in northern Germany apparently hunted swans and ducks and fished for perch and pike.[34] Little, however, is known about the particular plant foods the European Neandertals may have consumed; the remains of plants are unlikely to survive thousands of years in a nonarid environment.

In Africa, too, early *Homo sapiens* varied in how they got food. For example, we know that the people living at the mouth of the Klasies River in South Africa ate shellfish as well as meat from small grazers such as antelopes and large grazers such as eland and buffalo.[35] But archaeologists disagree about how the Klasies River people got their meat when they began to occupy the caves in the area.

Richard Klein thinks they hunted both large and small game. Klein speculates that because the remains of eland of all ages have been found in Cave 1 at the Klasies River site, the people there probably hunted the eland by driving them into corrals or other traps, where animals of all ages could be killed. Klein thinks that buffalo were hunted differently. Buffalo tend to charge attackers, which would make it difficult to drive them into traps. Klein believes that, because bones from mostly very young and very old buffalo are found in the cave, the hunters were able to stalk and kill only the most vulnerable animals.[36]

Lewis Binford thinks the Klasies River people hunted only small grazers and scavenged the eland and buffalo meat from the kills of large carnivores. He argues that sites should contain all or almost all of the bones from animals that were hunted. According to Binford, since more or less complete skeletons are found only from small animals, the Klasies River people were not, at first, hunting all the animals they used for food.[37]

But new evidence suggests that people were hunting big game as much as 400,000 years ago. Wooden spears that old were recently found in Germany in association with stone tools and the butchered remains of more than ten wild horses. The heavy spears resemble modern aerodynamic javelins, which suggests they would have been thrown at large animals such as horses, not at small animals. This new evidence strongly suggests that hunting, not just scavenging, may be older than archaeologists once thought.[38]

FUNERAL AND OTHER RITUALS?

Some Neandertals appear to have been deliberately buried. At Le Moustier, the skeleton of a boy 15 or 16 years old was found with a beautifully fashioned stone axe near his hand. At La Ferrassie, five children and two adults were apparently interred together in a family plot. These finds, along with several at Shanidar cave in Iraq, have aroused speculation about the possibility of funeral rituals.

The most important evidence at Shanidar consists of pollen around and on top of a man's body. Pollen analysis suggests that the flowers included ancestral forms of modern grape hyacinths, bachelor's buttons, hollyhocks, and yellow flowering groundsels. John Pfeiffer speculated about this find:

> A man with a badly crushed skull was buried deep in the cave with special ceremony. One spring day about 60,000 years ago members of his family went

As this reconstruction illustrates, Neandertals may have been the first humans to purposely bury their dead.

out into the hills, picked masses of wild flowers, and made a bed of them on the ground, a resting place for the deceased. Other flowers were probably laid on top of his grave; still others seem to have been woven together with the branches of a pinelike shrub to form a wreath.[39]

Can we be sure? Not really. All we really know is that there was pollen near and on top of the body. It could have gotten there because humans put flowers in the grave, or it could have gotten there for other, even accidental, reasons. Some scholars have argued that other Shanidar burials are actually the remains of people who were trapped under rockfalls within the cave and killed—they were not deliberately buried at all, but rather buried accidentally.[40]

Neandertals may have taken part in other rituals as well, but, like funeral rituals, the evidence is ambiguous. At Drachenloch cave in the Swiss Alps, for example, a stone-lined pit holding the stacked skulls of seven cave bears was found in association with a Neandertal habitation. Why preserve these skulls? One reason might be for rituals intended to placate or control bears. Cave bears were enormous—some nearly nine feet tall—and competed with Neandertals for prime cave living sites. Perhaps the Neandertals preserved the skulls of bears they killed in the cave as a way of honoring or appeasing either the bears or their spirits. But, as with funeral rituals, the evidence is not completely persuasive. In our own society some may hang a deer or moose head on the wall without any associated ritual. At this point we cannot say for certain whether or not Neandertals engaged in ritual behavior.[41]

◆ The Emergence of Modern Humans

Cro-Magnon humans, who appear in western Europe about 35,000 years ago, were once thought to be the earliest specimens of modern humans, or *Homo sapiens sapiens.* (The Cro-Magnons are named after the rock shelter in France where they were first found, in 1868.[42]) But we now know that modern-looking humans appeared earlier outside of Europe. As of now, the oldest unambiguous fossils classified as *H. sapiens* come from Africa. Some of these fossils, discovered in one of the Klasies River mouth caves, are possibly as old as 100,000 years.[43] Other *Homo sapiens* fossils of about the same age have been found in Border cave in South Africa, and a find at Omo in Ethiopia may be an early *H. sapiens.*[44] Remains of anatomically modern humans (*Homo sapiens sapiens*) found at two sites in Israel, at Skhul and Qafzeh, which used to be thought to date back 40,000 to 50,000 years, may be 90,000 years old.[45] There are also anatomically modern human finds in Borneo, at Niah, from about 40,000 years ago and in Australia, at Lake Mungo, from about 30,000 years ago.[46]

These modern-looking humans differed from the Neandertals and other early *H. sapiens* in that they had higher, more bulging foreheads, thinner and lighter bones, smaller faces and jaws, chins (the bony protuberances that remain after projecting faces recede), and only slight brow ridges (or no ridges at all; see Figure 8–2).

THEORIES ABOUT THE ORIGINS OF MODERN HUMANS

Two theories about the origins of modern humans continue to be debated among anthropologists. One, which can be called the *single-origin theory,* suggests that modern humans emerged in just one part of the Old World and then spread to other parts, replacing Neandertals. (Africa is generally thought to be the place of modern humans' origin.) The second theory, which has been called the multiregional theory, suggests that modern humans evolved in various parts of the Old World after *Homo erectus* spread out of Africa.[47]

SINGLE-ORIGIN THEORY According to the single-origin theory, the Neandertals did not evolve into modern humans. Rather, Neandertals became extinct after 35,000 years ago because they were replaced by modern humans. The presumed place of origin of the first modern humans has varied over the years as new fossils have been discovered. In the 1950s, the source population was presumed to be Neandertals in the Near East, who were referred to as "generalized" or "progressive" Neandertals. Later, when earlier *Homo sapiens* were found in Africa, paleoanthropologists postulated that modern humans emerged first in Africa and then moved to the Near East and from there to Europe and Asia. Single-origin theorists think that the originally small population of *H. sapiens sapiens* had some biological or cultural advantage, or both, that allowed them to spread and replace Neandertals.

The main evidence for the single-origin theory comes from the mtDNA of living peoples. In 1987, Rebecca Cann and her colleagues presented evidence that the mtDNA from people in the United States, New Guinea, Africa, and East Asia showed differences suggesting that their common ancestor lived only 200,000 years ago. Cann and colleagues further claimed that, since the amount of variation among individuals was greatest in African populations, the common ancestor of all lived in Africa.[48] (It is generally the case that people living in a homeland exhibit more variation than any emigrant descendant population.) Thus was born what the media called the "mitochondrial Eve" and the "Eve hypothesis" for the origins of modern humans. Of course, there wasn't just one "Eve"; there must have been more than one of her generation with similar mtDNA.

There were many problems with early mtDNA studies, but over the years those problems have been addressed and new and better mtDNA analyses have been performed. Most scholars now agree that the mtDNA of modern humans shows a remarkably small degree of variation (in fact less than half the variation found in most chimpanzee populations), which strongly suggests that we all share a very recent, common ancestry.[49] More detailed analyses of mtDNA diversity in modern humans have allowed scholars to identify the ancestral roots of contemporary populations around the world, and these analyses also point to modern human origins in East Africa and a subsequent spread out of that region.[50]

Evidence for an East African origin of modern humans and the subsequent expansion also comes from research on variation in the Y chromosome. The Y chromosome is the chromosome that determines whether a person is male. A female inherits an X chromosome from both her mother and father, while a male inherits an X chromosome from his mother and a Y chromosome from his father. Only men have a Y chromosome, and since there is only one copy in any given man, the Y chromosome is the only nuclear chromosome that, like mtDNA, does not undergo recombination. While the Y chromosome can be affected by selection, it is thought that most variation in the Y chromosome, like variation in mtDNA, is caused by random mutations. Variation in the Y chromosome can therefore be analyzed in much the same way as variation in mtDNA.[51]

The results of research on variation in the Y chromosome mirror those on variation in mtDNA to a remarkable extent. Analysis of Y chromosome variation points to Africa as the source of modern humans, and suggests an exodus from Africa of modern humans. One of the major differences between mtDNA studies and those employing the Y chromosome is in the dating of the most recent common ancestor. As noted above, studies of mtDNA suggest the most recent common ancestor lived about 200,000 years ago, while studies of the Y chromosome suggest the most recent ancestor lived only about 100,000 years ago.[52] Additional research, including new research on variation in nuclear DNA, may help to resolve these differences. For now, however, it seems clear that the modern human gene pool has a single, and fairly recent, origin in Africa.[53]

The mtDNA analyses of Neandertals, and the archaeological evidence suggesting that Neandertals and modern humans lived without apparent interaction in Europe and the Near East, also tend to support the single-origin theory. However, the lack of unambiguous *Homo sapiens* skeletal material from Africa in the 150,000–200,000-year-ago time range makes it impossible as yet to support the single-origin theory through the fossil record. Even if we had such evidence, it would not necessarily question the validity of the multiregional theory of human origins.

MULTIREGIONAL THEORY According to the multiregional theory, *Homo erectus* populations in various parts of the Old World gradually evolved into anatomically modern-looking humans. The theorists espousing this view believe that the "transitional" or "archaic" *H. sapiens* and the Neandertals represent phases in the gradual development of more "modern" anatomical features. Indeed, as we have noted, some of these theorists see so much continuity between *Homo erectus* and modern humans that they classify *Homo erectus* as *Homo sapiens erectus*.

Continuity is the main evidence used by the multiregional theorists to support their position. In several parts of the world there seem to be clear continuities in distinct skeletal features between *Homo erectus* and *Homo sapiens*. For example, *Homo erectus* fossils from China tend to have broader faces with more horizontal cheekbones than specimens from elsewhere in the world, traits that also appear in modern Chinese populations.[54] Southeast Asia provides more compelling evidence, according to multiregional theorists. There, a number of traits—relatively thick cranial bones, a receding forehead, an unbroken brow ridge, facial prognathism, relatively large cheekbones, and relatively large molars—appear to persist from *Homo erectus* through modern populations (see Figure 8–6).[55] But others suggest that these traits cannot be used to establish a unique continuation from *Homo erectus* in Southeast Asia because these traits are found in modern humans all over the world. And still others argue that the traits are not as similar as the multiregional theorists claim.[56]

In support of their position, multiregional theorists argue that the mtDNA and Y chromosome evidence supports multiregional evolution rather than a single-origin of modern humans, that genetic variation in modern humans may reflect the emigration of *Homo erectus* out of Africa rather than the emigration of *Homo sapiens sapiens*. This

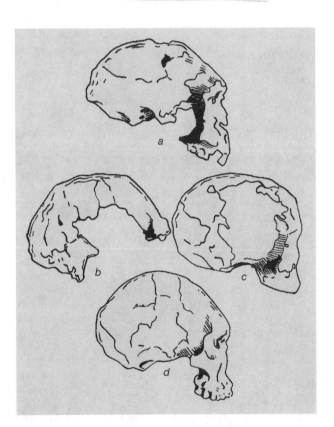

Figure 8–6 *Fossil Evidence for Regional Continuity*

Continuity in southeast Asian and Australian populations: Skulls of (a) Homo erectus, *(b) early* Homo sapiens, *and (d) modern* Homo sapiens, *all from southeast Asia and Australia, have similar foreheads, brow ridges, and occipital and facial shapes, while skulls from Africa, represented here by (c), an early* Homo sapiens, *have different forms. The similarity in southeast Asian and Australian populations over more than 500,000 years argues for regional continuity rather than replacement.*

interpretation would mean that the accepted rates of mutation in both mtDNA and the Y chromosome are wrong, that both actually mutate much more slowly than currently thought.[57] However, this interpretation is contradicted by established correlations between differences in mtDNA among human groups known to have colonized New Guinea and Australia at particular points in time, which seem to fit the accepted rate of mutation, and with the divergence between humans and apes, the date of which also seems to accord with the accepted faster rate of mtDNA mutation.

To explain why human evolution would proceed gradually and in the same direction in various parts of the Old World, multiregional theorists point to cultural improvements in cutting-tool and cooking technology that occurred all over the Old World. These cultural improvements may have relaxed the prior natural selection for heavy bones and musculature in the skull. The argument is that unless many plant and animal foods were cut into small pieces and thoroughly cooked in hearths or pits that were efficient thermally, they would be hard to chew and digest. Thus people would have needed robust jaws and thick skull bones to support the large muscles that enabled them to cut and chew their food. But robust bone and muscle would no longer be needed after people began to cut and cook more effectively.[58]

INTERMEDIATE THEORIES The single-origin and multiregional theories are not the only possible interpretations of the available fossil record. There is also the intermediate interpretation that there may have been some replacement of one population by another, some local continuous evolution, and some interbreeding between early modern humans, who spread out of Africa, and populations encountered in North Africa, Europe, and Asia.[59] As the biologist Alan Templeton has noted, the debates over a single-origin versus multiregional evolution "are based on the myth that replacement of one physical feature in a fossil series with another feature can only be created by one population replacing another (by exterminating them, for example), but such fossil patterns could be a reflection of one genotype replacing another through gene flow and natural selection. Morphological replacement should not be equated with population replacement when one is dealing with populations that can interbreed."[60]

What Happened to the Neandertals?

Regardless of which theory (single-origin, multiregional, or intermediate) is correct, it seems clear that Neandertals and modern humans (*H. sapiens sapiens*) coexisted in Eu-

ANTHROPOLOGICAL ORIGINALS
Testing Theories and Hypotheses about Modern Human Origins

Why is the study of human evolution so contentious? Partly it's because the evidence is fragmentary, but David Frayer suggests that a large part of the answer is that researchers do not specify clear hypotheses so that we can compare alternative theories.

The study of human evolution has always had a reputation for being a contentious subject. There is a long history of debates about the general course of human evolution, the details of the evolutionary process, the authenticity of the fossils, the reliability of their dates, and even the relevance of the fossils themselves for answering evolutionary questions. In some respects, paleoanthropology is no more acrimonious than re-

search on crickets or about black holes, but the academic battles in paleoanthropology are more often reported in the popular literature, making it seem like there is constant bickering about ideas and theories. In another respect, the "bone wars," as one journalist called them, often persist because there is incomplete information due to a spotty and fragmentary fossil record. Even if paleoanthropologists wanted to reach an agreement on some issues, the incompleteness of the fossil record often allows it to be read in multiple ways and these inevitably lead to controversy. Still another source of troubles is the inability to frame hypotheses in ways that allow unambiguous testing and refutation. This is

important since the primary mechanism for resolving scientific disagreements is through rejecting hypotheses on the basis of available data.

CD-ROM Anthropological Originals 8

Source: David W. Frayer, "Testing Theories and Hypotheses about Modern Human Origins," in Peter N. Peregrine, Carol R. Ember, and Melvin Ember, eds., *Physical Anthropology: Original Readings in Method and Practice* (Upper Saddle River, NJ: Prentice Hall, 2002), pp. 174-189; also in Carol R. Ember and Melvin Ember, eds., *New Directions in Anthropology* (Upper Saddle River, NJ: Prentice Hall, CD-ROM, 2003).

rope and the Near East for at least 20,000 years, and maybe as long as 60,000 years. What happened to the Neandertals? Three answers have generally been considered. First, they interbred with modern humans and the unique Neandertal characteristics slowly disappeared from the interbreeding population. Second, they were killed off by modern humans. Third, they were driven to extinction due to competition with modern humans. Let's take a look at each of these scenarios.

INTERBREEDING The interbreeding scenario seems the most probable, yet evidence supporting it is weak. If modern humans and Neandertals interbred, we should be able to find "hybrid" individuals in the fossil record. In fact, a group of scholars has argued that an Upper Paleolithic skeleton from Portugal demonstrates a combination of modern human and Neandertal features.[61] The finding remains controversial, however, because it is a child's skeleton (approximately 4 years old) and its Neandertal-like features have not been corroborated by other scholars. More significantly, if the interbreeding hypothesis is correct, then the mtDNA analysis we have discussed several times in this chapter must be wrong. On the other hand, recent research on Neandertal tools suggests that some Neandertal groups adopted new techniques of tool manufacture that are thought to be uniquely associated with modern humans[62] (we discuss these in more detail in the next chapter). If Neandertals were learning from modern humans, then the idea that they could have interbred and perhaps been absorbed within the modern human population gains credibility.

GENOCIDE The genocide scenario, that modern humans killed off Neandertals, has appeal as a sensational story, but little evidence. Not a single "murdered" Neandertal has ever been found, and one might wonder, in a fight between the powerful Neandertals and the more gracile modern humans, who might get the better of whom.

EXTINCTION Finally, the extinction scenario, that Neandertals simply could not compete with modern humans, seems to have the best archaeological support. As we discussed earlier, there appear to be "refugee" populations of Neandertals in Iberia as recently as perhaps 30,000 years ago. The "retreat" of Neandertals from the Near East, eastern Europe, and finally western Europe following the movement of modern humans into the region seems to support the "refugee" interpretation.[63] More importantly, physical anthropologist Erik Trinkaus has argued, based on both physical characteristics of the Neandertal skeleton and their apparent patterns of behavior, that Neandertals were less efficient hunters and gatherers than modern humans.[64] If this is true, a modern human group would have been able to live and reproduce more easily than a Neandertal group in the same territory, and this would likely drive the Neandertals away. When there were no new territories to run to, the Neandertals would go extinct—precisely what the archaeological record seems to suggest.[65]

But were modern humans and their cultures really that much more efficient than Middle Paleolithic cultures? As we will see in the next chapter, the Upper Paleolithic does seem to mark a watershed in the evolution of human culture, allowing humans to expand their physical horizons throughout the world and their intellectual horizons into the realms of art and ritual.

 CD-ROM Flashcards Chapter 8

 ## Summary

1. Most anthropologists agree that *Homo erectus* began to evolve into *Homo sapiens* after about 500,000 years ago. But there is disagreement about how and where the transition occurred. The mixed traits of the transitional fossils include large cranial capacities (well within the range of modern humans), together with low foreheads and large brow ridges, which are characteristic of *H. erectus* specimens. The earliest definite *H. sapiens,* who did not look completely like modern humans, appeared about 100,000 years ago.

2. *Homo sapiens* have been found in many parts of the Old World—in Africa and Asia as well as in Europe. Some of these *H. sapiens* may have lived earlier than the Neandertals of Europe. There is still debate over whether the Neandertals in western Europe became extinct or survived and were ancestral to the modern-looking people who lived in western Europe after about 40,000 years ago.

3. The period of cultural history associated with the Neandertals is traditionally called the Middle Paleolithic in Europe and the Near East and dates from about 300,000 to about 40,000 years ago. For Africa, the term Middle Stone Age is used. The assemblages of flake tools from this period are generally referred to as Mousterian in Europe and the Near East and as post-Acheulian in Africa. Compared with an Acheulian assemblage, a Mousterian tool assemblage has a smaller proportion of large hand axes and cleavers and a larger proportion of small flake tools such as scrapers. Some Mousterian sites show signs of intentional burial.

4. Fossil remains of fully modern-looking humans, *Homo sapiens sapiens,* have been found in Africa, the Near East, Asia, and Australia, as well as in Europe. The oldest of these fossils have been found in South Africa and may be 50,000 to 100,000 years old.

5. Two theories about the origins of modern humans continue to be debated among anthropologists. One, the *single-origin theory,* suggests that modern humans emerged in just one part of the Old World—the Near East and, more recently, Africa have been the postulated places of origin—and spread to other parts of the Old World, superseding Neandertals. The second theory, the *multiregional theory,* suggests that modern

humans emerged in various parts of the Old World, becoming the varieties of humans we see today.

Glossary Terms

Cro-Magnon

Homo heidelbergensis

Homo neandertalensis

Homo sapiens sapiens

Levalloisian method

Middle Paleolithic

Mousterian tool assemblage

Neandertal

Critical Questions

1. If the single-origin or "out-of-Africa" theory were correct, by what mechanisms could *Homo sapiens* have been able to replace *Homo erectus* and *Homo neandertalensis* populations?

2. If modern human traits emerged in *Homo erectus* populations in different areas more or less at the same time, what mechanisms would account for similar traits emerging in different regions?

3. How do Middle Paleolithic cultures differ from Lower Paleolithic cultures?

Internet Exercises

1. Learn about how the face of a Neandertal child was reconstructed by visiting the Computer-Assisted Paleoanthropology site at http://www.ifi.unizh.ch/staff/zolli/CAP/Main.htm.

2. Visit the Smithsonian Institution page on *Homo heidelbergensis* at http://www.mnh.si.edu/anthro/humanorigins/ha/heid.htm.

3. Visit the Neandertals and Modern Humans page at http://www.neanderthal-modern.com. Follow the regional links and compare and contrast several of the regions in terms of the archaeological and fossil material that has been recovered.

4. Visit the Neanderthal Museum (http://www.neanderthal.de/e_thal/fs_2.htm) and explore the

presentation of Neandertals and their culture. Compare the interpretation of the Neandertals with the one presented in this chapter.

Suggested Reading

KLEIN, J., AND TAKAHATA, N. *Where Do We Come From?: The Molecular Evidence for Human Descent.* New York: Springer Verlag, 2002. An easy-to-read introduction to molecular genetics and the ways in which paleoanthropologists use genetic evidence to understand human evolution.

MELLARS, P. *The Neanderthal Legacy: An Archaeological Perspective from Western Europe.* Princeton, NJ: Princeton University Press, 1996. Focuses on the archaeological rather than the fossil record of Neandertals, and includes detailed discussions of Neandertal tool kits and archaeological sites.

PEREGRINE, P. N., EMBER, C. R., AND EMBER, M., EDS. *Physical Anthropology: Original Readings in Method and Practice.* Upper Saddle River, NJ: Prentice Hall, 2002; also in Carol R. Ember and Melvin Ember, eds., *New Directions in Anthropology* Upper Saddle River, NJ: Prentice Hall, CD-ROM, 2003. Especially relevant to this chapter are D. W. Frayer, "Testing Theories and Hypotheses about Modern Human Origins"; A. Kramer, "The Natural History and Evolutionary Fate of *Homo erectus*"; N. Minugh-Purvis, "Neandertal Growth: Examining Developmental Adaptations in Earlier *Homo sapiens*"; and I. Tattersall, "Paleoanthropology and Evolutionary Theory."

STRINGER, C. *In Search of the Neanderthals: Solving the Puzzle of Human Origins.* London: Thames and Hudson, 1993. A comprehensive and detailed account of research on the Neandertals.

TATTERSALL, I. *The Last Neanderthal: The Rise, Success, and Mysterious Extinction of Our Closest Human Relatives.* Boulder, CO: Westview, 1999. An easy to read, up-to-date overview of the Neandertals, with wonderful illustrations.

TRINKAUS, E., AND SHIPMAN, P. *The Neandertals: Changing the Image of Mankind.* New York: Knopf, 1993. An interesting history of research on the Neandertals along with a clear discussion of current interpretations.

WELLS, S. *The Journey of Man: A Genetic Odyssey.* Princeton, NJ: Princeton University Press. An easy-to-follow introduction to molecular genetics.

THE CONCEPT OF CULTURE

13

CHAPTER OUTLINE

We all consider ourselves to be unique individuals with our own set of personal opinions, preferences, habits, and quirks. Indeed, each of us *is* unique; and yet most of us share the feeling that it *is* wrong to eat dogs, the belief that bacteria or viruses cause illness, the habit of sleeping on a bed. We share many such feelings, beliefs, and habits with most of the people who live in our society. We hardly ever think about the ideas and customs we share, but they constitute what anthropologists refer to as "North American culture."

We tend not to think about our culture because it is so much a part of us that we take it for granted. But when we become aware that other peoples have different feelings from ours, different beliefs, and different habits, we begin to think of how we share certain ideas and customs. We would never even think of the possibility of eating dog meat if we were not aware that people in some other societies commonly do so. We would not realize that our belief in germs was cultural if we were not aware that people in some societies think that illness is caused by witchcraft or evil spirits. We could not become aware that it is our custom to sleep on beds if we were not aware that people in many societies sleep on the floor or on the ground. It is only when we compare ourselves with people in other societies that we become aware of cultural differences and similarities. This is, in fact, the way that anthropology as a profession began. When Europeans began to explore and move to faraway places, they were forced to confront the sometimes striking facts of cultural variation.

◆ Defining Features of Culture

In everyday usage, the word *culture* refers to a desirable quality we can acquire by attending a sufficient number of plays and concerts and visiting art museums and galleries. The anthropologist, however, has a different definition, as Ralph Linton explained:

> *Culture* refers to the total way of life of any society, not simply to those parts of this way which the society regards as higher or more desirable. Thus culture, when applied to our own way of life, has nothing to do with playing the piano or reading Browning. For the social scientist such activities are simply elements within the totality of our culture. This totality also includes such mundane activities as washing dishes or driving an automobile, and for the purposes of cultural studies these stand quite on a par with "the finer things of life." It follows that for the social scientist there are no uncultured societies or even individuals. Every society has a culture, no matter how simple this culture may be, and every human being is cultured, in the sense of participating in some culture or other.[1]

Culture, then, refers to innumerable aspects of life. Some anthropologists think of culture as the rules or ideas

behind behavior.[2] Most anthropologists define **culture** as the set of learned behaviors, beliefs, attitudes, values, and ideals that are characteristic of a particular society or population.

CULTURE IS COMMONLY SHARED

If only one person thinks or does a certain thing, that thought or action represents a personal habit, not a pattern of culture. For a thought or action to be considered cultural, it must be commonly shared by some population or group of individuals. Even if some behavior is not commonly practiced, it is cultural if most people think it is appropriate. The idea that marriage should involve only one man and only one woman is cultural in our society. Most North Americans share this idea and act accordingly when they marry. The role of president or prime minister is not widely shared—after all, there is only one such person at a time—but the role is cultural because most inhabitants of a country with such a position agree that it should exist, and its occupant is generally expected to exhibit certain behaviors. We usually share many values, beliefs, and behaviors with our families and friends (although anthropologists are not particularly concerned with this type of cultural group). We commonly share cultural characteristics with segments of our population whose ethnic or regional origins, religious affiliations, and occupations are the same as or similar to our own. We have certain practices, beliefs, and feelings in common with most North Americans, and we share certain characteristics with people beyond our society who have similar interests (such as rules for international sporting events) or similar roots (as do the various English-speaking nations).

When we talk about the commonly shared customs of a society, which constitute the central concern of cultural anthropology, we are referring to *a culture*. When we talk about the commonly shared customs of a group within a society, which are a central concern of sociology, we are referring to a **subculture.** And when we study the commonly shared customs of some group that includes different societies, we are talking about a phenomenon for which we do not have a single word—for example, as when we refer to *Western culture* (the cultural characteristics of societies in or derived from Europe) or the *culture of poverty* (the presumed cultural characteristics of poor people the world over).

We must remember that even when anthropologists refer to something as cultural, there is always individual variation, which means that not everyone in a society shares a particular cultural characteristic of that society. For example, it is cultural in North American society for adults to live apart from their parents. But not all adults in our society do so, nor do all adults wish to do so. The custom of living apart from parents is considered cultural because most adults practice that custom. As Edward Sapir noted in the late 1930s, in every society studied by anthropologists—in the simplest as well as the most complex—individuals do not all think and act the same.[3] As we discuss later, individual variation is the source of new culture.[4]

CULTURE IS LEARNED

Not all things shared generally by a population are cultural. The typical hair color of a population is not cultural, nor is eating. For something to be considered cultural, it must be learned as well as shared. A typical hair color (unless dyed) is not cultural because it is genetically determined. Humans eat because they must; but what and when and how they eat are learned and vary from culture to culture. Most North Americans do not consider dog meat edible, and indeed the idea of eating dogs horrifies us. But in China, as in some other societies, dog meat is considered delicious. In our society, many people consider a baked ham to be a holiday dish. In several societies of the Middle East, however, including those of Egypt and Israel, eating the meat of a pig is forbidden by sacred writings.

To some extent, all animals exhibit learned behaviors, some of which may be shared by most individuals in a population and may therefore be considered cultural. But different animal species vary in the degree to which their shared behaviors are learned or are instinctive. The sociable ants, for instance, despite all their patterned social behavior, do not appear to have much, if any, culture. They divide their labor, construct their nests, form their raiding columns, and carry off their dead—all without having been taught to do so and without imitating the behavior of other ants. In contrast, much of the behavior of humans appears to be culturally patterned.

We are increasingly discovering that our closest biological relatives, the monkeys and the apes, not only learn a

Much of culture is learned by children imitating their parents and other role models.

wide variety of behaviors on their own, they also learn from each other. Some of their learned responses are as basic as those involved in maternal care; others are as frivolous as the taste for candy. Frans de Waal reviewed seven long-term studies of chimpanzees and identified at least 39 behaviors that were clearly learned from others.[5] When shared and socially learned, these behaviors could be described as cultural. For example, as we discuss in more detail in the chapter on communication and language, vervet monkeys learn to use a certain call in the presence of circling eagles, which prey on the monkeys. The call seems to mean "Watch out—there are eagles around!" Its meaning seems to be shared or understood by the group, because they all respond similarly—they look up—when one individual sounds the call.

The proportion of an animal's life span occupied by childhood seems to reflect the degree to which the animal depends on learned behavior for survival. Monkeys and apes have relatively long childhoods compared to other animals. Humans have by far the longest childhood of any animal, reflecting our great dependence on learned behavior. Although humans may acquire much learned behavior by trial and error and imitation, as do monkeys and apes, most human learned behavior is probably acquired with the aid of spoken, symbolic language.

LANGUAGE All people known to anthropologists, regardless of their kind of society, have had a complex system of spoken, symbolic communication, what we call *language.* Language is *symbolic* in that a word or phrase can represent what it stands for, *whether or not that thing is present.*

This symbolic quality of language has tremendous implications for the transmission of culture. It means that a human parent can tell a child that a snake, for example, is dangerous and should be avoided. The parent can then describe the snake in great detail—its length, diameter, color, texture, shape, and means of locomotion. The parent can also predict the kinds of places where the child is likely to encounter snakes and explain how the child can avoid them. Should the child encounter a snake, then, he or she will probably recall the symbolic word for the animal, remember as well the related information, and so avoid danger. If symbolic language did not exist, the parent would have to wait until the child actually saw a snake and then, through example, show the child that such a creature is to be avoided. Without language, we probably could not transmit or receive information so efficiently and rapidly, and thus would not be heir to so rich and varied a culture.

To sum up, we may say that something is cultural if it is a learned behavior, belief, attitude, value, or ideal generally shared by the members of a group. Traditionally, anthropologists have usually been concerned with the cultural characteristics of a **society,** by which they mean a group of people who occupy a particular territory and speak a common language not generally understood by neighboring peoples. By this definition, societies may or may not necessarily correspond to countries or nations. There are many countries, particularly the newer ones, that have within their boundaries different peoples speaking mutually unintelligible languages. By our definition of society, such countries are composed of many different societies and cultures. Also, by our definition of society, some societies may even include more than one country or nation. For example, we would have to say that Canada and the United States form a single society because the two groups generally speak English, live next to each other, and share many common beliefs, values, and practices. That is why we refer to "North American culture" in this chapter. Not everyone would agree that Canada and the United States form a single society; some would prefer to consider the United States and Canada two different societies because they are separate political entities.

Given that a society refers to a group of people who occupy a particular territory and speak a common language not generally understood by neighboring peoples, when an anthropologist speaks about a culture, she or he is usually referring to that set of learned and shared beliefs, values, and behaviors generally characteristic of a particular society.

Attitudes That Hinder the Study of Cultures

Many of the Europeans who first traveled to faraway places were revolted or shocked by customs they observed. Such reactions are not surprising. People commonly feel that their own behaviors and attitudes are the correct ones and that people who do not share those patterns are immoral or inferior. The person who judges other cultures solely in terms of his or her own culture is **ethnocentric**—that is, he or she holds an attitude called **ethnocentrism.** Most North Americans would think that eating dogs or insects is disgusting, but they clearly do not feel the same way about eating beef. Similarly, they would react negatively to child betrothal, lip plugs, or digging up the bones of the dead.

Our own customs and ideas may appear bizarre or barbaric to an observer from another society. Hindus in India, for example, would consider our custom of eating beef both primitive and disgusting. In their culture, the cow is a sacred animal and may not be slaughtered for food. In many societies a baby is almost constantly carried by someone, in someone's lap, or asleep next to others.[6] People in such societies may think it is cruel of us to leave babies alone for long periods of time, often in devices that resemble cages (cribs and playpens). Even our most ordinary customs—the daily rituals we take for granted—might seem thoroughly absurd when viewed from an outside perspective. An observer of our society might justifiably take notes on certain strange behaviors that seem quite ordinary to us, as the following description shows:

> The daily body ritual performed by everyone includes a mouth-rite. Despite the fact that these people are so punctilious about the care of the mouth, this rite involves a practice which strikes the uninitiated stranger as revolting. It was reported to me that

the ritual consists of inserting a small bundle of hog hairs into the mouth, along with certain magical powders, and then moving the bundle in a highly formalized series of gestures. In addition to the private mouth-rite, the people seek out a holy-mouth man once or twice a year. These practitioners have an impressive set of paraphernalia, consisting of a variety of augers, awls, probes, and prods. The use of these objects in the exorcism of the evils of the mouth involves almost unbelievable ritual torture of the client. The holy-mouth man opens the client's mouth and, using the above mentioned tools, enlarges any holes which decay may have created in teeth. Magical materials are put into these holes. If there are no naturally occurring holes in the teeth, large sections of one or more teeth are gouged out so that the supernatural substance can be applied. In the client's view, the purpose of these ministrations is to arrest decay and to draw friends. The extremely sacred and traditional character of the rite is evident in the fact that the natives return to the holy-mouth man year after year, despite the fact that their teeth continue to decay.[7]

We are likely to protest that to understand the behaviors of a particular society—in this case, our own—the observer must try to find out what the people in that society say about why they do things. For example, the observer might find out that periodic visits to the "holy-mouth man" are for medical, not magical, purposes. Indeed, the observer, after some questioning, might discover that the "mouth-rite" has no sacred or religious connotations whatsoever. Ethnocentrism hinders our understanding of the customs of other people and, at the same time, keeps us from understanding our own customs. If we think that everything we do is best, we are not likely to ask why we do what we do or why "they" do what "they" do.

Ethnocentrism is common, but we may not always glorify our own culture. Other ways of life may sometimes seem more appealing. Whenever we are weary of the complexities of civilization, we may long for a way of life that is "closer to nature" or "simpler" than our own. For instance, a young North American whose parent is holding two or three jobs just to provide the family with bare necessities might briefly be attracted to the life-style of the !Kung of the Kalahari Desert in the 1950s. The !Kung shared their food and therefore were often free to engage in leisure activities during the greater part of the day. They obtained all their food by men hunting animals and women gathering wild plants. They had no facilities for refrigeration, so sharing a large freshly killed animal was clearly more sensible than hoarding meat that would soon rot. Moreover, the sharing provided a kind of social security system for the !Kung. If a hunter was unable to catch an animal on a certain day, he could obtain food for himself and his family from someone else in his band. Then, at some later date the game he caught would provide food for the family of another, unsuccessful hunter. This system of sharing also ensured that persons too young or too old to help with the collecting of food would still be fed.

ANTHROPOLOGICAL ORIGINALS
The Nandi of Kenya

Touching is not always sexual: Anthropologists have to learn *not* to judge behavior in another culture in terms of their own culture. Regina Oboler and her husband Leon were at first confused by same-sex touching behavior that they observed in Kenya. But they soon came to understand that touching someone of the same sex, intimate as it may seem to us, is not necessarily sexual. In fact, it may be just the opposite.

Shortly after our arrival in Nairobi, a Kenyan couple from our research institute invited us to dinner. Over drinks, I [Regina] sat with Georgia on one bench, and Leon [her husband] sat with John on the other. "Have another drink," Georgia said brightly as she

draped her arm around my shoulders, stroking my arm, and leaning close across me to fill my glass. On the other side of the table, I noted that John's hand was on Leon's thigh as he inquired about his favorite authors. On the North American continent, we'd be enacting a swingers' seduction scene—but in Kenya, this body language has no such meaning. In fact, the ideas that connect touching and sexuality are almost the opposite of Euro-American norms. A naïve American visitor to Nairobi could easily assume that it's a gay paradise on the basis of numerous same-sex couples strolling the sidewalks hand-in-hand. This would be totally wrong. The Kenyan attitude toward homosexuality is less tolerant than North Americans'.

Holding hands or touching intimately in public is a way of declaring the *absence* of any possibility of a sexual relationship. If people are sexually interested in each other, they will refrain from touching. Husbands and wives are never seen touching in public.

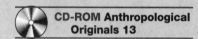

CD-ROM Anthropological Originals 13

Source: Regina Smith Oboler, "Nandi: From Cattle-Keepers to Cash-Crop Farmers," in Melvin Ember and Carol R. Ember, eds., *Portraits of Culture: Ethnographic Originals,* in Carol R. Ember and Melvin Ember, eds., *New Directions in Anthropology* (Upper Saddle River, NJ: Prentice Hall, CD-ROM, 2003).

Could we learn from the !Kung? Perhaps we could in some respects, but we must not glorify their way of life either or think that their way of life might be easily imported into our own society. Other aspects of !Kung life would not appeal to many North Americans. For example, when the nomadic !Kung decided to move their camps, they had to carry all the family possessions, substantial amounts of food and water, and all young children below age 4 or 5. This is a sizable burden to carry for any distance. The !Kung traveled about 1,500 miles in a single year.[8] Thus, for them being nomadic meant that families could not have many possessions. It is unlikely that most North Americans would find the !Kung way of life enviable in all respects.

Both ethnocentrism and its opposite, the glorification of other cultures, hinder effective anthropological study.

Cultural Relativism

In the 1870s, the early days of anthropology, the prevailing view was that culture develops in a uniform and progressive manner; this belief is called **early evolutionism.** For example, Lewis Henry Morgan postulated that the family evolved in six stages. The first was a "horde living in promiscuity"; the highest, or last, stage was the monogamous family. In almost every evolutionary sequence postu-

lated by Morgan and other early evolutionists, the traits of Western cultures were thought to be at the highest, most progressive stage, and many non-Western cultures were thought to represent earlier stages of evolution. Not only were these early ideas based on very poor evidence of the details of ethnography (for example, the custom of marriage turns out to be universal), they were also based on a good deal of ethnocentrism.

One of the leading opponents of evolutionism in the early twentieth century was Franz Boas. He and many of his students—like Ruth Benedict, Melville Herskovits, and Margaret Mead—stressed that the early evolutionists did not sufficiently understand the details of the cultures they theorized about, nor did they understand the context in which these customs appeared. They challenged the attitude that Western cultures were obviously superior.[9]

The anthropological attitude that a society's customs and ideas should be described objectively and understood in the context of that society's problems and opportunities became known as **cultural relativism.** Does cultural relativism mean that the actions of another society, or of our own, should not be judged? Does our insistence on objectivity mean that anthropologists should not make moral judgments about the cultural phenomena they observe and try to explain? Does it mean that anthropologists should not try to bring about change? Not necessarily. While the concept of cultural relativism remains an important

Because we are ethnocentric about many things, it is often difficult to criticize our own customs, some of which might be shocking to a member of another society. The elderly in America often spend their days alone. In contrast, the elderly in Japan often live in a three-generational family.

anthropological tenet, anthropologists differ in their interpretation of the principle of cultural relativism.

Many anthropologists are now uncomfortable with the strong form of cultural relativism advocated by Benedict and Herskovits in the 1930s and 1940s, that morality differs in every society and that all patterns of culture are equally valid. What if the people practice slavery, torture, or genocide? If the strong doctrine of relativism is adhered to, then cultural practices such as these are not to be judged, and we should not try to eliminate them. A weaker form of cultural relativism asserts that anthropologists should strive for objectivity in describing a people, and in their attempts to understand the reasons for cultural behavior they should be wary of superficial or quick judgment. Tolerance should be the basic mode unless there is strong reason to behave otherwise.[10] The weak version of cultural relativity does not preclude anthropologists from making judgments or from trying to change behavior they think is harmful. But judgments need not, and should not, preclude accurate description and explanation in spite of any judgments we might have.

But now that we have defined what is cultural, we must ask a further question: How does an anthropologist go about deciding which particular behaviors, values, and beliefs of individuals are cultural?

 **Describing a Culture**

INDIVIDUAL VARIATION

Describing a particular culture might seem relatively uncomplicated at first. You simply observe what the people in that society do and then record their behavior. But consider the substantial difficulties you might encounter. How would you decide which people to observe? And what would you conclude if each of the first dozen people you observed or talked to behaved quite differently in the same situation? Admittedly, you would be unlikely to encounter such extreme divergence of behaviors. Yet there would tend to be significant individual variation in the actual behaviors observed, even when individuals were responding to the same generalized situation and conforming to cultural expectations.

To understand better how an anthropologist might make sense of diverse behaviors, let us examine the diversity at a professional football game in the United States. When people attend a football game, various members of the crowd behave differently while "The Star-Spangled Banner" is being played. As they stand and listen, some people remove their hats; a child munches popcorn; a

CURRENT RESEARCH AND ISSUES
Human Rights and Cultural Relativity

The news increasingly reports what we consider violations of human rights the world over. Examples range from jailing people for expressing political ideas to ethnic massacre. But faced with criticism from the West, people in other parts of the world are saying that the West should not dictate its ideas about human rights to other countries. Indeed, many countries say they have different codes of ethics. Are we in the Western countries being ethnocentric by taking our own cultural ideas and applying them to the rest of the world? Should we instead employ the strong version of the concept of cultural relativism, considering each culture on its own terms? But if we do that, it may not be possible to have a universal standard of human rights.

What we do know is that all cultures have ethical standards, but they do not always emphasize the same things. So, for example, some cultures emphasize individual political rights; others emphasize political order. Some cultures emphasize protection of individual property; others emphasize the sharing or equitable distribution of resources. People in the United States may have freedom to dissent and the right not to have property taken away, but they can be deprived of health insurance or of food if they lack the money to buy them. Cultures also vary markedly in the degree to which they have equal rights for minorities and women. In some societies women are killed when a husband dies or when they disobey a father or brother.

A strong case against the concept of cultural relativism is made by Elizabeth Zechenter. She points out that cultural relativists claim there are no universal principles of morality, but insist on tolerance for all cultures. If tolerance is one universal principle, why shouldn't there be others? She also suggests that the concept of cultural relativism is often used to justify traditions desired by the dominant and powerful. She points to a case in 1996 in Algeria where two teenage girls were raped and murdered because they violated the fundamentalist edict against attending school. Are those girls any less a part of the culture than the fundamentalists? Would it make any difference if most Algerian women supported the murders? Would that make it right? Zechenter does not believe that international treaties such as the Universal Declaration of Human Rights impose uniformity among diverse cultures. Rather, they seek to create a floor below which no society is supposed to fall.

Can the concept of cultural relativism be reconciled with the concept of an international code of human rights? Probably not completely. Paul Rosenblatt recognizes the dilemma but nonetheless thinks that something has to be done to stop torture and "ethnic cleansing," among other practices. He makes the case that "to the extent that it is easier to persuade people whose viewpoints and values one understands, relativism can be a tool for change . . . a relativist's awareness of the values and understanding of the elite makes it easier to know what arguments would be persuasive. (For example, in a society in which the group rather than the individual has great primacy, it might be persuasive to try to show how respect for individual rights benefits the group.)" What do you think?

Sources: Elizabeth M. Zechenter, "In the Name of Culture: Cultural Relativism and the Abuse of the Individual," *Journal of Anthropological Research*, 53 (1997): 319–47; Paul C. Rosenblatt, "Human Rights Violations across Cultures," in Carol R. Ember, Melvin Ember, and Peter N. Peregrine, eds., *Research Frontiers in Anthropology*, in Carol R. Ember and Melvin Ember, eds., *New Directions in Anthropology* (Upper Saddle River, NJ: Prentice Hall, CD-ROM, 2003). ◎

veteran of the armed forces stands at attention; a teenager searches the crowd for a friend; and the coaches take a final opportunity to intone secret chants and spells designed to sap the strength of the opposing team. Yet, despite these individual variations, most of the people at the game respond in a basically similar manner: Nearly everyone stands silently, facing the flag. Moreover, if you go to several football games, you will observe that many aspects of the event are notably similar. Although the plays will vary from game to game, the rules of the game are never different, and although the colors of the uniforms of the teams are different, the players never appear on the field dressed in swimsuits.

Although the variations in individual reactions to a given stimulus are theoretically limitless, in fact they tend to fall within easily recognizable limits. The child listening to the anthem may continue to eat popcorn but will probably not do a rain dance. Similarly, it is unlikely that the coaches will react to that same stimulus by running onto the field and embracing the singer. Variations in behavior,

In deciding what is cultural behavior, anthropologists look for commonalities, but there is always individual variation. Here, during the playing of the national anthem before the start of a game, most of the crowd, but not all, is facing forward and placing a hand over the heart.

then, are confined within socially acceptable limits, and it is part of the anthropologist's goal to find out what those limits are. She or he may note, for example, that some limitations on behavior have a practical purpose: A spectator who disrupts the game by wandering onto the field would be required to leave. Other limitations are purely traditional. In our society it is considered proper for a man to remove his overcoat if he becomes overheated, but others would undoubtedly frown upon his removing his trousers even if the weather were quite warm. Using such observations, the anthropologist discovers the customs and the ranges of acceptable behavior that characterize the society under study.

By focusing on the range of customary behavior, discovered by observing or asking about individual variation, the anthropologist is able to describe cultural characteristics of a group. For example, an anthropologist interested in describing courtship and marriage in our society would initially encounter a variety of behaviors. The anthropologist may note that one couple prefers to go to a movie on a first date, whereas another couple chooses to go bowling; some couples have very long engagements, and others never become engaged at all; some couples emphasize religious rituals in the marriage ceremony, but others are married by civil authorities; and so on. Despite this variability, the anthropologist, after further observation and interviewing, might begin to detect certain regularities in court-

ing practices. Although couples may do many different things on their first and subsequent dates, they nearly always arrange the dates by themselves; they try to avoid their parents when on dates; they often manage to find themselves alone at the end of a date; they put their lips together frequently; and so forth. After a series of more and more closely spaced encounters, a man and woman may decide to declare themselves publicly as a couple, either by announcing that they are engaged or by revealing that they are living together or intend to do so. Finally, if the two of them decide to marry, they must in some way have their union recorded by the civil authorities.

In our society a person who wishes to marry cannot completely disregard the customary patterns of courtship. If a man saw a woman on the street and decided he wanted to marry her, he could conceivably choose a quicker and more direct form of action than the usual dating procedure. He could get on a horse, ride to the woman's home, snatch her up in his arms, and gallop away with her. In Sicily, until the last few decades such a couple would have been considered legally married, even if the woman had never met the man before or had no intention of marrying. But in our society, any man who acted in such a fashion would be arrested and jailed for kidnapping and would probably have his sanity challenged. Such behavior would not be acceptable in our society. Although individual behaviors may vary, most social behavior falls within culturally acceptable limits.

CULTURAL CONSTRAINTS

The noted French sociologist Emile Durkheim stressed that culture is something *outside* us exerting a strong coercive power on us. We do not always feel the constraints of our culture because we generally conform to the types of conduct and thought it requires. Standards or rules about what is acceptable behavior are referred to by social scientists as **norms.** The importance of a norm usually can be judged by how members of a society respond when the norm is violated.

Cultural constraints are of two basic types, *direct* and *indirect.* Naturally, the direct constraints are the more obvious. For example, if you choose to wear a casual shorts outfit to a wedding, you will probably be subject to some ridicule and a certain amount of social isolation. But if you choose to wear nothing, you may be exposed to a stronger, more direct cultural constraint—arrest for indecent exposure. Although indirect forms of cultural constraint are less obvious than direct ones, they are no less effective. Durkheim illustrated this point when he wrote, "I am not obliged to speak French with my fellow-countrymen, nor to use the legal currency, but I cannot possibly do otherwise. If I tried to escape this necessity, my attempt would fail miserably."[11] In other words, if Durkheim had decided he would rather speak Serbo-Croatian than French, nobody would have tried to stop him. But no one would have understood him either. And although he would not have been put into prison for trying to buy groceries with Icelandic money, he would have had difficulty convincing the local merchants to sell him food. In a series of classic experiments on conformity, Solomon Asch revealed how strong cultural constraints can be. Asch coached the majority of a group of college students to give deliberately incorrect answers to questions involving visual stimuli. A "critical subject," the one student in the room who was not so coached, had no idea that the other participants would purposely misinterpret the evidence presented to them. Asch found that in one-third of the experiments, the critical subjects consistently allowed their own correct perceptions to be distorted by the obviously incorrect statements of the others. And in another 40 percent of the experiments, the critical subject yielded to the opinion of the group some of the time.[12]

The existence of social or cultural constraints, however, is not necessarily incompatible with individuality. Cultural constraints are usually exercised most forcefully around the limits of acceptable behavior. Thus, there is often a broad range of behavior within which individuals can exercise their uniqueness. And individuals do not always give in to the wishes of the majority. In the Asch experiments, many individuals, about one-fourth of the critical subjects, consistently retained their independent opinions in the face of complete disagreement with the majority.

IDEAL VERSUS ACTUAL CULTURAL PATTERNS

Every society has ideas (values and norms) about how people in particular situations ought to feel and behave. In everyday terms we speak of these ideas as *ideals;* in anthropology we refer to them as *ideal cultural patterns.* These patterns tend to be reinforced through cultural constraints. But we all know that people do not always behave according to the standards they express. If they did, there would be no need for direct or indirect constraints. Some of our ideal patterns differ from actual behavior because the ideal is outmoded—that is, it is based on the way society used to be. (Consider the ideal of "free enterprise," that industry should be totally free of governmental regulation.) Other ideal patterns may never have been actual patterns and may represent merely what people would like to see as correct behavior.

To illustrate the difference between ideal and actual culture, consider the idealized belief, long cherished in North America, that everybody is "equal before the law," that everybody should be treated in the same way by the police and courts. Of course, we know that this is not always true. The rich, for example, may receive less jail time and be sent to nicer prisons. Nevertheless, the ideal is still part of our culture; most of us continue to believe that the law should be applied equally to all.

HOW TO DISCOVER CULTURAL PATTERNS

There are two basic ways in which an anthropologist can discover cultural patterns. When dealing with customs that are overt or highly visible within a society—for example,

our custom of sending children to school—the investigator can determine the existence of such practices by direct observation and by interviewing some knowledgeable people. (We'll discuss in the next chapter how the ethnographer could decide who is knowledgeable.) When dealing with a particular sphere of behavior that encompasses many individual variations, or when the people studied are unaware of their pattern of behavior, the anthropologist should collect information from a sample of individuals in order to establish what the cultural pattern is.

One example of a cultural pattern that most people in a society are not aware of is how far apart people stand when they are having a conversation. Yet there is considerable reason to believe that unconscious cultural rules govern such behavior. These rules become obvious when we interact with people who have different rules. We may experience considerable discomfort when another person stands too close (indicating too much intimacy) or too far (indicating unfriendliness). Edward Hall reported that Arabs customarily stand quite close to others, close enough, as we have noted, to be able to smell the other person. In interactions between Arabs and North Americans, then, the Arabs will move closer at the same time that the North Americans back away.[13]

If we wanted to arrive at the cultural rule for conversational distance between casual acquaintances, we could study a sample of individuals from a society and determine the *modal response,* or *mode.* The mode is a statistical term that refers to the most frequently encountered response in a given series of responses. So, for the North American pattern of casual conversational distance, we would plot the actual distance for many observed pairs of people. Some pairs may be 2 feet apart, some 2.5, and some 4 feet apart. If we count the number of times every particular distance is observed, these counts provide what we call a *frequency distribution.* The distance with the highest frequency is the *modal pattern.* Very often the frequency distribution takes the form of a *bell-shaped curve,* as shown in Figure 13–1. There the characteristic being measured is plotted on the

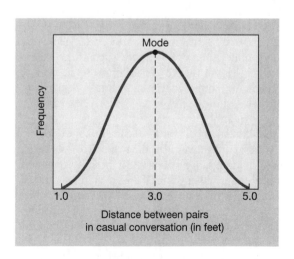

Figure 13–1 *Frequency Distribution Curve*

Distance between people conversing varies cross-culturally. The faces of the Rajput Indian men on the left are much closer than the faces of the American women on the right.

horizontal axis (in this case, the distance between conversational pairs), and the number of times each distance is observed (its frequency) is plotted on the vertical axis. If we were to plot how a sample of North American casual conversational pairs is distributed, we would probably get a bell-shaped curve that peaks at around 3 feet.[14] Is it any wonder, then, that we sometimes speak of keeping others "at arm's length"?

Frequency distributions may be calculated on the basis of behaviors exhibited or responses given by all the members of a particular population. But studying everybody is rarely necessary. Instead, most social scientists rely on a subset, or sample, that is believed to be representative of the larger population. The best way to ensure that a sample is representative is to choose a **random sample**—that is, give all individuals an equal chance of being selected for study. If a sample is random, it probably will include examples of all frequent variations of behavior or response exhibited in the society or community in roughly the proportions in which they actually occur.

Because it is relatively easy to make generalizations about public aspects of a culture, such as the existence of executive, legislative, and judicial branches in the U.S. government, or about widely shared norms or behaviors, which almost anyone can identify correctly, random sampling is often not necessary. But in dealing with aspects of culture that are more private, difficult to put into words, or unconscious, the investigator may have to observe or interview a random sample of people in order to generalize correctly about whether or not there are cultural patterns. The reason is that most people may not be aware of others' private behavior and thoughts, such as sexual attitudes and behavior, nor are they aware of unconscious cultural patterns, such as conversational distance. The fact that something is less readily observed publicly or harder to put into words does not imply that it is less likely to be shared. However, it is harder to discover those aspects of culture.

Although we may be able to discover by interviews and observation that a behavior, thought, or feeling is widely shared within a society, how do we establish that something commonly shared is learned, so that we can call it cultural? Establishing that something is or is not learned may be difficult. Because children are not reared apart from adult caretakers, the behaviors they exhibit as part of their genetic inheritance are not clearly separated from those they learn from others around them. We suspect that particular behaviors and ideas are learned if they vary from society to society. And we suspect purely genetic determinism when particular behaviors or ideas are found in all societies. For example, as we will see in the chapter on language, children the world over seem to acquire language at about the same age, and the structure of their early utterances seems to be similar. These facts suggest that human children are born with an innate grammar. However, although early childhood language seems similar the world over, the particular languages spoken by adults in different societies show considerable variability. This variability suggests that particular languages have to be learned. Similarly, if the courtship patterns of one society differ markedly from those of another, we can be fairly certain that those courtship patterns are learned and therefore cultural.

◆ Some Assumptions about Culture

CULTURE IS GENERALLY ADAPTIVE

There are some cultural behaviors that, if carried to an extreme, would decrease the chances of survival of a particular society. For example, certain tribes in New Guinea view women as essentially unclean and dangerous individuals with whom physical contact should be as limited as possible. Suppose the men in one such tribe decided to avoid contact, including sexual contact, with women completely. Clearly, we would not expect such a society to survive for long. Although this example may appear extreme, it indicates that customs that diminish the survival chances of a society are not likely to persist. Either the people clinging to those customs will become extinct, taking the customs with them, or the customs will be replaced, thereby possibly helping the people to survive. By either process, **maladaptive customs**—those that diminish the chances of survival and reproduction—are likely to disappear. The customs of a society that enhance survival and reproductive success are **adaptive** and are likely to persist. Hence, we assume that if a society has survived long enough to be described in the annals of anthropology (the "ethnographic record"), much, if not most, of its cultural repertoire is adaptive, or was at one time.

When we say that a custom is adaptive, however, we mean it is adaptive only with respect to a specific physical and social environment. What may be adaptive in one environment may not be adaptive in another. Therefore, when we ask why a society may have a particular custom, we really are asking if that custom makes sense as an adaptation to that society's particular environmental conditions.

Many cultural behaviors that would otherwise appear incomprehensible to us may be understandable as a society's response to its environment. For example, we might express surprise at certain societies' postpartum sex taboos that prohibit women from engaging in sexual intercourse until their 2-year-olds are ready to be weaned. But in the tropical areas where such taboos exist, they may represent a people's way of adjusting to their physical environment. If there were no such taboo and a mother had another baby soon, she could no longer continue to nurse the older baby. Without its mother's milk, the older child might succumb to *kwashiorkor,* a severe protein-deficiency disease that is common in those tropical areas. The taboo, then, may serve to give infants a better chance to survive.[15] Thus, the long postpartum sex taboo may be an adaptive custom. In nontropical areas where kwashiorkor is not a problem, the same taboo may not be advantageous.

Just as culture represents an adjustment to the physical environment and to biological demands, it may also represent an adjustment to the social environment, that is, to neighboring peoples. For example, we do not know for sure why the Hopi Indians of what is now the state of Arizona began building their settlements on the tops of mesas. They must have had strong reasons for doing so, because there are many difficulties in building on such sites—the problem of hauling water long distances to the settlements, for instance. It is possible that the Hopi chose to locate their villages on mesa tops for defensive reasons when Athapaskan-speaking groups of Indians (the Navajo and Apache) moved into the Hopi area. In other words, the Hopi may have adjusted their living habits to their social environment.

A given custom represents one society's adaptation to its environment; it does not represent all possible adaptations. Different societies may choose different means of adjusting to the same situation. Thus, among some South American Indian societies where people's diets are low in protein, there is no long postpartum sex taboo, but induced abortion is reported to be a common practice. This practice may serve the same function of spacing out live births and thereby preventing too early weaning of children. The Hopi Indians, when suddenly confronted by the Navajo and Apache, clearly had to take some action to protect themselves. But instead of building their settlements on easily defended mesa tops, they could conceivably have developed a standing army.

Why a society develops a particular response to a problem always requires explanation. The choice may depend largely on whether a particular response is possible, given the existing cultural repertoire. For example, in the Hopi case, a standing army would not have been a likely response to the problem of invaders because the Hopi economy probably could not have supported any large group of full-time specialists such as soldiers. As we shall see in the chapter on food-getting, full-time specialists have to be fed by the regular production of more food than the people involved in food production generally need, and such a level of food production did not exist among the Hopi. The strategy of moving their dwellings to easily defended mesa tops may have been the easiest option.

Although we may assume that societies surviving long enough to be described have had many more adaptive culture traits than maladaptive traits, that does not mean that all culture traits are adaptive. Some, if not many, traits may be neutral in terms of adaptation. That is, they may have no direct relationship to reproductive success. Consider, for example, rules about what to wear at weddings and funerals, how to set the table, and how far to stand from someone. Perhaps someone will uncover survival and reproductive consequences of these shared behaviors, but probably they are neutral in terms of survival. Such neutral traits may once have had adaptive consequences, or they may never have had any.

We must remember that a society is not forced to adapt its culture to changing environmental circumstances. Even in the face of changed circumstances, people may choose not to change their customs. For example, the Tapirapé of central Brazil did not alter their custom of limiting the number of births, even though they suffered severe population losses after contact with Europeans and their diseases. The Tapirapé population fell to fewer than 100 people from over 1,000. Clearly they were on the way to extinction, yet they continued to value small families. Not only did they believe that a woman should have no more than three children, but they took specific steps to achieve this limitation. They practiced infanticide if twins were born, if the third child was of the same sex as the first two children, and if the possible fathers broke certain taboos during pregnancy or in the child's infancy.[16]

Of course, it is also possible that a people will behave maladaptively even if they try to alter their behavior. After all, although people may alter their behavior according to what they perceive will be helpful to them, what they perceive to be helpful may not prove to be adaptive.

CULTURE IS MOSTLY INTEGRATED

When we hear of an unfamiliar cultural pattern, our natural response is to try to imagine how that pattern would work in our own society. We might wonder, for example, what would happen if North American women adopted a long postpartum sex taboo—say, one year of abstinence after the birth of a baby. Such a question is purely whimsical, for the customs of one culture cannot easily be grafted onto another culture. A long postpartum sex taboo presupposes a lack of effective birth-control methods, but our society already has many such methods. Moreover, a long postpartum sex taboo could conceivably affect important aspects of our culture, such as the idea that a happy marriage is a sexy one. The point is that with such a taboo imposed on it, our culture would no longer be the same. Too many aspects of the culture would have to be changed to accommodate the new behavior. This is so because our culture is mostly integrated.

In saying that a culture is mostly *integrated*, we mean that the elements or traits that make up that culture are not just a random assortment of customs but are mostly adjusted to or consistent with one another. One reason anthropologists believe that culture tends to be integrated is that culture is generally adaptive. If certain customs are more adaptive in particular settings, then those "bundles" of traits will generally be found together under similar conditions. For example, the !Kung, as we have mentioned, subsisted by hunting wild animals and gathering wild plants. They were also nomadic, had very small communities, had few material possessions, and shared food within their bands. As we will see, these cultural traits usually occur together when people depend on hunting and gathering for their food.

A culture may also tend to be integrated for psychological reasons. The *traits* of a culture—attitudes, values, ideals, and rules for behavior—are stored, after all, in the brains of individuals. Research in social psychology has suggested that people tend to modify beliefs or behaviors that are not cognitively or conceptually consistent with other information.[17] We do not expect cultures to be completely integrated, just as we do not expect individuals to be completely consistent. But if a tendency toward cognitive consistency is found in humans, we might expect that at least some aspects of a culture would tend to be integrated for that reason.

How this pressure for consistency works is not hard to imagine. Children, for example, seem to be very good at remembering *all* the things their parents say. If they ask for something and the parents say no, they may say, "But you said I could yesterday." This pressure for consistency may even make parents change their minds! Of course, not everything one wants to do is consistent with the rest of one's desires, but there surely is pressure from within and without to make it so.

Humans are also capable of rational decision making; they can usually figure out that certain things are not easy to do because of other things they do. For example, if a society has a long postpartum sex taboo, we might expect that most people in the society could figure out that it would be easier to observe the taboo if husband and wife did not sleep in the same bed. Or if people drive on the left side of the road, as in England, it is easier and less dangerous to drive a car with a steering wheel on the right because that placement allows you to judge more accurately how close you are to cars coming at you from the opposite direction.

Consistency or integration of culture traits may also be produced by less conscious psychological processes. As we discuss in the chapters on psychology and culture, religion and magic, and the arts, people may generalize (transfer) their experiences from one area of life to another. For example, where children are taught that it is wrong to express anger toward family and friends, it turns out that folktales parallel the child rearing; anger and aggression in the folktales tend to be directed only toward strangers, not toward family and friends. It seems as if the expression of anger is too frightening, or maladaptive, to be expressed close to home, even in folktales.

The tendency for a culture to be integrated, then, may be cognitively and emotionally, as well as adaptively, induced.

CULTURE IS ALWAYS CHANGING

When you examine the history of a society, it is obvious that its culture has changed over time. Some of the shared behaviors, beliefs, and values that were common at one time are modified or replaced at another time. In North American society, we only have to consider our attitudes toward sex and marriage to realize that a lot of our culture has changed recently. The impetus for change may come from within the society or from without. From within, the unconscious or conscious pressure for consistency will produce culture change if enough people adjust old behavior and thinking to new. Change can also occur if people try to invent better ways of doing things. Michael Chibnik suggests that people who confront a new problem conduct mental or small "experiments" to decide how to behave. These experiments may give rise to new cultural traits.[18]

A good deal of culture change may be stimulated by changes in the external environment. For example, if people move into an arid area, they will either have to give up farming or develop a system of irrigation. In the modern world, changes in the social environment are probably more frequent stimuli for culture change than changes in the physical environment. Many North Americans, for example, started to think seriously about conserving energy and about using sources of energy other than oil only after oil supplies from the Middle East were curtailed in 1973 and 1974. Different societies have often affected each other, and a significant amount of the radical and rapid culture change that has occurred in the last few hundred years has been due to the colonial expansion of Western societies into other areas of the world. Native Americans, for instance, were forced to alter their life-styles drastically when they were driven off their lands and confined to reserva-

APPLIED ANTHROPOLOGY
Why the Bedouin Do Not Readily Settle Down

Most countries of the world today want to "develop." They want to increase their crop yields and their exports, build major roads and irrigation projects, and industrialize. Anthropologists interested in development have pointed out that many development schemes have failed in part because they do not adequately consider the culture of the people whose lives they affect. Thus, the international agencies that lend money have increasingly turned for advice to anthropologists to help plan and evaluate development projects.

Governments often view traditional ways of life negatively and fail to recognize that the old ways of life may be adaptive. Because culture is integrated, people cannot be expected to change an aspect of culture that is central to their lives. It is not that people do not want to change, but change is unlikely if it doesn't integrate well with other aspects of their life-style.

In many countries of the Middle East, governments want the Bedouin—people who herd animals over vast stretches of semiarid grassland—to settle down. Governments have tried to settle them by force or by enticements, but time after time settlement schemes have failed. In retrospect, such failures are not surprising. The Bedouin continue to try to herd animals near newly constructed settlements, but such grazing often results in human-made deserts near the settlements, so the settle-

ments are abandoned. The traditional Bedouin pattern of herding animals depends on mobility. When the animals eat the tops of the grasses in a particular place, the people need to move on. When water starts drying up in one location, the herds need to be moved. Overgrazing near a settlement and plowing land in a semiarid environment can lead to quick erosion of the soil and the loss of plant cover. After the failure of many settlement schemes, governments may try to encourage a return to more traditional methods of grazing.

It is not that the Bedouin are reluctant to change in all respects. Many Bedouin readily gave up relying on camels for transport in favor of trucks. Trucks are a modern adaptation, yet they still allow mobility. Now the Bedouin are able to get water from wells and transport water to their animals by truck. The adoption of trucks led to other changes in Bedouin life. Small animals can be more readily transported to new pastures by truck, so many Bedouin have given up their dependence on camels and shifted to sheep and goat herding. Money is required to buy trucks and pay for gasoline and repairs, so more time is spent working for wages in temporary jobs.

In the 1980s, Dawn Chatty was asked by the government of Oman to help design a project to extend basic social services to the Bedouin without coercing them to alter their way of life. It isn't often that

governments fund in-depth studies to understand the needs of the people being affected, but Chatty was able to persuade the Oman government that such a study was necessary as a first step. With United Nations funding, she began to survey the people to evaluate their needs. The government wanted some action right away, so the project soon incorporated a mobile health unit that could begin a program of primary care as well as immunization against measles, whooping cough, and polio. After a period of evaluation, the project team also recommended an annual distribution of tents, the establishment of dormitories so children could live at schools, a new system of water delivery, and veterinary and marketing assistance.

Unfortunately, a development project often ends without any guarantee that health and other services will continue to be provided. As Chatty found out, long-term change is not as easy to achieve as short-term change. Along with other applied anthropologists, she continues to push for what Michael Cernea called "putting people first."

Sources: Dawn Chatty, *Mobile Pastoralists: Development Planning and Social Change in Oman* (New York: Columbia University Press, 1996); Michael M. Cernea, ed., *Putting People First: Sociological Variables in Development,* 2nd ed. (New York: Oxford University Press, 1991), p. 7.

tions. In the chapter on culture change and globalization, we discuss the major patterns of culture change in the modern world, much of it affected by the expansion of the West.

If we assume that cultures are more than random collections of behaviors, beliefs, and values—that they tend to

be adaptive, integrated, and changing—then the similarities and differences between them should be understandable. That is, we can expect that similar circumstances within or outside the culture will give rise to, or favor, similar cultural responses. Although we may assume that cultural variation is understandable, the task of discovering which particular circumstances favor which particular patterns is a large and difficult one. In the chapters that follow, we hope to convey the main points of what anthropologists think they know about aspects of cultural variation and what they do not know. We frequently describe particular cultures to illustrate aspects of cultural variation. When we do so, the reader should understand that the culture described is probably not the same now, since the sources of our material always refer to some previous time.[19] The !Kung of the 1990s are not necessarily like the !Kung of the 1950s.

 CD-ROM Flashcards Chapter 13

 # Summary

1. Despite very strong individual differences, the members of a particular society closely agree in their responses to certain phenomena because they share common beliefs, attitudes, values, ideals, and behaviors, which constitute their culture.

2. Culture may be defined as the learned behaviors, beliefs, attitudes, values, and ideals generally shared by the members of a group.

3. The size of the group within which cultural traits are shared can vary from a particular society or a segment of that society to a group that transcends national boundaries. When anthropologists refer to a culture, they usually are referring to the cultural patterns of a particular society—that is, a particular territorial population speaking a language not generally understood by neighboring territorial populations.

4. A defining feature of culture is that it is learned. Although other animals exhibit some cultural behavior, humans are unusual in the number and complexity of the learned patterns that they transmit to their young. And they have a unique way of transmitting their culture: through spoken, symbolic language.

5. Ethnocentrism and its opposite—the glorification of other cultures—impede anthropological inquiry. An important tenet in anthropology is the principle of cultural relativism: the attitude that a society's customs and ideas should be studied objectively and understood in the context of that society's culture. But when it comes to some cultural practices such as torture, slavery, or genocide, most anthropologists can no longer adhere to the strong form of cultural relativism that asserts that all cultural practices are equally valid.

6. Anthropologists seek to discover the customs and ranges of acceptable behavior that constitute the culture of a society under study. In doing so, they focus on general or shared patterns of behavior rather than on individual variations. When dealing with practices that are highly visible, or with beliefs that are almost unanimous, the investigator can rely on observation or on a few knowledgeable persons. With less obvious behaviors or attitudes, the anthropologist must collect information from a sample of individuals. The mode of a frequency distribution can then be used to express the cultural pattern.

7. Every society develops a series of ideal cultural patterns that represent what most members of the society believe to be the correct behavior in particular situations. A society's ideal cultural patterns, however, do not always agree with its actual cultural patterns.

8. One important factor that limits the range of individual variation is the culture itself, which acts directly or indirectly as a constraint on behavior. The existence of cultural constraints, however, is not necessarily incompatible with individuality.

9. Several assumptions are frequently made about culture. First, culture is generally adapted to the particular conditions of its physical and social environment. What may be adaptive in one environment may not be adaptive in another. Some cultural traits may be neutral in terms of adaptation, some may merely have been adaptive in the past, and still others may be maladaptive. Second, culture is mostly integrated, in that the elements or traits that make up the culture are mostly adjusted to or consistent with one another. Third, culture is always changing.

 # Glossary Terms

adaptive customs	maladaptive customs
cultural relativism	norms
culture	random sample
early evolutionism	society
ethnocentric	subculture
ethnocentrism	

 # Critical Questions

1. Would it be adaptive for a society to have everyone adhere to the cultural norms?

2. Why does culture change more rapidly in some societies than in others?

3. Does the concept of cultural relativism promote international understanding, or does it hinder attempts to have international agreement on acceptable behavior, such as human rights?

 # Internet Exercises

1. Culture change can come about when enough individuals start altering their behavior. Young people in the United States have increasingly altered their bodies by

piercing the ears, eyebrows, lips, and other body parts. It is too soon to say whether this trend may become widely shared. As this on-line exhibit on body alteration shows, many cultures employ piercing, tattooing, and painting of the body. Explore http://www.upenn.edu/museum/Exhibits/bodmodintro.html. Why do you think body piercing has become more common?

2. What are your thoughts on cultural relativism and human rights? If you would like to know what some anthropologists think, read the two articles at http://www.cs.org/publications/featuredarticles/1998/fluerhlobban.htm and http://www.bgu.ac.il/humphrey/seminar/moha.htm. What is the basic dilemma between these two concepts?

3. An important part of anthropological knowledge is understanding how people view their own culture. With the World Wide Web, it is now possible for people to make information about their own culture available. Visit the site of the Hopi Tribe Cultural Preservation Office: http://www.nau.edu/%7Ehcpo-p/. What does this site tell you about what the Hopi consider important?

 ## Suggested Reading

DE VITA, P., AND ARMSTRONG, D., Eds. *Distant Mirrors: America as a Foreign Culture,* 3rd ed. Belmont, CA: Wadsworth, 2001. Nineteen foreign scholars look at the culture of the United States. Their perceptions challenge persons who were born in the United States to look at their culture from a new perspective.

EMBER, M., AND EMBER, C. R., Eds. *Portraits of Culture: Ethnographic Originals.* In C. R. Ember and M. Ember, eds., *New Directions in Anthropology.* Upper Saddle River, NJ: Prentice Hall, CD-ROM, 2003. A series of original mini-ethnographies, each describing a different culture and written by someone with firsthand experience in that culture. Each piece provides a portrait of the culture, including how it has recently changed.

HALL, E. T., AND HALL, M. R. *Hidden Differences: Doing Business with the Japanese.* New York: Doubleday, 1990. When people from different cultures interact, their difficulties often stem from hidden, unstated cultural rules of how to behave. On the basis of extensive interviews in the United States and Japan, the authors analyze these hidden communications.

KROEBER, A. L. *The Nature of Culture.* Chicago: University of Chicago Press, 1952. A collection of papers on the nature of culture by a distinguished pioneer in North American anthropology.

SPIRO, M. "On the Strange and the Familiar in Recent Anthropological Thought." In C. R. Ember, M. Ember, and P. N. Peregrine, eds., *Research Frontiers in Anthropology,* in C. R. Ember and M. Ember, eds., *New Directions in Anthropology.* Upper Saddle River, NJ: Prentice Hall, CD-ROM, 2003. The author discusses the controversy about whether it is possible in anthropology to make "the strange familiar." Are cultures so diverse and so fundamentally different that it is not really possible for an outsider to understand or describe them?

WERNER, O., AND SCHOEPFLE, G. M. *Systematic Fieldwork.* Volume 1: Foundations of Ethnography and Interviewing. Newbury Park, CA: Sage, 1987. A detailed presentation and discussion of the methods used to discover patterns of culture on the basis of fieldwork.

COMMUNICATION AND LANGUAGE

CHAPTER OUTLINE

Few of us can remember when we first became aware that words signified something. Yet that moment was a milestone for us, not just in the acquisition of language but in becoming acquainted with all the complex, elaborate behavior that constitutes our culture. Without language, the transmission of complex traditions would be virtually impossible, and each person would be trapped within his or her own world of private sensations.

Helen Keller, left deaf and blind by illness at the age of 19 months, gives a moving account of the afternoon she first established contact with another human being through words:

> [My teacher] brought me my hat, and I knew I was going out into the warm sunshine. This thought, if a wordless sensation may be called a thought, made me hop and skip with pleasure.
>
> We walked down the path to the well house, attracted by the fragrance of the honeysuckle with which it was covered. Someone was drawing water and my teacher placed my hand under the spout. As the cool stream gushed over one hand she spelled into the other the word water, first slowly, then rapidly. Suddenly I felt a misty consciousness as of something forgotten—a thrill of returning thought; and somehow the mystery of language was revealed to me. I knew then that w-at-e-r meant the wonderful cool something that was flowing over my hand. That living word awakened my soul, gave it light, hope, joy, set it free! There were barriers still, it is true, barriers that could in time be swept away.
>
> I left the well house eager to learn. Everything had a name, and each name gave birth to a new thought. As we returned to the house every object which I touched seemed to quiver with life. That was because I saw everything with the strange, new sight that had come to me.[1]

◆ Communication

Against all odds, Helen Keller had come to understand the essential function that language plays in all societies—namely, that of communication. The word *communicate* comes from the Latin verb *communicare,* "to impart," "to share," "to make *common.*" We communicate by agreeing, consciously or unconsciously, to call an object, a movement, or an abstract concept by a common name. For example, speakers of English have agreed to call the color of grass green, even though we have no way of comparing precisely how two persons actually experience this color. What we share is the agreement to call similar sensations green. Any system of language consists of publicly accepted symbols by which individuals try to share private experiences.

NONVERBAL HUMAN COMMUNICATION

As we all know from experience, the spoken word does not communicate all that we know about a social situation. We can usually tell when someone says, "It was good to meet you," whether he or she really means it. We can tell if people are sad from their demeanor, even if they just say, "I'm fine," in response to the question "How are you?"

Obviously, our communication is not limited to spoken language. We communicate directly through facial expression, body stance, gesture, and tone of voice and indirectly through systems of signs and symbols, such as writing, algebraic equations, musical scores, dancing, painting, code flags, and road signs. As Anthony Wilden put it, "every act, every pause, every movement in living and social systems is also a message; silence is communication; short of death it is impossible for an organism or person not to communicate."[2] How can silence be a communication? Silence may reflect companionship, as when two people work side by side on a project, but silence can also communicate unfriendliness. An anthropologist can learn a great deal from what people in a society do not talk about. For example, in India, sex is not supposed to be talked about. HIV infection is spreading very fast in India, so the unwillingness of people to talk about sex makes it extraordinarily difficult for medical anthropologists and health professionals to do much to reduce the rate of spread.[3]

Some nonverbal communication appears to be universal in humans. For example, humans the world over appear to understand facial expression in the same way; that is, they are able to recognize a happy, sad, surprised, angry, disgusted, or afraid face. How the face is represented in art appears to evoke similar feelings in many different cultures. As we explore later in the arts chapter, masks intended to be frightening have sharp, angular features and inward- and downward-facing eyes and eyebrows. But nonverbal communication is also culturally variable. In the chapter on the concept of culture, we discussed how the distance between people standing together is culturally variable. In the realm of facial expression, different cultures have different rules about the emotions that are acceptable to express. One study compared how Japanese and Americans express emotion. Individuals from both groups were videotaped while they were shown films intended to evoke feelings of fear and disgust. When the subjects saw the films by themselves, without other people present, they showed the same kinds of facial expressions of fear and disgust. But there was a cultural effect too. When an authority figure was present during the videotaping, the Japanese subjects tried to mask their negative feelings with a half-smile more often than did the Americans.[4] Many gestures are culturally variable. In some cultures an up and down nod of the head means "yes," in others it means "no."

Despite all the various systems of communication available to us, we must recognize the overriding importance of spoken or vocal language. It is probably the major transmitter of culture, allowing us to share and pass on our complex configuration of attitudes, beliefs, and patterns of behavior.

NONHUMAN COMMUNICATION

Systems of communication are not unique to human beings, nor is communication by sound. Other animal species communicate in a variety of ways. One way is by

Research suggests that many human emotions are expressed in the same ways all over the world. Can you guess what emotions are being expressed by these faces?

sound. A bird may communicate by a call that "this is my territory"; a squirrel may utter a cry that leads other squirrels to flee from danger. Another means of animal communication is odor. An ant releases a chemical when it dies, and its fellows then carry it away to the compost heap. Apparently the communication is highly effective; a healthy ant painted with the death chemical will be dragged to the

funeral heap again and again. Another means of communication, body movement, is used by bees to convey the location of food sources. Karl von Frisch discovered that the black Austrian honeybee—by choosing a round dance, a wagging dance, or a short, straight run—can communicate not only the precise direction of the source of food but also its distance from the hive.[5]

One of the biggest scholarly debates is the degree to which nonhuman animals, particularly nonhuman primates, differ from humans in their capacity for language. Some scholars see so much discontinuity that they postulate that humans must have acquired (presumably through mutation) a specific genetic capability for language. Others see much more continuity between humans and nonhuman primates and point to research that shows much more cognitive capacity in nonhuman primates than previously thought possible. They point out that the discontinuity theorists are constantly raising the standards for the capacities thought necessary for language.[6] For example, in the past, only human communication was thought to be symbolic. But recent research suggests that some monkey and ape calls in the wild are also symbolic.

When we say that a communication (call, word, sentence) is *symbolic,* we mean at least two things. First, the communication has meaning even when its *referent* (whatever is referred to) is not present. Second, the meaning is arbitrary; the receiver of the message could not guess its meaning just from the sound(s) and does not know the meaning instinctively. In other words, symbols have to be learned. There is no compelling or "natural" reason that the word *dog* in English should refer to a smallish four-legged omnivore that is the bane of letter carriers.

Vervet monkeys in Africa are not as closely related to humans as are African apes. Nevertheless, scientists who have observed vervet monkeys in their natural environment consider at least three of their alarm calls to be symbolic because each of them *means* (refers to) a different kind of predator—eagles, pythons, or leopards—and monkeys react differently to each call. For example, they look up when they hear the "eagle" call. Experimentally, in the absence of the referent, investigators have been able to evoke the normal reaction to a call by playing it back electronically. Another indication that the vervet alarm calls are symbolic is that infant vervets appear to need some time to learn the referent for each. When they are very young, infants apply a particular call to more animals than adult vervets apply the call to. So, for example, infant vervets will often make the eagle warning call when they see any flying bird. The infants learn the appropriate referent apparently through adult vervets' repetition of infants' "correct" calls; in any case, the infants gradually learn to restrict the call to eagles. This process is probably not too different from the way a North American infant in an English-speaking family first applies the "word" *dada* to all adult males and gradually learns to restrict it to one person.[7]

All of the nonhuman vocalizations we have described so far enable individual animals to convey messages. The sender gives a signal that is received and "decoded" by the receiver, who usually responds with a specific action or reply. How is human vocalization different? Since monkeys and apes appear to use symbols at least some of the time, it is not appropriate to emphasize symbolism as the distinctive feature of human language. However, there is a significant quantitative difference between human language and other primates' systems of vocal communication. All human languages employ a much larger set of symbols.

Another often-cited difference between human and nonhuman vocalizations is that the other primates' vocal systems are *closed*—that is, different calls are not combined to produce new, meaningful utterances. In contrast, human languages are *open* systems, governed by complex rules about how sounds and sequences of sounds can be combined to produce an infinite variety of meanings.[8] For example, an English speaker can combine *care* and *full* (*careful*) to mean one thing, then use each of the two elements in other combinations to mean different things. *Care* can be used to make *carefree, careless,* or *caretaker; full* can be used to make *powerful* or *wonderful.* And because language is a system of shared symbols, it can be re-formed into an infinite variety of expressions and be understood by all who share these symbols. In this way, for example, T. S. Eliot could form a sentence never before formed—"In the room the women come and go/talking of Michelangelo"[9]—and the sense of his sentence, though not necessarily his private meaning, could be understood by all speakers of English.

While no primatologist disputes the complexity and infinite variety with which human languages can combine sounds, the dichotomy of closed versus open distinction has been called into question by research on cotton-top tamarins, pygmy marmosets, capuchin monkeys, and rhesus macaques. These nonhuman primates do combine calls in orderly sequences.[10]

Another trait thought to be unique to humans is the ability to communicate about past or future events. But Sue Savage-Rumbaugh has observed wild bonobos leaving what appear to be messages to other bonobos to follow a trail. They break off vegetation where trails fork and point the broken plants in the direction to follow.

Perhaps most persuasive are the recent successful attempts to teach apes to communicate with humans and with each other using human-created signs. These successes have led many scholars to question the traditional assumption that the gap between human and other animal communication is enormous. Even a parrot, which has a small brain, has been taught to communicate with a human trainer in ways once thought impossible. Alex (the parrot) can correctly answer questions in English about what objects are made of, how many objects of a particular type there are, and even what makes two objects the same or different.[11] When he is not willing to continue a training session, Alex says: "I'm sorry . . . Wanna go back."[12] Chimpanzees Washoe and Nim and the gorilla Koko were taught hand signs based on American Sign Language (ASL; used by the hearing impaired in the United States). The chimpanzee Sarah was trained with plastic symbols. Subsequently, many chimpanzees were trained on symbol keyboards connected to computers. For example, Sherman and Austin began to communicate with each other about actions they were intending to do, such as the types of tools they needed to solve a problem. And they were able to classify items into categories, such as "food" and "tools." Some of the best examples of linguistic ability come from a chimpanzee named Kanzi. In contrast to other apes, Kanzi initially learned symbols just by watching his mother being taught, and he spontaneously began using the computer symbols to communicate with humans, even indicating his intended actions. Kanzi did not need rewards or to have his

Researcher Joyce Butler teaching Nim, a chimpanzee, the sign for "drink."

hands put in the right position. And he understood a great deal of what was spoken to him in English. For example, when he was 5 years old, Kanzi heard someone talk about throwing a ball in the river, and he turned around and did so. Kanzi has come close to having a primitive English grammar when he strings symbols together.[13] If chimpanzees and other primates have the capacity to use non-spoken language and even to understand spoken language, then the difference between humans and nonhumans may not be as great as people used to think.

Are these apes really using language in some minimal way? Many investigators do agree about one thing—nonhuman primates have the ability to "symbol," to refer to something (or a class of things) with an arbitrary "label" (gesture or sequence of sounds).[14] For example, the gorilla Koko (with a repertoire of about 375 signs) extended the sign for *drinking straw* to plastic tubing, hoses, cigarettes, and radio antennae. Washoe originally learned the sign *dirty* to refer to feces and other soil and then began to use it insultingly, as in "dirty Roger," when her trainer Roger Fouts refused to give her things she wanted. Even the mistakes made by the apes suggest that they are using signs symbolically, just as words are used in spoken language. For example, the sign *cat* may be used for dog if the animal learned *cat* first (just as the Embers' daughter Kathy said "dog" to all pictures of four-footed animals, including elephants, when she was 18 months old).

When we discuss the structure of sounds (phonology) later in this chapter, we will see that every human language has certain ways of combining sounds and ways of not combining those sounds. Apes do not have anything comparable to linguistic rules for allowed and not allowed combinations of sounds. In addition, humans have many kinds of discourse. We make lists and speeches, tell stories, argue, and recite poetry. Apes do none of these things.[15] But apes do have at least some of the capacities for language. Therefore, understanding their capacities may help us better understand the evolution of human language.

◈ The Origins of Language

How long humans have had spoken language is not known. Some think that the earliest *Homo sapiens,* perhaps 100,000 years ago, may have had the beginnings of language. Others believe that language developed only in the last 40,000 years or so, with the emergence of modern humans. Because the only unambiguous remains of language are found on written tablets, and the earliest stone tablets date back only about 5,000 years,[16] pinpointing the emergence of earliest languages remains speculative. Theories about when language developed are based on nonlinguistic information such as when cranial capacity expanded dramatically, when complex technology and symbolic artifacts (such as art) started to be made, and when the anatomy of the throat, as inferred from fossil remains, began to resemble what we see in modern humans.

Perhaps the majority of scholars believe that spoken language was a radical departure from communication that preceded it. However, as we have noted, based on observations of nonhuman primates in the wild and in the laboratory, many primatologists have questioned whether there is an enormous gap between nonhuman primate and human communicational capacities. In fact, some think that all the brain prerequisites for language were in place before the evolutionary split between apes and humans, and they view the emergence of spoken language as a quantitative rather than a qualitative difference.[17] These two points of view have led to lively debate.

Noam Chomsky and other theoreticians of grammar suggest that there is an innate *language-acquisition device* in the human brain, as innate to humans as call systems are to other animals.[18] If humans are unique in having an innate capacity for language, then some mutation or series of mutations had to be favored in human evolution, not before the human line separated from apes. Whether such a mechanism in fact exists is not clear. But we do know that the actual development of individual language is not completely biologically determined; if it were, all human beings would speak the same brain-generated language. Instead, about 4,000 to 5,000 mutually unintelligible languages have been identified. More than 2,000 of them were still spoken as of recently, most by peoples who did not traditionally have a system of writing.

Can we learn anything about the origins of language by studying the languages of nonliterate and technologically simpler societies? The answer is no, because such languages are not simpler or less developed than ours. The sound systems, vocabularies, and grammars of technologically simpler peoples are in no way inferior to those of peoples with more complex technology.[19] Of course, people in other societies, and even some people in our own society, will not be able to name the sophisticated machines used in our society. All languages, however, have the potential for doing so. As we will see later in this chapter, all languages possess the amount of vocabulary their speakers need, and all languages expand in response to cultural changes. A language that lacks terminology for some of our conveniences may have a rich vocabulary for events or natural phenomena that are of particular importance to the people in that society.

If there are no primitive languages, and if the earliest languages have left no traces that would allow us to reconstruct them, does that mean we cannot investigate the origins of language? Some linguists think that understanding the way children acquire language, which we discuss shortly, can help us understand the origins of language. Recently, other linguists have suggested that an understanding of how creole languages develop will also tell us something about the origins of language.

CREOLE LANGUAGES

Some languages developed in various areas where European colonial powers established commercial enterprises that relied on imported labor, generally slaves. The laborers in one place often came from several different societies and in the beginning would speak with their masters and with each other in some kind of *pidgin* (simplified) version of the masters' language. Pidgin languages lack many of the building blocks found in the languages of whole societies, building blocks such as prepositions (*to, on,* and so forth) and auxiliary verbs (designating future and other tenses). Many pidgin languages developed into and were replaced by so-called *creole languages,* which incorporate much of the vocabulary of the masters' language but also have a grammar that differs from it and from the grammars of the laborers' native languages.[20]

Derek Bickerton argues that there are striking grammatical similarities in creole languages throughout the world. This similarity, he thinks, is consistent with the idea that some grammar is inherited by all humans. Creole languages, therefore, may resemble early human languages. All creoles use intonation instead of a change in word order to ask a question. The creole equivalent of the question "Can you fix this?" would be "You can fix this?" The creole version puts a rising inflection at the end; in contrast, the English version reverses the subject and verb without much inflection at the end. All creoles express the future and the past in the same grammatical way, by the use of particles (such as the English *shall*) between subject and verb, and they all employ double negatives, as in the Guyana English creole "Nobody no like me."[21]

It is possible that many other things about language are universal, that all languages are similar in many respects, because of the way humans are "wired" or because people in all societies have similar experiences. For example, names for frogs may usually contain *r* sounds because frogs make them.[22]

CHILDREN'S ACQUISITION OF LANGUAGE

Apparently a child is equipped from birth with the capacity to reproduce all the sounds used by the world's languages and to learn any system of grammar. The language the child learns is the one spoken by the parents or caretakers.

Children's acquisition of the structure and meaning of language has been called the most difficult intellectual achievement in life. If that is so, it is pleasing to note that they accomplish it with relative ease and vast enjoyment. Many believe that this "difficult intellectual achievement" may in reality be a natural response to the capacity for language that is one of humans' genetic characteristics. All over the world children begin to learn language at about the same age, and in no culture do children wait until they are 7 or 10 years old. By 12 or 13 months of age, children are able to name a few objects and actions, and by 18 to 20 months they can make one key word stand for a whole sentence: "Out!" for "Take me out for a walk right now";

ANTHROPOLOGICAL ORIGINALS
The Haitians of the Caribbean

All languages are complex, in different ways: Anthropological linguists have to remind people that no languages are primitive or simple. For example, creole languages (like Haitian Creole) are not degraded forms of introduced languages, spoken only by the lower classes of a colonial society. Rather, creoles are like all languages that have been in use for some time. All are complex; all have developed a lot of ways to express whatever the people speaking the language want to express.

Outsiders have traditionally misunderstood the language situation of Haiti. It has often been stated that the elite speaks French, and the masses speak some sort of degraded version of French called *patois* or Creole. Anthropological linguists wring their hands in despair at such notions. All languages that have been in use for more than a couple of generations are structurally and functionally complex enough to handle all the descriptive, emotional, and expressive needs of the people speaking the particular language. The language of Haiti, the language spoken by *all* Haitians, is properly referred to as Haitian Creole. For much of the modern history of Haiti, however, the official language of government, business, and education has been French, even though only about 8 percent of the people speak French consis-

tently. The reason for the usage of French is that members of the educated elite have found that they can exclude the masses from competing for scarce jobs by requiring knowledge of the French language for positions in government and business.

CD-ROM Anthropological Originals 15

Source: Robert Lawless, "Haitians: From Political Repression to Chaos," in Melvin Ember and Carol R. Ember, eds., *Portraits of Culture: Ethnographic Originals,* in Carol R. Ember and Melvin Ember, eds., *New Directions in Anthropology* (Upper Saddle River, NJ: Prentice Hall, CD-ROM, 2003).

"Juice!" for "I want some juice now." Evidence suggests that children acquire the concept of a word as a whole, learning sequences of sounds that are stressed or at the ends of words (for example, "raffe" for giraffe). Even hearing-impaired children learning signs in ASL tend to acquire and use signs in a similar fashion.[23]

Children the world over tend to progress to two-word sentences at about 18 to 24 months of age. In their sentences they express themselves in "telegraph" form—using nounlike words and verblike words but leaving out the seemingly less important words. So a two-word sentence such as "Shoes off" may stand for "Take my shoes off," or "More milk" may stand for "Give me more milk, please."[24] They do not utter their two words in random order, sometimes saying "off" first, other times saying "shoes" first. If a child says "Shoes off," then he or she will also say "Clothes off" and "Hat off." They seem to select an order that fits the conventions of adult language, so they are likely to say "Daddy eat," not "Eat Daddy." In other words, they tend to put the subject first, as adults do. And they tend to say "Mommy coat" rather than "Coat Mommy" to indicate "Mommy's coat."[25] Adults do not utter sentences such as "Daddy eat," so children seem to know a lot about how to put words together with little or no direct teaching from their caretakers. Consider the 5-year-old who, confronted with the unfamiliar "Gloria in Excelsis," sings quite happily, "Gloria eats eggshells." To make the words fit the structure of English grammar is more important than to make the words fit the meaning of the Christmas pageant.

If there is a basic grammar imprinted in the human mind, we should not be surprised that children's early and later speech patterns seem to be similar in different languages. We might also expect children's later speech to be similar to the structure of creole languages. And it is, according to Derek Bickerton.[26] The "errors" children make in speaking are consistent with the grammar of creoles. For example, English-speaking children 3 to 4 years old tend to ask questions by intonation alone, and they tend to use double negatives, such as "I don't see no dog," even though the adults around them do not speak that way and consider the children's speech "wrong."

But some linguists argue that the evidence for an innate grammar is weak because children the world over do not develop the same grammatical features at similar ages. For example, word order is a more important determinant of meaning in English than in Turkish; the endings of words are more important in Turkish. The word at the beginning of the sentence in English is likely to be the subject. The word with a certain ending in Turkish is the likely subject. Consistent with this difference, English-speaking children learn word order earlier than Turkish children do.[27]

Future research on children's acquisition of language and on the structure of creole languages may bring us closer to an understanding of the origins of human language. But even if much of grammar is universal, we still need to understand how and why the thousands of languages in the world vary, which brings us to the conceptual tools linguists have had to invent in order to study languages.

◆ Descriptive Linguistics

In every society children do not need to be taught "grammar" to learn how to speak. They begin to grasp the essential structure of their language at a very early age, without direct instruction. If you show English-speaking children a picture of one "gork" and then a picture of two of these creatures, they will say there are two "gorks." Somehow they know that adding an *s* to a noun means more than one. But they do not know this consciously, and adults may not either. One of the most surprising features of human language is that meaningful sounds and sound sequences are combined according to rules that often are not consciously known by the speakers.

These rules should not be equated with the "rules of grammar" you were taught in school so that you would speak "correctly." Rather, when linguists talk about rules, they are referring to the patterns of speaking that are discoverable in actual speech. Needless to say, there is some overlap between the actual rules of speaking and the rules taught in school. But there are rules that children never hear about in school, because their teachers are not linguists and are not aware of them. When linguists use the term *grammar,* they are *not* referring to the prescriptive rules that people are supposed to follow in speaking. Rather, *grammar* to the linguist consists of the actual, often unconscious principles that predict how most people talk. As we have noted, young children may speak two-word sentences that conform to a linguistic rule, but their speech is hardly considered "correct."

Discovering the mostly unconscious rules operating in a language is a very difficult task. Linguists have had to invent special concepts and methods of transcription (writing) to permit them to describe: (1) the rules or principles that predict how sounds are made and how they are used

A lot of language instruction is by pointing to something and saying what it is.

(slightly varying sounds are often used interchangeably in words without creating a difference in meaning—this aspect of language is called **phonology**); (2) how sound sequences (and sometimes even individual sounds) convey meaning and how meaningful sound sequences are strung together to form words (this aspect is called **morphology**); and (3) how words are strung together to form phrases and sentences (this aspect is called **syntax**).

Understanding the language of another people is an essential part of understanding the culture of that people. Although sometimes what people say is contradicted by their observed behavior, there is little doubt that it is hard to understand the beliefs, attitudes, values, and worldview of a people without understanding their language and the nuances of how that language is used. Even behavior, which theoretically one can observe without understanding language, usually cannot be readily understood without interpretation. Imagine that you see people go by a certain rock and seemingly walk out of their way to avoid it. Suppose they believe that an evil spirit resides there. How could you possibly know that without being able to ask and to understand their answer?

PHONOLOGY

Most of us have had the experience of trying to learn another language and finding that some sounds are exceedingly difficult to make. Although the human vocal tract theoretically can make a very large number of different sounds—**phones,** to linguists—each language uses only some of them. It is not that we cannot make the sounds that are strange to us; we just have not acquired the habit of making those sounds. And until the sounds become habitual for us, they continue to be difficult to form.

Finding it difficult to make certain sounds is only one of the reasons we have trouble learning a "foreign" language. Another problem is that we may not be used to combining certain sounds or making a certain sound in a particular position in a word. Thus, English speakers find it difficult to combine z and d, as Russian speakers often do (because we never do so in English), or to pronounce words in Samoan, a South Pacific language, that begin with the sound English speakers write as *ng,* even though we have no trouble putting that sound at the end of words, as in the English *sing* and *hitting.*

In order to study the patterning of sounds, linguists who are interested in *phonology* have to write down speech utterances as sequences of sound. This task would be almost impossible if linguists were restricted to using their own alphabet (say, the one we use to write English), because other languages use sounds that are difficult to represent with the English alphabet or because the alphabet we use in English can represent a particular sound in different ways. (English writing represents the sound f by f as in *food,* but also as gh in *tough* and ph in *phone.*) In addition, in English different sounds may be represented by the same letter. English has 26 letters but more than 40 significant sounds (sounds that can change the meaning of a word).[28] To overcome these difficulties in writing sounds

with the letters of existing writing systems, linguists have developed systems of transcription with special alphabets in which each symbol represents only one particular sound.

Once linguists have identified the sounds or phones used in a language, they try to identify which sounds affect meaning and which sounds do not. One way is to start with a simple word like *lake* and change the first sound to r to make the word *rake.* The linguist will ask if this new combination of sounds means the same thing. An English speaker would say *lake* means something completely different from *rake.* These minimal contrasts enable linguists to identify a **phoneme** in a language—a sound or set of sounds that makes a difference in meaning in that language.[29] So the sound l in *lake* is different phonemically from the sound r in *rake.* The ways in which sounds are grouped together into phonemes vary from language to language. We are so used to phonemes in our own language that it may be hard to believe that the contrast between r and l may not make a difference in meaning in some languages. For example, in Samoan, l and r can be used interchangeably in a word without changing the meaning (therefore, these two sounds belong to the same phoneme in Samoan). So Samoan speakers may say "Leupena" sometimes and "Reupena" at other times when they are referring to someone who in English would be called "Reuben."

English speakers may joke about languages that "confuse" l and r, but they are not usually aware that we do the same thing with other sets of sounds. For example, in English, the word we spell *and* may be pronounced quite differently by two different English speakers without changing the meaning, and no one would think that a different word was spoken. We can pronounce the a in *and* as in the beginning of the word *air,* or we can pronounce it as the a in *bat.* If you say those varying a sounds and try to think about how you are forming them in your mouth, you will realize that they are two different sounds. English speakers might recognize a slight difference in pronunciation but pay little or no attention to it because the two ways to pronounce the a in *and* do not change the meaning. Now think about l and r. If you form them in your mouth, you will notice that they are only slightly different with respect to how far the tongue is from the ridge behind the upper front teeth. Languages do tend to consider sounds that are close as belonging to the same phoneme, but why they choose some sounds and not others to group together is not yet fully understood.

Some recent research suggests that infants may learn early to ignore meaningless variations of sound (those that are part of the same phoneme) in the language they hear at home. It turns out that as early as 6 months of age, infants "ignore" sound shifts within the same phoneme of their own language, but they "hear" a sound shift within the phoneme of another language. Researchers are not sure how babies learn to make the distinction, but they seem to acquire much of the phonology of their language very early indeed.[30]

After discovering which sounds are grouped into phonemes, linguists can begin to discover the sound sequences that are allowed in a language and the usually unconscious rules that predict those sequences. For example, words in English rarely start with three nonvowel sounds. But when they do, the first sound or phone is always an *s*, as in *strike* and *scratch*.[31] (Some other words in English may start with three consonants but only two sounds are involved, as in *chrome*, where the *ch* stands for the sound in *k*.) Linguists' descriptions of the patterning of sounds (phonology) in different languages may allow them to investigate why languages vary in their sound rules.

Why, for example, are two or more consonants strung together in some languages, whereas in other languages vowels are *almost* always put between consonants? The Samoan language now has a word for "Christmas" borrowed from English, but the borrowed word has been changed to fit the rules of Samoan. In the English word, two consonants come first, *k* and *r*, which we spell as *ch* and *r*. The Samoan word is *Kerisimasi* (pronounced as if it were spelled Keh-ree-see-mah-see). It has a vowel after each consonant, or five consonant-vowel syllables.

Why do some languages like Samoan alternate consonants and vowels more or less regularly? Recent cross-cultural research suggests three predictors of this variation. One predictor is a warmer climate. Where people live in warmer climates, the typical syllable is likely to be a consonant-vowel syllable. Linguists have found that consonant-vowel syllables provide the most contrast in speech. Perhaps when people converse outdoors at a distance, which they are likely to do in a warmer climate, they need more contrast between sounds to be understood. A second predictor of consonant-vowel alternation is literacy. Languages that are written have fewer consonant-vowel syllables. If communication is often in written form, meaning does not have to depend so much on contrast between adjacent sounds. A third (indeed the strongest) predictor of consonant-vowel alternation is the degree to which babies are held in close body contact by others. Societies with a great deal of such baby-holding have a lot of consonant-vowel syllables. Later, in the chapter on the arts, you will read about research that relates baby-holding to a societal preference for regular rhythm in music. The theory is that when babies are held in close body contact for much of the day, they begin to associate regular rhythm with pleasurable experiences. The baby senses the regular rhythm of the caretaker's heartbeats or the caretaker's rhythmic work, and the reward value of that experience generalizes to a preference for all regular rhythms in adult life, including apparently a regular consonant-vowel alternation in adult speech. Compare the rhythm of the Samoan word *Kerisimasi* with the English word *Christmas*.[32]

MORPHOLOGY

A phoneme in a language usually does not mean something by itself. Usually phonemes are combined with other phonemes to form a meaningful sequence of sounds. *Morphology* is the study of sequences of sounds that have meaning. Often these meaningful sequences of sounds make up what we call *words*, but a word may be composed of a number of smaller meaningful units. We take our words so much for granted that we do not realize how complicated it is to say what words are. People do not usually pause very much between words when they speak; if we did not know our language, a sentence would seem like a continuous stream of sounds. This is how we first hear a foreign language. It is only when we understand the language and write down what we say that we separate (by spaces) what we call words. But a word is really only an arbitrary sequence of sounds that has a meaning; we would not "hear" words as separate units if we did not understand the language spoken.

Because anthropological linguists traditionally investigated unwritten languages, sometimes without the aid of interpreters, they had to figure out which sequences of sounds conveyed meaning. And because words in many languages can often be broken down into smaller meaningful units, linguists had to invent special words to refer to those units. Linguists call the smallest unit of language that has a meaning a **morph.** Just as a phoneme may have one or more phones, one or more morphs with the same meaning may make up a **morpheme.** For example, the prefix *in-*, as in *indefinite*, and the prefix *un-*, as in *unclear,* are morphs that belong to the morpheme meaning *not.* Although some words are single morphs or morphemes (for example, *for* and *giraffe* in English), many words are a combination of morphs, generally prefixes, roots, and suffixes. Thus *cow* is one word, but the word *cows* contains two meaningful units—a root (*cow*) and a suffix (pronounced like *z*) meaning more than one. The **lexicon** of a language, which a dictionary approximates, consists of words and morphs and their meanings.

It seems likely that the intuitive grasp children have of the structure of their language includes a recognition of morphology. Once they learn that the morph /-z/ added to a noun-type word indicates more than one, they plow ahead with *mans, childs;* once they grasp that the morpheme class pronounced /-t/ or /-d/ or /-ed/ added to the end of a verb indicates that the action took place in the past, they apply that concept generally and invent *runned, drinked, costed.* They see a ball roll near*er* and near*er,* and they transfer that concept to a kite, which goes upp*er* and upp*er.* From their mistakes as well as their successes, we can see that children understand the regular uses of morphemes. By the age of 7, they have mastered many of the irregular forms as well—that is, they learn which morphs of a morpheme are used when.

The child's intuitive grasp of the dependence of some morphemes on others corresponds to the linguist's recognition of free morphemes and bound morphemes. A *free* morpheme has meaning standing alone—that is, it can be a separate word. A *bound* morpheme displays its meaning only when attached to another morpheme. The morph pronounced /-t/ of the bound morpheme meaning *past tense* is attached to the root *walk* to produce *walked;* but the /-t/ cannot stand alone or have meaning by itself.

In English, the meaning of an utterance (containing a subject, verb, object, and so forth) usually depends on the order of the words. "The dog bit the child" is different in

APPLIED ANTHROPOLOGY
Can Languages Be Kept from Extinction?

Not only animal and plant species are endangered; many peoples and their languages are too. In the last few hundred years, and continuing in some places today, Western expansion and colonization have led to the depopulation and extinction of many native societies, mainly as a result of introduced disease and campaigns of extermination. Thus, many languages disappeared with the peoples that spoke them. More than 50 aboriginal languages in Australia of approximately 200 disappeared relatively quickly as a result of massacre and disease.

Today native languages are endangered more by the fact that they are not being passed on to children. Political and economic dominance by speakers of Western languages undoubtedly plays an enormous role in this process. First, schooling is usually conducted in the dominant language. Second, when another culture is dominant, the children themselves may prefer to speak in the language perceived to have higher prestige; indeed, parents sometimes encourage this ten-

dency. Almost all the languages of aboriginal Australia are now gone. This is a worldwide trend. Michael Krauss, a linguist who tracks disappearing languages, estimates that 90 percent of the world's languages are endangered. Here is another example: Only 2 of the 20 native Alaskan languages are currently being taught to children, who therefore speak English only.

What can be done? Krauss, who is particularly interested in native Alaskan languages, is trying to do something. With help from the state government of Alaska, Krauss is developing materials on native languages to help teachers promote bilingual education as a way of preserving native languages. A very different approach has been taken by H. Russell Bernard, who believes that "to keep a language truly alive we must produce authors." With the help of computer technology, which allows reconfiguring a keyboard to produce special characters for sounds, Bernard has taught native speakers to write their native languages directly on computers. These texts then be-

come the basis for dictionaries. So far, more than 80 people, speaking 12 endangered languages, have become authors in Mexico and South America. Although these authors may not be using the standardized characters used by linguists to represent sounds, they are producing "written" materials that might otherwise be lost forever. These texts provide more than just information about language. In their works the authors convey ideas about curing illness, acquiring food, raising children, and settling disputes.

We are not sure when humans first developed spoken language. But the enormous linguistic diversity on this planet took a long time to develop. Unfortunately, it may take only a short time for that diversity to become a thing of the past.

Sources: Seth Shulman, "Nurturing Native Tongues," *Technology Review,* May/June 1993, 16; Janet Holmes, *An Introduction to Sociolinguistics* (London: Longman, 1992), pp. 61–62.

---

meaning from "The child bit the dog." But in many other languages, the grammatical meaning of an utterance does not depend much, if at all, on the order of the words. Rather, meaning may be determined by how the morphs in a word are ordered. For example, in Luo, a language of East Africa, the same bound morpheme may mean the subject or object of an action. If the morpheme is the prefix to a verb, it means the subject; if it is the suffix to a verb, it means the object. Another way that grammatical meaning may be conveyed is by altering or adding a bound morpheme to a word to indicate what part of speech it is. For example, in Russian, the word for "mail" when it is the subject of a sentence is pronounced something like "pawchtah." When "mail" is used as the object of a verb, as in "I gave her the mail," the ending of the word changes to "pawchtoo." And if I say, "What was in the mail?" the word becomes "pawchtyeh."

Some languages have so many bound morphemes that they might express as a complex but single word what is considered a sentence in English. For example, the English sentence "He will give it to you" can be expressed in Wishram, a Chinookan dialect that was spoken along the Columbia River in the Pacific Northwest, as *acimluda* (a-c-i-m-l-ud-a, literally "will-he-him-thee-to-give-will"). Note that the pronoun *it* in English is gender-neutral; Wishram requires that *it* be given a gender, in this case, "him."[33]

SYNTAX

Because language is an open system, we can make up meaningful utterances that we have never heard before. We are constantly creating new phrases and sentences. Just as they do for morphology, speakers of a language seem to have an intuitive grasp of *syntax*—the rules that predict how phrases and sentences are generally formed. These "rules" may be partly learned in school, but children know many of them even before they get to school. In adulthood, our understanding of morphology and syntax is so intuitive that we can even understand a nonsense sentence, such as this famous one from Lewis Carroll's *Through the Looking Glass:*

> 'Twas brillig, and the slithy toves
> Did gyre and gimble in the wabe

Simply from the ordering of the words in the sentence, we can surmise which part of speech a word is, as well as its function in the sentence. *Brillig* is an adjective; *slithy* an adjective; *toves* a noun and the subject of the sentence; *gyre* and *gimble* verbs; and *wabe* a noun and the object of a prepositional phrase. Of course, an understanding of morphology helps too. The *-y* ending in *slithy* is an indication that the latter is an adjective, and the *-s* ending in *toves* tells us that we most probably have more than one of these creatures.

In addition to producing and understanding an infinite variety of sentences, speakers of a language can tell when a sentence is not "correct" without consulting grammar books. For example, an English speaker can tell that "Child the dog the hit" is not an acceptable sentence but "The child hit the dog" is fine. There must, then, be a set of rules underlying how phrases and sentences are constructed in a language.[34] Speakers of a language know these implicit rules of syntax but are not usually consciously aware of them. The linguist's description of the syntax of a language tries to make these rules explicit.

◆ Historical Linguistics

The field of **historical linguistics** focuses on how languages change over time. Written works provide the best data for establishing such changes. For example, the following passage from Chaucer's *Canterbury Tales,* written in the English of the 14th century, has recognizable elements but is different enough from modern English to require a translation.

> A Frere ther was, a wantowne and a merye,
> A lymytour, a ful solempne man.
> In alle the ordres foure is noon that kan
> So muche of daliaunce and fair language.
> He hadde maad ful many a mariage
> Of yonge wommen at his owene cost.
> Unto his ordre he was a noble post.
> Ful wel biloued and famulier was he
> With frankeleyns ouer al in his contree,
> And with worthy wommen of the toun;
> For he hadde power of confessioun,
> As seyde hymself, moore than a curat,
> For of his ordre he was licenciat.

> A Friar there was, wanton and merry,
> A limiter [a friar limited to certain districts], a full solemn [very important] man.

> In all the orders four there is none that knows
> So much of dalliance [flirting] and fair [engaging] language.
> He had made [arranged] many a marriage
> Of young women at his own cost.
> Unto his order he was a noble post [pillar].
> Full well beloved and familiar was he
> With franklins [wealthy landowners] all over his country
> And also with worthy women of the town;
> For he had power of confession,
> As he said himself, more than a curate,
> For of his order, he was a licentiate [licensed by the Pope].[35]

In this passage we can recognize several changes. Many words are spelled differently today, and in some cases, meaning has changed: *Full,* for example, would be translated today as *very.* What is less evident is that changes in pronunciation have occurred. For example, the *g* in *mariage* (marriage) was pronounced *zh,* as in the French from which it was borrowed, whereas now it is usually pronounced like either *g* in *George.*

Because languages spoken in the past leave no traces unless they were written, and most of the languages known to anthropology were not written by their speakers, you might think that historical linguists can study linguistic change only by studying written languages such as English. But that is not the case. Linguists can reconstruct changes that have occurred by comparing contemporary languages that are similar. Such languages show phonological, morphological, and syntactical similarities because they usually derive from a common ancestral language. For example, Romanian, Italian, French, Spanish, and Portuguese have many similarities. On the basis of these similarities, linguists can reconstruct what the ancestral language was like and how it changed into what we call the Romance languages. Of course, these reconstructions can easily be tested and confirmed because we know from many surviving writings what the ancestral language, Latin, was like; and we know from documents how Latin diversified as the Roman Empire expanded. Thus, common ancestry is frequently the reason why neighboring, and sometimes even separated, languages show patterns of similarity.

But languages can be similar for other reasons too. Contact between speech communities, often with one group dominant over another, may lead one language to borrow from the other. For example, English borrowed a lot of vocabulary from French after England was conquered by the French-speaking Normans in A.D. 1066. Languages may also show similarities even though they do not derive from a common ancestral language and even though there has been no contact or borrowing between them. Such similarities may reflect common or universal features of human cultures or human brains or both. (As we noted earlier in the chapter, the grammatical similarities exhibited by creole languages may reflect how the human brain is "wired.") Finally, even unrelated and separated languages may show some similarities because of the phenomenon of convergence; similarities can develop because some processes of linguistic change may have only a few possible outcomes.

LANGUAGE FAMILIES AND CULTURE HISTORY

Latin is the ancestral language of the Romance languages. We know this from documentary (written) records. But if the ancestral language of a set of similar languages is not known from written records, linguists still can reconstruct many features of that language by comparing the derived languages. (Such a reconstructed language is called a **protolanguage.**) That is, by comparing presumably related languages, linguists can become aware of the features that many of them have in common, features that were probably found in the common ancestral language. The languages that derive from the same protolanguage are called a *language family.* Most languages spoken today can be grouped into fewer than 30 families. The language family that English belongs to is called *Indo-European,* because it includes most of the languages of Europe and some of the languages of India. About 50 percent of the world's more than 4 billion people speak Indo-European languages.[36] Another very large language family, now spoken by more than a billion people, is Sino-Tibetan, which includes the languages of northern and southern China as well as those of Tibet and Burma.

The field of historical linguistics got its start in 1786, when a British scholar living in India, Sir William Jones, noticed similarities between Sanskrit, a language spoken and written in ancient India, and classical Greek, Latin, and more recent European languages.[37] In 1822, Jakob Grimm, one of the brothers Grimm of fairy-tale fame, formulated rules to describe the sound shifts that had occurred when the various Indo-European languages diverged from each other. So, for example, in English and the other languages in the Germanic branch of the Indo-European family, *d* regularly shifted to *t* (compare the English *two* and *ten* with the Latin *duo* and *decem*) and *p* regularly shifted to *f* (English *father* and *foot,* Latin *pater* and *pes*). Scholars generally agree that the Indo-European languages derive from a language spoken 5,000 to 6,000 years ago.[38] The ancestral Indo-European language, many of whose features have now been reconstructed, is called *proto-Indo-European,* or *PIE* for short. Figure 15–1 shows the branches and some existing languages of the family.

Where did PIE originate? Some linguists believe that the approximate location of a protolanguage is suggested by the words for plants and animals in the derived languages. More specifically, among these different languages, the words that are **cognates**—that is, words that are similar in sound and meaning—presumably refer to plants and animals that were present in the original homeland. So if we know where those animals and plants were located 5,000 to 6,000 years ago, we can guess where PIE people lived. Among all the cognates for trees in the Indo-European languages, Paul Friedrich has identified 18 that he believes were present in the eastern Ukraine in 3000 B.C. On this basis he suggests that the eastern Ukraine was the PIE homeland.[39] Also consistent with this hypothesis is the fact that the Balto-Slavic subfamily of Indo-European, which

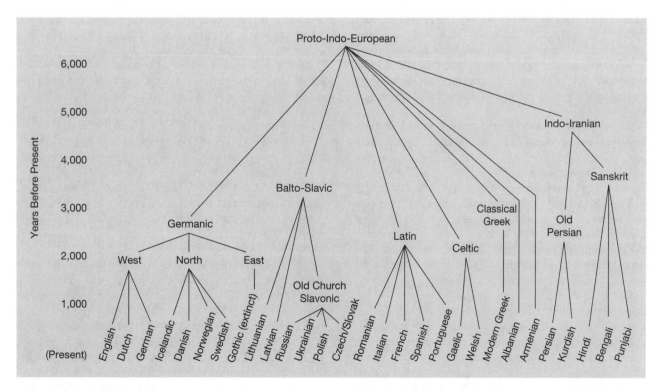

Figure 15–1 *Major Branches and Languages of the Indo-European Language Family*

includes most of the languages in and around the former Soviet Union, has the most tree names (compared with other subfamilies) that are similar to the reconstructed form in proto-Indo-European.[40]

Marija Gimbutas thinks we can even identify the proto-Indo-Europeans archaeologically. She believes that the PIE people were probably the people associated with what is known as the Kurgan culture (5000 to 2000 B.C.), which spread out from the Ukraine around 3000 B.C. The Kurgan people were herders, raising horses, cattle, sheep, and pigs. They also relied on hunting and grain cultivation. Burials suggest differences in wealth and special status for men.[41] Why the Kurgan and linguistically similar people were able to expand to many places in Europe and the Near East is not yet clear. Some have suggested that horses and horse-drawn wagons and perhaps horseback riding provided important military advantages.[42] In any case, it is clear that many Kurgan cultural elements were distributed after 3000 B.C. over a wide area of the Old World.

Colin Renfrew disagrees with the notion that the Ukraine was the homeland of PIE. He thinks that PIE is 2,000 to 3,000 years older than Kurgan culture and that the PIE people lived in a different place. Renfrew locates the PIE homeland in eastern Anatolia (Turkey) in 7000 to 6000 B.C., and he suggests, on the basis of archaeological evidence, that the spread of Indo-European to Europe and what is now Iran, Afghanistan, and India accompanied the spread of farming to those areas.[43]

Just as some historical linguists and archaeologists have suggested when and where the PIE people may have lived originally and how they may have spread, other linguists and archaeologists have suggested culture histories for other language families. For example, the Bantu languages in Africa (spoken by perhaps 100 million people) form a subfamily of the larger Niger-Congo family of languages. Bantu speakers currently live in a wide band across the center of Africa and down the eastern and western sides of southern Africa. All of the Bantu languages presumably derive from people who spoke proto-Bantu. But where was their homeland?

As in the case of proto-Indo-European, different theories have been proposed. But most historical linguists now agree with Joseph Greenberg's suggestion that the origin of Bantu was in what is now the Middle Benue area of eastern Nigeria.[44] The point of origin is presumably where there is the greatest diversity of related languages and **dialects** (varying forms of a language); it is assumed that the place of origin has had the most time for linguistic diversity to develop, compared with an area only recently occupied by a related language. For example, England has more dialect diversity than New Zealand or Australia.

Why were the Bantu able to spread so widely over the last few thousand years? Anthropologists have only begun to guess.[45] Initially, the Bantu probably kept goats and practiced some form of agriculture and thereby were able to spread, displacing hunter-gatherers in the area. As the Bantu speakers expanded, they began to cultivate certain cereal crops and herd sheep and cattle. Around this time,

after 1000 B.C., they also began to use and make iron tools, which may have given them significant advantages. In any case, by 1,500 to 2,000 years ago, Bantu speakers had spread throughout central Africa and into the northern reaches of southern Africa. But speakers of non-Bantu languages still live in eastern, southern, and southwestern Africa.

◆ The Processes of Linguistic Divergence

The historical or comparative linguist hopes to do more than record and date linguistic divergence. Just as the physical anthropologist may attempt to develop explanations for human variation, so the linguist investigates the possible causes of linguistic variation. Some of the divergence undoubtedly comes about gradually. When groups of people speaking the same language lose communication with one another because they become separated, either physically or socially, they begin to accumulate small changes in phonology, morphology, and syntax (which occur continuously in any language). Eventually, if the separation continues, the former dialects of the same language will become separate languages; that is, they will become mutually unintelligible, as German and English now are.

Geographic barriers, such as large bodies of water, deserts, and mountains, may separate speakers of what was once the same language, but distance by itself can also produce divergence. For example, if we compare dialects of English in the British Isles, it is clear that the regions farthest away from each other are the most different linguistically (compare the northeast of Scotland and London).[46] In northern India, hundreds of semi-isolated villages and regions developed hundreds of local dialects. Today, the inhabitants of each village understand the dialects of the surrounding villages and, with a little more difficulty, the dialects of the next circle of villages. But slight dialect shifts accumulate village by village, and it seems as if different languages are being spoken at the opposite ends of the region, which are separated by more than a thousand miles.[47]

Even where there is little geographic separation there may still be a great deal of dialect differentiation because of social distance. So, for example, the spread of a linguistic feature may be halted by "racial," religious, or social class differences that inhibit communication.[48] In the village of Khalapur in northern India, John Gumperz found substantial differences in speech between the Untouchables and other groups. Members of the Untouchables have work contacts with members of other groups but no friendships.[49] Without friendships and the easy communication between friends, dialect differentiation can readily develop.

Whereas isolation brings gradual divergence between speech communities, contact results in greater resemblance. This effect is particularly evident when contact between mutually unintelligible languages introduces borrowed words, which usually name some new item borrowed from the other culture—*tomato, canoe, sushi,* and so on. Bilingual groups within a culture may also introduce foreign words, especially when the mainstream language has no real equivalent. Thus, *salsa* has come into English, and *le weekend* into French.

Conquest and colonization often result in extensive and rapid borrowing, if not linguistic replacement. The Norman conquest of England introduced French as the language of the new aristocracy. It was 300 years before the educated classes began to write in English. During this time the English borrowed words from French and Latin, and the two languages—English and French—became more alike than they would otherwise have been. About 50 percent of the English general vocabulary originated in French. As this example suggests, different social classes may react to language contact differentially. For example, English aristocrats eventually called their meat "pork" and "beef" (derived from the French words), but the people who raised the animals and prepared them for eating continued (at least for a while) to refer to the meat as "pig" and "bull," the original Anglo-Saxon words.

In those 300 years of extensive contact, the grammar of English remained relatively stable. English lost most of its inflections or case endings, but it adopted little of the French grammar. In general, the borrowing of words, particularly free morphemes,[50] is much more common than the borrowing of grammar.[51] As we might expect, borrowing by one language from another can make the borrowing language more different from its *sibling languages* (those derived from a common ancestral language) than it would otherwise be. Partly as a result of the French influence, the

The word *sushi* has been borrowed in North America to identify a Japanese style of food.

English vocabulary looks quite different from the languages to which it is actually most similar in terms of phonology and grammar—German, Dutch, and the Scandinavian languages.

Relationships between Language and Culture

Some attempts to explain the diversity of languages have focused on the possible interactions between language and other aspects of culture. On the one hand, if it can be shown that a culture can affect the structure and content of its language, then it would follow that linguistic diversity derives at least in part from cultural diversity. On the other hand, the direction of influence between culture and language might work in reverse: Linguistic features and structures might affect other aspects of the culture.

CULTURAL INFLUENCES ON LANGUAGE

One way a society's language may reflect its corresponding culture is in **lexical content,** or vocabulary. Which experiences, events, or objects are singled out and given words may be a result of cultural characteristics.

BASIC WORDS FOR COLORS, PLANTS, AND ANIMALS Early in the twentieth century many linguists pointed to the lexical domain (vocabulary) of color words to illustrate the supposed truth that languages vary arbitrarily or without apparent reason. Different languages not only had different numbers of basic color words (from 2 to 12 or so; for example, the words *red, green,* and *blue* in English), but they also, it was thought, had no consistency in the way they classified or divided the colors of the spectrum. But findings from a comparative (cross-linguistic) study contradicted these traditional presumptions about variation in the number and meaning of basic color words. On the basis of their study of at first 20 and later over 100 languages, Brent Berlin and Paul Kay found that languages did not encode color in completely arbitrary ways.[52]

Although different languages do have different numbers of basic color words, most speakers of any language are very likely to point to the same color chips as the best representatives of particular colors. For example, people the world over mean more or less the same color when they are asked to select the best "red." Moreover, there appears to be a nearly universal sequence by which basic color words are added to a language.[53] If a language has just two basic color words, its speakers will always refer to "black" (or dark) hues and "white" (or light) hues. If a language has three basic color words, the third word will nearly always be "red." The next category to appear is either "yellow" or "grue" (green/blue); then different words for green and blue; and so on. To be sure, we usually do not see the process by which basic color words are added to a language. But we can infer the usual sequence because, for example, if a language has a word for "yellow," it will almost always have a word for "red," whereas having a word for "red" does not mean that the language will have a word for "yellow."

What exactly is a *basic* color word? All languages, even the ones with only two basic color terms, have many different ways of expressing how color varies. For example, in English we have words such as turquoise, blue-green, scarlet, crimson, and sky blue. Linguists do not consider these to be basic color words. In English the basic color words are *white, black, red, green, yellow, blue, brown, pink, purple, orange,* and *gray.* One feature of a basic color word is that it consists of a single morph; it cannot include two or more units of meaning. This feature eliminates combinations such as *blue-green* and *sky blue.* A second feature of a basic color word is that the color it represents is not generally included in a higher-order color term. For example, scarlet and crimson are usually considered variants of red, turquoise a variant of blue. A third feature is that basic terms tend to be the first-named words when people are asked for color words. Finally, for a word to be considered a basic color word, many individual speakers of the language have to agree on the central meaning (in the color spectrum) of the word.[54]

Why do different societies (languages) vary in number of basic color terms? Berlin and Kay suggest that the number of basic color terms in a language increases with technological specialization as color is used to decorate and distinguish objects.[55] Cross-linguistic variation in the number of basic color terms does not mean that some languages make more color distinctions than others. Every language could make a particular distinction by combining words (for example, "fresh leaf" for green); a language need not have a separate basic term for that color.

There may also be many basic color terms because of a biological factor.[56] Peoples with darker (more pigmented) eyes seem to have more trouble distinguishing colors at the dark (blue-green) end of the spectrum than do peoples with lighter eyes. It might be expected, then, that peoples who live nearer the equator (who tend to have darker eyes, presumably for protection against damaging ultraviolet radiation) would tend to have fewer basic color terms. And they do.[57] Moreover, it seems that both cultural and biological factors are required to account for cross-linguistic variation in the number of basic color terms. Societies tend to have six or more such terms (with separate terms for blue and green) only when they are relatively far from the equator and only when their cultures are more technologically specialized.[58] As we will see in later chapters, technological specialization tends to go with larger communities, more centralized governments, occupational specialization, and more social inequality. Societies with such traits are often referred to in a shorthand way as more "complex," which should not be taken to mean "better."

Echoing Berlin and Kay's finding that basic color terms seem to be added in a more or less universal sequence, Cecil Brown has found what seem to be developmental sequences in other lexical domains. Two such domains are

general, or *life-form,* terms for plants and for animals. Life-form terms are higher-order classifications. All languages have lower-order terms for specific plants and animals. For example, English has words such as *oak* and *pine, sparrow,* and *salmon.* English speakers make finer distinctions too—*pin oak* and *white pine, white-throated sparrow,* and *red salmon.* But why in some languages do people have a larger number of general terms such as *tree, bird,* and *fish?* It seems that these general terms show a universal developmental sequence too. That is, general terms seem to be added in a somewhat consistent order. After "plant" comes a term for "tree"; then one for "grerb" (small, green, leafy, nonwoody plant); then "bush" (for plants between tree and grerb in size); then "grass"; then "vine."[59] The life-form terms for animals also seem to be added in sequence: after "animal" comes a term for "fish," then "bird," then "snake," then "wug" (for small creatures other than fish, birds, and snakes—for example, worms and bugs), then "mammal."[60]

More complex societies tend to have a larger number of general, or life-form, terms for plants and animals than do simpler societies, just as they tend to have a larger number of basic color terms. Why? And do all realms or domains of vocabulary increase in size as social complexity increases? If we look at the total vocabulary of a language (as can be counted in a dictionary), more complex societies do have larger vocabularies.[61] But we have to remember that complex societies have many kinds of specialists, and dictionaries will include the terms used by such specialists. If we look instead at the nonspecialist **core vocabulary** of languages, it seems that all languages have a core vocabulary of about the same size.[62] Indeed, although some domains increase in size with social complexity, some remain the same and still others decrease. An example of a smaller vocabulary domain in complex societies is that of specific names for plants. Urban North Americans may know general terms for plants, but they know relatively few names for specific plants. The typical individual in a small-scale society can commonly name 400 to 800 plant species; a typical person in our own and similar societies may be able to name only 40 to 80.[63] The number of life-form terms is larger in societies in which ordinary people know less about particular plants and animals.[64]

The evidence now available strongly supports the idea that the vocabulary of a language reflects the everyday distinctions that are important in the society. Those aspects of environment or culture that are of special importance will receive greater attention in the language.

GRAMMAR Most of the examples we could accumulate would show that a culture influences the names of things visible in its environment. Evidence for cultural influence on the grammatical structure of a language is less extensive. Harry Hoijer draws attention to the verb categories in the language of the Navajo, a traditionally nomadic people. These categories center mainly in the reporting of events, or "eventings," as he calls them. Hoijer notes that in "the reporting of actions and events, and the framing of substantive concepts, Navajo emphasizes movement and specifies the nature, direction, and status of such movement in considerable detail."[65] For example, Navajo has one category for eventings that are in motion and another for eventings that have ceased moving. Hoijer concludes that the emphasis on events in the process of occurring reflects the Navajo's nomadic experience over the centuries, an experience also reflected in their myths and folklore.

A linguistic emphasis on events may or may not be generally characteristic of nomadic peoples; as yet, no one has investigated the matter cross-culturally or comparatively. But there are indications that systematic comparative research would turn up other grammatical features that are related to cultural characteristics. For example, many languages lack the possessive transitive verb we write as "have," as in "I have." Instead, the language may say something such as "it is to me." A cross-cultural study has suggested that a language may develop the verb "have" after the speakers of that language have developed a system of private property or personal ownership of resources.[66] As we shall see later, in the chapter on economic systems, the concept of private property is far from universal and tends to occur only in complex societies with social inequality. In contrast, many societies have some kind of communal ownership, by kin groups or communities. How people talk about owning seems to reflect how they own; societies that lack a concept of private property also lack the verb "have."

LINGUISTIC INFLUENCES ON CULTURE: THE SAPIR-WHORF HYPOTHESIS

There is general agreement that culture influences language. But there is less agreement about the opposite possibility—that language influences other aspects of culture. Edward Sapir and Benjamin Lee Whorf suggested that language is a force in its own right, that it affects how individuals in a society perceive and conceive reality. This suggestion is known as the *Sapir-Whorf hypothesis.*[67] In comparing the English language with Hopi, Whorf pointed out that English-language categories convey discreteness with regard to time and space, but Hopi does not. English has a discrete past, present, and future, and things occur at a definite time. Hopi expresses things with more of an idea of ongoing processes without time being apportioned into fixed segments. According to Ronald Wardhaugh, Whorf believed that these language differences lead Hopi and English speakers to see the world differently.[68]

As intriguing as that idea is, the relevant evidence is mixed. Linguists today do not generally accept the view that language coerces thought, but some suspect that particular features of language may facilitate certain patterns of thought.[69] The influences may be clearest in poetry and metaphors, where words and phrases are applied to other than their ordinary subjects, as in "all the world's a stage."[70] One of the serious problems in testing the Sapir-Whorf hypothesis is that researchers need to figure out how to separate the effects of other aspects of culture from the effects of language.

One approach that may reveal the direction of influence between language and culture is to study how children in different cultures (speaking different languages) develop concepts as they grow up. If language influences the formation of a particular concept, we might expect that children will acquire that concept earlier in societies where the languages emphasize that concept. For example, some languages make more of gender differences than others. Do children develop gender identity earlier when their language emphasizes gender? (Very young girls and boys seem to believe they can switch genders by dressing in opposite-sex clothes, suggesting that they have not yet developed a stable sense that they are unchangeably girls or boys.) Alexander Guiora and his colleagues have studied children growing up in Hebrew-speaking homes (Israel), English-speaking homes (the United States), and Finnish-speaking homes (Finland). Hebrew has the most gender emphasis of the three languages; all nouns are either masculine or feminine, and even second-person and plural pronouns are differentiated by gender. English emphasizes gender less, differentiating by gender only in the third-person singular (*she* or *her* or *hers, he* or *him* or *his*). Finnish emphasizes gender the least; although some words, such as *man* and *woman*, convey gender, differentiation by gender is otherwise lacking in the language. Consistent with the idea that language may influence thought, Hebrew-speaking children acquire the concept of stable gender identity the earliest on the average, Finnish-speaking children the latest.[71]

Another approach is to predict from language differences how people may be expected to perform in experiments. Comparing the Yucatec Mayan language and English, John Lucy predicted that English speakers might recall the *number* of things presented more than Yucatec Mayan speakers. For most classes of nouns, English requires a linguistic way of indicating whether something is singular or plural. You cannot say "I have dog" (no indication of number), but must say "I have a dog," "I have dogs," or "I have one (two, three, several, many) dogs." Yucatec Maya, like English, can indicate a plural, but allows the noun to be neutral with regard to number. For example, the translated phrase there-is-dog-over-there (*yàan pèek té'elo'*) can be left ambiguous about whether there is one or more than one dog. In English, the same ambiguity would occur in the sentence "I saw deer over there," but English does not often allow ambiguity for animate or inanimate nouns.[72] In a number of experiments, Yucatec Mayan and American English speakers were equally likely to recall the objects in a picture, but they differed in how often they described the number of a particular object in the picture. Yucatec Mayan speakers did so less often, consistent with their language's lack of insistence on indicating number.[73] So the salience of number in the experiments was probably a consequence of how the languages differ. Of course, it is possible that salience of number is created by some other cultural feature, such as dependence on money in the economy.

◆ The Ethnography of Speaking

Traditionally, linguists concentrated on trying to understand the structure of a language, the usually unconscious rules that predict how the people of a given society typically speak. In recent years, many linguists have begun to study how people in a society vary in how they speak. This type of linguistic study, *sociolinguistics*, is concerned with the *ethnography of speaking*—that is, with cultural and subcultural patterns of speech variation in different social contexts.[74] The sociolinguist might ask, for example, what kinds of things one talks about in casual conversation with a stranger. A foreigner may know English vocabulary and grammar well but may not know that one typically chats with a stranger about the weather or where one comes from, and not about what one ate that day or how much money one earns. A foreigner may be familiar with much of the culture of a North American city, but if that person divulges the real state of his or her health and feelings to the first person who says, "How are you?" he or she has much to learn about "small talk" in North American English.

Strangers in many cultures shake hands when they meet; friends touch each other more warmly. How we speak to others also differs according to the degree of friendship.

Similarly, North Americans tend to get confused in societies where greetings are quite different from ours. People in some other societies may ask as a greeting, "Where are you going?" or "What are you cooking?" Some Americans may think such questions are rude; others may try to answer in excruciating detail, not realizing that only vague answers are expected, just as we don't really expect a detailed answer when we ask people how they are.

SOCIAL STATUS AND SPEECH

That a foreign speaker of a language may know little about the small talk of that language is but one example of the sociolinguistic principle that what we say and how we say it are not wholly predictable by the rules of our language. Who we are socially and whom we are talking to may greatly affect what we say and how we say it.

In a study interviewing children in a New England town, John Fischer noted that in formal interviews, children were likely to pronounce the ending in words such as *singing* and *fishing*, but in informal conversations they said *"singin'"* and *"fishin'."* Moreover, he noted that the phenomenon also appeared to be related to social class; children from higher-status families were less likely to drop the ending than were children from lower-status families. Subsequent studies in English-speaking areas tend to support Fischer's observations with regard to this speech pattern. Other patterns are observed as well. For example, in Norwich, England, lower classes tend to drop the *h* in words such as *hammer,* but in all classes the pattern of dropping the *h* increases in casual situations.[75]

Research has shown that English people from higher-class backgrounds tend to have more *homogeneous* speech, conforming more to what is considered standard English (the type of speech heard on television or radio), whereas people from lower-class backgrounds have very *heterogeneous* speech, varying in their speaking according to the local or dialect area they come from.[76] In some societies, social status differences may be associated with more marked differentiation of words. Clifford Geertz, in his study of Javanese, showed that the vocabularies of the three rather sharply divided groups in Javanese society—peasants, townspeople, and aristocrats—reflect their separate positions. For example, the concept *now* is expressed differently in these three groups. A peasant will use *saiki* (considered the lowest and roughest form of the word); a townsman will use *saniki* (considered somewhat more elegant); and an aristocrat will use *samenika* (the most elegant form).[77]

Status relationships between people can also influence the way they speak to each other. Terms of address are a good example. In English, forms of address are relatively simple. One is called either by a first name or by a title (such as *Doctor,* or *Professor, Ms., Mister*) followed by a last name. A study by Roger Brown and Marguerite Ford indicates that terms of address in English vary with the nature of the relationship between the speakers.[78] The reciprocal use of first names generally signifies an informal or intimate relationship between two persons. A title and last name used reciprocally usually indicates a more formal or businesslike relationship between individuals who are roughly equal in status. Nonreciprocal use of first names and titles in English is reserved for speakers who recognize a marked difference in status between them. This status difference can be a function of age, as when a child refers to her mother's friend as Mrs. Miller and is in turn addressed as Sally, or can be due to occupational hierarchy, as when a person refers to his boss as Ms. Ramirez and is in turn addressed as Joe. In some cases, generally between boys and between men, the use of the last name alone represents a middle ground between the intimate and the formal usages.

GENDER DIFFERENCES IN SPEECH

In many societies the speech of men differs from the speech of women. The variation can be slight, as in our own society, or more extreme, as with the Carib Indians in the Lesser Antilles of the West Indies, among whom women and men use different words for the same concepts.[79] In Japan, males and females use entirely different words for numerous concepts (for example, the male word for water is *mizu*, the female version is *ohiya*), and females often add the polite prefix *o-* (females will tend to say *ohasi* for chopsticks; males will tend to say *hasi*).[80] In the United States and other Western societies, there are differences in the speech of females and males, but they are not as dramatic as in the Carib and Japanese cases. For example, earlier we noted the tendency for the *g* to be dropped in words such as *singing* when the situation is informal and when the social class background is lower. But there is also a gender difference. Women are more likely than men to keep the *g* sound and less likely than men to drop the *h* in words such as *happy*. In Montreal, women are less likely than men to drop the *l* in phrases such as *il fait* ("he does") or in the idiom *il y a* ("there is/are").[81]

Gender differences occur in intonation and in phrasing of sentences as well. Robin Lakoff found that in English women tend to answer questions with sentences that have rising inflections at the end instead of a falling intonation associated with a firm answer. Women also tend to add questions to statements, such as "They caught the robber last week, didn't they?"[82]

One explanation for the gender differences, particularly with regard to pronunciation, is that women in many societies may be more concerned than men with being "correct."[83] (Not in the linguist's sense; it is important to remember that linguists do not consider one form of speech more correct than another, just as they do not consider one dialect superior to another. All are equally capable of expressing a complex variety of thoughts and ideas.) In societies with social classes, what is considered more correct by the average person may be what is associated with the upper class. In other societies, what is older may be considered more correct. For example, in the Native American language of Koasati, which used to be spoken in Louisiana, males and females used different endings in certain verbs. The differences seemed to be disappearing in the 1930s,

when the research on Koasati was done. Young girls had begun to use the male forms and only older women still used the female forms. Koasati men said that the women's speech was a "better" form of speech.[84] Gender differences in speech may parallel some of the gender differences noted in other social behavior (as we will see in the chapter on sex, gender, and culture): Girls are more likely than boys to behave in ways that are acceptable to adults.

There are not enough studies to know just how common it is for women to exhibit more linguistic "correctness." We do know of some instances where it is not the case. For example, in a community in Madagascar where people speak Merina, a dialect of Malagasy, it is considered socially correct to avoid explicit directives. So instead of directly ordering an action, a Merina speaker will try to say it indirectly. Also, it is polite to avoid negative remarks, such as expressing anger toward someone. In this community, however, it is women, not men, who often break the rules; women speak more directly and express anger more often.[85] This difference may be related to the fact that women are more involved in buying and selling in the marketplace.

Some researchers have questioned whether it is correctness that is at issue. Rather, we may be dealing in these examples with unequal prestige and power. Women may try to raise their status by conforming more to standard speech. When they answer a question with a rising inflection, they may be expressing uncertainty and a lack of power. Alternatively, perhaps women want to be more cooperative conversationalists. Speaking in a more "standard" fashion is consistent with being more likely to be understood by others. Answering a question with another question leads to continued conversation.[86]

MULTILINGUALISM AND CODESWITCHING

For many people the ability to speak more than one language is a normal part of life. One language may be spoken at home and another in school, the marketplace, or government. Or more than one language may be spoken at home if family members come from different cultures and still other languages are spoken outside. Some countries explicitly promote multilingualism. For example, Singapore has four official languages—English, Mandarin (one of the Chinese languages), Tamil, and Malay. English is stressed for trade, Mandarin as the language of communication with most of China, Malay as the language of the general region, and Tamil as the language of an important ethnic group. Moreover, most of the population speaks Hokkien, another Chinese language. Education is likely to be in English and Mandarin.[87]

What happens when people who know two or more languages communicate with each other? Very often you find them **codeswitching,** using more than one language in the course of conversing.[88] Switching can occur in the middle of a Spanish-English bilingual sentence, as in "No van a bring it up in the meeting" ("They are not going to bring it up in the meeting").[89] Or switching can occur when the topic or situation changes, such as from social

NEW PERSPECTIVES ON GENDER
Does the English Language Promote Sexist Thinking?

Does English promote sexist thinking, or does the language merely reflect gender inequalities that already exist? For those who wish to promote gender equality, the answers to these questions are important because if language influences thought (along the lines put forward by Edward Sapir and Benjamin Whorf), then linguistic change will be necessary in order to bring about change in the culture of gender. If it is the other way around, that is, if language reflects inequality, then social, economic, and political changes have to come before we can expect substantial linguistic change to occur.

Leaving aside for the moment which changes first, how does English represent gender inequity? Consider the following written by Benjamin Lee Whorf: "Speech is the best show man puts on. . . . Language helps man in his thinking." While *man* in English techni-

cally refers to all humans and *his* technically refers to the thinking of a single person of either gender, the frequent use of such words could convey the idea that males are more important. Similarly, do the words *chairman, policeman, businessman, salesman* convey that males are supposed to have those jobs? What is conveyed when there are two words for the two genders, as in *actor* and *actress* and *hero* and *heroine*? Usually the base word is male and the suffix is added for the female form. Does the suffix convey that the female form is an afterthought or less important?

It is not just the structure of the language that may convey gender inequity. There are also differences in usage and metaphor. Although there is a female and male form for someone who has lost a spouse (*widow* and *widower*), many people will say "Sally is Henry's widow" but hardly anyone would

say "Henry is Sally's widower." Why? Is it considered more important that a woman was formerly attached to a man than that a man was formerly attached to a woman? Given this usage, it is not surprising that *widow* (the female form) is the basic term in this case, *widower* (the male form) the derived term. And how come in the pairs *sir/madam, master/mistress, wizard/witch*, the female version has acquired negative connotations? Why are so many animal images applied to women? They may be described as *chicks, henpeckers, cows, dogs, bitches, kittens, birds.*

Coming back to the original questions, how would we know whether language promotes sexism or sexism influences language? One way to find out is to do experimental studies, such as the one conducted by Fatemeh Khosroshashi. Some individuals were asked to read texts written with

---

talk to schoolwork. Why do speakers of more than one language sometimes switch? Although speakers switch for a lot of different reasons, what is clear is that the switching is not a haphazard mix that comes from laziness or ignorance. Codeswitching involves a great deal of knowledge of two or more languages and an awareness of what is considered appropriate or inappropriate in the community. For example, in the Puerto Rican community in New York City, codeswitching within the same sentence seems to be common in speech among friends, but if a stranger who looks like a Spanish speaker approaches, the language will shift entirely to Spanish.[90] (We discuss interethnic communication more in the chapter on applied anthropology.)

Although each community may have its own rules for codeswitching, variations in practice may need to be understood in terms of the broader political and historical context. For example, German speakers in Transylvania, where Romanian is the national language, hardly ever codeswitch to Romanian. Perhaps the reason is that, before the end of World War II, German speakers were a privileged economic group who looked down upon landless Romanians and their language. Under socialism, the Ger-

man speakers lost their economic privilege, but they continued to speak German among themselves. In the rare cases that Romanian is used among German speakers, it tends to be associated with low-status speech, such as singing bawdy songs. The opposite situation occurred in a Hungarian region of German-speaking Austria. The people of this agricultural region, annexed to Austria in 1921, were fairly poor peasant farmers. After World War II, business expansion began to attract labor from rural areas, so many Hungarians eagerly moved into jobs in industry. German was seen by the younger generations as a symbol of higher status and upward mobility; not surprisingly, codeswitching between Hungarian and German became part of their conversations. Indeed, in the third generation, German has become the language of choice, except when speaking to the oldest Hungarians. The Hungarian-Austrian situation is fairly common in many parts of the world, where the language of the politically dominant group ends up being "linguistically dominant."[91]

CD-ROM Flashcards Chapter 15

(continued)

man and *he* and *his* referring to people; others were asked to read texts with more gender-neutral phrasing. Individuals were subsequently asked to draw pictures to go with the texts. The ones who read the texts with more male terminology drew more accompanying pictures of men, strongly suggesting that the use of the terms *man, he,* and *his* conveyed the thought that the people in the text were men, not women, *because* of the vocabulary used. We need more such studies to help address the intellectual question of which comes first, linguistic or nonlinguistic culture.

It would be important to know whether societies with more "male-oriented" language are more male-dominated than are societies without such distinctions. We don't have that kind of comparative research yet. But one study by Robert and Ruth Munroe looked at the *proportion* of female and male nouns in ten languages (six Indo-European, four other than Indo-European) in which nouns have gender. Although none of those societies could be described as having a female bias, the Munroes were able to ask whether those societies with less male bias in social customs (for example, all children are equally likely to inherit property) have a higher proportion of female nouns than male nouns (more female than male nouns). The answer appears to be yes. Although this study does not reveal what came first, studies like it are important if we want to discover how language differences may be related to other aspects of culture. If male-oriented languages are not related to male dominance, then it is not likely that sexist thinking is a consequence of language.

On the assumption that language may influence thought, many are pushing for changes in the way English is used, if not structured. It is hard to get English speakers to adopt a gender-neutral singular pronoun to replace *he.* Attempts to do so go back to the eighteenth century and include suggestions of *tey, thon, per,* and *s/he.* Although these efforts have not succeeded, the way English is written and spoken has begun to change. Words or phrases such as *chair* (or *chairperson*), *police officer, sales assistant* (*salesperson*) have begun to replace their former *man* versions. If Whorf were writing his sentence now, it probably would be written: "Speech is the best show humans put on.... Language helps people think."

Sources: Janet Holmes, *An Introduction to Sociolinguistics,* 2nd ed. (London: Longman, 2001), pp. 305–16; Suzanne Romaine, *Language in Society: An Introduction to Sociolinguistics* (Oxford: Oxford University Press, 1994), pp. 105–16; Richard Wardhaugh, *An Introduction to Sociolinguistics,* 4th ed. (Oxford: Blackwell, 2002), p. 317; Robin Lakoff, "Language and Woman's Place," *Language in Society,* 2 (1973): 45–80; Fatemeh Khosroshashi, "Penguins Don't Care, but Women Do: A Social Identity Analysis of a Whorfian Problem," *Language in Society,* 18 (1989): 505–25; Robert L. Munroe and Ruth H. Munroe, "A Cross-Cultural Study of Sex, Gender and Social Structure," *Ethnology,* 8 (1969): 206–11.

Summary

1. The essential function language plays in all societies is that of communication. Although human communication is not limited to spoken language, such language is of overriding importance because it is the primary vehicle through which culture is shared and transmitted.

2. Systems of communication are not unique to humans. Other animal species communicate in a variety of ways—by sound, odor, body movement, and so forth. The ability of chimpanzees and gorillas to learn and use sign language suggests that symbolic communication is not unique to humans. Still, human language is distinctive as a communication system in that its spoken and symbolic nature permits an infinite number of combinations and recombinations of meaning.

3. Descriptive (or structural) linguists try to discover the rules of phonology (the patterning of sounds), morphology (the patterning of sound sequences and words), and syntax (the patterning of phrases and sentences) that predict how most speakers of a language talk.

4. By comparative analysis of cognates and grammar, historical linguists test the notion that certain languages derive from a common ancestral language, or protolanguage. The goals are to reconstruct the features of the protolanguage, to hypothesize how the offspring languages separated from the protolanguage or from each other, and to establish the approximate dates of such separations.

5. When two groups of people speaking the same language lose communication with each other because they become separated either physically or socially, they begin to accumulate small changes in phonology, morphology, and syntax. If the separation continues, the two former dialects of the same language will eventually become separate languages—that is, they will become mutually unintelligible.

6. Whereas isolation brings about divergence between speech communities, contact results in greater resemblance. This effect is particularly evident when contact

between mutually unintelligible languages introduces borrowed words, most of which name some new item borrowed from the other culture.

7. Some attempts to explain the diversity of languages have focused on the possible interaction between language and other aspects of culture. On the one hand, if it can be shown that a culture can affect the structure and content of its language, then it would follow that linguistic diversity derives at least in part from cultural diversity. On the other hand, the direction of influence between culture and language might work in reverse; the linguistic structures might affect other aspects of the culture.

8. In recent years, some linguists have begun to study variations in how people actually use language when speaking. This type of linguistic study, called sociolinguistics, is concerned with the ethnography of speaking—that is, with cultural and subcultural patterns of speaking in different social contexts.

 Glossary Terms

codeswitching	morpheme
cognates	morphology
core vocabulary	phone
dialect	phoneme
historical linguistics	phonology
lexical content	protolanguage
lexicon	syntax
morph	

 Critical Questions

1. Why might natural selection have favored the development of true language in humans but not in apes?
2. Would the world be better off with many different languages spoken or with just one universal language?
3. Can you think of some new behavior or way of thinking that led people to adopt or invent new vocabulary or some new pattern of speech?

Internet Exercises

1. Search the site http://whyfiles.org/ for articles about language. Summarize an article of your choice.
2. Explore http://www.friesian.com/egypt.htm to learn the pronunciation of some ancient Egyptian language. Based on what you discover on this site, provide a brief description of the terms *ideogram* and *pictogram*.

3. Read the introduction on the Bemba language and Cherokee on the site http://www.yourdictionary.com/grammars.html, which has some grammars of different languages on the Web.
4. Read about endangered languages at http://www.yourdictionary.com/elr/index.html. Read about the Rosetta Project, an attempt to preserve languages for posterity, at http://www.rosettaproject.org.

 Suggested Reading

AKMAJIAN, A., DEMERS, R. A., AND HARNISH, R. M. *Linguistics: An Introduction to Language and Communication,* 5th ed. Cambridge, MA: MIT Press, 2001. After reviewing the structure of human language, the authors survey research on topics including language use, language acquisition in children, and language and the brain.

BLOUNT, B. G., ED. *Language, Culture, and Society: A Book of Readings,* 2nd ed. Prospect Heights, IL: Waveland, 1995. A book of readings that includes some of the most influential developments in the study of language and culture from the 1910s through the 1990s.

BROWN, C. H., AND WITKOWSKI, S. R. "Language Universals," Appendix B. In D. Levinson and M. J. Malone, eds., *Toward Explaining Human Culture: A Critical Review of the Findings of Worldwide Cross-Cultural Research.* New Haven, CT: HRAF Press, 1980. A review of studies of universals in human languages, including universals in phonology and grammar. Focuses especially on developmental sequences in the lexicon or vocabulary.

FOLEY, W. A. *Anthropological Linguistics: An Introduction.* Malden, MA: Blackwell, 1997. A broad introduction to the particular concerns of linguistic studies in anthropology.

HILL, J. "Do Apes Have Language?" In C. R. Ember, M. Ember, and P. N. Peregrine, eds. *Research Frontiers in Anthropology,* in C. R. Ember and M. Ember, eds., *New Directions in Anthropology.* Upper Saddle River, NJ: Prentice Hall, CD-ROM, 2003. A discussion of the differences and similarities between human and ape language.

KING, BARBARA, ED. *The Origins of Language.* Santa Fe, NM: School of American Research, 1999. This work grew out of a conference where scholars from different disciplines came together to evaluate how primate studies could help understand the origins of language.

SAPIR, E. *Language: An Introduction to the Study of Speech.* New York: Harcourt Brace Jovanovich, 1949 (originally published 1921). A classic nontechnical introduction to the study of human languages and how they vary. Also discusses the relations between language and thought.

WARDHAUGH, R. *An Introduction to Sociolinguistics,* 4th ed. Oxford: Blackwell, 2001. This introduction deals with the relationship between language and society and covers, among other topics, linguistic variation related to variation in status, ethnicity, and gender; multilingualism; creole languages; the possible influences of language on society; and attempts to change language.

ECONOMIC SYSTEMS

CHAPTER OUTLINE

- ◆ The Allocation of Resources

- ◆ The Conversion of Resources

- ◆ The Distribution of Goods and Services

When we think of economics, we think of things and activities involving money. We think of the costs of goods and services, such as food, rent, haircuts, and movie tickets. We may also think of factories, farms, and other enterprises that produce the goods and services we need, or think we need. In industrial societies, workers may stand before a moving belt for eight hours, tightening identical bolts that glide by. For this task they are given bits of paper that may be exchanged for food, shelter, and other goods or services. But many societies—indeed, most that are known to anthropology—did not have money or the equivalent of the factory worker. Still, all societies have economic systems, whether or not they involve money. All societies have customs specifying how people gain access to natural resources; customary ways of transforming or converting those resources, through labor, into necessities and other desired goods and services; and customs for distributing and perhaps exchanging goods and services.

As we shall see in this chapter, a great deal of the cross-cultural variation in economic systems is related to how a society gets its food. However, other aspects of the culture also affect the economic system. These other influences, which we cover in subsequent chapters, include the presence or absence of social (class and gender) inequality, family and kinship groups, and the political system.

The Allocation of Resources

NATURAL RESOURCES: LAND

Every society has access to natural resources—land, water, plants, animals, minerals—and every society has cultural rules for determining who has access to particular resources and what can be done with them. In societies like the United States, where land and many other things may be bought and sold, land is divided into precisely measurable units, the borders of which may be visible or invisible. Relatively small plots of land and the resources on them are usually owned by individuals. Large plots of land ae generally owned collectively. The owner may be a government agency, such as the National Park Service, which owns land on behalf of the entire population of the United States. Or the owner may be a corporation—a private collective of shareholders. In the United States, property ownership entails a more or less exclusive right to use land or other resources (called *usufruct*) in whatever ways the owner wishes, including the right to withhold or prevent use by others. In the United States and many other societies, property ownership also includes the right to "alienate" property—that is, to sell, give away, bequeath, or destroy the resources owned. This type of property ownership is often referred to as a *private property* system.

Private property in regard to land is unknown to most food collectors and most horticulturalists. There is no individual ownership of land or ownership by a group of unrelated people. If there is collective ownership, it is always by groups of related people (kinship groups) or by territorial groups (bands or villages). Land is not bought and sold.

Society specifies what is considered property and the rights and duties associated with that property.[1] These specifications are social in nature, for they may be changed over time. For example, France declared all its beaches to be public, thereby stating, in effect, that the ocean shore is not a resource that can be owned by an individual. As a result, all the hotels and individuals that had fenced off portions of the best beaches for their exclusive use had to remove the barriers. Even in countries with private property, such as the United States, people cannot do anything that they want with their property. Federal, state, and local governments have adopted legislation to prevent the pollution of the air and the water supply. Such regulation may be new, but the rights of ownership in the United States have been limited for some time. For example, land may be taken by the government for use in the construction of a highway; compensation is paid, but the individual cannot prevent confiscation. Similarly, people are not allowed to burn their houses or to use them as brothels or munitions arsenals. In short, even with an individualistic system of ownership, property is not entirely private.

How societies differ in their rules for access to land and other natural resources seems to be related in part to how they differ in food-getting. Let us now examine how food collectors, horticulturalists, pastoralists, and intensive agriculturalists structure rights to land in different ways. We look at traditional patterns first. As we shall note later, traditional rights to land have been considerably affected by state societies that have spread to and colonized native societies in the New World, Africa, and Asia.

FOOD COLLECTORS As we have noted, members of food-collecting societies generally do not own land individually. The reason is probably that land itself has no intrinsic value for food collectors; what is of value is the presence of game and wild plant life on the land. If game moves away or food resources become less plentiful, the land is less valuable. Therefore, the greater the possibility that the wild food supply in a particular locale will fluctuate, the less desirable it is to parcel out small areas of land to individuals and the more advantageous it is to make land ownership communal. The Hadza of Tanzania, for example, do not believe that they have exclusive rights over the land on which they hunt. Any member of the group can hunt, gather, or draw water wherever he or she likes.[2]

Although food collectors rarely practice anything resembling individual ownership of land or other resources, there is considerable variation in the extent of communal ownership. In some societies, such as the Hadza, groups do not claim or defend particular territories. In fact, the Hadza do not even restrict use of their land to members of their own language group. But the Hadza are somewhat unusual. It is more common in food-collecting societies for a group of individuals, usually kin, to "own" land. To be sure, such ownership is not usually exclusive; typically some degree of access is provided to members of neighboring bands.[3]

At the other extreme, local groups in some foraging societies try to maintain exclusive rights to particular territories.

The Owens Valley Paiute in the California part of the Great Basin lived all year in permanent villages along streams. A group of villagers claimed and defended a particular territory against intruders, who may or may not have been other Owens Valley Paiute.

Why have some food collectors been more territorial than others? One suggestion is that when the plants and animals collected are predictably located and abundant, groups are more likely to be sedentary and to try to maintain exclusive control over territories. In contrast, when plant and animal resources are unpredictable in location or amount, territoriality will tend to be minimal.[4] Territorial food collectors appear to have predictably located resources *and* more permanent villages, so it is hard to know which factor is more important in determining whether territory will be defended.

HORTICULTURALISTS Like food collectors, most horticulturalists do not have individual or family ownership of land. This may be because rapid depletion of the soil necessitates letting some of the land lie fallow for a period of years or abandoning an area after a few years and moving to a new location. There is no reason for individuals or families to claim permanent access to land that, given available technology, is not usable permanently. But, unlike food collectors, horticulturalists do allocate particular plots of land to individuals or families for their use, although these individuals or families do not own the land in our sense of potentially permanent ownership.

Among the Mundurucu of Brazil, the village controls the rights to use land. People in the community can hunt and fish where they like, and they have the right to clear a garden plot wherever land belonging to the community is not being used. Gardens can be cultivated for only two years before the soil is exhausted; then the land reverts to the community. The Mundurucu distinguish between the land and the produce on the land, so that a person who cultivates the land owns the produce. Similarly, the person who kills an animal or catches a fish owns it, no matter where it was obtained. But because all food is shared with others, it does not really matter who owns it. Rights to land became more individualized when Mundurucu men began to tap rubber trees for sale. Rights to a particular path in the forest where trees were tapped could not be bought and sold, but the rights could be inherited by a son or son-in-law.[5]

PASTORALISTS The territory of pastoral nomads usually far exceeds that of most horticultural societies. Since their wealth ultimately depends on mobile herds, uncultivated pasture for grazing, and water for drinking, pastoralists must combine the adaptive potential of both food collectors and horticulturalists. Like food collectors, they must know the potential of their territory, which can extend as much as 1,000 miles, so that they are assured supplies of grass and water. And, like horticulturalists, they must move on when a resource is exhausted (in this case, until grass renews itself). Also like horticulturalists, they depend for subsistence on human manipulation of a natural resource—animals—as opposed to the horticulturalists' land.

A Surui village in the Amazon with cleared land for horticulture in the foreground and the surrounding rainforest in the background.

CURRENT RESEARCH AND ISSUES
Does Communal Ownership Lead to Economic Disaster?

A common idea in Western thought is that when land or other resources are held in common, serious damage results because individuals do not see it in their own interest to protect those resources. In a paper called "The Tragedy of the Commons," Garrett Hardin suggested that if animals are grazed on common land, it is economically rational for individual animal owners to graze as many animals as possible, since they do not incur the pasture costs. According to Hardin, tragedy results because pasture is degraded by overgrazing, and productivity falls. Similarly, why shouldn't a fisher take as much fish as possible from the ocean, a kind of commons, and not worry about the consequences? On the other hand, if the resource is privately owned, individuals might try to conserve their resources because degrading

those resources will cost them in the long run by decreasing their yields. The theory, then, is that in order to minimize costs and maximize yields, private owners will find it rational to conserve their resources.

Is it really true that communal ownership tends to result in overexploitation of resources and lower yields, and private ownership tends to result in conservation of resources and higher yields? We do not have enough studies yet to generalize, but we do know about instances where communal grazing lands have been more productive than private grazing lands in comparable climates. For example, the Borana of Ethiopia, who have communal grazing, produce more animal protein per acre at lower cost than Australian cattle ranches, although the climates are similar. And there are instances, such as the over-

grazing in the Great American Desert (described in the box "The Effect of Food-Getting on the Environment" in the preceding chapter), where private ownership did lead to degradation of the environment.

We have to remember that communal ownership does not mean that anyone can graze animals or fish at any time. Communities and kin groups often govern rights to pasturage or fishing, and only members of the group have rights of access and use. As we saw in the last chapter, pastoralists such as the Basseri have well-defined, socially arranged travel routes, moving their herds when conditions demand. For traditional pastoralists, mobility is often the key to prevent overgrazing. Similarly, many groups that fish have strict rules regulating access to fishing grounds, and some have conservation rules as well. For example, the

---

Because land is only good if there is sufficient pasture and water, there would be considerable risk to individuals or families to own land. So, like most foragers and horticulturalists, community members generally have free access to pasture land.[6] Although grazing land tends to be communally held, it is customary among pastoralists for animals to be owned by individuals.[7] Fredrik Barth argued that if animals were not so owned, the whole group might be in trouble because the members might be tempted to eat up their productive capital—their animals—in bad times. When animals are owned individually, a family whose herd drops below the minimum number of animals necessary for survival can drop out of nomadic life, at least temporarily, and work for wages in sedentary agricultural communities. But in so doing, such a family does not jeopardize other pastoral families. On the other hand, if the fortunate were to share their herds with the unfortunate, all might approach bankruptcy. Thus, Barth argued, individual ownership is adaptive for a pastoral way of life.[8]

John Dowling questioned that interpretation. As he pointed out, pastoral nomads are not the only ones who have to save some of their "crop" for future production. Horticulturalists also must save some of their crop, in the

form of seeds or tubers, for future planting. But horticulturalists generally lack private ownership of productive resources, so the necessity to save for future production cannot explain private ownership of animals in pastoral societies. Dowling suggested that private ownership will develop only in pastoral societies that depend on selling their products to nonpastoralists.[9] Thus, it may be the opportunity to sell their products as well as their labor that explains both the possibility of dropping out of nomadic life and the private ownership of animals among most pastoralists.

INTENSIVE AGRICULTURALISTS Individual ownership of land resources—including the right to use the resources and the right to sell or otherwise dispose of them—is common among intensive agriculturalists. The development of such ownership is partly a result of the possibility of using land season after season, which gives the land more or less permanent value. But the concept of individual ownership is also partly a political and social matter. So, for example, the occupation and cultivation of frontier land in the United States was transformed by law into individual ownership. Under the Homestead Act of

(continued)

Palauans of Micronesia usually allow only members of a cluster of villages to fish in the adjacent lagoon waters inside the fringing reef. Traditionally, people took only what they could eat, and there were "laws" governing the times that people could fish for certain species.

Restricted access to communal property may be the main way that pastoralists and fishers prevent degradation of their environment. Some groups, such as the Palauans, clearly have conservation rules. But we do not know how many pastoralists and fishers have such rules. For example, the Ponam of New Guinea do not appear to conserve fish resources, even though they restrict access to their communal fishing territories. They do value the prestige associated with generosity, and consequently they try to collect more fish than they need in order to give some away.

Development and commercialization may be more important than private versus communal ownership in leading to overgrazing or overfishing, at least initially. In Palau, which had traditional conservation practices, serious overfishing became a problem apparently only when people started to sell fish to Japanese colonists for imported trade goods. Some of those goods (nets and motors) helped to make fishing easier. Eventually, overfishing resulted in reduced catches and increased costs of fishing, and the Palauans had to buy much of their fish in imported cans. In arid areas of the Sahel in Africa, development may have led to pastoral overgrazing. Boreholes were built by development agencies to increase the water supply, but this practice often made people reluctant to move to new grazing land, so local land was overgrazed. In addition, the development of irrigation agriculture nearby decreased the amount of land available for pasturage.

So which is more likely in general to lead to conservation, com-munal ownership or private ownership? We cannot say yet. We need more systematic comparisons of many cases of the two types of systems to tell us.

Sources: Garrett Hardin, "The Tragedy of the Commons," *Science,* 162 (1968): 1243–48; Bonnie M. McCay and James M. Acheson, "Introduction," and James G. Carrier, "Marine Tenure and Conservation in Papua New Guinea," in Bonnie M. McCay and James M. Acheson, eds., *The Question of Commons: The Culture and Ecology of Communal Resources* (Tucson: University of Arizona Press, 1987); Michael M. Horowitz, "Donors and Deserts: The Political Ecology of Destructive Development in the Sahel," in Rebecca Huss-Ashmore and Solomon H. Katz, eds., *African Food Systems in Crisis. Part Two. Contending with Change* (New York: Gordon and Breach, 1990); R. E. Johannes, *Words of the Lagoon: Fishing and Marine Lore in the Palau District of Micronesia* (Berkeley: University of California Press, 1981); Robert Dirks, "Hunger and Famine," in Carol R. Ember, Melvin Ember, and Peter N. Peregrine, eds., *Research Frontiers in Anthropology,* in Carol R. Ember and Melvin Ember, eds., *New Directions in Anthropology* (Upper Saddle River, NJ: Prentice Hall, CD-ROM, 2003); John J. Poggie, personal communication, 1994.

1862, if a person cleared a 160-acre piece of land and farmed it for five years, the federal government would consider that person the owner of the land. This practice is similar to the custom in some societies by which a kin group, a chief, or a community is obligated to assign a parcel of land to anyone who wishes to farm it. The difference is that once the American homesteader had become the owner of the land, the laws of the country gave the homesteader the right to dispose of it at will by selling or giving it away. Once individual ownership of land has become established, property owners may use their economic, and hence political, power to pass laws that favor themselves. In the early years of the United States, only property owners could vote.

Private individual ownership is usually associated with intensive agriculture, but not always. As we mentioned in the preceding chapter, intensive agriculture is usually associated with more complex political systems and with differences in wealth and power, so we need to understand the larger political and social context in order to understand fully particular systems of land allocation. For example, under the feudal and manor systems in much of medieval Europe, land and protection were granted by a higher aris-tocrat to a lower aristocrat (vassal) in exchange for military service and other obligations. If the vassal had no heirs, the land reverted to the higher aristocrat. Most of the farming was done by commoners—tenants and serfs. Tenants were granted land by the lord of a manor in return for labor, a portion of the crops, and military service when needed. Tenancy could be passed on to the children, and tenants technically were free to leave, but it was not easy to leave. Serfs, who had similar obligations to the lord of the manor, were bound to the land and could not leave, but neither could they be ejected. In recent times, some communist and socialist nations with intensive agriculture formed agricultural collectives. For example, after World War II, the small farm holdings in a village in Bulgaria named Zamfirovo were incorporated into a village cooperative. Most of the villagers worked as laborers on the new cooperative, but every household was allocated a small plot by the cooperative on which to grow its own grain, vegetables, and grapes. These plots were fairly productive, and Westerners often attributed their productivity to private enterprise. But the cooperative provided much of the labor needed to plant and plow these plots, so they could hardly be considered private property. In 1989, after the over-

Fences usually indicate private ownership.

throw of the communist regime, the cooperative was dissolved, and the land was divided and sold to private owners.[10]

COLONIALISM, THE STATE, AND LAND RIGHTS

Almost universally around the world, colonial conquerors and settlers have taken land away from the natives or aborigines. Even if the natives were given other land in exchange, as in Brazil and the United States, these reservations were often, if not always, poorer in potential than the original land. (If the reservation land hadn't been poorer in quality, the settlers would have taken it for themselves.) In addition, the new centralized governments often tried to change how land was owned by the natives, almost always in the direction of individual or private ownership. If kin groups or larger social entities owned the land, it would be more difficult for the settlers to get the natives to give it up, either by sale or threat. Individual owners could be dispossessed more easily.[11]

The newcomers who benefited from these forced changes were not always people of European background, but they were always people from expanding state societies. Beginning in the late fifteenth century, the expanding groups came mostly from Western Europe. But in recent times, as well as in the millennia before and after the time of Christ, conquerors and settlers have come from India, China, Japan, Arabia, Scandinavia, Russia, and other countries. This is not to say that native peoples in Africa, Asia, and the New World were never guilty of conquering and exploiting others on their continents or elsewhere. They were. The Aztecs in Mexico and Central America, the native kingdoms in West Africa after about 800 years ago, and the Arabs after the rise of Islam were just some of the ex-

panding state societies of the past, before the rise of the West. Wherever there have been "civilized" (urban) societies, there have been imperialism and colonialism.

In North America, the British recognized the principle that lands not ceded to the crown would be Indian hunting grounds, but such recognition of rights by the British and then by the United States remained in force only as long as the various Indian groups remained numerous enough to constitute a threat to the settlers. President Andrew Jackson, for example, called for removal of all eastern Native American groups to "permanent" settlements west of the Mississippi. Some 90,000 people were removed. But as settlers moved west, the reservations were often reduced in size. Government agents usually assumed that communal forms of ownership were detrimental to progress and enacted laws to assign land to individuals.[12] In much of colonial Africa, governments ceded land to European-owned companies for development. Reserves were established for large native populations, who then were invariably forced to work as laborers on European-owned plantations and in European-owned mines. In Kenya, for example, Europeans, who constituted less than 1 percent of the population, acquired access to or control of 20 percent of the land, mostly in the highlands, where there was the greatest potential for commercial production of tea and coffee.[13]

The taking of land by state authorities does not just happen with colonialism and imperialism. Indigenous revolutionary movements have collectivized land, as in Russia, or broken up large private landholdings, as in Mexico. Typically, state authorities do not like communal land-use systems. Mobile pastoralists are particularly viewed unfavorably by state authorities, because their mobility makes them difficult to control. Governments usually try to settle pastoralists or break up communally-held pasture into small units.[14]

TECHNOLOGY

In order to convert resources to food and other goods, every society makes use of a technology, which includes tools, constructions (such as fish traps), and required skills (such as how and where to set up a fish trap). Societies vary considerably in their technologies and in the way access to technology is allocated. For example, food collectors and pastoralists typically have fairly small tool kits. They must limit their tools, and their material possessions in general, to what they can comfortably carry with them. As for access to technology, food collectors and horticulturalists generally allow equal opportunity. In the absence of specialization, most individuals have the skills to make what they need. But in an industrial society like our own, the opportunity to acquire or use a particular technology (which may be enormously expensive as well as complex) is hardly available to all. Most of us may be able to buy a drill or a hammer, but few of us can buy the factory that makes it.

The tools most needed by food collectors are weapons for the hunt, digging sticks, and receptacles for gathering and carrying. Andaman Islanders used bows and arrows for hunting game and large fish. Australian aborigines developed two types of boomerangs: a heavy one for a straight throw in killing game and a light, returning one for playing games or for scaring birds into nets strung between trees. The Semang of Malaya used poisoned darts and blowguns. The Mbuti of the Congo still trap elephants and buffalo in deadfalls and nets. Of all food collectors, the Inuit probably had the most sophisticated weapons, including harpoons, compound bows, and ivory fishhooks. Yet the Inuit also had relatively fixed settlements with available storage space and dog teams and sleds for transportation.[15] Among food collectors, tools are considered to belong to the person who made them. There is no way of gaining superiority over others through possession of tools, because whatever resources for toolmaking are available to one are available to all. In addition, the custom of sharing applies to tools as well as to food. For example, Elizabeth Thomas, speaking of the !Kung, said, "The few possessions that Bushmen have are constantly circulating among the members of their groups."[16]

Pastoralists, like food collectors, are somewhat limited in their possessions, for they too are nomadic. But pastoralists can use their animals to carry some possessions. Each family owns its own tools, clothes, and perhaps a tent, as well as its own livestock. The livestock are the source of other needed articles, for the pastoralists often trade their herd products for the products of the townspeople. Horticulturalists, on the other hand, are more self-sufficient than pastoralists. The knife for slashing and the hoe or stick for digging are their principal farming tools. What a person makes is considered his or her own, yet everyone is often obligated to lend tools to others. In Chuuk society, the owner of a canoe has first use of it; the same is true for farming implements. Yet if a close relative needs the canoe and finds it unused, the canoe may be taken without permission. A distant relative or neighbor must ask permission to borrow any tools, but the owner may not refuse. If owners were to refuse, they would risk being scorned and refused if they were to need tools later.

Societies with intensive agriculture and industrialized societies are likely to have tools made by specialists, which means that tools must be acquired by trade or purchase. Probably because complex tools cost a considerable amount of money, they are less likely than simple tools to be shared except by those who contributed to the purchase price. For example, a diesel-powered combine requires a large amount of capital for its purchase and upkeep. The person who has supplied the capital is likely to regard the machine as individual private property and to regulate its use and disposal. The owner must then use the machine to produce enough surplus to pay for its cost and upkeep as well as for its replacement. The owner may rent the machine to neighboring farmers during slack periods to obtain a maximum return on the investment.

Expensive equipment, however, is not always individually owned in societies with intensive agriculture or industrialized economies. Even in capitalist countries, there may be collective ownership of machines by cooperatives or co-ownership with neighbors.[17] Governments often own very expensive equipment or facilities that benefit some productive group as well as the public: Airports benefit airlines and travelers; highways benefit truckers, commuters, and travelers; dams benefit power and water companies as well as the consumers of water. Such resources are owned collectively by the whole society. Rights of use depend on the facility. Anyone can use a highway, but only contributing municipalities can draw upon the water in a dam. Other productive resources in industrial societies, such as factories or service companies, may be owned jointly by shareholders, who purchase a portion of a corporation's assets in return for a proportionate share of its earnings. The proportion of technology and facilities owned by various levels of government also reflects the type of political-economic system—socialist and communist countries have more public ownership than do capitalist countries.

The Conversion of Resources

In all societies, resources have to be transformed or converted through labor into food, tools, and other goods. These activities constitute what economists call *production*. In this section, after briefly reviewing different types of production, we examine what motivates people to work, how societies divide up the work to be done, and how they organize work. As we shall see, some aspects of the conversion of natural resources are culturally universal, but there is also an enormous amount of cultural variation.

TYPES OF ECONOMIC PRODUCTION

At the times they were first described, most of the societies known to anthropology had a *domestic*—family or kinship—mode of production. People labored to get food and to produce shelter and implements for themselves and their kin. Usually families had the right to exploit productive resources and control the products of their labor. Even part-time specialists, such as potters, could still support themselves without that craft if they needed to. At the other extreme are *industrial* societies, where much of the work is based on mechanized production, as in factories but also in mechanized agriculture. Because machines and materials are costly, only some individuals (capitalists), corporations, or governments can afford the expenses of production. Therefore, most people in industrial societies labor for others as wage earners. Although wages can buy food, people out of work lose their ability to support themselves, unless they are protected by welfare payments or unemployment insurance. Then there is the *tributary* type of production system, found in nonindustrial societies in which most people still produce their own food but an elite or aristocracy controls a portion of production (including the products of specialized crafts). The feudal societies of medieval Western Europe were examples of tributary production, as was czarist Russia under serfdom.[18]

Many people have suggested that our own and other developed economies are now moving from *industrialism* to *postindustrialism*. In many areas of commerce, computers have radically transformed the workplace. Computers

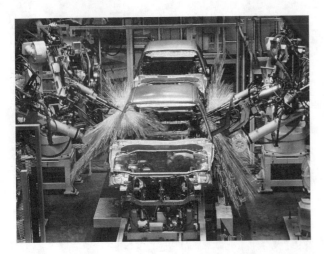

Robots, not people, assemble automobile bodies in South Africa.

"drive" machines and robots, and much of the manual work required in industry is disappearing. Businesses are now more knowledge- and service-oriented. Information is more accessible with telecommunication, so much so that *telecommuting* has entered our vocabulary to describe how people can now work (for wages) at home. This economic transformation has important implications for both home life and the workplace. With inexpensive home computers and speedy data transmission by telephone and other means, more and more people are able to work at home. In addition, when information and knowledge become more important than capital equipment, more and more people can own and have access to the productive resources of society.[19] If "who owns what" partly determines who has political and other influence, the wider ownership of resources that is possible in postindustrial society may eventually translate into new, more democratic political forms and processes.

INCENTIVES FOR LABOR

Why do people work? Probably all of us have asked ourselves this question. Our concern may not be why other people are working, but why we have to work. Clearly, part of the answer is that work is necessary for survival. Although there are always some able-bodied adults who do not work as much as they should and rely on the labor of others, no society would survive if most able-bodied adults were like that. In fact, most societies probably succeed in motivating most people to want to do (and even enjoy) what they have to do. But are the incentives for labor the same in all societies? Anthropologists think the answer is both yes and no. One reason people may work is because they must. But why do people in some societies apparently work *more* than they must?

We can be fairly certain that a particular and often-cited motive—the profit motive, or the desire to exchange something for more than it costs—is not universal or always the dominant motive. There can be no profit motive among people who produce food and other goods primarily for

their own consumption, as do most food collectors, most horticulturalists, and even some intensive agriculturalists. Such societies have what we call a *subsistence economy,* not a money or commercial economy. Anthropologists have noticed that people in subsistence economies (with a domestic mode of production) often work less than people in commercial economies (with tributary or industrial modes of production). Indeed, food collectors appear to have a considerable amount of leisure time, as do many horticulturalists. It has been estimated, for example, that the men of the horticultural Kuikuru tribe in central Brazil spent about three and a half hours a day on subsistence. It appears that the Kuikuru could have produced a substantial surplus of manioc, their staple food, by working 30 minutes more a day.[20] Yet they and many other peoples do not produce more than they need. Why should they? They cannot store a surplus for long because it would rot; they cannot sell it because there is no market nearby; and they do not have a political authority that might collect it for some purpose. Although we often think "more is better," a food-getting strategy with such a goal might even be disastrous, especially for food collectors. The killing of more animals than a group could eat might seriously jeopardize the food supply in the future, because overhunting could reduce reproduction among the hunted animals.[21] Horticulturalists might do well to plant a little extra, just in case part of the crop failed, but a great deal extra would be a tremendous waste of time and effort.

It has been suggested that when resources are converted primarily for household consumption, people will work harder if they have more consumers in the household. That is, when there are few able-bodied workers and a proportionately large number of consumers (perhaps because there are many young children and old people), the workers have to work harder. But when there are proportionately more workers, they can work less. This idea is called *Chayanov's rule.*[22] Alexander Chayanov found this relationship in data on rural Russians before the Russian Revolution.[23] But it appears to work in other places too. For example, Michael Chibnik found support for Chayanov's rule when he compared data from 12 communities in 5 areas of the world. The communities ranged in complexity from New Guinea horticulturalists to commercial Swiss farmers. Although Chayanov restricted his theory to farmers who mostly produced food for their own consumption and did not hire labor, Chibnik's analysis suggests that Chayanov's rule applies even for hired labor.[24]

But there appear to be many societies, even with subsistence economies, in which some people work harder than they need to just for their own families' subsistence. What motivates them to work harder? It turns out that many subsistence economies are not oriented just to household consumption. Rather, sharing and other transfers of food and goods often go well beyond the household, sometimes including the whole community or even groups of communities, as we will see later in this chapter. In such societies, social rewards come to those who are generous, who give things away. Thus, people who work harder than they have to for subsistence may be motivated to do so because they gain respect or esteem thereby.[25] In many societies too, as we shall see in subsequent chapters, extra food and goods may be needed at times for special purposes and occasions; goods and services may be needed to arrange and celebrate marriages, to form alliances, and to perform rituals and ceremonies (including what we would call sporting events). Thus, how the culture defines what one works for and what is needed may go beyond what is necessary.

In commercial economies such as our own—where foods, other goods, and services are sold and bought—people seem to be motivated to keep any extra income for themselves and their families. Extra income is converted into bigger dwellings, more expensive furnishings and food, and other elements of a "higher" standard of living. But the desire to improve one's standard of living is probably not the only motive operating. Some people may work partly to satisfy a need for achievement,[26] or because they find their work enjoyable. In addition, just as in precommercial societies, some people may work partly to gain respect or influence by giving some of their income away. Not only do we respect philanthropists and movie stars for giving to charities; our society encourages such giving by making it an allowable tax deduction. Still, the emphasis on giving in commercial societies is clearly less developed than in subsistence economies. We consider charity by the religious or rich appropriate and even admirable, but we would think it foolish or crazy for people to give so much away that they become poverty-stricken.

FORCED LABOR

Thus far we have mostly discussed *voluntary labor*—voluntary in the sense that no formal organization within the society compels people to work and punishes them for not working. Social training and social pressure are powerful enough to persuade an individual to perform some useful task. In both food-collecting and horticultural societies, individuals who can stand being the butt of jokes about laziness will still be fed. At most, they will be ignored by the other members of the group. There is no reason to punish them and no way to coerce them to do the work expected of them.

More complex societies have ways of forcing people to work for the authorities, whether those authorities be kings or presidents. An indirect form of forced labor is taxation. The average tax in the United States (local, state, and federal) is about 33 percent of income, which means that the average person works four months out of the year for the various levels of government. If a person decides not to pay the tax, the money will be taken forcibly or the person may be put in prison.

Money is the customary form of tax payment in a commercial society. In a politically complex but nonmonetary society, persons may pay their taxes in other ways—by performing a certain number of hours of labor or by giving up a certain percentage of what they produce. The **corvée**, a system of required labor, existed in the Inca Empire in the central Andes before the Spanish conquest. Each male commoner was assigned three plots of land to work: a tem-

The Great Wall of China, like many monumental works in ancient societies, was built with forced labor.

ple plot, a state plot, and his own plot. The enormous stores of food that went into state warehouses were used to supply the nobles, the army, the artisans, and all other state employees. If labor became overabundant, the people were still kept occupied; it is said that one ruler had a hill moved to keep some laborers busy. In addition to subsistence work for the state, Inca commoners were subject to military service, to duty as personal servants for the nobility, and to other "public" service.[27]

The draft, or compulsory military service, is also a form of corvée, in that a certain period of service is required, and failure to serve can be punished by a prison term or involuntary exile. Emperors of China had soldiers drafted to defend their territory and to build the Great Wall along the northern borders of the empire. The wall extends over 1,500 miles, and thousands were drafted to work on it. Slavery is the most extreme form of forced work, in that slaves have little control over their labor. Because slaves constitute a category or class of persons in many societies, we discuss slavery more fully in the chapter on social stratification.

DIVISION OF LABOR

All societies have some division of labor, some customary assignment of different kinds of work to different kinds of people. Universally, males and females and adults and children do not do the same kinds of work. In a sense, then, division of labor by gender and age is a kind of universal specialization of labor. Many societies known to anthropology divide labor only by gender and age; other societies have more complex specialization.

BY GENDER AND AGE   All societies make use of gender differences to some extent in their customary assignment of labor. In the chapter on sex, gender, and culture, we discuss the division of labor by gender in detail.

ANTHROPOLOGICAL ORIGINALS
The Yanomamö of Venezuela and Brazil

You don't have to be paid to consider it work: What is work? In our society, we are accustomed to think of anything that we get paid for is work, and work usually takes place outside the home. But what about the societies that have "subsistence economies"? They don't have money. They don't have jobs. And they don't get paid. Does this mean that they don't have work? Of course not. Every society has to have ways of making a living, and what the people do to stay alive is work. But who does it?

The question of whether men or women work more can only be answered if we have a reasonable definition of work. Generally, economic anthropologists define work as all of those activities required to directly maintain and enhance survival and reproduction. Thus, it includes rather obvious activities

such as the provisioning and preparing of food, construction and repair of tools and shelter, and the acquisition and management of fuel (or firewood, in the case of the Yanomamö). If we used this definition of work, Yanomamö women work about twelve minutes per day more than men, but the difference is not statistically significant. This finding is rather interesting since in the vast majority of horticultural tribal populations on which we have time allocation data, women work significantly more than men. The only societies in which men work significantly more than women are hunters and gatherers. That Yanomamö men and women work approximately equally is therefore consistent with the point made earlier: that they can be best characterized as foraging horticulturalists since their time allocation patterns

fall between horticulturalists and hunter-gatherers. . . . When I include direct child care activities (carrying, feeding, nursing, holding, etc.), female work time increases by forty-three minutes per day while male work time increases by only eight minutes per day. If child care activities are added to conventionally defined labor, then Yanomamö women work more than men.

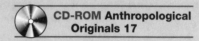

CD-ROM Anthropological Originals 17

Source: Raymond B. Hames, "Yanomamö: Varying Adaptations for Foraging Horticulturalists," in Melvin Ember and Carol R. Ember, eds., *Portraits of Culture: Ethnographic Originals,* in Carol R. Ember and Melvin Ember, eds., *New Directions in Anthropology* (Upper Saddle River, NJ: Prentice Hall, CD-ROM, 2003).

Age is also a universal basis for division of labor. Clearly, children cannot do work that requires a great deal of strength. But in many societies girls and boys contribute much more in labor than do children in our own society. For example, they help in animal tending, weeding, and harvesting and do a variety of domestic chores such as child care, fetching water and firewood, and cooking and cleaning. In agricultural communities in the Ivory Coast, children's tasks mirror the tasks of same-sex adults (see Figure 17–1). In some societies, a child 6 years old is considered old enough to be responsible for a younger sibling for a good part of the day.[28] Animal tending is often important work for children. Children in some societies spend more time at this task than adults.[29]

Why do children do so much work in some societies? If adults, particularly mothers, have heavy workloads, and children are physically and mentally able to do the work, a good part of the work is likely to be assigned to children.[30] As we have seen, food producers probably have more work than food collectors, so we would expect that children would be likely to work more where there is herding and farming. Consistent with this expectation, Patricia Draper

and Elizabeth Cashdan found differences in children's work between nomadic and settled !Kung. Even though recently settled !Kung have not switched completely from food collection to food production, children's as well as adults' activities have changed considerably. The children living in nomadic camps had virtually no work at all; adults did all the gathering and hunting. But the settled children were given lots of chores, ranging from helping with animals to helping with the harvest and food processing.[31]

What we have said about the !Kung should not imply that children in foraging societies always do little work. For example, among the Hadza of Tanzania, children between the ages of 5 and 10 are able to get one-third to one-half of their calories as they forage with their mothers. The Hadza also have more children than the !Kung.[32] Is there a relationship between children's work and fertility? When children in a society do a great deal of work, parents may value them more and may consciously want to have more children.[33] This may be one of the reasons why birth rates are especially high in intensive agricultural societies where workloads are very high.[34]

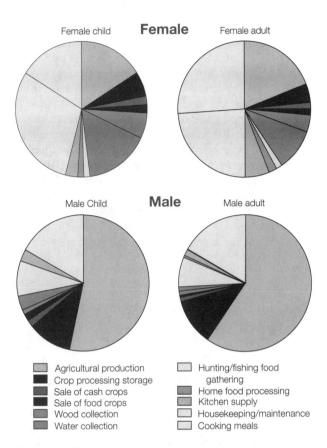

Female child **Female** Female adult

Male Child **Male** Male adult

- ▢ Agricultural production
- ▢ Crop processing storage
- ▢ Sale of cash crops
- ▢ Sale of food crops
- ▢ Wood collection
- ▢ Water collection
- ▢ Hunting/fishing food gathering
- ▢ Home food processing
- ▢ Kitchen supply
- ▢ Housekeeping/maintenance
- ▢ Cooking meals

Figure 17–1 *A Comparison of the Proportion of Work Tasks Done by Adults and Children*

Source: From James A. Levine, Robert Weisell, Simon Chevassus, Claudio D. Martinez, and Barbara Burlingame. "The Distribution of Work Tasks for Male and Female Children and Adults Separated by Gender" in "Looking at Child Labor," *Science 296* (10 May 2002): 1025.

In some societies, work groups are formally organized on the basis of age. Among the Nyakyusa of southeastern Africa, for example, cattle are the principal form of wealth, and boys 6 to 11 years old herd the cattle for their parents' village. The boys join together in herding groups to tend the cattle of their fathers and of any neighboring families that do not have a son of herding age.[35]

BEYOND GENDER AND AGE In societies with relatively simple technologies, there is little specialization of labor beyond that of gender and age. But as a society's technology becomes more complex and it is able to produce large quantities of food, more of its people are freed from subsistence work to become specialists in some other tasks—canoe builders, weavers, priests, potters, artists, and the like.

In contrast with food collectors, horticultural societies may have some part-time specialists. Some people may devote special effort to perfecting a particular skill or craft—pottery making, weaving, house building, doctoring—and in return for their products or services be given food or other gifts. Among some horticultural groups, the entire village may specialize part time in making a particular product, which can then be traded to neighboring people.

With the development of intensive agriculture, full-time specialists—potters, weavers, blacksmiths—begin to appear. The trend toward greater specialization reaches its peak in industrialized societies, where workers develop skills in one small area of the economic system. The meaninglessness and dehumanizing effect of much of industrialized work was depicted by Charlie Chaplin in the film *Modern Times.* When his character left the factory after repeatedly tightening the same kind of bolt all day long, he could not stop his arms from moving, as if they were still tightening bolts. In societies with full-time occupational specialization, different jobs are usually associated with differences in prestige, wealth, and power, as we shall see in the chapter on social stratification.

THE ORGANIZATION OF LABOR

The degree to which labor has to be organized reaches its peak in industrial societies, which have great occupational specialization and complex political organization. The coordination required to produce an automobile on an assembly line is obvious; so is the coordination required to collect taxes from every wage earner.

In many food-collecting and horticultural societies there is little formal organization of work. Work groups tend to be organized only when productive work requires it and to dissolve when they are no longer needed. Furthermore, the groups so organized often have changing composition and leadership; participation tends to be individualistic and voluntary.[36] Perhaps this flexibility is possible because when virtually everyone has the same work to do, little instruction is needed, and almost anyone can assume leadership. Still, some types of work require more organization than others. Hunting big game usually requires coordinated efforts by a large number of hunters; so might catching fish in large nets. For example, on Moala, a Fijian island in the Pacific, net fishing is a group affair. Saturday is the most popular day for communal netting. A party of 20 to 30 women wade out on the reef and make a semicircle of nets. At a signal from an experienced woman, usually the chief's wife, the women move together at the ends, forming a circle. After the fish are caught in the nets, the women bite them on the backs of their heads to kill them and put them in baskets that they carry ashore. A larger fish drive is undertaken by the village, or several villages, around Christmas. The day before, more than 100 people make a "sweep," some 1,600 yards long, from coconut fronds. The next day, the men, women, and children all participate in the surround, catching thousands of fish.[37]

Kinship ties are an important basis for work organization, particularly in nonindustrial societies. For example, among the horticultural Kapauku of western New Guinea, the male members of a village are a kin group, and all work together to build drainage ditches, large fences, and bridges.[38] With increasing technological complexity, the basis of work organization begins to shift to more formally organized groups.[39] In modern industrial societies, the predominant basis of organization is the *contract*—the agreement between employers and employees whereby the latter perform a specified amount of work for a specified amount of wages. Although the arrangement may be entered into voluntarily, laws and the power of the state enforce the obligation of the parties to abide by the contract.

MAKING DECISIONS ABOUT WORK

Food collectors ignore many of the plant and animal species in their environment, choosing to go after only some. Why? The people may say that some animals are taboo whereas others are delicious. But where do such customary beliefs come from? Are they adaptive? And if there are no customary preferences for certain plants and animals, how can we explain why a food collector will go after certain foods and ignore others on a particular day? Food producers also make choices constantly. For example, a farmer has to decide when to plant, what to plant, how much to plant, when to harvest, how much to store, how much to give away or sell. Researchers have tried to explain why certain economic decisions become customary and why individuals make certain economic choices in their everyday lives.

A frequent source of ideas about choices is **optimal foraging theory,** which was developed originally by students of animal behavior and which has been applied to decision making by food collectors. Optimal foraging theory assumes that individuals seek to maximize the returns, in calories and nutrients, on their labor in deciding which animals and plants to hunt or collect. Natural selection should favor optimal foraging because "good" decisions would increase the chances of survival and reproduction. Research in different food-collecting societies supports the optimal foraging model.[40] For example, the Aché of eastern Paraguay consistently prefer to hunt peccaries (wild piglike mammals) rather than armadillos. Although peccaries take much longer to find and are harder to kill than armadillos, a day spent hunting peccaries yields more than 4,600 calories per hour of work, whereas hunting armadillos yields only about 1,800 calories an hour.[41] Other factors in addition to calorie yield, such as predictability of resources, may also influence which foods are collected. For example, the !Kung of the Kalahari Desert depend largely on mongongo nuts, even though these nuts yield fewer calories per hour of work than does meat. But mongongo nuts in season are more dependable than game is. Once a group of !Kung hikes to a grove of ripe mongongo nuts, they know they can obtain food there until the supply is exhausted; they are not as certain of getting game when they seek it.[42]

How does a farmer decide whether to plant a particular crop and how much land and labor to devote to it? Christina Gladwin and others suggested that farmers make decisions in steps, with each choice point involving a yes or no answer. For example, in the high-altitude region of Guatemala, farmers could choose to plant about eight crops, or combinations of them, such as corn and beans, which grow together well. A farmer will quickly exclude some choices because of the answers to certain questions: Can I afford the seed and fertilizer? Can this crop be watered adequately? Is the altitude appropriate? And so on. If any of the answers is no, the crop is not planted. By a further series of yes or no decisions, farmers presumably decide which of the remaining possibilities will be planted.[43]

Individuals may not always be able to state clearly their rules for making decisions, nor do they always have complete knowledge about the various possibilities, particularly when some of the possibilities are new. That does not mean, however, that economic choices cannot be predicted or explained by researchers. For example, Michael Chibnik found that men in two villages in Belize, in Central America, were not able to say why they devoted more or less time to working for wages versus growing crops. But their behavior was still predictable. Older men grew crops because wage labor was more physically demanding; and in the village with a higher cost of living, men were more likely to work for wages.[44]

◆ The Distribution of Goods and Services

Goods and services are distributed in all societies by systems that, however varied, can be classified under three general types: reciprocity, redistribution, and market or commercial exchange.[45] The three systems often coexist in a society, but one system usually predominates. The predominant system seems to be associated with the society's food-getting technology and, more specifically, its level of economic development.

RECIPROCITY

Reciprocity consists of giving and taking without the use of money; it mainly takes the form of gift giving or generalized reciprocity. There may also be exchanges of equal value (trade) or balanced reciprocity, without the use of money.[46]

GENERALIZED RECIPROCITY When goods or services are given to another, without any apparent expectation of a return gift, we call it **generalized reciprocity.** Generalized reciprocity sustains the family in all societies. Parents give food, clothing, and labor to children because they want to or perhaps feel obliged to, but they do not usually calculate exactly how their children will reciprocate years later. In this sense, all societies have some kind of generalized reciprocity. But some societies depend on it almost entirely to distribute goods and services.

Lorna Marshall recounted how the !Kung divided an eland brought to a site where five bands and several visitors were camping—more than 100 people in all. The owner of the arrow that had first penetrated the eland was, by custom, the owner of the meat. He first distributed the forequarters to the two hunters who had aided him in the kill. After that, the distribution depended on kinship: Each hunter shared with his wives' parents, wives, children, parents, and siblings, and they in turn shared with their kin. Sixty-three gifts of raw meat were recorded, after which further sharing of raw and cooked meat was begun. The !Kung distribution of large game—clearly, generalized reciprocity—is common among foragers. But giving away is not limited to game. For example, when Marshall left the band that had sponsored her in 1951, she gave each woman in the band a present of enough cowrie shells to make a necklace—one large shell and 20 small ones. When she returned in 1952, there were no cowrie-shell necklaces and hardly a single shell among the people in the band. Instead, the shells appeared by ones and twos in the ornaments of the people of neighboring bands.[47]

Although generalized reciprocity may seem altruistic or unselfish, researchers have suggested that giving may in fact benefit the givers in various ways. For example, parents who help their children may not only perpetuate their genes (the ultimate biological benefit) but may also be likely to receive care and affection from their grown-up children when the parents are old. And giving parents may be happier and enjoy life more than nongiving parents. So, in the shorter as well as the longer run, givers may derive economic and psychological benefits, in addition to reproductive benefits.

Parent-child giving may seem easy to understand, but giving beyond the family is more of a problem. Why do some societies rely more on generalized reciprocity than others, particularly beyond the family? Sharing may be most likely when people are not sure they can get the food and water they need. In other words, sharing may be most likely if resources are unpredictable. So a !Kung band may share its water with other bands because they may have water now but not in the future. A related group in the Kalahari, the G//ana,[48] has been observed to share less than other groups. It turns out that the resources available to the G//ana are more predictable, because the G//ana supplement their hunting and gathering with plant cultivation and goat herding. Cultivated melons (which store water) appear to buffer the G//ana against water shortages, and goats to buffer them against shortages of game. Thus, whereas the !Kung distribute the meat right after a kill, the G//ana dry it and then store it in their houses.[49]

The idea that unpredictability favors sharing may also explain why some foods are more often shared than others. Wild game, for example, is usually unpredictable; when hunters go out to hunt, they cannot be sure that they will come back with meat. Wild plants, on the other hand, are more predictable; gatherers can be sure when they go out that they will come back with at least some plant foods. In any case, it does appear that game tends to be shared by food collectors much more than wild plant foods.[50] Even among people who depend largely on horticulture, such as the Yanomamö of Venezuela and Brazil, food items that are less predictably obtained (hunted game and fish) are shared more often than the more predictably obtained garden produce.[51] But while meat is shared more than plant food, foraged or cultivated plants are often shared by horticulturalists. Why? Sharing plant food may be advantageous to horticulturalists who are some distance from their gardens because they may not have to go as often. And sharing may solidify a social relationship so that other families will help in times of need, such as sickness or accident that makes it hard to work.[52] Does food sharing increase the food supply for an individual? Calculations for the Aché of eastern Paraguay, who get most of their food from hunting when they go on food-collecting trips, suggest that the average individual gets more food when food is shared. Even the males who actually do the hunting get more, although the benefits are greater for the females and children on the trip.[53] Mathematically, the risk that an individual food collector will not find enough food on a particular day will be appreciably reduced if at least six to eight adult collectors share the food they collect. Food-collecting bands may often contain only 25 to 30 people, which is about the size that is needed to ensure that there are six to eight adult collectors.[54]

Although giving things to others may be expected in some societies, this does not necessarily mean that everyone does so willingly or without some social pressure. For example, the !Kung call "far-hearted" anyone who does not give gifts, and they express their disapproval openly. The necessity to reduce tensions, to avoid envy and anger, and to keep all social relations peaceful, not only within their own band but among all !Kung bands, creates continuing cross-currents of obligation and friendship. These are maintained, renewed, or established through the generalized reciprocity of gift giving. In a sense, one can say that in exchange for a gift, one gains prestige or perhaps "social credit" for a potential return at some indefinite time in the future. But this gain clearly is not based on explicit return considerations. Among the !Kung as well as other foraging groups, a person who does not hunt will still get a share of meat.

Day-to-day unpredictability is one thing; more prolonged scarcity is another. What happens to a system of generalized reciprocity when resources are scarce because of a drought or other disaster? Does the ethic of giving break down? Evidence from a few societies suggests that the degree of sharing may actually *increase* during the period of food shortage.[55] For example, in describing the Netsilik Inuit, Asen Balikci said, "Whenever game was abundant, sharing among non-relatives was avoided, since every family was supposedly capable of obtaining the necessary catch. In situations of scarcity, however, caribou meat was more evenly distributed throughout camp."[56] Sharing may increase during mild scarcity because people can minimize their deprivation, but generalized reciprocity may be strained by extreme scarcity. Ethnographic evidence from a few societies suggests that during famine, when individuals are actually dying from hunger, sharing may be limited to the household.[57]

Researchers generally have difficulty explaining sharing because they assume that, other things being equal, individuals would tend to be selfish. Most of the ideas about sharing have postulated that sharing is, in fact, advantageous to individuals in certain circumstances. And it is in those circumstances that societies have found ways to make sharing a moral issue or to otherwise make non-sharers extremely uncomfortable. However, some recent and intriguing evidence suggests that cooperation may evoke plea-

Sharing can occur even in a socially stratified society. Here we see men in a village in Yunnan, China, cutting the meat from a steer into 72 portions for the families of the village.

sure. Researchers studying brain activity in women, who are playing a game allowing either cooperative or greedy strategies, found to their surprise that cooperation made certain areas of the brain light up. These areas are normally associated with pleasure, such as when eating desserts. If this finding holds up in other circumstances and populations, cooperation may be more "natural" than we think.[58]

BALANCED RECIPROCITY Balanced reciprocity is explicit and short term in its expectations of return. It involves either an immediate exchange of goods or services or an agreed-upon exchange over a limited period of time. The !Kung, for instance, trade with the Tswana Bantu: a gemsbok hide for a pile of tobacco, five strings of beads made from ostrich eggshells for a spear, three small skins for a good-sized knife.[59] In the 1600s, the Iroquois of the North American Northeast traded deerskin to Europeans for brass kettles, iron hinges, steel axes, woven textiles, and guns.[60] The !Kung and Iroquois acquired trade goods by balanced reciprocity, but such exchanges were not crucial to their economies.

In contrast, some societies depend much more heavily on balanced reciprocity. For example, the Efe, who hunt and gather in the Ituri forest of central Africa, get most of their calories from manioc, peanuts, rice, and plaintains grown by another group—the agricultural Lese. Efe men and women provide labor to the Lese, and in exchange receive a portion of the harvest as well as goods such as metal pots and spears.[61] Pastoralists, too, are rarely self-sufficient, as we mentioned in the preceding chapter. They have to trade their pastoral products to agriculturalists to get the grain and other things they need. Balanced reciprocity may mostly involve labor. Cooperative work parties exchange or balance gifts of labor. A cooperative work party, or *kuu*, among the Kpelle of Liberia may number from 6 to 40 persons, all of whom are generally relatives or friends. In addition to promising return work on a particular date, each farmer rewards the work party's hard day's labor by providing a feast and sometimes rhythmic music to work by.[62]

When we say that an exchange is balanced, we do not mean to imply that the things exchanged are exactly equivalent in value or that the exchange is purely economic. In the absence of a money economy, where there is no explicit standard by which value can be judged, there is no way to assess value objectively. The point is that the parties in balanced reciprocity are freely giving each other the respective goods and services they each want; they are not coerced into doing so, so presumably they are not conceiving of the exchange as unbalanced.[63] And when something is valued, it may be valued for other than economic reasons. The exchange itself may also be fun, adventuresome, or aesthetically pleasing, or it may enhance social relationships.

Because exchanges can have different motivations, they can have different meanings. Consequently, some economic anthropologists now want to distinguish between gift and commodity exchanges. *Gift exchanges* are personal and involve the creation or perpetuation of some kind of enduring relationship between people and groups. In our society, the exchange of dinner invitations or Christmas gifts is motivated by social considerations; we are not interested only in the actual food or objects received. As we shall see shortly, some of the exchanges involved in the famous *kula* ring seem mostly to be motivated by the desire to establish or cement trade partnerships. In contrast, *commodity exchanges,* which can occur even in the absence of money, focus on the objects or services received—the transaction itself is the motive. When the transaction is completed, the relationship between the parties involved usually ends.[64]

The Kula Ring   The horticultural Trobriand Islanders, who live off the eastern coast of New Guinea, worked out an elaborate scheme for trading ornaments, food, and other necessities with the people of neighboring islands. The trade is essential, for some of the islands are small and rocky and cannot produce enough food to sustain their inhabitants, who specialize instead in canoe building, pottery making, and other crafts. Other islands produce far more yams, taro, and pigs than they need. According to Uberoi, the trade in necessary items is carefully hidden beneath the panoply of the *kula* **ring,** the ceremonial exchange of valued shell ornaments classically described by Bronislaw Malinowski.[65]

Two kinds of ornaments are involved in the ceremonial exchanges—white shell armbands (*mwali*), which travel

CD-ROM Activity III-1

around the circle of islands in a counterclockwise direction, and red shell necklaces (*soulava*), which travel in a clockwise direction (see Figure 17–2). The possession of one or more of these ornaments allows a man to organize an expedition to the home of one of his trading partners on another island. The high point of an expedition is the ceremonial giving of the valued *kula* ornaments. Each member of the expedition receives a shell ornament from his trading partner and then remains on the island for two or three days as the guest of that person. During the visit the trading of necessities goes on. Some of the exchange takes the form of gift giving between trading partners. There is also exchange or barter between expedition members and others on the island. By the time the visitors leave, they have accomplished a year's trading, without seeming to do so.

But the practical advantages of the *kula* ring are not the only gains. There may be purely social ones, for goods are traded with ease and enjoyment. A trading expedition takes on the flavor of adventure rather than business. Many

of the traditions of the islands are kept alive: Myth, romance, ritual, and history are linked to the circulating ornaments, especially the larger, finer pieces, which are well known and recognized as heirlooms. The *kula* ring also permits wide ownership of valuables. Instead of possessing one valued object permanently, a man is able to possess many valued things within his lifetime, each for a year or so. Each object, when it is received, arouses enthusiasm in a way that one lifelong possession could not.[66]

Whatever the reasons for the origin of the *kula* ring, which may date back nearly 2,000 years, it continued to be an important institution after Papua New Guinea became an independent country. For example, active participation in the *kula* ring helped candidates in the 1960s and the 1970s to be elected to the national parliament.[67]

The *kula* is not the only form of exchange in Trobriand life. For example, on the two days following a burial, the kin of the deceased give yams, taro, and valuables to those who helped care for the deceased before death, to those who participated in the burial ceremonies, and to those who came to mourn the deceased. After these initial exchanges, the hamlet settles into mourning. Women from other hamlets bring food to the people in mourning, and the mourning women prepare bundles of banana leaves and weave skirts of banana fiber for later distribution. Husbands help their wives accumulate valuables to "buy" extra bundles of banana leaves. Then the women's mortuary ceremony is held. It is very competitive—each of the mourning women tries to distribute the most bundles and skirts. As many as 5,000 bundles and 30 skirts might be distributed by one mourning woman in a single day. Each of these giveaways completes a balanced reciprocity: The giver is

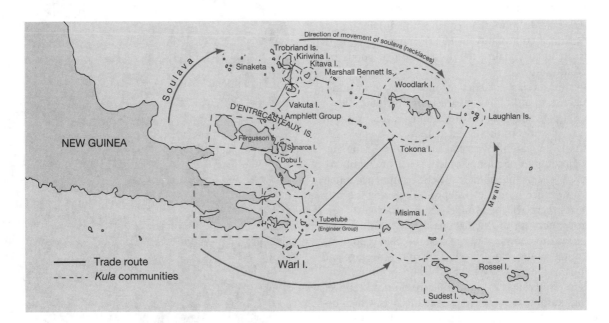

Figure 17–2 *The* **Kula** *Ring*

In the kula *ring, red shell necklaces* (soulava) *travel in a clockwise direction; white shell armbands* (mwali) *travel counterclockwise. The solid lines show the overseas trade routes. The dashed circles identify the* (kula) *communities, and the dashed rectangles show the areas indirectly affected by the* kula.

reciprocating for gifts of goods and services received in the past. A woman's brothers gave her yams and taro during the year. She gives her brothers' wives bundles or skirts, which are also given to those who helped make the special mourning skirts and to those who brought or cooked food during the mourning period.[68]

Sometimes the line between generalized and balanced reciprocity is not so clear. Consider our gift giving at Christmas. Although such gift giving may appear to be generalized reciprocity, there may be strong expectations of balance. Two friends or relatives may try to exchange presents of fairly equal value, based on calculations of what last year's gift cost. If a person receives a $5 present when he or she gave a $25 present, that person will be hurt and perhaps angry. On the other hand, a person who receives a $500 present when he or she gave a $25 present may well be dismayed.

KINSHIP DISTANCE AND TYPE OF RECIPROCITY

Most food-collecting and horticultural societies depend on some form of reciprocity for the distribution of goods and labor. Marshall Sahlins suggested that the form of the reciprocity depends largely on the kinship distance between persons. Generalized reciprocity may be the rule for family members and close kinsmen. Balanced reciprocity may be practiced among equals who are not closely related. Persons who would consider it inappropriate to trade with their own families will trade with neighboring groups.[69] In general, the importance of reciprocity declines with economic development.[70] In societies with intensive agriculture, and even more so in industrialized societies, reciprocity distributes only a small proportion of goods and services.

RECIPROCITY AS A LEVELING DEVICE

Reciprocal gift giving may do more than equalize the distribution of goods within a community, as in the !Kung's sharing. It may also tend to equalize the distribution of goods between communities.

Many Melanesian societies in and near New Guinea have the custom of holding pig feasts in which 50, 100, or even 2,000 pigs are slaughtered. Andrew Vayda, Anthony Leeds, and David Smith suggested that these enormous feasts, though apparently wasteful, are just one of the outcomes of a complex of cultural practices that are highly advantageous. The people of these societies cannot accurately predict how much food they will produce during the year. Some years there will be bumper crops, other years very poor crops, because of fluctuations in the weather. So it might be wise to overplant just in case the yield is poor. Yet overplanting results in overproduction during average and exceptionally good years. What can be done with this extra food? Root crops such as yams and taro do not keep well over long periods, so any surplus is fed to pigs, which become, in effect, food-storing repositories. Pigs are then available for needed food during lean times. But if there are several years of surpluses, pigs can become too much of a good thing. Pigs wanting food can destroy yam and taro patches. When the pig population grows to menacing pro-

portions, a village may invite other villages to a gigantic feast that results in a sharp reduction of the pig population and keeps the fields from being overrun. Over the years the pig feasts serve to equalize the food consumption, and especially the protein consumption, of all the villages that participate in the feasts.[71] Thus, the custom of pig feasts may be a way for villages to "bank" surplus food by storing up "social credit" with other villages, which will return that credit in subsequent feasts.

In some Melanesian societies, the pig feasts foster an element of competition among the men who give them. "Big men" may try to bolster their status and prestige by the size of their feasts. A reputation is enhanced not by keeping wealth but by giving it away. A similar situation existed among many Native American groups of the Pacific Northwest, where a chief might attempt to enhance his status by holding a **potlatch.** At a potlatch, a chief and his group would give away blankets, pieces of copper, canoes, large quantities of food, and other items to their guests. The host chief and his group would later be invited to other potlatches.

The competitive element in the potlatch appears to have intensified after contact with Europeans. Because of the fur trade, the number of trade goods increased, and so more items could be given away. Possibly more important was

A man on the Northwest Pacific coast (southeastern Alaska) wears a "potlatch hat" showing how many potlatches he has had.

the population decline among the Indians, caused by diseases such as smallpox that were introduced by European traders. Distant relatives of chiefs who had no direct heirs might compete for the right to the title, each attempting to give away more than the others.[72] Chiefs may also have attempted to attract men to their half-empty villages by spectacular giveaways.[73] Decimated groups might have coalesced in order to maintain the potlatching. For example, when the Tlingit population declined to a low in the 1910s, kin groups coalesced in order to assemble enough resources for a potlatch.[74] Although the potlatch system seems wasteful in that goods were often destroyed in the competition, the system probably also served to equalize the distribution of goods among competing groups.

The Pomo Indians of central California had another way to bank credit for previous generosity. A village with an overabundance of fish or acorns might invite another village to a feast. In return for surplus fish or acorns, the guests would give the host village a certain number of beads. Before beginning the journey to the feast, the chief of the guest village would obtain from each family as many strings of beads as possible. After a few days of feasting at the host village, the chief would trade the beads for the supply of surplus fish or acorns. Each member of the visiting village would be given an equal share of the food, regardless of how many beads had been contributed. But the members of a village would not be invited to a feast unless they brought beads to trade, and they could not obtain beads unless they had given food away themselves sometime in the past. Thus, giving away food and receiving beads in return served as a means of storing social credit for times of scarcity. Later, if food was scarce in the former host village, the villagers could use the beads they had acquired by giving in the past to obtain food from another village with a surplus. The trade feasts, then, had the effect of equalizing the consumption of food not only within a village but over a fairly widespread area.[75]

On one level of analysis, the Melanesian pig feasts, the Pacific Northwest potlatches, and the Pomo trade feasts were all reciprocal exchanges between communities or villages. But these exchanges were not just intercommunity versions of reciprocal gift giving between individuals. Because these feasts were organized by people who collected goods, they also involved another mode of distribution, which anthropologists call *redistribution*.

REDISTRIBUTION

Redistribution is the accumulation of goods or labor by a particular person, or in a particular place, for the purpose of subsequent distribution. Although redistribution is found in all societies, it becomes an important mechanism only in societies that have political hierarchies—that is, chiefs or other specialized officials and agencies. In all societies, there is some redistribution, at least within the family. Members of the family pool their labor or products or income for the common good. But in many societies, there is little or no redistribution beyond the family. It seems that redistribution on a territorial basis emerges when there is a

political apparatus to coordinate centralized collection and distribution of goods or to mobilize labor for some public purpose.

In the African state of Bunyoro, in western Uganda, for example, the king (called the *mukama*) retained much of the wealth for himself and his close kin. The *mukama* had the authority to grant the use of land and all other natural resources to his subordinate chiefs, and they in turn granted it to the common people. In return, everyone was required to give the *mukama* large quantities of food, crafts, and even labor services. The *mukama* then redistributed these goods and services, in theory at least, to all the people. The *mukama* was praised with names that emphasized his generosity: *Agutamba* ("he who relieves distress") and *Mwebingwa* ("he to whom the people run for help"). But it is clear that much of what the king redistributed did not find its way back to the common people, who produced the bulk of the goods. Instead, the wealth was distributed largely according to rank within the state.[76]

Other redistribution systems are more equal. For example, among the Buin of Melanesia, "the chief is housed, dressed, and fed exactly like his bondsman."[77] Even though the chief owns most of the pigs, everyone shares equally in the consumption of the wealth. In general, where redistribution is important, as in societies with higher levels of productivity, the wealthy are more likely than the poor to benefit from the redistributions.[78]

Why do redistribution systems develop? Elman Service suggested that they develop in agricultural societies that contain subregions suited to different kinds of crops or natural resources. Food collectors can take advantage of environmental variation by moving to different areas. With agriculture, the task is more difficult; it might be easier to move different products across different regions.[79] If the demand for different resources or products becomes too great, reciprocity between individuals might become awkward. So it might be more efficient to have someone—a chief, perhaps—coordinate the exchanges. We saw in the Pomo trade feasts that, although whole communities appeared to be engaged in reciprocal exchanges, the collection of surplus food and beads was handled by village chiefs.

Marvin Harris agreed that redistribution becomes more likely with agriculture, but for a somewhat different reason. He argued that competitive feasting, as in New Guinea, is adaptive because it encourages people to work harder to produce somewhat more than they need. Why would this feature be adaptive? Harris argued that with agriculture, people really have to produce more than they need so that they can protect themselves against crises such as crop failure. The groups that make feasts may be indirectly ensuring themselves against crises by storing up social credit with other villages, who will reciprocate by making feasts for them in the future. On the other hand, inducements to collect more than they need may not be advantageous to food-collecting groups, who might lose in the long run by overcollecting.[80]

MARKET OR COMMERCIAL EXCHANGE

When we think of markets we usually think of bustling colorful places where goods are bought and sold. The exchanges usually involve money. In our own society we have supermarkets and the stock market and other places for buying and selling that we call shops, stores, and malls. In referring to **market** or **commercial exchange,** economists and economic anthropologists are referring to exchanges or transactions in which the "prices" are subject to supply and demand, whether or not the transactions actually occur in a marketplace.[81] Market exchange involves not only the exchange (buying and selling) of goods but also transactions of labor, land, rentals, and credit.

On the surface, many market exchanges resemble balanced reciprocity. One person gives something and receives something in return. How, then, does market exchange differ from balanced reciprocity? It is easy to distinguish market exchange from balanced reciprocity when money is directly involved, since reciprocity is defined as not involving money. But market exchange need not always involve money directly.[82] For example, a landowner grants a tenant farmer the right to use the land in exchange for a portion of the crop. So, to call a transaction market exchange, we have to ask whether supply and demand determine the price. If a tenant farmer gave only a token gift to the landowner, we would not call it market exchange, just as a Christmas gift to a teacher is not payment for teaching. If tenants, however, are charged a large portion of their crops when the supply of land is short, or if landowners lower their demands when few people want to tenant-farm, then we would call the transactions market or commercial exchange.

KINDS OF MONEY Although market exchange need not involve money, most commercial transactions, particularly nowadays, do involve what we call money. Some anthropologists define money according to the functions and characteristics of the **general-purpose money** used in our own and other complex societies, for which nearly all goods, resources, and services can be exchanged. According to this definition, money performs the basic functions of serving as an accepted medium of exchange, a standard of value, and a store of wealth. As a medium of exchange, it allows all goods and services to be valued in the same objective way; we say that an object or service is worth so much money. Also, money is nonperishable, and therefore savable or storable, and almost always transportable and divisible, so transactions can involve the buying and selling of goods and services that differ in value.

Although money can technically be anything, the first money systems used rare metals such as gold and silver. These metals are relatively soft and therefore can be melted and shaped into standard sizes and weights. The earliest standardized coins we know of are said to have been made by the Lydians in Asia Minor and the Chinese, in the 7th century A.D. It is important to realize that money has little or no intrinsic value; rather, it is society that determines its value. In the United States today, paper bills, bank checks, and credit and debit cards are fully accepted as money, and money is increasingly transferred electronically.

General-purpose money is used both for commercial transactions (buying and selling) and for noncommercial transactions (payment of taxes or fines, personal gifts, contributions to religious and other charities). General-purpose money provides a way of condensing wealth: Gold dust or nuggets are easier to carry around than bushels of wheat; paper bills, a checkbook, and plastic cards are handier than a herd of sheep or goats.

In many societies, money is not an all-purpose medium of exchange. Many peoples whose food production per capita is not sufficient to support a large population of nonproducers of food have **special-purpose money.** This consists of objects of value for which only some goods and services can be exchanged on the spot or through balanced reciprocity. In some parts of Melanesia, pigs are assigned value in terms of shell money—lengths of shells strung together in units each roughly as long as the distance covered by a man's outstretched arms. According to its size, a pig will be assigned a value in tens of such units up to 100.[83] But shell money cannot be exchanged for all the goods or services a person might need. Similarly, a Pacific Northwest native could exchange food, but not most other goods and services, for a "gift of wealth," such as blankets. The gift was a "receipt" that entitled the person to receive an equal amount of food, but little else, later.

DEGREES OF COMMERCIALIZATION Most societies were not commercialized at all, or only barely so, when first described in the ethnographic record by explorers, missionaries, and anthropologists. That is, most societies as first described did not rely on market or commercial exchange to distribute goods and services. But commercial exchange has become the dominant form of distribution in the modern world. Most societies of the ethnographic past are now incorporated into larger nation-states; for example, the Trobriand Islanders and other societies in Melanesia are now districts in the nation of Papua New Guinea. Selling today goes far beyond the nation-state. The world is now a multinational market.[84]

But there is considerable variation in the degree to which societies today depend on market or commercial exchange. Many societies still allocate land without purchase and distribute food and other goods primarily by reciprocity and redistribution, participating only peripherally in market exchange. These are societies in transition; their traditional subsistence economies are becoming commercialized. Among the Luo of western Kenya, for example, most rural families still have land that was allocated to them by their kin groups. The food they eat they mostly produce themselves. But many men also work for wages—some nearby, others far away in towns and cities, where they spend a year or two. These wages are used to pay government taxes, to pay for children's schooling, and to buy commercially produced items, such as clothes, kerosene lamps, radios, fish from Lake Nyanza, tea, sugar, and coffee. Occasionally, families sell agricultural surpluses or craft items such as reed mats. Economies such as that of the

APPLIED ANTHROPOLOGY
Impact of the World System—Deforestation of the Amazon

When we speak of the economic system of a people, we must keep in mind that probably no group has ever been completely isolated from outside economic, political, social, or environmental events. In the modern world, with the expanding demand and opportunity of a growing world market economy, even the most self-sufficient groups cannot avoid the effects of their connections to the outside world.

Consider the great rain forest drained by the Amazon River and its tributaries. Covering more than a billion acres, it is not only the home to many largely self-sufficient indigenous cultures; it also supports about 50 percent of all the earth's plants and animals. Yet the Amazon forest and other tropical forests are disappearing at an alarming rate because of their increased use. Some have suggested that the world demand for wood, hamburger, and gold is largely responsible for the diminution of the Amazon forest.

Like many tropical forests, the Amazon has large numbers of desirable hardwood trees. Forests in Africa and Asia are already largely depleted, so the demand for wood from the Amazon has grown considerably. In addition, the Amazon Development Agency in Brazil has offered incentives to clear forest for cattle ranching, which can provide hamburger to fast-food restaurants. There is little concern that a few seasons of overgrazing can make it impossible even for grasses to grow in the soils of the former forest.

The indigenous people often find themselves in a land squeeze, with loggers, cattle ranchers, and miners trying to encroach on their territory. With less land, food-getting and traditional economic practices are in jeopardy. But it is naive to assume that the indigenous people are interested only in maintaining their traditional economies. They often accept the dilemma of economic development: They might lose some land, but selling rights to loggers and miners brings in money, which they can use to buy things they need and want. Development experts and applied anthropologists are searching for ways to achieve development without destroying or degrading the environment. For example, indigenous groups are encouraged to gather Brazil nuts, a wild but renewable resource, for sale. Others are encouraged to harvest latex (natural rubber) and hearts of palm. Medicinal plants have economic value to multinational pharmaceutical and biotechnical companies, which have discovered that the conservation of biodiversity may be economically advantageous to themselves as well as to the local people and to scientists who want to study the diversity.

Can development be sustainable? That is, are resources (such as hardwoods) renewable, so that both economic productivity and the environment can be protected? Even if some kind of sustainable development is possible, organizing it may require concerted effort by all involved, which requires participation by all in decision making. Whether we like it or not, economic development and the desire for it are not going to go away. But we need to do more than applaud or bemoan economic development. In particular, we need research that reveals what impact particular changes will have on people, other animals, plants, and the environment. Most of all, for the sake of human rights, we need to listen to the people whose lives will be most affected, to understand their needs as well as those of the developers.

Sources: Marguerite Holloway, "Sustaining the Amazon," *Scientific American,* July 1993, 91–99; Emilio F. Moran, *Through Amazon Eyes: The Human Ecology of Amazonian Populations* (Iowa City: University of Iowa Press, 1993); Robert Winterbottom, "The Tropical Forestry Plan: Is It Working?" in Pamela J. Puntenney, ed., *Global Ecosystems: Creating Options through Anthropological Perspectives, NAPA Bulletin* 15 (1995): 60–70.

rural Luo are not fully commercialized, but they may become so in the future. In the chapter on culture change and globalization we discuss some of the implications and effects of this transition to a more commercialized economy—a transition that is a worldwide phenomenon.

What anthropologists call *peasant economies* are somewhat more commercialized than transitional subsistence economies such as that of the Luo. Although **peasants** also produce food largely for their own consumption, they regularly sell part of their surplus (food, other goods, or labor) to others, and land is one of the commodities they buy, rent, and sell. But, although their production is somewhat commercialized, peasants still are not like the fully commercialized farmers in industrialized societies, who rely on the market to exchange all or almost all of their crops for all or almost all of the goods and services they need.

In fully commercialized societies such as our own, market or commercial exchange dominates the economy;

prices and wages are regulated, or at least significantly affected, by the forces of supply and demand. A modern industrial or postindustrial economy may involve international as well as national markets in which everything has a price, stated in the same money terms—natural resources, labor, goods, services, prestige items, religious and ceremonial items. Reciprocity is reserved for family members and friends or remains behind the scene in business transactions. Redistribution, however, is an important mechanism. It is practiced in the form of taxation and the use of public revenue for transfer payments and other benefits to low-income families—welfare, social security, health care, and so on. But commercial exchange is the major way goods and services are distributed.

WHY DO MONEY AND MARKET EXCHANGE DEVELOP?

Most economists think that money is invented in a society, or copied from another society, when trade increases and barter becomes increasingly inefficient. The more important or frequent trade is, the more difficult it is to find a person who can give something you want and wants something you have to give. Money makes it easy to trade. It is a valuable that may be exchanged for *anything,* and so it is an efficient medium of exchange when trade becomes important. In contrast, many anthropologists do not link the origins of money or market exchange to the necessities of trade. Instead, they link the origins of money to various noncommercial "payments," such as the *kula* valuables, the Pomo beads, and the taxes that have to be paid to a political authority. All of the available explanations of money suggest that money will be found mostly in societies at higher levels of economic development; and indeed it is. When simpler societies have money, dominant and more complex societies have usually introduced it.[85]

Most theories about the development of money and market exchange assume that producers have regular surpluses they want to exchange. But why do people produce surpluses in the first place? Perhaps they are motivated to produce extra only when they want to obtain goods from a distance and the suppliers of such goods are not well known to them, making reciprocity less likely as a way to obtain those goods. So some theorists suggest that market exchange begins with external, or intersocietal, trade; kin would not likely be involved, so transactions would involve bargaining, and therefore market exchange, by definition. Finally, some argue that as societies become more complex and more densely populated, social bonds between individuals become less kinlike and friendly, and therefore reciprocity becomes less likely.[86] Perhaps this is why traders in developing areas are often foreigners or recent immigrants.[87]

In any case, Frederic Pryor's cross-cultural research supports the notion that all types of market exchange—goods, labor, land, and credit—are more likely with higher levels of economic productivity. Pryor also found that market exchange of goods appears at lower levels of economic development than market exchange of labor and credit; market exchange of land, probably because it is associated with private property (individual ownership), appears mostly at the highest levels of productivity. Perhaps surprisingly,

Fiesta sponsors spend a great deal of money for food and drink as well as for musicians and dancers. Here we see a fiesta in Oaxaca, Mexico.

smaller societies tend to have more market exchange or trade with other societies. Larger societies can presumably get more of what they need from inside the society; for example, until recently China had relatively little foreign trade throughout much of its history.[88]

POSSIBLE LEVELING DEVICES IN COMMERCIAL ECONOMIES As we will see in the next chapter, societies that depend substantially on market or commercial exchange tend to have marked differences in wealth among the people. Nonetheless, there may be mechanisms that lessen the inequality, that act at least partially as leveling devices. Some anthropologists have suggested that the fiesta complex in highland Indian communities of Latin America may be a mechanism that tends to equalize income.[89] In these peasant villages, fiestas are held each year to celebrate important village saints. The outstanding feature of this system is the extraordinary amount of money and labor a sponsoring family must contribute. Sponsors must hire ritual specialists, pay for church services, musicians, and costumes for dancers, and cover the complete cost of food and drink for the entire community. The costs incurred can very easily amount to a year's wages.[90]

Some anthropologists have suggested that, although the richer Indians who sponsor fiestas are clearly distributing a good deal of wealth to the poorer members of their own and other communities, the fiestas do not really level wealth at all. First, true economic leveling would entail the redistribution of important productive resources such as land or animals; the fiesta only temporarily increases the general level of consumption. Second, the resources expended by the sponsors are usually extra resources that have been accumulated specifically for the fiesta, which is why the sponsors are always appointed in advance. Third, and perhaps most important, the fiestas do not seem to have reduced long-term wealth distinctions within the villages.[91]

In nations such as ours, can the income tax and the social-assistance programs it pays for, such as welfare and disaster relief, be thought of as leveling devices? Theoretically, our tax system is supposed to work that way, by taxing higher incomes at higher rates. But we know that in fact it doesn't. Those in higher income brackets can often deduct an appreciable amount from their taxable incomes and therefore pay taxes at a relatively low rate. Our tax system may help some to escape extreme poverty, but, like the fiesta system, it has not eliminated marked distinctions in wealth.

 CD-ROM Flashcards Chapter 17

 Summary

1. All societies have economic systems, whether or not these involve the use of money. All societies have customs specifying access to natural resources; customary ways of transforming or converting those resources, through labor, into necessities and other desired goods and services; and customs for distributing and perhaps exchanging goods and services.

2. Regulation of access to natural resources is a basic factor in all economic systems. The concept of individual or private ownership of land—including the right to use its resources and the right to sell or otherwise dispose of them—is common among intensive agriculturalists. In contrast, food collectors, horticulturalists, and pastoralists generally lack individual ownership of land. Among pastoral nomads, however, animals are considered family property and are not usually shared.

3. Every society makes use of a technology, which includes tools, constructions, and required skills. Even though food collectors and horticulturalists tend to think of tools as "owned" by the individuals who made them, the sharing of tools is so extensive that individual ownership does not have much meaning. Among intensive agriculturalists, toolmaking tends to be a specialized activity. Tools tend not be shared, except mainly by those who have purchased them together.

4. Incentives for labor vary cross-culturally. Many societies produce just for household consumption; if there are more consumers, producers work harder. In some subsistence economies, people may work harder to obtain the social rewards that come from giving to others. Forced labor generally occurs only in complex societies.

5. Division of labor by gender is universal. In many nonindustrial societies, large tasks are often accomplished through the cooperative efforts of a kinship group. Such cooperation is not as prevalent in industrialized societies. In general, the more technically advanced a society is, the more surplus food it produces and the more some of its members engage in specialized work.

6. The organization of labor reaches its peak in complex societies; work groups tend to be formally organized, and sometimes there is an enforced obligation to participate. In food-collecting and horticultural societies, in contrast, there is little formal organization of work.

7. Goods and services are distributed in all societies by systems that can be classified under three types: reciprocity, redistribution, and market or commercial exchange. Reciprocity is giving and taking without the use of money and generally assumes two forms: generalized reciprocity and balanced reciprocity. Generalized reciprocity is gift giving without any immediate or planned return. In balanced reciprocity, individuals exchange goods and services immediately or in the short term.

8. Redistribution is the accumulation of goods or labor by a particular person, or in a particular place, for the purpose of subsequent distribution. It becomes an important mechanism of distribution only in societies with political hierarchies.

9. Market or commercial exchange, where "prices" depend on supply and demand, tends to occur with increasing levels of economic productivity. Especially nowadays, market exchange usually involves an all-purpose medium of exchange—money. Most societies today are at least partly commercialized; the world is becoming a single market system.

 ## Glossary Terms

balanced reciprocity	optimal foraging theory
corvée	peasants
generalized reciprocity	potlatch
general-purpose money	reciprocity
kula ring	redistribution
market or commercial exchange	special-purpose money

 ## Critical Questions

1. What conditions might enable us to achieve a world of sustainable resources?
2. What are the possible effects of a postindustrial economy in which a large proportion of the population has inexpensive access to computers and information?
3. Do you expect any appreciable change in the amount of resources privately owned in the future? State your reasons.

 ## Internet Exercises

1. For an introduction to economic anthropology, visit one of the organizations devoted exclusively to this field. Look up the Society for Economic Anthropology on one of the Web search engines and read about a past or upcoming professional meeting.
2. The issue of sustainable development is a complex one. Explore some of the current thoughts and ongoing debates on the subject at http://www.un.org/esa/sustdev/. What are some of the topics discussed at this site that are of direct relevance to this chapter?
3. Find at least four labor-related sources on Africa on the Internet, for example, at http://www-sul.stanford.edu/depts/ssrg/africa/labor.html. Briefly summarize your findings.
4. Money is an important concept. Visit http://www.ex.ac.uk/~RDavies/arian/amser/chrono.html to learn about the monetary systems of ancient times. Read the information in the earliest time period to learn about the earliest uses of money.

 ## Suggested Reading

BLANTON, R. E. "Variation in Economy." In C. R. Ember and M. Ember, eds., *Cross-Cultural Research for Social Science,* in C. R. Ember and M. Ember, eds., *New Directions in Anthropology.* Upper Saddle River, NJ: Prentice Hall, CD-ROM, 2003. A brief survey for undergraduates of the concepts and challenges involved in cross-cultural comparisons of variations in economic systems.

CASHDAN, E., ED. *Risk and Uncertainty in Tribal and Peasant Economies.* Boulder, CO: Westview, 1990. The contributors to this volume discuss the various ways people in nonindustrial societies respond to unpredictable variation in the environment.

HUNT, R. C., AND GILMAN, A., EDS. *Property in Economic Context.* Lanham, MD: University Press of America, 1998. This book focuses on how property is variably defined in selected societies, including precapitalist societies known from history and archaeology and modern colonial situations described by ethnographers.

OSTROM, E., BURGER, J., FIELD, C. B., NORGAARD, R. B., AND POLICANSKY, D. "Revisiting the Commons: Local Lessons, Global Challenges." *Science,* April 9, 1999, 278–282. This article discusses new insights on the destruction of resources held in common, and the conditions most likely to favor sustainable uses of common-pool resources.

PRYOR, F. L. *The Origins of the Economy: A Comparative Study of Distribution in Primitive and Peasant Economies.* New York: Academic Press, 1977. A large cross-cultural study of variation in distribution systems and their possible determinants.

The Society for Economic Anthropology publishes a series of monographs on economic anthropology. The series can be found at http://nautarch.tamu.edu/anth/sea/volumes.htm. Recent volumes include *Economic Development: An Anthropological Approach* (J. F. Cohen and N. Dannhaeuser, eds.), *Theory in Economic Anthropology* (J. Ensminger, ed.), *At the Interface: The Household and Beyond* (D. Small and N. Tannenbaum, eds.), *Property in Economic Context* (R. C. Hunt and A. Gilman, eds.), and *Economic Analysis Beyond the Local System* (R. E. Blanton, P. N. Peregrine, D. Winslow, and T. D. Hall, eds.).

SOCIAL STRATIFICATION: CLASS, ETHNICITY, AND RACISM

18

CHAPTER OUTLINE

Along-enduring value in the United States is the belief that "all men are created equal." These famous words from the American Declaration of Independence do not mean that all people are equal in wealth or status but rather that all (including women nowadays) are supposed to be equal before the law. Equality before the law is the ideal. But the ideal is not always the actuality. Some people have advantages in legal treatment, and they generally also tend to have advantages of other kinds, including economic advantages. Without exception, recent and modern industrial and postindustrial societies such as our own are *socially stratified*—that is, they contain social groups such as families, classes, or ethnic groups that have unequal access to important advantages such as economic resources, power, and prestige.

Hasn't such inequality always existed? Anthropologists, based on firsthand observations of recent societies, would say not. To be sure, even the simplest societies (in the technological sense) have some differences in advantages based on age or ability or gender—adults have higher status than children, the skilled more than the unskilled, men more than women (we discuss gender stratification in the next chapter). But anthropologists would argue that *egalitarian* societies exist where *social groups* (e.g., families) have more or less the same access to rights or advantages. As we noted in the last chapter, the economic systems of many food collectors and horticulturalists promote equal access to economic resources for all families in the community. Moreover, such societies also tend to emphasize the sharing of food and other goods, which tends to equalize any small inequalities in resources between families. Until about 10,000 years ago, all human societies depended on food they hunted, gathered, and/or fished. And so we might expect that egalitarianism characterized most of human history. That is indeed what archaeology suggests. Substantial inequality generally appears only with permanent communities, centralized political systems, and intensive agriculture, which are cultural features that began to appear in the world only in the last 10,000 years. Before that time, then, most societies were probably egalitarian. In the world today, egalitarian societies have all but disappeared because of two processes—the global spread of commercial or market exchange and the voluntary or involuntary incorporation of many diverse people into large centralized political systems. In modern societies, some groups have more advantages than others. These groups may include *ethnic* groups. That is, ethnic diversity is almost always associated with differential access to advantages. When ethnic diversity is also associated with differences in physical features such as skin color, the social stratification may involve *racism,* the belief that some "racial" groups are inferior.

Systems of social stratification are strongly linked to the customary ways in which economic resources are allocated, distributed, and converted through labor into goods and services. So we would not expect much inequality if all people had relatively equal access to economic resources. But stratification cannot be understood solely in terms of economic resources; there are other benefits such as prestige and power that may be unequally distributed. We first examine how societies vary in their systems of stratification. Then we turn to possible explanations of why they vary.

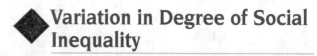

Variation in Degree of Social Inequality

Societies vary in the extent to which social groups, as well as individuals, have unequal access to advantages. In this chapter we are concerned with differential or unequal access to three types of advantages: wealth or economic resources, power, and prestige. As we saw in the preceding chapter, *economic resources* may range from hunting or fishing grounds to farmland to money; the different social groups in a society may or may not have unequal access to these resources. *Power,* a second but related advantage, is the ability to make others do what they do not want to do; power is influence based on the threat of force. When groups in a society have rules or customs that give them unequal access to wealth or resources, they generally also have unequal access to power. So, for example, when we speak of a "company town" in the United States, we are referring to the fact that the company that employs most of the residents of the town usually has considerable control over them. Finally, there is the advantage of *prestige.* When we speak of prestige, we mean that someone or some group is accorded particular respect or honor. Even if it is true that there is always unequal access by individuals to prestige (because of differences in age, gender, or ability), there are some societies in the ethnographic record that have no social groups with unequal access to prestige.

Thus, anthropologists conventionally distinguish three types of society in terms of the degree to which different social groups have unequal access to advantages: *egalitarian, rank,* and *class societies* (see Table 18–1). Some societies in the ethnographic record do not fit easily into any of these three types; as with any classification scheme, some cases seem to straddle the line between types.[1] **Egalitarian societies** contain no social groups with greater or lesser access to economic resources, power, or prestige. **Rank societies** do not have very unequal access to economic resources or to power, but they do contain social groups with unequal access to prestige. Rank societies, then, are partly stratified. **Class societies** have unequal access to all three advantages—economic resources, power, and prestige.

Egalitarian Societies

Egalitarian societies can be found not only among foragers such as the !Kung, Mbuti, Australian aborigines, Inuit, and Aché, but also among horticulturalists such as the Yanomamö and pastoralists such as the Lapps. An important point to keep in mind is that egalitarian does not mean that all people within such societies are the same. There will always be differences among individuals in age and

Table 18–1 Stratification in Three Types of Societies

	SOME SOCIAL GROUPS HAVE GREATER ACCESS TO:			
Type of Society	Economic Resources	Power	Prestige	Examples
Egalitarian	No	No	No	!Kung, Mbuti, Australian aborigines, Inuit, Aché, Yanomamö
Rank	No	No	Yes	Samoans, Tahiti, Trobriand Islands, Ifaluk
Class/caste	Yes	Yes	Yes	United States, Canada, Greece, India, Inca

gender and in such abilities or traits as hunting skill, perception, health, creativity, physical prowess, attractiveness, and intelligence. According to Morton Fried, egalitarian means that within a given society "there are as many positions of prestige in any given age/sex grade as there are persons capable of filling them."[2] For instance, if a person can achieve high status by fashioning fine spears, and if many persons in the society fashion such spears, then many acquire high status as spear makers. If high status is also acquired by carving bones into artifacts, and if only three people are considered expert carvers of bones, then only those three achieve high status as carvers. But the next generation might produce eight spear makers and 20 carvers. In an egalitarian society, the number of prestigious positions is adjusted to fit the number of qualified candidates. We would say, therefore, that such a society is not socially stratified.

There are, of course, differences in position and prestige arising out of differences in ability. Even in an egalitarian society, differential prestige exists. But, although some persons may be better hunters or more skilled artists than others, there is still *equal access* to status positions for people of the same ability. Any prestige gained by achieving high status as a great hunter, for instance, is neither transferable nor inheritable. Because a man is a great hunter, it is not assumed that his sons are also great hunters. There also may be individuals with more influence, but it cannot be inherited, and there are no groups with appreciably more influence over time. An egalitarian society keeps inequality at a minimal level.

Any differences in prestige that do exist are not related to economic differences. Egalitarian groups depend heavily on *sharing*, which ensures equal access to economic resources despite differences in acquired prestige. For instance, in some egalitarian communities, some members achieve higher status through hunting. But even before the hunt begins, how the animal will be divided and distributed among the members of the band has already been decided according to custom. The culture works to separate the status achieved by members—recognition as great hunters—from actual possession of the wealth, which in this case would be the slain animal.

Just as egalitarian societies do not have social groups with unequal access to economic resources, they also do not have social groups with unequal access to power. As we will see later in the chapter on political organization, unequal access to power by social groups seems to occur only in state societies, which have full-time political officials and marked differences in wealth. Egalitarian societies use a number of customs to keep leaders from dominating others. Criticism and ridicule can be very effective. The Mbuti of central Africa shout down an overassertive leader. When a Hadza man tried to get people to work for him, other Hadza made fun of him. Disobedience is another strategy. If a leader tries to command, people just ignore the command. In extreme cases, a particularly domineering leader may be killed by community agreement; this behavior was reported among the !Kung and the Hadza. Finally, particularly among more nomadic groups, people may just move away from a leader they don't like. The active attempts to put down upstarts in many egalitarian societies prompts Christopher Boehm to suggest that dominance comes naturally to humans. Egalitarian societies work hard to reverse that tendency.[3] The Mbuti provide an example of a society almost totally equal: "Neither in ritual, hunting, kinship nor band relations do they exhibit any discernable inequalities of rank or advantage."[4] Their hunting bands have no leaders, and recognition of the achievement of one person is not accompanied by privilege of any sort. Economic resources such as food are communally shared, and even tools and weapons are frequently passed from person to person. Only within the family are rights and privileges differentiated.

Foraging societies with extensive sharing of resources are more readily labeled egalitarian as compared with some pastoral societies where households may vary considerably in the number of animals they own. Should we consider a pastoral society with unequal distribution of animals egalitarian? Here there is controversy. One important issue is whether unequal ownership persists through time—that is, inherited. If vagaries of weather, theft, and gifts of livestock to relatives make livestock ownership fluctuate over time, wealth differences may mostly be temporary. A second important issue is whether the inequalities in livestock ownership make any difference in the ease of acquiring other "goods," such as prestige and political power. If wealth in livestock is ephemeral and is not associated with differential access to prestige and power, then some anthropologists would characterize such pastoral societies as egalitarian.[5] It is easy to imagine how an egalitarian society with

The dwellings in a Plains Indian camp were more or less the same as is typically the case where social stratification is minimal.

some wealth differences, as opposed to one with no wealth differences, could become a rank or a class society. All you would need is a mechanism for retaining more wealth in some families over time.

Rank Societies

Most societies with social *ranking* practice agriculture or herding, but not all agricultural or pastoral societies are ranked. Ranking is characterized by social groups with unequal access to prestige or status but *not* significantly unequal access to economic resources or power. Unequal access to prestige is often reflected in the position of chief, a rank to which only some members of a specified group in the society can succeed.

Unusual among rank societies were the nineteenth-century Native Americans who lived along the northwestern coast of the United States and the southwestern coast of Canada. An example were the Nimpkish, a Kwakiutl group.[6] These societies were unusual because their economy was based on food collecting. But huge catches of salmon—which were preserved for year-round consumption—enabled them to support fairly large and permanent villages. These societies were similar to food-producing societies in many ways, not just in their development of social ranking. Still, the principal means of proving one's high status was to give wealth away. The tribal chiefs celebrated solemn rites by grand feasts called *potlatches* at which they gave gifts to every guest.[7]

In rank societies, the position of chief is at least partly hereditary. The criterion of superior rank in some Polynesian societies, for example, was genealogical. Usually the eldest son succeeded to the position of chief, and different kinship groups were differentially ranked according to their genealogical distance from the chiefly line. In rank societies, chiefs are often treated with deference by people of lower rank. For example, among the Trobriand Islanders of Melanesia, people of lower rank must keep their heads lower than a person of higher rank. So, when a chief is standing, commoners must bend low. When commoners have to walk past a chief who happens to be sitting, he may rise and they will bend. If the chief chooses to remain seated, they must crawl.[8]

While there is no question that chiefs in a rank society enjoy special prestige, there is some controversy over whether they really do not also have material advantages. Chiefs may sometimes look as if they are substantially richer than commoners, for they may receive many gifts and have larger storehouses. In some instances, the chief may even be called the "owner" of the land. However, Marshall Sahlins maintains that the chief's storehouses only house temporary accumulations for feasts or other redistributions. And although the chief may be designated the "owner" of the land, others have the right to use the land. Furthermore, Sahlins suggests that the chief in a rank society lacks power because he usually cannot make people give him gifts or force them to work on communal projects. Often the chief can encourage production only by working furiously on his own cultivation.[9]

This picture of economic equality in rank societies is beginning to be questioned. Laura Betzig studied patterns of food sharing and labor on Ifaluk, a small atoll in the Western Carolines.[10] Chiefly status is inherited geneaologically in the female line, although most chiefs are male. (In the sex, gender, and culture chapter, we discuss why political leaders are usually male, even in societies structured around women.) As in other chiefly societies, Ifaluk chiefs

In societies with rank and class, deference is usually shown to political leaders, as in the case of this Fon chief in the lowlands of Cameroon, Africa.

are accorded deference. For example, during collective meals prepared by all the island women, chiefs were served first and were bowed to. The Ifaluk chiefs are said to control the fishing areas. Were the catches equitably distributed? Betzig measured the amount of fish each household got. All the commoners received an equal share, but the chiefs got extra fish; their households got twice as much per person as other households. Did the chiefs give away more later?

Theoretically, it is generosity that is supposed to even things out, but Betzig found that the gifts from chiefs to other households did not equal the amount the chiefs received from others. Furthermore, while everyone gave to the chiefs, the chiefs gave mostly to their close relatives. On Ifaluk, the chiefs did not work harder than others; in fact, they worked less. Is this true in other societies conventionally considered to be rank societies? We do not know. However, we need to keep in mind that the chiefs in Ifaluk were not noticeably better off either. If they lived in palaces with servants, had elaborate meals, or were dressed in fine clothes and jewelry, we would not need measures of food received or a special study to see if the chiefs had greater access to economic resources, because their wealth would be obvious. But rank societies may not have had as much economic equality as we used to think.

Class Societies

In class societies, as in rank societies, there is unequal access to prestige. But, unlike rank societies, class societies are characterized by groups of people that have substantially greater or lesser access to economic resources and power. That is, not every social group has the same opportunity to obtain land, animals, money, or other economic benefits or the same opportunity to exercise power that other groups have. Fully stratified or class societies range from somewhat open to virtually closed class, or *caste,* systems.

OPEN CLASS SYSTEMS

A **class** is a category of persons who all have about the same opportunity to obtain economic resources, power, and prestige. Different classes have differing opportunities. We call class systems *open* if there is some possibility of moving from one class to another. Since the 1920s, there have been many studies of classes in towns and cities in the United States. Researchers have produced profiles of these different communities—known variously as Yankee City, Middletown, Jonesville, and Old City—all of which support the premise that the United States has distinguishable,

ANTHROPOLOGICAL ORIGINALS
The Tlingit of Southern Alaska

Nearly all societies in the modern world have classes, even if they used to be egalitarian: Many societies, particularly those that depended on the collection of wild foods, did not have social inequality. Now nearly all are socially stratified; they have classes—groups such as families and ethnic groups with unequal access to wealth and power. Usually there are names for the classes, just like we may refer to people as "working class," "middle class," and "upper class." The Tlingit of Southern Alaska traditionally depended on fishing, hunting, and gathering. From the nineteenth century on, they increasingly participated in commercial production and exchange, and social ranking and named classes developed.

Persons were not only differentiated according to their household, clan, and moiety, but also according to class. The class system developed as some families acquired greater wealth through production, trade, and ceremonial exchanges. Every Tlingit was conscious of belonging to a social class. A Tlingit belonged to either (1) the high class—*anyaddi*; (2) the commoner class—*kanachideh*; (3) the low class—*nitckakaku*; or (4) the classless category of slaves—*gux*. Social class was significant in Tlingit society because it determined with whom one played as a child, to whom one was married as a youth, and to whom one sent invitations to attend potlatches as an adult. High- and low-class children were not permitted to play

together for fear that a low-class child might severely injure a child of a higher class and would not be able to provide proper compensation. Marriages were arranged within one's social class to promote stability and security. Only high-class people were invited to other villages for potlatches, because they were financially able to participate in the exchange of wealth items.

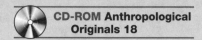

CD-ROM Anthropological Originals 18

Source: Kenneth Tollefson, "Tlingit: Chiefs Past and Present," in Melvin Ember and Carol R. Ember, eds., *Portraits of Culture: Ethnographic Originals,* in Carol R. Ember and Melvin Ember, eds., *New Directions in Anthropology* (Upper Saddle River, NJ: Prentice Hall, CD-ROM, 2003).

though somewhat open, social classes. Both W. Lloyd Warner and Paul Lunt's Yankee City study[11] and Robert and Helen Lynd's Middletown study[12] concluded that the social status or prestige of a family is generally correlated with the occupation and wealth of the head of the family. Class systems are by no means confined to the United States. They are found in all nations of the modern world.

Although class status is not fully determined at birth in open class societies, there is a high probability that most people will stay close to the class into which they were born and will marry within that class. Classes tend to perpetuate themselves through the inheritance of wealth. John Brittain suggested that, in the United States, the transfer of money through bequests accounts for much of the wealth of the next generation. As we might expect, the importance of inheritance seems to increase at higher levels of wealth. That is, the wealth of richer people comes more from inheritance than does the wealth of not-so-rich people.[13]

Other mechanisms of class perpetuation may be more subtle, but they are still powerful. In the United States there are many institutions that make it possible for an upper-class person to have little contact with other classes. Private day and boarding schools put upper-class children in close contact mostly with others of their class. Attending these schools makes it more likely they will get into universities

with higher prestige. Debutante balls and exclusive private parties ensure that young people meet "the right people." Country clubs, exclusive city clubs, and service in particular charities continue the process of limited association. People of the same class also tend to live in the same neighborhood. Before 1948, explicit restrictions kept certain groups out of particular neighborhoods, but after the U.S. Supreme Court ruled such discrimination unconstitutional, more subtle methods were developed. For instance, zoning restrictions may prohibit multiple-family dwellings in a town or neighborhood and lots below a certain acreage.[14]

Identification with a social class begins early in life. In addition to differences in occupation, wealth, and prestige, social classes vary in many other ways, including religious affiliation, closeness to kin, ideas about child rearing, job satisfaction, leisure-time activities, style of clothes and furniture, and (as noted in the chapter on communication and language) even in styles of speech.[15] People from each class tend to be more comfortable with those from the same class; they talk similarly and are more likely to have similar interests and tastes.

Class boundaries, though vague, have been established by custom and tradition; sometimes they have been reinforced by the enactment of laws. Many of our laws serve to

A private boarding school in New Jersey whose students are mostly from wealthy families.

protect property and thus tend to favor the upper and upper-middle classes. The poor, in contrast, seem to be disadvantaged in our legal system. The crimes the poor are most likely to commit are dealt with harshly by the courts, and poor people rarely have the money to secure effective legal counsel.

In open class systems it is not always clear how many classes there are. In Stanley Barrett's study of "Paradise," Ontario, some people thought that in the past there were only two classes. One person said, "There was the hierarchy, and the rest of us." Another said that there were three classes: "The people with money, the in-between, and the ones who didn't have anything." Many said there were four: "The wealthy businessmen, the middle class, blue collar workers, and the guys that were just existing."[16] A few insisted that there were five classes. With the breakdown of the old rigid class structure, there are more people in the middle. As in the United States, there is now an ideology of "classlessness"—most people tend to put themselves in the middle. However, objective evidence indicates a continuing multiple class system.[17]

DEGREE OF OPENNESS   Some class systems are more open than others; that is, it is easier in some societies to move from one class position to another. Social scientists typically compare the class of a person with the class of his or her parent or parents to measure the degree of mobility. Although most people aspire to move up, mobility also includes moving down. Obtaining more education, particularly a university education, is one of the most effective ways to move upward in contemporary societies. For example, in the United States, college-educated individuals have on average 60 percent more income than those without a college education.[18] In fact, in many countries educational attainment predicts one's social class better than parents' occupation does.[19]

How do the United States and Canada compare with other countries in degree of class mobility? Canada and Sweden have more mobility than the United States, France, and Britain. Japan and Italy have less mobility. If we focus on the ease of moving into the highest class, Italy, France, Spain, Germany, and Japan are more difficult than Britain and the United States.[20]

Class openness also varies over time. In the study of "Paradise," Ontario, Barrett found that the rigid stratification system of the 1950s opened up considerably as new people moved into the community. No one disputed who belonged to the elite in the past. They were of British background, lived in the largest houses, had new cars, and vacationed in Florida. Moreover, they controlled all the leadership positions in the town. By the 1980s, though, the leaders came mostly from the middle and working classes.[21]

DEGREE OF INEQUALITY   Degree of class mobility, however, is not the same as degree of economic inequality. For example, Japan, Italy, and Germany have less mobility than the United States, but less inequality (see below). Degree of inequality can vary considerably over time. In the United States, inequality has fluctuated considerably from the 1900s to the present. The greatest inequality was just before the 1929 stock market crash, when the top 1 percent had 42.6 percent of all the wealth. The least inequality was in the mid-1970s after the stock market declined by 42 percent. Then the top 1 percent controlled 17.6 percent of the wealth.

Change over time in the degree of inequality sometimes appears to have economic causes; for example, the 1929 crash made the wealthy less wealthy. But some of the change over time is due to shifts in public policy. During the New Deal of the 1930s, tax changes and work programs shifted more income to ordinary people; in the 1980s, tax cuts for the wealthy helped the rich get richer. In the 1990s, the rich continued to get richer and the poor got poorer.[22] One way of calculating the disparity between rich and poor is to use the ratio of income held by the top fifth of the households divided by the income held by the bottom fifth. Comparatively speaking, the United States presently has more inequality than any of the countries in Western Europe, with a ratio of 9 to 1 (see Figure 18–1). That is, the top 20 percent of U.S. households controls 9 times the wealth controlled by the bottom 20 percent. Norway, on the other hand, has a ratio of about 3.5 to 1. And Germany has a ratio of about 4.5 to 1. The degree of inequality in the United States exceeds that of India, with a ratio of about 5.5 to 1. South Africa and Brazil are among the most unequal countries, with ratios of 22 to 1 and 24 to 1, respectively.

CASTE SYSTEMS

Some societies have classes that are virtually closed called castes. A **caste** is a ranked group in which membership is determined at birth, and marriage is restricted to members of one's own caste. The only way you can belong is by being born into the group; and since you cannot marry outside the group, your children cannot acquire another caste status either. In India, for example, there are several thousand hereditary castes. Although the precise ranking of these thousands of groups is not clear, there appear to be four main levels of hierarchy. The castes in India are often thought to be associated with different occupations, but that is not quite true. Most Indians live in rural areas and have agricultural occupations, but their castes vary widely.[23]

Castes may exist in conjunction with a more open class system. Indeed, in India today, members of a low caste who can get wage-paying jobs, chiefly those in urban areas, may improve their social standing in the same ways available to people in other class societies. In general, however, they still cannot marry someone in a higher caste, so the caste system is perpetuated.

Questions basic to all stratified societies, and particularly to a caste society, were posed by John Ruskin, a nineteenth-century British essayist: "Which of us . . . is to do the hard and dirty work for the rest—and for what pay? Who is to do the pleasant and clean work, and for what pay?"[24] In India those questions have been answered by the caste system, which mainly dictates how goods and services are exchanged, particularly in rural areas.[25] Who is to do the hard and dirty work for the rest of society is clearly established: A large group of Untouchables forms the bottom of the hierarchy. Among the Untouchables are subcastes such as the Camars, or leatherworkers, and the Bhangis, who traditionally are sweepers. At the top of the hierarchy, performing the pleasant and clean work of priests, are the Brahmans. Between the two extremes are thousands of castes and subcastes. In a typical village, the potter makes clay drinking cups and large water vessels for the entire village population. In return, the principal landowner gives him a house site and supplies him twice yearly with grain. Some other castes owe the potter their services: The barber cuts his hair; the sweeper carries away his rubbish; the washer washes his clothes; the Brahman performs his children's weddings. The barber serves every caste in the village except the Untouchables; he, in turn, is served by half of the others. He has inherited the families he works for, along with his father's occupation. All castes help at harvest and at weddings for additional payment, which sometimes includes a money payment.

This description is, in fact, an idealized picture of the caste system of India. In reality, the system operates to the advantage of the principal landowning caste—sometimes the Brahmans and sometimes other castes. Also, it is not carried on without some resentment; signs of hostility are shown toward the ruling caste by the Untouchables and other lower castes. The resentment does not appear to be

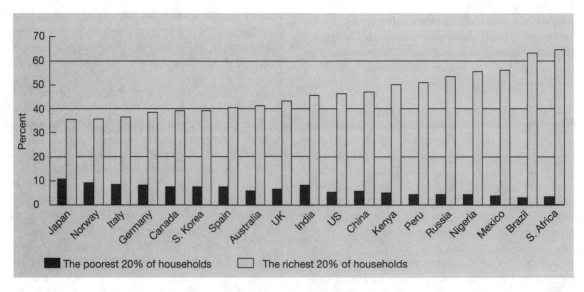

Figure 18–1 *Proportion of National Income Earned by the Richest 20 Percent of Households Compared with the Poorest 20 Percent: Selected Country Comparisons.*

Source: These data are abstracted from *2001 World Development Indicators.* Washington, DC: The World Bank, 2001, pp. 70–73.

against the caste system as such. Instead, the lower castes exhibit bitterness at their own low status and strive for greater equality. For instance, one of the Camars' traditional services is to remove dead cattle; in return, they can have the meat to eat and the hide to tan for their leather-working. Because handling dead animals and eating beef are regarded as unclean acts, the Camars of one village refused to continue this service. Thus, they lost a source of free hides and food in a vain attempt to escape unclean status.

Since World War II, the economic basis of the caste system in India has been undermined somewhat by the growing practice of giving cash payment for services. For instance, the son of a barber may be a teacher during the week, earning a cash salary, and confine his haircutting to weekends. But he still remains in the barber caste (Nai) and must marry within that caste.

Perpetuation of the caste system is ensured by the power of those in the upper castes, who derive three main advantages from their position: economic, prestige, and sexual gains. The economic gain is the most immediately apparent. An ample supply of cheap labor and free services is maintained by the threat of sanctions. Lower-caste members may have their use of a house site withdrawn; they may be refused access to the village well or to common grazing land for animals; or they may be expelled from the village. Prestige is also maintained by the threat of sanctions; the higher castes expect deference and servility from the lower castes. The sexual gain is less apparent but equally real. The high-caste male has access to two groups of females, those of his own caste and those of lower castes. High-caste females are kept free of the "contaminating"

touch of low-caste males because low-caste males are allowed access only to low-caste women. Moreover, the constant reminders of ritual uncleanness serve to keep the lower castes "in their place." Higher castes do not accept water from Untouchables, sit next to them, or eat at the same table with them.

Japan also had a caste group within a class society. Now called *burakumin* (instead of the pejorative *Eta*), this group traditionally had occupations that were considered unclean.[26] Comparable to India's Untouchables, they were a hereditary, endogamous (in-marrying) group. Their occupations were traditionally those of farm laborer, leather-worker, and basket weaver; their standard of living was very low. The burakumin are physically indistinguishable from other Japanese.[27] Discrimination against the burakumin was officially abolished by the Japanese government in 1871, but it was not until the twentieth century that the burakumin began organizing to bring about change. These movements appear to be paying off as more active steps have been taken recently by the Japanese government to alleviate discrimination and poverty. As of 1995, 73 percent of burakumin marriages were with non-burakumin. In public opinion polls, two-thirds of burakumin now said that they had not encountered discrimination. However, most burakumin still live in segregated neighborhoods where unemployment, crime, and alcoholism rates are high.[28]

We turn now to some situations where the caste system appears to be associated with differences in physical appearance. In Rwanda, a country in east-central Africa, a longtime caste system was overthrown, first by an election and then by a revolution in 1959 to 1960. Three castes had existed, each distinguished from the others by physical appearance and occupation.[29] It is believed that the three castes derived from three different language groups who came together through migration and conquest. Later, however, they began to use a common language, although remaining endogamous and segregated by hereditary occupations. The taller and leaner ruling caste, the Tutsi, constituted about 15 percent of the population. They were the landlords and practiced the prestigious occupation of herding. The shorter and stockier agricultural caste, the Hutu, made up about 85 percent of the population. As tenants of the Tutsi, they produced most of the country's food. The much shorter Twa, accounting for less than 1 percent of the population, were foragers who formed the lowest caste.

Colonial rule, first by the Germans and then by the Belgians after World War I, strengthened Tutsi power. When the Hutu united to demand more of the rewards of their labor in 1959, the king and many of the Tutsi ruling caste were driven out of the country. The Hutu then established a republican form of government and declared independence from Belgium in 1962. In this new government, however, the forest-dwelling Twa were generally excluded from full citizenship. In 1990, Tutsi rebels invaded from Uganda, and attempts were made to negotiate a multiparty government. However, civil war continued, and in 1994 alone over a million people, mostly Tutsi, were killed.

Commercialization and new technologies have increased social mobility in India despite the continuing importance of caste.

Almost 2 million refugees, mostly Hutu, fled to Zaire as the Tutsi-led rebels established a new government.[30]

In the United States, African Americans used to have more of a castelike status determined partly by the inherited characteristic of skin color. Until recently, some states had laws prohibiting an African American from marrying a European American. When interethnic marriage did occur, children of the union were often regarded as having lower status than European American children, even though they may have had blond hair and light skin. In the South, where treatment of African Americans as a caste was most apparent, European Americans refused to eat with African Americans or sit next to them at lunch counters, on buses, and in schools. Separate drinking fountains and toilets reinforced the idea of ritual uncleanness. The economic advantages and gains in prestige enjoyed by European Americans are well documented.[31] In the following sections, on slavery and racism and inequality, we discuss the social status of African Americans in more detail.

SLAVERY

Slaves are persons who do not own their own labor, and as such they represent a class. We may associate slavery with a few well-known examples, such as ancient Egypt, Greece, and Rome or the southern United States, but slavery has existed in some form in almost every part of the world at one time or another, in simpler as well as in more complex societies. Slaves are often obtained from other cultures directly: kidnapped, captured in war, or given as tribute. Or they may be obtained indirectly as payment in barter or trade. Slaves sometimes come from the same culture; one became a slave as payment of a debt, as a punishment for a crime, or even as a chosen alternative to poverty. Slave societies vary in the degree to which it is possible to become freed from slavery.[32] Sometimes the slavery system has been a closed class, or caste, system; sometimes a relatively open class system. In different slave-owning societies, slaves have had different, but always some, legal rights.[33]

In ancient Greece, slaves often were conquered enemies. Because city-states were constantly conquering one another or rebelling against former conquerors, slavery was a threat to everyone. After the Trojan War, the transition of Hecuba from queen to slave was marked by her cry, "Count no one happy, however fortunate, before he dies."[34] Nevertheless, Greek slaves were considered human beings, and they could even acquire some higher-class status along with freedom. Andromache, Hecuba's daughter-in-law, was taken as slave and concubine by one of the Greek heroes. When his legal wife produced no children, Andromache's slave son became heir to his father's throne. Although slaves had no rights under law, once they were freed, either by the will of their master or by purchase, they and their descendants could become assimilated into the dominant group. In other words, slavery in Greece was not seen as the justified position of inferior people. It was regarded, rather, as an act of fate—"the luck of the draw"—that relegated one to the lowest class in society.

Among the Nupe, a society in central Nigeria, slavery was of quite another type.[35] The methods of obtaining slaves—as part of the booty of warfare and, later, by purchase—were similar to those of Europeans, but the position of the slaves was very different. Mistreatment was rare. Male slaves were given the same opportunities to earn money as other dependent males in the household—younger brothers, sons, or other relatives. A slave might be given a garden plot of his own to cultivate, or he might be given a commission if his master was a craftsman or a tradesman. Slaves could acquire property, wealth, and even slaves of their own. But all of a slave's belongings went to the master at the slave's death.

Manumission—the granting of freedom to slaves—was built into the Nupe system. If a male slave could afford the marriage payment for a free woman, the children of the resulting marriage were free; the man himself, however, remained a slave. Marriage and concubinage were the easiest ways out of bondage for a slave woman. Once she had produced a child by her master, both she and the child had free status. The woman, however, was only figuratively free; if a concubine, she had to remain in that role. As might be expected, the family trees of the nobility and the wealthy were liberally grafted with branches descended from slave concubines.

The most fortunate slaves among the Nupe were the house slaves. They could rise to positions of power in the household as overseers and bailiffs, charged with law enforcement and judicial duties. (Recall the Old Testament story of Joseph, who was sold into slavery by his brothers. Joseph became a household slave of the pharaoh and rose to the position of second in the kingdom because he devised an ingenious system of taxation.) There was even a titled group of Nupe slaves, the Order of Court Slaves, who were trusted officers of the king and members of an elite. Slave status in general, though, placed one at the bottom of the social ladder. In the Nupe system, few slaves, mainly princes from their own societies, ever achieved membership in the titled group.

In the United States, slavery originated as a means of obtaining cheap labor, but the slaves soon came to be regarded as deserving of their low status because of their alleged inherent inferiority. Because the slaves were from Africa and dark-skinned, some European Americans justified slavery and the belief in "black" people's inferiority by quoting Scripture out of context ("They shall be hewers of wood and drawers of water"). Slaves could not marry or make any other contracts, nor could they own property. In addition, their children were also slaves, and the master had sexual rights over the female slaves. Because the status of slavery was determined by birth in the United States, slaves constituted a caste. During the days of slavery, therefore, the United States had both a caste and a class system. And even after the abolition of slavery, as we have noted, some castelike elements remained.

As for why slavery may have developed in the first place, cross-cultural research is as yet inconclusive. We do know, however, that slavery is not an inevitable stage in economic development, contrary to what some have assumed. In

CURRENT RESEARCH AND ISSUES
Is Global Inequality Increasing?

When people support themselves by what they collect and produce themselves, as most people did until a few thousand years ago, it is difficult to compare the standards of living of different societies because we cannot translate what people have into market or monetary value. It is only where people are at least partly involved in the world market economy that we can measure the standard of living in monetary terms. Today this comparison is possible for most of the world. Many people in most societies depend on buying and selling for a living; and the more people who depend on international exchange, the more possible it is to compare them in terms of standard economic indicators. We do not have such indicators for all the different societies, but we do have them for many countries. Those indicators suggest that the degree of economic inequality in the world is not only very substantial but has generally increased over time.

To convey just how economically unequal the world is, consider this. Surveying households in 91 countries, Branko Milanovic calculated that the richest 1 percent of people in the world have as much total income as 57 percent of the people at the bottom. Over one billion people on earth live on less than one U.S. dollar a day. This level of inequality exceeds the degree of inequality within any individual country. The disparities are not just in terms of income; there are vast inequalities in literacy, access to clean water, and mortality from a wide range of diseases.

Global inequality has increased substantially in the last three decades. To measure the changes, we can compare the ratio between the richest and poorest fifths over time. In 1997, the ratio was 70.4 to 1, which is calculated by dividing the income for the top fifth by the income for the bottom fifth. That ratio has increased since the 1970s, when the ratio was 33.7 to 1. Higher inequality over time does not necessarily mean that the poor are worse off than before; it is possible that the rich can get much richer and the poor remain the same. However, it does seem that the poor have gotten poorer and the rich have gotten richer. Between 1988 and 1993 Milanovic calculated that the real incomes of the bottom 5 percent dropped by 25 percent, while the incomes of the richest 20 percent grew by about 12 percent.

If the world as a whole is seeing improvements in technology and economic development, why is inequality in the world increasing? As we shall see later, in the chapter on culture change and globalization, it is often the rich within a society who benefit most from new technology, at least initially. They are not only the most likely to be able to afford it, they also are the only ones who can afford to take the risks that it involves. The same may be true for nations. Those that already have capital are more likely than the poorer nations to take advantage of improvements in technology. In addition, the poorer countries generally have the highest rates of population growth, so income per capita can fall if population increases faster than the rate of economic development. Economists tell us that a developing country may, at least initially, experience an increase in inequality, - but the inequality often decreases over time. Will the inequalities among countries also decrease as the world economy develops further?

The picture is not entirely bleak. It is true that the disparity between rich and poor countries has increased in recent years, but it is also true that the world economy has improved in some respects. The United Nations has computed a "human development index" for 114 countries, combining measures of life expectancy, literacy, and a measure of per capita purchasing power. According to this index, all countries but Zambia have improved over a period of 30 years, many of them substantially. For example, a child in the world today can expect to live 8 more years than 30 years ago. Literacy has increased from 47 percent in 1970 to 73 percent in 1999. The most progress has occurred in East Asia and the Pacific; the least in sub-Saharan Africa. World leaders at the United Nations Millennium Declaration have committed themselves to a number of goals by the year 2015, including halving the proportion of people living in extreme poverty and halving the proportion of people suffering from hunger. Even if those goals are achieved, much more will remain to be done if we are to achieve a more equal world.

Sources: Human Development Report 2001, published for the United Nations Development Programme (New York: Oxford University Press, 2001), pp. 9–25; Branko Milanovic, "True World Income Distribution, 1988 and 1993: First Calculation Based on Household Surveys Alone." *The Economic Journal,* 112 (2002): 51–92; *State of the World 1994: A Worldwatch Institute Report on Progress toward a Sustainable Society* (New York: Norton, 1994), pp. 1–8; Peter Donaldson, *Worlds Apart: The Economic Gulf between Nations* (London: British Broadcasting Corporation, 1971); Philips Foster, *The World Food Problem: Tackling the Causes of Undernutrition in the Third World* (Boulder, CO: Lynne Rienner, 1992), pp. 149–51.

other words, slavery is not found mainly in certain economies, such as those dependent on intensive agriculture. Unlike the United States until the Civil War, many societies with intensive agriculture did not develop any variety of slavery. Also, the hypothesis that slavery develops where available resources are plentiful but labor is scarce is not supported by the cross-cultural evidence. All we can say definitely is that slavery does not occur in developed or industrial economies; either it disappears or it was never present in them.[36]

Racism and Inequality

Racism is the belief that some "races" are inferior to others. In a society composed of people with noticeably different physical features, such as differences in skin color, racism is almost invariably associated with social stratification. Those "races" considered inferior make up a larger proportion of the lower social classes or castes. Even in more open class systems, where individuals from all backgrounds can achieve higher status positions, individuals from "racial" groups deemed inferior may be subject to discrimination in housing or may be more likely to be searched or stopped by the police.

In some societies, such as the United States, the idea that humans are divided into "races" is taken so much for granted that people are asked for their "race" on the census. Most Americans probably assume that "races" are real, meaningful categories, reflecting important biological variation. But that is not necessarily the case. You may have noticed that we put "races" in quotes. We have done so deliberately because most anthropologists are persuaded that "race" is a meaningless concept as applied to humans. To understand why we say that, we first need to consider what the concept of *race* means in biology.

RACE AS A CONSTRUCT IN BIOLOGY

While all members of a species can potentially interbreed with others, most reproduction takes place within smaller groups or breeding populations. Through time, populations inhabiting different geographic regions may develop some differences in biological traits. Biologists may then classify different geographic populations into different *varieties,* or **races.** If the term *race* is understood to be just a shorthand or classificatory way in which biologists describe variation within a species from one population to the next, the concept of race would probably not be controversial. But, as applied to humans, racial classifications have often been thought to imply that some "races" are innately inferior to others.

The misuse and misunderstanding of the term *race,* and its association with racist thinking, are two of the reasons that many anthropologists and others have suggested that the concept of race may hinder the search to explain the development of biological differences in humans. In any case, racial classifications are not scientifically useful in that search because different populations are not clearly classifiable into discrete groups that can be defined in terms of the presence or absence of particular sets of biological traits.[37] Population A may have a higher frequency of trait X than population B, but in regard to the frequency of trait Y the two populations may not be distinguishable. So biological characteristics in humans often vary from one population to another in uncorrelated ways. This situation makes racial classification a very arbitrary undertaking when it comes to humans. Compare the number of "races" that different classifiers have come up with. The number of distinguished racial categories has varied from as few as 3 to more than 37.[38]

How can groups be clearly divided into "races" if most adaptive biological traits show gradual, but not always correlated, differences from one region to a neighboring region?[39] Skin color is a good example. Darker skin appears to protect the body from damaging ultraviolet radiation, and natural selection seems to have favored individuals with darker skin in environments with more sunlight. In the area around Egypt, there is a gradient of skin color as you move from north to south in the Nile Valley. Skin generally becomes darker closer to the equator (which is south) and lighter closer to the Mediterranean. Other adaptive traits may not have north-south gradients, because the environmental predictors may be distributed differently. Nose shape varies with humidity, but clines in humidity do not particularly correspond to variation in latitude. So the gradient for nose shape would not be the same as the gradient for skin color.

Because adaptive traits tend to be distributed in **clines,** or gradients of varying frequencies, there is no line you could draw on a world map that would separate "white" from "black" people, or "whites" from "Asians."[40] Only traits that are neutral in terms of adaptation or natural selection will tend to cluster in regions.[41] It should also be noted that the traits we have mentioned are superficial surface features. Human populations do vary biologically in many ways, but it is important to realize that few of these ways are correlated with each other.

RACE AS A SOCIAL CATEGORY

If race, in the opinion of many biological anthropologists, is not a particularly useful device for classifying humans, how come it is so widely used as a category in various societies? Anthropologists suggest the reasons are social. That is, racial classifications are social categories to which individuals are assigned, by themselves and others, to separate "our" group from others. We have seen that people tend to be *ethnocentric,* to view their culture as better than other cultures. Racial classifications may reflect the same tendency to divide "us" from "them," except that the divisions are supposedly based on biological differences.[42] The "them" are almost always viewed as inferior to "us."

We know that racial classifications have often been, and still are, used by certain groups to justify discrimination, exploitation, or genocide. The "Aryan race" was supposed to be the group of blond-haired, blue-eyed, white-skinned people whom Adolf Hitler wanted to dominate the world,

"Race" is a social, not biological, category. Individuals labeled "black" vary enormously in physical features. There is more genetic variation within a "race" than between "races."

to which end he and others attempted to destroy as many members of the Jewish "race" as they could. (It is estimated that 6 million Jews and others were murdered in what is now called the Holocaust.[43]) But who were the Aryans? Technically, Aryans are any people, including the German-speaking Jews in Hitler's Germany, who speak one of the Indo-European languages. The Indo-European languages include such disparate modern tongues as Greek, Spanish, Hindi, Polish, French, Icelandic, German, Gaelic, and English. And many Aryans speaking these languages have neither blond hair nor blue eyes. Similarly, all kinds of people may be Jews, whether or not they descend from the ancient Near Eastern population that spoke the Hebrew language. There are light-skinned Danish Jews and darker Jewish Arabs. One of the most orthodox Jewish groups in the United States is based in New York City and is composed entirely of African Americans.

The arbitrary and social basis of most racial classifications becomes apparent when you compare how they differ from one place to another. Consider, for example, what used to be thought about the "races" in South Africa. Under apartheid, which was a system of racial segregation and discrimination, someone with mixed "white" and "black" ancestry was considered "colored." However, when important people of African ancestry (from other countries) would visit South Africa, they were often considered "white." Chinese were considered "Asian"; but the Japanese, who were important economically to South Africa, were considered "white."[44] In some parts of the United States, laws against interracial marriage continued in force through the 1960s. You would be considered a "negro" if you had an eighth or more "negro" ancestry (if one or

more of your eight grandparents were "negro"). So only a small amount of "negro" ancestry made a person "negro." But a small amount of "white" ancestry did not make a person "white." Biologically speaking, this makes no sense, but socially it was another story.[45]

If people of different "races" are viewed as inferior, they are almost inevitably going to end up on the bottom of the social ladder in a socially stratified society. Discrimination will keep them out of the better-paying or higher-status jobs and in neighborhoods that are poorer. As the box "Unequal in Death" shows, people of different "races" also suffer from differential access to health care and have more health problems.

Ethnicity and Inequality

If "race" is not a scientifically useful category because people cannot be clearly divided into different "racial" categories based on sets of physical traits, then "racial" classifications such as "black" and "white" in the United States might better be described as *ethnic* classifications. How else can we account for the following facts? Groups that now in the United States are thought of as "white" were earlier thought of as belonging to inferior "races." For example, in the latter half of the nineteenth century, newspapers would often talk about the new immigrants from Ireland as belonging to the Irish "race." Similarly, before World War II, Jews were thought of as a separate "racial" group, and only became "white" afterwards.[46] It is hard to escape the idea that changes in "racial" classification occurred as the Irish, Jews, and other immigrant groups became more accepted by the majority in the United States.[47]

It is apparent that *ethnic groups* and *ethnic identities* emerge as part of a social and political process. The process of defining **ethnicity** usually involves a group of people emphasizing common origins and language, shared history, and selected cultural difference such as a difference in religion. Those doing the defining can be outside or inside the ethnic group. Outsiders and insiders often perceive ethnic groups differently. In a country with one large core majority group, often the majority group doesn't think of itself as an ethnic group. Rather, they consider only the minority groups to have ethnic identities. For example, in the United States it is not common for the majority to call themselves European Americans, but other groups may be called African Americans, Asian Americans, or Native Americans. The minority groups, on the other hand, may have different named identities.[48] Asian Americans may identify themselves more specifically as Japanese Americans, Korean Americans, Chinese Americans, or Hmong. The majority population often uses derogatory names to identify people who are different. The majority may also tend to lump people of diverse ethnicities together. Naming a group establishes a boundary between it and other ethnic groups.[49]

Ethnic identity may be manipulated, by insiders and by outsiders, in different situations. A particularly repressive

APPLIED ANTHROPOLOGY
Unequal in Death: African Americans Compared with European Americans

Everyone dies of something. Yet, if you consider cardiovascular disease, the leading cause of death in the United States, it turns out that after controlling for the effects of age and gender, African Americans die more often from that disease than European Americans. The same kind of disparity occurs also with almost every other major cause of death—cancer, cirrhosis of the liver, diabetes, injuries, infant mortality, and homicide. Medical anthropologists and health policy researchers want to know why. Without such understanding, it is hard to know how to reduce the disparity.

One reason may be subtle discrimination by the medical profession itself. For example, a European American with chest pain in the United States is more likely than an African American to be given an angiogram, a medical procedure that injects radioactive dye into the heart to look for deficits in blood flow through the coronary arteries that supply blood to the heart. And even if coronary heart disease is detected by an angiogram, an African American is less likely to receive bypass surgery. Thus, the death rate from cardiovascular disease may be higher for African Americans than for European Americans because of unequal medical care.

Yet, while some difference in mortality may be due to disparity in medical treatment, this could only be part of the picture. African Americans may be more prone to cardiovascular disease because they are about twice as likely as European Americans to have high rates of hypertension (high blood pressure). But why the disparity in hypertension? Three possible explanations, not mutually exclusive, are discussed in the research literature.

The first is a possible difference in genetics. The second is a difference in life-style. The third is class difference.

Most of the Africans that came to the Americas were forcibly taken as slaves between the sixteenth and nineteenth centuries, largely from West Africa. In one comparative study of hypertension, African Americans had much higher blood pressure than Africans in Nigeria and Cameroon, even in urban areas. People with African ancestry in the Caribbean were in the middle of the range. Life-style differences were also vast—the West Africans had plenty of exercise, were lean, and had low-fat and low-salt diets. Any possible difference in genes would seem to be insignificant. Jared Diamond has suggested that individuals who could retain salt would have been most likely to survive the terrible conditions of the sailing ships that brought slaves to the New World. Many died from diarrhea and dehydration (salt-depleting conditions) on those voyages. Retention of salt would have been a genetic advantage then, but disadvantageous in places such as the United States with high-salt, high-fat diets. Critics of this theory suggest that salt-depleting diseases were not the leading causes of death in the slave voyages; tuberculosis and violence were more frequent causes of death. Furthermore, critics say that the slave-ship theory would predict little genetic diversity in African American populations with respect to hypertension, but in fact there is great diversity.

Hypertension could be related also to differences in life-style and wealth. As we noted in the section on racism and inequality, African Americans in the United States are disproportionately poorer. Study after study has noted that healthier life-style habits are generally correlated with higher positions on the socioeconomic ladder. Moreover, individuals from higher social positions are more likely to have health insurance and access to care in superior hospitals. But even after correcting for factors such as obesity, physical activity, and social class, the health differential persists—African Americans still have a much higher incidence of hypertension than European Americans.

William Dressler suggests that stress is another possible cause of higher rates of hypertension. Despite increased economic mobility in recent years, African Americans are still subject to prejudice and may consequently have more stress even if they have higher income. Stress is related to higher blood pressure. In a color-conscious society, a very dark-skinned individual walking in a wealthy neighborhood at night may be thought not to live there and may be stopped by the police. If Dressler is correct, darker-skinned African Americans who have objective indicators of higher status should have much higher blood pressure than would be expected from their relative education, age, body mass, or social class alone. And that seems to be true. Racism may affect health.

Sources: William W. Dressler, "Health in the African American Community: Accounting for Health Inequalities," *Medical Anthropological Quarterly* 7 (1993): 325–45; Richard S. Cooper, Charles N. Rotimi, and Ryk Ward, "The Puzzle of Hypertension in African-Americans," *Scientific American,* February 1999, 56–63; Jared Diamond, "The Saltshaker's Curse—Physiological Adaptations That Helped American Blacks Survive Slavery May Now Be Predisposing Their Descendants to Hypertension," *Natural History* (10), October 1991.

regime that emphasizes nationalism and loyalty to the state may not only suppress the assertiveness of ethnic claims; it may also act to minimize communication among people who might otherwise embrace the same ethnic identity.[50] More democratic regimes may allow more expression of difference and celebrate ethnic difference. However, manipulation of ethnicity does not come just from the top. It may be to the advantage of minority groups to lobby for more equal treatment as a larger entity, such as Asian American, rather than as Japanese, Chinese, Hmong, Filipino, or Korean American. Similarly, even though there are hundreds of American Indian groups, originally speaking different languages, there may be political advantages for all if they are treated as Native Americans.

In many multiethnic societies, ethnicity and diversity are things to be proud of and celebrated. Shared ethnic identity often makes people feel comfortable with similar people and gives them a strong sense of belonging. Still, ethnic differences in multiethnic societies are usually associated with inequities in wealth, power, and prestige. In other words, ethnicity is part of the system of *stratification.*

Although there are some people who believe that inequities are deserved, the origins of ethnic stereotypes, prejudice, and discrimination usually follow from historical and political events that give some groups dominance over others. For example, even though there were many early stories of help given by native peoples to the English settlers in the 17th century in the land now known as North America, the English were the invaders, and negative stereotypes about native peoples developed to justify taking their land and their lives. Referring to the negative stereotypes of Native Americans that developed, J. Milton Yinger said: "One would almost think that it had been the Indian who had invaded Europe, driven back the inhabitants, cut their population to one-third of its original size, unilaterally changed treaties, and brought the dubious glories of firewater and firearms."[51]

Similarly, as we noted in the section on slavery, African slaves were initially acquired as cheap labor, but inhumane treatment of slaves was justified by beliefs about their inferiority. Unfortunately, stereotypes can become self-fulfilling prophesies, especially if those discriminated against come to believe the stereotypes. It is easy to see how this can happen. If there is a widespread belief that a group is inferior, and that group is given inferior schools and little chance for improvement or little chance for a good job, the members of that group may acquire few skills and not try hard. The result is often a vicious cycle.[52]

And yet, the picture is not all bleak. Change has occurred. The ethnic identity forged by a minority group can help promote political activism, such as the nonviolent civil rights movement in the United States in the 1960s. That activism, helped by some people in the more advantaged groups, helped break down many of the legal barriers and segregationist practices that reinforced inequality.

The traditional barriers in the United States have mostly been lifted in recent years, but the "color line" has not disappeared. African Americans are found in all social classes, but they remain underrepresented in the wealthiest group and overrepresented at the bottom. Discrimination may be lessened, but it is still not gone. In research done with matched pairs of "whites" and "blacks" applying for jobs or for housing, discrimination is still evident.[53] Thus, African Americans may have to be better than others to get promoted, or it may be assumed that they got ahead just because they were African American and were hired because of affirmative action programs. European Americans often expect African Americans to be "ambassadors," to be called on mainly for knowledge about how to handle situations involving other African Americans. African Americans may work with others, but they usually go home to African American neighborhoods. Or they may live in mixed neighborhoods and experience considerable isolation. Few African Americans can completely avoid the anguish of racism.[54]

The Emergence of Stratification

Anthropologists are not certain why social stratification developed. Nevertheless, they are reasonably sure that higher levels of stratification emerged relatively recently in human history. Archaeological sites dating before about 8,000 years ago do not show extensive evidence of inequality. Houses do not appear to vary much in size or content, and different communities of the same culture are similar in size and otherwise. Signs of inequality appear first in the Near East, about 2,000 years after agriculture emerged in that region. Inequality in burial suggests inequality in life. Particularly telling are unequal child burials. It is unlikely that children could achieve high status by their own achievements. So when archaeologists find statues and ornaments only in some children's tombs, as at the 7,500-year-old site of Tell es-Sawwan in Iraq,[55] the grave goods suggest that those children belonged to a higher-ranking family or a higher class.

Another indication that stratification is a relatively recent development in human history is the fact that certain cultural features associated with stratification also developed relatively recently. For example, most societies that depend primarily on agriculture or herding have social classes.[56] Agriculture and herding developed within the past 10,000 years, so we may assume that most food collectors in the distant past lacked social classes. Other recently developed cultural features associated with class stratification include fixed settlements, political integration beyond the community level, the use of money as a medium of exchange, and the presence of at least some full-time specialization.[57]

In 1966, the comparative sociologist Gerhard Lenski suggested that the trend since 8,000 years ago toward increasing inequality was reversing. He argued that inequalities of power and privilege in industrial societies—measured in terms of the concentration of political power and the distribution of income—are less pronounced than inequalities in complex preindustrial societies. Technology in

Shantytown near city's richest neighborhood: the center of Buenos Aires, Argentina.

and the larger the agricultural surplus, the greater the scope and complexity of the distribution system. The status of the chief, who serves as redistributing agent, is enhanced. Sahlins argued that the differentiation between distributor and producer inevitably gives rise to differentiation in other aspects of life:

> First, there would be a tendency for the regulator of distribution to exert some authority over production itself—especially over productive activities which necessitate subsidization, such as communal labor or specialist labor. A degree of control of production implies a degree of control over the utilization of resources, or, in other words, some preeminent property rights. In turn, regulation of these economic processes necessitates the exercise of authority in interpersonal affairs; differences in social power emerge.[61]

Sahlins later rejected the idea that a surplus leads to chiefships, postulating instead that the relationship may be the other way around—that is, leaders encourage the development of a surplus so as to enhance their prestige through feasts, potlatches, and other redistributive events.[62] Of course, both trajectories are possible—surpluses may generate stratification, and stratification may generate surpluses; they are not mutually exclusive.

Lenski's theory of the causes of stratification is similar to Sahlins's original idea. Lenski, too, argued that production of a surplus is the stimulus in the development of stratification, but he focused primarily on the conflict that arises over control of that surplus. Lenski concluded that the distribution of the surplus will be determined on the basis of power. Thus, inequalities in power promote unequal access to economic resources and simultaneously give rise to inequalities in privilege and prestige.[63]

The "surplus" theories of Sahlins and Lenski do not really address the question of why the redistributors or leaders will want, or be able, to acquire greater control over resources. After all, the redistributors or leaders in many rank societies do not have greater wealth than others, and custom seems to keep things that way. One suggestion is that as long as followers have mobility, they can vote with their feet by moving away from leaders they do not like. But when people start to make more permanent "investments" in land or technology (for example, irrigation systems or weirs for fishing), they are more likely to put up with a leader's aggrandizement in exchange for protection.[64] Another suggestion is that access to economic resources becomes unequal only when there is population pressure on resources in rank or chiefdom societies.[65] Such pressure may be what induces redistributors to try to keep more land and other resources for themselves and their families.

C. K. Meek offered an example of how population pressure in northern Nigeria may have led to economic stratification. At one time, a tribal member could obtain the right to use land by asking permission of the chief and presenting him with a token gift in recognition of his higher status. But by 1921, the reduction in the amount of available land had led to a system under which applicants

industrialized societies is so complex, he suggested, that those in power are compelled to delegate some authority to subordinates if the system is to work. In addition, a decline in the birth rate in industrialized societies, coupled with the need for skilled labor, has pushed the average wage of workers far above the subsistence level, resulting in greater equality in the distribution of income. Finally, Lenski also suggested that the spread of the democratic ideology, and particularly its acceptance by elites, has significantly broadened the political power of the lower classes.[58] A few studies have tested and supported Lenski's hypothesis that inequality has decreased with industrialization. In general, nations that are highly industrialized exhibit a lower level of inequality than nations that are only somewhat industrialized.[59] But, as we have seen, even the most industrialized societies may still have an enormous degree of inequality.

Why did social stratification develop in the first place? On the basis of his study of Polynesian societies, Marshall Sahlins suggested that an increase in agricultural productivity results in social stratification.[60] According to Sahlins, the degree of stratification is directly related to the production of a surplus, which is made possible by greater technological efficiency. The higher the level of productivity

offered the chief large payments for scarce land. As a result of these payments, farms came to be regarded as private property, and differential access to such property became institutionalized.[66]

Future research by archaeologists, sociologists, historians, and anthropologists should provide more understanding of the emergence of social stratification in human societies and how and why it may vary in degree.

 CD-ROM Flashcards Chapter 18

 # Summary

1. Without exception, recent and modern industrial and postindustrial societies such as our own are socially stratified—that is, they contain social groups such as families, classes, or ethnic groups that have unequal access to important advantages, such as economic resources, power, and prestige. Anthropologists, based on firsthand observations, would say that such inequality has not always existed among the societies they have studied. While even the simplest societies (in the technological sense) have some differences in advantages based on age or ability or gender—adults have higher status than children, the skilled more than the unskilled, men more than women (we discuss gender stratification in the next chapter)—anthropologists would argue that egalitarian societies exist where social groups (e.g., families) have more or less the same access to rights or advantages.

2. The presence or absence of customs or rules that give certain groups unequal access to economic resources, power, and prestige can be used to distinguish three types of societies. In egalitarian societies, social groups do not have unequal access to economic resources, power, or prestige; they are unstratified. In rank societies, social groups do not have very unequal access to economic resources or power, but they do have unequal access to prestige. Rank societies, then, are partially stratified. In class societies, social groups have unequal access to economic resources, power, and prestige. They are more completely stratified than are rank societies.

3. Stratified societies range from somewhat open class systems to caste systems, which are extremely rigid, since caste membership is fixed permanently at birth.

4. Slaves are persons who do not own their own labor; as such, they represent a class and sometimes even a caste. Slavery has existed in various forms in many times and places, regardless of "race" and culture. Sometimes slavery is a rigid and closed, or caste, system; sometimes it is a relatively open class system.

5. Within a society composed of people from widely divergent backgrounds and different physical features, such as skin color, racism is almost invariably associated with social stratification. Those "races" considered inferior make up a larger proportion of the lower social classes or castes. In the opinion of many biological anthropologists, "race" is not a scientifically useful device for classifying humans. "Racial" classifications should be recognized for what they mostly are—social categories to which individuals are assigned, by themselves and others, on the basis of supposedly shared biological traits.

6. In multiethnic societies, ethnic differences are usually associated with inequities in wealth, power, and prestige. In other words, ethnicity is part of the system of stratification.

7. Social stratification appears to have emerged relatively recently in human history, about 8,000 years ago. This conclusion is based on archaeological evidence and on the fact that certain cultural features associated with stratification developed relatively recently.

8. One theory suggests that social stratification developed as productivity increased and surpluses were produced. Another suggestion is that stratification can develop only when people have "investments" in land or technology and therefore cannot move away from leaders they do not like. A third theory suggests that stratification emerges only when there is population pressure on resources in rank societies.

 # Glossary Terms

caste	manumission
class	race
class society	racism
cline	rank society
egalitarian society	slaves
ethnicity	

 # Critical Questions

1. What might be the social consequences of large differences in wealth?
2. Is an industrial or a developed economy incompatible with a more egalitarian distribution of resources?
3. In a multiethnic society, does ethnic identity help or hinder social equality?
4. Why do you suppose the degree of inequality has decreased in some countries in recent years?

 # Internet Exercises

1. The web site at http://www.globalpolicy.org/socecon/inequal/indexinq.htm provides links to sources describing worldwide inequality. Check out one link dealing with that subject and summarize what you read.

2. Read the U.S. Census Bureau's report on the changes in inequality in the United States from 1947 to 1998 at http://www.census.gov/hhes/www/p60204.html. Pay particular attention to the figures, look at the text and graphs on changes in income inequality over time, and read the explanation of why inequality may have increased over time.

3. Read the accounts of a few people who were traded as slaves. Go to http://www.ukans.edu/carrie/docs/texts/canadian_slaves.html. Summarize the narrative on Edward Hicks. What are your thoughts?

Suggested Reading

COHEN, M. N. *Culture of Intolerance: Chauvinism, Class, and Racism in the United States.* New Haven, CT: Yale University Press. 1998. The author discusses the cultural blinders in the United States that promote intolerance, racism, and inequality.

KLASS, M. "Is There 'Caste' Outside of India?" In C. R. Ember and M. Ember, eds., *Cross-Cultural Research for Social Science,* in C. R. Ember and M. Ember, eds., *New Directions in Anthropology.* Upper Saddle River, NJ: Prentice Hall, CD-ROM, 2003. A discussion of what caste is like in contemporary Hindu India and whether anything like it is found in other societies.

MONTAGU, A. *Man's Most Dangerous Myth: The Fallacy of Race,* 6th ed. Walnut Creek: AltaMira Press, 1997. Beginning with the first edition published in 1942 at the height of Nazism, Montagu challenged the ideas that "race" is a useful scientific concept and that "race" determines human behavior. A very readable and thorough review of the biological and social evidence.

PEREGRINE, P. N. "Variation in Stratification." In C. R. Ember and M. Ember, eds., *Cross-Cultural Research for Social Science,* in C. R. Ember and M. Ember, eds., *New Directions in Anthropology.* Upper Saddle River, NJ: Prentice Hall, CD-ROM, 2003. A discussion, with examples, of egalitarian, rank, and class-stratified societies, and what may account for the variation.

PRYOR, F. L. *The Origins of the Economy: A Comparative Study of Distribution in Primitive and Peasant Economies.* New York: Academic Press, 1977. A large cross-cultural study of variation in distribution systems and their possible determinants. Chapter 8, on the varieties of slavery, is particularly relevant to this chapter.

YINGER, M. J. *Ethnicity: Source of Strength? Source of Conflict?* Albany: State University Press of New York, 1994. A wide-ranging treatment of ethnicity that discusses some of the things we need to know to respond to the importance of ethnicity in the world today. Of special relevance to this chapter is the discussion of the relationship between ethnicity and stratification.

SEX, GENDER, AND CULTURE

19

CHAPTER OUTLINE

- Physique and Physiology

- Gender Roles

- Relative Contributions to Subsistence

- Political Leadership and Warfare

- The Relative Status of Women

- Personality Differences

- Sexuality

We all know that humans come in two major varieties—female and male. The contrast between them is one of the facts of life we share with most animal species. But the fact that males and females always have different organs of reproduction does not explain why males and females may also differ in other physical ways. After all, there are many animal species—such as pigeons, gulls, and laboratory rats—in which the two sexes differ little in appearance.[1] Thus, the fact that we are a species with two sexes does not really explain why human females and males typically look different. Also, the fact that humans reproduce sexually does not explain why human males and females should differ in behavior or be treated differently by society. Yet no society we know of treats females and males in exactly the same way; indeed, females usually have fewer advantages than males. That is why in the last chapter we were careful to say that egalitarian societies have no *social groups* with unequal access to resources, power, and prestige. But within social groups (for example, families), even egalitarian societies usually allow males greater access to economic resources, power, and prestige.

Because many of the differences between females and males may reflect cultural expectations and experiences, many researchers now prefer to speak of **gender differences,** reserving the term **sex differences** for purely biological differences.[2] Unfortunately, biological and cultural influences are not always clearly separable, so it is sometimes hard to know which term to use. As long as societies treat males and females differently, we may not be able to separate the effects of biology from the effects of culture, and both may be present. As we focus our discussion on differences and similarities between females and males, keep in mind that not all cultures conceive of gender as including just two categories. Sometimes "maleness" and "femaleness" are thought of as opposite ends of a continuum, or there might be three or more categories of gender, such as "female," "male," and "other."[3]

In this chapter we discuss what we know cross-culturally about how and why females and males may differ physically, in gender roles, and in personality. We also discuss how and why sexual behavior and attitudes about sex vary from culture to culture.

 Physique and Physiology

As we noted at the outset, males and females of many animal species cannot readily be distinguished. Although they differ in chromosome makeup and in their external and internal organs of reproduction, they do not differ otherwise. In contrast, humans are **sexually dimorphic**—that is, the females and males of our species are generally different in size and appearance. Females have proportionately wider pelvises. Males typically are taller and have heavier skeletons. Females have a larger proportion of their body weight in fat; males have a larger proportion of body weight in muscle. Males typically have greater grip strength, propor-

tionately larger hearts and lungs, and greater aerobic capacity (greater intake of oxygen during strenuous activity).

There is a tendency in our society to view "taller" and "more muscled" as better, which may reflect the bias toward males in our culture. Natural selection may have favored these traits in males but different ones in females. For example, because females bear children, selection may have favored earlier cessation of growth, and therefore less ultimate height, in females so that the nutritional needs of a fetus would not compete with a growing mother's needs.[4] (Females achieve their ultimate height shortly after puberty, but boys continue to grow for years after puberty.) Similarly, there is some evidence that females are less affected than males by nutritional shortages, presumably because they tend to be shorter and have proportionately more fat.[5] Natural selection may have favored those traits in females because they resulted in greater reproductive success.

CD-ROM Video Activity 1

Both female and male athletes can build up their muscle strength and increase their aerobic work capacity through training. Given that fact, then, cultural factors, such as how much a society expects and allows males and females to engage in muscular activity, could influence the degree to which females and males differ muscularly and in aerobic capacity. Similar training may account for the recent trend toward decreasing differences between females and males in certain athletic events, such as marathons and swim meets. Even when it comes to female and male physique and physiology, then, what we see may be the result of both culture and genes.[6]

◆ **Gender Roles**

PRODUCTIVE AND DOMESTIC ACTIVITIES

In the chapter on economic systems, we noted that all societies assign or divide labor somewhat differently between females and males. Because role assignments have a clear cultural component, we speak of them as **gender roles.** What is of particular interest here about the gender division of labor is not so much that every society has different work for males and females but rather that so many societies divide up work in similar ways. The question, then, is why there are universal or near-universal patterns in such assignments.

Table 19–1 summarizes the worldwide patterns. We note which activities are performed by which gender in all or almost all societies, which activities are usually performed by one gender, and which activities are commonly assigned to either gender or both. Does the distribution of activities in the table suggest why females and males generally do different things?

Training can greatly increase muscle strength and aerobic capacity.

One possible explanation may be labeled the **strength theory.** The greater strength of males and their superior capacity to mobilize their strength in quick bursts of energy (because of their greater aerobic work capacity) have commonly been cited as the reason for the universal or near-universal patterns in the division of labor by gender. Certainly, activities that require lifting heavy objects (hunting large animals, butchering, clearing land, working with stone, metal, or lumber), throwing weapons, and running with great speed (as in hunting) may generally be performed best by males. And none of the activities females usually perform, with the possible exception of collecting firewood, seems to require the same degree of physical strength or quick bursts of energy. But the strength theory is not completely convincing, if only because it cannot readily explain all the observed patterns. For example, it is not clear that the male activities of trapping small animals, collecting wild honey, or making musical instruments require much physical strength.

Another possible explanation of the worldwide patterns in division of labor can be called the **compatibility-with-child-care theory.** The argument here is that women's tasks tend to be those that are compatible with child care. Although males can take care of infants, most traditional societies rely on breast-feeding of infants, which men

cannot do. (In most societies, women breast-feed their children for two years on the average.) Women's tasks may be those that do not take them far from home for long periods, that do not place children in potential danger if they are taken along, and that can be stopped and resumed if an infant needs care.[7]

The compatibility theory may explain why *no* activities other than infant care are listed in the right-hand column of Table 19–1. That is, it may be that there are practically no universal or near-universal women-only activities because until recently most women have had to devote much of their time to nursing and caring for infants, as well as caring for other children. The compatibility theory may also explain why men usually perform tasks such as hunting, trapping, fishing, collecting honey, lumbering, and mining. Those tasks are dangerous for infants to be around, and in any case would be difficult to coordinate with infant care.[8]

Finally, the compatibility theory may also explain why men seem to take over certain crafts in societies with full-time specialization. Although the distinction is not shown in Table 19–1, crafts such as making baskets, mats, and pottery are women's activities in noncommercial societies but tend to be men's activities in societies with full-time craft specialists.[9] Similarly, weaving tends to be a female activity unless it is produced for trade.[10] Why should commercial activities change the gender division of labor? Full-time specialization and production for trade may increase incompatibility with child care. Cooking is a good example in our own society. Women may be fine cooks, but chefs and bakers tend to be men, even though women traditionally do most of the cooking at home. Women might be more likely to work as cooks and chefs if they could leave their babies and young children in safe places to be cared for by other people.

But the compatibility theory does not explain why men usually prepare soil for planting, make objects out of wood, or work bone, horn, and shell. All of those tasks could probably be stopped to tend to a child, and none of them is any more dangerous to children nearby than is cooking. Why, then, do males tend to do them? The **economy-of-effort theory** may help explain patterns that cannot readily be explained by the strength and compatibility theories. For example, it may be advantageous for men to make musical instruments because men generally collect the hard materials involved (for example, by lumbering).[11] And because they collect those materials, men may be more knowledgeable about the physical properties of the materials and so more likely to know how to work with them. The economy-of-effort interpretation also suggests that it would be advantageous for one gender to perform tasks that are located near each other. Thus, if women have to be near home to take care of young children, it would be economical for them to perform other chores that are located in or near the home.

A fourth explanation of division of labor is the **expendability theory.** This theory suggests that men, rather than women, will tend to do the dangerous work in a society because men are more expendable, because the loss of

Table 19–1   Worldwide Patterns in the Division of Labor by Gender

TYPE OF ACTIVITY	MALES ALMOST ALWAYS	MALES USUALLY	EITHER GENDER OR BOTH	FEMALES USUALLY	FEMALES ALMOST ALWAYS
Primary subsistence activities	Hunt and trap animals, large and small	Fish Herd large animals Collect wild honey Clear land and prepare soil for planting	Collect shellfish Care for small animals Plant crops Tend crops Harvest crops Milk animals	Gather wild plants	

Secondary subsistence and household activities		Butcher animals	Preserve meat and fish	Care for children
				Cook
				Prepare
				   vegetable food
				   drinks
				   dairy products
				Launder
				Fetch water
				Collect fuel
					Care for infants

Other	Lumber
	Mine and quarry
	Make
	   boats
	   musical
	      instruments
	   bone, horn, and
	      shell objects
	Engage in combat
		Build houses
		Make
		   nets
		   rope
		Exercise political leadership
			Prepare skins
			Make
			   leather products
			   baskets
			   mats
			   clothing
			   pottery
				Spin yarn	

Source: Mostly adapted from George P. Murdock and Caterina Provost, "Factors in the Division of Labor by Sex: A Cross-Cultural Analysis," *Ethnology,* 12 (1973): 203–25. The information on political leadership and warfare comes from Martin K. Whyte, "Cross-Cultural Codes Dealing with the Relative Status of Women," *Ethnology,* 17 (1978): 217. The information on child care comes from Thomas S. Weisner and Ronald Gallimore, "My Brother's Keeper: Child and Sibling Caretaker," *Current Anthropology,* 18 (1977): 169–80.

men is less disadvantageous reproductively than the loss of women. If some men lose their lives in hunting, deep-water fishing, mining, quarrying, lumbering, and the like, reproduction need not suffer as long as most fertile women have sexual access to men—for example, if the society permits two or more women to be married to the same man.[12] When would anybody, male or female, be willing to do dangerous work? Perhaps only when society glorifies those roles and endows them with high prestige and other rewards.

Although the various theories, singly or in combination, seem to explain much of the division of labor by gender, there are some unresolved problems. Critics of the strength theory have pointed out that in some societies women do engage in very heavy labor.[13] If women in some societies can develop the strength to do such work, perhaps strength is more a function of training than traditionally has been believed.

The compatibility theory also has some problems. It suggests that labor is divided to conform to the requirements of child care. But sometimes it seems the other way around. For example, women who spend a good deal of

time in agricultural work outside the home often ask others to watch and feed their infants while they are unavailable to nurse.[14] Consider, too, the mountain areas of Nepal, where agricultural work is incompatible with child care; heavy loads must be carried up and down steep slopes, fields are far apart, and labor takes up most of the day. Yet women do this work anyway and leave their infants with others for long stretches of time.[15]

Furthermore, in some societies women hunt—one of the activities most incompatible with child care and generally not done by women. Many Agta women of the Philippines regularly hunt wild pig and deer; women alone or in groups kill almost 30 percent of the large game.[16] The women's hunting does not seem to be incompatible with child care. Women take nursing babies on hunting trips, and the women who hunt do not have lower reproductive rates than the women who choose not to hunt. Agta women may find it possible to hunt because the hunting grounds are only about a half-hour from camp, the dogs that accompany the women assist in the hunting and protect the women and babies, and the women generally hunt in groups, so others can help carry babies as well as

Maasai women can do house construction and babytending at the same time.

carcasses. Hunting by women is also fairly common among forest foragers in central Africa. Aka women participate in and sometimes lead in organizing cooperative net-hunting, in which an area is circled and animals are flushed out and caught in nets. Women spend approximately 18 percent of their time net-hunting, which is more than men do.[17]

As the cases just described suggest, we need to know a lot more about labor requirements. More precisely, we need to know exactly how much strength is required in particular tasks, exactly how dangerous those tasks are, and whether a person could stop working at a task to care for a child. So far, we have mostly guesses. When there is more systematically collected evidence on such aspects of particular tasks, we will be in a better position to evaluate the theories we have discussed. In any case, it should be noted that none of the available theories implies that the worldwide patterns of division of labor shown in Table 19–1 will persist. As we know from our own and other industrial societies, when machines replace human strength, when women have fewer children, and when women can assign child care to others, a strict gender division of labor begins to disappear.

◆ Relative Contributions to Subsistence

In our society, the stereotype of the husband is that he is the breadwinner in the family; the wife is the manager of the house and children. As we know, the stereotype is more myth than reality. In addition to the many women who are single parents, many married women—in the United States, more than 50 percent—now work outside the home. Among married women with children 6 to 17 years old, more than 70 percent are employed.[18] The concept of "breadwinner" in our society emphasizes the person—traditionally, the male—who "brings in the bread" (food or money to buy it) from the outside. In focusing on the breadwinner, however, we may minimize the contributions of the person who works primarily inside the home.

How should we decide who contributes more to subsistence? Most anthropologists distinguish between **primary subsistence activities** and **secondary subsistence activities** (see Table 19–1). The primary activities are the food-getting activities: gathering, hunting, fishing, herding, and agriculture. Many of the secondary activities involve preparing and processing food for eating or storing. We know a considerable amount about how, and possibly why, women's and men's relative contributions to primary subsistence activities vary cross-culturally. We know much less about contributions to secondary subsistence activities. Researchers have focused mostly on primary subsistence activities, and they usually measure how much each gender's work in these activities contributes to the diet, in terms of caloric intake. Alternatively, contribution to primary subsistence activities—generally outside activities, away from the home—can be measured in terms of time spent doing them. Measures of caloric versus time contribution, however, can yield very different results. As we saw in the chapter on getting food, more time is spent by the Yanomamö in hunting than in horticulture, but horticulture yields more calories.

In some societies women traditionally have contributed more to the economy than men by any measure. For example, among the Tchambuli of New Guinea in the 1930s, the women did all the fishing—going out early in the morning by canoe to their fish traps and returning when the sun was hot. Some of the catch was traded for sago (a starch) and sugarcane, and it was the women who went on the long canoe trips to do the trading.[19]

The stereotype of husband as breadwinner no longer fits our society, but it does fit the Toda of India. As they were described early in the twentieth century, they depended for subsistence almost entirely on the dairy products of their water buffalo, either by using the products directly or by selling them for grain. Women were not allowed to have anything to do with dairy work; only men tended the buffalo and prepared the dairy products. Women's work was largely household work. Women prepared the purchased grain for cooking, cleaned house, and decorated clothing.[20]

A survey of a wide variety of societies has revealed that both women and men typically contribute to primary food-getting activities, but men usually contribute more in terms of calories.[21] Women are almost always occupied with infant- and child-care responsibilities in most societies, so it is not surprising that men usually do most of the primary food-getting work, which generally has to be done away from the home.

In societies that depend on hunting, fishing, and herding—generally male activities—for most of their calories, men usually contribute more than women.[22] For example, among the Inuit, who traditionally depended mostly on hunting and fishing, and among the Toda, who depended mostly on herding, men did most of the primary subsistence work. But the predominant type of food-getting is not always predictive. Among the Tchambuli, who depended mostly on fishing, women did most of the work. In societies that depend on gathering, primarily women's work, women tend to do most of the food-getting, in terms of calories. The !Kung are an example. But most societies known to anthropology depend primarily on agriculture, not on hunting or gathering, for their calories. And, with the exception of clearing land and preparing the soil, which are usually men's tasks, the work of planting, crop tending (weeding, irrigating), and harvesting is done by men or women or both (see Table 19–1). So we need some explanation of why women do most of the agricultural work in some societies and men in others. Different patterns predominate in different areas of the world. In Africa south of the Sahara, women generally do most of the agricultural work. But in much of Asia and Europe and the areas around the Mediterranean, men do more.[23] In some societies women contribute more, in terms of calories, to primary subsistence activities than do men.

One explanatory factor is the kind of agriculture. Many writers have pointed out that with intensive agriculture, particularly plow agriculture, men's caloric contribution to primary subsistence tends to be much higher than women's. In horticultural societies, in contrast, women's contribution is relatively high compared with men's. Women usually contribute the most when horticulture is practiced, either root and tree crop horticulture or shifting/slash-and-burn cultivation. According to Ester Boserup, when population increases and there is pressure to make more intensive use of the land, cultivators begin to use the plow and irrigation, and males start to do more.[24] But it is not clear why.

Why should women not continue to contribute a lot to agriculture just because plows are used? In trying to answer this question, most researchers shift to considering how much time males and females spend in various agricultural tasks, rather than estimating the total caloric contribution of females versus males. The reason for this shift is that gender contribution to agriculture varies substantially over the various phases of the production sequence, as well as from one crop to another. Thus, the total amount of time females versus males work at agricultural tasks is easier to estimate than how much each gender contributes to the diet in terms of calories. How would caloric contribution be judged, for example, if men do the clearing and plowing, women do the planting and weeding, and both do the harvesting?

One suggestion about why males contribute more to agriculture when the plow is used is that plow agriculture involves a great deal of labor input in the clearing and preparation phases of cultivation and at the same time minimizes subsequent weeding time. Men usually clear land anyway, but clearing is a more time-consuming process if intensive agriculture is practiced. It has been estimated that in one district in Nigeria, 100 days of work are required to clear one acre of virgin land for plowing by tractor; only 20 days are required to prepare the land for shifting cultivation. Weeding is a task that probably can be combined with child care, and perhaps for that reason it may have been performed mostly by women previously.[25] But the fact that men do the plowing, which may take a lot of time, does not explain why women do relatively fewer agricultural tasks, including weeding, in societies that have the plow.[26]

Another explanation for why women contribute less time than men to intensive agriculture is that household chores increase with intensive agriculture and thus limit the time women can spend in the fields. Intensive agriculturalists typically rely heavily on grain crops, which take much more work to make edible. Cereal grains (corn, wheat, oats) are usually dried before storing and thus take a long time to cook if they are left whole. More cooking requires more time to collect water and firewood (usually women's work) and more time to clean pots and utensils. A variety of techniques can reduce cooking time (such as soaking, grinding, or pounding), but the process that speeds up cooking the most—grinding—is itself time-consuming (unless done by machine). Finally, household work may increase substantially with intensive agriculture because women in such societies have more children than women in horticultural societies. If household work increases in these ways, it is easy to understand why women cannot contribute more time than men, or as much time as men, to intensive agriculture. But women's contribution, although less than men's, is nonetheless substantial; they seem to work outside the home four and a half hours a day, seven days a week, on the average.[27]

Grinding corn is very time-consuming hard work. Women near Lake Titicaca in Peru grind corn between two large stones.

We still have not explained why women contribute so much to horticulture in the first place. They may not have as much household work as intensive agricultural women, but neither do the men. Why, then, don't men do relatively more in horticulture also? One possibility is that in horticultural societies men are often drawn away from cultivation into other types of activities. There is evidence that if males are engaged in warfare when primary subsistence work has to be done, the women must do that work.[28] Men may also be withdrawn from primary subsistence work if they have to work in distant towns and cities for wages or if they periodically go on long-distance trading trips.[29]

When women contribute a lot to primary food-getting activities, we might expect their behavior and attitudes concerning children to be affected. Several cross-cultural studies suggest that this expectation is correct. In societies with a high female contribution to primary subsistence (in terms of contributing calories), infants are fed solid foods earlier (so that other persons besides mothers can feed them) than in societies with a low female contribution.[30] Girls are likely to be trained to be industrious (probably to help their mothers), and girl babies are more valued.[31]

It is important to realize that what we conclude about gender contribution to subsistence depends largely on how we measure it. Most of our discussion until now has focused on contribution to primary subsistence activities. If we change our perspective for a moment and count all kinds of work, we see a different picture of men's versus women's contribution to making a living. Adding up all work time, including activities outside the home (mostly food-getting activities) and activities inside the home (mostly preparing and cooking food), we find that women typically work more total hours per day than men in both intensive agricultural and horticultural societies.[32]

◆ Political Leadership and Warfare

In almost every known society, men rather than women are the leaders in the political arena. One cross-cultural survey found that, in about 85 percent of the surveyed societies, only men were leaders. In the societies in which some women occupied leadership positions, the women were either outnumbered by or less powerful than the male leaders.[33] If we look at countries, not cultures, women on the average make up only around 10 percent of the representatives in national parliaments or legislative bodies.[34] Whether or not we consider warfare to be part of the political sphere of life, we find an almost universal dominance of males in that arena. In 87 percent of the world's societies, women never participate actively in war.[35] (See the box "Why Do Some Societies Allow Women to Participate in Combat?" for a discussion of women in combat in the remaining 13 percent of societies.)

Women as well as men serve on political councils in many Coast Salish communities. Here we see a swearing-in ceremony for the Special Chief's Council in Sardis, British Columbia.

NEW PERSPECTIVES ON GENDER
Why Do Some Societies Allow Women to Participate in Combat?

U.S. women can serve in the military but are usually excluded from combat. Some women feel that such exclusion is unfair and decreases their chances of promotion in the military. Other people, including some women, insist that female participation in combat would be detrimental to military performance or is inappropriate for women.

Why, then, do some societies allow women to be warriors? The psychologist David Adams compared about 70 societies studied by anthropologists to try to answer that question. Although most societies exclude women from war, Adams found that women are active warriors, at least occasionally, in 13 percent of the sample societies. In native North America, such societies included the Comanche, Crow, Delaware, Fox, Gros Ventre, and Navajo. In the Pacific, there were active warrior women among the Maori of New Zealand, on Majuro Atoll in the Marshall Islands, and among the Orokaiva of New Guinea. In none of these societies were the warriors usually women, but women were allowed to engage in combat if they wanted to.

How are the societies with women warriors different from those that exclude women from combat? They differ in one of two ways. Either they conduct war only against people in other societies (this is called "purely external"

war) or they marry within their own community. Adams argues that these two conditions, which are not particularly common, preclude the possibility of conflicts of interest between wives and husbands, and therefore women can be permitted to engage in combat because their interests are the same as their husbands'. Because marriages in most cases involve individuals from the same society, husbands and wives will have the same loyalties if the society has purely external war. And even if war occurs between communities and larger groups in the same society (what we call "internal" war), there will be no conflict of interest between husband and wife if they both grew up in the same community. In contrast, there is internal war at least occasionally in most societies, and wives usually marry in from other communities. In this situation, there may often be a conflict of interest between husband and wife; if women were to engage in combat, they might have to fight against their fathers, paternal uncles, and brothers. And wouldn't we expect the wives to try to warn kin in their home communities if the husbands planned to attack them? Indeed, the men's likely fear of their wives' disloyalty would explain why women in these societies are forbidden to make or handle weapons or go near meetings in which war plans are discussed.

Many countries today engage in

purely external war; so other things being equal, we would not expect conflicts of interest to impede women's participation in combat. Therefore, extrapolating from Adams's findings, we might expect that the barriers against female participation in combat will disappear completely. But other conditions may have to be present before women and men participate equally in combat. In Adams's study, not all societies with purely external war or intracommunity marriage had women warriors. So we may also have to consider the degree to which the society seeks to maximize reproduction (and therefore protect women from danger) and the degree to which the society depends on women for subsistence during wartime.

There are other related questions to explore: Does military participation by women increase women's participation in politics? Does the presence of war in a society decrease or increase women's political participation? Does women's participation in politics or in the military change the nature of war?

Source: Excerpted from David B. Adams, "Why There Are So Few Women Warriors," in _Behavior Science Research,_ 18 (1983): 196–212. Copyright © 1983. Reprinted by permission of Sage Publications, Inc.

Even in _matrilineal_ societies, which seem to be oriented around women (see the chapter on marital residence and kinship), men usually occupy political positions. For example, among the Iroquois of what is now New York State, women had control over resources and a great deal of influence, but men, not women, held political office. The highest political body among the League of the Iroquois, which comprised five tribal groups, was a council of 50

male chiefs. Although women could not serve on the council, they could nominate, elect, and impeach their male representatives. Women also could decide between life and death for prisoners of war, forbid the men of their households to go to war, and intervene to bring about peace.[36]

Why have men (at least so far) almost always dominated the political sphere of life? Some scholars have suggested that men's role in warfare gives them the edge in all kinds of political leadership, particularly because they control weapons, an important resource.[37] But evidence suggests that force is rarely used to obtain leadership positions;[38] superior strength is not the deciding factor. Still, warfare may be related to political leadership for another reason. Warfare clearly affects survival, and it occurs regularly in most societies. Therefore, decision making about war may be among the most important kinds of politics in most societies. If so, then the persons who know the most about warfare should be making the decisions about it.

To explain why males and not females usually engage in fighting, let us refer to three of the possible explanations of the worldwide patterns in the gender division of labor. Warfare, like hunting, probably requires strength (for throwing weapons) and quick bursts of energy (for running). And certainly combat is one of the most dangerous and uninterruptible activities imaginable, hardly compatible with child care. Also, even if they do not at the time have children, women may generally be kept out of combat because their potential fertility is more important to a population's reproduction and survival than their potential usefulness as warriors.[39] So the strength theory, the compatibility theory, and the expendability theory might all explain the predominance of men in warfare.

Two other factors may be involved in male predominance in politics. One is the generally greater height of men. Why height should be a factor in leadership is unclear, but studies suggest that taller persons are more likely to be leaders.[40] Finally, there is the possibility that men dominate politics because they get around more in the outside world than do women. Men's activities typically take them farther from home; women tend to work more around the home. If societies choose leaders at least in part because of what they know about the larger world, then men will generally have some advantage. In support of this reasoning, Patricia Draper found that in !Kung bands that had settled down, women no longer engaged in long-distance gathering, and they lost much of their former influence in decision making.[41] Involvement in child care may also detract from such influence. In a study of village leadership among the Kayapo of Brazil, Dennis Werner found that women with heavy child-care burdens were less influential than women not as involved in child care; perhaps they had fewer friends and missed many details of what was going on in the village.[42]

These various explanations suggest why men generally dominate politics, but we still need to explain why women participate in politics more in some societies than in others. Marc Ross investigated this question in a cross-cultural survey of 90 societies.[43] In that sample, the degree of female participation in politics varied considerably. For example, among the Mende of Sierra Leone, women regularly held high office, but among the Azande of Zaire, women took no part in public life. One factor that appeared to predict the exclusion of women from politics was the organization of communities around male kin. As we will see later, when they marry, women usually have to leave their communities and move to their husband's place. If women are "strangers" in a community with many related males, then

the males will have political advantages because of their knowledge of community members and past events.

The Relative Status of Women

There are probably as many definitions of status as there are researchers interested in the topic. To some, the relative status of the sexes means how much importance society confers on females versus males. To others, it means how much power and authority men and women have relative to each other. And to still others, it means what kinds of rights women and men possess to do what they want to do. In any case, many social scientists are asking why the status of women appears to vary from one society to another. Why do women have few rights and little influence in some societies and more of each in other societies? In other words, why is there variation in degree of **gender stratification?**

In the small Iraqi town of Daghara, women and men live very separate lives.[44] In many respects, women appear to have very little status. Like women in much of the Islamic world, women in Daghara live their lives mostly in seclusion, staying in their houses and interior courtyards. If women must go out, which they can do only with male approval, they must shroud their faces and bodies in long black cloaks. These cloaks must be worn in mixed company, even at home. Women are essentially excluded from political activities. Legally, they are considered to be under the authority of their fathers and husbands. Even the sexuality of women is controlled. There is strict emphasis on virginity before marriage. Because women are not permitted even casual conversations with strange men, the possibilities for extramarital or even premarital relationships are very slight. In contrast, hardly any sexual restrictions are imposed on men.

But some societies, such as the Mbuti, seem to approach equal status for males and females. Like most food collectors, the Mbuti have no formal political organization to make decisions or to settle disputes. Public disputes occur, and both women and men take part in the uproar that is part of such disputes. Not only do women make their positions known, but their opinions are often heeded. Even in domestic quarrels involving physical violence between husband and wife, others usually intervene to stop them, regardless of who hit whom first.[45] Women control the use of dwellings; they usually have equal say over the disposal of resources they or the men collect, over the upbringing of their children, and about whom their children should marry. One of the few signs of inequality is that women are somewhat more restricted than men with respect to extramarital sex.[46]

There are many theories about why women have relatively high or low status. One of the most common is that women's status will be high when they contribute substantially to primary subsistence activities. According to this theory, then, women should have very little status when

New Perspectives on Gender
Women's Electoral Success on the Northwest Coast

Political life has changed dramatically since first contact with Europeans for most Native American groups, including the Coast Salish of western Washington State and British Columbia. With impetus from the U.S. and Canadian governments, each of the recognized Coast Salish communities now has an elected council. But who is getting elected? Even though women did not have much of a role in traditional politics, now the Coast Salish groups are electing a lot of women. From the 1960s to the 1980s, women held over 40 percent of the council seats in the 12 Washington State groups, and in the 1990s women held 28 percent of the seats in the 50 British Columbian groups. The proportion of women on the councils varies from 6 percent among the Tulalip to 62 percent among the Stillaguamish. What accounts for the women's electoral success? And why does that success vary from one group to another, even though the groups are closely related culturally?

According to Bruce Miller, who did a comparative study of women's electoral success in Coast Salish communities, women generally have more of a political role now perhaps because new economic opportunities in the service and technical sectors allow women to contribute more to the household economy. But why do women win proportionately more council seats in some communities than in others? Miller found that women win proportionately more seats in communities with less income, the least income derived from fishing, and the smallest populations. Why should lower household income predict more electoral success for women? Miller suggests that it is not so much the amount of income but rather the degree to which women (compared with men) contribute to household income. In groups with economic difficulties, the jobs women are able to get play a vital role in the household. Women were helped by federally funded programs such as the War on Poverty to acquire technical skills and jobs. Simultaneously, many men in some communities lost their jobs in logging and agriculture.

But a high dependence on fishing income seems to favor men politically. Families that operate vessels with a large drawstring net to catch fish at sea can make hundreds of thousands of dollars a year. Such fishing is predominantly done by men, and where there is such lucrative fishing, the successful men dominate the councils. Even though women may have jobs too, their income is not as great as the successful fisherman's.

Why should women be more successful politically in smaller communities? Miller suggests that women have a better chance to be known personally when the community is small, even though working outside the home in technical or service jobs cuts down on the time women can devote to tribal ceremonials and other public events.

Does female income relative to male and community size help explain the relative political success of women elsewhere? We do not know yet, but subsequent research may help us find out.

Source: Bruce G. Miller, "Women and Politics: Comparative Evidence from the Northwest Coast," *Ethnology,* 31 (1992): 367–82. ◉

food-getting depends largely on hunting, herding, or intensive agriculture. A second theory suggests that where warfare is especially important, men will be more valued and esteemed than women. A third theory suggests that where there are centralized political hierarchies, men will have higher status. The reasoning in this theory is essentially the same as the reasoning in the warfare theory: Men usually play the dominant role in political behavior, so men's status should be higher wherever political behavior is more important or frequent. Finally, there is the theory that women will have higher status where kin groups and couples' place of residence after marriage are organized around women.

One of the problems in evaluating these theories is that decisions have to be made about the meaning of *status.*

Does it mean value? Rights? Influence? And do all these aspects of status vary together? Cross-cultural research by Martin Whyte suggests that they do not. For each sample society in his study, Whyte rated 52 items that might be used to define the relative status of the sexes. These items included such things as which sex can inherit property, who has final authority over disciplining unmarried children, and whether the gods in the society are male, female, or both. The results of the study indicate that very few of these items are related. Therefore, Whyte concluded, we cannot talk about status as a single concept. Rather, it seems more appropriate to talk about the relative status of women in different spheres of life.[47]

Even though Whyte found no necessary connection between one aspect of status and another, he decided to ask

In November 2001, after the Taliban government fell, women in Kabul, Afghanistan no longer had to wear a head-to-toe veil.

whether some of the theories correctly predict why some societies have many, as opposed to few, areas in which the status of women is high. Let us turn first to the ideas that are not supported by the available cross-cultural evidence. The idea that generally high status derives from a greater caloric contribution to primary subsistence activities is not supported at all.[48] Women in intensive agricultural societies (who contribute less than men to primary subsistence) do tend to have lower status in many areas of life, just as in the Iraqi case described earlier. But in societies that depend mostly on hunting (where women also do little of the primary subsistence work), women seem to have higher status, which contradicts the theoretical expectation. Similarly, there is no consistent evidence that a high frequency of warfare generally lowers women's status in different spheres of life.[49]

What does predict higher status for women in many areas of life? Although the results are not strong, there is some support in Whyte's study for the theory that where kin groups and marital residence are organized around women, women have somewhat higher status. (We discuss these features of society more fully in the chapter on marital residence and kinship.) The Iroquois are a good example. Even though Iroquois women could not hold political office, they had considerable authority within and beyond the household. Related women lived together in longhouses with husbands who belonged to other kin groups. In the longhouse, the women's authority was clear, and they could ask objectionable men to leave. The women controlled the allocation of the food they produced. Allocation could influence the timing of war parties, since men could not undertake a raid without provisions. Women were involved in the selection of religious leaders, half of whom were women. Even in politics, although women could not speak or serve on the council, they largely controlled the selection of councilmen and could institute impeachment proceedings against those to whom they objected.[50]

A generally lower status for women does appear to be found in societies with political hierarchies.[51] Lower status for women appears to be associated with other indicators of cultural complexity as well as political hierarchies. Societies with social stratification, plow and irrigation agriculture, large settlements, private property, and craft specialization tend to have lower status for women. One type of influence for women increases with cultural complexity—informal influence. But, as Whyte pointed out, informal influence may simply reflect a lack of *real* influence.[52] Why cultural complexity is associated with women having less authority in the home, less control over property, and more restricted sexual lives is not yet understood.

Western colonialism also appears to have been generally detrimental to women's status, perhaps because Westerners were accustomed to dealing with men. There are plenty of examples of Europeans restructuring landownership around men and teaching men modern farming techniques, even in places where women were usually the farmers. In addition, men more often than women could earn cash through wage labor or through sales of goods (such as furs) to Europeans.[53] Although the relative status of men and women may not have been equal before the Europeans arrived, colonial influences seem generally to have undermined the position of women.

We are beginning to understand some of the conditions that may enhance or decrease certain aspects of women's status. If we can understand which of these conditions are most important, society may, if it wants to, be able to reduce gender inequality.[54]

 ## Personality Differences

Reporting on three tribes in New Guinea, Margaret Mead said that "many, if not all, of the personality traits we have called masculine or feminine are as lightly linked to sex as are the clothing, the manners, and the form of head-dress that a society at a given period assigns to either sex."[55] In other words, she suggested that there were *no* universal or near-universal personality differences between the sexes. Rather, societies were free to create any such differences. She described Arapesh females and males as essentially alike: Both sexes were gentle, cooperative, and nurturing. She also described the Mundugumor males and females as similar, but in this case both sexes exhibited violence and aggression. Finally, she described the Tchambuli as having substantial female-male differences in temperament, but opposite to what we might expect. The women were domineering, practical, and impersonal and were the chief economic providers; the men were sensitive and delicate and devoted their time to their appearance and to artistic pursuits.

But research conducted in recent years does not support Mead's view that there are no consistent sex differences in temperament. On the contrary, some sex differences in behavior occur consistently and in diverse societies. This does not mean that Mead was wrong about the three New Guinea societies she studied. It is possible that they were unusual cases. Nancy McDowell reanalyzed Mead's Mundugumor notes and studied a group of related neighboring people; she found no reason to doubt Mead's conclusion that female and male temperaments were similar.[56] It is also possible that Mead might have found some gender differences if she had employed the kinds of observation techniques that have

been used in recent field studies. Such studies systematically record the minute details of behavior of a substantial number of males and females. Any conclusions about female-male differences in aggressiveness, for example, are based on actual counts of the number of times a particular individual tried to hurt or injure another person in a fixed amount of observation time. Almost all of these differences are subtle and a matter of degree, not a matter of a behavior being present or absent in females or males.

Which differences in personality are suggested by these systematic studies? Most of them have observed children in different cultural settings. The most consistent difference is in the area of aggression; boys try to hurt others more frequently than girls do. In an extensive comparative study of children's behavior, the Six Cultures project, this difference showed up as early as 3 to 6 years of age.[57] A more recent cross-cultural comparison of four cultures supports the sex difference in aggression.[58] Research done in the United States is consistent with the cross-cultural findings.[59] In a large number of observational and experimental studies, boys exhibited more aggression than girls.

Other female-male differences have turned up with considerable consistency, but we have to be cautious in accepting them, either because they have not been documented as well or because there are more exceptions. There seems to be a tendency for girls to exhibit more responsible behavior, including nurturance (trying to help others). Girls seem more likely to conform to adult wishes and commands. Boys try more often to exert dominance over others in order to get their own way. In play, boys and girls show a preference for their own gender. Boys seem to play in large groups, girls in small ones. And boys seem to maintain more distance between each other than girls do.[60]

If we assume that these differences are consistent across cultures, how can we explain them? Many writers and researchers believe that because certain female-male differences are so consistent, they are probably rooted in the biological differences between the two sexes. Aggression is one of the traits talked about most often in this connection, particularly because this male-female difference appears so early in life.[61] But an alternative argument is that societies bring up boys and girls differently because they almost universally require adult males and females to perform different types of roles. If most societies expect adult males to be warriors or to be prepared to be warriors, shouldn't we expect most societies to encourage or idealize aggression in males? And if females are almost always the caretakers of infants, shouldn't we also expect societies generally to encourage nurturant behaviors in females?

Researchers tend to adopt either the biological or the socialization view, but it is possible that both kinds of causes are important in the development of gender differences. For example, parents might turn a slight genetic difference into a large gender difference by maximizing that difference in the way they socialize boys versus girls.

It is difficult for researchers to distinguish the influence of genes and other biological conditions from the influence of socialization. We have research indicating that as early as birth, parents treat boy and girl infants differently.[62] In

"It's a guy thing."

spite of the fact that objective observers can see no major "personality" differences between girl and boy infants, parents often claim to.[63] But parents may unconsciously want to see differences and may therefore produce them in socialization. So even early differences could be learned rather than genetic. Remember, too, that researchers cannot do experiments with people; for example, parents' behavior cannot be manipulated to find out what would happen if boys and girls were treated exactly the same way.

However, there is considerable experimental research on aggression in nonhuman animals. These experiments suggest that the hormone androgen is partly responsible for higher levels of aggression. For example, in some experiments, females injected with androgen at about the time the sexual organs develop (before or shortly after birth) behave more aggressively when they are older than do females without the hormone. These results may or may not apply to humans of course, but some researchers have investigated human females who were "androgenized" in the womb because of drugs given to their mothers to prevent miscarriage. By and large the results of these studies are similar to the experimental studies—androgenized human females show similar patterns of higher aggression.[64] Some scholars take these results to indicate that biological differences between males and females are responsible for the male-female difference in aggression;[65] others suggest that even these results are not conclusive, because females who get more androgen show generally disturbed metabolic systems, and general metabolic disturbance may itself increase aggressiveness. Furthermore, androgen-injected females may look more like males because they develop male-like genitals; therefore, they may be treated like males.[66]

Is there any evidence that socialization differences may account for differences in aggression? Although a cross-cultural survey of ethnographers' reports on 101 societies does show that more societies encourage aggression in boys than in girls, most societies show no difference in aggression training.[67] The few societies that do show differences in aggression training can hardly account for the widespread sex differences in actual aggressiveness. But the survey does not necessarily mean that there are no consistent differences in aggression training for boys and girls. All it shows is that there are no *obvious* differences. For all we know, the learning of aggression and other "masculine" traits by boys could be produced by subtle types of socialization.

One possible type of subtle socialization that could create gender differences in behavior is the chores children are assigned. It is possible that little boys and girls learn to behave differently because their parents ask them to do different kinds of work. Beatrice and John Whiting reported from the Six Cultures project that in societies where children were asked to do a great deal of work, they generally showed more responsible and nurturant behavior. Because girls are almost always asked to do more work than boys, they may be more responsible and nurturant for this reason alone.[68] If this reasoning is correct, we should find that if boys are asked to do girls' work, they will learn to behave more like girls.

A study of Luo children in Kenya supports this view.[69] Girls were usually asked to baby-sit, cook, clean house, and fetch water and firewood. Boys were usually asked to do very little because boys' traditional work was herding cattle, and most families in the community studied had few cattle. But for some reason more boys than girls had been born, and many mothers without girls at home asked their sons to do girls' chores. Systematic behavior observations showed that much of the behavior of the boys who did girls' work was intermediate between the behavior of other boys and the behavior of girls. The boys who did girls' work were more like girls in that they were less aggressive, less domineering, and more responsible than other boys, even when they weren't working. So it is possible that task assignment has an important influence on how boys and girls learn to behave. These and other subtle forms of socialization need to be investigated more thoroughly.

MISCONCEPTIONS ABOUT DIFFERENCES IN BEHAVIOR

Before we leave the subject of behavior differences, we should note some widespread beliefs about them that are not supported by research. Some of these mistaken beliefs are that girls are more dependent than boys, that girls are more sociable, and that girls are more passive. The results obtained by the Six Cultures project cast doubt on all these notions.[70] First, if we think of dependency as seeking help and emotional support from others, girls are generally no more likely to behave this way than boys. To be sure, the results do indicate that boys and girls have somewhat different styles of dependency. Girls more often seek help and contact; boys more often seek attention and approval. As for sociability, which means seeking and offering friendship, the Six Cultures results showed no reliable differences between the sexes. Of course, boys and girls may be sociable in different ways because boys generally play in larger groups than girls. As for the supposed passivity of girls, the evidence is also not particularly convincing. Girls in the Six Cultures project did not consistently withdraw from aggressive attacks or comply with unreasonable demands. The only thing that emerged as a female-male difference was that older girls were less likely than boys to respond to aggression with aggression. But this finding may not reflect passivity as much as the fact that girls are less aggressive than boys, which we already knew.

So some of our common ideas about female-male differences are unfounded. Others, such as those dealing with aggression and responsibility, cannot be readily dismissed and should be investigated further.

As we noted, an observed difference in aggression does not mean that males are aggressive and females are not. Perhaps because males are generally more aggressive, aggression in females has been studied less often. For that reason, Victoria Burbank focused on female aggression in an Australian aborigine community she calls Mangrove. During the 18 months that she was there, Burbank observed some act of aggression almost every other day. Consistent with the cross-cultural evidence, men initiated

ANTHROPOLOGICAL ORIGINALS
Andean Mestizos

Gender inequality exists everywhere, even sometimes in breast-feeding: Among Andean Mestizos, mothers used to think that 8 months was the ideal age to stop breast-feeding girls, whereas 24 months was ideal for boys. Even though these ideals were not always acted on, on average girls were weaned 10 months earlier than boys. People said this was because girls overly breast-fed would grow up to be too sexual, which was a bad thing. But there seems to be an unintended consequence of girls being breast-fed for a shorter time than boys: a higher death rate for girls between the ages of one and three years.

[The women and their husbands] offer two cultural scenarios to predict the fate of an overly breastfed, and therefore overly-sexual and aggressive, daughter's fate. The first is that her strong drives will lead her to rebel against her parents and seek sexual partners before she is married. This notion is widespread in mestizo culture, and arises from a value on premarital chastity imported from the Spanish (and, indeed, circum-Mediterranean) cultural insistence on female honor. . . .

The second scenario predicts that her strong sexuality will burden such a girl in the future with numerous pregnancies. Neither of these "fates" is viewed positively, so women are convinced that, even though it gives them pain, they do their daughters a favor by weaning them early, saving them from negative consequences in their future adult lives.

Why should breast-feeding (or the lack of it) be related to infant mortality levels? In the highlands, respiratory and gastrointestinal diseases are the leading causes of death among infants and young children. These factors interact with high levels of parasitic infestation in rural areas lacking potable water and effective sanitation. Human milk at all stages of lactation that have been studied continues to contain immunoglobulins and other antimicrobial factors that are particularly effective against respiratory and gastrointestinal diseases. These immune factors especially aid and protect newborns, whose own immune mechanisms are not mature. An early switch to environmental foods may increase the probability that some weaned infants will succumb to disease.

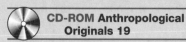
CD-ROM Anthropological Originals 19

Source: Lauris A. McKee, "Andean Mestizos: Growing Up Female and Male," in Melvin Ember and Carol R. Ember, eds., *Portraits of Culture: Ethnographic Originals,* in Carol R. Ember and Melvin Ember, eds., *New Directions in Anthropology* (Upper Saddle River, NJ: Prentice Hall, CD-ROM, 2003).

aggression more often than women, but women were initiators about 43 percent of the time. The women of Mangrove engaged in almost all the same kinds of aggression as men did, including fighting, except that it tended not to be as lethal as male violence. Lethal weapons were most often used by men; when women fought with weapons, they mostly used sticks, not spears, guns, or knives. Burbank points out that, in contrast to Western cultures, female aggression is not viewed as unnatural or deviant but rather as a natural expression of anger.[71]

◈ Sexuality

In view of the way the human species reproduces, it is not surprising that sexuality is part of our nature. But no society we know of leaves sexuality to nature; all have at least some rules governing "proper" conduct. There is much variation from one society to another in the degree of sexual activity permitted or encouraged before marriage, outside marriage, and even within marriage. And societies vary markedly in their tolerance of nonheterosexual sexuality.

CULTURAL REGULATIONS OF SEXUALITY: PERMISSIVENESS VERSUS RESTRICTIVENESS

All societies seek to regulate sexual activity to some degree, and there is a lot of variation cross-culturally. Some societies allow premarital sex; others forbid it. The same is true for extramarital sex. In addition, a society's degree of restrictiveness is not always consistent throughout the life span or for all aspects of sex. For example, a number of societies ease sexual restrictions somewhat for adolescents, and many become more restrictive for adults.[72] Then, too, societies change over time. Our own society has traditionally been restrictive, but until recently—before the emergence of the AIDS epidemic—more permissive attitudes were gaining acceptance.

PREMARITAL SEX The degree to which sex before marriage is approved or disapproved of varies greatly from society to society. The Trobriand Islanders, for example, approved of and encouraged premarital sex, seeing it as an important preparation for later marriage roles. Both girls and boys were given complete instruction in all forms of sexual expression at the onset of puberty and were allowed plenty of opportunity for intimacy. Some societies not only allow premarital sex on a casual basis but specifically encourage trial marriages between adolescents. Among the Ila-speaking peoples of central Africa, at harvest time girls were given houses of their own where they could play at being wife with the boys of their choice. It is said that among these people virginity did not exist beyond the age of 10.[73]

On the other hand, in many societies premarital sex was discouraged. For example, among the Tepoztlan Indians of Mexico, a girl's life became "crabbed, cribbed, confined" from the time of her first menstruation. She was not to speak to or encourage boys in the least way. To do so would be to court disgrace, to show herself to be crazy. The responsibility of guarding the chastity and reputation of one or more daughters of marriageable age was often a burden for the mother. One mother said she wished her 15-year-old daughter would marry soon because it was inconvenient to "spy" on her all the time.[74] In many Muslim societies, a girl's premarital chastity was tested after her marriage. After the wedding night, blood-stained sheets were displayed as proof of the bride's virginity.

Cultures do not remain the same; attitudes and practices can change markedly over time, as in the United States. In the past, sex was generally delayed until after marriage; in the 1990s, most Americans accepted or approved of premarital sex.[75]

EXTRAMARITAL SEX   Extramarital sex is not uncommon in many societies. In about 69 percent of the world's societies men have extramarital sex more than occasionally, and in about 57 percent so do women. The frequency of such sexual activity is higher than we might expect, given that only a slight majority of societies (54 percent) say they allow extramarital sex for men, and only a small number (11 percent) say they allow it for women.[76]

In several societies, then, there is quite a difference between the restrictive code and actual practice. The Navajo of the 1940s were said to forbid adultery, but young married men under the age of 30 had 27 percent of their heterosexual contacts with women other than their wives.[77] And although people in the United States in the 1970s almost overwhelmingly rejected extramarital sex, 41 percent of married men and about 18 percent of married women had had extramarital sex. In the 1990s, proportionately more men and women reported that they had been faithful to their spouses.[78] Cross-culturally, most societies have a double standard with regard to men and women, with restrictions considerably greater for women.[79] A substantial number of societies openly accept extramarital relationships. The Chukchee of Siberia, who often traveled long distances, allowed a married man to engage in sex with his host's wife, with the understanding that he would offer the same hospitality when the host visited him.[80]

SEX IN MARRIAGE   There is as much variety in the way coitus is performed as there is in sexual attitudes in general. Privacy is a nearly universal requirement. But, whereas a North American will usually find privacy in the bedroom, many other peoples are obliged to go out into the bush. The Siriono of Bolivia, for example, had as many as 50 hammocks 10 feet apart in their small huts.[81] In some cultures coitus often occurs in the presence of others, who may be sleeping or simply looking the other way.

Time and frequency of coitus also vary. Night is generally preferred, but some peoples, such as the Rucuyen of Brazil and the Yapese of the Pacific Caroline Islands, specifically opted for day. The Chenchu of India believed that a child conceived at night might be born blind. People in most societies abstain from intercourse during menstruation, during at least part of pregnancy, and for a period after childbirth. The Lesu, a people of New Ireland, an island off New Guinea, prohibited all members of the community from engaging in sex between the death of any member and burial.[82] Some societies prohibit sexual relations before various activities, such as hunting, fighting, planting, brewing, and iron smelting. Our own society is among the most lenient regarding restrictions on coitus within marriage, imposing only rather loose restraints during mourning, menstruation, and pregnancy.

Some cultures are more relaxed about sexuality than others. Does public sculpture reflect that? A park in Oslo, Norway, is dedicated to sculptures by Gustav Vigeland.

HOMOSEXUALITY   The range in permissiveness or restrictiveness toward homosexual relations is as great as that for any other kind of sexual activity. Among the Lepcha of the Himalayas, a man was believed to become homosexual if he ate the flesh of an uncastrated pig. But the Lepcha said that homosexual behavior was practically unheard of, and they viewed it with disgust.[83] Perhaps because many societies deny that homosexuality exists, little is known about homosexual practices in the restrictive societies. Among the permissive ones, there is variation in the pervasiveness of homosexuality. In some societies homosexuality is accepted but limited to certain times and certain individuals. For example, among the Papago of the southwestern United States there were "nights of saturnalia" in which homosexual tendencies could be expressed. The Papago also had many male transvestites, who wore women's clothing, did women's chores, and, if not married, could be visited by men.[84] A woman did not have the same freedom of expression. She could participate in the saturnalia feasts but only with her husband's permission, and female transvestites were nonexistent.

Homosexuality occurs even more widely in other societies. The Siwans of North Africa expected all males to engage in homosexual relations. In fact, fathers made arrangements for their unmarried sons to be given to an older man in a homosexual arrangement. Siwan custom limited a man to one boy. Fear of the government made this a secret matter, but before 1909 such arrangements were made openly. Almost all men were reported to have engaged in a homosexual relationship as boys; later, when they were between 16 and 20, they married girls.[85] Among the most extremely prohomosexual societies, the Etoro of New Guinea preferred homosexuality to heterosexuality. Heterosexuality was prohibited as many as 260 days a year and was forbidden in or near the house and gardens. Male homosexuality, on the other hand, was not prohibited at any time and was believed to make crops flourish and boys become strong.[86]

REASONS FOR RESTRICTIVENESS

Before we deal with the question of why some societies are more restrictive than others, we must first ask whether all forms of restrictiveness go together. The research to date suggests that societies that are restrictive with regard to one aspect of heterosexual sex tend to be restrictive with regard to other aspects. Thus, societies that frown on sexual expression by young children also punish premarital and extramarital sex.[87] Furthermore, such societies tend to insist on modesty in clothing and are constrained in their talk about sex.[88] But societies that are generally restrictive about heterosexuality are not necessarily restrictive about homosexuality. Societies restrictive about premarital sex are neither more nor less likely to restrict homosexuality. In the case of extramarital sex, the situation is somewhat different. Societies that have a considerable amount of male homosexuality tend to disapprove of males having extramarital heterosexual relationships.[89] If we are going to explain restrictiveness, then, it appears we have to consider heterosexual and homosexual restrictiveness separately.

Let us consider homosexual restrictiveness first. Why do homosexual relationships occur more frequently in some societies, and why are some societies intolerant of such relationships? There are many psychological interpretations of why some people become interested in homosexual relationships, and many of these interpretations relate the phenomenon to early parent-child relationships. So far, the research has not yielded any clear-cut predictions, although several cross-cultural predictors about male homosexuality are intriguing.

One such finding is that societies that forbid abortion and infanticide for married women (most societies permit these practices for illegitimate births) are likely to be intolerant of male homosexuality. This and other findings are consistent with the point of view that homosexuality is less tolerated in societies that would like to increase population. Such societies may be intolerant of all kinds of behaviors that minimize population growth. Homosexuality would have this effect, if we assume that a higher frequency of homosexual relations is associated with a lower frequency of heterosexual relations. The less frequently heterosexual relations occur, the lower the number of conceptions there might be. Another indication that intolerance may be related to a desire for population growth is that societies with famines and severe food shortages are more likely to allow homosexuality. Famines and food shortages suggest population pressure on resources; under these conditions, homosexuality and other practices that minimize population growth may be tolerated or even encouraged.[90]

The history of the Soviet Union may provide some other relevant evidence. In 1917, in the turmoil of revolution, laws prohibiting abortion and homosexuality were revoked and reproduction was discouraged. But in the period 1934 to 1936 the policy was reversed. Abortion and homosexuality were again declared illegal, and homosexuals were arrested. At the same time, awards were given to mothers who had more children.[91] Population pressure may also explain why our own society has become somewhat more tolerant of homosexuality recently. Of course, population pressure does not explain why certain individuals become homosexual or why most individuals in some societies engage in such behavior, but it might explain why some societies view such behavior more or less permissively.

Let us turn now to heterosexual behavior. What kinds of societies are more permissive than others? Although we do not yet understand the reasons, we do know that greater restrictiveness toward premarital sex tends to occur in more complex societies—societies that have hierarchies of political officials, part-time or full-time craft specialists, cities and towns, and class stratification.[92] It may be that as social inequality increases and various groups come to have differential wealth, parents become more concerned with preventing their children from marrying "beneath them." Permissiveness toward premarital sexual relationships might lead a person to become attached to someone not considered a desirable marriage partner. Even worse, from the family's point of view, such "unsuitable" sexual liaisons might result in a pregnancy that could make it impossible for a girl to marry "well." Controlling mating, then, may be a way of trying to control property. Consistent with this view is the finding that virginity is emphasized in rank and stratified societies, in which families are likely to exchange goods and money in the course of arranging marriages.[93]

The biological fact that humans depend on sexual reproduction does not by itself help explain why females and males differ in so many ways across cultures, or why societies vary in the way they handle male and female roles. We are only beginning to investigate these questions. When we eventually understand more about how and why females and males are different or the same in roles, personality, and sexuality, we may be better able to decide how much we want the biology of sex to shape our lives.

 CD-ROM Flashcards Chapter 19

 ## Summary

1. That humans reproduce sexually does not explain why males and females tend to differ in appearance and behavior, and to be treated differently, in all societies.

2. All or nearly all societies assign certain activities to females and other activities to males. These worldwide gender patterns of division of labor may be explained by male-female differences in strength, by differences in compatibility of tasks with child care, or by economy-of-effort considerations and/or the expendability of men.

3. Perhaps because women almost always have infant- and child-care responsibilities, men in most societies contribute more to primary subsistence activities, in terms of calories. But women contribute substantially to primary subsistence activities in societies that depend heavily on gathering and horticulture and in which warfare occurs while primary subsistence work has to be done. When primary and secondary subsistence work are counted, women typically work more hours than men. In most societies men are the leaders in the political arena, and warfare is almost exclusively a male activity.

4. The relative status of women compared with that of men seems to vary from one area of life to another. Whether women have relatively high status in one area does not necessarily indicate that they will have high status in another. Less complex societies, however, seem to approach more equal status for males and females in a variety of areas of life.

5. Recent field studies have suggested some consistent female-male differences in personality: Boys tend to be more aggressive than girls, and girls seem to be more responsible and helpful than boys.

6. Although all societies regulate sexual activity to some extent, societies vary considerably in the degree to which various kinds of sexuality are permitted. Some societies allow both masturbation and sex play among children, whereas others forbid such acts. Some societies allow premarital sex; others do not. Some allow extramarital sex in certain situations; others forbid it generally.

7. Societies that are restrictive toward one aspect of heterosexual sex tend to be restrictive with regard to other aspects. And more complex societies tend to be more restrictive toward premarital heterosexual sex than less complex societies.

8. Societal attitudes toward homosexuality are not completely consistent with attitudes toward sexual relationships between the sexes. Societal tolerance of homosexuality is associated with tolerance of abortion and infanticide and with famines and food shortages.

Glossary Terms

compatibility-with
  child-care theory

economy-of-effort theory

expendability theory

gender differences

gender roles

gender stratification

primary subsistence
  activities

secondary subsistence
  activities

sex differences

sexual dimorphism

strength theory

 ## Critical Questions

1. Would you expect female-male differences in personality to disappear in a society with complete gender equality in the workplace?

2. Under what circumstances would you expect male-female differences in athletic performance to disappear?

3. What conditions make the election of a female head of state most likely?

 ## Internet Exercises

1. Check out women's work in Sierra Leone at http://www.fao.org/news/factfile/ff9719-e.htm or http://www.fao.org/news/factfile/ff9718-e.htm. What impressed you most?

2. The global gender gap is addressed at http://www.undp.org/trustfunds/TTFGender091101E.PDF. Write a brief summary of what you found.

3. Visit http://www.swc-cfc.gc.ca/ to learn about the status of women and their changing role in Canada. Write a brief summary on the current issues this Web page addresses. Go to http://www.swc-cfc.gc.ca/publish/egei/egeibck-e.html for more specific information on economic equality indicators.

Suggested Reading

BRETTELL, C. B., AND SARGENT, C. F., eds. *Gender in Cross-Cultural Perspective,* 3rd ed. Upper Saddle River, NJ: Prentice Hall, 2000. A book of readings that draws on the classics as well as the recent gender literature on various topics, including women and men in prehistory, the cultural construction of masculinity and femininity, and the impact of colonialism, the state, and globalization on gender issues.

BROUDE, G. J. "Variations in Sexual Attitudes, Norms and Practices." In C. R. Ember and M. Ember, eds., *Cross-Cultural Research for Social Science,* in C. R. Ember and M. Ember, eds., *New Directions in Anthropology.* Upper Saddle River, NJ: Prentice Hall, CD-ROM, 2003. An exploration of the ways in which cultures vary in their sexual attitudes and practices and the possible reasons for the variation.

EMBER, C. R. "Universal and Variable Patterns of Gender Difference." In C. R. Ember and M. Ember, eds. *Cross-Cultural Research for Social Science* in C. R. Ember and M. Ember, eds. *New Directions in Anthropology.* Upper Saddle River, NJ: Prentice Hall, 2003. A review of what we know and do not know about sex and gender differences cross-culturally and a critical evaluation of the theories that might explain the universal and variable patterns.

EMBER, C. R., AND EMBER, M. EDS. Encyclopedia of Sex and Gender: Men and Women in the World's Cultures. 2 vols. New York: Kluwer Academic/Plenum, 2004. In comparative overviews and portraits of cultures around the world, the anthropologists and other scholars who contributed to this encyclopedia describe and discuss cultural variation in cultural constructions of gender, gender roles and how girls and boys are reared, gender status, gender issues over the life cycle, the relationships between men and women, and sexuality.

GOLDSTEIN, J. S. *War and Gender: How Gender Shapes the War System and Vice Versa.* New York: Cambridge University Press, 2001. A book that describes and explains the cross-cultural consistency and variation of gender roles in war, and the effect of war on ideas of masculinity.

MACCOBY, E. E. *The Two Sexes: Growing Up Apart, Coming Together.* Cambridge, MA: Belknap Press of Harvard University Press, 1998. This book describes the vast changes in men's and women's relationships that have occurred in recent years, in spite of the ways boys and girls are generally socialized and in spite of possible sex differences in hormones and brain function.

SCHLEGEL, A. "The Status of Women." In C. R. Ember and M. Ember, eds., *Cross-Cultural Research for Social Science,* in C. R. Ember and M. Ember, eds., *New Directions in Anthropology.* Upper Saddle River, NJ: Prentice Hall, CD-ROM, 2003. A critical discussion of the comparative research on variation in women's status with an analysis of different kinds of equality and inequality in four ethnographic cases.

WOMACK, M., AND MARTI, J., eds. *The Other Fifty Percent: Multicultural Perspectives on Gender Relations.* Prospect Heights, IL: Waveland, 1993. A collection of 24 articles about women in different societies and their roles in marriage, economic decision making, politics, and religion.

MARRIAGE AND THE FAMILY

CHAPTER OUTLINE

Whatever a society's attitudes toward male-female relationships, one such relationship is found in all societies—marriage. Why marriage is customary in every society we know of is a classic and perplexing question, and one we attempt to deal with in this chapter.

The universality of marriage does not mean that everyone in every society gets married. It means only that most, usually nearly all, people in every society get married at least once in their lifetime. In addition, when we say that marriage is universal, we do not mean that marriage and family customs are the same in all societies. On the contrary, there is much variation from society to society in how one marries, whom one marries, and even how many persons a person can be married to simultaneously. The only cultural universal about marriage is that no society permits people to marry parents, brothers, or sisters.

Families also are universal. All societies have parent-child social groups, although the form and size of family may vary from one society to another. Some societies have large extended families with two or more related parent-child groups; others have smaller independent families. Today, marriage is not always the basis for family life. One-parent families are becoming increasingly common in our own and other societies. Marriage has not disappeared in these places—it is still customary to marry—but more individuals are choosing now to have children without being married.

 Marriage

When anthropologists speak of marriage, they do not mean to imply that couples everywhere must get marriage certificates or have wedding ceremonies, as in our own society. **Marriage** merely means a socially approved sexual and economic union, usually between a woman and a man. It is presumed, by both the couple and others, to be more or less permanent, and it subsumes reciprocal rights and obligations between the two spouses and between spouses and their future children.[1]

It is a socially approved sexual union in that a married couple does not have to hide the sexual nature of their relationship. A woman might say, "I want you to meet my husband," but she could not say, "I want you to meet my lover" without causing some embarrassment in most societies. Although the union may ultimately be dissolved by divorce, couples in all societies begin marriage with some idea of permanence in mind. Implicit too in marriage are reciprocal rights and obligations. These may be more or less specific and formalized regarding matters of property, finances, and child rearing.

Marriage entails both a sexual and an economic relationship, as George Peter Murdock noted:

> Sexual relations can occur without economic cooperation, and there can be a division of labor between men and women without sex. But marriage unites the economic and the sexual.[2]

As we will see, the event that marks the commencement of marriage varies in different societies. A Winnebago bride, for example, knew no formal ritual such as a wedding ceremony. She went with her groom to his parents' house, took off her "wedding" clothes and finery, gave them to her mother-in-law, received plain clothes in exchange, and that was that.[3]

THE NAYAR "EXCEPTION"

There is one group of people in the ethnographic literature that did not have marriage, as we have defined it. In the nineteenth century, a caste group in southern India called the Nayar seems to have treated sex and economic relations between men and women as things separate from marriage. About the time of puberty, Nayar girls took ritual husbands. The union was publicly established in a ceremony during which the husband tied a gold ornament around the neck of his bride. But from that time on, he had

An elite couple in Phnom Penh, Cambodia steps onto a carpet with money on it to celebrate their wedding.

no more responsibility for her. Usually, he never saw her again.

The bride lived in a large household with her family, where she was visited over the subsequent years by other "husbands." One might be a passing guest, another a more regular visitor; it did not matter, providing the "husband" met the caste restrictions and was approved by her kin group. He came at night and left the following day. If a regular visitor, he was expected to make small gifts of cloth, betel nuts, and hair and bath oil. If the father of her child, or one of a group who might be, he was expected to pay the cost of the midwife. But at no time was he responsible for the support of the woman or her child, nor did he have any say in the upbringing of his biological children. Rather, her blood relatives retained such responsibilities.[4]

Whether or not the Nayar had marriage depends, of course, on how we choose to define marriage. Certainly, Nayar marital unions involved no regular sexual component or economic cooperation, nor did they involve important reciprocal rights and obligations. According to our definition, then, the Nayar did not have marriage. But the Nayar were not a separate society—only a caste group whose men specialized in soldiering. The Nayar situation seems to have been a special response to the problem of extended male absence during military service. In more recent times, military service has ceased to be a common occupation of the Nayars, and stable married relationships have become the norm.[5] Because the Nayar were not a separate society, they are not really an exception to our statement that marriage, as we have defined it, has been customary in all societies known to anthropology.

Rare Types of Marriage

In addition to the usual male-female marriages, some societies recognize marriages between persons of the same biological sex. But such marriages are not typical in any known society and do not fit the usual type of marriage. First, the unions are not between a male and a female. Second, they are not necessarily sexual unions, as we will see. But these "marriages" are socially approved unions, usually modeled after regular marriages, and they often entail a considerable number of reciprocal rights and obligations. Sometimes the marriages involve an individual who is considered a "woman" or "man," even though "she" or "he" is not that sex biologically. For example, the Cheyenne Indians allowed married men to take **berdaches**, or male transvestites, as second wives.[6] (The term *two-spirits* is often used now instead of *berdache*.)

Although it is not clear that the Cheyenne male-male marriages involved homosexual relationships, it is clear that temporary homosexual marriages did occur among the Azande of Africa. Before the British took control over what is now Sudan, Azande warriors who could not afford wives often married "boy-wives" to satisfy their sexual needs. As in normal marriages, gifts (although not as substantial) were given by the "husband" to the parents of his boy-wife. The husband performed services for the boy's parents and could sue any other lover of the boy in court

for adultery. The boy-wives not only had sexual relations with their husbands but also performed many of the chores female wives traditionally performed for their husbands.[7]

Female-female marriages are reported to have occurred in many African societies, but there is no evidence of any sexual relationship between the partners. It seems, rather, that female-female marriages were a socially approved way for a woman to take on the legal and social roles of a father and husband.[8] For example, among the Nandi, a pastoral and agricultural society of Kenya, about 3 percent of the marriages are female-female marriages. Such marriages appear to be a Nandi solution to the problem of a regular marriage's failure to produce a male heir to property. The Nandi solution is to have the woman, even if her husband is still alive, become a "husband" to a younger female and "father" the younger woman's children. The female husband provides the marriage payments required for obtaining a wife, renounces female work, and takes on the obligations of the husband to that woman. Although no sexual relations are permitted between the female husband and the new wife (or between the female husband and her own husband), the female husband arranges a male consort so that the new wife can have children. Those children, however, consider the female husband to be their father because she (or more aptly the gender role "he") is the socially designated father. If asked who their father is, a child of such a marriage will name the female who is the husband.[9]

◆ Why Is Marriage Universal?

Because all societies practice female-male marriage as we have defined it, we can assume that the custom is adaptive. But saying that does not specify exactly how it may be adaptive. Several interpretations have traditionally been offered to explain why all human societies have the custom of marriage. Each suggests that marriage solves problems found in all societies—how to share the products of a gender division of labor; how to care for infants, who are dependent for a long time; and how to minimize sexual competition. To evaluate the plausibility of these interpretations, we must ask whether marriage provides the best or the only reasonable solution to each problem. After all, we are trying to explain a custom that is presumably a universal solution. The comparative study of other animals, some of which have something like marriage, may help us to evaluate these explanations.

Gender Division of Labor

We noted in the preceding chapter that every society known to anthropology has had a gender division of labor. Males and females in every society perform different economic activities. This gender division of labor has often been cited as a reason for marriage.[10] As long as there is a division of labor by gender, society has to have some mechanism by which women and men share the products of their labor. Marriage would be one way to solve that problem. But it seems unlikely that marriage is the only possible solution. The hunter-gatherer rule of sharing could be extended to include all the products brought in by both women and men. Or a small group of men and women, such as brothers and sisters, might be pledged to cooperate economically. Thus, although marriage may solve the problem of sharing the fruits of a division of labor, it clearly is not the only possible solution.

Prolonged Infant Dependency

Humans exhibit the longest period of infant dependency of any primate. The child's prolonged dependence places the greatest burden on the mother, who is the main child caregiver in most societies. The burden of prolonged child care by human females may limit the kinds of work they can do. They may need the help of a man to do certain types of work, such as hunting, that are incompatible with child care. Because of this prolonged dependency, it has been suggested, marriage is necessary.[11] But here the argument becomes essentially the same as the division-of-labor argument, and it has the same logical weakness. It is not clear why a group of women and men, such as a hunter-gatherer band, could not cooperate in providing for dependent children without marriage.

Sexual Competition

Unlike most other female primates, the human female may engage in intercourse at any time throughout the year. Some scholars have suggested that more or less continuous female sexuality may have created a serious problem—considerable sexual competition between males for females. It is argued that society had to prevent such competition in order to survive, that it had to develop some way of minimizing the rivalry among males for females in order to reduce the chance of lethal and destructive conflict.[12]

There are several problems with this argument. First, why should continuous female sexuality make for more sexual competition in the first place? One might argue the other way around. There might be more competition over the scarcer resources that would be available if females were less frequently interested in sex. Second, males of many animal species, even some that have relatively frequent female sexuality (as do many of our close primate relatives), do not show much aggression over females. Third, why couldn't sexual competition, even if it existed, be regulated by cultural rules other than marriage? For instance, society might have adopted a rule whereby men and women circulated among all the opposite-sex members of the group, each person staying a specified length of time with each partner. Such a system presumably would solve the problem of sexual competition. On the other hand, such a system might not work particularly well if individuals came to prefer certain other individuals. Jealousies attending those attachments might give rise to even more competition.

Other Mammals and Birds: Postpartum Requirements

None of the theories we have discussed explains convincingly why marriage is the only or the best solution to a particular problem. Also, we now have some comparative evidence on mammals and birds that casts doubt on those theories.[13] How can evidence from other animals help us evaluate theories about human marriage? If we look at the animals that, like humans, have some sort of stable female-male mating, as compared with those that are completely promiscuous, we can perhaps see what sorts of factors may predict male-female bonding in the warm-blooded animal species. Most species of birds, and some mammals such as wolves and beavers, have "marriage." Among 40 mammal and bird species, none of the three factors discussed above—division of labor, prolonged infant dependency, and greater female sexuality—predicts or is correlated strongly with male-female bonding. With respect to division of labor by sex, most other animals have nothing comparable to a humanlike division of labor, but many have stable female-male matings anyway. The two other supposed factors—prolonged infant dependency and female sexuality—predict just the opposite of what we might expect. Mammal and bird species that have longer dependency periods or more female sexuality are less likely to have stable matings.

Does anything predict male-female bonding? One factor does among mammals and birds, and it may also help explain human marriage. Animal species in which females can simultaneously feed themselves and their babies after birth (*postpartum*) tend not to have stable matings; species in which postpartum mothers cannot feed themselves and their babies at the same time tend to have stable matings. Among the typical bird species, a mother would have difficulty feeding herself and her babies simultaneously. Because

"I do love you. But, to be perfectly honest, I would have loved any other lovebird who happened to turn up."

(Rothco Cartoons)

the young cannot fly for a while and must be protected in a nest, the mother risks losing them to other animals if she goes off to obtain food. But if she has a male bonded to her (as most bird species do), he can bring back food or take a turn watching the nest. Among animal species that have no postpartum feeding problem, babies almost immediately after birth are able to travel with the mother as she moves about to eat (as do grazers such as horses), or the mother can transport the babies as she moves about to eat (as do baboons and kangaroos). We think the human female has a postpartum feeding problem. When humans lost most of their body hair, babies could not readily travel with the mother by clinging to her fur. And when humans began to depend on certain kinds of food-getting that could be dangerous (such as hunting), mothers could not engage in such work with their infants along.

Even if we assume that human mothers have a postpartum feeding problem, we still have to ask if marriage is the most likely solution to the problem. We think so, because other conceivable solutions probably would not work as well. For example, if a mother took turns baby-sitting with another mother, neither might be able to collect enough food for both mothers and the two sets of children dependent on them. But a mother and father share the same set of children, and therefore it would be easier for them to feed themselves and their children adequately. Another possible solution is no pair bonding at all, just a promiscuous group of males and females. But in that kind of arrangement, we think, a particular mother probably would not always be able to count on some male to watch her baby when she had to go out for food or to bring her food when she had to watch her baby. Thus, it seems to us that the problem of postpartum feeding by itself helps to explain why some animals, including humans, have relatively stable male-female bonds. Of course, there is still the question of whether research on other animals can be applied to human beings. We think it can, but not everybody will agree.

◆ How Does One Marry?

When we say that marriage is a socially approved sexual and economic union, we mean that all societies have some way of marking the onset of a marriage, but the ways of doing so vary considerably. For reasons that we don't fully understand, some cultures mark marriages by elaborate rites and celebrations; others mark marriages in much more informal ways. And most societies have economic transactions before, during, or even after the onset of the marriages.

MARKING THE ONSET OF MARRIAGE

Many societies have ceremonies marking the beginning of marriage. But others, such as the Taramiut Inuit, the Trobriand Islanders of the South Pacific, and the Kwoma of New Guinea, use different social signals to indicate that a marriage has taken place. Among the Taramiut Inuit, the betrothal is considered extremely important and is arranged between the parents at or before the time their children reach puberty. Later, when the youth is ready, he moves in with his betrothed's family for a trial period. If all goes well—that is, if the girl gives birth to a baby within a year or so—the couple are considered married. At this time, the wife goes with her husband to his camp.[14]

In keeping with the general openness of their society's attitudes toward sexual matters, a Trobriand couple advertise their desire to marry "by sleeping together regularly, by showing themselves together in public, and by remaining with each other for long periods at a time."[15] When a girl accepts a small gift from a boy, she demonstrates that her parents favor the match. Before long, she moves to the boy's house, takes her meals there, and accompanies her husband all day. Then the word goes around that the two are married.[16]

The Kwoma of New Guinea practice a trial marriage followed by a ceremony that makes the couple husband and wife. The girl lives for a while in the boy's home. When the boy's mother is satisfied with the match and knows that her son is too, she waits for a day when he is away from the house. Until that time, the girl has been cooking only for herself, and the boy's food has been prepared by his womenfolk. Now the mother has the girl prepare his meal. The young man returns and begins to eat his soup. When the first bowl is nearly finished, his mother tells him that his betrothed cooked the meal, and his eating it means that he is now married. At this news, the boy customarily rushes out of the house, spits out the soup, and shouts, "Faugh! It tastes bad! It is cooked terribly!" A ceremony then makes the marriage official.[17]

Among those societies that have ceremonies marking the onset of marriage, feasting is a common element. It expresses publicly the unification of the two families by marriage. The Reindeer Tungus of Siberia set a wedding date after protracted negotiations between the two families and their larger kin groups. Go-betweens assume most of the responsibility for the negotiating. The wedding day opens with the two kin groups, probably numbering as many as 150 people, pitching their lodges in separate areas and offering a great feast. After the groom's gifts have been presented, the bride's dowry is loaded onto reindeer and carried to the groom's lodge. There the climax of the ceremony takes place. The bride takes the wife's place— that is, at the right side of the entrance of the lodge—and members of both families sit in a circle. The groom enters and follows the bride around the circle, greeting each guest, while the guests, in their turn, kiss the bride on the mouth and hands. Finally, the go-betweens spit three times on the bride's hands, and the couple are formally husband and wife. More feasting and revelry bring the day to a close.[18]

In many cultures, marriage includes ceremonial expressions of hostility. One form of this custom is the trading of insults between kin groups, such as occurs on the Polynesian atoll of Pukapuka. Mock fights are staged in many societies. On occasion, hostility can have genuinely aggressive overtones, as among the Gusii of Kenya:

> Five young clansmen of the groom come to take the bride and two immediately find the girl and post themselves at her side to prevent her escape, while the others receive the final permission of her parents. When it has been granted the bride holds onto the house posts and must be dragged outside by the young men. Finally she goes along with them, crying and with her hands on her head.[19]

But the battle is not yet over. Mutual antagonism continues right onto the marriage bed, even up to and beyond coitus. The groom is determined to display his virility; the bride is equally determined to test it. "Brides," Robert and Barbara LeVine remarked, "are said to take pride in the length of time they can hold off their mates." Men can also win acclaim. If the bride is unable to walk the following day, the groom is considered a "real man."[20] Such expressions of hostility usually occur in societies in which the two sets of kin are actual or potential rivals or enemies. In many societies, it is common to marry women from "enemy" villages.

As this example suggests, marriage ceremonies often symbolize important elements of the culture. Whereas the Gusii ceremony may symbolize hostility between the two families, in other societies the ceremony may promote harmony between the families. For example, on the Polynesian island of Rotuma, a female clown is an important part of the ceremony. She is responsible for creating an enjoyable, joking atmosphere that facilitates interaction between the two sides.[21]

ECONOMIC ASPECTS OF MARRIAGE

"It's not man that marries maid, but field marries field, vineyard marries vineyard, cattle marry cattle." In its down-to-earth way, this German peasant saying indicates that in many societies marriage involves economic considerations. In our culture, economic considerations may or may not be explicit. However, in about 75 percent of the societies known to anthropology,[22] one or more explicit economic transactions take place before or after the marriage. The economic transaction may take several forms: bride price, bride service, exchange of females, gift exchange, dowry, or indirect dowry. The distribution of those forms among societies that have economic marriage transactions is shown in Figure 20–1.

BRIDE PRICE Bride price or bride wealth is a gift of money or goods from the groom or his kin to the bride's kin. The gift usually grants the groom the right to marry the bride and the right to her children. Of all the forms of economic transaction involved in marriage, bride price is the most common. In one cross-cultural sample, 44 percent of the societies with economic transactions at marriage practiced bride price; in almost all of those societies the bride price was substantial.[23] Bride price occurs all over the world but is especially common in Africa and Oceania.

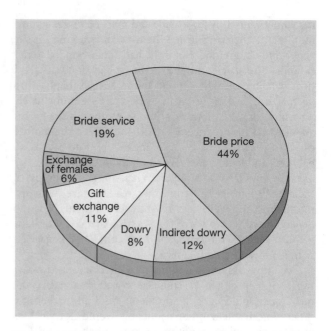

Figure 20–1 *Distribution of Economic Marriage Transactions among Societies That Have Them*

Note that there are societies in the ethnographic record (25 percent) that lack any substantial economic transactions at marriage.

Source: Based on data from Alice Schlegel and Rohn Eloul, "Marriage Transactions: Labor, Property, and Status," *American Anthropologist* 90 (1988): 291–309.

Payment can be made in different currencies; livestock and food are two of the more common. With the increased importance of commercial exchange, money has increasingly become part of the bride price payments. Among the Nandi, the bride price consists of about five to seven cattle, one or two sheep and goats, cowrie shells, and money equivalent to the value of one cow. Even in unusual female-female marriages, the female "husband" must pay a bride price to arrange the marriage and be considered the "father."[24]

The Subanun of the Philippines have an expensive bride price—several times the annual income of the groom plus three to five years of bride service (described in the next section).[25] Among the Manus of the Admiralty Islands off New Guinea, a groom requires an economic backer, usually an older brother or an uncle, if he is to marry, but it will be years before he can pay off his debts. Depending on the final bride price, payments may be concluded at the time of the marriage, or they may continue for years afterward.[26]

Despite the connotations that bride price may have for us, the practice does not reduce a woman to the position of slave—although it is associated, as we shall see, with relatively low status for women. The bride price may be important to the woman and her family. Indeed, the fee they receive can serve as a security. If the marriage fails through no fault of hers and the wife returns to her kin, the family might not return the bride price to the groom. On the other hand, the wife's kin may pressure her to remain with her husband, even though she does not wish to, because

ANTHROPOLOGICAL ORIGINALS
The Yapese of Micronesia

Marriage is not the same everywhere: Why people are considered married varies from culture to culture. It even varies in this country. The only thing that's true about marriages in North America is that there is some recognition by society that two people are "married." In many societies, a marriage becomes public or acknowledged without any kind of formal ceremony, and without any recognition by the authorities—similar to what is called "living together" in North America. This was the way it was on Yap in the Pacific.

Elder Yapese report that they often had several affairs before they found a satisfying relationship. When the excitement of a new love grew cold, each looked to other partners for that elusive ecstasy of love. Much of the joy was found in the process of courtship, and young people were reluctant to enter marriage until they were in their mid-twenties or even thirties.

Marriage was precipitated by two major concerns: weariness of the necessity of continual clandestine encounters after dark accompanied by a desire to live together, and pregnancy. Once a couple established a more or less permanent commitment to each other, they began to talk about marriage. Women were sometimes the most reluctant to marry because of the heavy burden and responsibility that followed. Once they agreed, however, the marriage became public when the man brought his lover home and announced to his father that they wanted to marry. Fathers rarely refused such a request. The typical response was for a man to go with his son to the house of the girl's father to offer a piece of shell money to obtain approval of the marriage. When her father accepted the shell, the marriage was recognized and the couple established their own household at the home of the young man.

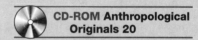
CD-ROM Anthropological Originals 20

Source: Sherwood G. Lingenfelter, "Yap: Changing Roles of Men and Women," in Melvin Ember and Carol R. Ember, eds., *Portraits of Culture: Ethnographic Originals,* in Carol R. Ember and Melvin Ember, eds., *New Directions in Anthropology* (Upper Saddle River, NJ: Prentice Hall, CD-ROM, 2003).

they do not want to return the bride price or are unable to do so. A larger bride price is associated with more difficulty in obtaining a divorce.[27]

What kinds of societies are likely to have the custom of bride price? Cross-culturally, societies with bride price are likely to practice horticulture and lack social stratification. Bride price is also likely where women contribute a great deal to primary subsistence activities[28] and where they contribute more than men to all kinds of economic activities.[29] Although these findings might suggest that women are highly valued in such societies, recall that the status of women relative to men is not higher in societies in which women contribute a lot to primary subsistence activities. Indeed, bride price is likely to occur in societies in which men make most of the decisions in the household,[30] and decision making by men is one indicator of lower status for women.

BRIDE SERVICE **Bride service,** which is the next most common type of economic transaction at marriage—occurring in about 19 percent of the societies with economic transactions—requires the groom to work for the bride's family, sometimes before the marriage begins, sometimes after. Bride service varies in duration. In some societies it lasts for only a few months; in others, as long as several years. Among the North Alaskan Eskimo, for example, the boy works for his in-laws after the marriage is arranged. To fulfill his obligation, he may simply catch a seal for them. The marriage may be consummated at any time while he is in service.[31] In some societies, bride service sometimes substitutes for bride price. An individual might give bride service in order to reduce the amount of bride price required. Native North and South American societies were likely to practice bride service, particularly if they were egalitarian food collectors.[32]

EXCHANGE OF FEMALES Of the societies that have economic transactions at marriage, 6 percent have the custom whereby a sister or female relative of the groom is exchanged for the bride. Among these societies are the Tiv of West Africa and the Yanomamö of Venezuela-Brazil. These societies tend to be horticultural, egalitarian, and to have a relatively high contribution of women to primary subsistence.[33]

GIFT EXCHANGE Gift exchange, which involves the exchange of gifts of about equal value by the two kin groups about to be linked by marriage, occurs somewhat more often than the exchange of females (about 11 percent of those with economic transactions).[34] For example, among the Andaman Islanders, as soon as a boy and girl indicate their intention to marry, their respective sets of parents cease all communication and begin sending gifts of food and other objects to each other through a third party. This arrangement continues until the marriage is completed and the two kin groups are united.[35]

DOWRY   A **dowry** is usually a substantial transfer of goods or money from the bride's family to the bride.[36] Unlike the types of transactions we have discussed so far, the dowry, which occurs in about 8 percent of the societies with economic transactions, is usually not a transaction between the kin of the bride and the kin of the groom. A family has to have wealth to give a dowry, but because the goods go to the bride, no wealth comes back to the family that gave the dowry. Payment of dowries was common in medieval and Renaissance Europe, where the size of the dowry often determined the desirability of the daughter. The custom is still practiced in parts of Eastern Europe and in sections of southern Italy and France, where land is often the major item provided by the bride's family. Parts of India also practice the dowry.

In contrast to societies with bride price, societies with dowry tend to be those in which women contribute relatively little to primary subsistence activities, there is a high degree of social stratification, and a man is not allowed to be married to more than one woman simultaneously.[37] Why does dowry tend to occur in these types of societies? One theory suggests that the dowry is intended to guarantee future support for a woman and her children, even though she will not do much primary subsistence work. Another theory is that the dowry is intended to attract the best bridegroom for a daughter in monogamous societies with a high degree of social inequality. The dowry strategy is presumed to increase the likelihood that the daughter and her children will do well reproductively. Both theories are supported by recent cross-cultural research, with the

second predicting dowry better.[38] But many stratified societies (including our own) in which women and men have only one spouse at a time do not practice dowry. Why this is so still needs to be explained.

INDIRECT DOWRY   The dowry is provided by the bride's family to the bride. But sometimes the payments to the bride originate from the groom's family. Because the goods are sometimes first given to the bride's father, who passes most if not all of them to her, this kind of transaction is called **indirect dowry**.[39] Indirect dowry occurs in about 12 percent of the societies in which marriage involves an economic transaction. For example, among the Basseri of southern Iran, the groom's father assumes the expense of setting up the couple's new household. He gives cash to the bride's father, who uses at least some of the money to buy his daughter household utensils, blankets, and rugs.[40]

◆ Restrictions on Marriage: The Universal Incest Taboo

Hollywood and its press agents notwithstanding, marriage is not always based solely on mutual love, independently discovered and expressed by the two life-partners-to-be. Nor is it based on sex or wealth alone. Even when love, sex, and economics are contributing factors, regulations specify whom one may or may not marry. Perhaps the most rigid regulation, found in *all* cultures, is the **incest taboo,** which prohibits sexual intercourse or marriage between some categories of kin.

The most universal aspect of the incest taboo is the prohibition of sexual intercourse or marriage between mother and son, father and daughter, and brother and sister. No society in recent times has permitted either sexual intercourse or marriage between those pairs. A few societies in the past, however, did permit incest, mostly within the

The bride's brother at a wedding in Baghdad, Iraq, shows the dowry to the groom.

royal and aristocratic families, though generally it was forbidden to the rest of the population. For example, the Incan and Hawaiian royal families allowed marriage within the family. Probably the best-known example of allowed incest involved Cleopatra of Egypt.

It seems clear that the Egyptian aristocracy and royalty indulged in father-daughter and brother-sister marriages. Cleopatra was married to two of her younger brothers at different times.[41] The reasons seem to have been partly religious—a member of the family of the pharaoh, who was considered a god, could not marry any "ordinary" human—and partly economic, for marriage within the family kept the royal property undivided. In the Egyptian case, between 30 B.C. and A.D. 324, incest was allowed not just in the royal family; an estimated 8 percent of commoner marriages were brother-sister marriages.[42]

But, despite these exceptions, the fact remains that no culture we know of today permits or accepts incest within the nuclear family. Why is the familial incest taboo universal? Several explanations have been suggested.

CHILDHOOD-FAMILIARITY THEORY

The childhood-familiarity theory, suggested by Edward Westermarck, was given a wide hearing in the early 1920s. Westermarck argued that persons who have been closely associated with each other since earliest childhood, such as siblings, are not sexually attracted to each other and therefore would avoid marriage with each other.[43] This theory was subsequently rejected because of evidence that some children were sexually interested in their parents and siblings. Studies have suggested, however, that there might be something to Westermarck's theory.

Yonina Talmon investigated marriage patterns among the second generation of three well-established collective communities (*kibbutzim*) in Israel. In these collectives,

children live with many members of their peer group in quarters separate from their families. They are in constant interaction with their peers, from birth to maturity. The study revealed that among 125 couples, there was "not one instance in which both mates were reared from birth in the same peer group,"[44] despite parental encouragement of marriage within the peer group. Children reared in common not only avoided marriage, they also avoided any sexual relations among themselves.

Talmon stated that the people reared together firmly believed that overfamiliarity breeds sexual disinterest. As one of them told her, "We are like an open book to each other. We have read the story in the book over and over again and know all about it."[45] Talmon's evidence reveals not only the onset of disinterest and even sexual antipathy among children reared together, but a correspondingly heightened fascination with newcomers or outsiders, particularly for their "mystery."

Arthur Wolf's study of the Chinese in northern Taiwan also supports the idea that something about being reared together produces sexual disinterest. Wolf focused on a community still practicing the Chinese custom of *t'ung-yang-hsi,* or "daughter-in-law raised from childhood."

> When a girl is born in a poor family . . . she is often given away or sold when but a few weeks or months old, or one or two years old, to be the future wife of a son in the family of a friend or relative which has a little son not betrothed in marriage. . . . The girl is called a "little bride" and taken home and brought up in the family together with her future husband.[46]

Wolf's evidence indicates that this arrangement is associated with sexual difficulties when the childhood "couple" later marry. Informants implied that familiarity results in disinterest and lack of stimulation. As an indication of

Children on an Israeli kibbutz live together as well as go to school together.

their disinterest, these couples produce fewer offspring than spouses not raised together, they are more likely to seek extramarital sexual relationships, and they are more likely to get divorced.[47]

The Talmon and Wolf studies suggest, then, that children raised together are not likely to be sexually interested in each other when they grow up. Such disinterest is consistent with Westermarck's notion that the incest taboo may be more an avoidance of certain matings than a prohibition of them. There is one other piece of evidence consistent with this explanation of the incest taboo. Hilda and Seymour Parker compared two samples of fathers: those who had sexually abused their daughters and those who supposedly had not.[48] To maximize their similarities otherwise, the Parkers selected the two samples of fathers from the same prisons and psychiatric facilities. The Parkers found that the fathers who had committed incest with their daughters were much more likely than the other sample of fathers to have had little to do with bringing up their daughters, because they were not at home or hardly at home during the daughters' first three years of life. In other words, the fathers who avoided incest had been more closely associated with their daughters in childhood. That finding is consistent with Westermarck's suggestion that the incest taboo is a result of familiarity in childhood.

Although Westermarck was talking about the development of sexual aversion during early childhood, some researchers have asked how the childhood-familiarity theory could explain the extension of incest taboos to first cousins. The familiarity argument implies that first-cousin marriage should be prohibited in societies in which first cousins grow up together in the same community. But that is not the case. Such societies are not more likely to prohibit first-cousin marriage.[49]

Even if there is something about familiarity in childhood that normally leads to sexual disinterest,[50] we still are left with the question of why societies have to prohibit marriages that would voluntarily be avoided because of disinterest. And why do many couples remain actively interested in each other sexually after years of marriage?

FREUD'S PSYCHOANALYTIC THEORY

Sigmund Freud proposed that the incest taboo is a reaction against unconscious, unacceptable desires.[51] He suggested that the son is attracted to his mother (as the daughter is to her father) and as a result feels jealousy and hostility toward his father. But the son knows that these feelings cannot continue, for they might lead the father to retaliate against him; therefore, they must be renounced or repressed. Usually the feelings are repressed and retreat into the unconscious. But the desire to possess the mother continues to exist in the unconscious, and, according to Freud, the horror of incest is a reaction to, or a defense against, the forbidden unconscious impulse.

Although Freud's theory may account for the aversion felt toward incest, or at least the aversion toward parent-child incest, it does not explain why society needs an ex-

plicit taboo, particularly on brother-sister incest. Nor does it account for the findings of sexual disinterest we discussed in connection with the Westermarck hypothesis.

FAMILY-DISRUPTION THEORY

The family-disruption theory, often associated with Bronislaw Malinowski,[52] can best be summed up as follows: Sexual competition among family members would create so much rivalry and tension that the family could not function as an effective unit. Because the family must function effectively for society to survive, society has to curtail competition within the family. The familial incest taboo is thus imposed to keep the family intact.

But there are inconsistencies in this approach. Society could have shaped other rules about the sexual access of one member of the family to another that would also eliminate potentially disruptive competition. Also, why would brother-sister incest be so disruptive? As we noted, such marriages did exist in ancient Egypt. Brother-sister incest would not disrupt the authority of the parents if the children were allowed to marry when mature. The family-disruption theory, then, does not explain the origin of the incest taboo.

COOPERATION THEORY

The cooperation theory was proposed by the early anthropologist Edward B. Tylor and was elaborated by Leslie A. White and Claude Lévi-Strauss. It emphasizes the value of the incest taboo in promoting cooperation among family groups and thus helping communities to survive. As Tylor saw it, certain operations necessary for the welfare of the community can be accomplished only by large numbers of people working together. In order to break down suspicion and hostility between family groups and make such cooperation possible, early humans developed the incest taboo to ensure that individuals would marry members of other families. The ties created by intermarriage would serve to hold the community together. Thus, Tylor explained the incest taboo as an answer to the choice "between marrying out and being killed out."[53]

The idea that marriage with other groups promotes cooperation sounds plausible, but is there evidence to support it? After all, there are societies such as the Gusii in which marriage is often between hostile groups. But is that society an exception? Does marriage promote cooperation? Because people in all recent societies marry outside the family, we cannot test the idea that such marriages promote cooperation more than marriages within the family. We can, however, ask whether other kinds of out-marriage, such as marriage with other communities, promote cooperation with those communities. The evidence on that question does not support the cooperation theory. There is no greater peacefulness between communities when marriages are forbidden within the community and always arranged with other communities than when they are not.[54]

But even if marriage outside the family promoted cooperation with other groups, why would it be necessary to prohibit all marriages within the family? Couldn't families have required some of their members to marry outside the family if they thought it necessary for survival but permitted incestuous marriages when such alliances were not needed? Although the incest taboo might enhance cooperation between families, the need for cooperation does not adequately explain the existence of the incest taboo in all societies; other customs might also promote alliances. Furthermore, the cooperation theory does not explain the sexual aspect of the incest taboo. Societies could conceivably allow incestuous sex and still insist that children marry outside the family.

INBREEDING THEORY

One of the oldest explanations for the incest taboo, the inbreeding theory, focuses on the potentially damaging consequences of inbreeding or marrying within the family. People within the same family are likely to carry the same harmful recessive genes. Inbreeding, then, will tend to produce offspring who are more likely to die early of genetic disorders than are the offspring of unrelated spouses. For many years this theory was rejected because, on the basis of dog-breeding practices, it was thought that inbreeding need not be harmful. The inbreeding practiced to produce prize-winning dogs, however, is not a good guide to whether inbreeding is harmful; dog breeders don't count the runts they cull when they try to breed for success in dog shows. We now have a good deal of evidence, from humans as well as other animals, that the closer the degree of inbreeding, the more harmful the genetic effects.[55]

Genetic mutations occur frequently. Although many pose no harm to the individuals who carry a single recessive gene, matings between two persons who carry the same gene often produce offspring with a harmful or lethal condition. Close blood relatives are much more likely than unrelated individuals to carry the same harmful recessive gene. So if close relatives mate, their offspring have a higher probability than the offspring of nonrelatives of inheriting the harmful trait.

One study compared children produced by familial incest with children of the same mothers produced by nonincestuous unions. About 40 percent of the incestuously produced children had serious abnormalities, compared with about 5 percent of the other children.[56] Matings between other kinds of relatives not as closely related also show harmful, but not as harmful, effects of inbreeding. These results are consistent with inbreeding theory. The likelihood that a child will inherit a double dose of a harmful recessive gene is lower the more distantly the child's parents are related. Also consistent with inbreeding theory is the fact that rates of abnormality are consistently higher in the offspring of uncle-niece marriages (which are allowed in some societies) than in the offspring of cousin marriages; for the offspring of uncle-niece marriages, the likelihood of inheriting a double dose of a

harmful recessive is twice that for the offspring of first cousins.[57]

Although most scholars acknowledge the harmful effects of inbreeding, some question whether people in former days would have deliberately invented or borrowed the incest taboo because they knew that inbreeding was biologically harmful. William Durham's cross-cultural survey suggests that they did. Ethnographers do not always report the perceived consequences of incest, but in 50 percent of the reports Durham found, biological harm to the offspring was mentioned.[58] For example, Raymond Firth reported on the Tikopia, who live on an island in the South Pacific:

> The idea is firmly held that unions of close kin bear with them their own doom, their *mara*. . . . The idea [*mara*] essentially concerns barrenness. . . . The peculiar barrenness of an incestuous union consists not in the absence of children, but in their illness or death, or some other mishap. . . . The idea that the offspring of a marriage between near kin are weakly and likely to die young is stoutly held by these natives and examples are adduced to prove it.[59]

So, if the harm of inbreeding was widely recognized, people may have deliberately invented or borrowed the incest taboo.[60] But whether or not people actually recognized the harmfulness of inbreeding, the demographic consequences of the incest taboo would account for its universality, since reproductive and hence competitive advantages probably accrued to groups practicing the taboo. Thus, although cultural solutions other than the incest taboo might provide the desired effects assumed by the family-disruption theory and the cooperation theory, the incest taboo is the only possible solution to the problem of inbreeding.

As is discussed toward the end of the next section, a society may or may not extend the incest taboo to first cousins. That variation is also predictable from inbreeding theory, which provides additional support for the idea that the incest taboo was invented or borrowed to avoid the harmful consequences of inbreeding.

◆ Whom Should One Marry?

Probably every child in our society knows the story of Cinderella—the poor, downtrodden, but lovely girl who accidentally meets, falls in love with, and eventually marries a prince. It is a charming tale, but as a guide to mate choice in our society it is misleading. The majority of marriages simply do not occur in so free and coincidental a way in any society. In addition to the incest taboo, societies often have rules restricting marriage with other persons, as well as preferences about which other persons are the most desirable mates.

Even in a modern, urbanized society such as ours, where theoretically mate choice is free, people tend to marry within their own class and geographic area. For example,

CURRENT RESEARCH AND ISSUES
The Husband-Wife Relationship: Variation in Love, Intimacy, and Sexual Jealousy

Americans believe that love should be a basis of marriage. Does this ideal characterize most societies? We know the answer to that question: No. In fact, in many places romantic love is believed to be a poor basis for marriage and is strongly discouraged. However, even though romantic love may not be a basis for marriage everywhere, it does occur almost everywhere. A recent cross-cultural survey suggests that about 88 percent of the world's societies show signs of romantic love—accounts of personal longing, love songs or love depicted in folklore, elopement because of affection, and passionate love described by informants quoted in ethnographies. So if love is nearly universal, why is it often discouraged as a basis for marriage?

Three conditions appear to predict such discouragement. One is that the husband and wife live in an extended family. In this situation, the family seems more concerned with how the in-marrying person gets along with others, and less concerned with whether the husband and wife love each other. A second condition predicting the discouragement of romantic love as a basis for marriage is that one of the spouses does most of the primary subsistence work or earns most of the couple's income. Third, romantic love is unlikely when men have more sexual freedom than women. In general, then, romantic love is discouraged as a basis for marriage under conditions of inequality—if one of the spouses is highly dependent on the other or the other's kin or the

woman has fewer sexual rights than the man.

Intimacy is different from romantic love. It refers to how close the married couple are to each other—eating together, sleeping in the same bed, spending their leisure time together, as well as having frequent sex. In some societies couples are together a lot; in others they spend very little time together. Foraging societies seem on average to have more intimacy between couples than more complex herding and agricultural societies, but the reason is not entirely clear. A high involvement in war also seems to detract from intimacy between couples.

When it comes to sexual jealousy, men are far more likely to be violent than women. Anthropologists with a biological orientation

---

studies in the United States consistently indicate that a person is likely to marry someone who lives close by.[61] Neighborhoods are frequently made up of people from similar class backgrounds, so it is unlikely that many of these alliances are Cinderella stories.

ARRANGED MARRIAGES

In an appreciable number of societies, marriages are arranged; negotiations are handled by the immediate families or by go-betweens. Sometimes betrothals are completed while the future partners are still children. This was formerly the custom in much of Hindu India, China, Japan, and eastern and southern Europe. Implicit in the arranged marriage is the conviction that the joining together of two kin groups to form new social and economic ties is too important to be left to free choice and romantic love.

An example of a marriage arranged for reasons of prestige comes from Clellan Ford's study of the Kwakiutl of British Columbia. Ford's informant described his marriage as follows:

> When I was old enough to get a wife—I was about 25—my brothers looked for a girl in the same position that I and my brothers had. Without my consent, they picked a wife for me—Lagius' daughter.

The one I wanted was prettier than the one they chose for me, but she was in a lower position than me, so they wouldn't let me marry her.[62]

In many places arranged marriages are beginning to disappear, and couples are beginning to have more say about their marriage partners. As recently as 1960, marriages were still arranged on the Pacific island of Rotuma, and sometimes the bride and groom did not meet until the wedding day. Today weddings are much the same, but couples are allowed to "go out" and have a say about whom they wish to marry.[63] In a small Moroccan town, arranged marriages are still the norm, although a young man may ask his mother to make a marriage offer to a particular girl's parents, who may ask her whether she wants to accept the marriage offer. But dating is still not acceptable, so getting acquainted is hard to arrange.[64]

EXOGAMY AND ENDOGAMY

Marriage partners often must be chosen from outside one's own kin group or community; this is known as a rule of **exogamy.** Exogamy can take many forms. It may mean marrying outside a particular group of kin or outside a particular village or group of villages. Often, then, spouses come from a distance. For example, in Rani Khera, a village in India, 266 married women had come from about 200

(continued)

point out that fathers always have some uncertainty about whether their children are theirs, so males are much more likely for that reason alone to try to guard against rival males. But how can we account for the considerable variation in jealousy from one society to another? It does seem that the more a society emphasizes the importance of getting married, the more it limits sex to the marriage relationship, the more it emphasizes property, and the more its males appear to exhibit sexual jealousy.

How are these various aspects of marriage related to each other? Does romantic love as a basis for marriage increase or decrease sexual jealousy? Does romantic love predict intimacy, or is romantic love more likely with less frequent contact between the spouses? We are still far from understanding how these different aspects are related. All we know is that an em-

The Valentine, as in this 19th century British card, symbolizes romantic love.

phasis on love and intimacy does not preclude marital violence or marital dissolution.

───

Sources: Lewellyn Hendrix, "Varieties of Marital Relationships," in Carol R. Ember and Melvin Ember, eds., *Cross-Cultural Research for Social Science,* in Carol R. Ember and Melvin Ember, eds., *New Directions in Anthropology* (Upper Saddle River, NJ: Prentice Hall, CD-ROM, 2003); William R. Jankowiak and Edward F. Fischer, "A Cross-Cultural Perspective on Romantic Love," *Ethnology,* 31 (1992): 149–55; Victor C. de Munck and Andrey Korotayev, "Sexual Equality and Romantic Love: A Reanalysis of Rosenblatt's Study on the Function of Romantic Love," *Cross-Cultural Research,* 33 (1999): 265–73.

different villages averaging between 12 and 24 miles away; 220 local women had gone to 200 other villages to marry. As a result of these exogamous marriages, Rani Khera, a village of 150 households, was linked to 400 other nearby villages.[65] When there are rules of exogamy, violations are often believed to cause harm. On the islands of Yap in Micronesia, people who are related through women are referred to as "people of one belly." The elders say that if two people from the same kinship group married, they would not have any female children and the group would die out.[66]

The spouses in some arranged marriages in the state of Madhya Pradesh, India are children.

People in societies with very low population densities often have to travel considerable distances to meet mates. A study of foragers and horticulturalists found a clear relationship between population density and the distance between the communities of the husband and wife—the lower the density, the greater the marriage distance. Because foragers generally have lower densities than horticulturalists, they generally have further to go to find mates. Among the !Kung, for instance, the average husband and wife had lived 65 kilometers (40 miles) from each other before they were married.[67]

A rule of **endogamy** obliges a person to marry within some group. The caste groups of India traditionally have been endogamous. The higher castes believed that marriage with lower castes would "pollute" them, and such unions were forbidden. Caste endogamy is also found in some parts of Africa. In East Africa, a Masai warrior would never stoop to marry the daughter of an ironworker, nor would a former ruling caste Tutsi in Rwanda, in central Africa, think of marrying a person from the hunting caste Twa.

COUSIN MARRIAGES

Kinship terminology for most people in the United States does not differentiate between types of cousins. In some other societies such distinctions may be important, particularly with regard to first cousins; the terms for the different kinds of first cousin may indicate which cousins are suitable marriage partners (sometimes even preferred mates) and which are not. Although most societies prohibit marriage with all types of first cousins,[68] some societies allow and even prefer particular kinds of cousin marriage.

Cross-cousins are children of siblings of the opposite sex; that is, a person's cross-cousins are father's sisters' children and mother's brothers' children. **Parallel cousins** are children of siblings of the same sex; a person's parallel cousins, then, are father's brothers' children and mother's sisters' children. The Chippewa Indians used to practice cross-cousin marriage, as well as cross-cousin joking. With his female cross-cousins, a Chippewa man was expected to exchange broad, risqué jokes, but he would not do so with his parallel cousins, with whom severe propriety was the rule. In general, in any society in which cross-cousin marriage is allowed but parallel-cousin is not, there is a joking relationship between a man and his female cross-cousins. This attitude contrasts with the formal and very respectful relationship the man maintains with female parallel cousins. Apparently, the joking relationship signifies the possibility of marriage, whereas the respectful relationship signifies the extension of the incest taboo to parallel cousins.

When first-cousin marriage is allowed or preferred, it is usually with some kind of cross-cousin. Parallel-cousin marriage is fairly rare, but Muslim societies usually prefer such marriages, allowing other cousin marriages as well. The Kurds, who are mostly Sunni Muslims, prefer a young man to marry his father's brother's daughter (for the young woman this would be her father's brother's son). The father

and his brother usually live near each other, so the woman will stay close to home in such a marriage. The bride and groom are also in the same kin group, so marriage in this case also entails kin group endogamy.[69]

What kinds of societies allow or prefer first-cousin marriage? There is evidence from cross-cultural research that cousin marriages are most apt to be permitted in relatively large and densely populated societies. Perhaps this is because the likelihood of such marriages, and therefore the risks of inbreeding, are minimal in those societies. Many small, sparsely populated societies, however, permit or even sometimes prefer cousin marriage. How can these cases be explained? They seem to cast doubt on the interpretation that cousin marriage should be prohibited in sparsely populated societies, in which marriages between close relatives are more likely just by chance and the risks of inbreeding should be greatest. It turns out that most of the small societies that permit cousin marriage have lost a lot of people to epidemics. Many peoples around the world, particularly in the Pacific and in North and South America, suffered severe depopulation in the first generation or two after contact with Europeans, who introduced diseases (such as measles, pneumonia, and smallpox) to which the native populations had little or no resistance. Such societies may have had to permit cousin marriage in order to provide enough mating possibilities among the reduced population of eligible mates.[70]

LEVIRATE AND SORORATE

In many societies, cultural rules oblige individuals to marry the spouse of deceased relatives. **Levirate** is a custom whereby a man is obliged to marry his brother's widow. **Sororate** obliges a woman to marry her deceased sister's husband. Both customs are exceedingly common, being the obligatory form of second marriage in a majority of societies known to anthropology.[71]

Among the Chukchee of Siberia, levirate obliges the next oldest brother to become the successor husband. He cares for the widow and children, assumes the sexual privileges of the husband, and unites the deceased's reindeer herd with his own, keeping it in the name of his brother's children. If there are no brothers, the widow is married to a cousin of her first husband. The Chukchee regard the custom more as a duty than as a right. The nearest relative is obliged to care for a woman left with children and a herd.[72]

◆ How Many Does One Marry?

We are accustomed to thinking of marriage as involving just one man and one woman at a time—**monogamy**—but most societies known to anthropology have allowed a man to be married to more than one woman at the same time—**polygyny.** At any given time, however, the majority of men in societies permitting polygyny are married monogamously; few or no societies have enough women to permit most men to have at least two wives. Polygyny's mirror image—one woman being married to more than one man at the same time, called **polyandry**—is practiced in very few societies. Polygyny and polyandry are the two types of **polygamy**, or plural marriage. **Group marriage**, in which more than one man is married to more than one woman at the same time, sometimes occurs but is not customary in any known society. The four possible forms of marriage are illustrated in Table 20–1.

POLYGYNY

The Old Testament has many references to men with more than one wife simultaneously: King David and King Solomon are just two examples of men polygynously married. Just as in the society described in the Old Testament, polygyny in many societies is a mark of a man's great wealth or high status. In such societies only the very wealthy can, and are expected to, support more than one wife. Some Muslim societies, especially Arabic-speaking ones, still view polygyny in this light. But a man does not always have to be wealthy to be polygynous; indeed, in some societies in which women are important contributors to the economy, it seems that men try to have more than one wife in order to become wealthier.

Among the Siwai, a society in the South Pacific, status is achieved through feast giving. Pork is the main dish at these feasts, so the Siwai associate pig raising with prestige. This great interest in pigs sparks an interest in wives, because in Siwai society women raise the food needed to raise pigs. Thus, although having many wives does not in itself confer status among the Siwai, the increase in pig herds that may result from polygyny is a source of prestige for the owner.[73]

Polygynously married Siwai men do seem to have greater prestige, but they complain that a household with multiple wives is difficult. Sinu, a Siwai, described his plight:

> There is never peace for a long time in a polygynous family. If the husband sleeps in the house of one wife, the other one sulks all the next day. If the man is so stupid as to sleep two consecutive nights in the house of one wife, the other one will refuse to cook for him, saying, "So-and-so is your wife; go to her for food. Since I am not good enough for you to sleep with, then my food is not good enough for you to eat." Frequently the co-wives will quarrel and fight. My uncle formerly had five wives at one time and the youngest one was always raging and fighting the others. Once she knocked an older wife senseless and then ran away and had to be forcibly returned.[74]

Jealousy between co-wives is reported in many polygynous societies, but it seems not to be present in some. For example, Margaret Mead reported that married life among the Arapesh of New Guinea, even in the polygynous marriages, was "so even and contented that there is nothing to relate of it at all."[75] Why might there be little or no jealousy between co-wives in a society? One possible reason is that a man is married to two or more sisters—**sororal polygyny**; it seems that sisters, having grown up together, are more likely to get along and cooperate as co-wives than are co-wives who are not also sisters—**nonsororal polygyny**. Other customs may also lessen jealousy between co-wives:

1. Co-wives who are not sisters tend to have separate living quarters; sororal co-wives almost always live together. Among the Plateau Tonga in Africa, who practice nonsororal polygyny, the husband shares his personal goods and his favors among his wives, who live in separate dwellings, according to principles of strict equality. The Crow Indians practiced sororal polygyny, and co-wives usually shared a tepee.

2. Co-wives have clearly defined equal rights in matters of sex, economics, and personal possessions. For example, the Tanala of Madagascar require the husband to spend a day with each co-wife in succession. Failure to do so constitutes adultery and entitles the slighted wife to sue for divorce and alimony of up to one-third of the husband's property. Furthermore, the land is shared equally among all the women, who expect the husband to help with its cultivation when he visits them.

3. Senior wives often have special prestige. The Tonga of Polynesia, for example, grant to the first wife the status of "chief wife." Her house is to the right of her husband's and is called "the house of the father." The other wives are called "small wives," and their houses are to the left of the husband's. The chief wife has the right to be consulted before the small wives, and her husband is expected to sleep under her roof before and after a journey. Although this rule might seem to enhance the jealousy of the secondary wives, later wives are usually favored somewhat because they tend to be younger and more attractive. By this custom, then, the first wife may be compensated for her loss of physical attractiveness by increased prestige.[76]

We must remember that, although jealousy is commonly mentioned in polygynous marriages, people who practice polygyny think it has considerable advantages. In a study conducted by Philip and Janet Kilbride in Kenya, female as well as male married people agreed that polygyny

---

Table 20–1 Four Possible Forms of Marriage		
FORM OF MARRIAGE	**MALES**	**FEMALES**
Monogamy	△	= ○
Polygamy		
Polygyny	△	= ○ + ○ +
Polyandry	△ + △ +	= ○
Group marriage	△ + △ +	= ○ + ○ +

△ represents male; ○, female; and =, marriage.

Polygyny is practiced by some in this country, even though it is prohibited by law.

had economic and political advantages. Because they tend to be large, polygynous families provide plenty of farm labor and extra food that can be marketed. They also tend to be influential in their communities and are likely to produce individuals who become government officials.[77] And in South Africa, Connie Anderson found that women choose to be married to a man with other wives because the other wives could help with child care and household work, provide companionship, and allow more freedom to come and go. Some women said they chose polygynous marriages because there was a shortage of marriageable males.[78]

How can we account for the fact that polygyny is allowed and often preferred in most of the societies known to anthropology? Ralph Linton suggested that polygyny derives from a general male primate urge to collect females.[79] But if that were so, then why wouldn't all societies allow polygyny? Other explanations of polygyny have been suggested. We restrict our discussion here to those that statistically and strongly predict polygyny in worldwide samples of societies.

One theory is that polygyny will be permitted in societies that have a long **postpartum sex taboo.**[80] In these societies, a couple must abstain from intercourse until their child is at least a year old. John Whiting suggested that couples abstain from sexual intercourse for a long time after their child is born for health reasons. A Hausa woman reported:

> A mother should not go to her husband while she has a child she is suckling. If she does, the child gets thin; he dries up, he won't be strong, he won't be healthy. If she goes after two years it is nothing, he is already strong before that, it does not matter if she conceives again after two years.[81]

The symptoms the woman described seem to be those of *kwashiorkor.* Common in tropical areas, kwashiorkor is a protein-deficiency disease that occurs particularly in children suffering from intestinal parasites or diarrhea. By observing a long postpartum sex taboo, and thereby ensuring

that her children are widely spaced, a woman can nurse each child longer. If a child gets protein from mother's milk during its first few years, the likelihood of contracting kwashiorkor may be greatly reduced. Consistent with Whiting's interpretation is the fact that societies with low-protein staples (those whose principal foods are root and tree crops such as taro, sweet potatoes, bananas, and breadfruit) tend to have a long postpartum sex taboo. Societies with long postpartum sex taboos also tend to be polygynous. Perhaps, then, a man's having more than one wife is a cultural adjustment to the taboo. As a Yoruba woman said,

> When we abstain from having sexual intercourse with our husband for the two years we nurse our babies, we know he will seek some other woman. We would rather have her under our control as a co-wife so he is not spending money outside the family.[82]

Even if we agree that men will seek other sexual relationships during the period of a long postpartum sex taboo, it is not clear why polygyny is the only possible solution to the problem. After all, it is conceivable that all of a man's wives might be subject to the postpartum sex taboo at the same time. Furthermore, there may be sexual outlets outside marriage.

Another explanation of polygyny is that it is a response to an excess of women over men. Such an imbalanced sex ratio may occur because of the prevalence of warfare in a society. Because men and not women are generally the warriors, warfare almost always takes a greater toll of men's lives. Given that almost all adults in noncommercial societies are married, polygyny may be a way of providing spouses for surplus women. Indeed, there is evidence that societies with imbalanced sex ratios in favor of women tend to have both polygyny and high male mortality in warfare. Conversely, societies with balanced sex ratios tend to have both monogamy and low male mortality in warfare.[83]

A third explanation is that a society will allow polygyny when men marry at an older age than women. The argument is similar to the sex ratio interpretation. Delaying the age of marriage for men would produce an artificial, though not an actual, excess of marriageable women. Why marriage for men is delayed is not clear, but the delay does predict polygyny.[84]

Is one of these explanations better than the others, or are all three factors—long postpartum sex taboo, an imbalanced sex ratio in favor of women, and delayed age of marriage for men—important in explaining polygyny? One way of trying to decide among alternative explanations is to do what is called a *statistical-control analysis,* which allows us to see if a particular factor still predicts when the effects of other possible factors are removed. In this case, when the possible effect of sex ratio is removed, a long postpartum sex taboo no longer predicts polygyny and hence is probably not a cause of polygyny.[85] But both an actual excess of women and a late age of marriage for men seem to be strong predictors of polygyny. Added together, these two factors predict even more strongly.[86]

POLYANDRY

George Peter Murdock's "World Ethnographic Sample" included only four societies (less than 1 percent of the total) in which polyandry, or the marriage of several men to one woman, was practiced.[87] When the husbands are brothers we call it **fraternal polyandry;** if they are not brothers, it is **nonfraternal polyandry.** Some Tibetans, the Toda of India, and the Sinhalese of Sri Lanka have practiced fraternal polyandry. Among the Tibetans who practice fraternal polyandry, biological paternity seems to be of no particular concern; there is no attempt to link children biologically to a particular brother, and all children are treated the same.[88]

One possible explanation for the practice of polyandry is a shortage of women. The Toda practiced female infanticide;[89] the Sinhalese had a shortage of women but denied the practice of female infanticide.[90] A correlation between shortage of women and polyandry would account for why polyandry is so rare in the ethnographic record; an excess of men is rare cross-culturally.

Another possible explanation is that polyandry is an adaptive response to severely limited resources. Melvyn Goldstein studied Tibetans who live in the northwestern corner of Nepal, above 12,000 feet in elevation. Cultivable land is extremely scarce there, with most families having less than an acre. The people say they practice fraternal polyandry in order to prevent the division of a family's farm and animals. Instead of dividing up their land among them and each taking a wife, brothers preserve the family farm by sharing a wife. Although not recognized by the Tibetans, their practice of polyandry minimizes population growth. There are as many women as men of marriageable age. But about 30 percent of the women do not marry, and, although these women do have some children, they have far fewer than married women. Thus, the practice of polyandry minimizes the number of mouths to feed and therefore maximizes the standard of living of the polyandrous family. In contrast, if the Tibetans practiced monogamy and almost all women married, the birth rate would be much higher and there would be more mouths to feed with the severely limited resources.[91]

 CD-ROM Video Activity 2

 # The Family

Although family form varies from one society to another and even within societies, all societies have families. A **family** is a social and economic unit consisting minimally of one or more parents and their children. Members of a family always have certain reciprocal rights and obligations, particularly economic ones. Family members usually live in one household, but common residence is not a defining feature of families. In our society, children may live away while they go to college. Some members of a family may deliberately set up separate households in order to manage multiple business enterprises while maintaining economic unity.[92] In simpler societies, the family and the household tend to be indistinguishable; it is only in more complex societies, and in societies becoming dependent on commercial exchange, that some members of a family may live elsewhere.[93]

The family provides a learning environment for children. Although some animals, such as fish, do take care of themselves after birth or hatching, no mammal is able to care for itself at birth, and a human is exceptional in that he or she is unable to do so until many years later. Since humans mature late biologically, they have few if any inborn or instinctive responses that will simplify adjustment to their surroundings. Consequently, they have to learn a repertoire of beliefs and habits (most of which are cultural) in order to become functioning adults in society. A family cares for and protects children while they acquire the cultural behavior, beliefs, and values necessary for their own, and their society's, survival.

 **CD-ROM Video Activities 3 & 4**

VARIATION IN FAMILY FORM

Most societies have families that are larger than the single-parent family (the parent in such families is usually the mother, in which case the unit is called the **matrifocal family**), the monogamous (single-couple) family (called the **nuclear family**), or the polygamous (usually polygynous) family. The **extended family** is the prevailing form of family in more than half the societies known to anthropology.[94] It may consist of two or more single-parent, monogamous, polygynous, or polyandrous families linked by a blood tie. Most commonly, the extended family consists of a married couple and one or more of the married children, all living in the same house or household. The constituent nuclear families are normally linked through the parent-child tie. An extended family, however, is sometimes composed of families linked through a sibling tie. Such a family might consist of two married brothers, their wives, and their children. Extended families may be very large, containing many relatives and including three or four generations.

EXTENDED-FAMILY HOUSEHOLDS

In a society composed of extended-family households, marriage does not bring as pronounced a change in lifestyle as it does in our culture, where the couple typically moves to a new residence and forms a new, and basically independent, family unit. In extended families, the newlyweds are assimilated into an existing family unit. Margaret Mead described such a situation in Samoa:

> In most marriages there is no sense of setting up a new and separate establishment. The change is felt in the change of residence for either husband or wife and in the reciprocal relations which spring up between the two families. But the young couple live in the main household, simply receiving a bamboo pillow, a mosquito net and a pile of mats for their bed. . . . The wife works with all the women of the household and waits on all the men. The husband shares

CURRENT RESEARCH AND ISSUES
One-Parent Families: Why the Recent Increase?

Not only is the custom of marriage almost universal, but in most societies known to anthropology most people marry. And they usually remarry if they divorce. This means that, except for the death of a spouse or temporarily during times of divorce or separation, one-parent families are relatively uncommon in most societies.

In many Western countries, however, there has been a dramatic increase recently in the percentage of one-parent families, most of which (about 90 percent) are female-headed families. For example, in the 1960s about 9 percent of families in the United States were one-parent families, but in the mid-1980s the figure jumped to about 24 percent. Whereas Sweden once led the Western countries in percentage of one-parent families—about 13 percent in the 1970s—the United States now has the highest percentage.

Before we examine the reasons for the increase, we need to consider that there are a variety of ways to become a one-parent family. First, many one-parent families result from the divorce or separation of two-parent families. Second, many one-parent families result from births out of wedlock. In addition, some result from the death of a spouse and others from the decision by a single person to have a child.

Many researchers suggest that the ease of divorce is largely responsible for the increase in one-parent families. On the face of it, this explanation seems plausible. But it is flawed. In many countries during the late 1960s and early 1970s, changes in the law made getting a divorce much easier, and the percentage of one-parent families did rise after that. But why did so many countries ease divorce restrictions at the same time? Did attitudes about marriage change first? A high divorce rate by itself will make for a higher percentage of one-parent households only if individuals do not remarry quickly. In the United States, for example, remarriage rates did decline sharply in the mid-1960s, particularly among younger, better educated women, and so the percentage of one-parent households may have risen for that reason. In many other countries, divorce rates stabilized in the 1980s, but the percentage of one-parent families still increased. Thus, easier divorce does not fully explain the increase in number of one-parent families.

Although some parents are clearly choosing to stay single, many might prefer to marry if they could find an appropriate spouse. In some countries, and among some ethnic groups within some countries, there are many fewer males than females, and sometimes a high proportion of the males have poor economic prospects. In the former Soviet Union, there are many more women than men because males are more likely to have died from war, alcoholism, and accidents. The United States does not have such a skewed sex ratio, but in some neighborhoods, particularly

the enterprises of the other men and boys. Neither in personal service given or received are the two marked off as a unit.[95]

A young couple in Samoa, as in other societies with extended families, generally has little decision-making power over the governing of the household. Often the responsibility of running the household rests with the senior male. Nor can the new family accumulate its own property and become independent; it is a part of the larger corporate structure:

So the young people bide their time. Eventually, when the old man dies or retires, they will own the homestead, they will run things. When their son grows up and marries, he will create a new subsidiary family, to live with them, work for the greater glory of *their* extended family homestead, and wait for them to die.[96]

The extended family is more likely than the independent nuclear family to perpetuate itself as a social unit. In contrast with the independent nuclear family, which by definition disintegrates with the death of the senior members (the parents), the extended family is always adding junior families (monogamous or polygamous or both), whose members eventually become the senior members when their elders die.

POSSIBLE REASONS FOR EXTENDED-FAMILY HOUSEHOLDS

Why do most societies known to anthropology commonly have extended-family households? Extended-family households are found most frequently in societies with sedentary agricultural economies, so economic factors may play a role in determining household type. M. F. Nimkoff and

(continued)

poor neighborhoods, there are very high mortality rates for young males. And many males in such neighborhoods do not have work. One study by Daniel Lichter and his colleagues estimated that for every 100 African American women between the ages of 21 and 28, there were fewer than 80 available African American men. If we count only men who are employed full or part time, the number of available men per 100 women drops below 50. So there may be considerable merit to the argument that one-parent families (usually headed by women) will be likely when a spouse (particularly an employed one) is hard to find.

Another popular explanation for the rise in number of one-parent families is that, in contrast to the past, women can manage without husbands because of support from the state. This scenario seems to fit Sweden, where unmarried and divorced mothers receive many social supports and allowances for maternity and educational leave. But Iceland has few social supports from the government and yet has the highest rate of out-of-wedlock births of all the Scandinavian countries. In the United States, the welfare argument fails to predict changes over time. The program called Aid to Families with Dependent Children provided aid largely to single mothers. If the theory about government help were correct, increases in such aid would generally predict increases in the percentage of mother-headed households. But, in fact, during the 1970s the percentage of families receiving aid and the value of aid decreased, while the percentage of mother-headed households increased. In the 1980s it was more difficult to go "on welfare," but the percentage of mother-headed households increased anyway.

Women might be more able to manage alone if they have high-paying employment, and therefore we might expect more one-parent families by choice, as more women enter the job market. But, although this may explain the choices of some women, recent research finds that employed women generally are *more* rather than less likely to marry.

In any case, there seems to be a general association between commercial economies and the possibility of one-parent families. Is there something about subsistence economies that promotes marriage and something about commercial economies that detracts from it? Although marriage is not universally based on love or companionship, it entails a great deal of economic and other kinds of interdependence, particularly in not-so-commercial economies. Market economies allow other possibilities; goods and services can be bought and sold, and governments may take over functions normally handled by kin and family. So the one-parent family is likely to remain an option—either a choice or a necessity—for some people.

Sources: Alisa Burns and Cath Scott, *Mother-Headed Families and Why They Have Increased* (Hillsdale, NJ: Lawrence Erlbaum Associates, 1994); David Popenoe, *Disturbing the Nest: Family Change and Decline in Modern Societies* (New York: Aldine, 1988); Daniel T. Lichter, Diane K. McLaughlin, George Kephart, and David J. Landry, "Race and the Retreat from Marriage: A Shortage of Marriageable Men?" *American Sociological Review*, 57 (1992): 781–99.

Russell Middleton suggested how agricultural life, as opposed to hunting-gathering life, may favor extended families among agriculturalists. The extended family may be a social mechanism that prevents the economically ruinous division of family property in societies in which property such as cultivated land is important. Conversely, the need for mobility in hunter-gatherer societies may make it difficult to maintain extended-family households. During certain seasons, the hunter-gatherers may be obliged to divide into nuclear families that scatter into other areas.[97]

But agriculture is only a weak predictor of extended-family households. Many agriculturalists lack them, and many nonagricultural societies have them. A different theory is that extended-family households come to prevail in societies that have incompatible activity requirements—that is, requirements that cannot be met by a mother or a father in a one-family household. In other words, extended-family households are generally favored when the work a mother has to do outside the home (cultivating fields or gathering foods far away) makes it difficult for her also to care for her children and do other household tasks. Similarly, extended families may be favored when the required outside activities of a father (warfare, trading trips, or wage labor far away) make it difficult for him to do the subsistence work required of males. There is cross-cultural evidence that societies with such incompatible activity requirements are more likely to have extended-family households than societies with compatible activity requirements, regardless of whether or not the society is agricultural. Even though they have incompatible activity requirements, however, societies with commercial or monetary exchange may not have extended-family households. In commercial societies, a family may be able to obtain the necessary help by "buying" the required services.[98]

Of course, even in societies with money economies, not everyone can buy required services. Those who are poor

Three generations of a Chinese American family celebrate a grandchild's first birthday

may need to live in extended families, and extended-family living may become more common even in the middle class when the economy is depressed. As a popular magazine noted,

> Whatever happened to the all-American nuclear family—Mom, Pop, two kids and a cuddly dog, nestled under one cozy, mortgaged roof? What happened was an economic squeeze: layoffs, fewer jobs for young people, more working mothers, a shortage of affordable housing and a high cost of living. Those factors, along with a rising divorce rate, a trend toward later marriages and an increase in the over sixty-five population, all hitting at once, are forcing thousands of Americans into living in multigenerational families.[99]

In many societies there are kin groups even larger than extended families. The next chapter discusses the varieties of such groupings.

 CD-ROM Flashcards Chapter 20

 # Summary

1. All societies known today have the custom of marriage. Marriage is a socially approved sexual and economic union usually between a man and a woman that is presumed to be more or less permanent and that subsumes reciprocal rights and obligations between the two spouses and between the spouses and their children.

2. The way marriage is socially recognized varies greatly; it may involve an elaborate ceremony or none at all. Variations include childhood betrothals, trial-marriage periods, feasting, and the birth of a baby.

3. Marriage arrangements often include an economic element. The most common form is the bride price, in which the groom or his family gives an agreed-upon amount of money or goods to the bride's family. Bride service exists when the groom works for the bride's family for a specified period. In some societies, a female from the groom's family is exchanged for the bride; in others, gifts are exchanged between the two families. A dowry is a payment of goods or money by the bride's family, usually to the bride. Indirect dowry is provided by the groom's family to the bride, sometimes through the bride's father.

4. No society in recent times has allowed sex or marriage between brothers and sisters, mothers and sons, or fathers and daughters.

5. Every society tells people whom they cannot marry, whom they can marry, and sometimes even whom they should marry. In quite a few societies, marriages are arranged by the couple's kin groups. Implicit in arranged marriages is the conviction that the joining of two kin groups to form new social and economic ties is too important to be left to free choice and romantic love. Some societies have rules of exogamy, which require marriage outside one's own kin group or community; others have rules of endogamy, requiring marriage within one's group. Although most societies prohibit all first-cousin marriages, some permit or prefer marriage with cross-cousins (children of siblings of the opposite sex) and parallel cousins (children of siblings of the same sex). Many societies have customs providing for the remarriage of widowed persons. Levirate is a custom whereby a man marries his brother's widow. Sororate is the practice whereby a woman marries her deceased sister's husband.

6. We think of marriage as involving just one man and one woman at a time (monogamy), but most societies allow a man to be married to more than one woman at a time (polygyny). Polyandry, the marriage of one woman to several husbands, is rare.

7. The prevailing form of family in most societies is the extended family. It consists of two or more single-parent, monogamous (nuclear), polygynous, or polyandrous families linked by blood ties.

Glossary Terms

berdache

bride price (or bride wealth)

bride service

cross-cousins

dowry

endogamy

exogamy

extended family

family

fraternal polyandry

group marriage

incest taboo

indirect dowry

levirate

marriage

matrifocal family

monogamy

nonfraternal polyandry

nonsororal polygyny

nuclear family

parallel cousins

polyandry

polygamy

polygyny

postpartum sex taboo

sororal polygyny

sororate

Critical Questions

1. Will it remain customary in our society to marry? Why do you think it will or will not?
2. Do you think extended-family households will become more common in our society? Why?
3. Why is polyandry so much less common than polygyny?

Internet Exercises

1. Go to http://www.census.gov/apsd/www/statbrief/ and read at least one article on child care in the United States. How might child care in the United States be different if people mostly lived in extended-family households?

2. Explore marriage patterns in one of the ethnographic examples given in the Kinship and Social Organization tutorial at http://www.umanitoba.ca/faculties/arts/anthropology/tutor/.

3. In the pamphlet *A Basic Guide to Cross-Cultural Research* (http://www.yale.edu/hraf/basiccc.html) read about how extended-family households might be measured in a cross-cultural study. You can start with "Measures." If you don't understand some of the concepts, back up to the section "What's the Question?"

Suggested Reading

EMBER, M., AND EMBER, C. R. *Marriage, Family, and Kinship: Comparative Studies of Social Organization.* New Haven, CT: HRAF Press, 1983. A collection of reprinted cross-cultural and cross-species studies testing possible explanations for some aspects of human social organization. Relevant to this chapter are the studies of male-female bonding, the incest taboo, polygyny, and the extended family.

HENDRIX, L. "Varieties of Marital Relationships." In C. R. Ember and M. Ember, eds., *Cross-Cultural Research for Social Science,* in C. R. Ember and M. Ember, eds., *New Directions in Anthropology.* Upper Saddle River, NJ: Prentice Hall, CD-ROM, 2003. A recent review of what is known cross-culturally about love, intimacy, jealousy, violence, and fear of sex within the marital relationship, as well as the conditions under which divorce rates are high.

MURDOCK, G. P. *Social Structure.* New York: Macmillan, 1949. A classic cross-cultural analysis of variation in social organization. Chapters 1, 2, 9, and 10—on the nuclear family, composite forms of the family, the regulation of sex, and incest taboos and their extensions—are particularly relevant.

PASTERNAK, B. "Family and Household: Who Lives Where, Why Does It Vary, and Why Is It Important?" In C. R. Ember and M. Ember, eds., *Cross-Cultural Research for Social Science,* in C. R. Ember and M. Ember, eds., *New Directions in Anthropology.* Upper Saddle River, NJ: Prentice Hall, CD-ROM, 2003.

PASTERNAK, B., EMBER, C. R., AND EMBER, M. *Sex, Gender and Kinship: A Cross-Cultural Perspective.* Upper Saddle River, NJ: Prentice Hall, 1997. A review and discussion of cross-cultural studies of sex, gender, marriage, family, and kinship. See particularly Chapters 4–9 and 11.

POLITICAL LIFE: SOCIAL ORDER AND DISORDER

CHAPTER OUTLINE

For people in the United States, the phrase *political life* has many connotations. It may call to mind the various branches of government: the executive branch, from the president on the national level to governors on the state level to mayors on the local level; legislative institutions, from Congress to state legislatures to city councils; and administrative bureaus, from federal government departments to local agencies.

Political life may also evoke thoughts of political parties, interest groups, lobbying, campaigning, and voting. In other words, when people living in the United States think of political life, they may think first of "politics," the activities (not always apparent) that influence who is elected or appointed to political office, what public policies are established, how they get established, and who benefits from those policies.

But in the United States and in many other countries, *political life* involves even more than government and politics. Political life also involves ways of preventing or resolving troubles and disputes both within and outside the society. Internally, a complex society such as ours may employ mediation or arbitration to resolve industrial disputes, a police force to prevent crimes or track down criminals, and courts and a penal system to deal with lawbreakers as well as with social conflict in general. Externally, such a society may establish embassies in other nations and develop and utilize its armed forces both to maintain security and to support domestic and foreign interests.

By means of all these informal and formal political mechanisms, complex societies establish social order and minimize, or at least deal with, social disorder.

Formal governments have become more and more widespread around the world over the last 100 years, as powerful colonizing countries have imposed political systems upon others or as people less formally organized realized that they needed governmental mechanisms to deal with the larger world. But many societies known to anthropology did not have political officials or political parties or courts or armies. Indeed, the band or village was the largest autonomous political unit in 50 percent of the societies in the ethnographic record, as of the times they were first described. And those units were only informally organized; that is, they did not have individuals or aencies formally authorized to make and implement policy or resolve disputes. Does this mean they did not have political life? If we mean political life as we know it in our own society, then the answer has to be that they did not. But if we look beyond our formal institutions and mechanisms—if we ask what functions these institutions and mechanisms perform—we find that all societies have had political activities and beliefs to create and maintain social order and cope with social disorder.

Many of the kinds of groups we discussed in the three previous chapters, on families, descent groups, and associations, have political functions. But when anthropologists talk about *political organization* or *political life*, they are particularly focusing on activities and beliefs pertaining to *territorial groups*. Territorial groups, in whose behalf political activities may be organized, range from small communities, such as bands and villages, to large communities, such as towns and cities, to multilocal groups, such as districts or regions, entire nations, or even groups of nations.

As we shall see, the different types of political organization, as well as how people participate in politics and how they cope with conflict, are often strongly linked to variation in food-getting, economy, and social stratification.

◆ Variation in Types of Political Organization

Societies in the ethnographic record vary in *level of political integration*—that is, the largest territorial group on whose behalf political activities are organized—and in the degree to which political authority is centralized or concentrated in the integrated group. When we describe the political integration of particular societies, we focus on their traditional political systems. In many societies known to anthropology, the small community (band or village) was traditionally the largest territorial group on whose behalf political activities were organized. The authority structure in such societies did not involve any centralization; there was no political authority whose jurisdiction included more than one community. In other societies political activities were traditionally organized sometimes on behalf of a multilocal group, but there was no permanent authority at the top. And in still other societies political activities were often traditionally organized on behalf of multilocal territorial groups, and there was a centralized or supreme political authority at the top. In the modern world, however, every society has been incorporated into some larger, centralized political system.

Elman Service suggested that most societies can be classified into four principal types of political organization: bands, tribes, chiefdoms, and states.[1] Although Service's classification does not fit all societies, it is a useful way to show how societies vary in trying to create and maintain social order. We often use the present tense in our discussion, because that is the convention in ethnographic writing, but the reader should remember that most societies that used to be organized at the band, tribe, or chiefdom level are now incorporated into larger political entities. With a handful of exceptions, there are no politically autonomous bands or tribes or chiefdoms in the world any more.

BAND ORGANIZATION

Some societies were composed of fairly small and usually nomadic groups of people. Each of these groups is conventionally called a **band** and is politically autonomous. That is, in **band organization** the local group or community is the largest group that acts as a political unit. Because most recent food collectors had band organization, some anthropologists contend that this type of political organization characterized nearly all societies before the development of agriculture, or until about 10,000 years ago. But we have to remember that almost all of the described food-collecting societies are or were located in marginal environments; and almost all were affected by more dominant societies nearby.[2] So it is possible that what we call "band organization" may not have been typical of food collectors in the distant or prehistoric past.

Bands are typically small, with less than 100 people usually, often considerably less. Each small band occupies a large territory, so population density is low. Band size often varies by season, with the band breaking up or recombining according to the food resources available at a given time and place. Inuit bands, for example, are smaller in the winter, when food is hard to find, and larger in the summer, when there is sufficient food to feed a larger group.

Political decision making within the band is generally informal. The "modest informal authority"[3] that does exist can be seen in the way decisions affecting the group are made. Because the formal, permanent office of leader typically does not exist, decisions such as when camp has to be moved or how a hunt is to be arranged are either agreed upon by the community as a whole or made by the best-qualified member. Leadership, when it is exercised by an individual, is not the consequence of bossing or throwing one's weight about. Each band may have its informal **headman**, or its most proficient hunter, or a person most accomplished in rituals. There may be one person with all these qualities, or several persons, but such a person or persons will have gained status through the community's recognition of skill, good sense, and humility. Leadership, in other words, stems not from power but from influence, not from office but from admired personal qualities.

In Inuit bands, each settlement may have its headman, who acquires his influence because the other members of the community recognize his good judgment and superior skills. The headman's advice concerning the movement of the band and other community matters is generally heeded, but he possesses no permanent authority and has no power to impose sanctions of any kind. Inuit leaders are male, but men often consult their wives in private, and women who hunt seem to have more influence than those who do not.[4] In any case, leadership exists only in a very restricted sense, as among the Iglulik Inuit, for example:

> Within each settlement . . . there is as a rule an older man who enjoys the respect of the others and who decides when a move is to be made to another hunting center, when a hunt is to be started, how the spoils are to be divided, when the dogs are to be fed . . . He is called *isumaitoq*, "he who thinks." It is not always the oldest man, but as a rule an elderly man who is a clever hunter or, as head of a large family, exercises great authority. He cannot be called a chief; there is no obligation to follow his counsel; but they do so in most cases, partly because they rely on his experience, partly because it pays to be on good terms with this man.[5]

A summary of the general features of band organization can be found in Table 23–1. Note, however, that there are exceptions to these generalizations. For example, not all known food collectors are organized at the band level or have all the features of a band type of society. Classic exceptions are the Native American societies of the Northwest Pacific coast, who had enormous resources of salmon and other fish, relatively large and permanent villages, and political organization beyond the level of the typical band societies in the ethnographic record.

 CD-ROM Activity III-m

TRIBAL ORGANIZATION

When local communities mostly act autonomously but there are kinship groups (such as clans or lineages) or associations (such as age-sets) that can potentially integrate several local groups into a larger unit (**tribe**), we say that the society has **tribal organization**. Unfortunately, the term *tribe* is sometimes used to refer to an entire society; that is, an entire language group may be called a tribe. But a tribal type of political system does not usually permit the entire society to act as a unit; all the communities in a tribal society may be linked only occasionally for some political (usually military) purpose. Thus, what distinguishes tribal from band political organization is the presence in the former of some multilocal, but not usually societywide, integration. The multilocal integration, however, is *not permanent*, and it is *informal* in the sense that it is not headed by political officials. Frequently, the integration is called into play only when an outside threat arises; when the threat disappears, the local groups revert to self-sufficiency.[6] Tribal organization may seem fragile—and, of course, it usually is—but the fact that there are social ways to integrate local groups into larger political entities means that societies with tribal organization are militarily a good deal more formidable than societies with band organization.

Societies with tribal political organization are similar to band societies in their tendency to be egalitarian (see Table 23–1). At the local level, informal leadership is also characteristic. In those tribal societies where kinship provides the basic framework of social organization, the elders of the local kin groups tend to have considerable influence; where age-sets are important, a particular age-set is looked to for leadership. But, in contrast to band societies, societies with tribal organization generally are food producers. And because cultivation and animal husbandry are generally more productive than hunting and gathering, the population density of tribal societies is generally higher, local groups are larger, and the way of life is more sedentary than in hunter-gatherer bands.

KINSHIP BONDS Frequently communities are linked to each other by virtue of belonging to the same kin group, usually a unilineal group such as a lineage or clan. A **segmentary lineage system** is one type of tribal integration based on kinship. A society with such a system is composed of segments, or parts, each similar to the others in structure and function. Every local segment belongs to a hierarchy of lineages stretching farther and farther back ge-

Table 23–1 Suggested Trends in Political Organization and Other Social Characteristics

TYPE OF ORGANIZATION	HIGHEST LEVEL OF POLITICAL INTEGRATION	SPECIALIZATION OF POLITICAL OFFICIALS	PREDOMINANT MODE OF SUBSISTENCE	COMMUNITY SIZE AND POPULATION DENSITY	SOCIAL DIFFERENTATION	MAJOR FORM OF DISTRIBUTION
Band	Local group or band	Little or none: informal leadership	Food collecting	Very small communities, very low density	Egalitarian	Mostly reciprocity
Tribe	Sometimes multilocal group	Little or none: informal leadership	Extensive (shifting) agriculture and/or herding	Small communities, low density	Egalitarian	Mostly reciprocity
Chiefdom	Multilocal group	Some	Extensive or intensive agriculture and/or herding	Large communities, medium density	Rank	Reciprocity and redistribution
State	Multilocal group, often entire, language group	Much	Intensive agriculture and herding	Cities and towns, high density	Class and caste	Mostly market exchange

167

In many egalitarian societies, leadership shifts informally from one person to another. In much of New Guinea there is more competition for achieving "big" status. On Vanatinai the women compete as well as the men, so there are "big women" as well as "big men." Here a "big woman" paints the face of her cousin's widow for a feast honoring the dead man.

nealogically. The hierarchy of lineages, then, unites the segments into larger and larger genealogical groups. The closer two groups are genealogically, the greater their general closeness. In the event of a dispute between members of different segments, people related more closely to one contestant than to another take the side of their nearest kinsman.

The Tiv of northern Nigeria offer a classic example of a segmentary lineage system, one that happens to link all the Tiv into a single genealogical structure or tribe. The Tiv are a large society, numbering more than 800,000. Figure 23–1 is a representation of the Tiv lineage structure as described by Paul Bohannan. In the figure, there are four levels of lineages. Each of the smallest lineages, symbolized by *a* through *h*, is in turn embedded in more inclusive lineages. So minimal lineages *a* and *b* are together in lineage *1*. Lineages *1* and *2* are embedded in lineage *A*. Territorial organization follows lineage hierarchy. As shown in the bottom of the figure, the most closely related lineages have territories near each other. Minimal lineages *a* and *b* live next to each other; their combined territory is the territory of their higher-order lineage, *1*. Lineage *A* in turn has a territory that is differentiated from lineage *B*. All of Tivland is said to descend from one ancestor, represented by *I*.[7]

Tiv lineage organization is the foundation of Tiv political organization. A look at Figure 23–1 helps to explain how. A dispute between lineages (and territories) *a* and *b*

remains minor, since no more than "brother" segments are involved. But a dispute between *a* and *c* involves lineages *1* and *2* as well, with the requirement that *b* assist *a* and *d* support *c*. This process of mutual support, called **complementary opposition**, means that segments will unite only in a confrontation with some other group. Groups that will fight with each other in a minor dispute might coalesce at some later time against a larger group.

The segmentary lineage system was presumably very effective in allowing the Tiv to intrude into new territory and take land from other tribal societies with smaller descent groups. Individual Tiv lineage segments could call on support from related lineages when faced with border troubles. Conflicts within the society—that is, between segments—especially in border areas, were often turned outward, "releasing internal pressure in an explosive blast against other peoples."[8]

Segmentary lineage systems may have military advantages even when they do not unite the entire society. A classic example is the Nuer of the Upper Nile region, who had tribal, but not societywide, organization because of their segmentary lineages. In the early 1800s, the Nuer had a territory of about 8,700 square miles and the neighboring Dinka had ten times that much. But by 1890, the Nuer had cut a 100-mile swath through Dinka territory, increasing

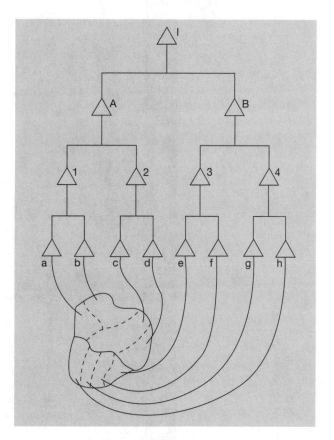

Figure 23–1 *Tiv Lineage Segments and Their Territories*

Source: Adapted from Paul Bohannan, "The Migration and Expansion of the Tiv," *Africa*, 24 (1954):3.

Nuer territory to 35,000 square miles. Even though the Nuer and Dinka were culturally very similar, the segmentary lineage organization of the Nuer seems to have given them a significant military advantage in their incursions into Dinka territory.[9]

A segmentary lineage system may generate a formidable military force, but the combinations of manpower it produces are temporary, forming and dissolving as the occasion demands.[10] Tribal political organization does not make for a political system that more or less permanently integrates a number of communities.

AGE-SET SYSTEMS   In the previous chapter we described age-set systems in general. Here we discuss how age-sets can function as the basis of a tribal type of political organization, as among the Karimojong of northeastern Uganda.[11]

The Karimojong age-set system has an important bearing on day-to-day tribal life. As herders, Karimojong adults are often separated from their usual settlements. Herders will meet, mingle for a while, then go their separate ways, but each may call upon other members of his age-set wherever he goes. The age-set system is important among the Karimojong because it immediately allocates to each individual a place in the system and thereby establishes for him an appropriate pattern of response. A quarrel in camp will be settled by the representatives of the senior age-set who are present, regardless of which section of the tribe they may belong to.

Among the Karimojong, political leaders are not elected from among the elders of a particular age-set, nor are they appointed; they acquire their positions informally. Usually a man's background, and the ability he has demonstrated in public debates over a period of time, will result in his being considered by the men of his neighborhood to be their spokesman. His function is to announce what course of action seems required in a particular situation, to initiate that action, and then to coordinate it after it has begun.

Most political leaders exercise their authority within the local sphere because the pastoral nature of the Karimojong economy, with its dispersed groups and movement from one feeding ground to another, offers no alternative. From time to time an elder may acquire the status of a prophet and be awarded respect and obedience on a tribal scale. He will be called upon to lead sacrifices (to avert misfortune), to undertake rainmaking (to bring prosperity), and so on. Yet even a prophet's prestige and authority do not warrant him a position of overlord or chief.[12]

CHIEFDOM ORGANIZATION

Whereas a tribe has some informal mechanism that can integrate more than one community, a **chiefdom** has some *formal* structure that integrates more than one community into a political unit. The formal structure could consist of a council with or without a *chief*, but most commonly there is a person—the **chief**—who has higher rank or authority than others. Most societies at the chiefdom level of organization contain more than one multicommunity political

unit or chiefdom, each headed by a district chief or a council. There may also be more than one level of chief beyond the community, such as district chiefs and higher-level chiefs. Compared with tribal societies, societies with chiefdoms are more densely populated and their communities more permanent, partly as a consequence of their generally greater economic productivity (see Table 23–1).

The position of chief, which is sometimes hereditary and generally permanent, bestows high status on its holder. Most chiefdoms have social ranking and accord the chief and his family greater access to prestige. The chief may redistribute goods, plan and direct the use of public labor, supervise religious ceremonies, and direct military activities on behalf of the chiefdom. In South Pacific chiefdoms, the chiefs carried out most of these duties. In Fijian chiefdoms, for example, the chief was responsible for the redistribution of goods and the coordination of labor:

> [The chief] could summon the community's labor on his own behalf, or on behalf of someone else who requested it, or for general purposes. . . . Besides his right to summon labor he accumulated the greater proportion of the first fruits of the yam crop . . . and he benefited from other forms of food presentation, or by the acquisition of special shares in ordinary village distribution. . . . Thus, the paramount [chief] would collect a significant part of the surplus production of the community and redistribute it in the general welfare.[13]

In contrast to leaders in tribal societies, who generally have to earn their privileges by their personal qualities, hereditary chiefs are said to have those qualities in their "blood." A high-ranking chief in Polynesia, that huge triangular area of islands in the South Pacific, inherited special religious power called *mana*. *Mana* sanctified his rule and protected him.[14] Chiefs in Polynesia had so much religious power that the missionaries could convert people to Christianity only after their chiefs had been converted.[15]

In most chiefdoms, the chiefs did not have the power to compel people to obey them; people would act in accordance with the chief's wishes because the chief was respected and often had religious authority. But in the most complex paramount chiefdoms, such as those of Hawaii and Tahiti, the chiefs seemed to have more compelling sanctions than the "power" of respect or *mana*. Substantial amounts of goods and services collected by the chiefs were used to support subordinates, including specialists, such as high priests, political envoys, and warriors who could be sent to quell rebellious factions.[16] When redistributions do not go to everybody—when chiefs are allowed to keep items for their own purposes—and when a chief begins to use armed force, the political system is on the way to becoming what we call a state.

STATE ORGANIZATION

A **state**, according to one more or less standard definition, is "an autonomous political unit, encompassing many communities within its territory and having a centralized

Presenting *kava,* a special drink, to a chief in Fiji.

government with the power to collect taxes, draft men for work or war, and decree and enforce laws."[17] States, then, have a complex, centralized political structure that includes a wide range of permanent institutions with legislative, executive, and judicial functions and a large bureaucracy. Central to this definition is the concept of legitimate force used to implement policies both internally and externally. In states, the government tries to maintain a monopoly on the use of physical force.[18] This monopoly can be seen in the development of formal and specialized instruments of social control: a police force, a militia, a standing army.

Just as a particular society may contain more than one band, tribe, or chiefdom, so may it contain more than one state. The contiguously distributed population speaking a single language may or may not be politically unified in a single state. Ancient Greece was composed of many city-states; so, too, was Italy until the 1870s. German speakers are also not politically unified; Austria and Germany are separate states, and Germany itself was not politically unified until the 1870s. We say that a society has **state organization** when it is composed of one or more political units that are states.

A state may include more than one society. Multisociety states often are the result of conquest or colonial control when the dominant political authority, itself a state, imposes a centralized government over a territory with many different societies and cultures, as the British did in Nigeria and Kenya. Nearly all of the multisociety states that emerged after World War II were the results of successful independence movements against colonial powers.[19] Most have retained their political unity despite the fact that they contain many different societies. For example, Nigeria remains unified despite a civil war; the eastern section called Biafra (mostly populated by people of Ibo culture) tried unsuccessfully 35 years ago to secede, and subsequently there has been serious conflict among some of the constituent societies. Multisociety or multiethnic states may also form voluntarily, in reaction to external threat. Switzerland comprises cantons, each of which speaks mainly French, German, Italian, or Romansch; the various cantons confederated originally to shake off control by the Holy Roman Empire. But some states have lost their unity recently, including the former Union of Soviet Socialist Republics (USSR) and much of Yugoslavia.

In addition to their strictly political features, state-organized societies are generally supported by intensive agriculture. The high productivity of the agriculture allows for the emergence of cities, a high degree of economic and other kinds of specialization, and market or commercial exchange. In addition, state societies usually have class stratification (see Table 23–1).

When states come into existence, people's access to scarce resources is radically altered. So, too, is their ability to not listen to leaders: You cannot refuse to pay taxes and go unpunished. Of course, the rulers of a state do not maintain the social order by force alone. The people must believe, at least to some extent, that those in power have a legitimate right to govern. If the people think otherwise, history suggests that those in power may eventually lose their ability to control. Witness the recent downfall of Communist parties throughout most of Eastern Europe and the former Soviet Union.

So force and the threat of force are not enough to explain the legitimacy of power, and the inequities that occur

All governments, even state societies, ultimately depend on the people's sense of legitimacy. This toppled statue of Lenin symbolizes the breakup of the Soviet Union and the overthrow of the Communist party.

commonly, in state societies. But then what does? There are various theories. The rulers of early states often claimed divine descent to buttress their legitimacy, but this claim is rare nowadays. Another theory is that if parents teach their children to accept all authority, such lessons may generalize to the acceptance of political authority. Some analysts think that people accept state authority for no good reason; the rulers are just able to fool them. Finally, some theorists think that states must provide people with real or rational advantages; otherwise people would not think that the rulers deserve to exercise authority. Legitimacy is not an all-or-none phenomenon; it varies in degree. Why it has varied, in different times and places, remains a classic question in the social sciences, including anthropology, as well as in philosophy and other humanistic disciplines.[20]

A state society can retain its legitimacy, or at least its power, for a long time. For example, the Roman Empire was a complex state society that dominated the Mediterranean and Near East for hundreds of years. It began as a city-state that waged war to acquire additional territory. At its height, the Roman Empire embraced more than 55 million people;[21] the capital city of Rome had a population of well over a million.[22] The empire included parts of what are now Great Britain, France, Spain, Portugal, Germany, Rumania, Turkey, Greece, Armenia, Egypt, Israel, and Syria.

Another example of a state society was the kingdom of Nupe in West Africa, now part of the nation-state of Nigeria. As is characteristic of state societies, Nupe society was rigidly stratified. At the top of the social system was the king, or *etsu*. Beneath the king, members of the royal family formed the highest aristocratic class. Next in order were two other classes of nobility, the local chiefs and the military leaders. At the bottom were the commoners, who had neither prestige nor power and no share in political authority.

The Nupe king possessed ultimate authority in many judicial matters. Minor disputes and civil cases were handled by local village councils, but serious criminal cases were the prerogative of the king. Such cases, referred to as "crimes for the king," were brought before the royal court by the king's local representatives. The king and his counselors judged the cases and determined suitable punishments.

The most powerful influence of the state over the Nupe people was in the area of taxation. The king was given the power to impose taxes and collect them from every household. Payment was made either in money (cowrie shells originally and, later, British currency) or certain gifts, such as cloth, mats, and slaves. Much of the revenue collected was kept by the king, and the remainder was shared with his local representatives and lords. In return for the taxes they paid, the people received security—protection against invasion and domestic disorder.[23]

FACTORS ASSOCIATED WITH VARIATION IN POLITICAL ORGANIZATION

The kinds of political organization we call band, tribal, chiefdom, and state are points on a continuum of levels of political integration or unification, from small-scale local autonomy to large-scale regional unification. There also is variation in political authority, from a few temporary and informal political leaders to large numbers of permanent, specialized political officials, from the absence of coercive political power to the monopoly of public force by a central authority. These aspects of variation in political organization are generally associated with shifts from food collection to more intensive food production, from small to large communities, from low to high population densities, from an emphasis on reciprocity to redistribution to market exchange, and from egalitarian to rank to fully stratified class societies.

The associations just outlined, which seem to be confirmed by the available cross-cultural evidence, are summarized in Table 23–1. With regard to the relation between level of subsistence technology and political complexity, one cross-cultural study employing a small random sample of societies found that the greater the importance of agriculture in a society, the larger the population that is politically unified and the greater the number and types of political officials.[24] A massive cross-cultural survey reported a similar trend: The more intensive the agriculture, the greater the likelihood of state organization; conversely, societies with no more than local political institutions are likely to depend on hunting, gathering, and fishing.[25]

With regard to community size, the first of these studies also suggested that the larger the leading community, the wider the range of political officials in the society.[26] Robert Textor presented a similar finding: Societies with state organization tend to have cities and towns, whereas those with only local political organization are more likely to have communities with an average population of fewer than 200 persons.[27] Cross-cultural research also tends to confirm that societies with higher levels of political integration are more likely to exhibit social differentiation, especially in the form of class distinctions.[28]

Does this evidence provide us with an explanation for why political organization varies? Clearly, the data indicate that several factors are associated with political development, but exactly why changes in organization occur is not yet understood. Although economic development may be a necessary condition for political development,[29] that relation does not fully explain why political organization should become more complex just because the economy can support it. Some theorists have suggested that competition between groups may be a more important reason for political consolidation. For example, Elman Service suggested competition as a reason why a society might change from a band level of political organization to a tribal level. Band societies are generally hunter-gatherers. With a changeover to agriculture, population density and competition between groups may increase. Service believed that such competition would foster the development of some informal organization beyond the community—namely, tribal organization—for offense and defense.[30] Indeed, as we saw in the chapters on residence and kinship and associations, both unilineal kinship groups and age-set systems seem to be associated with warfare.

Among agriculturalists, defensive needs might also be the main reason for switching from informal multivillage political organization to more formal chiefdom organization. Formally organized districts are probably more likely to defeat autonomous villages or even segmentary lineage systems.[31] In addition, there may be economic reasons for political development. With regard to chiefdoms, Service suggested that chiefdoms will emerge when redistribution between communities becomes important or when large-scale coordinated work groups are required. The more im-

portant these activities are, the more important—and hence more "chiefly"—the organizer and his family presumably become.[32] But redistribution is far from a universal activity of chiefs.[33]

Theory and research on the anthropology of political development have focused mostly on the high end of the scale of political complexity, and particularly on the origins of the first state societies. Those earliest states apparently rose independently of one another, after about 3500 B.C., in what are now southern Iraq, Egypt, northwestern India, northern China, and central Mexico. As we discussed in the chapter on the origins of cities and states, several theories have been proposed to explain the rise of the earliest states, but no one theory seems to fit all the known archaeological sequences culminating in early state formation. The reason may be that different conditions in different places favored the emergence of centralized government. The state, by definition, implies the power to organize large populations for collective purposes. In some areas, the impetus may have been the need to organize necessary local or long-distance trade or both. In other areas, the state may have emerged as a way to control defeated populations that could not flee. In still other instances, other factors or a combination of factors may have fostered the development of states. It is still not clear what the specific conditions were that led to the emergence of the state in each of the early centers.[34]

◆ The Spread of State Societies

For whatever reasons the earliest states developed, the state level of political development has come to dominate the world. Societies with states have larger communities and higher population densities than do band, tribal, and chiefdom societies. They also have armies that are ready to fight at almost any time. State systems that have waged war against chiefdoms and tribes have almost always won, and the result has usually been the political incorporation of the losers. For example, the British and, later, the U.S. colonization of much of North America led to the defeat and incorporation of many Native American societies.

The defeat and incorporation of the Native Americans was at least partly due to the catastrophic depopulations they suffered because of epidemic diseases, such as smallpox and measles, that European colonists introduced. Catastrophic depopulation was commonly the outcome of the first contacts between Euro-Americans and the natives of North and South America, as well as the natives of the far islands in the Pacific. People in the New World and the Pacific had not been exposed, and therefore were not resistant, to the diseases the Euro-Americans carried with them when they began to colonize the world. Before the expansion of Europeans, the people of the New World and the Pacific had been separated for a long time from the people and diseases on the geographically continuous landmass we separate into Europe, Africa, and Asia. Smallpox, measles, and the other former scourges of Europe had largely become childhood diseases that most individuals of European ancestry survived.[35]

Whether by depopulation, conquest, or intimidation, the number of independent political units in the world has decreased strikingly in the last 3,000 years, and especially in the last 200 years. Robert Carneiro estimated that in 1000 B.C., there may have been between 100,000 and 1 million separate political units in the world; today there are fewer than 200.[36] In the ethnographic record, about 50 percent of the 2,000 or so societies described within the last 150 years had only local political integration. That is, the highest level of political integration in one out of two fairly recent societies was the local community.[37] Thus, most of the decrease in the number of independent political units has occurred fairly recently.

But the recent secessions from the former Soviet Union and Yugoslavia and other separatist movements around the world suggest that ethnic rivalries may make for departures from the trend toward larger and larger political units. Ethnic groups that have been dominated by others in multinational states may opt for political autonomy, at least for a while. On the other hand, the separate nations of Western Europe are becoming more unified every day, both politically and economically. So the trend toward larger and larger political units may be continuing, even if there are departures from it now and then.

Extrapolating from past history, a number of investigators have suggested that the entire world will eventually come to be politically integrated, perhaps as soon as the twenty-third century and no later than A.D. 4850.[38] Only the future will tell if this prediction will come true. And only the future will tell if further political integration in the world will occur peacefully—with all parties agreeing—or by force or the threat of force, as has happened so often in the past.

Variation in Political Process

Anthropologists are increasingly interested in the politics, or political processes, of the societies they study: who acquires influence or power, how they acquire it, and how political decisions are made. But even though we have descriptive accounts of politics in many societies, there is still little comparative or cross-cultural research on what may explain variation in politics.[39]

GETTING TO BE A LEADER

In those societies that have hereditary leadership, which is common in rank societies and in state societies with monarchies, rules of succession usually establish how leadership is inherited. Such leaders are often identifiable in some obviously visible way; they may be permanently marked or tattooed, as in chiefdoms in Polynesia, or they may wear elaborate dress and insignia, as in class-stratified societies (see the discussion of body adornment in the chapter on the arts). But for societies whose leaders are *chosen*, either as informal leaders or as political officials, we need a lot more research to understand why some kinds of people are chosen over others.

A few studies have investigated the personal qualities of leaders in tribal societies. One study, conducted among the Mekranoti-Kayapo of central Brazil, found that leaders, in contrast to followers, tend to be rated by their peers as higher in intelligence, generosity, knowledgeability, ambitiousness, and aggressiveness. Leaders also tend to be older and taller. And despite the egalitarian nature of Mekranoti society (at least with respect to sharing resources), sons of leaders are more likely than others to become leaders.[40]

Research in another Brazilian society, the Kagwahiv of the Amazon region, suggests another personal quality of

The European Union (EU) had integrated 15 countries in various ways by the end of the year 2000. For example, the EU now had a common currency and coinage, the Euro.

leaders: They seem to have positive feelings about their fathers and mothers.[41] In many respects, studies of leaders in the United States show them to be not that different from their counterparts in Brazil. But there is one major difference: Mekranoti and Kagwahiv leaders are not wealthier than others; in fact, they give their wealth away. U.S. leaders are generally wealthier than others.[42]

"BIG MEN"   In some egalitarian tribal societies, the quest for leadership seems quite competitive. In parts of New Guinea and South America, "big men" compete with other ambitious men to attract followers. Men who want to compete must show that they have magical powers, success in gardening, and bravery in war. But, most important, they have to collect enough goods to throw big parties at which the goods are given away. Big men have to work very hard to attract and keep their followings, for dissatisfied followers can always join other aspiring men.[43] The wives of big men are often leaders too. Among the Kagwahiv, for example, a headman's wife is usually the leader of the women in the community; she is responsible for much of the planning for feasts and often distributes the meat at them.[44]

Although the phenomenon of big men leaders is common throughout New Guinea, researchers are beginning to see variation in the type and extent of "bigmanship" in different areas of New Guinea. For example, in the southern Highlands, groups of men (not just big men) may engage in large-scale giveaways, so big men are not so different from ordinary men. In the northwestern Highlands, on the other hand, big men stand out from other men in striking ways. They make policy for groups of people and organize collective events, they have substantial access to pigs or to valuables acquired in exchanges, and they have control over a substantial amount of labor (more than one wife and fellow kin).[45]

We know that some big men are "bigger" than others, but how does a man get to be a big man? Among the Kumdi-Engamoi, a central Highlands group, a man who wants to be considered a *wua nium* (literally, a "great-important-wealthy man") needs to have many wives and daughters, because the amount of land controlled by a man and how much can be produced on that land depend on the number of women in his family. The more wives he has, the more land he is given to cultivate. He must also be a good speaker. Everyone has the right to speak and give speeches, but to get to be known as a big man requires speaking well and forcefully and knowing when to sum up a consensus. It usually takes a man until his thirties or forties to acquire more than one wife and to make his name through exchanges. When a man wants to inaugurate an exchange, he needs to get shells and pigs from his family and relatives. Once he has achieved a reputation as a *wua nium*, he can keep it only if he continues to perform well—that is, if he continues to distribute fairly, make wise decisions, speak well, and conduct exchanges.[46]

"BIG WOMEN"   In contrast to most of mainland New Guinea, the islands off the southeastern coast are charac-

terized by matrilineal descent. But, like the rest of New Guinea, the islands also have a shifting system of leadership in which people compete for "big" status. Here, though, the people competing are women as well as men, and so there are "big women" as well as "big men." On the island of Vanatinai, for example, women and men compete with each other to exchange valuables. Women lead canoe expeditions to distant islands to visit male as well as female exchange partners, women mobilize relatives and exchange partners to mount large feasts, and the women get to keep the ceremonial valuables exchanged, at least for a while.[47]

The prominence of women on Vanatinai may be linked to the disappearance of warfare—the colonial powers imposed peace; we call this "pacification." Interisland exchanges became frequent when war became rarer in the early 20th century, giving women and men more freedom to travel. For men, but not women, war provided a path to leadership; champion warriors would acquire great renown and influence. It is not that women did not participate in war; they did, which is unusual cross-culturally, but a woman could not become a war leader. Now, in the absence of war, women have an opportunity through exchanges to become leaders, or "big women."

In one respect, however, women have less of an opportunity to acquire influence now. There are local government councils now, but all the councillors are male. Why? Some women were nominated for the posts, but they withdrew in embarrassment because they could not speak English. Big men or big women do not automatically have a path to these new positions; it is mostly young males who know English who become the councillors. But this situation may change. With the opening of a government primary school in 1984, both girls and boys are learning English, so women in the future may be more likely to achieve leadership by becoming councillors.

POLITICAL PARTICIPATION

The political scientist Marc Ross conducted cross-cultural research on variation in degree of political participation. As Ross phrased the research question: "Why is it that in some polities there are relatively large numbers of persons involved in political life, while in others political action is the province of very few?"[48]

Political participation in preindustrial societies ranges from widespread to low or nonexistent. In 16 percent of the societies examined, there is widespread participation; decision-making forums are open to all adults. The forums may be formal (councils and other governing bodies) or informal. Next in degree of political participation are societies (37 percent) that have widespread participation by some but not all adults (men but not women, certain classes but not others). Next are societies (29 percent) that have some but not much input by the community. Finally, 18 percent of the societies have low or nonexistent participation, which means that leaders make most decisions, and involvement of the average person is very limited.

Degree of political participation seems to be high in small-scale societies, as well as in modern democratic nation-states, but not in between (feudal states and preindustrial empires). Why? In small-scale societies leaders do not have the power to force people to act; thus a high degree of political participation may be the only way to get people to go along with decisions. In modern democracies, which have many powerful groups outside the government—corporations, unions, and other associations are examples—the central authorities may only theoretically have the power to force people to go along; in reality, they rely mostly on voluntary compliance. For example, the U.S. government failed when it tried with force (Prohibition, 1920 to 1933) to stop the manufacture, transport, and sale of alcoholic beverages. Another factor may be early family experiences.

Recently some scholars have suggested that the type of family people are raised in predicts the degree of political participation in a society. A large extended family with multiple generations tends to be hierarchical, with the older generations having more authority. Children may learn that they have to obey and subordinate their wishes to their elders. Societies with polygyny also seem to have less political participation. The ways of interacting in the family may carry over to the political sphere.[49]

A high degree of political participation seems to have an important consequence. In the modern world, democratically governed states rarely go to war with each other.[50] So, for example, the United States invaded three countries—Grenada, Panama, and Iraq—between 1980 and 2003 but no democracies. Similarly, it appears that more participatory, that is, more "democratic," political units in the ethnographic record fight with each other significantly less often than do less participatory political units, just as seems to be the case among modern nation-states.[51] Does this mean that democracies are more peaceful in general? Here there is more controversy. Judging by the frequency of war, modern democratic states do not look very different from autocratic states in their tendency to go to war. However, if you look at the severity of war as measured by casualty rates, democratic societies do look less warlike.[52] Exactly why more participation or more democracy is likely to lead to peace remains to be established. But there are policy implications of the relationship, which we explore in the chapter on global social problems.

◆ Resolution of Conflict

As we noted in the beginning of this chapter, political life involves more than the making of policy, its administration, and its enforcement. Political life also involves the resolution of conflict, which may be accomplished peacefully by avoidance, community action, mediation or the negotiation of compromises, apology, appeal to supernatural forces, or adjudication by a third party. As we shall see, the procedures used usually vary with degree of social complexity; decisions by third parties are more likely in hierarchical societies.[53] But peaceful solutions are not always possible, and disputes may erupt into violent conflict. When

violence occurs within a political unit in which disputes are usually settled peacefully, we call such violence *crime,* particularly when committed by an individual. When the violence occurs between groups of people from separate political units—groups between which there is no procedure for settling disputes—we usually call such violence *warfare.* When violence occurs between subunits of a population that had been politically unified, we call it *civil war.*

PEACEFUL RESOLUTION OF CONFLICT

Most modern industrialized states have formal institutions and offices, such as police, district attorneys, courts, and penal systems, to deal with minor disputes and more serious conflicts that may arise in society. All these institutions generally operate according to **codified laws**—that is, a set of explicit, usually written, rules stipulating what is permissible and what is not. Transgression of the law by individuals gives the state the right to take action against them. The state has a monopoly on the legitimate use of force in the society, for it alone has the right to coerce subjects into agreement with regulations, customs, political edicts, and procedures.

Many societies lack such specialized offices and institutions for dealing with conflict. Yet, because all societies have peaceful, regularized ways of handling at least certain disputes, some anthropologists speak of the *universality of law.* E. Adamson Hoebel, for example, stated the principle as follows:

> Each people has its system of social control. And all but a few of the poorest of them have as a part of the control system a complex of behavior patterns and institutional mechanisms that we may properly treat as law. For, "anthropologically considered, law is merely one aspect of our culture—the aspect which employs the force of organized society to regulate individual and group conduct and to prevent redress or punish deviations from prescribed social norms."[54]

Law, then, whether informal as in simpler societies, or formal as in more complex societies, provides a means of dealing peacefully with whatever conflicts develop. That does not mean that conflicts are always resolved peacefully. But that also does not mean that people cannot learn to resolve their conflicts peacefully. The fact that there are societies with little or no violent conflict means that it may be possible to learn from them; it may be possible to discover how to avoid violent outcomes of conflicts. How come South Africa could move relatively peacefully from a society dominated by people from Europe to one with government and civil rights shared by all groups? On the other hand, Bosnia had very violent conflict between ethnic groups and needed intervention by outside parties to keep the warring sides apart.[55]

AVOIDANCE Violence can often be avoided if the parties to a dispute voluntarily avoid each other or are sepa-

CURRENT RESEARCH AND ISSUES
Democracy and Economic Development: How and Why Are They Related?

The subsistence economies traditionally studied by anthropologists are becoming more and more commercialized as people increasingly produce goods and services for a market. And the pace of economic development is quickening, particularly in places that until recently lacked industrial wage labor, as their economies are increasingly integrated into the same world system. What effect, if any, does economic development have on political participation? Can we speculate about the future on the basis of comparative research?

Most of the comparative research on the relationship between economic development and political participation has been cross-national, comparing data on different countries. Some countries are more democratic than others, on the basis of such characteristics as contested elections, an elected head of state, an elected powerful legislature, and the protection of civil liberties. In capitalist countries, more democracy is generally associated with higher levels of economic development, as measured by indicators such as per capita output; in countries that are not very industrialized, there is little democracy at the national level. Why should more democracy be associated with more economic development? The prevailing opinion is that economic development increases the degree of social equality in the country, and the more equality among interest groups, the more they demand participation in the political process, and hence the more democracy. Or, to put this theory another way, as the economy develops, the more what we might call the middle and working classes can demand rewards and power, and therefore the less power the elite can retain.

What about the societies usually studied by anthropologists, what we call the cross-cultural or ethnographic record? We know that some of the highest levels of political participation occur in the least complex societies, such as foraging societies. Many adults in such societies have a say in decisions, and leadership is informal; leaders can retain their roles only if people voluntarily go along with them. Concentrated power and less political participation are more likely in chiefdoms and states than in band and tribal societies. The more hierarchical chiefdoms and states usually depend on agriculture, particularly intensive agriculture, which can produce more goods and services per capita than foraging economies can. So the relationship between economic development and political participation in the ethnographic record is *opposite* to what we find cross-nationally. That is, the more economic development, the less political participation, in the societies studied by anthropologists. Why should this be so? It seems that social equality *decreases* with economic development in the ethnographic record (which does not include many industrialized societies). In that record, an economically developed society is likely to have features such as plowing, fertilizers, and irrigation, which make permanent cultivation of the fields and permanent communities possible. Such intensive agricultural activity is more conducive to concentrated wealth than is hunter-gatherer subsistence or shifting cultivation (horticulture). Thus, in the ethnographic record, the more economically developed societies have more social inequality and therefore less democracy.

The two sets of findings, the cross-national and the cross-cultural, are not that hard to reconcile. Social and economic inequality appears to work against democracy and extensive political participation. Social inequality increases with the switch from foraging to agriculture. But social inequality decreases with the switch from preindustrial agriculture to high (industrial) levels of economic development. Political participation decreases with the first switch and increases with the second, because social inequality first increases and then decreases.

So what does comparative research suggest about the future? If the middle and working classes feel they are not getting a fair return on their labor, their demands should increase. The elite may be willing to satisfy those increased demands; if they do, their power will be reduced. In either case, unless the elite try to retain their power at any cost, there should be more political participation and more democracy, at least in the long run.

Sources: Kenneth A. Bollen, "Liberal Democracy: Validity and Method Factors in Cross-National Measures," *American Journal of Political Science*, 37 (1993): 1207–30; Edward N. Muller, "Economic Determinants of Democracy," and Melvin Ember, Carol R. Ember, and Bruce Russett, "Inequality and Democracy in the Anthropological Record," pp. 133–55 and 110–30, respectively, in Manus I. Midlarsky, ed., *Inequality, Democracy, and Economic Development* (Cambridge: Cambridge University Press, 1997); Marc Howard Ross, "Political Participation," in Carol R. Ember and Melvin Ember, eds., *Cross-Cultural Research for Social Science*, in Carol R. Ember and Melvin Ember, eds., *New Directions in Anthropology* (Upper Saddle River, NJ: Prentice Hall, CD-ROM, 2003).

rated until emotions cool down. Anthropologists have frequently remarked that foragers are particularly likely to make use of this technique. People may move to other bands or move their dwellings to opposite ends of camp. Shifting horticulturalists may also split up when conflicts get too intense. Avoidance is obviously easier in societies, such as band societies, that are nomadic or seminomadic and in which people have temporary dwellings. And avoidance is more feasible when people live independently and self-sufficiently (for example, in cities and suburbs).[56] But even if conditions in such societies may make avoidance easier, we still need to know why some societies use avoidance more than confrontation as a way of resolving conflict.

COMMUNITY ACTION Societies have found various ways of resolving disputes peacefully. One such way involves action by a group or the community as a whole; collective action is common in simpler societies that lack powerful authoritarian leaders.[57] Many Inuit societies, for example, frequently resolve disputes through community action. Within local groups, kinship ties are not particularly emphasized, and the family is regarded as autonomous in most matters. They believe that spirits, particularly if displeased, can determine much of a person's fate. Consequently, people carry out their daily tasks within a complex system of taboos. This system is so extensive that the Inuit, at least in the past, may have had no need for a formal set of laws.

Nevertheless, conflicts do arise and have to be resolved. Accordingly, *principles* act as guides to the community in settling trouble cases. An individual's failure to heed a taboo or to follow the suggestions of a shaman leads to expulsion from the group, because the community cannot accept a risk to its livelihood. A person who fails to share goods voluntarily will find them confiscated and distributed to the community, and he or she may be executed in the process. A single case of murder, as an act of vengeance (usually because of the abduction of a wife or as part of a blood feud), does not concern the community, but repeated murders do. Franz Boas gave a typical example:

> There was a native of Padli by the name Padlu. He had induced the wife of a native of Cumberland Sound to desert her husband and follow him. The deserted husband, meditating revenge . . . visited his friends in Padli, but before he could accomplish his intention of killing Padlu, the latter shot him. . . . A brother of the murdered man went to Padli to avenge the death . . . but he also was killed by Padlu. A third native of Cumberland Sound, who wished to avenge the death of his relatives, was also murdered by him.
>
> On account of these outrages the natives wanted to get rid of Padlu, but yet they did not dare to attack him. When the *pimain* (headman) of the Akudmurmuit learned of these events he started southward and *asked every man in Padli whether Padlu should be killed. All agreed;* so he went with the latter deer hunting . . . and . . . shot Padlu in the back.[58]

The killing of an individual is the most extreme action a community can take—we call it *capital punishment*. The community as a whole or a political official or a court may decide to administer such punishment, but capital punishment seems to exist in nearly all societies, from the simplest to the most complex.[59] It is often assumed that capital punishment deters crime. If it did, we would expect the abolition of capital punishment to be followed by an increase in homicide rates. But that does not seem to happen. A cross-national study indicated that the abolition of capital punishment tends to be followed by a decrease in homicide rates.[60]

NEGOTIATION AND MEDIATION In many conflicts, the parties to a dispute may come to a settlement themselves by **negotiation**. There aren't necessarily any rules for how they will do so, but any solution is "good" if it restores peace.[61] Sometimes an outside or third party is used to help bring about a settlement between the disputants. We call it **mediation** when the outside party tries to help bring about a settlement, but that third party does not have the formal authority to force a settlement. Both negotiation and mediation are likely when the society is relatively egalitarian and it is important for people to get along.[62]

Among the Nuer of East Africa, a pastoral and horticultural people, disputes within the community can be settled with the help of an informal mediator called the "leopard-skin chief." This man is not a political chief but a mediator. His position is hereditary, has religious overtones, and makes its holder responsible for the social well-being of the district. Matters such as cattle stealing rarely come to the attention of the leopard-skin chief; the parties involved usually prefer to settle in their own private way. But if, for example, a murder has been committed, the culprit will go at once to the house of the leopard-skin chief. Immediately the chief cuts the culprit's arm so that blood flows; until the cut has been made the murderer may not eat or drink. If the murderer is afraid of vengeance by the slain man's family, he will remain at the house of the leopard-skin chief, which is considered sanctuary. Then, within the next few months, the chief attempts to mediate between the parties to the crime.

The chief elicits from the slayer's kin that they are prepared to pay compensation to avoid a feud, and he persuades the dead man's kin that they ought to accept compensation, usually in the form of cattle. During this period neither party may eat or drink from the same vessels as the other, and they may not, therefore, eat in the house of the same third person. The chief then collects the cattle—some 40 to 50 beasts—and takes them to the dead man's home, where he performs various sacrifices of cleansing and atonement.[63]

Throughout the process, the chief acts as a go-between. He has no authority to force either party to negotiate, and he has no power to enforce a solution once it has been arrived at. However, he is able to take advantage of the fact that because both disputants belong to the same community and are anxious to avoid a blood feud, they usually are willing to come to terms.

RITUAL RECONCILIATION—APOLOGY The desire to restore a harmonious relationship may also explain

ANTHROPOLOGICAL ORIGINALS
The Iroquois of North America

Political unification may result in less internal war: If the Iroquois Confederacy is a guide, people may decide on the political unification of formerly independent polities when they want to abolish war.

The date of the establishment of the Iroquois Confederacy will probably always be uncertain. It does seem likely that it predated, possibly by as much as a century and a half, initial contacts of the Iroquois with Europeans. The elaborate oral tradition of the confederacy's founding exists in numerous variants. Here just the bare bones of this exciting story are presented.

Deganawida was born to a Huron virgin on the Bay of Quinté on the Canadian side of Lake Ontario. Hearing of the endless wars of blood-revenge ravaging the peoples to the south of that lake, he determined to take a message of peace to those peoples. In the Mohawk country he converted the fierce cannibal, Hiawatha, to

the cause of peace. (Those familiar with Longfellow's epic should be cautioned that the Iroquoian Hiawatha had his name stolen by the New England poet and attributed to the Ojibwa culture hero Nanabush. Longfellow's hero bears no relation to the Hiawatha of Iroquois tradition.) Some variants of this story suggest Degana-wida had a speech impediment, hence Hiawatha became his speaker in councils. The Mohawk, Oneida, Cayuga, and Seneca pledged to join the Great Peace, but the Onondaga held out. Leading them was terrible sorcerer Thadodaho, with seven crooks in his body and snakes entangled in his hair. The Onondaga were persuaded to join with the recognition that Thadodaho was first (although still equal) among the confederacy chiefs, that the Onondaga would have more positions on the confederacy council than any of the other nations, that the Onondaga would be "firekeepers" for the confederacy whose council would regularly meet at Onon-

daga, and that the wampum keeper for the confederacy would be one of the Onondaga chiefs. [Wampum are sacred strings or belts of shell beads.] . . .

The Great Peace was established at a council attended by fifty chiefs called by Deganawida. The fifty positions remain, and each individual on assuming the "antlers of office" (a metaphor for holding chiefly positions) takes the name or title of his predecessor. Hence the names of the fifty founders of the confederacy continue. These Confederacy chiefs were strictly civil positions: as peace chiefs the members of the council were not allowed to go to war.

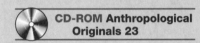
CD-ROM Anthropological Originals 23

Source: Thomas Abler, "Iroquois: The Tree of Peace and the War Kettle," in Melvin Ember and Carol R. Ember, eds., *Portraits of Culture: Ethnographic Originals*, in Carol R. Ember and Melvin Ember, eds., *New Directions in Anthropology* (Upper Saddle River, NJ: Prentice Hall, CD-ROM, 2003).

---

ceremonial apologies. An apology is based on deference—the guilty party shows obeisance and asks for forgiveness. Such ceremonies tend to occur in recent chiefdoms.[64] Among the Fijians of the South Pacific, there is a strong ethic of harmony and mutual assistance, particularly within a village. When a person offends someone of higher status, the offended person and other villagers begin to avoid, and gossip about, the offender. If the offender is sensitive to village opinion, he or she will perform a ceremony of apology called *i soro*. One of the meanings of *soro* is "surrender." In the ceremony the offender keeps her or his head bowed and remains silent while an intermediary speaks, presents a token gift, and asks the offended person for forgiveness. The apology is rarely rejected.[65]

OATHS AND ORDEALS   Still another way of peacefully resolving disputes is through oaths and ordeals, both of which involve appeals to supernatural power. An **oath** is

the act of calling upon a deity to bear witness to the truth of what one says. An **ordeal** is a means used to determine guilt or innocence by submitting the accused to dangerous or painful tests believed to be under supernatural control.[66]

Oaths, as one would expect, vary widely in content, according to the culture in which they are found. The Rwala Bedouin, for example, do the following:

In serious disputes the judge requires the *msabba* oath, so called from the seven lines drawn with a saber on the ground. The judge first draws a circle with a saber, then its diameter; then he intersects with five vertical lines, inviting the witness to step inside and, facing south, to swear: "A false oath is the ruin of the descendants, for he who [swears falsely] is insatiable in his desire [of gain] and does not fear for his Lord."[67]

Scarcely is the oath finished when the witness jumps out of the circle and, full of rage, runs at his opponent, who has made him swear. The people at the trial have to hold him until he calms down.

A common kind of ordeal, found in almost every part of the world, is scalding. Among the Tanala of Madagascar, the accused person, having first had his hand carefully examined for protective covering, has to reach his hand into a cauldron of boiling water and grasp, from underneath, a rock suspended there. He then plunges his hand into cold water, has it bandaged, and is led off to spend the night under guard. In the morning his hand is unbandaged and examined. If there are blisters, he is guilty.

Oaths and ordeals have also been practiced in Western societies. Both were common in medieval Europe. Even today, in our own society, vestiges of oaths can be found. Children can be heard to say, "Cross my heart and hope to die," and witnesses in courts of law are obliged to swear to tell the truth.

Why do some societies use oaths and ordeals? John Roberts suggested that their use tends to be found in fairly complex societies in which political officials lack sufficient power to make and enforce judicial decisions or would make themselves unnecessarily vulnerable were they to attempt to do so. So the officials may use oaths and ordeals to let the gods decide guilt or innocence. When political officials gain more power, oaths and ordeals seem to decline or disappear.[68] In contrast, smaller and less complex societies probably have no need for elaborate mechanisms such as courts and oaths and ordeals to ascertain guilt. In such societies, everyone is aware of what crimes have been committed and who the guilty parties probably are.

ADJUDICATION, COURTS, AND CODIFIED LAW

We call it **adjudication** when a third party acting as judge makes a decision that the disputing parties have to accept. Judgment may be rendered by one person (a judge), a panel of judges, a jury, or a political agent or agency (a chief, a royal personage, a council). Courts are often open to an audience, but they need not be. Judges and courts may rely on codified law and stipulated punishments, but codified law is not necessary for decisions to be made. Our own society relies heavily on codified law and courts to resolve disputes peacefully, but courts often, if not usually, rely on precedent—that is, the outcomes of previous, similar cases. Codified laws and courts are not limited to Western societies. From the late 17th to the early 20th centuries, for example, the Ashanti of West Africa had a complex political system with elaborate legal arrangements. The Ashanti state was a military-based empire possessing legal codes that resembled those of many ancient civilizations.[69]

The most effective sanction underpinning Ashanti law and its enforcement was the intense respect—almost religious deference—accorded the wishes of the ancestors and also the elders as custodians of the ancestral tradition. Ashanti law was based on a concept of natural law, a belief that there is an order of the universe whose principles lawmakers should follow in the decisions they make and in the regulations they design. Criminal and religious law were merged by the Ashanti. Crimes, especially homicide, cursing of a chief, cowardice, and sorcery, were regarded as sins

against the ancestral spirits. In Ashanti court procedure, elders examined and cross-examined witnesses as well as parties to the dispute. There were also quasi-professional advocates, and appeals against a verdict could be made directly to a chief. Particularly noteworthy was the emphasis on intent when assessing guilt. Drunkenness constituted a valid defense for all crimes except murder and cursing a chief, and a plea of insanity, if proved, was upheld for all offenses.

Ashanti punishments could be severe. Physical mutilation, such as slicing off the nose or an ear—even castration in sexual offenses—was often employed. Fines were more frequent, however, and death sentences could often be commuted to banishment and confiscation of goods.

Why do some societies have codified systems and others do not? One explanation, advanced by E. Adamson Hoebel, A. R. Radcliffe-Brown, and others, is that in small, closely knit communities there is little need for formal legal guidelines because competing interests are minimal. Hence, simple societies need little codified law. There are relatively few matters to quarrel about, and the general will of the group is sufficiently well known and demonstrated frequently enough to deter transgressors.

This point of view is echoed in Richard Schwartz's study of two Israeli settlements. In one communal kibbutz, a young man aroused a good deal of community resentment because he had accepted an electric teakettle as a gift. It was the general opinion that he had overstepped the code about not having personal possessions, and he was so informed. Accordingly, he gave the kettle to the communal infirmary. Schwartz observed that "no organized enforcement of the decision was threatened, but had he disregarded the expressed will of the community, his life . . . would have been made intolerable by the antagonism of public opinion."[70]

In this community, where people worked and ate together, not only did everyone know about transgressions, but a wrongdoer could not escape public censure. Thus, public opinion was an effective sanction. In another Israeli community, however, where individuals lived in widely separated houses and worked and ate separately, public opinion did not work as well. Not only were community members less aware of problems, but they had no quick way of making their feelings known. As a result, they established a judicial body to handle trouble cases.

Larger, more heterogeneous and stratified societies are likely to have more frequent disputes, which at the same time are less visible to the public. Individuals in stratified societies are generally not so dependent on community members for their well-being and hence are less likely to know of, or care about, others' opinions. It is in such societies that codified laws and formal authorities for resolving disputes develop—in order, perhaps, that disputes may be settled impersonally enough so that the parties can accept the decision and social order can be restored.

A good example of how more formal systems of law develop is the experience of towns in the American West during the gold-rush period. These communities were literally swamped by total strangers. The townsfolk, having no con-

NEW PERSPECTIVES ON GENDER
New Courts Allow Women to Address Grievances in Papua New Guinea

In most societies in New Guinea, women did not traditionally participate in the resolution of disputes. And they could not bring actions against men. But when village courts were introduced, women began to go to court to redress offenses against them.

In colonial times, the introduced Western-style courts followed Western law, primarily Australian and British common law, not native customary law. After Papua New Guinea became an independent country, those courts remained in place. The lowest of the courts, called Local Courts, were located in town centers, often far from villages, so villagers rarely brought cases to them. But in 1973 a new kind of court was created. Called Village Courts, they were designed to settle local disputes in the villages, using a blend of customary law (relying on compromise) and Western law. In contrast to the Local Courts, magistrates in the Village Courts were not outsiders but were selected from the pool of traditional and local leaders who knew the local people.

When Richard Scaglion studied changes in Village Courts among the Abelam from 1977 to 1987, he noticed a shift toward the increased use of these courts by women. In 1977 most of the complainants were male, but by 1987 most of them were female. In a wider study of court cases over many regions of Papua New Guinea, Scaglion and Rose Whittingham found that most of the cases in which women were the plaintiffs were attempts to redress sex-related offenses (sexual jealousy, rape, incest, domestic disputes) committed by males. Most disputes in New Guinea villages are settled informally by self-help or by appeal to a "big man"; the courts are appealed to only as a last resort. Serious sex-related cases are unlikely to be settled informally but, rather, in the Village Court. Apparently women do not believe that they can get satisfaction informally. So they go to the Village Court, where they win some sort of punishment for the defendant in about 60 percent of the cases, just about the same rate that men achieve when they bring a case seeking punishment.

Culture change introduced from the outside often works against native peoples. But Papuan New Guinea women have benefited from the new Village Court system, particularly in redressing grievances against males. The traditional system for resolving disputes was largely male-dominated (women could not be plaintiffs) and so the possibility of taking disputes to the new courts has given women some measure of legal equality with men.

Sources: Richard Scaglion, "Legal Adaptation in a Papua New Guinea Village Court," *Ethnology*, 29 (1990): 17–33; Richard Scaglion and Rose Whittingham, "Female Plaintiffs and Sex-Related Disputes in Rural Papua New Guinea," in S. Toft, ed., *Domestic Violence in Papua New Guinea*. Monograph No. 3 (Port Moresby, Papua New Guinea: Law Reform Commission, 1985), pp. 120–33.

Many societies have adopted courts to resolve disputes, as here in Papua New Guinea.

trol (authority) over these intruders because the strangers had no local ties, looked for ways to deal with the trouble cases that were continually flaring up. A first attempt at a solution was to hire gunslingers, who were also strangers, to act as peace officers or sheriffs, but this strategy usually failed. Eventually, towns succeeded in having federal authorities send in marshals backed by federal power.

Is there some evidence to support the theory that codified law is necessary only in larger, more complex societies? Data from a large, worldwide sample of societies suggest that codified law is associated with political integration beyond the local level. Murder cases, for example, are dealt with informally in societies that have only local political organization. In societies with multilocal political units, murder cases tend to be judged or adjudicated by specialized political authorities.[71] There is also some cross-cultural evidence that violence within a society tends to be less frequent when there are formal authorities (chiefs, courts) who have the power to punish murderers.[72] In general, adjudication or enforced decisions by outside authorities tend to occur in hierarchical societies with social classes and centralized power.[73]

VIOLENT RESOLUTION OF CONFLICT

People are likely to resort to violence when regular, effective alternative means of resolving a conflict are not available. Some societies consider violence between individuals to be appropriate under certain circumstances; we generally do not, and call it **crime**. When violence occurs between political entities such as communities, districts, or nations, we call it **warfare**. The type of warfare, of course, varies in scope and complexity from society to society. Sometimes a distinction is made among feuding, raiding, and large-scale confrontations.

Some scholars talk about a cultural pattern of violence. But are some cultures more violent than others? The answer seems to be yes. More often than not, societies with one type of violence have others. Societies with more war tend to have warlike sports, malevolent magic, severe punishment for crimes, high murder rates, feuding, and family violence. What might explain this tendency? One suggestion is that if war is frequent, the society may have to encourage boys to be aggressive, so that they can grow up to be effective warriors. But this socializing for aggression can spill over into other areas of life; high rates of crime and other violence may be inadvertent or unintended consequences of the encouragement of aggressiveness.[74]

INDIVIDUAL VIOLENCE Although at first it may seem paradoxical, violent behavior itself is often used to try to control behavior. In some societies it is considered necessary for parents to beat children who misbehave. They don't consider this criminal behavior or child abuse; they consider it punishment (see the discussion of family violence in the chapter on global social problems). Similar views may attach to interpersonal behavior between adults. If a person trespasses on your property or hurts someone in your family, some societies consider it appropriate or justified to kill or maim the trespasser. Is this social control, or is it just lack of control? Most societies have norms about when such "punishment" is or is not appropriate, so the behavior of anyone who contemplates doing something wrong, as well as the behavior of the person wronged, is likely to be influenced by the "laws" of their society. For example, systems of individual self-help are characteristic of egalitarian societies.[75] How is this different from "community action," which earlier we classified under peaceful resolution of conflict? Because community action is explicitly based on obtaining a consensus, it is likely to lead to the ending of a particular dispute. Individual action, or self-help, particularly if it involves violence, is not.

FEUDING Feuding is an example of how individual self-help may not lead to a peaceful resolution of conflict. **Feuding** is a state of recurring hostilities between families or groups of kin, usually motivated by a desire to avenge an offense—whether insult, injury, deprivation, or death—against a member of the group. The most common characteristic of the feud is that responsibility to avenge is carried by all members of the kin group. The killing of any member of the offender's group is considered appropriate revenge, because the kin group as a whole is regarded as responsible. Nicholas Gubser told of a feud within a Nunamiut Inuit community, caused by a husband's killing of his wife's lover, that lasted for decades. The Nunamiut take feuds seriously, as do many societies, especially when murder has been committed. Gubser described what happens when a man is killed:

> The closely related members of his kindred do not rest until complete revenge has been achieved. The immediate relatives of the deceased . . . recruit as much support from other relatives as they can. Their first action, if possible, is to kill the murderer, or maybe one of his closest kin. Then, of course, the members of the murderer's kindred are brought into the feud. These two kindreds may snipe at each other for years.[76]

Feuds are by no means limited to small-scale societies; they occur as frequently in societies with high levels of political organization.[77]

RAIDING **Raiding** is a short-term use of force, planned and organized, to realize a limited objective. This objective is usually the acquisition of goods, animals, or other forms of wealth belonging to another, often neighboring community.

Raiding is especially prevalent in pastoral societies, in which cattle, horses, camels, or other animals are prized and an individual's own herd can be augmented by theft. Raids are often organized by temporary leaders or coordinators whose authority may not last beyond the planning and execution of the venture. Raiding may also be organized for the purpose of capturing people. Sometimes people are taken to marry—the capture of women to be wives or concubines is fairly common[78]—or to be slaves. Slavery has been practiced in about 33 percent of the world's known societies, and war has been one way of obtaining slaves either to keep or to trade for other goods.[79]

LARGE-SCALE CONFRONTATIONS Individual episodes of feuds and raids usually involve relatively small numbers of persons and almost always an element of surprise. Because they are generally attacked without warning, the victims are often unable to muster an immediate defense. Large-scale confrontations, in contrast, involve a large number of persons and planning by both sides of strategies of attack and defense. Large-scale warfare is usually practiced among societies with intensive agriculture or industrialization. Only these societies possess a technology sufficiently advanced to support specialized armies, military leaders, strategists, and so on. But large-scale confrontations are not limited to state societies; they occur, for example, among the horticultural Dugum Dani of central New Guinea.

The military history of the Dani, with its shifting alliances and confederations, is reminiscent of that of Europe, although Dani battles involve far fewer fighters and less sophisticated weaponry. Among the Dani, long periods of ritual warfare are characterized by formal battles announced through a challenge sent by one side to the opposing side. If the challenge is accepted, the protagonists meet at the agreed-upon battle site to set up their lines. Fighting with spears, sticks, and bows and arrows begins at midmorning and continues either until nightfall or until rain intervenes. There may also be a rest period during the midday heat during which the two sides shout insults at each other or talk and rest among themselves.

The front line of battle is composed of about a dozen active warriors and a few leaders. Behind them is a second line, still within arrow range, composed of those who have just left the forward line or are preparing to join it. The third line, outside arrow range, is composed of noncombatants—males too old or too young to participate and those recovering from wounds. This third line merely watches the battle taking place on the grassy plain. On the hillsides far back from the front line, some of the old men help to direct ancestral ghosts to the battle by gouging a line in the ground that points in the direction of the battlefield.[80]

Yet, as total as large-scale confrontations may be, even warfare has cultural rules. Among the Dani, for instance, no fighting occurs at night, and weapons are limited to simple spears and bows and arrows. Similarly, in state societies, governments will sign "self-denying" pacts restricting the use of poison gas, germ warfare, and so forth. Unofficially, private arrangements are common. One has only to glance through the memoirs of national leaders of the two world wars to become aware of locally arranged truces, visits to one another's front positions, exchanges of prisoners of war, and so on.

EXPLAINING WARFARE

Most societies anthropology knows about have had warfare between communities or larger territorial groups. The vast majority of the societies in a recent cross-cultural study had at least occasional wars when they were first described, unless they had been pacified or incorporated by more dominant societies.[81] Yet relatively little research has been done on the possible causes of war and why it varies in type and frequency. For instance, why have some people fought a great deal, and others only infrequently? Why in some societies does warfare occur internally, within the society or language group?

We have answers, based on cross-cultural studies, to some of those questions. There is evidence that people in preindustrial societies go to war mostly out of fear, particularly a fear of expectable but unpredictable natural disasters (e.g., droughts, floods, locust infestations) that will destroy food resources. People may think they can protect themselves against such disasters ahead of time by taking things from defeated enemies. In any case, preindustrial societies with higher frequencies of war are very likely to have had a history of expectable but unpredictable disasters. The fact that chronic (annually recurring and therefore predictable) food shortages do not predict higher frequencies of war suggests that people go to war in an attempt to cushion the impact of the disasters they expect to occur in the future but cannot predict. Consistent with this tentative

Recent times have seen more international efforts to stop ethnic violence and restore peace, as in the NATO intervention in the former Yugoslavia. Here we see an exercise in Kosovo showing that troops from NATO countries can be rapidly deployed if necessary.

conclusion is the fact that the victors in war almost always take land or other resources from the defeated. And this is true for simpler as well as more complex preindustrial societies.[82] Might similar motives affect decisions about war and peace in the modern world?

We know that complex or politically centralized societies are likely to have professional armies, hierarchies of military authority, and sophisticated weapons.[83] But surprisingly, the frequency of warfare seems to be not much greater in complex societies than in simple band or tribal societies.[84] We have some evidence that warfare is unlikely to occur internally (within a society) if it is small in population (21,000 or fewer people) or territory; in a larger society there is a high likelihood of warfare within the society, between communities or larger territorial divisions.[85] In fact, complex societies, even if they are politically unified, are not less likely than simpler societies to have internal warfare.[86]

What about the idea that men in band and tribal societies may mostly go to war over women?[87] If this were true, those band and tribal societies with the most frequent wars should have shortages of women, and those with little or no war—less often than once in 10 years—should have more equal numbers of women and men. But the cross-cultural evidence clearly contradicts this theory. Band and tribal societies with more wars do not have fewer women.[88]

What, if anything, do we know about recent warfare between nation-states? Although many people think that military alliances lessen the chance of war, it turns out that nations formally allied with other nations do not necessarily go to war less often than nations lacking formal alliances. Countries that are allies are, of course, less likely to go to war with each other; however, alliances can drag dependent allies into wars they don't want.[89] Countries that are economically interdependent, that trade with each other for necessities, are less likely to go to war with each other.[90] Finally, military equality between nations, particularly when preceded by a rapid military buildup, seems to increase rather than lessen the chance of war between those nations.[91]

Clearly, these findings contradict some traditional beliefs about how to prevent war. Military buildups do not make war less likely, but trade does. What else may? We have already noted that participatory ("democratic") political systems are less likely to go to war with each other than are authoritarian political systems. Later, in the chapter on global social problems, we discuss how the results of the various cross-cultural studies may translate into policies that could minimize the risk of war in the world.

 CD-ROM Flashcards Chapter 23

 ## Summary

1. All societies have customs or procedures that, organized on behalf of territorial groups, result in decision making and the resolution of disputes. These ways of creating and maintaining social order and coping with social disorder vary from society to society.

2. Societies with a band type of political organization are composed of fairly small, usually nomadic groups. Each of these bands is politically autonomous, the band being the largest group that acts as a political unit. Authority within the band is usually informal. Societies with band organization generally are egalitarian hunter-gatherers. But band organization may not have been typical of food collectors in the distant past.

3. Societies with tribal organization are similar to those with band organization in being egalitarian. But in contrast with band societies, they generally are food producers, have a higher population density, and are more sedentary. Tribal organization is defined by the presence of groupings, such as clans and age-sets, that can integrate more than one local group into a larger whole.

4. The personal qualities of leaders in tribal societies seem to be similar to the qualities of leaders in the United States, with one major difference: U.S. leaders are generally wealthier than others in their society.

5. Chiefdom organization differs from tribal organization in having formal authority structures that integrate multicommunity political units. Compared with societies with tribal organization, societies with chiefdoms are more densely populated and their communities are more permanent. In contrast to "big men" in tribal societies, who generally have to earn their privileges by their personal qualities, chiefs generally hold their positions permanently. Most chiefdom societies have social ranking.

6. A state has been defined as a political unit composed of many communities and having a centralized government with the authority to make and enforce laws, collect taxes, and draft men for military service. In state societies, the government tries to maintain a monopoly on the use of physical force. In addition, states are generally characterized by class stratification, intensive agriculture (the high productivity of which presumably allows the emergence of cities), commercial exchange, a high degree of economic and other specialization, and extensive foreign trade. The rulers of a state cannot depend forever on the use or threat of force to maintain their power; the people must believe that the rulers are legitimate or have the right to govern.

7. Degree of political participation varies in the societies studied by anthropologists, just as among modern nation-states. Degree of political participation seems to be high in small-scale societies, as well as in modern democratic nation-states, but not in those in between, such as feudal states and preindustrial empires.

8. Many societies lack specialized offices and institutions for dealing with conflict. Yet all societies have peaceful, regularized ways of handling at least certain disputes. Avoidance, community action, and negotiation and mediation are more common in simpler societies. Ritual apology occurs frequently in chiefdoms. Oaths and ordeals tend to occur in complex societies in which political officials lack power to enforce judicial decisions.

Adjudication is more likely in stratified, more complex societies. Capital punishment seems to exist in nearly all societies, from the simplest to the most complex.

9. People are likely to resort to violence when regular, effective alternative means of resolving a conflict are not available. Violence can occur between individuals, within communities, and between communities. Violence that occurs between political entities such as communities, districts, or nations is generally referred to as warfare. The type of warfare varies in scope and complexity from society to society. Preindustrial societies with higher warfare frequencies are likely to have had a history of unpredictable disasters that destroyed food supplies. More often than not, societies with one type of violence have others.

 ## Glossary Terms

adjudication	negotiation
band	oath
band organization	ordeal
chief	raiding
chiefdom	segmentary lineage system
codified laws	state
complementary opposition	state organization
crime	tribal organization
feuding	tribe
headman	warfare
mediation	

Critical Questions

1. When, if ever, do you think the world will be politically unified? Why do you think so?
2. Why don't informal methods of social control work well in societies like our own? Why don't formal methods work better than they do?
3. What does research on war and violence suggest about how to minimize them?

 ## Internet Exercises

1. Visit http://valley.vcdh.virginia.edu and take a walking tour.
2. A political scientist, Rudy Rummel, has compiled data on genocide and, more generally, democide, by which he means the murder of any person or people by a government, including genocide, politicide, and mass murder. Go to his site, http://www.hawaii.edu/powerkills/. What kinds of governments commit the most democide? Keep in mind that you have to add

three zeros to most of his figures to see the number of people killed. In addition, read about the democratic peace clock and the projections about when violence in the world will diminish.

3. Learn about the UN international criminal tribunal to investigate genocide in Rwanda at http://www.ictr.org/.

 ## Suggested Reading

FRY, D. P., AND K. BJÖRKQVIST, EDS. *Cultural Variation in Conflict Resolution: Alternatives to Violence.* Mahwah, NJ: Lawrence Erlbaum Associates, 1997. The case studies in this book show that alternatives to violence exist in many societies, indicating that violence is not inevitable. If conflicts are often resolved without violence, it should be possible to discover the principles of nonviolent conflict resolution, which people could learn and practice.

HAAS, J., ED. *The Anthropology of War.* Cambridge: Cambridge University Press, 1990. The contributors to this volume discuss war in general and in particular places, focusing on explanatory models of warfare, origins versus persistence of warfare, and causes versus effects of warfare in nonstate societies.

MCGLYNN, F., AND TUDEN, A., EDS. *Anthropological Approaches to Political Behavior.* Pittsburgh: University of Pittsburgh Press, 1991. A compilation of articles that discuss political processes in a variety of societies. The editors provide an overview of the central concerns of political anthropology and its different approaches.

ROSS, M. H. "Political Participation." In C. R. Ember and M. Ember, eds., *Cross-Cultural Research for Social Science*, in C. R. Ember and M. Ember, eds., *New Directions in Anthropology.* Upper Saddle River, NJ: Prentice Hall, CD-ROM, 2003. This chapter, written especially for undergraduates, discusses variation in political participation (decision making and demand making) in societies and nations. The author also discusses why political participation varies.

SCAGLION, R. "Law and Society." In C. R. Ember and M. Ember, eds., *Cross-Cultural Research for Social Science*, in C. R. Ember and M. Ember, eds., *New Directions in Anthropology.* Upper Saddle River, NJ: Prentice Hall, CD-ROM, 2003. Written especially for undergraduates, this chapter reviews some of the comparative research on law and summarizes two approaches to the study of law in anthropology—the rule-centered approach and the processual approach.

STROUTHES, DANIEL P. *Law and Politics: A Cross-Cultural Encyclopedia.* Santa Barbara, CA: ABC-CLIO, 1995. A cross-cultural survey of law and politics, providing definitions of concepts and discussing important patterns observable around the world.

UPHAM, S., ED. *The Evolution of Political Systems: Sociopolitics in Small-Scale Sedentary Societies.* Cambridge: Cambridge University Press, 1990. The contributors to this volume offer different and sometimes contradictory ideas about political organization and change in sedentary societies. They explore fundamental questions such as how people come to give up local autonomy and equality for bigger, hierarchical political units.

RELIGION AND MAGIC

25

CHAPTER OUTLINE

- ◆ The Universality of Religion

- ◆ Variation in Religious Beliefs

- ◆ Variation in Religious Practices

- ◆ Religion and Adaptation

As far as we know, all societies have possessed beliefs that can be grouped under the term *religion*. These beliefs vary from culture to culture and from time to time. Yet, despite their variety, we shall define **religion** as any set of attitudes, beliefs, and practices pertaining to *supernatural power*, whether that power be forces, gods, spirits, ghosts, or demons.

In our society, we divide phenomena into the natural and the supernatural, but not all languages or cultures make such a neat distinction. Moreover, what is considered **supernatural**—powers believed to be not human or not subject to the laws of nature—varies from society to society. Some of the variation is determined by what a society regards as natural. For example, some illnesses commonly found in our society are believed to result from the natural action of bacteria and viruses. In other societies, and even among some people in our own society, illness is thought to result from supernatural forces, and thus it forms a part of religious belief.

Beliefs about what is, or is not, a supernatural occurrence also vary within a society at a given time or over time. In Judeo-Christian traditions, for example, floods, earthquakes, volcanic eruptions, comets, and epidemics were once considered evidence of supernatural powers intervening in human affairs. It is now generally agreed that they are simply natural occurrences—even though many still believe that supernatural forces may be involved. Thus, the line between the natural and the supernatural varies in a society according to what people believe about the causes of things and events in the observable world.

In many cultures, what we would consider religious is embedded in other aspects of everyday life. That is, it is often difficult to separate the religious or economic or political from other aspects of the culture. Such cultures have little or no specialization of any kind; there are no full-time priests, no purely religious activities. So the various aspects of culture we distinguish (for example, in the chapter titles of this book) are not separate and easily recognized in many societies, as they are in complex societies such as our own. However, it is sometimes difficult even for us to agree whether or not a particular custom of ours is religious. After all, the categorizing of beliefs as religious or political or social is a relatively new custom. The ancient Greeks, for instance, did not have a word for religion, but they did have many concepts concerning the behavior of their gods and their own expected duties to the gods.

When people's duties to their gods are linked with duty to their princes, it is difficult to separate religious from political ideas. As an example of our own difficulty in labeling a particular class of actions or beliefs as religious or social, consider our attitudes about wearing clothes. Is our belief that it is necessary to wear clothing, at least in the company of nonlovers, a religious principle, or is it something else? Recall that in Genesis, the wearing of clothes, or fig leaves, is distinctly associated with the loss of innocence: Adam and Eve, after eating the apple, covered their nakedness. Accordingly, when Christian missionaries first visited islands in the Pacific in the nineteenth century, they forced the native women to wear more clothes, particularly to cover their sexual parts. Were the missionaries' ideas about sex religious or social, or perhaps both?

The Universality of Religion

Religious beliefs and practices are found in all known contemporary societies, and archaeologists think they have found signs of religious belief associated with *Homo sapiens* who lived at least 60,000 years ago. People then deliberately buried their dead, and many graves contain the remains of food, tools, and other objects that were probably thought to be needed in an afterlife. Some of the artistic productions of modern humans after about 30,000 years ago may have been used for religious purposes. For example, sculptures of females with ample secondary sex characteristics may have been fertility charms. Cave paintings in which the predominant images are animals of the hunt may reflect a belief that the image had some power over events. Perhaps early humans thought that their hunting would be more successful if they drew images depicting good fortune in hunting. The details of religions practiced in the distant past cannot be recovered. Yet evidence of ritual treatment of the dead suggests that early people believed in the existence of supernatural spirits and tried to communicate with, and perhaps influence, them.

We may reasonably assume the existence of prehistoric religion and we have evidence of the universality of religion in historic times, so we can understand why the subject of religion has been the focus of much speculation, research, and theorizing. As long ago as the 5th century B.C., Herodotus made fairly objective comparisons among the religions of the 50 or so societies he traveled to from his home in Greece. He noted many similarities among their gods and pointed out evidence of diffusion of religious worship. During the 2,500 years since Herodotus's time, scholars, theologians, historians, and philosophers have speculated about religion. Some have claimed superiority for their own forms of religion; others have derided the naive simplicity of others' beliefs; and some have expressed skepticism concerning all beliefs.

Speculation about which religion is superior is not an anthropological concern. What is of interest to anthropologists is why religion is found in all societies and how and why it varies from society to society. Many social scientists—particularly anthropologists, sociologists, and psychologists—have offered theories to account for the universality of religion. Most think that religions are created by humans in response to certain universal needs or conditions. We consider four such needs or conditions here: a need for intellectual understanding, reversion to childhood feelings, anxiety and uncertainty, and a need for community.

CD-ROM Video Activity 8

THE NEED TO UNDERSTAND

One of the earliest social scientists to propose a major theory of the origin of religion was Edward Tylor. In Tylor's view, religion originated in people's speculation about dreams, trances, and death. The dead, the distant, those in the next house, animals—all seem real in dreams and trances. Tylor thought that the lifelike appearances of these imagined persons and animals suggest a dual existence for all things—a physical, visible body and a psychic, invisible soul. In sleep, the soul can leave the body and appear to other people; at death, the soul permanently leaves the body. Because the dead appear in dreams, people come to believe that the souls of the dead are still around.

Tylor thought that the belief in souls was the earliest form of religion; **animism** is the term he used to refer to belief in souls.[1] But many scholars criticized Tylor's theory for being too intellectual and not dealing with the emotional component of religion. One of Tylor's students, R. R. Marett, felt that Tylor's animism was too sophisticated an idea to be the origin of religion. Marett suggested that **animatism**—a belief in impersonal supernatural forces (for example, the power of a rabbit's foot)—preceded the creation of spirits.[2] A similar idea is that when people believe in gods, they are *anthropomorphizing*—attributing human characteristics and motivations to nonhuman, particularly supernatural, events.[3] Anthropomorphizing may be an attempt to understand what is otherwise incomprehensible and disturbing.

REVERSION TO CHILDHOOD FEELINGS

Sigmund Freud believed that early humans lived in groups each of which was dominated by a tyrannical man who kept all the women for himself.[4] Freud postulated that, on maturing, the sons were driven out of the group. Later they joined together to kill and eat the hated father. But then the sons felt enormous guilt and remorse, which they expressed (projected) by prohibiting the killing of a totem animal (the father-substitute). Subsequently, on ritual occasions, the cannibalistic scene was repeated in the form of a totem meal. Freud believed that these early practices gradually became transformed into the worship of deities or gods modeled after the father.

Freud's interpretation of the origin of religion is not accepted by most social scientists today. But there is widespread agreement with his idea that events in infancy can have long-lasting and powerful effects on beliefs and practices in adult life. Helpless and dependent on parents for many years, infants and children inevitably and unconsciously view their parents as all-knowing and all-powerful. When adults feel out of control or in need, they may unconsciously revert to their infantile and childhood feelings. They may then look to gods or magic to do what they cannot do for themselves, just as they looked to their parents to take care of their needs. As we shall see, there is evidence that feelings about the supernatural world parallel feelings in everyday life.

ANXIETY AND UNCERTAINTY

Freud thought that humans would turn to religion during times of uncertainty, but he did not view religion positively, believing that humans would eventually outgrow the need for religion. Others viewed religion more positively. Bronislaw Malinowski noted that people in all societies are faced with anxiety and uncertainty. They may have skills and knowledge to take care of many of their needs, but knowledge is not sufficient to prevent illness, accidents, and natural disasters. The most frightening prospect is death itself. Consequently, there is an intense desire for immortality. As Malinowski saw it, religion is born from the universal need to find comfort in inevitable times of stress. Through religious belief, people affirm their convictions that death is neither real nor final, that people are endowed with a personality that persists even after death. In religious ceremony, humans can commemorate and communicate with those who have died, and in these ways achieve some measure of comfort.[5]

Theorists such as William James, Carl Jung, Erich Fromm, and Abraham Maslow have viewed religion even more positively: Religion is not just a way of relieving anxiety; it is thought to be therapeutic. James suggested that religion provides a feeling of union with something larger than oneself,[6] and Jung suggested that it helps people resolve their inner conflicts and attain maturity.[7] Fromm proposed that religion gives people a framework of values,[8] and Maslow argued that it provides a transcendental understanding of the world.[9]

THE NEED FOR COMMUNITY

All those theories of religion agree on one thing: Whatever the beliefs or rituals, religion may satisfy psychological needs common to all people. But some social scientists believe that religion springs from society and serves social, rather than psychological, needs. Émile Durkheim, a French sociologist, pointed out that living in society makes humans feel pushed and pulled by powerful forces. These forces direct their behavior, pushing them to resist what is considered wrong, pulling them to do what is considered right. These are the forces of public opinion, custom, and law. Because they are largely invisible and unexplained, people would feel them as mysterious forces and therefore come to believe in gods and spirits. Durkheim suggested that religion arises out of the experience of living in social groups; religious belief and practice affirm a person's place in society, enhance feelings of community, and give people confidence. He proposed that society is really the object of worship in religion.

Consider how Durkheim explained totemism, so often discussed by early religious theorists. He thought that nothing inherent in a lizard, rat, or frog—animal totems for some Australian aboriginal groups—would be sufficient to make them *sacred*. The totem animal therefore must be a symbol. But a symbol of what? Durkheim noted that the people are organized into clans, and each clan has its own totem animal; the totem distinguishes one clan

CURRENT RESEARCH AND ISSUES
The Usefulness of Religion: Taboos among New England Fishermen

People who engage in risky activities may try to ensure their safety by carrying or wearing lucky charms. They believe the charms protect them by invoking the help of supernatural beings or forces. We might also believe we can protect ourselves by not doing some things. For example, baseball players on a hitting streak may choose not to change their socks or sweatshirt for the next game (to continue their luck). Or we obey a prohibition because we think that by doing so we can avoid supernatural punishment. For example, we may fast or give up certain foods for a period of time. Why? God knows!

Whether or not religious beliefs and practices can affect our success or reduce our risk, we may consider them useful or adaptive if they reduce our anxieties. And reducing anxiety might indirectly maximize our success. Doesn't an actor try to reduce his or her "stage fright" before a performance? Prohibitions (taboos) are perhaps particularly likely to be adaptive in this way. Consider some research on New England fishermen that suggests how their taboos, or "rituals of avoidance," may reduce anxiety.

John Poggie and Richard Pollnac interviewed a random sample of 108 commercial fishermen from three New England ports. They were trying to explain the number of taboos among the fishermen, as measured by asking them to describe all the superstitions related to fishing they could remember. The fishermen were often embarrassed when they talked about their ritual beliefs and practices. They would say they did not really believe in their taboos, but they admitted that they would not break them while fishing. The taboos prohibited saying or doing a certain thing, or something bad would happen. Most frequently mentioned were "Don't turn a hatch cover upside down," "Don't whistle on a boat," and "Don't mention the word pig on board." When the fishermen were asked what these taboos meant, they talked about personal safety and preventing bad luck.

The results of the study suggest that anxiety about personal danger while fishing is the main stimulus for the taboo behavior observed among the fishermen. For example, there are more taboos reported when the duration of exposure to danger is longer. Fishermen who go out just for the day report significantly fewer taboos than fishermen who go out for longer periods of time. And longer trips are clearly more dangerous because they are farther from shore. If there is a storm, the farther out you are, the more risk of disaster because you are exposed longer to rough seas. And it is more difficult to deal with illness, injury, breakdowns, and damage to the boat far from shore. Also consistent with the conclusion that the fishermen's taboos reduce anxiety is the fact that inshore fishermen (those who are after shellfish close to shore) report a significantly smaller number of taboos than offshore fishermen (who go out farther in trawlers).

On shore, the fishermen express some disbelief in the effectiveness of their taboos. (They are called "superstitions," you know!) But at sea it seems that the omnipresence of danger raises anxiety levels and discourages the fishermen from testing their disbelief. It won't hurt to practice the taboo at sea, they say, but it might hurt not to!

Sources: John J. Poggie, Jr., and Richard B. Pollnac, "Danger and Rituals of Avoidance among New England Fishermen," *MAST: Maritime Anthropological Studies,* 1 (1988): 66–78; John J. Poggie, Jr., Richard B. Pollnac, and Carl Gersuny, "Risk as a Basis for Taboos among Fishermen in Southern New England," *Journal for the Scientific Study of Religion,* 15 (1976): 257–62.

---

from another. So the totem is the focus of the clan's religious rituals and symbolizes both the clan and the clan's spirits. It is the clan with which people mostly identify, and it is the clan that is affirmed in ritual.[10]

Guy Swanson accepted Durkheim's belief that certain aspects or conditions of society generate the responses we call religious, but he thought that Durkheim was too vague about exactly what in society would generate the belief in spirits or gods. So what might? Swanson suggested that the belief in spirits derives from the existence of *sovereign*

groups in a society. These are the groups that have independent jurisdiction (decision-making powers) over some sphere of life—the family, the clan, the village, the state. Such groups are not mortal; they persist beyond the lifetimes of their individual members. According to Swanson, then, the spirits or gods that people invent personify or represent the powerful decision-making groups in their society. Just like sovereign groups in a society, the spirits or gods are immortal and have purposes and goals that supersede those of an individual.[11]

◆ Variation in Religious Beliefs

There is no general agreement among scholars as to why people need religion, or how spirits, gods, and other supernatural beings and forces come into existence. (Any or all of the needs we have discussed, psychological or social, may give rise to religious belief and practice.) Yet there is general recognition of the enormous variation in the details of religious beliefs and practices. Societies differ in the kinds of supernatural beings or forces they believe in and the character of those beings. They also differ in the structure or hierarchy of those beings, in what the beings actually do, and in what happens to people after death. Variation exists also in the ways in which the supernatural is believed to interact with humans.

TYPES OF SUPERNATURAL FORCES AND BEINGS

SUPERNATURAL FORCES Some supernatural forces have no personlike character. As we discussed earlier, Marett referred to such religious beliefs as animatism. For example, a supernatural, impersonal force called **mana,** after its Malayo-Polynesian name, is thought to inhabit some objects but not others, some people but not others. A farmer in Polynesia places stones around a field; the crops are bountiful; the stones have mana. During a subsequent year the stones may lose their mana and the crops will be poor. People may also possess mana, as, for example, the chiefs in Polynesia were said to do. However, such power is not necessarily possessed permanently; chiefs who were

There's room in the world for all religions—those who believe in rocks, those who believe in trees, those who believe in clouds . . .

© 1984 by Sidney Harris

unsuccessful in war or other activities were said to have lost their mana.

The word *mana* may be Malayo-Polynesian, but a similar concept is also found in our own society. We can compare mana to the power that golfers may attribute to some but, unhappily not all, of their clubs. A ballplayer might think a certain sweatshirt or pair of socks has supernatural power or force, and that more runs or points will be scored when they are worn. A four-leaf clover has mana; a three-leaf clover does not.

Objects, persons, or places can be considered **taboo.** Anthony Wallace distinguished mana from taboo by pointing out that things containing mana are to be touched, whereas taboo things are not to be touched, for their power can cause harm.[12] Thus, those who touch them may themselves become taboo. Taboos surround food not to be eaten, places not to be entered, animals not to be killed, people not to be touched sexually, people not to be touched at all, and so on. An Australian aborigine could not normally kill and eat the animal that was his totem; Hebrew tribesmen were forbidden to touch a woman during menstruation or for seven days afterward.

SUPERNATURAL BEINGS Supernatural beings fall within two broad categories: those of nonhuman origin, such as gods and spirits, and those of human origin, such as ghosts and ancestral spirits. Chief among the beings of nonhuman origin, **gods** are named personalities. They are often *anthropomorphic*—that is, conceived in the image of a person—although they are sometimes given the shapes of other animals or of celestial bodies, such as the sun or moon. Essentially, the gods are believed to have created themselves, but some of them then created, or gave birth to, other gods. Although some are seen as creator gods, not all peoples include the creation of the world as one of the acts of gods.

After their efforts at creation, many creator gods retire. Having set the world in motion, they are not interested in its day-to-day operation. Other creator gods remain interested in the ordinary affairs of human beings, especially the affairs of one small, chosen segment of humanity. Whether or not a society has a creator god, the job of running the creation is often left to lesser gods. The Maori of New Zealand, for example, recognize three important gods: a god of the sea, a god of the forest, and a god of agriculture. They call upon each in turn for help and try to get all three to share their knowledge of how the universe runs. The gods of the ancient Romans, on the other hand, specialized to a high degree. There were three gods of the plow, one god to help with the sowing, one for weeding, one for reaping, one for storing grain, one for manuring, and so on.[13]

Beneath the gods in prestige, and often closer to people, are multitudes of unnamed **spirits.** Some may be guardian spirits for people. Some, who become known for particularly efficacious work, may be promoted to the rank of named gods. Some spirits who are known to the people but are never invoked by them are of the hobgoblin type. Hobgoblins delight in mischief and can be blamed for any number of small mishaps; still other spirits take pleasure in deliberately working evil on behalf of people.

Many Native American groups believed in guardian spirits that had to be sought out, usually in childhood. For example, among the Sanpoil of northeastern Washington, boys and sometimes girls would be sent out on overnight vigils to acquire their guardians. Most commonly the spirits were animals, but they could also be uniquely shaped rocks, lakes, mountains, whirlwinds, or clouds. The vigil was not always successful. When it was, the guardian spirit appeared in a vision or dream, and always at first in human form. Conversation with the spirit would reveal its true identity.[14]

Ghosts and **ancestor spirits** are among the supernatural beings who were once human. The belief that ghosts or their actions can be perceived by the living is almost universal.[15] The near-universality of the belief in ghosts may not be difficult to explain. There are many cues in everyday experience that are associated with a loved one, and even after her or his death those cues might arouse the feeling that the dead person is still somehow present. The opening of a door or the smell of tobacco or cologne in a room may evoke the idea that the person is still present, if only for a moment. Then, too, loved ones live on in dreams. Small wonder, then, that most societies believe in ghosts. If the idea of ghosts is generated by these familiar associations, we might expect that ghosts in most societies would be close relatives and friends, not strangers—and they are.[16]

On the Day of the Dead in Michoacán, Mexico, it is believed that the spirits of the dead return for a visit.

Although the belief in ghosts is nearly universal, the spirits of the dead do not play an active role in the life of the living in all societies. In his cross-cultural study of 50 societies, Swanson found that people are likely to believe in active ancestral spirits where descent groups are important decision-making units. The descent group is an entity that exists over time, back into the past as well as forward into the future, despite the deaths of individual members.[17] The dead feel concern for the fortunes, the prestige, and the continuity of their descent group as strongly as the living. As a Lugbara elder (in northern Uganda in Africa) put it, "Are our ancestors not people of our lineage? They are our fathers and we are their children whom they have begotten. Those that have died stay near us in our homes and we feed and respect them. Does not a man help his father when he is old?"[18]

THE CHARACTER OF SUPERNATURAL BEINGS

Whatever type they may be, the gods or spirits venerated in a given culture tend to have certain personality or character traits. They may be unpredictable or predictable, aloof from or interested in human affairs, helpful or punishing. Why do the gods and spirits in a particular culture exhibit certain character traits rather than others?

We have some evidence from cross-cultural studies that the character of supernatural beings may be related to the nature of child training. Melford Spiro and Roy D'Andrade suggested that the god-human relationship is a projection of the parent-child relationship, in which case child-training practices might well be relived in dealings with the supernatural.[19] For example, if a child was nurtured immediately by her parents when she cried or waved her arms about or kicked, she might grow up expecting to be nurtured by the gods when she attracted their attention by performing a ritual. On the other hand, if her parents often punished her, she would grow up expecting the gods to punish her if she disobeyed them. William Lambert, Leigh Minturn Triandis, and Margery Wolf, in another cross-cultural study, found that societies with hurtful or punitive child-training practices are likely to believe that their gods are aggressive and malevolent; societies with less punitive child training are more likely to believe that the gods are benevolent.[20] These results are consistent with the Freudian notion that the supernatural world should parallel the natural. It is worth noting in this context that some peoples refer to the god as their father and to themselves as his children.

STRUCTURE OR HIERARCHY OF SUPERNATURAL BEINGS

The range of social structures in human societies from egalitarian to highly stratified has its counterpart in the supernatural world. Some societies have gods or spirits that are not ranked; one god has about as much power as another. Other societies have gods or spirits that are ranked in prestige and power. For example, on the Pacific islands of

Palau, which was a rank society, gods were ranked as people were. Each clan worshiped a god and a goddess that had names or titles similar to clan titles. Although a clan god was generally important only to the members of that clan, the gods of the various clans in a village were believed to be ranked in the same order that the clans were. Thus, the god of the highest-ranking clan was respected by all the clans of the village. Its shrine was given the place of honor in the center of the village and was larger and more elaborately decorated than other shrines.[21]

Although the Palauans did not believe in a high god or supreme being who outranked all the other gods, some societies do. Consider Judaism, Christianity, and Islam, which we call **monotheistic** religions. Although *monotheism* means "one god," most monotheistic religions actually include more than one supernatural being (e.g., demons, angels, the Devil). But the supreme being or high god, as the creator of the universe or the director of events (or both), is believed to be ultimately responsible for all events.[22] A **polytheistic** religion recognizes many important gods, no one of which is supreme.

Why do some societies have a belief in a high god and others do not? Recall Swanson's suggestion that people invent gods who personify the important decision-making groups in their society. He therefore hypothesized that societies with hierarchical political systems should be more likely to believe in a high god. In his cross-cultural study of 50 societies (none of which practiced any of the major world religions), he found that belief in a high god is strongly associated with three or more levels of "sovereign" (decision-making) groups. Of the 20 sample societies that had a hierarchy of three or more sovereign groups—for instance, family, clan, and chiefdom—17 possessed the idea of a high god. Of the 19 societies that had fewer than three levels of decision-making groups, only 2 had a high god.[23] Consistent with Swanson's findings, societies dependent on food production are more likely to have a belief in a high god than are food-collecting societies.[24] These results strongly suggest, then, that the realm of the gods parallels and may reflect the everyday social and political worlds.

INTERVENTION OF THE GODS IN HUMAN AFFAIRS

According to Clifford Geertz, it is when faced with ignorance, pain, and the unjustness of life that a person explains events by the intervention of the gods.[25] Thus, in Greek religion the direct intervention of Poseidon as ruler of the seas prevented Odysseus from getting home for ten years. In the Old Testament, the direct intervention of Yahweh caused the great flood that killed most of the people in the time of Noah. In other societies, people may search their memories for a violated taboo that has brought punishment through supernatural intervention.

In addition to unasked-for divine interference, there are numerous examples of requests for divine intervention, either for good for oneself and friends or for evil for others. Gods are asked to intervene in the weather and make the crops grow, to send fish to the fisherman and game to the

hunter, to find lost things, and to accompany travelers and prevent accidents. They are asked to stop the flow of lava down the side of a volcano, to stop a war, or to cure an illness.

The gods do not intervene in all societies. In some, they intervene in human affairs; in others, they are not the slightest bit interested; and in still others, they interfere only occasionally. We have little research on why gods are believed to interfere in some societies and not in others. We do, however, have some evidence suggesting when the gods will take an interest in the morality or immorality of human behavior. Swanson's study suggests that the gods are likely to punish people for immoral behavior when there are considerable differences in wealth in the society.[26] His interpretation is that supernatural support of moral behavior is particularly useful where inequalities tax the ability of the political system to maintain social order and minimize social disorder. Envy of others' privileges may motivate some people to behave immorally; the belief that the gods will punish such behavior might deter it.

LIFE AFTER DEATH

In many societies, ideas about an afterlife are vague and seemingly unimportant, but many other peoples have very definite and elaborate ideas of what happens after death. The Lugbara see the dead as joining the ancestors of the living and staying near the family homesite. They retain an interest in the behavior of the living, both rewarding and punishing them. The Zuni of the southwestern United States think the dead join the past dead, known as the *katcinas*, in a katcina village at the bottom of a nearby lake. There they lead a life of singing and dancing and bring rain to the living Zuni. Just as they are swift to punish the priest who fails in his duty, they also punish the people in masks who ineffectively impersonate the katcinas during the dance ceremonies.[27]

 CD-ROM Video Activity 9

The Chamulas have merged the ancient Mayan worship of the sun and moon with the Spanish conquerors' Jesus and Mary. Their vision of life after death contains a blending of the two cultures. All souls go to the underworld, where they live a humanlike life except that they are incapable of sexual intercourse. After the sun travels over the world, it travels under the underworld, so that the dead have sunlight. Only murderers and suicides are punished, being burned by the Christ-sun on their journey.[28]

Many Christians believe that the dead are divided into two groups: The unsaved are sent to everlasting punishment and the saved to everlasting reward. Accounts differ, but hell is often associated with torture by fire, heaven with mansions. Several societies see the dead as returning to earth to be reborn. The Hindus use this pattern of reincarnation to justify one's caste in this life and to promise eventual release from the pain of life through the attainment of *nirvana*, or inclusion into the One. The afterworld in many religions may resemble the everyday world, but we still lack comparative studies that show exactly how.

◆ Variation in Religious Practices

Beliefs are not the only elements of religion that vary from society to society. There is also variation in how people interact with the supernatural. The manner of approach to the supernatural varies from supplication—requests, prayers, and so on—to manipulation. And societies vary in the kinds of religious practitioners they have.

WAYS TO INTERACT WITH THE SUPERNATURAL

How to get in touch with the supernatural has proved to be a universal problem. Wallace identified a number of ways used by people the world over, though not necessarily all together, including, but not limited to, prayer (asking for supernatural help), physiological experience (doing things to the body and mind), simulation (manipulating imitations of things), feasts, and sacrifices.[29] Prayer can be spontaneous or memorized, private or public, silent or spoken. The Lugbara do not say the words of a prayer aloud, for doing so would be too powerful; they simply think about the things that are bothering them. The gods know all languages.

Doing things to the body or mind may involve drugs (hallucinogenics such as peyote or opiates) or alcohol; social isolation or sensory deprivation; dancing or running until exhausted; being deprived of food, water, and sleep; and listening to repetitive sounds such as drumming. Such behaviors may induce trances or altered states of consciousness.[30] Erika Bourguignon found that achieving these altered states, which she generally referred to as *trances,* is part of religious practice in 90 percent of the world's societies.[31] In some societies, trances are thought to

A worshipper making offerings at the feet of a statue in an Indian temple.

involve the presence of a spirit or power inside a person that changes or displaces that person's personality or soul. These types are referred to as possession trances. Other types of trances may involve the journey of a person's soul, experiencing visions, or transmitting messages from spirits. Possession trances are especially likely in societies that depend on agriculture and have social stratification, slavery, and more complex political hierarchies. Nonpossession trances are most likely to occur in food-collecting societies. Societies with moderate levels of social complexity have both possession and nonpossession trances.[32]

One puzzle is why there is a preponderance of women thought to be possessed. Alice Kehoe and Dody Giletti suggested that women are more likely than men to suffer from nutritional deficiencies because of pregnancy, lactation, and men's priority in gaining access to food. Calcium deficiency in particular can cause muscular spasms, convulsive seizures, and disorientation, all of which may foster the belief that an individual is possessed.[33] Douglas Raybeck and his colleagues suggest that women's physiology makes them more susceptible to calcium deficiency even with an equivalent diet. In addition, women are subject to more stress because they are usually less able to control their lives. Higher levels of stress, they suggest, lower the body's reserves of calcium.[34] Although intriguing, these suggestions need to be tested on individuals in field situations.

Voodoo employs simulation, or the imitation of things. Dolls are made in the likeness of an enemy and then are maltreated in hopes that the original enemy will experience pain and even death. Simulation is often employed during **divination,** or getting the supernatural to provide guidance. Many people in our society have their fortunes read in crystal balls, tea leaves, Ouija boards, or cards. Or they may choose a course of action by a toss of a coin or a throw of dice. All are variations of methods used in other cultures.

Omar Moore suggested that among the Naskapi hunters of Labrador, divination is an adaptive strategy for successful hunting. The Naskapi consult the diviner every three or four days when they have no luck in hunting. The diviner holds a caribou bone over the fire, as if the bone were a map, and the burns and cracks that appear in it indicate where the group should hunt. Moore, unlike the Naskapi, did not believe that the diviner really can find out where the animals will be; the cracks in the bones merely provide a way of randomly choosing where to hunt. Because humans are likely to develop customary patterns of action, they might be likely to look for game according to some plan. But game might learn to avoid hunters who operate according to a plan. Thus, any method of ensuring against patterning or predictable plans—any random strategy— may be advantageous. Divination by "reading" the bones would seem to be a random strategy. It also relieves any individual of the responsibility of deciding where to hunt, a decision that might arouse anger if the hunt failed.[35]

The eating of a sacred meal is found in many religions. For instance, Holy Communion is a simulation of the Last Supper. Australian aborigines, normally forbidden to eat their totem animal, have one totem feast a year at which they eat the totem. Feasts are often part of marriage and funeral ceremonies, as well as a fringe benefit of the sacrifice of food to the gods.

Some societies make sacrifices to a god in order to influence the god's action, either to divert anger or to attract goodwill. Characteristic of all sacrifices is that something of value is given up to the gods, whether it be food, drink, sex, household goods, or the life of an animal or person. Some societies feel that the god is obligated to act on their behalf if they make the appropriate sacrifice. Others use the sacrifice in an attempt to persuade the god, realizing there is no guarantee that the attempt will be successful.

Of all types of sacrifice, we probably think that the taking of human life is the ultimate. Nevertheless, human sacrifice is not rare in the ethnographic and historical records. Why have some societies practiced it? One cross-cultural study found that among preindustrial societies, those with full-time craft specialists, slavery, and the corvée are most likely to practice human sacrifice. The suggested explanation is that the sacrifice mirrors what is socially important: Societies that depend mainly on human labor for energy (rather than animals or machines) may think of a human life as an appropriate offering to the gods when people want something very important.[36]

MAGIC

All these modes of interacting with the supernatural can be categorized in various ways. One dimension of variation is how much people in society rely on pleading or asking or trying to persuade the supernatural to act on their behalf, as opposed to whether they believe they can compel the supernatural to help by performing certain acts. For example, prayer is asking; performing voodoo is presumably compelling. When people believe their action can compel the supernatural to act in some particular and intended way, anthropologists often refer to the belief and related practice as **magic.**

Magic may involve manipulation of the supernatural for good or for evil. Many societies have magical rituals designed to ensure good crops, the replenishment of game, the fertility of domestic animals, and the avoidance and cure of illness in humans. We tend to associate the belief in magic with societies simpler than our own. But as many as 80,000 people in the United States take magic seriously.[37] Many claim to be witches. An understanding of why magic appeals to some individuals but not others in our own society may help us explain why magic is an important part of religious behavior in many societies.

As we will see, the witch doctor and the shaman often employ magic to effect a cure. But the use of magic to bring about harm has evoked perhaps the most interest.

SORCERY AND WITCHCRAFT Sorcery and witchcraft are attempts to invoke the spirits to work harm against people. Although the words *sorcery* and *witchcraft* are often used interchangeably, they are also often distinguished. **Sorcery** may include the use of materials, objects, and medicines to invoke supernatural malevolence. **Witchcraft** may be said to accomplish the same ills by means of

thought and emotion alone. Evidence of witchcraft can never be found. This lack of visible evidence makes an accusation of witchcraft both harder to prove and harder to disprove.

To the Azande of Zaire, in central Africa, witchcraft was part of everyday living. It was not used to explain events for which the cause was known, such as carelessness or violation of a taboo, but to explain the otherwise unexplainable. A man is gored by an elephant. He must have been bewitched, because he had not been gored on other elephant hunts. A man goes to his beer hut at night, lights some straw, and holds it aloft to look at his beer. The thatch catches fire and the hut burns down. The man has been bewitched, for huts did not catch fire on hundreds of other nights when he and others did the same thing. Some of the pots of a skilled potter break; some of the bowls of a skilled carver crack. Witchcraft. Other pots, other bowls treated exactly the same have not broken.[38]

The witch craze in Europe during the sixteenth and seventeenth centuries and the witch trials in 1692 in Salem, Massachusetts, remind us that the fear of others, which the belief in witchcraft presumably represents, can increase and decrease in a society within a relatively short period of time. Many scholars have tried to explain these witch hunts. One factor often suggested is political turmoil, which may give rise to widespread distrust and a search for scapegoats. In the case of Europe during the sixteenth and seventeenth centuries, small regional political units were being incorporated into national states, and political allegiances were in flux. In addition, as Swanson noted, the commercial revolution and related changes were producing a new social class, the middle class, and "were promoting the growth of Protestantism and other heresies from Roman Catholicism."[39] In the case of Salem, the government of Massachusetts colony was unstable and there was much internal dissension. In 1692, the year of the witchcraft hysteria, Massachusetts was left without an English governor, and judicial practices broke down. These extraordinary conditions saw the accusation of a single person for witchcraft become the accusation of hundreds and the execution of 20 people. Swanson suggested that the undermining of legitimate political procedures may have generated the widespread fear of witches.[40]

It is also possible that epidemics of witchcraft accusation, as in Salem as well as other New England and European communities, may be the result of real epidemics—epidemics of disease. The disease implicated in Salem and elsewhere is the fungus disease called ergot, which can grow on rye plants. (The rye flour that went into the bread that the Salem people ate may have been contaminated by ergot.) It is now known that people who eat grain products contaminated by ergot suffer from convulsions, hallucinations, and other symptoms, such as crawling sensations in the skin. We also now know that ergot contains LSD, the drug that produces hallucinations and other delusions that resemble those occurring in severe mental disorders.

The presumed victims of bewitchment in Salem and other places had symptoms similar to victims of ergot poisoning today. They suffered from convulsions and the

In 1692 there was an epidemic of witchcraft accusations in Salem, Massachusetts. Some scholars have suggested that ergot poisoning may have made people act and feel as if they were bewitched.

Source: A witch trial at Salem, Massachusetts, in 1692. Lithograph, 19th century. The Granger Collection.

sensations of being pricked, pinched, or bitten. They had visions and felt as if they were flying through the air. We cannot know for sure that ergot poisoning occurred during those times when witchcraft accusations flourished. There is no direct evidence, of course, since the "bewitched" were not medically tested. But we do have some evidence that seems to be consistent with the ergot theory. Ergot is known to flourish on rye plants under certain climatic conditions—particularly a very cold winter followed by a cool, moist spring and summer. Tree-ring growth indicates that the early 1690s were particularly cold in eastern New England; and the outbreaks of witchcraft accusation in Europe seem to have peaked with colder winter temperatures.[41] Interestingly, too, when witchcraft hysteria was greatest in Europe, Europeans were using an ointment containing a skin-penetrating substance that we now know produces hallucinations and a vivid sensation of flying.[42] It may not be cause for wonder, then, that our popular image of witches is one of people flying through the air on broomsticks.

But whether or not epidemics of witchcraft hysteria are due to epidemics of ergot poisoning or episodes of political turmoil or both, we still have to understand why so many societies in the ethnographic record believe in witchcraft and sorcery in the first place. Why do so many societies believe that there are ways to invoke the spirits to work harm against people? One possible explanation, suggested by Beatrice Whiting, is that sorcery or witchcraft will be found in societies that lack procedures or judicial authorities to deal with crime and other offenses. Her theory is that all societies need some form of social control—some way of deterring most would-be offenders and of dealing with actual offenders. In the absence of judicial officials who, if present, might deter and deal with antisocial behavior, sorcery may be a very effective social-control mechanism. If you misbehave, the person you mistreated might cause you to become ill or even die. The cross-cultural evidence seems to support this theory. Sorcery is more important in societies that lack judicial authorities than in those that have them.[43]

TYPES OF PRACTITIONER

Individuals may believe that they can directly contact the supernatural, but almost all societies also have part-time or full-time religious or magical practitioners. Research suggests there are four major types of practitioner: shamans, sorcerers or witches, mediums, and priests. As we shall see, the number of types of practitioner in a society seems to vary with degree of cultural complexity.[44]

THE SHAMAN The word *shaman* may come from a language that was spoken in eastern Siberia. The **shaman** is usually a part-time male specialist who has fairly high status in his community and is often involved in healing.[45] We discuss the role of the shaman as healer in the chapter on medical anthropology. Here we focus on the methods used by shamans to help others.

The shaman enters into a trance, or some other altered state of consciousness, and then journeys to other worlds in order to get help from guardian or other spirits. Dreams may be used to provide insight or as a way for shamans to commune with spirits. People may seek help for practical matters, such as where to get food resources or whether to relocate, but solving a health problem is most often the goal of the shaman.[46] Shamans may also bring news from spirits, such as a warning about an impending disaster.[47]

Someone may receive a "call" to the role of shaman in recovering from an illness, through a vision quest, or in a dream. Shamans-in-training may enhance the vividness of their imagery by using hallucinogens, sleep or food deprivation, or engaging in extensive physical activity such as dancing. An important part of the process of being a shaman is learning to control the imagery and the spirit powers. Shamanistic training can take several years under the guidance of a master shaman.[48]

SORCERERS AND WITCHES In contrast with shamans, who have fairly high status, sorcerers and witches of both sexes tend to have very low social and economic status in their societies.[49] Suspected sorcerers and witches are usually feared because they are thought to know how to invoke the supernatural to cause illness, injury, and death. Because sorcerers use materials for their magic, evidence of sorcery can be found, and suspected sorcerers are often killed for their malevolent activities. Because witchcraft supposedly is accomplished by thought and emotion alone, it may be harder to prove that someone is a witch, but the difficulty of proving witchcraft has not prevented people from accusing and killing others for being witches.

MEDIUMS **Mediums** tend to be females. These part-time practitioners are asked to heal and divine while in possession trances—that is, when they are thought to be possessed by spirits. Mediums are described as having tremors, convulsions, seizures, and temporary amnesia.

PRIESTS **Priests** are generally full-time male specialists who officiate at public events. They have very high status and are thought to be able to relate to superior or high gods who are beyond the ordinary person's control. In most societies with priests, the people who get to be priests obtain their offices through inheritance or political appointment.[50] Priests are sometimes distinguished from other people by special clothing or a different hairstyle. The training of a priest can be vigorous and long, including fasting, praying, and physical labor, as well as learning the dogma and the

ANTHROPOLOGICAL ORIGINALS
The Sierra Otomí of Mexico

Shamans can heal because they can contact the supernatural: Where illness can be caused by sorcery, it could be counteracted by getting the supernatural to intervene. The gods can also be persuaded to control other evil forces that bring trouble into the world. But you need a special person to get them to act in your behalf. That person is the shaman.

Shamans are native healers who solve domestic conflicts, cure disease, and help the farmer bring the life forces back into his *milpa* [forest land cleared for cultivation]. They also act as ritual advisors at the *costumbres of the antiguas* [customs of the ancients]. Although shamans are also peasants, their shamanic work can keep them busy for weeks at a time. They may hire people or ask a kinsperson to do their farm work. Women as well as men can be shamans. Shamans work primarily with the *zaki* [spirit] of plant, animal, human, and superhuman beings. Each shaman has his or her particular style and particular specialties. In their rituals, shamans represent the zaki with figures cut out of paper.

Shamans are called upon when a family is particularly troubled by disease or psychological distress. Shamans make more house calls than Western doctors but normally receive their patients in their home oratories first. There they give "consultations" that bring patient, shaman, and superhuman beings into a therapeutic alliance. They may visit a house to clean it of evil airs, wandering troubled souls. They may counteract evil sorcery with rituals. They may suck evil magic out of the body of the sufferer. Above all, shamans are warriors on the side of the patient, attacking the evil besetting him, be it disease or envious neighbors.

CD-ROM Anthropological Originals 25

Source: James W. Dow, "Sierra Otomi: People of the Mexican Mountains," in Melvin Ember and Carol R. Ember, eds., *Portraits of Culture: Ethnographic Originals,* in Carol R. Ember and Melvin Ember, eds., *New Directions in Anthropology* (Upper Saddle River, NJ: Prentice Hall, CD-ROM, 2003).

ritual of his religion. Priests in the United States complete four years of theological school and sometimes serve first as apprentices under established priests. The priest does not receive a fee for his services but is supported by donations from parishioners or followers. Priests often have some political power as a result of their office—the chief priest is sometimes also the head of state or is a close adviser to the chief of state—and their material well-being is a direct reflection of their position in the priestly hierarchy.

It is the dependence on memorized ritual that both marks and protects the priest. If a shaman repeatedly fails to effect a cure, he will probably lose his following, for he has obviously lost the support of the spirits. But if a priest performs his ritual perfectly and the gods choose not to respond, the priest will usually retain his position and the ritual will preserve its assumed effectiveness. The nonresponse of the gods will be explained in terms of the people's unworthiness of supernatural favor.

PRACTITIONERS AND SOCIAL COMPLEXITY

More complex societies tend to have more types of religious or magical practitioners. If a society has only one type of practitioner, it is almost always a shaman; such societies tend to be nomadic or seminomadic food collectors. Societies with two types of practitioner (usually shaman-healers and priests) have agriculture. Those with three types of practitioner are agriculturalists or pastoralists with political integration beyond the community (the additional practitioner type tends to be either a sorcerer-witch or a medium). Finally, societies with all four types of practitioner have agriculture, political integration beyond the community, and social classes.[51]

◆ Religion and Adaptation

Following Malinowski, many anthropologists take the view that religions are adaptive because they reduce the anxieties and uncertainties that afflict all peoples. We do not really know that religion is the only means of reducing anxiety and uncertainty, or even that individuals or societies *have* to reduce their anxiety and uncertainty. Still, it seems likely that certain religious beliefs and practices have directly adaptive consequences. For example, the Hindu belief in the sacred cow has seemed to many to be the very opposite of a useful or adaptive custom. Their religion does not permit Hindus to slaughter cows. Why do the Hindus retain such a belief? Why do they allow all those cows to wander around freely, defecating all over the place, and not slaughter any of them? The contrast with our own use of cows could hardly be greater.

Marvin Harris suggested that the Hindu use of cows may have beneficial consequences that some other use of cows would not have. Harris pointed out that there may be a sound economic reason for not slaughtering cattle in India. The cows, and the males they produce, provide resources that could not easily be gotten otherwise. At the same time, their wandering around to forage is no strain on the food-producing economy.

The resources provided by the cows are varied. First, a team of oxen and a plow are essential for the many small farms in India. The Indians could produce oxen with fewer cows, but to do so they would have to devote some of their food production to the feeding of those cows. In the present system, they do not feed the cows, and even though poor nutrition makes the cows relatively infertile, males, which are castrated to make oxen, are still produced at no cost to the economy. Second, cow dung is essential as a cooking fuel and fertilizer. The National Council of Applied Economic Research estimated that an amount of dung equivalent to 45 million tons of coal is burned annually. Moreover, it is delivered practically to the door each day at no cost. Alternative sources of fuel, such as wood, are scarce or costly. In addition, about 340 million tons of dung are used as manure—essential in a country obliged to derive three harvests a year from its intensively cultivated land. Third, although Hindus do not eat beef, cattle that die naturally or are butchered by non-Hindus are eaten by the lower castes, who, without the upper-caste taboo against eating beef, might not get this needed protein. Fourth, the hides and horns of the cattle that die are used in India's enormous leather industry. Therefore, because the cows do not themselves consume resources needed by people and it would be impossible to provide traction, fuel, and fertilizer as cheaply by other means, the taboo against slaughtering cattle may be very adaptive.[52]

RELIGIOUS CHANGE AS REVITALIZATION

The long history of religion includes periods of strong resistance to change as well as periods of radical change. Anthropologists have been especially interested in the founding of new religions or sects. The appearance of new religions is one of the things that may happen when cultures are disrupted by contact with dominant societies. Various terms have been suggested for these religious movements—cargo cults, nativistic movements, messianic movements, millenarian cults. Wallace suggested that they are all examples of **revitalization movements,** efforts to save a culture by infusing it with a new purpose and new life.[53] We turn to examples of such movements from North America and Melanesia.

THE SENECA AND THE RELIGION OF HANDSOME LAKE The Seneca reservation of the Iroquois on the Allegheny River in New York State was a place of "poverty and humiliation" by 1799.[54] Demoralized by whiskey and dispossessed from their traditional lands, unable to compete with the new technology because of illiteracy and lack of training, the Seneca were at an impasse. In this setting, Handsome Lake, the 50-year-old brother of a chief, had the first of a number of visions. In them, he met with emissaries of the Creator who showed him heaven and hell and commissioned him to revitalize Seneca religion and society. This he set out to do for the next decade and a half. He used as his principal text the *Gaiwiio,* or "Good Word," a gospel that contains statements about the nature of

CURRENT RESEARCH AND ISSUES
One Appeal of Religion May Be the Wish for a Better World

There are many religions in the United States today, and new sects, often derisively called cults, emerge regularly. Few of us realize that nearly all of the major churches or religions in the world began as minority sects or cults. Indeed, some of the most established and prestigious Protestant churches were radical social movements at first. For example, what we now know as the United Church of Christ, which includes the Congregational Church, was founded by radicals in England who wanted church governance to be in the hands of the local congregation. Many of these radicals became the people we call Pilgrims, who had to flee to the New World. But they were very fundamentalist in their beliefs too; for example, as late as the 1820s, Congregationalist-dominated towns in Connecticut prohibited celebrations of Christmas outside of church because such celebrations were not mentioned in the Bible. Nowadays, Congregationalists are among the most liberal Protestants.

We should not be surprised to learn that most of the various Protestant churches today, including some considered very conservative, began as militant sects that set out to achieve a better world. After all, that's why we call them "Protestant." At first, the rebellion was against Rome and the Catholic Church. Later, sects developed in opposition to church and government hierarchies. And remember that Christianity itself began as a radical group in the hinterland of the Roman Empire. So new sects or cults were probably always political and social, as well as religious, movements. Recall that the word *millennium,* as used in discussions of religious movements, refers to a wished-for or expected future time when human life and society will be perfect and free of troubles; the world will then be prosperous and happy and peaceful. Nowadays, the wish for a better world may or may not be religiously inspired. Some people who seek a more perfect world believe that humans alone must achieve it.

How should we categorize this wish for a better world? Should we call it "conservative" because the imagined world may have existed in the past? If the imagined world does not yet exist, is it "radical" to believe it can be achieved? Maybe the wish for a more perfect world is neither conservative nor radical. Maybe it is just that people who are not satisfied with the world as it is think that something can be done to improve things, with or without divine assistance. However it will come, the "millennium" will be different from now, and better.

Ideas about the millennium, and the origins of new cults and religions, might best be viewed then as human hopes: Which ones do people have? Do they vary from culture to culture, and why? Are some hopes universal? And how might they be achieved?

Sources: Rodney Stark, *The Future of Religion: Secularization, Revival and Cult Formation* (Berkeley: University of California Press, 1985); G. W. Trompf, ed., *Cargo Cults and Millenarian Movements: Transoceanic Comparisons of New Religious Movements* (Berlin: Mouton de Gruyter, 1990).

religion and eternity and a code of conduct for the righteous. The *Gaiwiio* is interesting both for the influence of Quaker Christianity it clearly reveals[55] and for the way the new material was merged with traditional Iroquois religious concepts.

The first part of the "Good Word" has three main themes, one of which is the concept of an apocalypse. Handsome Lake offered many signs by which the faithful could recognize impending, cosmic doom. Great drops of fire would rain from the skies and a veil would be cast over the earth. False prophets would appear, witch women would openly cast spells, and poisonous creatures from the underworld would seize and kill those who had rejected the *Gaiwiio.* Second, the *Gaiwiio* emphasized sin. The great sins were disbelief in the "good way," drunkenness, witchcraft, and abortion. Sins had to be confessed and repented. Finally, the *Gaiwiio* offered salvation. Salvation could be won by following a code of conduct, attending certain important traditional rites, and performing public confession.

The second part of the *Gaiwiio* sets out the code of conduct. This code seems to orient the Seneca toward advantageous Euro-American practices without separating them from their culture. The code has five main sections:

1. *Temperance.* All Seneca leaders were fully aware of the social disorders arising out of abuse of liquor. Handsome Lake went to great lengths to illustrate and explain the harmfulness of alcohol.

2. *Peace and social unity.* Seneca leaders were to cease their futile bickering, and all were to be united in their approach to the larger society.

3. *Preservation of tribal lands.* Handsome Lake, fearing the piecemeal alienation of Seneca lands, was far ahead of his contemporaries in demanding a halt in land sales to non-Seneca.

4. *Proacculturation* (favoring external culture traits). Though individual property and trading for profit

A revitalization movement that became known as the Ghost Dance spread eastward from the Northwest in the 1870s to the 1890s. It was generally believed that if people did the dance correctly, ghosts would come to life with sufficient resources to allow the people to return to their old ways, and, as a result of some cataclysm, the whites would disappear.

Source: Ogallala Sioux performing the Ghost Dance at the Pine Ridge Indian Agency, South Dakota. Illustration by Frederic Remington, 1890. The Granger Collection.

were prohibited, the acquisition of literacy in English was encouraged so that people would be able to read and understand treaties and to avoid being cheated.

5. *Domestic morality.* Sons were to obey their fathers, mothers should avoid interfering with daughters' marriages, and husbands and wives should respect the sanctity of their marriage vows.

Handsome Lake's teaching seems to have led to a renaissance among the Seneca. Temperance was widely accepted, as were schooling and new farming methods. By 1801, corn yields had been increased tenfold, new crops (oats, potatoes, flax) had been introduced, and public health and hygiene had improved considerably. Handsome Lake himself acquired great power among his people. He spent the remainder of his life fulfilling administrative duties, acting as a representative of the Iroquois in Washington, and preaching his gospel to neighboring tribes. By the time of Handsome Lake's death in 1815, the Seneca clearly had undergone a dramatic rebirth, attributable at least in part to the new religion. Later in the century, some of Handsome Lake's disciples founded a church in his name that, despite occasional setbacks and political disputes, survives to this day.

Although many scholars believe cultural stress gives rise to these new religious movements, it is still important to understand exactly what the stresses are and how strong they have to become before a new movement emerges. Do different kinds of stresses produce different kinds of movements? And does the nature of the movement depend on the cultural elements already present? Let us consider some theory and research on the causes of the millenarian cargo cults that began to appear in Melanesia from about 1885 on.

CARGO CULTS The *cargo cults* can be thought of as religious movements "in which there is an expectation of, and preparation for, the coming of a period of supernatural bliss."[56] Thus, an explicit belief of the cargo cults was the notion that some liberating power would bring all the Western goods (cargo in pidgin English) the people might want. For example, around 1932, on Buka in the Solomon Islands, the leaders of a cult prophesied that a tidal wave would sweep away the villages and a ship would arrive with iron, axes, food, tobacco, cars, and arms. Work in the gardens ceased, and wharves and docks were built for the expected cargo.[57]

What may explain such cults? Peter Worsley suggested that an important factor in the rise of cargo cults and millenarian movements in general is the existence of oppression—in the case of Melanesia, colonial oppression. He suggested that the reactions in Melanesia took religious rather than political forms because they were a way of pulling together people who previously had no political unity and who lived in small, isolated social groups.[58] Other scholars, such as David Aberle, suggested that *relative deprivation* is more important than oppression in explaining the origins of cults; when people feel that they could have more, and they have less than what they used to have or less than others, they may be attracted to new cults.[59] Consistent with Aberle's general interpretation, Bruce Knauft's comparative study of cargo cults found that such cults were more important in Melanesian societies that had had decreasing cultural contact with the West, and presumably *decreasing* contact with valued goods, within the year prior to the cult's emergence.[60]

If the recent as well as distant past is any guide, we can expect religious belief and practice to be revitalized periodically, particularly during times of stress. Thus, we can expect the world to continue to have religious variation.

 CD-ROM Flashcards Chapter 25

 # Summary

1. Religion is any set of attitudes, beliefs, and practices pertaining to supernatural power. Such beliefs may vary within a culture as well as among societies, and they may change over time.

2. Religious beliefs are evident in all known cultures and are inferred from artifacts associated with *Homo sapiens* since at least 60,000 years ago.

3. Theories to account for the universality of religion suggest that humans create religion in response to certain universal needs or conditions, including a need for understanding, reversion to childhood feelings, anxiety or uncertainty, and a need for community.

4. There are wide variations in religious beliefs. Societies vary in the number and kinds of supernatural entities in which they believe. There may be impersonal supernatural forces (e.g., mana and taboo), supernatural beings of nonhuman origin (gods and spirits), and supernatural beings of human origin (ghosts and ancestor spirits). The religious belief system of a society may include any or all such entities.

5. Gods and spirits may be unpredictable or predictable, aloof from or interested in human affairs, helpful or punishing. In some societies, all gods are equal in rank; in others, there is a hierarchy of prestige and power among gods and spirits, just as among the humans in those societies.

6. A monotheistic religion is one in which there is one high god, as the creator of the universe or the director of events (or both); all other supernatural beings are either subordinate to, or function as alternative manifestations of, this god. A high god is generally found in societies with a high level of political development.

7. Faced with ignorance, pain, and injustice, people frequently explain events by claiming intervention by the gods. Such intervention has also been sought by people who hope it will help them achieve their own ends. The gods are likely to punish the immoral behavior of people in societies that have considerable differences in wealth.

8. Various methods have been used to attempt communication with the supernatural. Among them are prayer, taking drugs or otherwise affecting the body and mind, simulation, feasts, and sacrifices.

9. When people believe that their actions can compel the supernatural to act in a particular and intended way, anthropologists refer to the belief and related practice as magic. Sorcery and witchcraft are attempts to make the spirits work harm against people.

10. Almost all societies have part-time or full-time religious or magical practitioners. Recent cross-cultural research suggests that there are four major types of practitioner: shamans, sorcerers or witches, mediums, and priests. The number of types of practitioner seems to vary with degree of cultural complexity: the more complex the society, the more types of practitioner.

11. The history of religion includes periods of strong resistance to change and periods of radical change. One explanation for this cycle is that religious practices always originate during periods of stress. Religious movements have been called revitalization movements—efforts to save a culture by infusing it with a new purpose and new life.

 # Glossary Terms

ancestor spirits	polytheistic
animatism	priest
animism	religion
divination	revitalization movement
ghosts	shaman
gods	sorcery
magic	spirits
mana	supernatural
medium	taboo
monotheistic	witchcraft

 # Critical Questions

1. How does your conception of God compare with beliefs about supernatural beings in other religious systems?

2. What do you think is the future of religion?

3. Could any of the religious practices you know about be classified as magic? Are they associated with anxiety-arousing situations?

Internet Exercises

1. A project at Harvard University on pluralism is designed to study the growing diversity of religions in the United States. Go to the site **http://www.fas.harvard.edu/~pluralsm/**. Click on About the Project; then explore the online slide show.

2. To explore different religions and religious movements, visit the Web site at **http://religiousmovements.lib.virginia.edu/**. Read profiles about two religions (not your own) that you are not familiar with and two that you have never heard of.

3. Explore a site that gives some information about different religions in the Canadian province of Newfoundland at **http://www.ucs.mun.ca/~hrollman/indexjava.html**. Compare at least two religious traditions.

Suggested Reading

CHILD, A. B., AND CHILD, I. L. *Religion and Magic in the Life of Traditional Peoples.* Upper Saddle River, NJ: Prentice Hall, 1993. Based on a review of ethnographic data from all over the world, this book discusses the features common to traditional religions everywhere, as well as the factors that may account for variation in religion.

EMBER, M., AND EMBER, C. R., EDS. *Portraits of Culture: Ethnographic Originals.* In C. R. Ember and M. Ember, eds., *New Directions in Anthropology.* Upper Saddle River, NJ: Prentice Hall, CD-ROM, 2003. Several chapters deal extensively with religious belief and practice as seen in a particular culture; G. Brandon, "African-Americans: Getting into the Spirit"; J. W. Dow, "Sierra Otomí: People of the Mexican Mountains"; W. K. Powers and M. N. Powers, "Lakota: A Study in Cultural Continuity"; S. B. Schaefer, "Huichol: Becoming a Godmother"; J. R. Sosa, "Maya: The Sacred in Everyday Life."

MALINOWSKI, B. *Magic, Science and Religion and Other Essays.* Garden City, NY: Doubleday, 1954. A classic collection of papers representing some of Malinowski's work on ritual and religious behavior and the nature of primitive cults, magic, and faith.

MATLOCK, J. G. "Universals and Variation in Religious Belief and Practice." In C. R. Ember and M. Ember, eds., *Cross-Cultural Research for Social Science,* in C. R. Ember and M. Ember, eds., *New Directions in Anthropology.* Upper Saddle River, NJ: Prentice Hall, CD-ROM, 2003. A review of cross-cultural studies of religious diversity, suggesting how religious beliefs and practices change in response to changes in social and political organization and subsistence strategy.

SERED, S. S. *Priestess, Mother, Sacred Sister.* New York: Oxford University Press, 1994. This book discusses how and why women rather than men came to dominate the religion of some societies known to anthropology.

SWANSON, G. E. *The Birth of the Gods: The Origin of Primitive Beliefs.* Ann Arbor: University of Michigan Press, 1969. A pioneering cross-cultural study that explores the origins of religious beliefs and examines how various aspects of religion may be related to social and political organization.

CULTURE CHANGE AND GLOBALIZATION

27

CHAPTER OUTLINE

- ◆ How and Why Cultures Change

- ◆ Culture Change and Adaptation

- ◆ Types of Culture Change in the Modern World

- ◆ Globalization: Problems and Opportunities

- ◆ Ethnogenesis: The Emergence of New Cultures

- ◆ Cultural Diversity in the Future

Most of us are aware that "times have changed," especially when we compare our lives with those of our parents. Witness the recent changes in attitudes about sex and marriage, as well as the changes in women's roles. But such culture change is not unusual. Throughout history humans have replaced or altered customary behaviors and attitudes as their needs have changed. Just as no individual is immortal, no particular cultural pattern is impervious to change. Anthropologists, therefore, want to understand how and why culture change occurs.

Three general questions can be asked about culture change: What is the source of a new trait? Why are people motivated, unconsciously as well as consciously, to adopt it? And is the new trait adaptive? The source of the change may be inside or outside the society. That is, a new idea or behavior may originate within the society, or it may come from another society. With regard to motivation, people may adopt the new idea or behavior voluntarily, even if unconsciously, or they may be forced to adopt it. Finally, the outcome of culture change may or may not be beneficial. In this chapter, we first discuss the various processes of culture change in terms of the three dimensions of source, motivation, and outcome. Then we discuss some of the major types of culture change in the modern world. As we will see, these changes are associated largely with the expansion of Western societies over the last 500 years. In particular, we discuss *globalization*—the ongoing spread of cultural features around the world—and what it portends for the future of cultural diversity.

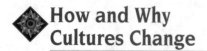

How and Why Cultures Change

Discoveries and inventions, which may originate inside or outside a society, are ultimately the sources of all culture change. But they do not necessarily lead to change. If an invention or discovery is ignored, no change in culture results. It is only when society accepts an invention or discovery and uses it regularly that we can begin to speak of culture change.

DISCOVERY AND INVENTION

The new thing discovered or invented, the innovation, may be an object—the wheel, the plow, the computer—or it may involve behavior and ideas—buying and selling, democracy, monogamy. According to Ralph Linton, a discovery is any addition to knowledge and an invention is a new application of knowledge.[1] Thus, a person might discover that children can be persuaded to eat nourishing food if the food is associated with an imaginary character who appeals to them. And then someone might exploit that discovery by inventing a character named Popeye who appears in a series of animated cartoons, acquiring miraculous strength by devouring cans of spinach.

UNCONSCIOUS INVENTION In discussing the process of invention, we should differentiate between various types of inventions. One type is the consequence of a society's setting itself a specific goal, such as eliminating tuberculosis or placing a person on the moon. Another type emerges less intentionally. This second process of invention is often referred to as *accidental juxtaposition* or *unconscious invention*. Linton suggested that some inventions, especially those of prehistoric days, were probably the consequences of literally dozens of tiny initiatives by "unconscious" inventors. These inventors made their small contributions, perhaps over many hundreds of years, without being aware of the part they were playing in bringing one invention, such as the wheel or a better form of hand ax, to completion.[2] Consider the example of children playing on a fallen log, which rolls as they walk and balance on it, coupled with the need at a given moment to move a slab of granite from a cave face. The children's play may have suggested the use of logs as rollers and thereby set in motion a series of developments that culminated in the wheel.

In reconstructing the process of invention in prehistoric times, however, we should be careful not to look back on our ancestors with a smugness generated by our more highly developed technology. We have become accustomed to turning to the science sections of our magazines and newspapers and finding, almost daily, reports of miraculous new discoveries and inventions. From our point of view, it is difficult to imagine such a simple invention as the wheel taking so many centuries to come into being. We are tempted to surmise that early humans were less intelligent than we are. But the capacity of the human brain has been the same for perhaps 100,000 years; there is no evidence that the inventors of the wheel were any less intelligent than we are.

INTENTIONAL INNOVATION Some discoveries and inventions arise out of deliberate attempts to produce a new idea or object. It may seem that such innovations are obvious responses to perceived needs. For example, during the Industrial Revolution there was a great demand for inventions that would increase productivity. James Hargreaves, in 18th-century England, is an example of an inventor who responded to an existing demand. Textile manufacturers were clamoring for such large quantities of spun yarn that cottage laborers, working with foot-operated spinning wheels, could not meet the demand. Hargreaves, realizing that prestige and financial rewards would come to the person who invented a method of spinning large quantities of yarn in a short time, set about the task and developed the spinning jenny.

But perceived needs and the economic rewards that may be given to the innovator do not explain why only some people innovate. We know relatively little about why some people are more innovative than others. The ability to innovate may depend in part on individual characteristics such as high intelligence and creativity. And creativity may be influenced by social conditions.

A study of innovation among Ashanti artist-carvers in Ghana suggests that creativity is more likely in some socioeconomic groups than in others.[3] Some carvers produced only traditional designs; others departed from tradition and produced "new" styles of carving. Two groups were found to innovate the most—the wealthiest and the poorest carvers. These two groups of carvers may tolerate risk more than the middle socioeconomic group. Innovative carving entails some risk because it may take more time and it may not sell. Wealthy carvers can afford the risk, and they may gain some prestige as well as income if their innovation is appreciated. The poor are not doing well anyway, and they have little to lose by trying something new.

Some societies encourage innovativeness more than others and this can vary substantially over time. Patricia Greenfield and her colleagues describe the changes in weaving in a Mayan community in the Zinacantán region of Chiapas, Mexico.[4] In 1969 and 1970, innovation was not valued. Rather, tradition was; there was the old "true way" to do everything, including how one dressed. There were only four simple weaving patterns, and virtually all males wore ponchos with the same pattern. By 1991, virtually no poncho was the same and the villagers had developed elaborate brocaded and embroidered designs. In a period of 20 years, innovation had increased dramatically. Two other things had also changed. The economy was more commercialized; textiles as well as other items were now bought and sold. The other change was a shift to a much less directed teaching style. Earlier, mothers would give highly structured instruction to their daughters, often with "four hands" on the loom. Later, girls were allowed to learn more by themselves, by trial-and-error, and they produced more abstract and varied designs.

WHO ADOPTS INNOVATIONS?   Once someone discovers or invents something, there is still the question of whether the innovation will be adopted by others. Many researchers have studied the characteristics of "early adopters." Such individuals tend to be educated, high in social status, upwardly mobile, and, if they are property owners, have large farms and businesses. The individuals who most need technological improvements—those who are less well off—are generally the last to adopt innovations. The theory is that only the wealthy can afford to take the substantial risks associated with new ways of doing things. In periods of rapid technological change, therefore, the gap between rich and poor is likely to widen because the rich adopt innovations sooner, and benefit more from them, than the poor.[5]

Does this imply that the likelihood of adopting innovations is a simple function of how much wealth a possible adopter possesses? Not necessarily. Frank Cancian reviewed several studies and found that upper-middle-class individuals show more conservatism than lower-middle-class individuals. Cancian suggested that when the risks are unknown, the lower-middle-class individuals are more receptive to innovation because they have less to lose. Later on, when the risks are better known—that is, as more people adopt the innovation—the upper-middle class catches up to the lower-middle.[6] So the readiness to accept

innovation, like the likelihood of creativity among Ashanti carvers, may not be related to socioeconomic position in a linear way.

The speed of accepting an innovation may depend partly on how new behaviors and ideas are typically transmitted in a society. In particular, is a person exposed to many versus few "teachers"? If children learn most of what they know from their parents or from a relatively small number of elders, then innovation will be slow to spread throughout the society, and culture change is likely to be slow. Innovations may catch on more rapidly if individuals are exposed to various teachers and other "leaders" who can influence many in a relatively short time. And the more peers we have, the more we might learn from them.[7] Perhaps this is why the pace of change appears to be so quick today. In societies like our own, and increasingly in the industrializing world, it is likely that people learn in schools from teachers, from leaders in their specialties, and from peers.

COSTS AND BENEFITS   An innovation that is technologically superior is not necessarily going to be adopted. There are costs as well as benefits for both individuals and large-scale industries. Take the computer keyboard. The keyboard used most often on computers today is called the QWERTY keyboard (named after the letters on the left side of the line of keys below the row of number keys). This keyboard was actually invented to slow typing speed down! Early typewriters had mechanical keys that jammed if the typist went too fast.[8] Computer keyboards don't have that problem, so an arrangement of keys that allowed faster typing would probably be better. Different keyboard configurations have been invented, but they haven't caught on. Most people probably would find it too hard or too time-consuming to learn a new style of typing, so the original style of keyboard persists.

In large-scale industries, technological innovations may be very costly to implement. A new product or process may require revamping a manufacturing or service facility and retraining workers. Before a decision is made to change, the costs of doing so are weighed against the potential benefits. If the market is expected to be large for a new product, the product is more likely to be produced. If the market is judged small, the benefits may not be sufficient inducement to change. Companies may also judge the value of an innovation by whether it could be copied by competitors. If the new innovation is easily copyable, the inventing company may not find the investment worthwhile. Although the market may be large, the inventing company may not be able to hold onto market share if other companies could produce the product quickly without having to invest in research and development.[9]

DIFFUSION

The source of new cultural elements in a society may also be another society. The process by which cultural elements are borrowed from another society and incorporated into the culture of the recipient group is called **diffusion.**

Americans have not adopted most features of Japanese culture, but the interest in sushi is spreading.

Borrowing sometimes enables a group to bypass stages or mistakes in the development of a process or institution. For example, Germany was able to accelerate its program of industrialization in the nineteenth century because it was able to avoid some of the errors made by its English and Belgian competitors by taking advantage of technological borrowing. Japan did the same somewhat later. Indeed, in recent years some of the earliest industrialized countries have fallen behind their imitators in certain areas of production, such as automobiles, televisions, cameras, and computers.

In a well-known passage, Linton conveyed the far-reaching effects of diffusion by considering the first few hours in the day of an American man in the 1930s. This man

> . . . awakens in a bed built on a pattern which originated in the Near East but which was modified in northern Europe before it was transmitted to America. He throws back covers made from cotton, domesticated in India, or linen, domesticated in the Near East, or silk, the use of which was discovered in China. All of these materials have been spun and woven by processes invented in the Near East. . . . He takes off his pajamas, a garment invented in India, and washes with soap invented by the ancient Gauls. He then shaves, a masochistic rite which seems to have derived from either Sumer or ancient Egypt.
>
> Before going out for breakfast he glances through the window, made of glass invented in Egypt, and if it is raining puts on overshoes made of rubber discovered by the Central American Indians and takes an umbrella, invented in southeastern Asia. . . .

On his way to breakfast he stops to buy a paper paying for it with coins, an ancient Lydian invention. . . . His plate is made of a form of pottery invented in China. His knife is of steel, an alloy first made in southern India, his fork a medieval Italian invention, and his spoon a derivative of a Roman original. . . . After his fruit (African watermelon) and first coffee (an Abyssinian plant) . . . he may have the egg of a species of bird domesticated in Indo-China, or thin strips of the flesh of an animal domesticated in Eastern Asia which have been salted and smoked by a process developed in northern Europe. . . .

While smoking (an American Indian habit) he reads the news of the day, imprinted in characters invented by the ancient Semites upon a material invented in China by a process invented in Germany. As he absorbs the accounts of foreign troubles he will, if he is a good conservative citizen, thank a Hebrew deity in an Indo-European language that he is 100 percent American.[10]

PATTERNS OF DIFFUSION There are three basic patterns of diffusion: direct contact, intermediate contact, and stimulus diffusion.

1. *Direct contact.* Elements of a society's culture may be first taken up by neighboring societies and then gradually spread farther and farther afield. The spread of the use of paper (a sheet of interlaced fibers) is a good example of extensive diffusion by direct contact. The invention of paper is attributed to the Chinese Ts'ai Lun in A.D. 105. Within 50 years, paper was being made in many places in central China. While the art of papermaking was kept secret for about 500 years, paper was distributed as a commodity to much of the Arab world through the markets at Samarkand. But when Samarkand was attacked by the Chinese in 751, a Chinese prisoner was forced to set up a paper mill. Paper manufacture then spread to the rest of the Arab world; it was first manufactured in Baghdad in A.D. 793, Egypt about A.D. 900, and Morocco about A.D. 1100. Papermaking was introduced as a commodity in Europe by Arab trade through Italian ports in the twelfth century. The Moors built the first European paper mill in Spain about 1150. The technical knowledge then spread throughout Europe with paper mills built in Italy in 1276, France 1348, Germany 1390, and England 1494.[11] In general, the pattern of accepting the borrowed invention was the same in all cases: Paper was first imported as a luxury, then in ever-expanding quantities as a staple product. Finally, and usually within one to three centuries, local manufacture began.

2. *Intermediate contact.* Diffusion by intermediate contact occurs through the agency of third parties. Frequently, traders carry a cultural trait from the society that originated it to another group. As an example of diffusion through intermediaries, Phoenician traders spread the alphabet, which may have been invented by another

Semitic group, to Greece. At times, soldiers serve as intermediaries in spreading a culture trait. European crusaders, such as the Knights Templar and the Knights of St. John, acted as intermediaries in two ways: They carried Christian culture to Muslim societies of North Africa and brought Arab culture back to Europe. In the nineteenth century, Western missionaries in all parts of the world encouraged natives to wear Western clothing. The result is that in Africa, the Pacific Islands, and elsewhere, native peoples can be found wearing shorts, suit jackets, shirts, ties, and other typically Western articles of clothing.

3. *Stimulus diffusion.* In stimulus diffusion, knowledge of a trait belonging to another culture stimulates the invention or development of a local equivalent. A classic example of stimulus diffusion is the Cherokee syllabic writing system created by a Native American named Sequoya so that his people could write down their

language. Sequoya got the idea from his contact with Europeans. Yet he did not adopt the English writing system; indeed, he did not even learn to write English. What he did was utilize some English alphabetic symbols, alter others, and invent new ones. All the symbols he used represented Cherokee syllables and in no way echoed English alphabetic usage. In other words, Sequoya took English alphabetic ideas and gave them a new, Cherokee form. The stimulus originated with Europeans; the result was peculiarly Cherokee.

THE SELECTIVE NATURE OF DIFFUSION Although there is a temptation to view the dynamics of diffusion as similar to a stone sending concentric ripples over still water, this would be an oversimplification of the way diffusion actually occurs. Not all cultural traits are borrowed as readily as the ones we have mentioned, nor do they usually expand in neat, ever-widening circles. Rather,

ANTHROPOLOGICAL ORIGINALS
The Eskimos of North Alaska

Culture change is usually selective: Many cultures in recent times have changed, sometimes drastically. But always some things about the old culture are retained despite contact with and experience in the outside world. How could it be otherwise? Some old ways may still be the best or preferred ways to do things. Traditional food is still preferred by many Eskimos, and they have to hunt and fish to get it.

The day after I arrived [in the North Alaska Eskimo village of Kivalina] I was invited to participate in a caribou hunt with three other men. I accepted, of course. Victor Swan told me to get in his sled. I was young and in reasonably good shape, and I responded that I preferred to trot alongside; I had read many times of how Eskimos traveled slowly across country with two to three dogs pulling a heavily loaded sled. However, I could not reconcile my book-based vision with the scene in front of me. Victor had fifteen dogs

hitched to an empty sled, and they were so enthused at the prospect of going that they were leaping five feet (one and a half meters) into the air and screaming with excitement. So I got in the sled. As soon as I did, Victor raised the hook that had held it and the dogs took off so fast that I fell flat on my back in the sled.

The hunt was unsuccessful because Dennis, who had been my partner during the hunt, had apparently made some tactical errors. Sitting around drinking coffee afterward, Leonard and Victor expressed some negative opinions about his actions. They spoke in Eskimo, but swore in English. Leonard, in particular, uttered amazing strings of profanity. I asked him where he learned to swear, and he responded that he had just retired from the U.S. Army after many years as a master sergeant. It also turned out that, after living for many years in Japan while in the Army, he could speak fluent Japanese, as well as English and Eskimo.

. . . What was going on here?

Were these people traditional Eskimos or modern Americans? On the one hand, they spoke almost exclusively in Eskimo among themselves. On the other hand, most of them could also speak English. They lived largely from hunting and fishing and ate traditional native foods almost exclusively, but most of the men also worked seasonally as carpenters, miners, longshoremen, or commercial fishermen in other parts of the state. . . . The answer to the question "Were these people traditional Eskimos or modern Americans?" is that they were both, or perhaps, neither.

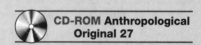

CD-ROM Anthropological Original 27

Source: Ernest S. Burch, Jr., "North Alaskan Eskimos: A Changing Way of Life," in Melvin Ember and Carol R. Ember, eds., *Portraits of Culture: Ethnographic Originals,* in Carol R. Ember and Melvin Ember, eds., *New Directions in Anthropology* (Upper Saddle River, NJ: Prentice Hall, CD-ROM, 2003).

diffusion is a selective process. The Japanese, for instance, accepted much from Chinese culture, but they also rejected many traits. Rhymed tonal poetry, civil service examinations, and foot binding, which were favored by the Chinese, were never adopted in Japan. The poetry form was unsuited to the structure of the Japanese language; the examinations were unnecessary in view of the entrenched power of the Japanese aristocracy; and foot binding was repugnant to a people who abhorred body mutilation of any sort.

Not only would we expect societies to reject items from other societies that are repugnant, we would also expect them to reject ideas and technology that do not satisfy some psychological, social, or cultural need. After all, people are not sponges; they don't automatically soak up the things around them. If they did, the amount of cultural variation in the world would be extremely small, which is clearly not the case. Diffusion is also selective because cultural traits differ in the extent to which they can be communicated. Elements of material culture, such as mechanical processes and techniques, and other traits, such as physical sports and the like, are not especially difficult to demonstrate. Consequently, they are accepted or rejected on their merits. But the moment we move out of the material context, we encounter real difficulties. Linton explained the problem in these words:

> Although it is quite possible to describe such an element of culture as the ideal pattern for marriage . . . it is much less complete than a description of basketmaking. . . .The most thorough verbalization has difficulty in conveying the series of associations and conditioned emotional responses which are attached to this pattern [marriage] and which gave it meaning and vitality within our own society. . . . This is even more true of those concepts which . . . find no direct expression in behavior aside from verbalization. There is a story of an educated Japanese who after a long discussion on the nature of the Trinity with a European friend . . . burst out with: "Oh, I see now, it is a committee."[12]

Finally, diffusion is selective because the overt form of a particular trait, rather than its function or meaning, frequently seems to determine how the trait will be received. For example, the enthusiasm in women for bobbed hair (short haircuts) that swept through much of North America in the 1920s never caught on among the Native Americans of northwestern California. To many women of European ancestry, short hair was a symbolic statement of their freedom. To Native American women, who traditionally cut their hair short when in mourning, it was a reminder of death.[13]

CD-ROM Video Activity 12

In the process of diffusion, then, we can identify a number of different patterns. We know that cultural borrowing is selective rather than automatic, and we can describe how a particular borrowed trait has been modified by the recip-

ient culture. But our current knowledge does not allow us to specify when one or another of these outcomes will occur, under what conditions diffusion will occur, and why it occurs the way it does.

ACCULTURATION

On the surface, the process of change called **acculturation** seems to include much of what we have discussed under the label of diffusion, since acculturation refers to the changes that occur when different cultural groups come into intensive contact. As in diffusion, the source of new cultural items is the other society. But more often than not, the term *acculturation* is used by anthropologists to describe a situation in which one of the societies in contact is much more powerful than the other. Thus, acculturation can be seen as a process of extensive cultural borrowing in the context of superordinate-subordinate relations between societies.[14] The borrowing may sometimes be a two-way process, but generally it is the subordinate or less powerful society that borrows the most. The concept of diffusion can then be reserved for the voluntary borrowing of cultural elements, in contrast with borrowing under external pressure, which characterizes acculturation.

External pressure for culture change can take various forms. In its most direct form—conquest or colonialization—the dominant group uses force or the threat of force to bring about culture change in the other group. For example, in the Spanish conquest of Mexico, the conquerors forced many of the native groups to accept Catholicism. Although such direct force is not always exerted in conquest situations, dominated peoples often have little choice but to change. Examples of such indirectly forced change abound in the history of Native Americans in the United States. Although the federal government made few direct attempts to force people to adopt American culture, it did drive many native groups from their lands, thereby obliging them to give up many aspects of their traditional ways of life. In order to survive, they had no choice but to adopt many of the dominant society's traits. When Native American children were required to go to schools, which taught the dominant society's values, the process was accelerated.

A subordinate society may acculturate to a dominant society even in the absence of direct or indirect force. The dominated people may elect to adopt cultural elements from the dominant society in order to survive in their changed world. Or, perceiving that members of the dominant society enjoy more secure living conditions, the dominated people may identify with the dominant culture in the hope that by doing so they will be able to share some of its benefits. For example, in Arctic areas many Inuit and Lapp groups seemed eager to replace dog sleds with snowmobiles without any coercion.[15]

But many millions of people never had a chance to acculturate after contact with Europeans. They simply died, sometimes directly at the hands of the conquerors, but probably more often as a result of the new diseases the Europeans inadvertently brought with them. Depopulation because of measles, smallpox, and tuberculosis was partic-

Spanish missionaries in the 16th century often forced natives in Mexico to convert to Catholicism.

ularly common in North and South America and on the islands of the Pacific. Those areas had previously been isolated from contact with Europeans and from the diseases of that continuous landmass we call the Old World—Europe, Asia, and Africa.[16]

The story of Ishi, the last surviving member of a group of Native Americans in California called the Yahi, is a moving testimonial to the frequently tragic effect of contact with Europeans. In the space of 22 years, the Yahi population was reduced from several hundred to near zero. The historical record on this episode of depopulation suggests that Euro-Americans murdered 30 to 50 Yahi for every Euro-American murdered, but perhaps 60 percent of the Yahi died in the ten years following their initial exposure to European diseases.[17]

Nowadays, many powerful nations—and not just Western ones—may seem to be acting in more humanitarian ways to improve the life of previously subjugated as well as other "developing" peoples. For better or worse, these programs, however, are still forms of external pressure. The tactic used may be persuasion rather than force, but most of the programs are nonetheless designed to bring about acculturation in the direction of the dominant societies' cultures. For example, the introduction of formal schooling cannot help but instill new values that may contradict traditional cultural patterns. And even health-care pro-grams may alter traditional ways of life by undermining the authority of shamans and other leaders and by increasing population beyond the number that can be supported in traditional ways. Confinement to "reservations" or other kinds of direct force are not the only ways a dominant society can bring about acculturation.

The process of acculturation also applies to immigrants, most of whom, at least nowadays, choose to leave one country for another. Immigrants are almost always a minority in the new country and therefore are in a subordinate position. If the immigrant's culture changes, it is almost always in the direction of the dominant culture. Immigrant groups vary considerably in the degree and speed with which they adopt the new culture and the social roles of the new society in which they live. An important area of research is explaining the variation in acculturation and assimilation. (*Assimilation* is a concept very similar to acculturation, but assimilation is a term more often used by sociologists to describe the process by which individuals acquire the social roles and culture of the dominant group.) Why do some immigrant groups acculturate or assimilate faster than others? A comparative study by Robert Schrauf assessed the degree to which immigrant groups coming to North America retained their native language over time. He looked at whether they lived in tightly knit communities, retained religious rituals, had separate schools and special festivals, visited their homeland, did not intermarry, or worked with others of their ethnic group. All of these factors might be expected to lead to retention of the native language (and presumably other cultural patterns), but only living in tightly knit communities and retaining religious rituals strongly predicted retaining the native language for a longer period of time.[18]

REVOLUTION

Certainly the most drastic and rapid way a culture can change is as a result of **revolution**—replacement, usually violent, of a country's rulers. Historical records, as well as our daily newspapers, indicate that people frequently rebel against established authority. Rebellions, if they occur, almost always occur in state societies, where there is a distinct ruling elite. They take the form of struggles between rulers and ruled, between conquerors and conquered, or between representatives of an external colonial power and segments of the native society. Rebels do not always succeed in overthrowing their rulers, so rebellions do not always result in revolutions. And even successful rebellions do not always result in culture change; the individual rulers may change, but customs or institutions may not. The sources of revolution may be mostly internal, as in the French Revolution, or partly external, as in the Russian-supported 1948 revolution in Czechoslovakia and the United States–supported 1973 revolution against President Allende in Chile.

The American War of Independence toward the end of the eighteenth century is a good example of a colonial rebellion, the success of which was at least partly a result of foreign intervention. The American rebellion was a war of

Revolutionary leaders are often from high-status backgrounds. Here we see a depiction of Patrick Henry giving his famous speech to the aristocratic landowners in the Virginia Assembly on March 23, 1775. Urging the Virginians to fight the British, Henry said that the choice was "liberty or death."

Source: Currier & Ives, "Give Me Liberty or Give Me Death!," 1775. Lithograph, 1876. © The Granger Collection, New York.

neighboring colonies against the greatest imperial power of the time, Great Britain. In the nineteenth century and continuing into the middle and later years of the twentieth century, there would be many other wars of independence, in Latin America, Europe, Asia, and Africa. We don't always remember that the American rebellion was the first of these anti-imperialist wars in modern times, and the model for many that followed. And just like many of the most recent liberation movements, the American rebellion was also part of a larger worldwide war, involving people from many rival nations. Thirty thousand German-speaking soldiers fought, for pay, on the British side; an army and navy from France fought on the American side. There were volunteers from other European countries, including Denmark, Holland, Poland, and Russia.

One of these volunteers was a man named Kosciusko from Poland, which at the time was being divided between Prussia and Russia. Kosciusko helped win a major victory for the Americans, and subsequently directed the fortification of what later became the American training school for army officers, West Point. After the war he returned to Poland and led a rebellion against the Russians, which was only briefly successful. In 1808 he published a *Manual on the Maneuvers of Horse Artillery,* which was used for many years by the American army. When he died he left money to buy freedom and education for American slaves. The executor of Kosciusko's will was Thomas Jefferson.

As in many revolutions, those who were urging revolution were considered "radicals." At a now famous debate in Virginia in 1775, delegates from each colony met at a Continental Congress. Patrick Henry put forward a resolution to prepare for defense against the British armed forces. The motion barely passed, by a vote of 65 to 60. Henry's speech is now a part of American folklore. He rose to declare that it was insane not to oppose the British and that he was not afraid to test the strength of the colonies against Great

Britain. Others might hesitate, he said, but he would have "liberty or death." The "radicals" who supported Henry's resolution included many aristocratic landowners, two of whom, George Washington and Thomas Jefferson, became the first and third occupants of the highest political office in what became the United States of America.[19]

Not all peoples who are suppressed, conquered, or colonialized eventually rebel against established authority. Why this is so, and why rebellions and revolts are not always successful in bringing about culture change, are still open questions. But some possible answers have been investigated. One historian who examined the classic revolutions of the past, including the American, French, and Russian revolutions, suggested some conditions that may give rise to rebellion and revolution:

1. *Loss of prestige of established authority,* often as a result of the failure of foreign policy, financial difficulties, dismissals of popular ministers, or alteration of popular policies. France in the 18th century lost three major international conflicts, with disastrous results for its diplomatic standing and internal finances. Russian society was close to military and economic collapse in 1917, after three years of World War I.

2. *Threat to recent economic improvement.* In France, as in Russia, those sections of the population (professional classes and urban workers) whose economic fortunes had only shortly before taken an upward swing were "radicalized" by unexpected setbacks, such as steeply rising food prices and unemployment. The same may be said for the American colonies on the brink of their rebellion against Great Britain.

3. *Indecisiveness of government,* as exemplified by lack of consistent policy, which gives the impression of being controlled by, rather than in control of, events. The frivolous arrogance of Louis XVI's regime and the

bungling of George III's prime minister, Lord North, with respect to the problems of the American colonies are examples.

4. *Loss of support of the intellectual class.* Such a loss deprived the prerevolutionary governments of France and Russia of any avowed philosophical support and led to their unpopularity with the literate public.[20]

The classic revolutions of the past occurred in countries that were industrialized only incipiently at best. For the most part, the same is true of the rebellions and revolutions in recent years; they have occurred mostly in countries we call "developing." The evidence from a worldwide survey of developing countries suggests that rebellions have tended to occur where the ruling classes depended mostly on the produce or income from land, and therefore were resistant to demands for reform from the rural classes that worked the land. In such agricultural economies, the rulers are not likely to yield political power or give greater economic returns to the workers, because to do so would eliminate the basis (landownership) of the rulers' wealth and power.[21]

Finally, a particularly interesting question is why revolutions sometimes, perhaps even usually, fail to measure up to the high hopes of those who initiate them. When rebellions succeed in replacing the ruling elite, the result is often the institution of a military dictatorship even more restrictive and repressive than the government that existed before. The new ruling establishment may merely substitute one set of repressions for another, rather than bring any real change to the nation. On the other hand, some revolutions have resulted in fairly drastic overhauls of societies.

The idea of revolution has been one of the central myths and inspirations of many groups both in the past and in the present. The colonial empire building of countries such as England and France created a worldwide situation in which rebellion became nearly inevitable. In numerous technologically underdeveloped lands, which have been exploited by more powerful countries for their natural resources and cheap labor, a deep resentment has often developed against the foreign ruling classes or their local clients. Where the ruling classes, native or foreign, refuse to be responsive to those feelings, rebellion becomes the only alternative. In many areas, it has become a way of life.

◆ Culture Change and Adaptation

The chapter on the concept of culture discussed the general assumption that most of the customary behaviors of a culture are probably adaptive, or at least not maladaptive, in that environment. A custom is adaptive if it increases the likelihood that the people practicing it will survive and reproduce. Even though customs are learned and not genetically inherited, cultural adaptation may be like biological adaptation or evolution in another respect. The frequency of certain genetic alternatives is likely to increase over time if those genetic traits increase their carriers' chances of survival and reproduction. Similarly, the frequency of a new learned behavior will increase over time and become customary in a population if the people with that behavior are most likely to survive and reproduce. Thus, if a culture is adapted to its environment, culture change should also be adaptive—not always, to be sure, but commonly.

One of the most important differences between cultural evolution and genetic evolution is that individuals often can decide whether or not to accept and follow the way their parents behave or think, whereas they cannot decide whether or not to inherit certain genes. When enough individuals change their behavior and beliefs, we say that the culture has changed. Therefore, it is possible for culture change to occur much more rapidly than genetic change.

A dramatic example of intentional cultural change was the adoption and later elimination of the custom of *sepaade* among the Rendille, a pastoral population that herds camels, goats, and sheep in the desert in northern Kenya. According to the *sepaade* tradition, some women had to wait to marry until all their brothers were married. These women could well have been over 40 by the time they married. The Rendille say that this tradition was a result of intense warfare between the Rendille and the Borana during the mid-nineteenth century. Attacked by Borana on horseback, the male warriors had to leave their camels unattended and the frightened camels fled. The daughters of one male age-set were appointed to look after the camels, and the *sepaade* tradition developed. In 1998, long after the warfare with the Borana ceased, the elders decided to free the *sepaade* from their obligation to postpone their own marriages. Interviews with the Rendille in the 1990s revealed that many individuals were fully aware of the reason for the tradition in the first place. Now, they said, there was peace, so there was no longer any reason for the *sepaade* tradition to continue.[22] The adoption of the *sepaade* is an example of culture change in a changing environment. But what if the environment is stable? Is culture change more or less likely? Robert Boyd and Peter Richerson have shown mathematically that when the environment is relatively stable and individual mistakes are costly, staying with customary modes of behavior (usually transmitted by parents) is probably more adaptive than changing.[23] But what happens when the environment, particularly the social environment, is changing? There are plenty of examples in the modern world: People have to migrate to new places for work; medical care leads to increased population so that land is scarcer; people have had land taken away from them and are forced to make do with less land; and so on.

It is particularly when circumstances change that individuals are likely to try ideas or behaviors that are different from those of their parents. Most people would want to adopt behaviors that are more suited to their present circumstances, but how do they know which behaviors are better? There are various ways to find out. One way is by experimenting, trying out various new behaviors. Another way is to evaluate the experiments of others. If a person who tries a new technique seems successful, we would expect that person to be imitated, just as we would expect people to stick with new behaviors they have personally tried and found successful. Finally, one might choose to do what most people in the new situation decide to do.[24]

Why one choice rather than another? In part, the choice may be a function of the cost or risk of the innovation. It is relatively easy, for example, to find out how long it takes to cut down a tree with an introduced steel ax, as compared with a stone ax. Not surprisingly, innovations such as a steel ax catch on relatively quickly because comparison is easy and the results clear-cut. But what if the risk is very great? Suppose the innovation involves adopting a whole new way of farming that you have never practiced before. You can try it, but you might not have any food if you fail. As we discussed earlier, risky innovations are likely to be tried only by those individuals who can afford the risk. Other people may then evaluate their success and adopt the new strategy if it looks promising. Similarly, if you migrate to a new area, say, from a high-rainfall area to a drier one, it may pay to look around to see what most people in the new place do; after all, the people in the drier area probably have customs that are adaptive for that environment.

We can expect, then, that the choices individuals make may often be adaptive ones. But it is important to note that adopting an innovation from someone in one's own society or borrowing an innovation from another society is not always or necessarily beneficial, either in the short or the long run. First, people may make mistakes in judgment, especially when some new behavior seems to satisfy a physical need. Why, for example, have smoking and drug use diffused so widely even though they are likely to reduce a person's chances of survival? Second, even if people are correct in their short-term judgment of benefit, they may be wrong in their judgment about long-run benefit. A new crop may yield more than the old crop for five consecutive years, but the new crop may fail miserably in the sixth year because of lower than normal rainfall or because the new crop depleted soil nutrients. Third, people may be forced by the more powerful to change, with few if any benefits for themselves.

Whatever the motives for humans to change their behavior, the theory of natural selection suggests that new behavior is not likely to become cultural or remain cultural over generations if it has harmful reproductive consequences, just as a genetic mutation with harmful consequences is not likely to become frequent in a population.[25] Still, we know of many examples of culture change that seem maladaptive—the switch to bottle-feeding rather than nursing infants, which may spread infection because contaminated water is used, or the adoption of alcoholic beverages, which may lead to alcoholism and early death. In the last few hundred years, the major stimulus to culture change, adaptive and maladaptive, has been the new social environment produced by the arrival of people from Western societies and the growth of a global economy.

Types of Culture Change in the Modern World

Many of the cultural changes in the world from A.D. 1500 to the present have been caused, directly or indirectly, by the dominance and expansion of Western societies.[26] Thus, much of the culture change in the modern world has been externally induced, if not forced. This is not to say that cultures are changing now only because of external pressures; but externally induced changes have been the changes most frequently studied by anthropologists and other social scientists. Most of the external pressures have come from Western societies, but not all. Far Eastern societies, such as Japan and China, have also stimulated culture change. And the expansion of Islamic societies after the eighth century A.D. made for an enormous amount of culture change in the Near East, Africa, Europe, and Asia.

COMMERCIALIZATION

One of the most important changes resulting from the expansion of Western societies is the increasingly worldwide dependence on commercial exchange. The borrowed customs of buying and selling may at first be supplementary to traditional means of distributing goods in a society. But as the new commercial customs take hold, the economic base of the receiving society alters. Inevitably, this alteration is accompanied by other changes, which have broad social, political, and even biological and psychological ramifications.

In examining contemporary patterns of change, however, we should bear in mind that commercialization has occurred in many parts of the world in the ancient past. The Chinese, Persians, Greeks, Romans, Arabs, Phoenicians, and Hindus were some of the early state societies that pushed commercial enterprises in other areas. We may cast some light on how and why some earlier cultures changed when we consider several questions: How, and why, does a contemporary society change from a subsistence to a commercial economic base? What are the resultant cultural changes? Why do they occur?

In general, the limited evidence available suggests that a previously noncommercial people may begin to sell and buy things simply in order to live, not just because they may be attracted by goods they can obtain only by commercial exchange. If the resources available to a group have been significantly reduced per person—because the group has been forced to resettle on a small "reservation" or because population has increased—the group may be likely to take advantage of any commercial opportunities that become available, even if such opportunities require considerably more work time and effort.[27]

MIGRATORY LABOR One way commercialization can occur is for some members of a community to move to a place that offers the possibility of working for wages. This happened in Tikopia, an island near the Solomon Islands

APPLIED ANTHROPOLOGY
Obesity, Hypertension, and Diabetes: Health Consequences of Modernization?

Contact with the West first brought medical devastation to many populations previously unexposed to European illnesses. However, with the acceptance of modern medical care throughout much of the developing world, infant mortality has declined and life expectancies have gone up. These achievements have largely come about because of the control of major epidemic diseases, such as smallpox (now eradicated), cholera, yellow fever, syphilis, and tuberculosis, as well as the inoculation of children against childhood diseases. Improvements in medical health are by no means uniform. The AIDS epidemic, which we discuss in the chapter on medical anthropology, is spreading throughout much of the world. Overall deaths from infectious diseases may have declined, but other health problems have increased. As more people survive into older ages, problems of hypertension, heart disease, cancer, and diabetes increase. Some of the increase in these chronic diseases is due to the aging of populations, but much of it appears to be due to changes in life-style that accompany modernization.

A good deal of research has focused on the Samoans of the South Pacific. As we noted in the chapter on food-getting, the Samoans traditionally depended on root and tree crop horticulture. As did many other people in the modern world, Samoans increasingly moved to urban areas, worked for wages, and started buying most of their food. Researchers reported substantial increases, within a relatively short time, in rates of hypertension, diabetes, and obesity across a wide range of age groups. For example, in 1990 about two-thirds of American Samoans were severely overweight, up substantially from the situation in the 1970s. And

Samoans from more rural areas show less hypertension and physiological signs of stress. Among the life-style changes thought to be responsible are less physical activity and changes in diet to low-fiber, high-calorie foods. Stress may also increase as more individuals buy material things and status goods without having the economic resources to support them.

What about genetic factors? Could some genetic predisposition be interacting with modernization to create obesity in the Samoan population? One possibility is referred to as the "thrifty" gene. The geneticist James Neel suggested that individuals who have very efficient metabolisms and who can store calories in fatty tissue are most apt to survive and reproduce in environments with frequent famines or chronic food shortages. In time, populations in such environments would have a high prevalence of individuals with "thrifty" genes. What happens, though, when such individuals no longer need to exercise much or have access to high-calorie foods? Neel suggested that adult-onset diabetes might result, a scenario that is consistent with the increase in diabetes in Samoa and other parts of Polynesia. It is also consistent with the increase in obesity and hypertension.

The "thrifty" gene theory does not just pertain to the Samoans and other Polynesian populations. Probably most human populations used to have to cope with food uncertainty in the past. If the food supply increases with modernization, but it is accompanied by a reduction in physical activity and a switch to high-calorie diets, then increases in obesity, diabetes, and hypertension may frequently accompany modernization. Understanding both biological and cul-

When food is not plentiful, the "thrifty gene" helps people survive on less. But when the food supply becomes plentiful and reliable, people may become overweight, as in the Marquesas.

tural factors is essential in helping populations adapt to conditions of urban life.

Sources: John S. Allen and Susan M. Cheer, "The Non-Thrifty Genotype," *Current Anthropology,* 37 (1996): 831–42; James R. Bindon and Douglas E. Crews, "Changes in Some Health Status Characteristics of American Samoan Men: Preliminary Observations from a 12-Year Follow-up Study," *American Journal of Human Biology,* 5 (1993): 31–37; James R. Bindon, Amy Knight, William W. Dressler, and Douglas E. Crews, "Social Context and Psychosocial Influences on Blood Pressure among American Samoans," *American Journal of Physical Anthropology,* 103 (1997): 7–18; Stephen T. McGarvey, "The Thrifty Gene Concept and Adiposity Studies in Biological Anthropology," *Journal of the Polynesian Society,* 103 (1994): 29–42; J. D. Pearson, Gary D. James, and Daniel E. Brown, "Stress and Changing Lifestyles in the Pacific: Physiological Stress Responses of Samoans in Rural and Urban Settings," *American Journal of Human Biology,* 5 (1993): 49–60; World Bank, *World Development Report 1995. Workers in an Integrating World* (Oxford: Oxford University Press, 1995).

in the South Pacific. In 1929, when Raymond Firth first studied the island, its economy was still essentially non-commercial—simple, self-sufficient, and largely self-contained.[28] Some Western goods were available but, with the exception of iron and steel in limited quantities, not sought after. Their possession and use were associated solely with Europeans. This situation changed dramatically with World War II. During the war, military forces occupied neighboring islands, and people from Tikopia migrated to those islands to find employment. In the period following the war, several large commercial interests extended their activities in the Solomons, thus creating a continued demand for labor. As a result, when Firth revisited Tikopia in 1952, he found the economic situation significantly altered.

More than 100 Tikopians had left the island to work for varying periods. The migrants wanted to earn money because they aspired to standards of living previously regarded as appropriate only to Europeans. Already, living conditions on Tikopia were changing. Western cooking and water-carrying utensils, mosquito nets, kerosene storm lamps, and so forth had come to be regarded as normal items in a Tikopia household.

The introduction of money into the economy of Tikopia not only altered the economic system but also affected other areas of life. Compared with the situation in 1929, land was under more intensive cultivation in 1952, with introduced manioc and sweet potatoes supplementing the old principal crop, taro. Pressures on the food supply resulting from improved living standards and an increased population seem to have weakened the ties of extended kinship. For example, the nuclear families constituting the extended family (the landholding and land-using unit in 1929) were not cooperating as much in 1952. In many cases, in fact, the land had actually been split up among the constituent nuclear families; land rights had become more individualized. People were no longer as willing to share with members of their extended family, particularly with respect to the money and goods acquired by working in the Solomons.

NONAGRICULTURAL COMMERCIAL PRODUCTION
Commercialization can also occur when a self-sufficient hunting or agricultural society comes to depend more and more on trading for its livelihood. Such a change is exemplified by the Mundurucú of the Amazon Basin, who largely abandoned general horticulture for commercial rubber production. A similar change may also be seen in the Montagnais of northeastern Canada, who came to depend increasingly on commercial fur trapping, rather than hunting, for subsistence. Robert Murphy and Julian Steward found that when modern goods from industrialized areas became available through trade, both the Mundurucú and the Montagnais devoted their energies to making specialized cash crops or other trade items. They did this to obtain other industrially made objects.[29] The primary socioeconomic change that occurred among the Mundurucú and the Montagnais was a shift from cooperative labor and community autonomy to individualized

Tea has become a major cash crop on the world market. A woman wears a big hat to shield herself from the sun as she picks tea leaves in West Java, Indonesia.

economic activity and a dependence on an external market.

Among the Mundurucú, for example, before close trading links were established, the native population and the Europeans had been in contact for some 80 years without the Mundurucú way of life being noticeably altered. The men did give up their independent military activities in order to perform as mercenaries for the Brazilians, but they continued to maintain their horticultural economy. Some trading took place with Brazilians, with the chief acting as agent for the village. Barter was the method of exchange. Traders first distributed their wares, ranging from cheap cottons to iron hatchets, trinkets, and so on; they returned about three months later to collect manioc, India rubber, and beans from the Mundurucú. At this time (1860), however, rubber was only a secondary item of commerce.

The rapidly growing demand for rubber from the 1860s onward increased the importance of Mundurucú-trader relationships. Traders now openly began to appoint agents, called *capitoes,* whose job it was to encourage greater rubber production. *Capitoes* were given economic privileges and hence power, both of which began to undercut the position of the traditional chief. In addition, the process of rubber collection itself began to alter Mundurucú social patterns by moving people away from their jungle-based communities.

Wild rubber trees are found only along rivers, which are often a considerable distance from the jungle habitat of the Mundurucú and can be exploited only during the dry season (late May to December). So the Mundurucú man who elected to gather rubber had to separate himself from his family for about half the year. Furthermore, rubber collecting is a solitary activity. Each tapper must work his territory, consisting of about 150 trees, daily, and he must live close to his trees because the work lasts all day. Therefore, the tapper usually lives alone or in a small group except during the rainy season, when he returns to his village.

At this stage in the commercialization process, the Mundurucú became increasingly dependent on goods supplied by the trader. Firearms were useless without regular quantities of gunpowder and lead or shot; clothing required needles and thread for repairs. But these items could be earned only through increased rubber production, which in turn led to greater dependency on the outside world. Inevitably, the ability to work with traditional materials and the desire to maintain traditional crafts disappeared. Metal pots took the place of clay ones, and manufactured hammocks replaced homemade ones. Gradually the village agricultural cycle ceased to be followed by all in the community so that rubber production would not suffer. The authority of the traditional chiefs was weakened as that of the *capitoes* was enhanced.

The point of no return was reached when significant numbers of Mundurucú abandoned the villages for permanent settlements near their individual territories of trees. These new settlements lacked the unity, the sense of community, of former village life. Property was held by nuclear families and carefully maintained in the interest of productivity.

With the discovery of gold, many Mundurucú young men have turned to panning for gold in rivers. The required equipment is simple, and gold is easier to transport and trade than rubber. Because gold can be sold for cash, which is then used for purchases, trading relationships are no longer so important. Cash is now used to buy transistor radios, tape recorders, watches, bicycles, and new kinds of clothing, in addition to firearms, metal pots, and tools. With money as a medium of exchange, the traditional emphasis on reciprocity has declined. Even food may now be sold to fellow Mundurucú, a practice that would have been unthinkable in the 1950s.[30]

SUPPLEMENTARY CASH CROPS A third way commercialization occurs is when people cultivating the soil produce a surplus above their subsistence requirements, which is then sold for cash. In many cases, this cash income must be used to pay rent or taxes. Under these circumstances, commercialization may be said to be associated with the formation of a peasantry. **Peasants** are rural people who produce food for their own subsistence, but they must also contribute or sell their surpluses to others, in towns and cities, who do not produce their own food.

Peasants first appeared with the emergence of state and urban civilizations about 5,000 to 6,000 years ago, and they have been associated with civilization ever since.[31] To say

that peasants are associated with urban societies perhaps needs some qualification. The contemporary, highly industrialized urban society has little need of peasants. Their scale of production is small and their use of land "uneconomic." A highly industrialized society with a large population of non-food producers requires mechanized agriculture. As a result, the peasant has passed, or is passing, out of all but the most peripheral existence in industrial countries. It is the preindustrial city, and the social organization it represents, that generate and maintain peasants. They cultivate land; they furnish the required quantity of food, rent, and profit on which the remainder of society, particularly the people in the cities, depends.

What changes does the development of a peasantry entail? In some respects there is little disturbance of the cultivator's (now peasant's) former way of life. The peasant still has to produce enough food to meet family needs, to replace what has been consumed, to cover a few ceremonial obligations (for example, the marriage of a child, village festivals, and funerals). But in other respects the peasant's situation is radically altered. For in addition to the traditional obligations—indeed, often in conflict with them—the peasant now has to produce extra crops to meet the requirements of a group of outsiders—landlords or officials of the state. These outsiders expect to be paid rent or taxes in produce or currency, and they are able to enforce their expectations because they control the military and the police.

INTRODUCTION OF COMMERCIAL AND INDUSTRIAL AGRICULTURE Commercialization can come about through the introduction of commercial agriculture, cultivation for sale rather than personal consumption. The system of agriculture may come to be industrialized. In other words, some of the production processes, such as plowing, weeding, irrigation, and harvesting, can be done by machine. Commercial agriculture is, in fact, often as mechanized as any manufacturing industry. Land is worked for the maximum return it will yield, and labor is hired and fired just as impersonally as in other industries.

E. J. Hobsbawm noted some of the developments that accompanied the introduction of commercial agriculture in eighteenth-century England and in continental Europe somewhat later.[32] The close, near-familial relationship between farmer and farm laborer disappeared, as did the once-personal connection between landlord and tenant. Land came to be regarded as a source of profit rather than a way of life. Fields were merged into single units and enclosed, and local grazing and similar privileges were reduced. Labor was hired at market rates and paid in wages. Eventually, as the emphasis on large-scale production for a mass market increased, machines began to replace farmers.

The introduction of commercial agriculture brings several important social consequences. Gradually, a class polarization develops. Farmers and landlords become increasingly separated from laborers and tenants, just as in the town the employer becomes socially separated from the employees. Gradually, too, manufactured items of all sorts are introduced into rural areas. Laborers migrate to urban centers in search of employment, often meeting even less sympathetic conditions there than exist in the country.

The changeover to commercial agriculture may result in an improved standard of living in the short and long run. But sometimes the switch is followed by a decline in the standard of living if the market price for the commercial crop declines. For example, the changeover of the farmer-herders of the arid *sertão* region of northeastern Brazil after 1940 to the production of sisal (a plant whose fibers can be made into twine and rope) seemed to be a move that could provide a more secure living in their arid environment. But when the world price for sisal dropped and the wages of sisal workers declined, many workers were forced to curtail the caloric intake of their children. The poorer people were obliged to save their now more limited food supplies for the money earners, at the expense of the children.[33]

Commercialization can start in various ways: People can begin to sell and buy because they begin to work near home or away for wages, or because they begin to sell nonagricultural products, surplus food, or cash crops (crops grown deliberately for sale). One type of commercialization does not exclude another; all types can occur in any society. However commercialization begins, it seems to have predictable effects on traditional economics. The ethic of generalized reciprocity declines, particularly with respect to giving money away. (Perhaps because it is nonperishable and hideable, money seems more likely than other goods to be kept for one's immediate family rather than shared with others.) Property rights become individualized rather than collective when people begin to buy and sell. And even in societies that were previously egalitarian, commercialization usually results in more unequal access to resources and hence a greater degree of social stratification.

RELIGIOUS CHANGE

Of course, commercialization is not the only type of culture change in the modern world. The growing influence of Western societies has also led to religious change in many places. Often, the change has been brought about intentionally through the efforts of missionaries, who have been among the first Westerners to travel to interior regions and out-of-the-way places. Missionaries have not met with equal success in all parts of the world. In some places, large portions of the native population have converted to the new religion with great zeal. In others, missionaries have been ignored, forced to flee, or even killed. We do not fully understand why missionaries have been successful in some societies and not in others. Yet, in many parts of the world, Western missionary activity has been a potent force for all kinds of cultural change. One possible reason is that missionaries offer resources that enable natives to minimize economic and other risks in the new, Western-dominated social environment.[34]

But aside from the direct effects of missionary work, contact with Westerners has often produced religious change in more indirect ways. In some native societies, contact with Westerners has led to a breakdown of social structure and the growth of feelings of helplessness and spiritual demoralization. In the chapter on religion and magic, we discussed how revitalization movements have arisen as apparent attempts to restore such societies to their former confidence and prosperity. We now examine the process of conversion on the island of Tikopia, as an example of religious change brought about by direct contact with missionaries.

CHRISTIANITY ON TIKOPIA   Tikopia was one of the few Polynesian societies to retain its traditional religious system into the first decades of the twentieth century. An Anglican mission was first established on the island in 1911. With it came a deacon and the founding of two schools for about 200 pupils. By 1929, approximately half the population had converted, and in the early 1960s almost all Tikopia gave at least nominal allegiance to Christianity.[35]

Traditional Tikopian belief embraced a great number of gods and spirits of various ranks who inhabited the sky, the water, and the land. One god in particular—the original creator and shaper of the culture—was given a place of special importance, but he was in no way comparable to the all-powerful God of Christianity. Unlike Christianity, Tikopian religion made no claim to universality. The Tikopian gods did not rule over all creation, only over Tikopia. It was thought that if one left Tikopia, one left the gods behind.

The people of Tikopia interacted with their gods and spirits primarily through religious leaders who were also the heads of descent groups. Clan chiefs presided over rituals associated with the everyday aspects of island life, such as house construction, fishing, planting, and harvesting. The chief was expected to intercede with the gods on the people's behalf, to persuade them to bring happiness and prosperity to the group. Indeed, when conditions were good it was assumed that the chief was doing his job well. When disaster struck, the prestige of the chief often fell in proportion. Why did the Tikopia convert to Christianity? Firth suggested several contributing factors.

First, the mission offered the people the prospect of acquiring new tools and consumer goods. Although conversion alone did not provide such benefits, attachment to the mission made them more attainable. Later, it became apparent that education, particularly in reading and writing English, was helpful in getting ahead in the outside world. Mission schooling became valued and provided a further incentive for adopting Christianity.

Second, conversion may have been facilitated by the ability of chiefs, as religious and political leaders, to bring over entire descent groups to Christianity. Should a chief decide to transfer his allegiance to Christianity, the members of his kin group usually followed him. In 1923, when Tafua, chief of the Faea district of Tikopia, converted to the new religion, he brought with him his entire group—nearly half the population of the island. The ability of the

People converted voluntarily to Christianity in 19th century Samoa. Children now line up for church on White Sunday, which occurs once a year.

chiefs to influence their kin groups, however, was both an asset and a hindrance to missionary efforts, since some chiefs steadfastly resisted conversion.

A final blow to traditional Tikopian religion came in 1955, when a severe epidemic killed at least 200 people in a population of about 1,700. According to Firth, "the epidemic was largely interpreted as a sign of divine discrimination," because three of the outstanding non-Christian religious leaders died.[36] Subsequently, the remaining non-Christian chiefs voluntarily converted to Christianity, and so did their followers. By 1966, all Tikopia, with the exception of one old woman, had converted to the new faith.

Although many Tikopians feel their conversion to Christianity has been a unifying, revitalizing force, the changeover from one religion to another has not been without problems. Christian missionaries on Tikopia have succeeded in eliminating the traditional Tikopian population-control devices of abortion, infanticide, and male celibacy. It is very possible that the absence of these controls will continue to intensify population pressure. The island, with its limited capacity to support life, can ill afford this outcome. Firth summed up the situation Tikopian society faced:

> In the history of Tikopia complete conversion of the people to Christianity was formerly regarded as a solution to their problems; it is now coming to be realized that the adoption and practice of Christianity itself represents another set of problems. As the Tikopia themselves are beginning to see, to be Christian Polynesians in the modern technologically and

industrially dominated world, even in the Solomon Islands, poses as many questions as it supplies answers.[37]

Unfortunately, not all native peoples have made the transition to Christianity as painlessly as the Tikopia. In fact, in most cases the record is dismal. All too frequently, missionary activity tends to destroy a society's culture and self-respect. It offers nothing in return but an alien, repressive system of values ill suited to the people's real needs and aspirations. Phillip Mason, a critic of European evangelists in Africa, pointed out some of the psychological damage inflicted by missionary activity.[38] The missionaries repeatedly stressed sin and guilt; they used the color black to represent evil and the color white to signify good; and they showed hostility toward pagan culture. Most damaging of all was their promise that the African, provided she or he adopted the European's ways, would gain access both to the European's heaven and to European society. But no matter how diligently Africans attempted to follow missionary precepts or climb the socioeconomic ladder, they were soon blocked from entry into European homes, clubs, and even churches and seminaries.

POLITICAL AND SOCIAL CHANGE

In addition to commercialization and religious change brought about by the expansion of Western and other countries, political changes have often occurred when a foreign system of government has been imposed. But, as recent events in the former Soviet Union and South Africa indicate, dramatic changes in a political system can also occur more or less voluntarily. Perhaps the most striking type of political change in recent years is the spread of participatory forms of government—"democracy."

To political scientists, democracy is usually defined in terms of voting by a substantial proportion of the citizenry, governments brought to power by periodic contested elections, a chief executive either popularly elected or responsible to an elected legislature, and often also civil liberties such as free speech. Depending on which criteria are used, only 12 to 15 countries qualified as democracies as of the beginning of the twentieth century. The number decreased after World War I, as emerging democratic institutions were replaced by dictatorships in Russia, Italy, Germany, central Europe, Japan, and elsewhere. After World War II, despite all the rhetoric associated with the founding of the United Nations, the picture was not much different. Some members of the new North Atlantic Treaty Organization (NATO) were not democracies, and neither were many members of the wider Western alliance system, in Latin America, the Middle East, and Asia.

It was not until the 1970s and 1980s that people, not just political scientists, started noticing that democracy was becoming more common in the world. By the early 1990s, President George Bush and then-candidate Bill Clinton were talking about the spread of the "democratic peace." As of 1992, about half of the countries in the world had more or less democratic governments, and others were in transition to democracy.[39] Social scientists do not yet understand why this change is happening. But it is possible that the global communication of ideas has a lot to do with it. Authoritarian governments can censor their own newspapers and prevent group meetings, but they really cannot stop the movement of ideas via telephone lines and the Internet. The movement of ideas, of course, does not explain the acceptance of those ideas. Why democracy has recently diffused to more countries than ever before still requires explanation.

Another frequent type of culture change in the modern world is increasing social stratification. Because of economic change, some groups become more privileged and powerful than others. For example, it has been suggested that the introduction of new technology may generally make for an increase in degree of social stratification.[40] When the snowmobile began to be used for herding by the Lapps, those who for various reasons could participate in the "snowmobile revolution" gained economic, social, and political advantages. But those who could not acquire the new machines tended to become an economically and generally deprived class—without machines *or* reindeer.[41]

◆ Globalization: Problems and Opportunities

Investment capital, people, and ideas are moving around the world at an ever faster rate.[42] Transportation now allows people and goods to circle the globe in days; telecommunications and the Internet make it possible to send a message around the world in seconds and minutes. Economic exchange is enormously more global and transnational. The word **globalization** is often used nowadays to refer to "the massive flow of goods, people, information, and capital across huge areas of the earth's surface."[43] The process of globalization has resulted in the worldwide spread of cultural features, particularly in the domain of economics and international trade. We buy from the same companies (that have factories all over the world), we sell our products and services for prices that are set by world market forces. We can eat pizza, hamburgers, curry, or

Democracy—contested elections with widespread voting—is spreading around the world. In this rural area of South Africa, people line up to vote.

sushi in most urban centers. In some ways, cultures are changing in similar directions. They have become more commercial, more urban, and more international. The job has become more important, and kinship less important, as people travel to and work in other countries, and return just periodically to their original homes. Ideas about democracy, the rights of the individual, alternative medical practices and religions, have become more widespread; people in many countries of the world watch the same TV shows, wear similar fashions, listen to the same or similar music. In short, people are increasingly sharing behaviors and beliefs with people in other cultures, and the cultures of the world are less and less things "with edges," as Paul Durrenberger says.[44]

Globalization is not new. The world has been global and interdependent since the 16th century.[45] What we currently call "globalization" is a more widespread version of what we used to call by various other names—diffusion, acculturation, colonialism, imperialism, commercialization. But globalization is now on a much grander scale; enormous amounts of international investment fuel world trade. Shifts in the world marketplace more than ever before may drastically affect a country's well-being. For example, 60 percent of Pakistan's industrial employment is in textile and apparel manufacturing, but serious unemployment resulted when that manufacturing was crippled by restrictive American import policies and fears about war between India and Afghanistan.[46]

As we have seen in this chapter, there are many negative effects of colonialism, imperialism, and globablization. Many native peoples in many places lost their land and have been forced to work for inadequate wages in mines and plantations and factories that are owned by foreign capitalists. Frequently, there is undernutrition if not starvation. But are there any positive consequences? As we discussed in the social stratification chapter, the "human development indicators" collected by the United Nations suggest an improvement in many respects, including increases in most countries in life expectancy and literacy. Much of the improvement in life expectancy is undoubtedly due to the spread of medicines developed in the advanced economies of the West. There is generally less warfare as colonial powers enforced pacification within the colonies that later became independent states. Most important, perhaps, has been the growth of middle classes all over the world, whose livelihoods depend on globalizing commerce. The middle classes in many countries have become strong and numerous enough to pressure governments for democratic reforms and the reduction of injustice.

World trade is the primary engine of economic development. Per capita income is increasing. Forty years ago, the countries of Asia were among the poorest countries in the world in terms of per capita income. Since then, because of their involvement in world trade, their incomes have risen enormously. In 1960, South Korea was as poor as India. Now its per capita income is 20 times higher than India's. Singapore is an even more dramatic example. In the late 1960s, its economy was a disaster. Today its per capita income is higher than Britain's.[47] Mexico used to be a place where North Americans built factories to produce garments for the North American market. Now its labor is no longer so cheap. But because it has easy access to the North American market and because its plentiful labor is acquiring the necessary skills, Mexico is now seeing the development of high-tech manufacturing with decent salaries.[48]

There is world trade also in people. Many countries of the world now export people to other countries. Mexico has done so for a long time. Virtually every family in a Bangladesh village depends on someone who works overseas and sends money home. Without those remittances, many would face starvation. The government encourages people to go abroad to work. Millions of people from Bangladesh are now overseas on government-sponsored work contracts.[49]

But does a higher per capita income mean that life has improved generally in a country? Not necessarily. As we also saw in the chapter on social stratification, inequality within countries can increase with technological improvements because the rich often benefit the most. In addition, economic wealth is increasingly concentrated in a relatively small number of countries. Obviously, then, not everyone is better off, even if on average most countries are doing better. Poverty has become more common as countries have become more unequal.

It is probably not possible to go back to a time when societies were not so dependent on each other, not so interconnected through world trade, not so dependent on commercial exchange. Even those who are most upset with globalization find it difficult to imagine that it is possible to return to a less connected world. For better or worse, the world is interconnected and will remain so. The question now is whether the average economic improvements in countries will eventually translate into economic improvements for most individuals.

◆ Ethnogenesis: The Emergence of New Cultures

Many of the processes that we have discussed—the expansion and domination by the West and other powerful nations, the deprivation of the ability of peoples to earn their livelihoods by traditional means, the imposition of schools or other methods to force acculturation, the attempts to convert people to other religions, and globalization—have led to profound changes in culture. But if culture change in the modern world has made cultures more alike, it has not eliminated all cultural differences. Indeed, people are still very variable culturally from one place to the next. New differences have also emerged. Often, in the aftermath of violent events such as depopulation, relocation, enslavement, and genocide by dominant powers, deprived peoples have created new cultures in a process called **ethnogenesis.**[50]

Some of the most dramatic examples of ethnogenesis come from areas where escaped slaves (called Maroons)

CURRENT RESEARCH AND ISSUES
Culture Change and Persistence in Communist China

In the years since the 1949 Communist takeover in China, the central government has initiated a variety of changes in family life. Many of these changes were literally forced; people who resisted them were often resettled or jailed. Ancestor worship and lineage organization were attacked or declared illegal. Most private property was abolished, undermining family loyalties. Why participate in family activities if there could be no economic reward? Still, the actions of the central government did not completely change family life. Even coercion has its limits.

The government may have wanted to restrict the family and kinship, but its investments in public health and famine relief reduced mortality, thereby strengthening family ties. Fewer infants died, more children lived long enough to marry, old age became more common—all of these developments allowed people in all social classes

to have larger and more complex networks of kin than were possible before 1949. To be sure, government policies undercut the power and authority of extended family patriarchs. But the new healthier conditions were conducive to large, multigenerational households with economic as well as social ties to other kin.

As China became more accessible to anthropologists and other researchers from abroad, many investigators came to study the variability and similarity in Chinese family life. Most of these studies focused on the dominant Han Chinese (the Han constitute about 95 percent of the total population of China); investigators have also studied many of the 55 "recognized" minority cultures in China. Burton Pasternak, a U.S. anthropologist, Janet Salaff, a Canadian sociologist, and Chinese sociologists studied four communities of Han who had moved outside the

Great Wall to colonize the Inner Mongolian frontier. (Inner Mongolia is part of China.) The results of their study suggest that, despite strong pressures from the government, what changes or persists in a culture mainly reflects what is possible ecologically and economically. A tradition of intensive agriculture cannot persist in the absence of sufficient watering. The government's insistence on one child per family cannot withstand a family's need for more children.

Han farmers who crossed the Great Wall were searching for a better life. They found difficulties in climate and soil that forced many to return home. But many adjusted to the grasslands and remained. Some continued to depend on farming on the fringes of the grasslands. Others farther out on the grasslands became herders. The Han who switched to herding are now in many respects more like the native Mongol herders than

created new cultures. Maroon societies emerged in the past few hundred years in a variety of New World locations, from the United States to the West Indies and northern parts of South America. One of the new cultures, now known as Aluku, emerged when slaves fled from coastal plantations in Suriname to the swampy interior country along the Cottica River. After a war with the Dutch colonists, this particular group moved to French Guiana. The escaped slaves, originating from widely varying cultures in Africa or born on Suriname plantations, organized themselves into autonomous communities with military headmen.[51] They practiced slash-and-burn cultivation, with women doing most of the work. Although settlements shifted location as a way of evading enemies, co-residence in a community and collective ownership of land became important parts of the emerging identities. Communities took on the names of the specific plantations from which their leaders had escaped. Principles of inheritance through the female line began to develop, and full-fledged

matriclans became the core of each village. Each village had its own shrine, the *faaka tiki,* where residents invoked the clan ancestors, as well as a special house where the deceased were brought to be honored and feted before being taken to the forest for burial. Clans also inherited avenging spirits with whom they could communicate through mediums.

The Aluku case is a clear example of ethnogenesis because the culture did not exist 350 years ago. It emerged and was created by people trying to adapt to circumstances not of their own making. In common with other cases of emerging ethnic identity, the Aluku came not only to share new patterns of behavior but also to see themselves as having a common origin (a common ancestor), a shared history, and a common religion.[52]

The emergence of the Seminole in Florida is another case of ethnogenesis. The early settlers who moved to what is now Florida and later became known as Seminole largely derived from the Lower Creek Kawita chiefdom. The Kawita chiefdom, like other southeastern Muskogean

(continued)

like Han or Mongol farmers. The gender division of labor among the Han pastoralists became much sharper than among the Han farmers since men are often far away with the herds. Pastoralist children, not that useful in herding because mistakes can be very costly, are more likely than farm children to stay in school for a long time. Perhaps because of the greater usefulness of children on the farm, Han farm families have more children than Han pastoralists. But both groups have more than one child per family. Herdsmen are less likely than farmers to need cooperative labor, so Han pastoralists are more likely to live as a neolocal independent family than as a patrilocal extended family (which was traditional). In short, the adjustment of the Han to the grasslands seems to be explained more by ecological requirements than by ethnic traditions.

Although an increasing number of Han have become more like Mongols in their pastoral adaptations, many Mongols have adopted an urban way of life and moved away from their pastoral life. The Chinese government was initially responsible for encouraging non-Mongols to move into Inner Mongolia, particularly into its new capital, Huhhot. At the same time, many Mongols moved from the grasslands and into the capital city. Chinese government policy was intended to make each non-Han ethnic group a minority in its traditional land, but the government paradoxically also tried to encourage minority ethnic pride in their traditional culture. So the city of Huhhot is filled with images of the traditional herding culture in its buildings and monuments.

As described by the anthropologist William Jankowiak, who studied the Mongols in the capital city of Huhhot, the results were not what the Chinese government intended. In many ways, to be sure, the urban Mongols had abandoned their traditional culture and assimilated to the dominant Han culture. But we see the force of ecology more than the hand of tradition in the outcome. Many Mongols in the city no longer speak the Mongol language. Parents find it difficult to get children to speak Mongol when they live among Han. And the scarcity of housing makes it difficult for the Mongols to form an ethnic enclave, or even live near kin as they did in the past. In contrast to life in the rural areas, which revolves around kinship, city life requires interacting with strangers as well as relatives. Indeed, nonkin are often more important to you than kin. As one person said to Jankowiak, "We hide from our cousins but not our friends."

Sources: Deborah Davis and Stevan Harrell, eds., *Chinese Families in the Post-Mao Era* (Berkeley: University of California Press, 1993); Burton Pasternak, "Han: Pastoralists and Farmers on a Chinese Frontier," in Melvin Ember and Carol R. Ember, eds., *Portraits of Culture: Ethnographic Originals,* in Carol R. Ember and Melvin Ember, eds., *New Directions in Anthropology* (Upper Saddle River, NJ: Prentice Hall, CD-ROM, 2003). William R. Jankowiak, "Urban Mongols: Ethnicity in Communist China," in Ember and Ember, eds., *Portraits of Culture.* ℗

---

chiefdoms, was a large, complex, multiethnic paramount chiefdom. Its ruler, Kawita, relied on allegiance and tribute from outlying districts; ritual and linguistic hegemony was imposed by the ruler.[53]

A combination of internal divisions among the Lower Creek, vacant land in northern Florida, and weak Spanish control over northern Florida apparently prompted dissidents to move away and settle in three different areas in Florida. Three new chiefdoms were established, essentially similar to those the settlers left and still under the supposed control of Kawita.[54] But the three chiefdoms began to act together under the leadership of Tonapi, the Talahassi chief. After 1780, over a period of 40 or so years, the three Seminole chiefdoms formally broke with Kawita. Not only was geographic separation a factor, but the political and economic interests of the Creek Confederacy and of the Seminole had diverged. For example, the Creek supported neutrality in the American Revolution, but the Seminole took the side of the British. It was during this time that the British encouraged slaves to escape by promising freedom in Florida. These Maroon communities allied themselves with the emerging Seminole. The composition of the Seminole population again changed dramatically after the War of 1812 and the Creek War of 1814.[55] First, a large number of Creek refugees, mostly Upper Creek Talapusa (who spoke a different Muskogean language), became Seminole. Second, the Seminole ranks were also expanded by a large number of escaped slaves and Maroons who fled when the Americans destroyed a British fort in 1816. Larger-scale political events continued to influence Seminole history. When the Americans conquered Florida, they insisted on dealing with one unified Seminole council, they removed the Seminole to a reserve in Florida, and later, after the second Seminole war, removed most of them to Oklahoma.[56]

It would seem from this and other cases that cultural identities can be shaped and reshaped by political and economic processes.

◈ Cultural Diversity in the Future

Measured in terms of travel time, the world today is much smaller than it has ever been. It is possible now to fly halfway around the globe in the time it took people less than a century ago to travel to the next state. In the realm of communication, the world is even smaller. We can talk to someone on the other side of the globe in a matter of minutes, we can send that person a message (by fax or Internet) in seconds, and through television we can see live coverage of events in that person's country. More and more people are drawn into the world market economy, buying and selling similar things and, as a consequence, altering the patterns of their lives in sometimes similar ways. Still, although modern transportation and communication facilitate the rapid spread of some cultural characteristics to all parts of the globe, it is highly unlikely that all parts of the world will end up the same culturally. Cultures are bound to retain some of their original characteristics or develop distinctive new adaptations. Even though television has diffused around the world, local people continue to prefer local programs when they are available. And even when people all over the world watch the same program, they may interpret it in very different ways. People are not just absorbing the messages they get; they often resist or revise them.[57]

Until recently, researchers studying culture change generally assumed that the differences between people of different cultures would become minimal. But in the last 30 years or so, it has become increasingly apparent that, although many differences disappear, many people are affirming ethnic identities in a process that often involves deliberately introducing cultural difference.[58] Eugeen Roosens describes the situation of the Huron of Quebec, who in the late 1960s seemed to have disappeared as a distinct culture. The Huron language had disappeared and the lives of the Huron were not obviously distinguishable from those of the French Canadians around them. The Huron then developed a new identity as they actively worked to promote the rights of indigenous peoples like themselves. That their new defining cultural symbols bore no resemblance to the past Huron culture is beside the point.

One fascinating possibility is that ethnic diversity and ethnogenesis may be a result of broader processes. Elizabeth Cashdan found that ethnic diversity appears to be related to environmental unpredictability, which is associated with distance from the equator.[59] There appear to be many more cultural groups nearer to the equator than in very northern and southern latitudes. Perhaps, Cashdan suggests, environmental unpredictability necessitates wider ties between social groups to allow cooperation in case local resources fail. This may minimize the likelihood of cultural divergence, that is, ethnogenesis. Hence there will be fewer cultures further from the equator.

Future research on culture change should increase our understanding of how and why various types of change are occurring. If we can increase our understanding of culture change in the present, we should be better able to understand similar processes in the past. We may be guided in our efforts to understand culture change by the large number of cross-cultural correlations that have been discovered between a particular cultural variation and its presumed causes.[60] All cultures have changed over time; variation is the product of differential change. Thus, the variations we see are the products of change processes, and the discovered predictors of those variations may suggest how and why the changes occurred.

The spread of new technology around the world will not make all cultural variation disappear.

 CD-ROM Flashcards Chapter 27

❋ Summary

1. Culture is always changing. Because culture consists of learned patterns of behavior and belief, cultural traits can be unlearned and learned anew as human needs change.

2. Discoveries and inventions, though ultimately the sources of all culture change, do not necessarily lead to change. Only when society accepts an invention or discovery and uses it regularly can culture change be said

to have occurred. Some inventions are probably the result of dozens of tiny, perhaps accidental, initiatives over a period of many years. Other inventions are consciously intended. Why some people are more innovative than others is still only incompletely understood. There is some evidence that creativity and a readiness to adopt innovations may be related to socioeconomic position.

3. The process by which cultural elements are borrowed from another society and incorporated into the culture of the recipient group is called diffusion. Three patterns of diffusion may be identified: diffusion by direct contact, in which elements of a culture are first taken up by neighboring societies and then gradually spread farther and farther afield; diffusion by intermediate contact, in which third parties, frequently traders, carry a cultural trait from the originating society to another group; and stimulus diffusion, in which knowledge of a trait belonging to another culture stimulates the invention or development of a local equivalent.

4. Cultural traits do not necessarily diffuse; that is, diffusion is a selective, not automatic, process. A society accepting a foreign cultural trait is likely to adapt it in a way that effectively harmonizes it with the society's own traditions.

5. When a group or society is in contact with a more powerful society, the weaker group is often obliged to acquire cultural elements from the dominant group. This process of extensive borrowing in the context of superordinate-subordinate relations between societies is called acculturation. In contrast with diffusion, acculturation comes about as a result of some sort of external pressure.

6. Perhaps the most drastic and rapid way a culture can change is by revolution—a usually violent replacement of the society's rulers. Rebellions occur primarily in state societies, where there is a distinct ruling elite. However, not all peoples who are suppressed, conquered, or colonized eventually rebel or successfully revolt against established authority.

7. Even though customs are not genetically inherited, cultural adaptation may be somewhat similar to biological adaptation. Traits (cultural or genetic) that are more likely to be reproduced (learned or inherited) are likely to become more frequent in a population over time. And if culture is generally adapted to its environment, then culture change should also be generally adaptive.

8. Many of the cultural changes observed in the modern world have been generated, directly or indirectly, by the dominance and expansion of Western societies. One of the principal changes resulting from the expansion of Western culture is the increasing dependence of much of the world on commercial exchange—that is, the proliferation of buying and selling in markets, usually accompanied by the use of money as the medium of exchange. The borrowed custom of buying and selling may at first be supplementary to traditional means of distributing goods, but as the new commercial customs take hold, the economic base of the receiving society alters. Inevitably, this alteration is accompanied by other changes, which have broad social, political, and even biological and psychological ramifications.

9. One way commercialization can occur is for members of a community to become migratory workers, traveling to a place nearby that offers the possibility of working for wages. Commercialization can also occur when a simple, self-sufficient hunting or agricultural society comes to depend more and more on trading for its livelihood. A third way commercialization occurs is when those cultivating the soil produce more than they require for subsistence. The surplus is then sold for cash. In many instances, this cash income must be used to pay rent or taxes; under such circumstances, commercialization may be said to be associated with the formation of a peasantry. A fourth way in which commercialization can come about is through the introduction of commercial agriculture, in which all the cultivated commodities are produced for sale rather than for personal consumption. Along with this change, the system of agriculture may be industrialized, with some of the production processes being done by machine.

10. The growing influence of Western societies has also led to religious change in many parts of the world. In many societies, such change has been brought about intentionally through the efforts of missionaries.

11. One of the most striking types of culture change in the modern world is the spread of democracies. Participatory political institutions are now found in a majority of the world's countries.

12. Globalization—the spread of cultural features around the world—is minimizing cultural diversity, but it is not eliminating it.

13. Ethnogenesis is the process by which new cultures are created.

 ## Glossary Terms

acculturation	globalization
diffusion	peasants
ethnogenesis	revolution

 ## Critical Questions

1. What kinds of cultural items might most easily be borrowed by another culture? Why do you think so?

2. The expansion of the West has had terrible consequences for many peoples. Have there been any beneficial consequences?

3. Why might an increasing understanding of cultural variation also provide an increasing understanding of culture change?

 Internet Exercises

1. While some political entities are breaking apart, others are integrating. How is Europe changing politically and economically? Look at the Web site on the European Parliament and summarize what it does (http://www .europarl.eu.int/). Also look at the site on the single European currency at http://europa.eu.int/euro/. What are the implications of an integrated Europe?

2. What are the gender problems associated with the English language as cited in the paper titled "Non-Sexist Language"? You may find this paper at http://www .stetson.edu/departments/history/nongenderlang .html. What changes could be made to English to make it gender neutral?

3. One organization dedicated to helping avoid the destruction of other cultures is Cultural Survival. Go to its Web site (http://www.culturalsurvival.org/ newpage/index.cfm) and read one or two articles.

4. Computers and the Internet are resulting in global culture change. Different groups of people, large and small, are able to present themselves to others around the world. Go to the site http://www.nativeculture. com/lisamitten/indians.html to find individual Native American Web sites. Look at one such site to see what they present about themselves.

 Suggested Reading

BERNARD, H. R., AND PELTO, P. J., EDS. *Technology and Social Change,* 2nd ed. Prospect Heights, IL: Waveland Press, 1987. This volume is concerned with the effects of intro-

duced Western technology on diverse cultures. Thirteen case studies were written especially for the volume; the editors provide concluding observations.

BODLEY, J. H. *Victims of Progress,* 4th ed. Mountain View, CA: Mayfield, 1998. An examination of the effects of industrial nations on tribal peoples. Emphasizes the imperialist and exploitative practices of expansionist nations, as well as the destructive consequences of imposed "progress."

BOYD, R., AND RICHERSON, P. J. *Culture and the Evolutionary Process.* Chicago: University of Chicago Press, 1996. Originally published, 1985. The authors develop mathematical models to analyze how genes and culture interact, under the influence of evolutionary processes, to produce the diversity we see in human cultures.

EMBER, M., AND EMBER, C. R., EDS. *Portraits of Culture: Ethnographic Originals.* In C. R. Ember and M. Ember, eds., *New Directions in Anthropology.* Upper Saddle River, NJ: Prentice Hall, CD-ROM, 2003. Most of the mini-ethnographies in this series discuss the changes in culture that have occurred in recent times.

GOLDSTONE, J. A. "The Comparative and Historical Study of Revolutions." *Annual Review of Sociology,* 8 (1982): 187–207. A review of theory and research on why revolutions have occurred, and why some succeeded, in the past and present.

HERBIG, P. A. *The Innovation Matrix: Culture and Structure Prerequisites to Innovation.* Westport, CT: Quorum Books, 1994. A discussion of the factors that may enable some societies to adapt and change more quickly than others.

MCNEILL, W. H. *Plagues and Peoples.* New York: Anchor Books/Doubleday, 1998. A historian suggests that epidemics have crucially affected the history of various societies all over the world.

ROGERS, E. M. *Diffusion of Innovations,* 5th ed. New York: Simon & Schuster, 2003. This book examines the roles of information and uncertainty in the spread of innovations, how different categories of people adopt innovations at different rates, and how change agents affect the process. A large literature is reviewed and synthesized.

GLOSSARY

Absolute Dating a method of dating fossils in which the actual age of a deposit or specimen is measured. Also known as chronometric dating.

Acclimatization impermanent physiological changes that people make when they encounter a new environment.

Acculturation the process of extensive borrowing of aspects of culture in the context of superordinate-subordinate relations between societies; usually occurs as the result of external pressure.

Acheulian a stone toolmaking tradition dating from 1.5 million years ago. Compared with the Oldowan tradition, Acheulian assemblages have more large tools created according to standardized designs or shapes. One of the most characteristic and prevalent tools in the Acheulian tool kit is the so-called hand axe, which is a teardrop-shaped bifacially flaked tool with a thinned sharp tip. Other large tools might have been cleavers and picks.

Achieved Qualities those qualities a person acquires during her or his lifetime.

Adapid a type of prosimian with many lemurlike features; appeared in the early Eocene.

Adaptation refers to genetic changes that allow an organism to survive and reproduce in a specific environment.

Adaptive Customs customs that enhance survival and reproductive success in a particular environment. Usually applied to biological evolution, the term is also often used by cultural anthropologists to refer to cultural traits that enhance reproductive success.

Adjudication the process by which a third party acting as judge makes a decision that the parties to a dispute have to accept.

Aegyptopithecus an Oligocene anthropoid and probably the best-known propliopithecid.

Affinal Kin one's relatives by marriage.

Age-Grade a category of persons who happen to fall within a particular, culturally distinguished age range.

Age-Set a group of persons of similar age and the same sex who move together through some or all of life's stages.

Agriculture the practice of raising domesticated crops.

AIDS (Acquired Immune Deficiency Syndrome) a recent lethal disease caused by the HIV virus.

Allele one member of a pair of genes.

Allen's Rule the rule that protruding body parts (particularly arms and legs) are relatively shorter in the cooler areas of a species' range than in the warmer areas.

Ambilineal Descent the rule of descent that affiliates an individual with groups of kin related to him or her through men or women.

Ancestor Spirits supernatural beings who are the ghosts of dead relatives.

Animatism a belief in supernatural forces.

Animism a term used by Edward Tylor to describe a belief in a dual existence for all things—a physical, visible body and a psychic, invisible soul.

Anthropoids one of the two suborders of primates; includes monkeys, apes, and humans.

Anthropological Linguistics the anthropological study of languages.

Anthropology a discipline that studies humans, focusing on the study of differences and similarities, both biological and cultural, in human populations. Anthropology is concerned with typical biological and cultural characteristics of human populations in all periods and in all parts of the world.

Applied (Practicing) Anthropology the branch of anthropology that concerns itself with applying anthropological knowledge to achieve practical goals, usually in the service of an agency outside the traditional academic setting.

^{40}Ar–^{39}Ar Dating used in conjunction with potassium-argon dating, this method gets around the problem of needing different rock samples to estimate potassium and argon. A nuclear reactor is used to convert the ^{39}Ar to ^{39}K, on the basis of which the amount of ^{40}K can be estimated. In this way, both argon and potassium can be estimated from the same rock sample.

Arboreal adapted to living in trees.

Archaeology the branch of anthropology that seeks to reconstruct the daily life and customs of peoples who lived in the past and to trace and explain cultural changes. Often lacking written records for study, archaeologists must try to reconstruct history from the material remains of human cultures. See also **Historical Archaeology.**

Archaic time period in the New World during which food production first developed.

Ardipithecus ramidus perhaps the first hominid, dating to some 4.5 million years ago. Its dentition combines apelike and australopithecine-like features, and its skeleton suggests it was bipedal.

Artifact any object made by a human.

Ascribed Qualities those qualities that are determined for a person at birth.

Association an organized group not based exclusively on kinship or territory.

Atlatl Aztec word for "spear-thrower."

Australopithecus genus of Pliocene and Pleistocene hominids.

Australopithecus aethiopicus an early robust australopithecine.

Australopithecus afarensis a species of *Australopithecus* that lived 4 million to 3 million years ago in East Africa and was definitely bipedal.

Australopithecus africanus a species of *Australopithecus* that lived between about 3 million and 2 million years ago.

Australopithecus anamensis a species of *Australopithecus* that lived perhaps 4.2 million years ago.

Australopithecus boisei an East African robust australopithecine species dating from 2.2 million to 1.3 million years ago with somewhat larger cranial capacity than *A. africanus*. No longer thought to be larger than other australopithecines, it is robust primarily in the skull and jaw, most strikingly in the teeth. Compared with *A. robustus*, *A. boisei* has even more features that reflect a huge chewing apparatus.

Australopithecus robustus a robust australopithecine species found in South African caves dating from about 1.8 million to 1 million years ago. Not as large in the teeth and jaws as *A. boisei*.

Avunculocal Residence a pattern of residence in which a married couple settles with or near the husband's mother's brother.

Balanced Reciprocity giving with the expectation of a straightforward immediate or limited-time trade.

Balancing Selection a type of selection that occurs when a heterozygous combination of alleles is positively favored even though a homozygous combination is disfavored.

Band a fairly small, usually nomadic local group that is politically autonomous.

Band Organization the kind of political organization where the local group or band is the largest territorial group in the society that acts as a unit. The local group in band societies is politically autonomous.

Behavioral Ecology the study of how all kinds of behavior may be related to the environment. The theoretical orientation involves the application of biological evolutionary principles to the behavior (including social behavior) of animals, including humans. Also called sociobiology, particularly when applied to social organization and social behavior.

Berdache a male transvestite in some Native American societies.

Bergmann's rule the rule that smaller-sized subpopulations of a species inhabit the warmer parts of its geographic range and larger-sized subpopulations the cooler areas.

Bifacial Tool a tool worked or flaked on two sides.

Bilateral Kinship the type of kinship system in which individuals affiliate more or less equally with their mother's and father's relatives; descent groups are absent.

Bilocal Residence a pattern of residence in which a married couple lives with or near either the husband's parents or the wife's parents.

Bilophodont having four cusps on the molars that form two parallel ridges. This is the common molar pattern of Old World monkeys.

Biological Anthropology See **Physical Anthropology.**

Biomedicine the dominant medical paradigm in Western societies today.

Bipedalism locomotion in which an animal walks on its two hind legs.

Blade a thin flake whose length is usually more than twice its width. In the blade technique of toolmaking, a core is prepared by shaping a piece of flint with hammerstones into a pyramidal or cylindrical form. Blades are then struck off until the core is used up.

Brachiators animals that move through the trees by swinging hand over hand from branch to branch. They usually have long arms and fingers.

Bride Price or Bride Wealth a substantial gift of goods or money given to the bride's kin by the groom or his kin at or before the marriage.

Bride Service work performed by the groom for his bride's family for a variable length of time either before or after the marriage.

Burin a chisel-like stone tool used for carving and for making such artifacts as bone and antler needles, awls, and projectile points.

Canines the cone-shaped teeth immediately behind the incisors; used by most primates to seize food and in fighting and display.

Carpolestes a mouse-sized arboreal creature living about 56 million years ago; a strong candidate for the common primate ancestor.

Cash Crop a cultivated commodity raised for sale rather than for personal consumption by the cultivator.

Caste a ranked group, often associated with a certain occupation, in which membership is determined at birth and marriage is restricted to members of one's own caste.

Catarrhines the group of anthropoids with narrow noses and nostrils that face downward. Catarrhines include monkeys of the Old World (Africa, Asia, and Europe), as well as apes and humans.

Ceramics objects shaped from clay and baked at high temperature (fired) to make them hard. Containers such as pots and jars are typical ceramics, though they can take on many forms and uses.

Cercopithecoids Old World monkeys.

Cerebral Cortex the "gray matter" of the brain; the center of speech and other higher mental activities.

Chief a person who exercises authority, usually on behalf of a multicommunity political unit. This role is generally found in rank societies and is usually permanent and often hereditary.

Chiefdom a political unit, with a chief at its head, integrating more than one community but not necessarily the whole society or language group.

Chromosomes paired rod-shaped structures within a cell nucleus containing the genes that transmit traits from one generation to the next.

Chronometric Dating see **Absolute Dating.**

Civilization urban society, from the Latin word for "city-state."

Clan a set of kin whose members believe themselves to be descended from a common ancestor or ancestress but cannot specify the links back to that founder; often designated by a totem. Also called a sib.

Class a category of persons who have about the same opportunity to obtain economic resources, power, and prestige.

Classificatory Terms kinship terms that merge or equate relatives who are genealogically distinct from one another; the same term is used for a number of different kin.

Class Society a society containing social groups that have unequal access to economic resources, power, and prestige.

Cline the gradually increasing (or decreasing) frequency of a gene from one end of a region to another.

Codeswitching using more than one language in the course of conversing.

Codified Laws formal principles for resolving disputes in heterogeneous and stratified societies.

Cognates words or morphs that belong to different languages but have similar sounds and meanings.

Commercial Exchange see **Market or Commercial Exchange.**

Commercialization the increasing dependence on buying and selling, with money usually as the medium of exchange.

Compatibility-with-Child-Care Theory an explanation for the gender division of labor that suggests that women's work will typically involve tasks that do not take women far from home for long periods, do not place children in potential danger if they are taken along, and can be stopped and resumed if an infant needs care.

Complementary Opposition the occasional uniting of various segments of a segmentary lineage system in opposition to similar segments.

Consanguineal Kin one's biological relatives; relatives by birth.

Conservation techniques used on archaeological materials to stop or reverse the process of decay.

Context the relationships between and among artifacts, ecofacts, fossils, and features.

Continental Drift the movement of the continents over the past 135 million years. In the early Cretaceous (ca. 135 million years ago) there were two "supercontinents"; *Laurasia,* which included North America and Eurasia, and *Gondwanaland,* which included Africa, South America, India, Australia, and Antarctica. By the beginning of the Paleocene (ca. 65 million years ago), Gondwanaland had broken apart, with South America drifting west away from Africa, India drifting east, and Australia and Antarctica drifting south.

Core Vocabulary nonspecialist vocabulary.

Corvée a system of required labor.

Cretaceous geological epoch 135 million to 65 million years ago, during which dinosaurs and other reptiles ceased to be the dominant land vertebrates and mammals and birds began to become important.

Crime violence not considered legitimate that occurs within a political unit.

Cro-Magnons humans who lived in western Europe about 35,000 years ago. Once thought to be the earliest specimens of modern-looking humans, or *Homo sapiens sapiens.* But it is now known that modern-looking humans appeared earlier outside of Europe; the earliest so far found lived in Africa.

Cross-Cousins children of siblings of the opposite sex. One's cross-cousins are father's sisters' children and mother's brothers' children.

Cross-Cultural Researcher an ethnologist who uses ethnographic data about many societies to test possible explanations of cultural variation.

Crossing-Over exchanges of sections of chromosomes from one chromosome to another.

Cultural Anthropology the study of cultural variation and universals.

Cultural Ecology the analysis of the relationship between a culture and its environment.

Cultural Relativism   the attitude that a society's customs and ideas should be viewed within the context of that society's problems and opportunities.

Cultural Resource Management (CRM)   the branch of applied anthropology that seeks to recover and preserve the archaeological record before programs of planned change disturb or destroy it.

Culture   the set of learned behaviors, beliefs, attitudes, values, and ideals that are characteristic of a particular society or population.

Culture History   a history of the cultures that lived in a given area over time. Until the 1950s building such culture histories was a primary goal of archaeological research.

Cuneiform   wedge-shaped writing invented by the Sumerians around 3000 B.C.

Descriptive or Structural Linguistics   the study of how languages are constructed.

Descriptive Term   kinship term used to refer to a genealogically distinct relative; a different term is used for each relative.

Dialect   a variety of a language spoken in a particular area or by a particular social group.

Diastema   a gap between the canine and first premolar found in apes.

Diffusion   the borrowing by one society of a cultural trait belonging to another society as the result of contact between the two societies.

Directional Selection   a type of natural selection that increases the frequency of a trait (the trait is said to be positively favored, or adaptive).

Diurnal   active during the day.

Divination   getting the supernatural to provide guidance.

DNA   deoxyribonucleic acid; a long, two-stranded molecule in the genes that directs the makeup of an organism according to the instructions in its genetic code.

Domestication   modification or adaptation of plants and animals for use by humans. When people plant crops, we refer to the process as cultivation. It is only when the crops cultivated and the animals raised have been modified—are different from wild varieties—that we speak of plant and animal domestication.

Dominant   the allele of a gene pair that is always phenotypically expressed in the heterozygous form.

Double Descent or Double Unilineal Descent   a system that affiliates an individual with a group of matrilineal kin for some purposes and with a group of patrilineal kin for other purposes.

Dowry   a substantial transfer of goods or money from the bride's family to the bride.

Dryopithecus   genus of ape from the later Miocene found primarily in Europe. It had thin tooth enamel and pointed molar-cusps very similar to those of the fruit-eating chimpanzees of today.

Early Evolutionism   the view that culture develops in a uniform and progressive manner.

Ecofacts   natural items that have been used by humans. Things such as the remains of animals eaten by humans or plant pollens found on archaeological sites are examples of ecofacts.

Economy-of-Effort Theory   an explanation for the gender division of labor that suggests that it may be advantageous for a gender to do tasks that follow in a production sequence (e.g., those who cut lumber make wooden objects; those who quarry stone make stone objects); it may also be advantageous for one gender to perform tasks that are located near each other (e.g., child care and other chores done in or near the home).

Egalitarian Society   a society in which all persons of a given age-sex category have equal access to economic resources, power, and prestige.

Ego   in the reckoning of kinship, the reference point or focal person.

Electron Spin Resonance Dating   like thermoluminescence dating, this technique measures trapped electrons from surrounding radioactive material. The material to be dated is exposed to varying magnetic fields in order to obtain a spectrum of the microwaves absorbed by the tested material. Because heat is not required for this technique, electron spin resonance is especially useful for dating organic materials, such as bone and shell, that decompose if heated.

Enculturation   see **Socialization.**

Endogamy   the rule specifying marriage to a person within one's own group (kin, caste, community).

Eocene   a geological epoch 55 million to 34 million years ago during which the first definite primates appeared.

Epipaleolithic   time period in the Near East during which food production first developed.

Ethnicity   the process of defining ethnicity usually involves a group of people emphasizing common origins and language, shared history, and selected aspects of cultural difference such as a difference in religion. Since different groups are doing the perceiving, ethnic identities often vary with whether one is inside or outside the group.

Ethnocentric   refers to judgment of other cultures solely in terms of one's own culture.

Ethnocentrism   the attitude that other societies' customs and ideas can be judged in the context of one's own culture.

Ethnogenesis   the creation of a new culture.

Ethnographer   a person who spends some time living with, interviewing, and observing a group of people so that he or she can describe their customs.

Ethnographic Analogy   method of comparative cultural study that extrapolates to the past from recent or current societies.

Ethnography   a description of a society's customary behaviors, beliefs, and attitudes.

Ethnohistorian   an ethnologist who uses historical documents to study how a particular culture has changed over time.

Ethnology   the study of how and why recent cultures differ and are similar.

Ethnomedicine   the health-related beliefs, knowledge, and practices of a cultural group.

Evolutionary Psychology   the study of how evolution may have produced lasting variation in the way humans behave, interact, and perceive the world.

Exogamy   the rule specifying marriage to a person from outside one's own group (kin or community).

Expendability Theory   an explanation for the gender division of labor that suggests that men, rather than women, will tend to do the dangerous work in a society because the loss of men is less disadvantageous reproductively than the loss of women.

Explanation   an answer to a why question. In science, there are two kinds of explanation that researchers try to achieve: associations and theories.

Extensive Cultivation   a type of horticulture in which the land is worked for short periods and then left to regenerate for some years before being used again. Also called shifting cultivation.

Falsification   showing that a theory seems to be wrong by finding that implications or predictions derivable from it are not consistent with objectively collected data.

Family   a social and economic unit consisting minimally of a parent and a child.

Fayum   a site southwest of Cairo, Egypt, where the world's best record of Oligocene primate fossils has been found.

Features   artifacts of human manufacture that cannot be removed from an archaeological site. Hearths, storage pits, and buildings are examples of features.

Feuding   a state of recurring hostility between families or groups of kin, usually motivated by a desire to avenge an offense against a member of the group.

Fieldwork   firsthand experience with the people being studied and the usual means by which anthropological information is obtained. Regardless of other methods (e.g., censuses, surveys) that anthropologists may use, fieldwork usually involves participant-observation for an extended period of time, often a year or more. See **Participant-Observation.**

Fission-Track Dating a chronometric dating method used to date crystal, glass, and many uranium-rich materials contemporaneous with fossils or deposits that are from 20 billion to 5 billion years old. This dating method entails counting the tracks or paths of decaying uranium-isotope atoms in the sample and then comparing the number of tracks with the uranium content of the sample.

Folklore includes all the myths, legends, folktales, ballads, riddles, proverbs, and superstitions of a cultural group. Generally, folklore is transmitted orally, but it may also be written.

Food Collection all forms of subsistence technology in which food-getting is dependent on naturally occurring resources—wild plants and animals.

Food Production the form of subsistence technology in which food-getting is dependent on the cultivation and domestication of plants and animals.

Foragers people who subsist on the collection of naturally occurring plants and animals. Also referred to as hunter-gatherers.

Foramen Magnum opening in the base of the skull through which the spinal cord passes en route to the brain.

Forensic Anthropology the use of anthropology to help solve crimes.

Fossils the hardened remains or impressions of plants and animals that lived in the past.

Fraternal Polyandry the marriage of a woman to two or more brothers at the same time.

F-U-N Trio fluorine (F), uranium (U), and nitrogen (N) tests for relative dating. All three minerals are present in groundwater. The older a fossil is, the higher its fluorine or uranium content will be and the lower its nitrogen content.

Gender Differences differences between females and males that reflect cultural expectations and experiences.

Gender Roles roles that are culturally assigned to genders.

Gender Stratification the degree of unequal access by the different genders to prestige, authority, power, rights, and economic resources.

Gene chemical unit of heredity.

Gene Flow the process by which genes pass from the gene pool of one population to that of another through mating and reproduction.

Generalized Reciprocity gift giving without any immediate or planned return.

General-Purpose Money a universally accepted medium of exchange.

Genetic Drift the various random processes that affect gene frequencies in small, relatively isolated populations.

Genotype the total complement of inherited traits or genes of an organism.

Genus a group of related species; pl., genera.

Ghosts supernatural beings who were once human; the souls of dead people.

Globalization the ongoing spread of goods, people, information, and capital around the world.

Gloger's Rule the rule that populations of birds and mammals living in warm, humid climates have more melanin (and therefore darker skin, fur, or feathers) than populations of the same species living in cooler, drier areas.

Gods supernatural beings of nonhuman origin who are named personalities; often anthropomorphic.

Gracile Australopithecines the earliest group of australopithecines, usually differentiated from the robust australopithecines (see below) by their lighter dentition and smaller faces.

Group Marriage marriage in which more than one man is married to more than one woman at the same time; not customary in any known human society.

Group Selection natural selection of group characteristics.

Half-Life The time it takes for half of the atoms of a radioactive substance to decay into atoms of a different substance.

Hand Axe a teardrop-shaped stone tool characteristic of Acheulian assemblages.

Hard Hammer a technique of stone tool manufacture where one stone is used to knock flakes from another stone. Flakes produced through hard hammer percussion are usually large and crude.

Headman a person who holds a powerless but symbolically unifying position in a community within an egalitarian society; may exercise influence but has no power to impose sanctions.

Heterozygous possessing differing genes or alleles in corresponding locations on a pair of chromosomes.

Hieroglyphics "picture writing," as in ancient Egypt and in Mayan sites in Mesoamerica (Mexico and Central America).

Historical Archaeology a specialty within archaeology that studies the material remains of recent peoples who left written records.

Historical Linguistics the study of how languages change over time.

Holistic refers to an approach that studies many aspects of a multifaceted system.

Hominids the group of hominoids consisting of humans and their direct ancestors. It contains at least two genera: *Homo* and *Australopithecus*.

Hominoids the group of catarrhines that includes both apes and humans.

Homo genus to which modern humans and their ancestors belong.

Homo erectus the first hominid species to be widely distributed in the Old World. The earliest finds are possibly 1.8 million years old. The brain (averaging 895–1,040 cc) was larger than that found in any of the australopithecines or *H. habilis* but smaller than the average brain of a modern human.

Homo habilis early species belonging to our genus, *Homo*, with cranial capacities averaging about 630–640 cc, about 50 percent of the brain capacity of modern humans. Dating from about 2 million years ago.

Homo heidelbergensis a transitional species between *Homo erectus* and *Homo sapiens*.

Homo neandertalensis the technical name for the Neandertals, a group of robust and otherwise anatomically distinct hominids that are close relatives of modern humans—so close that some believe they should be classified as *Homo sapiens neandertalensis*.

Homo rudolfensis early species belonging to our genus, *Homo*. Similar enough to *Homo habilis* that some paleoanthropologists make no distinction between the two.

Homo sapiens all living people belong to one biological species, *Homo sapiens*, which means that all human populations on earth can successfully interbreed. The first *Homo sapiens* may have emerged by 200,000 years ago.

Homo sapiens sapiens modern-looking humans, undisputed examples of which appeared about 50,000 years ago; may have appeared earlier.

Homozygous possessing two identical genes or alleles in corresponding locations on a pair of chromosomes.

Horticulture plant cultivation carried out with relatively simple tools and methods; nature is allowed to replace nutrients in the soil, in the absence of permanently cultivated fields.

Human Paleontology the study of the emergence of humans and their later physical evolution. Also called paleoanthropology.

Human Variation the study of how and why contemporary human populations vary biologically.

Hunter-Gatherers people who collect food from naturally occurring resources, that is, wild plants, animals, and fish. The phrase "hunter-gatherers" minimizes sometimes heavy dependence on fishing. Also referred to as foragers.

Hylobates the family of hominoids that includes gibbons and siamangs; often referred to as the lesser apes (as compared with the great apes such as gorillas and chimpanzees).

Hypotheses predictions, which may be derived from theories, about how variables are related.

Hypoxia a condition of oxygen deficiency that often occurs at high altitudes. The percentage of oxygen in the air is the same as at lower altitudes, but because the barometric pressure is lower, less oxygen is taken in with each breath. Often, breathing becomes more rapid, the heart beats faster, and activity is more difficult.

Incest Taboo prohibition of sexual intercourse or marriage between mother and son, father and daughter, and brother and sister.

Incisors the front teeth; used for holding or seizing food and preparing it for chewing by the other teeth.

Indirect Dowry goods given by the groom's kin to the bride (or her father, who passes most of them to her) at or before her marriage.

Indicator Artifacts and Ecofacts items that changed relatively rapidly and which, thus, can be used to indicate the relative age of associated items.

Indicator Fossils well-known fossils used to assign dates to rock strata.

Indirect Percussion a toolmaking technique common in the Upper Paleolithic. After shaping a core into a pyramidal or cylindrical form, the toolmaker can put a punch of antler or wood or another hard material into position and strike it with a hammer. Using a hammer-struck punch enabled the toolmaker to strike off consistently shaped blades.

Individual Selection natural selection of individual characteristics.

Insectivore the order or major grouping of mammals, including modern shrews and moles, that is adapted to feeding on insects.

Intensive Agriculture food production characterized by the permanent cultivation of fields and made possible by the use of the plow, draft animals or machines, fertilizers, irrigation, waterstorage techniques, and other complex agricultural techniques.

Kenyapithecus an apelike primate from the Middle Miocene found in East Africa. It had very thickly enameled teeth and robust jaws, suggesting a diet of hard, tough foods. Probably somewhat terrestrial.

Kindred a bilateral set of close relatives.

Knuckle Walking a locomotor pattern of primates such as the chimpanzee and gorilla in which the weight of the upper part of the body is supported on the thickly padded knuckles of the hands.

Kula **Ring** a ceremonial exchange of valued shell ornaments in the Trobriand Islands, in which white shell armbands are traded around the islands in a counterclockwise direction and red shell necklaces are traded clockwise.

Laws (Scientific) associations or relationships that are accepted by almost all scientists.

Levalloisian Method a method that allowed flake tools of a predetermined size to be produced from a shaped core. The toolmaker first shaped the core and prepared a "striking platform" at one end. Flakes of predetermined and standard sizes could then be knocked off. Although some Levallois flakes date from as far back as 400,000 years ago, they are found more frequently in Mousterian tool kits.

Levirate a custom whereby a man is obliged to marry his brother's widow.

Lexical Content vocabulary or lexicon.

Lexicon the words and morphs, and their meanings, of a language; approximated by a dictionary.

Lineage a set of kin whose members trace descent from a common ancestor through known links.

Lithics the technical name for tools made from stone.

Lower Paleolithic the period of the Oldowan and Acheulian stone tool traditions.

Magic the performance of certain rituals that are believed to compel the supernatural powers to act in particular ways.

Maladaptive Customs customs that diminish the chances of survival and reproduction in a particular environment. Usually applied to biological evolution, the term is often used by cultural anthropologists to refer to behavioral or cultural traits that are likely to disappear because they diminish reproductive success.

Mana a supernatural, impersonal force that inhabits certain objects or people and is believed to confer success and/or strength.

Manumission the granting of freedom to a slave.

Market or Commercial Exchange transactions in which the "prices" are subject to supply and demand, whether or not the transactions occur in a marketplace.

Marriage a socially approved sexual and economic union, usually between a man and a woman, that is presumed, both by the couple and by others, to be more or less permanent, and that subsumes reciprocal rights and obligations between the two spouses and their future children.

Matriclan a clan tracing descent through the female line.

Matrifocal Family a family consisting of a mother and her children.

Matrilineage a kin group whose members trace descend through known links in the female line from a common female ancestor.

Matrilineal Descent the rule of descent that affiliates an individual with kin of both sexes related to him or her through women only.

Matrilocal Residence a pattern of residence in which a married couple lives with or near the wife's parents.

Measure to describe how something compares with other things on some scale of variation.

Mediation the process by which a third party tries to bring about a settlement in the absence of formal authority to force a settlement.

Medium part-time religious practitioner who is asked to heal and divine while in a trance.

Meiosis the process by which reproductive cells are formed. In this process of division, the number of chromosomes in the newly formed cells is reduced by half, so that when fertilization occurs the resulting organism has the normal number of chromosomes appropriate to its species, rather than double that number.

Mesolithic the archaeological period in the Old World beginning about 12,000 B.C. Humans were starting to settle down in semipermanent camps and villages, as people began to depend less on big game (which they used to have to follow over long distances) and more on relatively stationary food resources such as fish, shellfish, small game, and wild plants rich in carbohydrates, proteins, and oils.

Messenger RNA a type of ribonucleic acid that is used in the cell to copy the DNA code for use in protein synthesis.

Microlith a small, razorlike blade fragment that was probably attached in a series to a wooden or bone handle to form a cutting edge.

Middle Paleolithic the time period of the Mousterian stone tool tradition.

Miocene the geological epoch from 24 million to 5.2 million years ago.

Mitosis cellular reproduction or growth involving the duplication of chromosome pairs.

Moiety a unilineal descent group in a society that is divided into two such maximal groups; there may be smaller unilineal descent groups as well.

Molars the large teeth behind the premolars at the back of the jaw; used for chewing and grinding food.

Monogamy marriage between only one man and only one woman at a time.

Monotheistic believing that there is only one high god and that all other supernatural beings are subordinate to, or are alternative manifestations of, this supreme being.

Morph the smallest unit of a language that has a meaning.

Morpheme one or more morphs with the same meaning.

Morphology the study of how sound sequences convey meaning.

Mousterian Tool Assemblage named after the tool assemblage found in a rock shelter at Le Moustier in the Dordogne region of southwestern France. Compared with an Acheulian assemblage, the Middle Paleolithic (40,000–300,000 years ago) Mousterian has a smaller proportion of large core tools such as hand axes and cleavers and a bigger proportion of small flake tools such as scrapers. Flakes were often altered or "retouched" by striking small flakes or chips from one or more edges.

Mutation   a change in the DNA sequence, producing an altered gene.

Natural Selection   the outcome of processes that affect the frequencies of traits in a particular environment. Traits that enhance survival and reproductive success increase in frequency over time.

Neandertal   the common name for the species *Homo neandertalensis*.

Negotiation   the process by which the parties to a dispute try to resolve it themselves.

Neolithic   originally meaning "the new stone age," now meaning the presence of domesticated plants and animals. The earliest evidence of domestication comes from the Near East about 8000 B.C.

Neolocal Residence   a pattern of residence whereby a married couple lives separately, and usually at some distance, from the kin of both spouses.

Nocturnal   active during the night.

Nonfraternal Polyandry   marriage of a woman to two or more men who are not brothers.

Nonsororal Polygyny   marriage of a man to two or more women who are not sisters.

Normalizing Selection   the type of natural selection that removes harmful genes that arose by mutation.

Norms   standards or rules about acceptable behavior in a society. The importance of a norm usually can be judged by how members of a society respond when the norm is violated.

Nuclear Family   a family consisting of a married couple and their young children.

Oath   the act of calling upon a deity to bear witness to the truth of what one says.

Obsidian   a volcanic glass that can be used to make mirrors or sharp-edged tools.

Occipital Torus   a ridge of bone running horizontally across the back of the skull in apes and some hominids.

Oldowan   the earliest stone toolmaking tradition, named after the tools found in Bed I at Olduvai Gorge, Tanzania; from about 2.5 million years ago. The stone artifacts include core tools and sharp-edged flakes made by striking one stone against another. Flake tools predominate. Among the core tools, so-called choppers are common.

Oligocene   the geological epoch 34 million to 24 million years ago during which definite anthropoids emerged.

Omnivorous   eating both meat and vegetation.

Omomyid   a type of prosimian with many tarsierlike features that appeared in the early Eocene.

Operational Definition   a description of the procedure that is followed in measuring a variable.

Opposable Thumb   a thumb that can touch the tips of all the other fingers.

Optimal Foraging Theory   the theory that individuals seek to maximize the returns (in calories and nutrients) on their labor in deciding which animals and plants they will go after.

Ordeal   a means of determining guilt or innocence by submitting the accused to dangerous or painful tests believed to be under supernatural control.

Orrorin tugenensis   an apparently bipedal primate dating to between 5.8 and 6 million years, making it possibly the earliest known hominid.

Paleoanthropologists   anthropologists who work in the field of paleoanthropology or human paleontology.

Paleoanthropology   see **Human Paleontology.**

Paleocene   the geological epoch 65 million to 55 million years ago.

Paleolithic   period of the early Stone Age, when flint, stone, and bone tools were developed and hunting and gathering were the means of acquiring food.

Paleomagnetic Dating   a method of dating archaeological and fossil deposits based on reversals and changes in the earth's magnetic field over time. By comparing the magnetic characteristics of a deposit to those known from the earth's past, a date when the deposit was formed can be determined.

Parallel Cousins   children of siblings of the same sex. One's parallel cousins are father's brothers' children and mother's sisters' children.

Parapithecids   small monkeylike Oligocene primates found in the Fayum area of Egypt.

Participant-Observation   living among the people being studied—observing, questioning, and (when possible) taking part in the important events of the group. Writing or otherwise recording notes on observations, questions asked and answered, and things to check out later are parts of participant-observation.

Pastoralism   a form of subsistence technology in which food-getting is based directly or indirectly on the maintenance of domesticated animals.

Patriclan   a clan tracing descent through the male line.

Patrilineage   a kin group whose members trace descent through known links in the male line from a common male ancestor.

Patrilineal Descent   the rule of descent that affiliates an individual with kin of both sexes related to him or her through men only.

Patrilocal Residence   a pattern of residence in which a married couple lives with or near the husband's parents.

Peasants   rural people who produce food for their own subsistence but who must also contribute or sell their surpluses to others (in towns and cities) who do not produce their own food.

Percussion Flaking   a toolmaking technique in which one stone is struck with another to remove a flake.

Personality   the distinctive way an individual thinks, feels, and behaves.

Personality Integration of Culture   the theory that personality or psychological processes may account for connections between certain aspects of culture.

Phenotype   the observable physical appearance of an organism, which may or may not reflect its genotype or total genetic constitution.

Phone   a speech sound in a language.

Phoneme   a sound or set of sounds that makes a difference in meaning to the speakers of the language.

Phonology   the study of the sounds in a language and how they are used.

Phratry   a unilineal descent group composed of a number of supposedly related clans (sibs).

Physical (Biological) Anthropology   the study of humans as biological organisms, dealing with the emergence and evolution of humans and with contemporary biological variations among human populations. Also called biological anthropology.

Platyrrhines   the group of anthropoids that have broad, flat-bridged noses, with nostrils facing outward; these monkeys are currently found only in the New World (Central and South America).

Pleistocene   a geological epoch that started 1.6 million years ago and, according to some, continues into the present. During this period, glaciers have often covered much of the earth's surface and humans became the dominant life form.

Plesiadipis   the most well known of the plesiadipiforms, possibly an archaic primate.

Pliocene   the geological epoch 5.2 million to 1.6 million years ago during which the earliest definite hominids appeared.

Political Economy   the study of how external forces, particularly powerful state societies, explain the way a society changes and adapts.

Polyandry   the marriage of one woman to more than one man at a time.

Polygamy   plural marriage; marriage to more than one spouse simultaneously.

Polygyny   the marriage of one man to more than one woman at a time.

Polyphony two or more melodies sung simultaneously.

Polytheistic recognizing many gods, none of whom is believed to be superordinate.

Pongids hominoids whose members include both the living and extinct apes.

Potassium-Argon (K-Ar) Dating a chronometric dating method that uses the rate of decay of a radioactive form of potassium (^{40}K) into argon (^{40}Ar) to date samples from 5,000 to 3 billion years old. The K-Ar method dates the minerals and rocks in a deposit, not the fossils themselves.

Postpartum Sex Taboo prohibition of sexual intercourse between a couple for a period of time after the birth of their child.

Potlatch a feast among Pacific Northwest Native Americans at which great quantities of food and goods are given to the guests in order to gain prestige for the host(s).

Practicing Anthropology see **Applied Anthropology**.

Prairie grassland with a high grass cover.

Prehensile adapted for grasping objects.

Prehistory the time before written records.

Premolars the teeth immediately behind the canines; used in chewing, grinding, and shearing food.

Pressure Flaking toolmaking technique whereby small flakes are struck off by pressing against the core with a bone, antler, or wooden tool.

Priest generally a full-time specialist, with very high status, who is thought to be able to relate to superior or high gods beyond the ordinary person's access or control.

Primary Institutions the sources of early experiences, such as family organization and subsistence techniques, that presumably help form the basic, or typical, personality found in a society.

Primary Subsistence Activities the food-getting activities: gathering, hunting, fishing, herding, and agriculture.

Primate a member of the mammalian order Primates, divided into the two suborders of prosimians and anthropoids.

Primatologists people who study primates.

Primatology the study of primates.

Probability Value (*p*-value) the likelihood that an observed result could have occurred by chance.

Proconsul the best-known genus of proto-apes from the Early Miocene.

Prognathic a physical feature that is sticking out or pushed forward, such as the faces in apes and some hominid species.

Projective Tests tests that utilize ambiguous stimuli; test subjects must project their own personality traits in order to structure the ambiguous stimuli.

Propliopithecids apelike anthropoids dating from the early Oligocene, found in the Fayum area of Egypt.

Prosimians literally "premonkeys," one of the two suborders of primates; includes lemurs, lorises, and tarsiers.

Protolanguage a hypothesized ancestral language from which two or more languages seem to have derived.

Quadrupeds animals that walk on all fours.

Race in biology, race refers to a subpopulation or variety species that differs somewhat in gene frequencies from other varieties of the species. All members of a species can interbreed and produce viable offspring. Many anthropologists do not think that the concept of race is usefully applied to humans because humans do not fall into geographic populations that can be easily distinguished in terms of different sets of biological or physical traits. Thus, race in humans is largely a culturally assigned category.

Rachis the seed-bearing part of a plant. In the wild variety the rachis shatters easily, releasing the seeds. Domesticated grains have a tough rachis, which does not shatter easily.

Racism the belief, without scientific basis, that one "race" is superior to others.

Radiocarbon (or Carbon-14, ^{14}C) Dating a dating method uses the decay of carbon-14 to date organic remains. It is reliable for dating once-living matter up to 50,000 years old.

Raiding a short-term use of force, generally planned and organized, to realize a limited objective.

Random Sample a sample in which all cases selected have had an equal chance to be included.

Rank Society a society that does not have any unequal access to economic resources or power, but with social groups that have unequal access to status positions and prestige.

Recessive an allele phenotypically suppressed in the heterozygous form and expressed only in the homozygous form.

Reciprocity giving and taking (not politically arranged) without the use of money.

Redistribution the accumulation of goods (or labor) by a particular person or in a particular place and their subsequent distribution.

Relative Dating a method of dating fossils that determines the age of a specimen or deposit relative to a known specimen or deposit.

Religion any set of attitudes, beliefs, and practices pertaining to supernatural power, whether that power rests in forces, gods, spirits, ghosts, or demons.

Revitalization Movement a new religious movement intended to save a culture by infusing it with a new purpose and life.

Revolution a usually violent replacement of a society's rulers.

Ribosome a structure in the cell used in making proteins.

Robust Australopithecines a later group of australopithecines usually differentiated from the gracile australopithecines (see above) by their heavier dentition and larger faces.

Rules of Descent rules that connect individuals with particular sets of kin because of known or presumed common ancestry.

Sagittal Crest a ridge of bone running along the top of the skull in apes and early hominids.

Sagittal Keel an inverted V-shaped ridge running along the top of the skull in *Homo erectus*.

Sahelanthropus tchadensis a hominoid found in Chad dating to around 7 million years ago.

Sampling Universe the list of cases to be sampled from.

Savanna tropical grassland.

Secondary Institutions aspects of culture, such as religion, music, art, folklore, and games, which presumably reflect or are projections of the basic, or typical, personality in a society.

Secondary Subsistence Activities activities that involve the preparation and processing of food either to make it edible or to store it.

Sedentarism settled life.

Segmentary Lineage System a hierarchy of more and more inclusive lineages; usually functions only in conflict situations.

Segregation the random sorting of chromosomes in meiosis.

Sex Differences the typical differences between females and males that are most likely due to biological differences.

Sexual Dimorphism a marked difference in size and appearance between males and females of a species.

Shaman a religious intermediary, usually part time, whose primary function is to cure people through sacred songs, pantomime, and other means; sometimes called witch doctor by Westerners.

Shifting Cultivation see **Extensive Cultivation**.

Sib see **Clan**.

Siblings a person's brothers and sisters.

Sickle-Cell Anemia (Sicklemia) a condition in which red blood cells assume a crescent (sickle) shape when deprived of oxygen, instead of the normal (disk) shape. The sickle-shaped red blood cells do not move through the body as readily as normal cells, and thus cause damage to the heart, lungs, brain, and other vital organs.

Sites locations where the material remains of human activity have been preserved in a way that archaeologists or paleoanthropologists can recover them.

Sivapithecus a genus of ape from the later Miocene known for its thickly enameled teeth, suggesting a diet of hard, tough, or gritty items. Found primarily in western and southern Asia and now thought to be ancestral to orangutans.

Slash-and-Burn a form of shifting cultivation in which the natural vegetation is cut down and burned off. The cleared ground is used for a short time and then left to regenerate.

Slaves a class of persons who do not own their own labor or the products thereof.

Socialization a term used by anthropologists and psychologists to describe the development, through the direct and indirect influence of parents and others, of children's patterns of behavior (and attitudes and values) that conform to cultural expectations.

Society a group of people who occupy a particular territory and speak a common language not generally understood by neighboring peoples. By this definition, societies do not necessarily correspond to nations.

Sociobiology see **Behavioral Ecology.**

Sociolinguistics the study of cultural and subcultural patterns of speaking in different social contexts.

Soft Hammer a technique of stone tool manufacture in which a bone or wood hammer is used to strike flakes from a stone.

Sorcery the use of certain materials to invoke supernatural powers to harm people.

Sororal Polygyny the marriage of a man to two or more sisters at the same time.

Sororate a custom whereby a woman is obliged to marry her deceased sister's husband.

Special-Purpose Money objects of value for which only some goods and services can be exchanged.

Speciation the development of a new species.

Species a population that consists of organisms able to interbreed and produce viable and fertile offspring.

Spirits unnamed supernatural beings of nonhuman origin who are beneath the gods in prestige and often closer to the people; may be helpful, mischievous, or evil.

State a form of political organization that includes class stratification, three or more levels of hierarchy, and leaders with the power to govern by force.

State Organization a society is described as having state organization when it includes one or more states.

Statistical Association a relationship or correlation between two or more variables that is unlikely to be due to chance.

Statistically Significant refers to a result that would occur very rarely by chance. The result (and stronger ones) would occur fewer than 5 times out of 100 by chance.

Steppe grassland with a dry, low grass cover.

Stratified an archaeological deposit that contains successive layers or strata.

Stratigraphy the study of how different rock formations and fossils are laid down in successive layers or strata. Older layers are generally deeper or lower than more recent layers.

Strength Theory an explanation for the gender division of labor suggesting that men's work typically involves tasks (like hunting and lumbering) requiring greater strength and greater aerobic work capacity.

Structural Linguistics see **Descriptive Linguistics.**

Subculture the shared customs of a subgroup within a society.

Subsistence Technology the methods humans use to procure food.

Supernatural believed to be not human or not subject to the laws of nature.

Syntax the ways in which words are arranged to form phrases and sentences.

Taboo a prohibition that, if violated, is believed to bring supernatural punishment.

Taphonomy the study of how natural processes form and disturb archaeological sites.

Taurodontism having teeth with an enlarged pulp cavity.

Taxonomy the classification of extinct and living organisms.

Terrestrial adapted to living on the ground.

Terrorism the use or threat of violence to create terror in others, usually for political purposes.

Theoretical Construct something that cannot be observed or verified directly.

Theories explanations of associations or laws.

Thermoluminescence Dating a dating technique that is well suited to samples of ancient pottery, brick, tile, or terra cotta, which (when they were made) were heated to a high temperature that released trapped electrons. Such an object continues over time to trap electrons from radioactive elements around it, and the electrons trapped after manufacture emit light when heated. Thus the age of the object can be estimated by measuring how much light is emitted when the object is heated.

Totem a plant or animal associated with a clan (sib) as a means of group identification; may have other special significance for the group.

Tribal Organization the kind of political organization in which local communities mostly act autonomously but there are kin groups (such as clans) or associations (such as age-sets) that can temporarily integrate a number of local groups into a larger unit.

Tribe a territorial population in which there are kin or nonkin groups with representatives in a number of local groups.

Typology a way of organizing artifacts in categories based on their particular characteristics.

Unifacial Tool a tool worked or flaked on one side only.

Unilineal Descent affiliation with a group of kin through descent links of one sex only.

Unilocal Residence a pattern of residence (patrilocal, matrilocal, or avunculocal) that specifies just one set of relatives that the married couple lives with or near.

Unisex Association an association that restricts its membership to one sex, usually male.

Universally Ascribed Qualities those ascribed qualities (age, sex) that are found in all societies.

Upper Paleolithic the time period associated with the emergence of modern humans and their spread around the world.

Uranium-Series Dating a technique for dating fossil sites that uses the decay of two kinds of uranium (^{235}U and ^{238}U) into other isotopes (such as ^{230}Th, thorium). Particularly useful in cave sites. Different types of uranium-series dating use different isotope ratios.

Variable a thing or quantity that varies.

Variably Ascribed Qualities those ascribed qualities (such as ethnic, religious, or social class differences) that are found only in some societies.

Vertical Clinging and Leaping a locomotor pattern characteristic of several primates, including tarsiers and galagos. The animal normally rests by clinging to a branch in a vertical position and uses its hind limbs alone to push off from one vertical position to another.

Warfare violence between political entities such as communities, districts, or nations.

Witchcraft the practice of attempting to harm people by supernatural means, but through emotions and thought alone, not through the use of tangible objects.

"Y-5" Pattern refers to the pattern of cusps on human molars. When looked at from the top, the cusps of the molars form a Y opening toward the cheek.

NOTES

CHAPTER 1

1. Gail G. Harrison, "Primary Adult Lactase Deficiency: A Problem in Anthropological Genetics," *American Anthropologist*, 77 (1975): 812–35; William H. Durham, *Coevolution: Genes, Culture and Human Diversity* (Stanford, CA: Stanford University Press, 1991), pp. 228–37.
2. F. C. Chen and W. H. Li, "Genomic Divergences between Humans and Other Hominoids and the Effective Population Size of the Common Ancestor of Humans and Chimpanzees," *American Journal of Human Genetics*, 68 (2001): 445–56.
3. E. Chambers, *Applied Anthropology: A Practical Guide*, rev. ed. (Prospect Heights, IL: Waveland, 1989), as referred to in Gilbert Kushner, "Applied Anthropology," in William G. Emener and Margaret Darrow, eds., *Career Explorations in Human Services* (Springfield, IL: Charles C Thomas, 1991).
4. Andrew W. Miracle, "A Shaman to Organizations," in Carol R. Ember, Melvin Ember, and Peter N. Peregrine, eds., *Research Frontiers in Anthropology* in Carol R. Ember and Melvin Ember, eds., *New Directions in Anthropology* (Upper Saddle River, NJ: Prentice Hall, CD-ROM, 2003); Kushner, "Applied Anthropology."
5. Leslie A. White, "The Expansion of the Scope of Science," in Morton H. Fried, ed., *Readings in Anthropology*, 2nd ed., vol. 1 (New York: Thomas Y. Crowell, 1968), pp. 15–24.
6. The exclamation point in the word !Kung signifies one of the clicking sounds made with the tongue by speakers of the !Kung language.
7. Edward T. Hall, *The Hidden Dimension* (Garden City, NY: Doubleday, 1966), pp. 144–53.

CHAPTER 2

1. Robert Martin, *Primate Origins and Evolution: A Phylogenetic Reconstruction* (Princeton, NJ: Princeton University Press, 1990), p. 42.
2. Robert Etienne, *Pompeii: The Day a City Died* (New York: Abrams, 1992).
3. Harold Dibble, P. Chase, S. McPherron, and A. Tuffreau, "Testing the Reality of a 'Living Floor' with Archaeological Data," *American Antiquity*, 62 (1997): 629–51.
4. Michael B. Schiffer, *Formation Processes of the Archaeological Record* (Albuquerque: University of New Mexico Press, 1987).
5. Glynn Isaac, ed., *Plio-Pleistocene Archaeology* (Oxford: Clarendon Press, 1997).
6. Brenda Fowler, *Iceman: Uncovering the Life and Times of a Prehistoric Man Found in an Alpine Glacier* (New York: Random House, 2000).
7. Anne Underhill, "Investigating Craft Specialization during the Longshan Period of China," in P. N. Peregrine, C. R. Ember, and M. Ember, eds., *Archaeology: Original Readings in Method and Practice*. Upper Saddle River, NJ: Prentice Hall, 2002.
8. R. H. Michel, P. E. McGovern, and V. R. Badler, "The First Wine and Beer: Chemical Detection of Ancient Fermented Beverages," *Analytical Chemistry*, 65 (1993): 408A–13A.
9. Carla Sinopoli, "Learning about the Past through Archaeological Ceramics: An Example from Yijayanagara, India," in P. N. Peregrine, C. R. Ember, and M. Ember, eds., *Archaeology: Original Readings in Method and Practice* (Upper Saddle River, NJ: Prentice Hall, 2002).

10. Thomas Wynn, "The Intelligence of Later Acheulean Hominids," *Man*, 14 (1979): 371–91.
11. Lawrence Keeley, "The Functions of Paleolithic Flint Tools," *Scientific American*, 237 (1977): 108–26.
12. Martin, *Primate Origins and Evolution*, p. 42.
13. Richard F. Kay, "Teeth," in Ian Tattersall, Eric Delson, and John van Couvering, eds., *Encyclopedia of Human Evolution and Prehistory* (New York: Garland, 1988), pp. 578, 571–78.
14. Bernard Wood, "Hominid Paleobiology: Recent Achievements and Challenges," in Corruccini and Ciochon, eds., *Integrative Paths to the Past* (Englewood Cliffs, NJ: Prentice Hall, 1994), pp. 153, 147–65.
15. Glenn C. Conroy, *Primate Evolution* (New York: Norton, 1990), pp. 76–77.
16. Peter N. Peregrine, "Social Change in the Woodland-Mississippian Transition: A Study of Household and Community Patterns in the American Bottom," *North American Archaeologist*, 13 (1992): 131–47.
17. Alan Bilsborough, *Human Evolution* (New York: Blackie Academic & Professional, 1992), pp. 21–22.
18. L.S.B. Leakey, *Olduvai Gorge, 1951–1961*, Volume I: *A Preliminary Report on the Geology and Fauna.* (Cambridge: Cambridge University Press, 1965), pp. 73–78.
19. Richard G. Klein, *The Human Career: Human Biological and Cultural Origins* (Chicago: University of Chicago, 1989), pp. 1–12.
20. Kenneth P. Oakley, "Analytical Methods of Dating Bones," in Don Brothwell and Eric Higgs, eds., *Science in Archaeology* (New York: Basic Books, 1963), p. 26.
21. Frank Hole and Robert F. Heizer, *An Introduction to Prehistoric Archeology*, 3rd ed. (New York: Holt, Rinehart & Winston, 1973), pp. 252–54.
22. F. H. Brown, "Methods of Dating," in Steve Jones, Robert Martin, and David Pilbeam, eds., *The Cambridge Encyclopedia of Human Evolution* (New York: Cambridge University Press, 1992), pp. 180, 470.
23. M. J. Aitken, *Thermoluminescence Dating* (London: Academic Press, 1985), pp. 1–4.
24. Ibid., pp. 191–202.
25. Ibid., pp. 4, 211–13.
26. John Kappelman, "The Attraction of Paleomagnetism," *Evolutionary Anthropology*, 2, no. 3 (1993): 89–99.
27. W. Gentner and H. J. Lippolt, "The Potassium-Argon Dating of Upper Tertiary and Pleistocene Deposits," in Don Brothwell and Eric Higgs, eds., *Science in Archaeology* (New York: Basic Books, 1963), pp. 72–84.
28. Klein, *The Human Career*, pp. 15–17.
29. Bilsborough, *Human Evolution*, pp. 23–24; Frank H. Brown, "Geochronometry," in Tattersall, Delson, and van Couvering, eds., *Encyclopedia of Human Evolution and Prehistory*, p. 225.
30. Brown, "Methods of Dating," pp. 182–83; Henry P. Schwarcz, "Uranium-Series Dating and the Origin of Modern Man," in Henry P. Schwarcz, *The Origin of Modern Humans and the Impact of Chronometric Dating* (Princeton, NJ: Princeton University Press, 1993), pp. 12–26.
31. Robert L. Fleischer, P. B. Price, R. M. Walker, and L. S. B. Leakey, "Fission-Track Dating of Bed I, Olduvai Gorge," *Science*, April 2, 1965, 72–74.
32. Robert L. Fleischer and Howard R. Hart, Jr., "Fission-Track Dating: Techniques and Problems," in W. A. Bishop and J. A.

Miller, eds., *Calibration of Hominid Evolution* (Toronto: University of Toronto Press, 1972), p. 474.

33. Fleischer et al., "Fission-Track Dating of Bed I, Olduvai Gorge."

34. Bruce G. Trigger, *A History of Archaeological Thought* (Cambridge: Cambridge University Press, 1989).

CHAPTER 8

1. Christopher Stringer, "Evolution of a Species," *Geographical Magazine*, 57 (1985): 601–607.

2. Ibid.

3. Philip Rightmire, "Human Evolution in the Middle Pleistocene: The Role of *Homo heidelbergensis*." *Evolutionary Anthropology*, 6 (1997): 281–27.

4. Ibid.; John G. Fleagle, *Primate Adaptation and Evolution*, 2nd ed. (San Diego: Academic Press, 1999), pp. 535–37.

5. Frank Spencer, "The Neandertals and Their Evolutionary Significance: A Brief Historical Survey," in Fred H. Smith and Frank Spencer, eds., *The Origins of Modern Humans* (New York: A. R. Liss, 1984), pp. 1–50.

6. Erik Trinkaus, "Pathology and the Posture of the La Chapelle-aux-Saints Neandertal," *American Journal of Physical Anthropology*, 67 (1985): 19–41.

7. Christopher B. Stringer, "Neandertals," in Ian Tattersall, Eric Delson, and John van Couvering, eds., *Encyclopedia of Human Evolution and Prehistory* (New York: Garland, 1988), p. 370.

8. Erik Trinkaus and Pat Shipman, "Neandertals: Images of Ourselves," *Evolutionary Anthropology*, 1, no. 6 (1993): 198, 194–201.

9. Fred H. Smith, "Fossil Hominids from the Upper Pleistocene of Central Europe and the Origin of Modern Humans," in Smith and Spencer, eds., *The Origins of Modern Humans*, p. 187.

10. Erik Trinkaus, "Western Asia," in Smith and Spencer, eds., *The Origins of Modern Humans*, pp. 251–53.

11. Matthias Krings, A. Stone, R. W. Schmitz, H. Krainitzki, M. Stoneking, and S. Paabo, "Neandertal DNA Sequences and the Origin of Modern Humans," *Cell*, 90 (1997): 19–30.

12. Rebecca Cann, "DNA and Human Origins," *Annual Review of Anthropology*, 17 (1988): 127–43.

13. Ibid.

14. Linda Vigilant, M. Stoneking, H. Harpending, K. Hawkes, and A. Wilson, "African Populations and the Evolution of Human Mitochondrial DNA," Science, 253 (1991): 1503–1507.

15. Krings et al., "Neandertal DNA Sequences and the Origin of Modern Humans."

16. Igor V. Ovchinnikov et al., "Molecular Analysis of Neanderthal DNA from the Northern Caucasus," *Nature* 404 (30 Mar. 2000): 490–494.

17. Ian Tattersall, *The Last Neanderthal* (Boulder, CO: Westview, 1999), pp. 115–16; Ann Gibbons, "The Riddle of Co-Existence," *Science*, 291 (2001): 1725–29.

18. Paul Mellars, *The Neanderthal Legacy* (Princeton, NJ: Princeton University Press, 1996), pp. 405–19.

19. Paul Mellars, "The Fate of the Neanderthals," *Nature*, 395 (1998): 539–40.

20. Lawrence Guy Strauss, "On Early Hominid Use of Fire," *Current Anthropology*, 30 (1989): 488–91.

21. Kathy D. Schick and Nicholas Toth, *Making Silent Stones Speak* (New York: Simon & Schuster, 1993), pp. 288–92.

22. Richard G. Klein, *The Human Career: Human Biological and Cultural Origins* (Chicago: University of Chicago Press, 1989), pp. 291–96.

23. Schick and Toth, *Making Silent Stones Speak*, pp. 288–92; John C. Whittaker, *Flintknapping: Making and Understanding Stone Tools* (Austin: University of Texas Press, 1994), pp. 30–31.

24. Klein, *The Human Career*, pp. 421–22.

25. Sally R. Binford and Lewis R. Binford, "Stone Tools and Human Behavior," *Scientific American*, April 1969, 70–84.

26. Paul R. Fish, "Beyond Tools: Middle Paleolithic Debitage Analysis and Cultural Inference," *Journal of Anthropological Research*, 37 (1981): 377.

27. Karl W. Butzer, "Geomorphology and Sediment Stratigraphy," in Ronald Singer and John Wymer, *The Middle Stone Age at Klasies River Mouth in South Africa* (Chicago: University of Chicago Press, 1982), p. 42.

28. David W. Phillipson, *African Archaeology*, 2nd ed. (Cambridge: Cambridge University Press, 1993), p. 63.

29. For the controversy about whether the inhabitants of the Dordogne Valley lived in their homesites year-round, see Lewis R. Binford, "Interassemblage Variability: The Mousterian and the 'Functional' Argument," in Colin Renfrew, ed., *The Explanation of Culture Change: Models in Prehistory* (Pittsburgh: University of Pittsburgh Press, 1973).

30. Schick and Toth, *Making Silent Stones Speak*, p. 292.

31. Richard G. Klein, "The Ecology of Early Man in Southern Africa," *Science*, July 8, 1977, 120.

32. Richard G. Klein, "Ice-Age Hunters of the Ukraine," *Scientific American*, June 1974, 96–105.

33. François Bordes, "Mousterian Cultures in France," *Science*, September 22, 1961, 803–10.

34. Thomas C. Patterson, *The Evolution of Ancient Societies: A World Archaeology* (Englewood Cliffs, NJ: Prentice Hall, 1981).

35. Phillipson, *African Archaeology*, p. 64.

36. Richard G. Klein, "The Stone Age Prehistory of Southern Africa," *Annual Review of Anthropology*, 12 (1983): 38–39.

37. Lewis R. Binford, *Faunal Remains from Klasies River Mouth* (Orlando, FL: Academic Press, 1984), pp. 195–97. To explain the lack of complete skeletons of large animals, Klein (see note 36) suggests that the hunters may have butchered the large animals elsewhere because they could carry home only small cuts.

38. John Noble Wilford, "Ancient German Spears Tell of Mighty Hunters of Stone Age," *New York Times*, March 4, 1997, p. C6.

39. John E. Pfeiffer, *The Emergence of Man*, 3rd ed. (New York: Harper & Row, 1978), p. 155.

40. Trinkaus, Eric, *The Shanidar Neandertals*. (New York: Academic, 1983).

41. Chase, Philip and Harold Dibble, "Middle Paleolithic Symbolism: A Review of Current Evidence and Interpretations," *Journal of Anthropological Archaeology* 6 (1987):263–269.

42. C. B. Stringer, J. J. Hublin, and B. Vandermeersch, "The Origin of Anatomically Modern Humans in Western Europe," in Smith and Spencer, eds., *The Origins of Modern Humans*, p. 107.

43. Singer and Wymer, *The Middle Stone Age at Klasies River Mouth in South Africa*, p. 149.

44. Günter Bräuer, "A Craniological Approach to the Origin of Anatomically Modern *Homo sapiens* in Africa and Implications for the Appearance of Modern Europeans," in Smith and Spencer, eds., *The Origins of Modern Humans*, pp. 387–89, 394; and Philip Rightmire, "*Homo sapiens* in Sub-Saharan Africa," in ibid., p. 320.

45. H. Valladas, J. L. Joron, G. Valladas, O. Bar-Yosef, and B. Vandermeersch, "Thermoluminescence Dating of Mousterian 'Proto-Cro-Magnon' Remains from Israel and the Origin of Modern Man," *Nature*, February 18, 1988, 614–16.

46. Stringer, Hublin, and Vandermeersch, "The Origin of Anatomically Modern Humans in Western Europe," p. 121.

47. For arguments supporting the single-origin theory, see the chapters by Günter Bräuer, F. Clark Howell, and C. B. Stringer et al. in Smith and Spencer, eds., *The Origins of Modern Humans*. For arguments supporting the multiregional theory, see the chapters by C. L. Brace et al., David W. Frayer, Fred H. Smith, and Milford H. Wolpoff et al. in the same volume.

48. Rebecca Cann, M. Stoneking, and A. C. Wilson, "Mitochondrial DNA and Human Evolution," *Nature*, 325 (1987): 31–36.

49. Vigilant et al., "African Populations and the Evolution of Human Mitochondrial DNA."

50. Mark Stoneking, "Recent African Origin of Human Mitochondrial DNA," in P. Donnelly and S. Tavaré, eds., *Progress in Population Genetics and Human Evolution* (New York: Springer), pp. 1–13.

51. Michael F. Hammer and Stephen L. Zegura, "The Role of the Y Chromosome in Human Evolutionary Studies." *Evolutionary Anthropology* 5 (1996):116–134.

52. Michael F. Hammer and Stephen L. Zegura, "The Human Y Chromosome Haplogroup Tree," *Annual Review of Anthropology* 31 (2002):303–321.

53. L. Luca Cavalli-Sforza and Marcus W. Feldman, "The Application of Molecular Genetic Approaches to the Study of Human Evolution." *Nature Genetics Supplement* 33 (2003):266–275.

54. Milford Wolpoff, *Paleoanthropology*, 2nd ed. (Boston: McGraw-Hill, 1999), pp. 501–504, 727–31; David Frayer, M. Wolpoff, A. Thorne, F. Smith, and G. Pope, "Theories of Modern Human Origins: The Paleontological Test," *American Anthropologist*, 95 (1993): 24–27.

55. Wolpoff, *Paleoanthropology*, pp. 735–43; Frayer et al., "Theories of Modern Human Origins," pp. 21–24.

56. Daniel E. Lieberman, "Testing Hypotheses about Recent Human Evolution from Skulls: Integrating Morphology, Function, Development, and Phylogeny," *Current Anthropology*, 36 (1995): 159–97.

57. Alan Templeton, "The 'Eve' Hypotheses: A Genetic Critique and Reanalysis," *American Anthropologist*, 95 (1993): 51–72.

58. Erik Trinkaus, "The Neandertals and Modern Human Origins," *Annual Review of Anthropology*, 15 (1986): 193–218.

59. Vinayak Eswaran, "A Diffusion Wave Out of Africa," *Current Anthropology* 43 (2002):749–774.

60. Alan R. Templeton, "Gene Lineages and Human Evolution," *Science*, May 31, 1996, 1363. See also Francisco J. Ayala, "The Myth of Eve: Molecular Biology and Human Origins," *Science*, December 22, 1995, 1930–36; and his subsequent communication in *Science*, November 29, 1996, 1354.

61. Cidalia Duarte, J. Mauricio, P. B. Pettitt, P. Souto, E. Trinkaus, H. van der Plicht, and J. Zilhao, "The Early Upper Paleolithic Human Skeleton from the Abrigo do Lagar Velho (Portugal) and Modern Human Emergence in Iberia," *Proceedings of the National Academy of Sciences of the United States* 96 (1999): 7604–7609.

62. Paul Bahn, "Neanderthals Emancipated," *Nature*, 394 (1998): 719–20.

63. Tattersall, *The Last Neanderthal*, pp. 198–203.

64. Erik Trinkaus, "The Neandertals and Modern Human Origins," *Annual Review of Anthropology*, 15 (1986): 193–218; see also Erik Trinkaus and W. W. Howells, "The Neanderthals," *Scientific* American, December 1979, 118–33.

65. Klein, Richard G., "Whither the Neanderthals?" *Science* 299 (7 Mar 2003):1525–1527.

CHAPTER 13

1. Ralph Linton, *The Cultural Background of Personality* (New York: Appleton-Century-Crofts, 1945), p. 30.

2. See, for example, Dorothy Holland and Naomi Quinn, eds., *Cultural Models in Language and Thought* (Cambridge: Cambridge University Press, 1987), p. 4.

3. Edward Sapir, "Why Cultural Anthropology Needs the Psychiatrist," *Psychiatry*, 1 (1938): 7–12; cited by Pertti J. Pelto and Gretel H. Pelto, "Intra-Cultural Diversity: Some Theoretical Issues," *American Ethnologist*, 2 (1975): 1.

4. Pelto and Pelto, "Intra-Cultural Diversity," pp. 14–15.

5. Frans de Waal, *The Ape and the Sushi Master: Cultural Reflections of a Primatologist* (New York: Basic Books, 2001), p. 269.

6. Barry Hewlett, "Diverse Contexts of Human Infancy," in Carol R. Ember and Melvin Ember, eds., *Cross-Cultural Research for Social Science*, in Carol R. Ember and Melvin Ember, eds., *New Directions in Anthropology* (Upper Saddle River, NJ: Prentice Hall, CD-ROM, 2003).

7. Horace Miner, "Body Rituals among the Nacirema," *American Anthropologist*, 58 (1956): 504–505, reproduced by permission of the American Anthropological Association from *American Anthropologist*, 58 (1956): 504–505. Although Miner is not a foreign visitor, he wrote this description in a way that shows how these behaviors might be seen from an outside perspective.

8. Richard B. Lee, "Population Growth and the Beginnings of Sedentary Life among the !Kung Bushmen," in Brian Spooner, ed., *Population Growth: Anthropological Implications* (Cambridge, MA: MIT Press, 1972), pp. 329–42.

9. For a more complete discussion, see Elizabeth M. Zechenter, "In the Name of Culture: Cultural Relativism and the Abuse of the Individual," *Journal of Anthropological Research*, 53 (1997): 325–27. See also additional essays in the special issue of the *Journal of Anthropological Research*, 53, no. 3 (1997), "Universal Human Rights versus Cultural Relativity," Terence Turner and Carole Nagengast, eds.

10. Elvin Hatch, "The Good Side of Relativism," *Journal of Anthropological Research*, 53 (1997): 371–81.

11. Émile Durkheim, *The Rules of Sociological Method*, 8th ed., trans. Sarah A. Soloway and John H. Mueller, ed. George E. Catlin (New York: Free Press, 1938 [originally published 1895]), p. 3.

12. Solomon Asch, "Studies of Independence and Conformity: A Minority of One against a Unanimous Majority," *Psychological Monographs*, 70 (1956): 1–70.

13. Edward T. Hall, *The Hidden Dimension* (Garden City, NY: Doubleday, 1966), pp. 159–60.

14. Ibid., p. 120.

15. John W. M. Whiting, "Effects of Climate on Certain Cultural Practices," in Ward H. Goodenough, ed., *Explorations in Cultural Anthropology: Essays in Honor of George Peter Murdock* (New York: McGraw-Hill, 1964), pp. 511–44.

16. Charles Wagley, "Cultural Influences on Population: A Comparison of Two Tupi Tribes," in Patricia J. Lyon, ed., *Native South Americans: Ethnology of the Least Known Continent* (Boston: Little, Brown, 1974), pp. 377–84.

17. Roger Brown, *Social Psychology* (New York: Free Press, 1965), pp. 549–609.

18. Michael Chibnik, "The Evolution of Cultural Rules," *Journal of Anthropological Research*, 37 (1981): 256–68.

19. Indeed, some of the cultures we cite may have been quite different before as well as after the time referred to. For example, the !Kung hunter-gatherers of southern Africa probably were not only hunter-gatherers in the past. There is evidence that the !Kung of the Kalahari Desert have switched from hunting and gathering to herding animals, and back again, many times in the past. See Carmel Schrire, "An Inquiry into the Evolutionary Status and Apparent Identity of San Hunter-Gatherers," *Human Ecology*, 8 (1980): 9–32.

CHAPTER 15

1. Helen Keller, *The Story of My Life* (New York: Dell, 1974 [originally published 1902]), p. 34.

2. Anthony Wilden, *The Rules Are No Game: The Strategy of Communication* (London: Routledge and Kegan Paul, 1987), p. 124; as referred to in Pia Christensen, Jenny Hockey, and Allison James, "Talk, Silence and the Material World: Patterns of Indirect Communication among Agricultural Farmers in Northern England," in Joy Hendry and C. W. Watson, eds., *An Anthropology of Indirect Communication* (London: Routledge, 2001), pp. 68–82.

3. Helen Lambert, "Not Talking about Sex in India: Indirection and the Communication of Bodily Intention," in Hendry and Watson, eds., *An Anthropology of Indirect Communication* (London: Routledge, 2001), pp. 51–67.

4. Paul Ekman and Dachner Keltner, "Universal Facial Expressions of Emotion: An Old Controversy and New Findings," in Ullica Segerstråle and Peter Molnar, eds., *Nonverbal Communication: Where Nature Meets Culture* (Mahwah, NJ: Lawrence Erlbaum, 1997), p. 32.

5. Karl von Frisch, "Dialects in the Language of the Bees," *Scientific American*, August 1962, 78–87.

6. Barbara J. King, "Introduction," in Barbara J. King, ed., *The Origins of Language: What Nonhuman Primates Can Tell Us* (Santa Fe, New Mexico: School of American Research Press, 1999), pp. 3–19; Kathleen R. Gibson and Stephen Jessee, "Language Evolution and Expansions of Multiple Neurological Processing Areas," in King, ed., *The Origins of Language*, pp. 189–190.

7. Robert M. Seyfarth and Dorothy L. Cheney, "How Monkeys See the World: A Review of Recent Research on East African Vervet Monkeys," in Charles T. Snowdon, Charles H. Brown, and Michael R. Petersen, eds., *Primate Communication* (New York: Cambridge University Press, 1982), pp. 242, 246.

8. C. F. Hockett and R. Ascher, "The Human Revolution," *Current Anthropology*, 5 (1964): 135–68.

9. T. S. Eliot, "The Love Song of J. Alfred Prufrock," in *Collected Poems, 1909–1962* (New York: Harcourt, Brace & World, 1963).

10. Charles T. Snowdon, "An Empiricist View of Language Evolution and Development," in King, ed., *The Origins of Language*, p. 81.

11. Irene Maxine Pepperberg, *The Alex Studies: Cognitive and Communicative Abilities of Grey Parrots* (Cambridge, MA: Harvard University Press, 1999).

12. Madhusree Mukerjee, "Field Notes: Interview with a Parrot," *Scientific American*, April 1996, 28.

13. E. S. Savage-Rumbaugh, "Language Training of Apes," in Steve Jones, Robert Martin, and David Pilbeam, eds., *The Cambridge Encyclopedia of Human Evolution* (Cambridge: Cambridge University Press, 1992), pp. 138–41.

14. Jane H. Hill, "Apes and Language," *Annual Review of Anthropology*, 7 (1978): 94; Jane H. Hill, "Do Apes Have Language?" in Carol R. Ember, Melvin Ember, and Peter N. Peregrine, eds., *Research Frontiers in Anthropology*, in Carol R. Ember and Melvin Ember, eds., *New Directions in Anthropology* (Upper Saddle River, NJ: Prentice Hall, CD-ROM, 2003).

15. Ibid. Hill, "Do Apes Have Language?"

16. Wayne M. Senner, "Theories and Myths on the Origins of Writing: A Historical Overview," in Wayne M. Senner, ed., *The Origins of Writing* (Lincoln: University of Nebraska Press, 1989), pp. 1–26.

17. See the following chapters in King, ed., *The Origins of Language*: Charles T. Snowdon, "An Empiricist View of Language Evolution and Development," pp. 79–114; Kathleen R. Gibson and Stephen Jessee, "Language Evolution and Expansions of Multiple Neurological Processing Areas," pp. 189–227; Robbins Burling, "Motivation, Conventionalization, and Arbitrariness in the Origin of Language," pp. 307–350; and Sherman Wilcox, "The Invention and Ritualization of Language," pp. 351–384.

18. See Noam Chomsky, *Reflections on Language* (New York: Pantheon, 1975).

19. Franklin C. Southworth and Chandler J. Daswani, *Foundations of Linguistics* (New York: Free Press, 1974), p. 312. See also Franz Boas, "On Grammatical Categories," in Dell Hymes, ed., *Language in Culture and Society: A Reader in Linguistics and Anthropology* (New York: Harper & Row, 1964 [originally published 1911]), pp. 121–23.

20. Derek Bickerton, "Creole Languages," *Scientific American*, July 1983, 116–22.

21. Ibid., p. 122.

22. Brent Berlin, *Ethnobiological Classification: Principles of Categorization of Plants and Animals in Traditional Societies* (Princeton, NJ: Princeton University Press, 1992); Terence E. Hays, "Sound Symbolism, Onomatopoeia, and New Guinea Frog Names," *Journal of Linguistic Anthropology*, 4 (1994): 153–74.

23. Lila R. Gleitman and Eric Wanner, "Language Acquisition: The State of the State of the Art," in Eric Wanner and Lila R. Gleitman, eds., *Language Acquisition: The State of the Art* (Cambridge: Cambridge University Press, 1982), pp. 3–48; Ben G. Blount, "The Development of Language in Children," in Ruth H. Munroe, Robert L. Munroe, and Beatrice B. Whiting, eds., *Handbook of Cross-Cultural Human Development* (New York: Garland, 1981), pp. 379–402.

24. Roger Brown, "The First Sentence of Child and Chimpanzee," in Thomas A. Sebeok and Jean Umiker-Sebeok, eds., *Speaking of Apes* (New York: Plenum, 1980), pp. 93–94.

25. Peter A. de Villiers and Jill G. de Villiers, *Early Language* (Cambridge, MA: Harvard University Press, 1979), p. 48; see also Wanner and Gleitman, eds., *Language Acquisition*.

26. Bickerton, "Creole Languages," p. 122.

27. Snowdon, "An Empiricist View of Language Evolution and Development," in King, ed., *The Origins of Language*, pp. 88–91; referring to the work of E. Bates and V. A. Marchman, "What Is and Is Not Universal in Language Acquisition," in F. Plum, ed. *Language, Communication, and the Brain* (New York: Raven Press, 1988), pp. 19–38.

28. David Crystal, *Linguistics* (Middlesex, England: Penguin, 1971), p. 168.

29. Ibid., pp. 100–101.

30. Maria Baringa, "Priming the Brain's Language Pump," *Science*, January 31, 1992, 535.

31. Adrian Akmajian, Richard A. Demers, and Robert M. Harnish, *Linguistics: An Introduction to Language and Communication*, 2nd ed. (Cambridge, MA: MIT Press, 1984), p. 136.

32. Robert L. Munroe, Ruth H. Munroe, and Stephen Winters, "Cross-Cultural Correlates of the Consonant-Vowel (CV) Syllable," *Cross-Cultural Research*, 30 (1996): 60–83; Melvin Ember and Carol R. Ember, "Cross-Language Predictors of Consonant-Vowel Syllables," *American Anthropologist*, 101 (1999): 730–42. The theory about the effect of baby-holding on consonant-vowel alternation is an extension of the theory that regular baby-holding encourages a preference for regular rhythm in music; see Barbara C. Ayres, "Effects of Infant Carrying Practices on Rhythm in Music," *Ethos*, 1 (1973): 387–404.

33. E. Sapir and M. Swadesh, "American Indian Grammatical Categories," in Hymes, ed., *Language in Culture and Society*, p. 103.

34. Akmajian, Demers, and Harnish, *Linguistics*, pp. 164–66.

35. Geoffrey Chaucer, *The Prologue to the Canterbury Tales, the Knightes Tale, the Nonnes Prestes Tale*, ed. Mark H. Liddell (New York: Macmillan, 1926), p. 8. Our modern English translation is based on the glossary in this book.

36. Akmajian, Demers, and Harnish, *Linguistics*, p. 356.

37. Philip Baldi, *An Introduction to the Indo-European Languages* (Carbondale: Southern Illinois University Press, 1983), p. 3.

38. Ibid., p. 12.

39. Paul Friedrich, *Proto-Indo-European Trees: The Arboreal System of a Prehistoric People* (Chicago: University of Chicago Press, 1970), p. 168.

40. Ibid., p. 166.

41. Marija Gimbutas, "An Archaeologist's View of PIE* in 1975," *Journal of Indo-European Studies*, 2 (1974): 293–95. See also Susan N. Skomal and Edgar C. Polomé, eds., *Proto-Indo-European: The Archaeology of a Linguistic Problem* (Washington, DC: Washington Institute for the Study of Man, 1987).

42. David Anthony, Dimitri Y. Telegin, and Dorcas Brown, "The Origin of Horseback Riding," *Scientific American*, December 1991, 94–100.

43. Colin Renfrew, *Archaeology and Language: The Puzzle of Indo-European Origins* (London: Jonathan Cape, 1987).

44. Joseph H. Greenberg, "Linguistic Evidence Regarding Bantu Origins," *Journal of African History*, 13 (1972): 189–216; see also D. W. Phillipson, "Archaeology and Bantu Linguistics," *World Archaeology*, 8 (1976): 71.

45. Phillipson, "Archaeology and Bantu Linguistics," p. 79.

46. Peter Trudgill, *Sociolinguistics: An Introduction to Language and Society*, rev. ed. (New York: Penguin, 1983), p. 34.

47. John J. Gumperz, "Speech Variation and the Study of Indian Civilization," *American Anthropologist*, 63 (1961): 976–88.

48. Trudgill, *Sociolinguistics*, p. 35.

49. John J. Gumperz, "Dialect Differences and Social Stratification in a North Indian Village," in *Language in Social Groups: Essays by John J. Gumperz*, selected and introduced by Anwar S. Dil (Stanford, CA: Stanford University Press, 1971), p. 45.

50. Uriel Weinreich, *Languages in Contact* (The Hague: Mouton, 1968), p. 31.

51. But see Sarah Grey Thomason and Terrence Kaufman, *Language Contact, Creolization, and Genetic Linguistics* (Berkeley: University of California Press, 1988), for a discussion of how grammatical changes due to contact may be more important than was previously assumed.

52. Brent Berlin and Paul Kay, *Basic Color Terms: Their Universality and Evolution* (Berkeley: University of California Press, 1969).

53. Ibid.

54. Ibid., pp. 5–6.

55. Ibid., p. 104; Stanley R. Witkowski and Cecil H. Brown, "Lexical Universals," *Annual Review of Anthropology*, 7 (1978): 427–51.

56. Marc H. Bornstein, "The Psychophysiological Component of Cultural Difference in Color Naming and Illusion Susceptibility," *Behavior Science Notes*, 8 (1973): 41–101.

57. Melvin Ember, "Size of Color Lexicon: Interaction of Cultural and Biological Factors," *American Anthropologist*, 80 (1978): 364–67.

58. Ibid.

59. Cecil H. Brown, "Folk Botanical Life-Forms: Their Universality and Growth," *American Anthropologist*, 79 (1977): 317–42.

60. Cecil H. Brown, "Folk Zoological Life-Forms: Their Universality and Growth," *American Anthropologist*, 81 (1979): 791–817.

61. Stanley R. Witkowski and Harold W. Burris, "Societal Complexity and Lexical Growth," *Behavior Science Research*, 16 (1981): 143–59.

62. Ibid.

63. Cecil H. Brown and Stanley R. Witkowski, "Language Universals," Appendix B, in David Levinson and Martin J. Malone, eds., *Toward Explaining Human Culture: A Critical Review of the Findings of Worldwide Cross-Cultural Research* (New Haven, CT: HRAF Press, 1980), p. 379.

64. Cecil H. Brown, "World View and Lexical Uniformities," *Reviews in Anthropology*, 11 (1984): 106.

65. Harry Hoijer, "Cultural Implications of Some Navaho Linguistic Categories," in Hymes, ed., *Language in Culture and Society*, p. 146.

66. Karen E. Webb, "An Evolutionary Aspect of Social Structure and a Verb 'Have'," *American Anthropologist*, 79 (1977): 42–49; see also Floyd Webster Rudmin, "Dominance, Social Control, and Ownership: A History and a Cross-Cultural Study of Motivations for Private Property," *Behavior Science Research*, 22 (1988): 130–60.

67. Edward Sapir, "Conceptual Categories in Primitive Languages," paper presented at the autumn meeting of the National Academy of Sciences, New Haven, CT, 1931, published in *Science*, 74 (1931): 578; see also John B. Carroll, ed., *Language, Thought, and Reality: Selected Writings of Benjamin Lee Whorf* (New York: Wiley, 1956), pp. 65–86.

68. Ronald Wardhaugh, *An Introduction to Sociolinguistics*, 4th ed. (Oxford: Blackwell, 2002), p. 222.

69. J. Peter Denny, "The 'Extendedness' Variable in Classifier Semantics: Universal Features and Cultural Variation," in Madeleine Mathiot, ed., *Ethnolinguistics: Boas, Sapir and Whorf Revisited* (The Hague: Mouton, 1979), p. 97.

70. Paul Friedrich, *The Language Parallax* (Austin: University of Texas Press, 1986).

71. Alexander Z. Guiora, Benjamin Beit-Hallahmi, Risto Fried, and Cecelia Yoder, "Language Environment and Gender Identity Attainment," *Language Learning*, 32 (1982): 289–304.

72. John A. Lucy, *Grammatical Categories and Cognition: A Case Study of the Linguistic Relativity Hypothesis* (Cambridge: Cambridge University Press, 1992), p. 46.

73. Ibid., pp. 85–148.

74. Dell Hymes, *Foundations in Sociolinguistics: An Ethnographic Approach* (Philadelphia: University of Pennsylvania Press, 1974), pp. 83–117.

75. John L. Fischer, "Social Influences on the Choice of a Linguistic Variant," *Word*, 14 (1958): 47–56; Wardhaugh, *An Introduction to Sociolinguistics*, 4th ed., research summarized in chapter 7, pp. 160–88.

76. Trudgill, *Sociolinguistics*, pp. 41–42.

77. Clifford Geertz, *The Religion of Java* (New York: Free Press, 1960), pp. 248–60; see also J. Joseph Errington, "On the Nature of the Sociolinguistic Sign: Describing the Javanese Speech Levels," in Elizabeth Mertz and Richard J. Parmentier, eds., *Semiotic Mediation: Sociocultural and Psychological Perspectives* (Orlando, FL: Academic Press, 1985), pp. 287–310.

78. Roger Brown and Marguerite Ford, "Address in American English," *Journal of Abnormal and Social Psychology*, 62 (1961): 375–85.

79. Wardhaugh, *An Introduction to Sociolinguistics*, 4th ed., p. 315.

80. Janet S. Shibamoto, "The Womanly Woman: Japanese Female Speech," in Susan U. Philips, Susan Steele, and Christine Tanz, eds., *Language, Gender, and Sex in Comparative Perspective* (Cambridge: Cambridge University Press, 1987), p. 28.

81. Janet Holmes, *An Introduction to Sociolinguistics*, 2nd ed. (London: Longman, 2001), p. 153.

82. Robin Lakoff, "Language and Woman's Place," *Language in Society*, 2 (1973): 45–80; Robin Tolmach Lakoff, "Why Can't a Woman Be Less Like a Man?" in Robin Tolmach Lakoff, ed., *Talking Power: The Politics of Language in Our Lives* (New York: Basic Books, 1990), pp. 198–214.

83. Wardhaugh, *An Introduction to Sociolinguistics*, 4th ed., p. 328; Holmes, *An Introduction to Sociolinguistics*, pp. 158–59; Trudgill, *Sociolinguistics*, pp. 87–88.

84. Mary R. Haas, "Men's and Women's Speech in Koasati," *Language*, 20 (1944): 142–49.

85. Elinor Keenan, "Norm-Makers, Norm-Breakers: Uses of Speech by Men and Women in a Malagasy Community," in Richard Bauman and Joel Sherzer, eds., Explorations in the Ethnography of Speaking, 2nd ed. (New York: Cambridge University Press, 1989), pp. 125–43.

86. Holmes, *An Introduction to Sociolinguistics*, p. 289.

87. Wardhaugh, *An Introduction to Sociolinguistics*, 4th ed., p. 100.

88. Monica Heller, "Introduction," in Monica Heller, ed., *Codeswitching: Anthropological and Sociolinguistic Perspectives* (Berlin: Mouton, 1988), p. 1.

89. Wardhaugh, *An Introduction to Sociolinguistics*, p. 107; citing an example from C. Pfaff, "Constraints on Language Mixing," *Language*, 55 (1979): 291–318.

90. Ibid., p. 108.

91. Susan Gal, "The Political Economy of Code Choice," in Heller, ed., *Codeswitching*, pp. 249–55.

CHAPTER 17

1. E. Adamson Hoebel, *The Law of Primitive Man* (New York: Atheneum, 1968 [originally published 1954]), pp. 46–63.

2. James Woodburn, "An Introduction to Hadza Ecology," in Richard B. Lee and Irven DeVore, eds., *Man the Hunter* (Chicago: Aldine, 1968), pp. 49–55.

3. Eleanor Leacock and Richard Lee, "Introduction," in Eleanor Leacock and Richard Lee, eds., *Politics and History in Band Societies* (Cambridge: Cambridge University Press, 1982), p. 8.

4. Rada Dyson-Hudson and Eric Alden Smith, "Human Territoriality: An Ecological Reassessment," *American Anthropologist*, 80 (1978): 121–41; Elizabeth Andrews, "Territoriality and Land Use among the Akulmiut of Western Alaska," in Ernest S. Burch, Jr., and Linda J. Ellanna, eds., *Key Issues in Hunter-Gatherer Research* (Oxford: Berg, 1994), pp. 65–92.

5. Robert F. Murphy, *Headhunter's Heritage: Social and Economic Change among the Mundurucú* (Berkeley: University of California Press, 1960), pp. 69, 142–43.

6. Philip Carl Salzman, "Pastoralism," in D. Levinson and M. Ember, eds., *Encyclopedia of Cultural Anthropology*, 4 vols. (New York: Henry Holt, 1996), volume 3, p. 902.

7. Not all pastoralists have individual ownership. For example, the Tungus of northern Siberia have kin group ownership of reindeer. See John H. Dowling, "Property Relations and Productive Strategies in Pastoral Societies," *American Ethnologist*, 2 (1975): 422.

8. Fredrik Barth, *Nomads of South Persia* (Oslo: Universitetsforlaget, 1964; Boston: Little, Brown, 1968), p. 124.

9. Dowling, "Property Relations and Productive Strategies in Pastoral Societies," pp. 419–26.

10. Gerald W. Creed, "Bulgaria: Anthropological Corrections to Cold War Stereotypes," in Melvin Ember and Carol R. Ember, eds., *Portraits of Culture: Ethnographic Originals*, in Carol R. Ember and Melvin Ember, eds., *New Directions in Anthropology* (Upper Saddle River, NJ: Prentice Hall, CD-ROM, 2003).

11. John H. Bodley, *Victims of Progress*, 3rd ed. (Mountain View, CA: Mayfield, 1990), pp. 77–93; Edwin N. Wilmsen, ed., *We Are Here: Politics of Aboriginal Land Tenure* (Berkeley: University of California Press, 1989), pp. 1–14.

12. Bodley, *Victims of Progress*, pp. 79–81.

13. Ibid., pp. 86–89.

14. Salzman, "Pastoralism," pp. 904–905.

15. Elman R. Service, *The Hunters*, 2nd ed. (Upper Saddle River, NJ: Prentice Hall, 1979), p. 10.

16. Elizabeth Marshall Thomas, *The Harmless People* (New York: Knopf, 1959), p. 22.

17. Lisa Gröger, "Of Men and Machines: Cooperation among French Family Farmers," *Ethnology*, 20 (1981): 163–75.

18. Stuart Plattner, "Marxism," in Stuart Plattner, ed., *Economic Anthropology* (Stanford, CA: Stanford University Press, 1989), pp. 379–96.

19. Jerald Hage and Charles H. Powers, *Post-Industrial Lives: Roles and Relationships in the 21st Century* (Newbury Park, CA: Sage, 1992).

20. Robert L. Carneiro, "Slash-and-Burn Cultivation among the Kuikuru and Its Implications for Settlement Patterns," in Yehudi Cohen, ed., *Man in Adaptation: The Cultural Present* (Chicago: Aldine, 1968), cited in Marshall Sahlins, *Stone Age Economics* (Chicago: Aldine, 1972), p. 68.

21. Marvin Harris, *Cows, Pigs, Wars and Witches: The Riddles of Culture* (New York: Random House, Vintage, 1975), pp. 127–28.

22. Sahlins, in *Stone Age Economics*, p. 87, introduced North American anthropology to Alexander Chayanov and coined the phrase Chayanov's rule.

23. Alexander V. Chayanov, *The Theory of Peasant Economy*, D. Thorner, B. Kerblay, and R. E. F. Smith, eds. (Homewood, IL: Richard D. Irwin, 1966), p. 78; for a discussion of Chayanov's analysis, see E. Paul Durrenberger, "Chayanov's Economic Analysis in Anthropology," *Journal of Anthropological Research*, 36 (1980): 133–48.

24. Michael Chibnik, "The Economic Effects of Household Demography: A Cross-Cultural Assessment of Chayanov's Theory," in Morgan D. MacLachlan, ed., *Household Economies and Their Transformations*, Monographs in Economic Anthropology No. 3 (Lanham, MD: University Press of America, 1987), pp. 74–106; Durrenberger, "Chayanov's Economic Analysis," also finds some support in an analysis of three northern Thailand groups. For a critique of the equation of Chayanov's rule with Chayanov's analysis, see Nicola Tannenbaum, "The Misuse of Chayanov: 'Chayanov's Rule' and Empiricist Bias in Anthropology," *American Anthropologist*, 86 (1984): 927–42.

25. Sahlins, *Stone Age Economics*, pp. 101–48.

26. David C. McClelland, *The Achieving Society* (New York: Van Nostrand, 1961).

27. Julian H. Steward and Louis C. Faron, *Native Peoples of South America* (New York: McGraw-Hill, 1959), pp. 122–25.

28. Beatrice B. Whiting and Carolyn P. Edwards, *Children of Different Worlds: The Formation of Social Behavior* (Cambridge, MA: Harvard University Press, 1988), p. 164.

29. Moni Nag, Benjamin N. F. White, and R. Creighton Peet, "An Anthropological Approach to the Study of the Economic Value of Children in Java and Nepal," *Current Anthropology*, 19 (1978): 295–96.

30. Whiting and Edwards, *Children of Different Worlds*, pp. 97–107.

31. Patricia Draper and Elizabeth Cashdan, "Technological Change and Child Behavior among the !Kung," *Ethnology*, 27 (1988): 348.

32. Nicholas Blurton Jones, Kristen Hawkes, and James F. O'Connell, "The Global Process and Local Ecology: How Should We Explain Differences between the Hadza and the !Kung?" in Susan Kent, *Cultural Diversity among Twentieth-century Foragers* (Cambridge: Cambridge University Press, 1996), pp. 166–69.

33. Nag, White, and Peet, "Anthropological Approach to the Study of the Economic Value of Children in Java and Nepal," p. 293; see also Candice Bradley, "The Sexual Division of Labor and the Value of Children," *Behavior Science Research*, 19 (1984–1985): 160–64.

34. Carol R. Ember, "The Relative Decline in Women's Contribution to Agriculture with Intensification," *American Anthropologist*, 85 (1983): 291–97.

35. Monica Wilson, *Good Company: A Study of Nyakyusa Age Villages* (Boston: Beacon Press, 1963 [originally published 1951]).

36. Stanley H. Udy, Jr., *Work in Traditional and Modern Society* (Upper Saddle River, NJ: Prentice Hall, 1970), pp. 35–37.

37. Marshall D. Sahlins, *Moala: Culture and Nature on a Fijian Island* (Ann Arbor: University of Michigan Press, 1962), pp. 50–52.

38. Leopold Pospisil, *The Kapauku Papuans of West New Guinea* (New York: Holt, Rinehart & Winston, 1963), p. 43.

39. Udy, *Work in Traditional and Modern Society*, pp. 35–39.

40. Eric Alden Smith, "Anthropological Applications of Optimal Foraging Theory: A Critical Review," *Current Anthropology*, 24 (1983): 626.

41. Kim Hill, Hillard Kaplan, Kristen Hawkes, and A. Magdalena Hurtado, "Foraging Decisions among Aché Hunter-Gatherers: New Data and Implications for Optimal Foraging Models," *Ethology and Sociobiology*, 8 (1987): 17–18.

42. Andrew Sih and Katharine A. Milton, "Optimal Diet Theory: Should the !Kung Eat Mongongos?" *American Anthropologist*, 87 (1985): 395–401.

43. Christina H. Gladwin, "A Theory of Real-Life Choice: Applications to Agricultural Decisions," in Peggy F. Barlett, ed., *Agricultural Decision Making: Anthropological Contributions to Rural Development* (New York: Academic Press, 1980), pp. 45–85.

44. Michael Chibnik, "The Statistical Behavior Approach: The Choice between Wage Labor and Cash Cropping in Rural Belize," in Peggy F. Barlett, ed., *Agricultural Decision Making: Anthropological Contributions to Rural Development* (New York: Academic Press, 1980), pp. 87–114.

45. Karl Polanyi, "The Economy as Instituted Process," in Karl Polanyi, Conrad Arensberg, and Harry W. Pearson, eds., *Trade and Market in the Early Empires* (New York: Free Press, 1957), pp. 243–70.

46. Sahlins, *Stone Age Economics*, pp. 188–96.

47. Lorna Marshall, "Sharing, Talking and Giving: Relief of Social Tensions among !Kung Bushmen," *Africa*, 31 (1961): 239–41.

48. The // sign in the name for the G//ana people symbolizes a click sound not unlike the sound we make when we want a horse to move faster.

49. Elizabeth A. Cashdan, "Egalitarianism among Hunters and Gatherers," *American Anthropologist*, 82 (1980): 116–20.

50. Hillard Kaplan and Kim Hill, "Food Sharing among Aché Foragers: Tests of Explanatory Hypotheses," *Current Anthropology*, 26 (1985): 223–46; Hillard Kaplan, Kim Hill, and A. Magdalena Hurtado, "Risk, Foraging and Food Sharing among the Aché," in Elizabeth Cashdan, ed., *Risk and Uncertainty in Tribal and Peasant Economies* (Boulder, CO: Westview, 1990), pp. 107–43; Michael Gurven, Kim Hill, and Hillard Kaplan, "From Forest to Reservation: Transitions in Food-sharing Behavior among the Aché of Paraguay," *Journal of Anthropological Research*, 58 (2002): 93–120, 114.

51. Raymond Hames, "Sharing among the Yanomamö. Part I. The Effects of Risk," in Cashdan, ed., *Risk and Uncertainty in Tribal and Peasant Economies*, pp. 89–105.

52. Gurven, Hill, and Kaplan, "From Forest to Reservation," p. 114.

53. Kaplan, Hill, and Hurtado, "Risk, Foraging and Food Sharing among the Aché."

54. Bruce Winterhalder, "Open Field, Common Pot: Harvest Variability and Risk Avoidance in Agricultural and Foraging Societies," in Cashdan, ed., *Risk and Uncertainty in Tribal and Peasant Economies*, pp. 67–87.

55. Kathleen A. Mooney, "The Effects of Rank and Wealth on Exchange among the Coast Salish," *Ethnology*, 17 (1978): 391–406.

56. Asen Balikci, *The Netsilik Eskimo* (Garden City, NY: Natural History Press, 1970), quoted in Mooney, "The Effects of Rank and Wealth on Exchange among the Coast Salish," p. 392.

57. Mooney, "Effects of Rank and Wealth on Exchange among the Coast Salish," p. 392.

58. Natalie Angier, "Why We're So Nice: We're Wired to Cooperate," Science Times in the *New York Times*, July 23, 2002, pp. F1, F8.

59. Marshall, "Sharing, Talking and Giving," p. 242.

60. Thomas S. Abler, "Iroquois: The Tree of Peace and the War Kettle," in Melvin Ember and Carol R. Ember, eds., *Portraits of Culture: Ethnographic Originals*, in Carol R. Ember and Melvin Ember, eds., *New Directions in Anthropology* (Upper Saddle River, NJ: Prentice Hall, CD-ROM, 2003).

61. Nadine Peacock and Robert Bailey, "Efe: Investigating Food and Fertility in the Ituri Rain Forest," in Ember and Ember, eds., *Portraits of Culture*.

62. James L. Gibbs, Jr., "The Kpelle of Liberia," in James L. Gibbs, Jr., ed., *Peoples of Africa* (New York: Holt, Rinehart & Winston, 1965), p. 223. But in other societies the food provided a work party may exceed the value of the labor provided, or there may not be any subsequent reciprocation of labor. Thus, an exchange of food for labor may not always be balanced. See Mahir Saul, "Work Parties, Wages, and Accumulation in a Voltaic Village," *American Ethnologist*, 10 (1983): 77–96.

63. Caroline Humphrey and Stephen Hugh-Jones, "Introduction: Barter, Exchange and Value," in Caroline Humphrey and Stephen Hugh-Jones, eds., *Barter, Exchange and Value: An Anthropological Approach* (New York: Cambridge University Press, 1992).

64. Richard E. Blanton, "Variation in Economy," in Carol R. Ember and Melvin Ember, eds., *Cross-Cultural Research for Social Science*, in Carol R. Ember and Melvin Ember, eds., *New Directions in Anthropology* (Upper Saddle River, NJ: Prentice Hall, CD-ROM, 2003); C. A. Gregory, *Gifts and Commodities* (New York: Academic Press, 1982).

65. J. P. Singh Uberoi, *The Politics of the Kula Ring: An Analysis of the Findings of Bronislaw Malinowski* (Manchester: University of Manchester Press, 1962).

66. Bronislaw Malinowski, "Kula: The Circulating Exchange of Valuables in the Archipelagoes of Eastern New Guinea," *Man*, 51, no. 2 (1920): 97–105; and Uberoi, *Politics of the Kula Ring*.

67. Jerry W. Leach, "Introduction," in Jerry W. Leach and Edmund Leach, eds., *The Kula: New Perspectives on Massim Exchange* (Cambridge: Cambridge University Press, 1983), pp. 12, 16.

68. Annette B. Weiner, *Women of Value, Men of Renown: New Perspectives in Trobriand Exchange* (Austin: University of Texas Press, 1976), pp. 77–117.

69. Sahlins, *Stone Age Economics*, pp. 196–204.

70. Frederic L. Pryor, *The Origins of the Economy: A Comparative Study of Distribution in Primitive and Peasant Economies* (New York: Academic Press, 1977), pp. 204, 276.

71. Andrew P. Vayda, Anthony Leeds, and David B. Smith, "The Place of Pigs in Melanesian Subsistence," in Viola E. Garfield, ed., *Symposium: Patterns of Land Utilization, and Other Papers*, Proceedings of the Annual Spring Meeting of the American Ethnological Society, 1961 (Seattle: University of Washington Press, 1962), pp. 69–74.

72. Philip Drucker, "The Potlatch," in George Dalton, ed., *Tribal and Peasant Economies: Readings in Economic Anthropology* (Garden City, NY: Natural History Press, 1967), pp. 481–93.

73. Harris, *Cows, Pigs, Wars and Witches*, p. 120.

74. Kenneth D. Tollefson, "Tlingit: Chiefs Past and Present," in Ember and Ember, eds., *Portraits of Culture*.

75. Andrew P. Vayda, "Pomo Trade Feasts," in George Dalton, ed., *Tribal and Peasant Economies: Readings in Economic Anthropology* (Garden City, NY: Natural History Press, 1967), pp. 494–500.

76. John Beattie, *Bunyoro: An African Kingdom* (New York: Holt, Rinehart & Winston, 1960).

77. R. C. Thurnwald, "Pigs and Currency in Buin: Observations about Primitive Standards of Value and Economics," *Oceania*, 5 (1934): 125.

78. Pryor, *Origins of the Economy*, pp. 284–86.

79. Elman R. Service, *Primitive Social Organization: An Evolutionary Perspective* (New York: Random House, 1962), pp. 145–46.

80. Harris, *Cows, Pigs, Wars and Witches*, pp. 118–21.

81. Stuart Plattner, "Introduction," in Stuart Plattner, ed., *Markets and Marketing*, Monographs in Economic Anthropology No. 4 (Lanham, MD: University Press of America, 1985), p. viii.

82. Pryor, *Origins of the Economy*, pp. 31–33.

83. Thurnwald, "Pigs and Currency in Buin," p. 122.

84. Plattner, "Introduction," p. xii.

85. Pryor, *Origins of the Economy*, pp. 153–83; James Stodder, "The Evolution of Complexity in Primitive Exchange," *Journal of Comparative Economics*, 20 (1995): 205, finds that monetary trade is more likely with capital-intensive agriculture.

86. Pryor, *Origins of the Economy*, pp. 109–11.

87. Brian L. Foster, "Ethnicity and Commerce," *American Ethnologist*, 1 (1974): 437–47.

88. Pryor, *Origins of the Economy*, pp. 125–48.

89. See, for example, Eric Wolf, "Types of Latin American Peasantry: A Preliminary Discussion," *American Anthropologist*, 57 (1955): 452–71; and Pedro Carrasco, "The Civil-Religious Hierarchy in Mesoamerican Communities: Pre-Spanish Background and Colonial Development," *American Anthropologist*, 63 (1961): 483–97.

90. Waldemar R. Smith, *The Fiesta System and Economic Change* (New York: Columbia University Press, 1977); and Marvin Harris, *Patterns of Race in the Americas* (New York: Walker, 1964).

91. Ibid.

CHAPTER 18

1. In an analysis of many native societies in the New World, Gary Feinman and Jill Neitzel argue that egalitarian and rank societies ("tribes" and "chiefdoms," respectively) are not systematically distinguishable. See their "Too Many Types: An Overview of Sedentary Prestate Societies in the Americas," in Michael B. Schiffer, ed., *Advances in Archaeological Method and Theory* (Orlando, FL: Academic Press, 1984), vol. 7, p. 57.

2. Morton H. Fried, *The Evolution of Political Society: An Essay in Political Anthropology* (New York: Random House, 1967), p. 33.

3. Christopher Boehm, "Egalitarian Behavior and Reverse Dominance Hierarchy," *Current Anthropology*, 34 (1993): 230–31; Christopher Boehm, *Hierarchy in the Forest: The Evolution of Egalitarian Behavior* (Cambridge, MA: Harvard University Press, 1999).

4. Michael G. Smith, "Pre-Industrial Stratification Systems," in Neil J. Smelser and Seymour Martin Lipset, eds., *Social Structure and Mobility in Economic Development* (Chicago: Aldine, 1966), p. 152.

5. See a discussion of the controversy in Philip Carl Salzman, "Is Inequality Universal?" *Current Anthropology*, 40 (1999): 31–61. Salzman takes the position that some pastoral societies are egalitarian.

6. See, for example, the description of a Kwakiutl group called the Nimpkish in Donald Mitchell, "Nimpkish: Complex Foragers on the Northwest Coast of North America," in Melvin Ember and Carol R. Ember, eds., *Portraits of Culture: Ethnographic Originals*, in Carol R. Ember and Melvin Ember, eds., *New Directions in Anthropology* (Upper Saddle River, NJ: Prentice Hall, CD-ROM, 2003).

7. Philip Drucker, *Cultures of the North Pacific Coast* (San Francisco: Chandler, 1965), pp. 56–64.

8. Elman R. Service, *Profiles in Ethnology*, 3rd ed. (New York: Harper & Row, 1978), p. 249.

9. Marshall Sahlins, *Social Stratification in Polynesia* (Seattle: University of Washington Press, 1958), pp. 80–81.

10. Laura Betzig, "Redistribution: Equity or Exploitation?" in Laura Betzig, Monique Borgerhoff Mulder, and Paul Turke, eds., *Human Reproductive Behavior* (Cambridge: Cambridge University Press, 1988), pp. 49–63.

11. W. Lloyd Warner and Paul S. Lunt, *The Social Life of a Modern Community* (New Haven, CT: Yale University Press, 1941).

12. Robert S. Lynd and Helen Merrell Lynd, *Middletown* (New York: Harcourt, Brace, 1929); and Robert S. Lynd and Helen Merrell Lynd, *Middletown in Transition* (New York: Harcourt, Brace, 1937).

13. John A. Brittain, *Inheritance and the Inequality of Material Wealth* (Washington, DC: Brookings Institution, 1978).

14. Stephen Richard Higley, *Privilege, Power, and Place: The Geography of the American Upper Class* (Lanham, MD: Rowman & Littlefield, 1995), pp. 1–47.

15. Michael Argyle, *The Psychology of Social Class* (New York: Routledge, 1994).

16. Stanley R. Barrett, *Paradise: Class, Commuters, and Ethnicity in Rural Ontario* (Toronto: University of Toronto Press, 1994), pp. 17–19, 34–35.

17. Ibid., p. 155.

18. Alexander Stille, "Grounded by an Income Gap," Arts and Ideas in the *New York Times*, December 15, 2001, pp. A17, A19.

19. Donald J. Treiman and Harry B. G. Ganzeboom, "Cross-National Comparative Status-Attainment Research," *Research in Social Stratification and Mobility*, 9 (1990): 117; David L. Featherman and Robert M. Hauser, *Opportunity and Change* (New York: Academic Press, 1978), pp. 4, 481.

20. Argyle, *Psychology of Social Class*, pp. 36–37, 178.

21. Barrett, *Paradise*, pp. 17, 41.

22. Kevin Phillips, *The Politics of Rich and Poor: Wealth and the American Electorate in the Reagan Aftermath* (New York: Random House, 1990); U.S. Bureau of the Census, *Statistical Abstract of the United States: 1993*, 113th ed. (Washington, DC: U.S. Government Printing Office, 1993); *New York Times International*, September 30, 1997, p. A26; David Cay Johnston, "Gap Between Rich and Poor Found Substantially Wider," *New York Times* (National), September 5, 1999, p. 16.

23. Morton Klass, "Is There 'Caste' Outside of India?" in Carol R. Ember and Melvin Ember, eds., *Cross-Cultural Research for Social Science*, in Carol R. Ember and Melvin Ember, eds., *New Directions in Anthropology* (Upper Saddle River, NJ: Prentice Hall, CD-ROM, 2003).

24. John Ruskin, "Of Kings' Treasures," in John D. Rosenberg, ed., *The Genius of John Ruskin: Selections from His Writings* (New York: Braziller, 1963), pp. 296–314.

25. See Oscar Lewis, with the assistance of Victor Barnouw, *Village Life in Northern India* (Urbana: University of Illinois Press, 1958).

26. Nicholas D. Kristof, "Japan's Invisible Minority: Better Off Than in Past, but Still Outcasts," *New York Times International*, November 30, 1995, p. A18.

27. For more information about caste in Japan, see Gerald D. Berreman, *Caste in the Modern World* (Morristown, NJ: General Learning Press, 1973), and "Race, Caste and Other Invidious Distinctions in Social Stratification," *Race*, 13 (1972): 403–14.

28. Nicholas D. Kristof, "Japan's Invisible Minority: Burakumin," *Britannica Online*, December 1997.

29. For more information about caste in Rwanda, see Berreman, *Caste in the Modern World*, and "Race, Caste and Other Invidious Distinctions in Social Stratification."

30. "Book of the Year (1995): World Affairs: RWANDA," and "Book of the Year (1995): Race and Ethnic Relations: Rwanda's Complex Ethnic History," *Britannica Online*, December 1997.

31. Gerald D. Berreman, "Caste in India and the United States," *American Journal of Sociology*, 66 (1960): 120–27.

32. Orlando Patterson, *Slavery and Social Death: A Comparative Study* (Cambridge, MA: Harvard University Press, 1982), pp. vii–xiii, 105.

33. Frederic L. Pryor, *The Origins of the Economy: A Comparative Study of Distribution in Primitive and Peasant Economies* (New York: Academic Press, 1977), p. 219.

34. Euripides, "The Trojan Women," in Edith Hamilton, trans., *Three Greek Plays* (New York: Norton, 1937), p. 52.

35. S. F. Nadel, *A Black Byzantium: The Kingdom of Nupe in Nigeria* (London: Oxford University Press, 1942). The Nupe abolished slavery at the beginning of the twentieth century.

36. Pryor, *Origins of the Economy*, pp. 217–47.

37. Jonathan Marks, "Black, White, Other: Racial Categories Are Cultural Constructs Masquerading as Biology," *Natural History*, December 1994, 33; Eugenia Shanklin, *Anthropology and Race* (Belmont, CA: Wadsworth, 1994), pp. 15–17.

38. Stephen Molnar, *Human Variation: Races, Types and Ethnic Groups*, 4th ed. (Upper Saddle River, NJ: Prentice Hall, 1998), p. 19.

39. C. Loring Brace, David P. Tracer, Lucia Allen Yaroch, John Robb, Kari Brandt, and A. Russell Nelson, "Clines and Clusters versus 'Race': A Test in Ancient Egypt and the Case of a Death on the Nile," *Yearbook of Physical Anthropology*, 36 (1993): 17–19.

40. Alison S. Brooks, Fatimah Linda Collier Jackson, and R. Richard Grinker, "Race and Ethnicity in America," *Anthro Notes* (National Museum of Natural History Bulletin for Teachers), 15, no. 3 (Fall 1993): 11.

41. Brace et al., "Clines and Clusters versus 'Race,'" p. 19.

42. Melvin D. Williams, "Racism: The Production, Reproduction, and Obsolescence of Social Inferiority," in Ember, Ember, and Peregrine, eds., *Research Frontiers in Anthropology*.

43. Saul S. Friedman, "Holocaust," in *Academic American* [now Grolier] *Encyclopedia*, vol. 10 (Princeton, NJ: Arete, 1980), p. 206.

44. Marc Howard Ross, "Ethnocentrism and Ethnic Conflict," in Ember, Ember, and Peregrine, eds., *Research Frontiers in Anthropology*.

45. Marks, "Black, White, Other," p. 32.

46. George J. Armelagos and Alan H. Goodman, "Race, Racism, and Anthropology," in Alan H. Goodman and Thomas L. Leatherman, eds., *Building a New Biocultural Synthesis: Political-Economic Perspectives on Human Biology* (Ann Arbor: University of Michigan Press, 1998), p. 365.

47. Orlando Patterson, review of *One Drop of Blood: The American Misadventure of Race* by Scott L. Malcomson, New York *Times Book Review*, October 22, 2000, pp. 15–16.

48. Manning Nash, *The Cauldron of Ethnicity in the Modern World* (Chicago: University of Chicago Press, 1989), p. 2.

49. Ibid., p. 10.

50. Fredrik Barth, "Enduring and Emerging Issues in the Analysis of Ethnicity," in Hans Vermeulen and Cora Govers, eds., *The Anthropology of Ethnicity* (Amsterdam: Het Spinhuis, 1994), p. 27.

51. J. Milton Yinger, *Ethnicity: Source of Strength? Source of Conflict?* (Albany: State University Press of New York, 1994), p. 169.

52. Ibid., pp. 169–71.

53. Ibid., pp. 216–17.

54. Lois Benjamin, *The Black Elite: Facing the Color Line in the Twilight of the Twentieth Century* (Chicago: Nelson-Hall, 1991); see also Melvin D. Williams, "Racism," in Ember, Ember, and Peregrine, eds., *Research Frontiers in Anthropology*.

55. Kent V. Flannery, "The Cultural Evolution of Civilizations," *Annual Review of Ecology and Systematics*, 3 (1972): 399–426.

56. Data from Robert B. Textor, comp., *A Cross-Cultural Summary* (New Haven, CT: HRAF Press, 1967).

57. Ibid.

58. Gerhard Lenski, *Power and Privilege: A Theory of Social Stratification* (Chapel Hill: University of North Carolina Press, 1984 [first published 1966]), pp. 308–18.

59. Treiman and Ganzeboom, "Cross-National Comparative Status-Attainment Research," p. 117; Phillips Cutright, "Inequality: A Cross-National Analysis," *American Sociological Review*, 32 (1967): 564.

60. Sahlins, *Social Stratification in Polynesia*.

61. Ibid., p. 4.

62. Marshall D. Sahlins, *Stone Age Economics* (Chicago: Aldine, 1972).

63. Lenski, *Power and Privilege*.

64. Antonio Gilman, "The Development of Social Stratification in Bronze Age Europe," *Current Anthropology*, 22 (1990): 1–23.

65. See Fried, *Evolution of Political Society*, p. 201ff.; and Michael J. Harner, "Scarcity, the Factors of Production, and Social Evolution," in Steven Polgar, ed., *Population, Ecology, and Social Evolution* (The Hague: Mouton, 1975), pp. 123–38.

66. C. K. Meek, *Land Law and Custom in the Colonies* (London: Oxford University Press, 1940), pp. 149–50.

CHAPTER 19

1. Lila Leibowitz, *Females, Males, Families: A Biosocial Approach* (North Scituate, MA: Duxbury, 1978), pp. 43–44.

2. Alice Schlegel, "Gender Issues and Cross-Cultural Research," *Behavior Science Research*, 23 (1989): 266; Cynthia Fuchs Epstein, *Deceptive Distinctions: Sex, Gender, and the Social Order* (New York: Russell Sage Foundation, 1988), pp. 5–6; Janet Saltzman Chafetz, *Gender Equity: An Integrated Theory of Stability and Change*, Sage Library of Social Research No. 176 (Newbury Park, CA: Sage, 1990), p. 28.

3. Sue-Ellen Jacobs and Christine Roberts, "Sex, Sexuality, Gender and Gender Variance," in Sandra Morgen, ed., *Gender and Anthropology: Critical Reviews for Research and Teaching* (Washington, DC: American Anthropological Association, 1989), pp. 438–62.

4. William A. Stini, "Evolutionary Implications of Changing Nutritional Patterns in Human Populations," *American Anthropologist*, 73 (1971): 1019–30.

5. David W. Frayer and Milford H. Wolpoff, "Sexual Dimorphism," *Annual Review of Anthropology*, 14 (1985): 431–32.

6. For reviews of theories and research on sexual dimorphism and possible genetic and cultural determinants of variation in degree of dimorphism over time and place, see Frayer and Wolpoff, "Sexual Dimorphism"; and J. Patrick Gray, *Primate Sociobiology* (New Haven, CT: HRAF Press, 1985), pp. 201–209, 217–25.

7. Judith K. Brown, "A Note on the Division of Labor by Sex," *American Anthropologist*, 72 (1970): 1074.

8. Among the Aché hunter-gatherers of Paraguay, women collect the type of honey produced by stingless bees (men collect other honey); this division of labor is consistent with the compatibility theory. See Ana Magdalena Hurtado, Kristen Hawkes, Kim Hill, and Hillard Kaplan, "Female Subsistence Strategies among the Aché Hunter-Gatherers of Eastern Paraguay," *Human Ecology*, 13 (1985): 23.

9. George P. Murdock and Caterina Provost, "Factors in the Division of Labor by Sex: A Cross-Cultural Analysis," *Ethnology*, 12 (1973): 213; Bryan Byrne, "Access to Subsistence Resources and the Sexual Division of Labor among Potters," *Cross-Cultural Research*, 28 (1994): 225–50.

10. Robin O'Brien, "Who Weaves and Why? Weaving, Loom Complexity, and Trade," *Cross-Cultural Research*, 33 (1999): 30–42.

11. Douglas R. White, Michael L. Burton, and Lilyan A. Brudner, "Entailment Theory and Method: A Cross-Cultural Analysis of

the Sexual Division of Labor," *Behavior Science Research,* 12 (1977): 1–24.

12. Carol C. Mukhopadhyay and Patricia J. Higgins, "Anthropological Studies of Women's Status Revisited: 1977–1987," *Annual Review of Anthropology,* 17 (1988): 473.

13. Brown, "Note on the Division of Labor by Sex," pp. 1073–78; and White, Burton, and Brudner, "Entailment Theory and Method," pp. 1–24.

14. Sara B. Nerlove, "Women's Workload and Infant Feeding Practices: A Relationship with Demographic Implications," *Ethnology,* 13 (1974): 201–14.

15. Nancy E. Levine, "Women's Work and Infant Feeding: A Case from Rural Nepal," *Ethnology,* 27 (1988): 231–51.

16. Madeleine J. Goodman, P. Bion Griffin, Agnes A. Estioko-Griffin, and John S. Grove, "The Compatibility of Hunting and Mothering among the Agta Hunter-Gatherers of the Philippines," *Sex Roles,* 12 (1985): 1199–209.

17. Andrew J. Noss and Barry S. Hewlett, "The Contexts of Female Hunting in Central Africa," *American Anthropologist,* 103 (2001): 1024–40.

18. John J. Macionis, *Sociology,* 4th ed. (Upper Saddle River, NJ: Prentice Hall, 1993), p. 362.

19. Margaret Mead, *Sex and Temperament in Three Primitive Societies* (New York: Mentor, 1950 [originally published 1935]), pp. 180–84.

20. W. H. R. Rivers, *The Todas* (Oosterhout, N.B., The Netherlands: Anthropological Publications, 1967 [originally published 1906]), p. 567.

21. Melvin Ember and Carol R. Ember, "The Conditions Favoring Matrilocal versus Patrilocal Residence," *American Anthropologist,* 73 (1971): 573, table 1.

22. Alice Schlegel and Herbert Barry III, "The Cultural Consequences of Female Contribution to Subsistence," *American Anthropologist,* 88 (1986): 142–50.

23. Ester Boserup, *Woman's Role in Economic Development* (New York: St. Martin's, 1970), pp. 22–25; see also Schlegel and Barry, "Cultural Consequences of Female Contribution to Subsistence," pp. 144–45.

24. Boserup, *Woman's Role in Economic Development,* pp. 22–25.

25. Ibid., pp. 31–34.

26. Carol R. Ember, "The Relative Decline in Women's Contribution to Agriculture with Intensification," *American Anthropologist,* 85 (1983): 286–87; data from Murdock and Provost, "Factors in the Division of Labor by Sex," p. 212; Candice Bradley, "Keeping the Soil in Good Heart: Weeding, Women and Ecofeminism," in Karen Warren, ed., *Ecofeminism: Multidisciplinary Perspectives* (Bloomington: Indiana University Press, 1995).

27. Ember, "Relative Decline in Women's Contribution to Agriculture with Intensification," pp. 287–93.

28. Ember and Ember, "Conditions Favoring Matrilocal versus Patrilocal Residence," pp. 579–80.

29. Ibid., p. 581; see also Peggy R. Sanday, "Toward a Theory of the Status of Women," *American Anthropologist,* 75 (1973): 1684.

30. Nerlove, "Women's Workload and Infant Feeding Practices," pp. 207–14.

31. Schlegel and Barry, "Cultural Consequences of Female Contribution to Subsistence," pp. 142–50.

32. Ember, "Relative Decline in Women's Contribution to Agriculture with Intensification," pp. 288–89.

33. Martin K. Whyte, "Cross-Cultural Codes Dealing with the Relative Status of Women," *Ethnology,* 17 (1978): 217.

34. Martha C. Nussbaum, "Introduction," in Martha C. Nussbaum and Jonathan Glover, *Women, Culture, and Development: A Study of Human Capabilities* (Oxford: Clarendon Press, 1995),

p. 2, based on data from Human Development Report (New York: United Nations Development Programme, 1993).

35. Whyte, "Cross-Cultural Codes"; and David B. Adams, "Why There Are So Few Women Warriors," *Behavior Science Research,* 18 (1983): 196–212.

36. Judith K. Brown, "Economic Organization and the Position of Women among the Iroquois," *Ethnohistory,* 17 (1970): 151–67.

37. Peggy R. Sanday, "Female Status in the Public Domain," in Michelle Z. Rosaldo and Louise Lamphere, eds., *Woman, Culture, and Society* (Stanford, CA: Stanford University Press, 1974), pp. 189–206; and William T. Divale and Marvin Harris, "Population, Warfare, and the Male Supremacist Complex," *American Anthropologist,* 78 (1976): 521–38.

38. Naomi Quinn, "Anthropological Studies on Women's Status," *Annual Review of Anthropology,* 6 (1977): 189–90.

39. Susan Brandt Graham, "Biology and Human Social Behavior: A Response to van den Berghe and Barash," *American Anthropologist,* 81 (1979): 357–60.

40. Dennis Werner, "Chiefs and Presidents: A Comparison of Leadership Traits in the United States and among the Mekranoti-Kayapo of Central Brazil," *Ethos,* 10 (1982): 136–48; and Ralph M. Stogdill, *Handbook of Leadership: A Survey of Theory and Research* (New York: Macmillan, 1974), cited in ibid.; see also W. Penn Handwerker and Paul V. Crosbie, "Sex and Dominance," *American Anthropologist,* 84 (1982): 97–104.

41. Patricia Draper, "!Kung Women: Contrasts in Sexual Egalitarianism in Foraging and Sedentary Contexts," in Rayna R. Reiter, ed., *Toward an Anthropology of Women* (New York: Monthly Review Press, 1975), p. 103.

42. Dennis Werner, "Child Care and Influence among the Mekranoti of Central Brazil," *Sex Roles,* 10 (1984): 395–404.

43. Marc H. Ross, "Female Political Participation: A Cross-Cultural Explanation," *American Anthropologist,* 88 (1986): 843–58.

44. This description is based on the fieldwork of Elizabeth and Robert Fearnea (1956 to 1958), as reported in M. Kay Martin and Barbara Voorhies, *Female of the Species* (New York: Columbia University Press, 1975), pp. 304–31.

45. Elsie B. Begler, "Sex, Status, and Authority in Egalitarian Society," *American Anthropologist,* 80 (1978): 571–88.

46. Ibid. See also Whyte, "Cross-Cultural Codes Dealing with the Relative Status of Women," pp. 229–32.

47. Martin K. Whyte, *The Status of Women in Preindustrial Societies* (Princeton, NJ: Princeton University Press, 1978), pp. 95–120. For a similar view, see Quinn, "Anthropological Studies on Women's Status."

48. Whyte, *Status of Women in Preindustrial Societies,* pp. 124–29, 145; see also Sanday, "Toward a Theory of the Status of Women."

49. Whyte, *Status of Women in Preindustrial Societies,* pp. 129–30.

50. Brown, "Economic Organization and the Position of Women among the Iroquois."

51. Whyte, *Status of Women in Preindustrial Societies,* pp. 135–36.

52. Ibid., p. 135.

53. Quinn, "Anthropological Studies on Women's Status," p. 85; see also Mona Etienne and Eleanor Leacock, eds., *Women and Colonization: Anthropological Perspectives* (New York: Praeger, 1980), pp. 19–20.

54. Chafetz, *Gender Equity,* pp. 11–19.

55. Mead, *Sex and Temperament in Three Primitive Societies,* p. 206.

56. Nancy McDowell, "Mundugumor: Sex and Temperament Revisited," in Melvin Ember and Carol R. Ember, eds., *Portraits of Culture: Ethnographic Originals,* in Carol R. Ember and Melvin Ember, eds., *New Directions in Anthropology* (Upper Saddle River, NJ: Prentice Hall, CD-ROM, 2003).

57. Beatrice B. Whiting and Carolyn P. Edwards, "A Cross-Cultural Analysis of Sex Differences in the Behavior of Children Aged

Three through Eleven," *Journal of Social Psychology,* 91 (1973): 171–88.

58. Robert L. Munroe, Robert Hulefeld, James M. Rodgers, Damon L. Tomeo, Steven K. Yamazaki, "Aggression among Children in Four Cultures," *Cross-Cultural Research,* 34 (2000): 8–9.

59. Eleanor E. Maccoby and Carol N. Jacklin, *The Psychology of Sex Differences* (Stanford, CA: Stanford University Press, 1974).

60. For a more extensive discussion of behavior differences and possible explanations of them, see Carol R. Ember, "A Cross-Cultural Perspective on Sex Differences," in Ruth H. Munroe, Robert L. Munroe, and Beatrice B. Whiting, eds., *Handbook of Cross-Cultural Human Development* (New York: Garland, 1981), pp. 531–80.

61. Whiting and Edwards, "Cross-Cultural Analysis of Sex Differences in the Behavior of Children Aged Three through Eleven."

62. For references to this research, see Ember, "Cross-Cultural Perspective on Sex Differences," p. 559.

63. J. Z. Rubin, F. J. Provenzano, and R. F. Haskett, "The Eye of the Beholder: Parents' Views on the Sex of New Borns," *American Journal of Orthopsychiatry,* 44 (1974): 512–19.

64. For a discussion of this evidence, see Lee Ellis, "Evidence of Neuroandrogenic Etiology of Sex Roles from a Combined Analysis of Human, Nonhuman Primate and Nonprimate Mammalian Studies," *Personality and Individual Differences,* 7 (1986): 525–27; Ember, "Cross-Cultural Perspective on Sex Differences," pp. 531–80.

65. For example, Ellis, in "Evidence of Neuroandrogenic Etiology of Sex Roles," considers the evidence for the biological view of aggression "beyond reasonable dispute."

66. For a discussion of other possibilities see Ember, "Cross-Cultural Perspective on Sex Differences."

67. Ronald P. Rohner, "Sex Differences in Aggression: Phylogenetic and Enculturation Perspectives," *Ethos,* 4 (1976): 57–72.

68. Beatrice B. Whiting and John W. M. Whiting (in collaboration with Richard Longabaugh), *Children of Six Cultures: A Psycho-Cultural Analysis* (Cambridge, MA: Harvard University Press, 1975); see also Beatrice B. Whiting and Carolyn P. Edwards, *Children of Different Worlds: The Formation of Social Behavior* (Cambridge, MA: Harvard University Press, 1988), p. 273.

69. Carol R. Ember, "Feminine Task Assignment and the Social Behavior of Boys," *Ethos,* 1 (1973): 424–39.

70. Whiting and Edwards, "Cross-Cultural Analysis of Sex Differences in the Behavior of Children Aged Three through Eleven," pp. 175–79; see also Maccoby and Jacklin, *The Psychology of Sex Differences.*

71. Victoria Katherine Burbank, *Fighting Women: Anger and Aggression in Aboriginal Society* (Berkeley: University of California Press, 1994).

72. David R. Heise, "Cultural Patterning of Sexual Socialization," *American Sociological Review,* 32 (1967): 726–39.

73. Clellan S. Ford and Frank A. Beach, *Patterns of Sexual Behavior* (New York: Harper, 1951), p. 191.

74. Oscar Lewis, *Life in a Mexican Village: Tepoztlan Revisited* (Urbana: University of Illinois Press, 1951), p. 397.

75. Reynolds Farley, *The New American Reality: Who We Are, How We Got Here, Where We Are Going* (New York: Russell Sage Foundation, 1996), p. 60.

76. Gwen J. Broude and Sarah J. Greene, "Cross-Cultural Codes on Twenty Sexual Attitudes and Practices," *Ethnology,* 15 (1976): 409–29.

77. Clyde Kluckhohn, "As an Anthropologist Views It," in A. Deutsch, ed., *Sex Habits of American Men* (Upper Saddle River, NJ: Prentice Hall, 1948), p. 101.

78. Morton Hunt, *Sexual Behavior in the 1970s* (Chicago: Playboy Press, 1974), pp. 254–57; Tamar Lewin, "Sex in America: Faithfulness in Marriage Is Overwhelming," *New York Times* (National), October 7, 1994, pp. A1, A18.

79. Gwen J. Broude, "Extramarital Sex Norms in Cross-Cultural Perspective," *Behavior Science Research,* 15 (1980): 184.

80. Ford and Beach, *Patterns of Sexual Behavior,* p. 114.

81. Ibid., p. 69.

82. Ibid., p. 76.

83. John Morris, *Living with Lepchas: A Book about the Sikkim Himalayas* (London: Heinemann, 1938), p. 191.

84. Ruth M. Underhill, *Social Organization of the Papago Indians* (New York: Columbia University Press, 1938), pp. 117, 186.

85. Mahmud M. 'Abd Allah, "Siwan Customs," *Harvard African Studies,* 1 (1917): 7, 20.

86. Raymond C. Kelly, "Witchcraft and Sexual Relations: An Exploration in the Social and Semantic Implications of the Structure of Belief," paper presented at the annual meeting of the American Anthropological Association, Mexico City, 1974.

87. Data from Robert B. Textor, comp., *A Cross-Cultural Summary* (New Haven, CT: HRAF Press, 1967).

88. William N. Stephens, "A Cross-Cultural Study of Modesty," *Behavior Science Research,* 7 (1972): 1–28.

89. Gwen J. Broude, "Cross-Cultural Patterning of Some Sexual Attitudes and Practices," *Behavior Science Research,* 11 (1976): 243.

90. Dennis Werner, "A Cross-Cultural Perspective on Theory and Research on Male Homosexuality," *Journal of Homosexuality,* 4 (1979): 345–62; see also Dennis Werner, "On the Societal Acceptance or Rejection of Male Homosexuality," M.A. thesis, Hunter College of the City University of New York, 1975, p. 36.

91. Werner, "Cross-Cultural Perspective on Theory and Research on Male Homosexuality," p. 358.

92. Data from Textor, comp., *A Cross-Cultural Summary.*

93. Alice Schlegel, "Status, Property, and the Value of Virginity," *American Ethnologist,* 18 (1991): 719–34.

CHAPTER 20

1. William N. Stephens, *The Family in Cross-Cultural Perspective* (New York: Holt, Rinehart & Winston, 1963), p. 5.

2. George Peter Murdock, *Social Structure* (New York: Macmillan, 1949), p. 8.

3. Stephens, *The Family in Cross-Cultural Perspective,* pp. 170–71.

4. E. Kathleen Gough, "The Nayars and the Definition of Marriage," *Journal of the Royal Anthropological Institute,* 89 (1959): 23–34; N. Prabha Unnithan, "Nayars: Tradition and Change in Marriage and Family," in Melvin Ember and Carol R. Ember, eds., *Portraits of Culture: Ethnographic Originals,* in Carol R. Ember and Melvin Ember, eds., *New Directions in Anthropology* (Upper Saddle River, NJ: Prentice Hall, CD-ROM, 2003).

5. Unnithan, "Nayars."

6. E. Adamson Hoebel, *The Cheyennes: Indians of the Great Plains* (New York: Holt, Rinehart & Winston, 1960), p. 77.

7. E. E. Evans-Pritchard, "Sexual Inversion among the Azande," *American Anthropologist,* 72 (1970): 1428–34.

8. Denise O'Brien, "Female Husbands in Southern Bantu Societies," in Alice Schlegel, ed., *Sexual Stratification: A Cross-Cultural View* (New York: Columbia University Press, 1977), pp. 109–26; see also Regina Smith Oboler, "Is the Female Husband a Man? Woman/Woman Marriage among the Nandi of Kenya," *Ethnology,* 19 (1980): 69–88.

9. Regina Smith Oboler, "Nandi: From Cattle-Keepers to Cash-Crop Farmers," in Ember and Ember, eds., *Portraits of Culture.*

10. Murdock, *Social Structure,* pp. 7–8.

11. Ibid., pp. 9–10.

12. See, for example, Ralph Linton, *The Study of Man* (New York: Appleton-Century-Crofts, 1936), pp. 135–36.

13. Melvin Ember and Carol R. Ember, "Male-Female Bonding: A Cross-Species Study of Mammals and Birds," *Behavior Science Research*, 14 (1979): 37–56.

14. Nelson H. Graburn, *Eskimos without Igloos* (Boston: Little, Brown, 1969), pp. 188–200.

15. Bronislaw Malinowski, *The Sexual Life of Savages in Northwestern Melanesia* (New York: Halcyon House, 1932), p. 77.

16. Ibid., p. 88.

17. John W. M. Whiting, *Becoming a Kwoma* (New Haven, CT: Yale University Press, 1941), p. 125.

18. Elman R. Service, *Profiles in Ethnology*, 3rd ed. (New York: Harper & Row, 1978).

19. Robert A. LeVine and Barbara B. LeVine, "Nyansongo: A Gusii Community in Kenya," in Beatrice B. Whiting, ed., *Six Cultures* (New York: Wiley, 1963), p. 65.

20. Ibid.

21. For an extensive discussion of the symbolism of Rotuman weddings, see Alan Howard and Jan Rensel, "Rotuma: Interpreting a Wedding," in Ember and Ember, eds., *Portraits of Culture*.

22. Alice Schlegel and Rohn Eloul, "A New Coding of Marriage Transactions," *Behavior Science Research*, 21 (1987): 119.

23. Alice Schlegel and Rohn Eloul, "Marriage Transactions: Labor, Property, and Status," *American Anthropologist*, 90 (1988): 295, table 1. We used the data to calculate the frequency of various types of economic transaction in a worldwide sample of 186 societies.

24. Oboler, "Nandi."

25. Charles O. Frake, "The Eastern Subanun of Mindanao," in George P. Murdock, ed., *Social Structure in Southeast Asia*, Viking Fund Publications in Anthropology No. 29 (Chicago: Quadrangle, 1960), pp. 51–64.

26. Margaret Mead, *Growing Up in New Guinea* (London: Routledge & Kegan Paul, 1931), pp. 206–208.

27. Monique Borgerhoff Mulder, Margaret George-Cramer, Jason Eshleman, and Alessia Ortolani, "A Study of East African Kinship and Marriage Using a Phylogenetically Based Comparative Method," *American Anthropologist*, 103 (2001): 1059–82.

28. Schlegel and Eloul, "Marriage Transactions," pp. 298–99.

29. Frederic L. Pryor, *The Origins of the Economy: A Comparative Study of Distribution in Primitive and Peasant Economies* (New York: Academic Press, 1977), pp. 363–64.

30. Ibid.

31. Robert F. Spencer, "Spouse-Exchange among the North Alaskan Eskimo," in Paul Bohannan and John Middleton, eds., *Marriage, Family and Residence* (Garden City, NY: Natural History Press, 1968), p. 136.

32. Schlegel and Eloul, "Marriage Transactions," pp. 296–97.

33. Ibid.

34. Ibid.

35. A. R. Radcliffe-Brown, *The Andaman Islanders: A Study in Social Anthropology* (London: Cambridge University Press, 1922), p. 73.

36. Jack Goody, "Bridewealth and Dowry in Africa and Eurasia," in Jack Goody and S. H. Tambiah, eds., *Bridewealth and Dowry* (Cambridge: Cambridge University Press, 1973), pp. 17–21.

37. Pryor, *Origins of the Economy*, pp. 363–65; Schlegel and Eloul, "Marriage Transactions," pp. 296–99.

38. Research is reported in Steven J. C. Gaulin and James S. Boster, "Dowry as Female Competition," *American Anthropologist*, 92 (1990): 994–1005. The first theory discussed herein is associated with Ester Boserup, *Woman's Role in Economic Development* (New York: St. Martin's, 1970). The second is put forward by Gaulin and Boster.

39. Schlegel and Eloul, in "Marriage Transactions," following Goody, "Bridewealth and Dowry in Africa and Eurasia," p. 20.

40. Fredrik Barth, *Nomads of South Persia* (Boston: Little, Brown, 1961), pp. 18–19; as reported in (and coded as indirect dowry by) Schlegel and Eloul, "New Coding of Marriage Transactions," p. 131.

41. Russell Middleton, "Brother-Sister and Father-Daughter Marriage in Ancient Egypt," *American Sociological Review*, 27 (1962): 606.

42. William H. Durham, *Coevolution: Genes, Culture, and Human Diversity* (Stanford, CA: Stanford University Press, 1991), pp. 293–94; citing research by K. Hopkins, "Brother-Sister Marriage in Roman Egypt," *Comparative Studies of Society and History*, 22 (1980): 303–54.

43. Edward Westermarck, *The History of Human Marriage* (London: Macmillan, 1894).

44. Yonina Talmon, "Mate Selection in Collective Settlements," *American Sociological Review*, 29 (1964): 492.

45. Ibid., p. 504.

46. Arthur Wolf, "Adopt a Daughter-in-Law, Marry a Sister: A Chinese Solution to the Problem of the Incest Taboo," *American Anthropologist*, 70 (1968): 864.

47. Arthur P. Wolf and Chieh-shan Huang, *Marriage and Adoption in China, 1845–1945* (Stanford, CA: Stanford University Press, 1980), pp. 159, 170, 185.

48. Hilda Parker and Seymour Parker, "Father-Daughter Sexual Abuse: An Emerging Perspective," *American Journal of Orthopsychiatry*, 56 (1986): 531–49.

49. Melvin Ember, "On the Origin and Extension of the Incest Taboo," *Behavior Science Research*, 10 (1975): 249–81; Durham, Coevolution, pp. 341–57.

50. For a discussion of mechanisms that might lead to sexual aversion, see Seymour Parker, "The Precultural Basis of the Incest Taboo: Toward a Biosocial Theory," *American Anthropologist*, 78 (1976): 285–305; see also Seymour Parker, "Cultural Rules, Rituals, and Behavior Regulation," *American Anthropologist*, 86 (1984): 584–600.

51. Sigmund Freud, *A General Introduction to Psychoanalysis* (Garden City, NY: Garden City Publishing, 1943 [originally published in German in 1917]).

52. Bronislaw Malinowski, *Sex and Repression in Savage Society* (London: Kegan Paul, Trench, Trubner, 1927).

53. Quoted in Leslie A. White, *The Science of Culture: A Study of Man and Civilization* (New York: Farrar, Straus, & Cudahy, 1949), p. 313.

54. Gay Elizabeth Kang, "Exogamy and Peace Relations of Social Units: A Cross-Cultural Test," *Ethnology*, 18 (1979): 85–99.

55. Curt Stern, *Principles of Human Genetics*, 3rd ed. (San Francisco: Freeman, 1973), pp. 494–95, as cited in Ember, "On the Origin and Extension of the Incest Taboo," p. 256. For a recent review of the theory and evidence, see Durham, *Coevolution*.

56. Eva Seemanova, "A Study of Children of Incestuous Matings," *Human Heredity*, 21 (1971): 108–28, as cited in Durham, *Coevolution*, pp. 305–309.

57. Durham, *Coevolution*, pp. 305–309.

58. Ibid., pp. 346–52.

59. Raymond Firth, *We, the Tikopia* (Boston: Beacon Press, 1957), pp. 287–88, cited (somewhat differently) in Durham, *Coevolution*, pp. 349–50.

60. A mathematical model of early mating systems suggests that people may have noticed the harmful effects of inbreeding once populations began to expand as a result of agriculture; people therefore may have deliberately adopted the incest taboo to solve the problem of inbreeding. See Ember, "On the Origin and Extension of the Incest Taboo." For a similar subsequent suggestion, see Durham, *Coevolution*, pp. 331–39.

61. William J. Goode, *The Family*, 2nd ed. (Upper Saddle River, NJ: Prentice Hall, 1982), pp. 61–62.

62. Clellan S. Ford, *Smoke from Their Fires* (New Haven, CT: Yale University Press, 1941), p. 149.

63. Howard and Rensel, "Rotuma."
64. Susan Schaefer Davis, "Morocco: Adolescents in a Small Town," in Ember and Ember, eds., *Portraits of Culture.*
65. W. J. Goode, *World Revolution and Family Patterns* (New York: Free Press, 1970), p. 210.
66. Sherwood G. Lingenfelter, "Yap: Changing Roles of Men and Women," in Ember and Ember, eds., *Portraits of Culture.*
67. Douglas H. MacDonald and Barry S. Hewlett, "Reproductive Interests and Forager Mobility," *Current Anthropology,* 40 (1999): 504–506.
68. Ember, "On the Origin and Extension of the Incest Taboo," p. 262, table 3.
69. Annette Busby, "Kurds: A Culture Straddling National Borders," in Ember and Ember, eds., *Portraits of Culture.*
70. Ember, "On the Origin and Extension of the Incest Taboo," pp. 260–69; see also Durham, *Coevolution,* pp. 341–57.
71. Murdock, *Social Structure,* p. 29.
72. Waldemar Bogoras, "The Chukchee," pt. 3, *Memoirs of the American Museum of Natural History,* 2 (1909), cited in Stephens, *The Family in Cross-Cultural Perspective,* p. 195.
73. Douglas Oliver, *A Solomon Island Society* (Cambridge, MA: Harvard University Press, 1955), pp. 352–53.
74. Ibid., pp. 223–24, quoted in Stephens, *The Family in Cross-Cultural Perspective,* p. 58.
75. Margaret Mead, *Sex and Temperament in Three Primitive Societies* (New York: New American Library, 1950 [originally published 1935]), p. 101.
76. The discussion of these customs is based on Stephens, *The Family in Cross-Cultural Perspective,* pp. 63–67.
77. Philip L. Kilbride and Janet C. Kilbride, "Polygyny: A Modern Contradiction?" in Philip L. Kilbride and Janet C. Kilbride, *Changing Family Life in East Africa: Women and Children at Risk* (University Park: Pennsylvania State University Press, 1990), pp. 202–206.
78. Connie M. Anderson, "The Persistence of Polygyny as an Adaptive Response to Poverty and Oppression in Apartheid South Africa," *Cross-Cultural Research,* 34 (2000): 102–103.
79. Linton, *The Study of Man,* p. 183.
80. John W. M. Whiting, "Effects of Climate on Certain Cultural Practices," in Ward H. Goodenough, ed., *Explorations in Cultural Anthropology: Essays in Honor of George Peter Murdock* (New York: McGraw-Hill, 1964), pp. 511–44.
81. Ibid., p. 518.
82. Ibid., pp. 516–17.
83. Melvin Ember, "Warfare, Sex Ratio, and Polygyny," *Ethnology,* 13 (1974): 197–206. Bobbi Low, in "Marriage Systems and Pathogen Stress in Human Societies," *American Zoologist,* 30 (1990): 325–39, has suggested that a high incidence of disease also may reduce the prevalence of "healthy" men. In such cases it may be to a woman's advantage to marry a "healthy" man even if he is already married, and it may be to a man's advantage to marry several unrelated women to maximize genetic variation (and disease resistance) among his children.
84. Melvin Ember, "Alternative Predictors of Polygyny," *Behavior Science Research,* 19 (1984–1985): 1–23. The statistical relationship between late age of marriage for men and polygyny was first reported by Stanley R. Witkowski, "Polygyny, Age of Marriage, and Female Status," paper presented at the annual meeting of the American Anthropological Association, San Francisco, 1975.
85. Ember, "Warfare, Sex Ratio, and Polygyny," pp. 202–205.
86. Ember, "Alternative Predictors of Polygyny." For other predictors of polygyny, see Douglas R. White and Michael L. Burton, "Causes of Polygyny: Ecology, Economy, Kinship, and Warfare," *American Anthropologist,* 90 (1988): 871–87; and Low, "Marriage Systems and Pathogen Stress in Human Societies."

87. Allan D. Coult and Robert W. Habenstein, *Cross Tabulations of Murdock's World Ethnographic Sample* (Columbia: University of Missouri Press, 1965); George Peter Murdock, "World Ethnographic Sample," *American Anthropologist,* 59 (1957): 664–87.
88. Melvyn C. Goldstein, "When Brothers Share a Wife," *Natural History,* March 1987, p. 39.
89. Stephens, *The Family in Cross-Cultural Perspective,* p. 45.
90. L. R. Hiatt, "Polyandry in Sri Lanka: A Test Case for Parental Investment Theory," *Man,* 15 (1980): 583–98.
91. Goldstein, "When Brothers Share a Wife," pp. 39–48. Formerly, in feudal Tibet, a class of serfs who owned small parcels of land also practiced polyandry. Goldstein suggested that a shortage of land would explain their polyandry too. See Melvyn C. Goldstein, "Stratification, Polyandry, and Family Structure in Central Tibet," *Southwestern Journal of Anthropology,* 27 (1971): 65–74.
92. For example, see Myron L. Cohen, *House United, House Divided: The Chinese Family in Taiwan* (New York: Columbia University Press, 1976).
93. Burton Pasternak, *Introduction to Kinship and Social Organization* (Upper Saddle River, NJ: Prentice Hall, 1976), p. 96.
94. Coult and Habenstein, *Cross Tabulations of Murdock's World Ethnographic Sample.*
95. Margaret Mead, *Coming of Age in Samoa* (New York: Morrow, 1928), quoted in Stephens, *The Family in Cross-Cultural Perspective,* pp. 134–35.
96. Ibid., p. 135.
97. M. F. Nimkoff and Russell Middleton, "Types of Family and Types of Economy," *American Journal of Sociology,* 66 (1960): 215–25.
98. Burton Pasternak, Carol R. Ember, and Melvin Ember, "On the Conditions Favoring Extended Family Households," *Journal of Anthropological Research,* 32 (1976): 109–23.
99. Jean Libman Block, "Help! They've All Moved Back Home!" *Woman's Day,* April 26, 1983, pp. 72–76.

CHAPTER 23

1. Elman R. Service, *Primitive Social Organization: An Evolutionary Perspective* (New York: Random House, 1962).
2. Carmel Schrire, "Wild Surmises on Savage Thoughts," in Carmel Schrire, ed., *Past and Present in Hunter-Gatherer Studies* (Orlando, FL: Academic Press, 1984), pp. 1–25; see also Eleanor Leacock and Richard Lee, "Introduction," in Eleanor Leacock and Richard Lee, eds., *Politics and History in Band Societies* (Cambridge: Cambridge University Press, 1982), p. 8.
3. Service, *Primitive Social Organization,* p. 109.
4. Jean L. Briggs, "Eskimo Women: Makers of Men," in Carolyn J. Matthiasson, *Many Sisters: Women in Cross-Cultural Perspective* (New York: Free Press, 1974), pp. 261–304.
5. Therkel Mathiassen, *Material Culture of the Iglulik Eskimos* (Copenhagen: Glydendalske, 1928), as quoted in E. M. Weyer, *The Eskimos: Their Environment and Folkways* (New Haven, CT: Yale University Press, 1932), p. 213.
6. Service, *Primitive Social Organization,* pp. 114–15.
7. Paul Bohannan, "The Migration and Expansion of the Tiv," *Africa,* 24 (1954): 3.
8. Marshall D. Sahlins, "The Segmentary Lineage: An Organization of Predatory Expansion," *American Anthropologist,* 63 (1961): 342.
9. Raymond C. Kelly, *The Nuer Conquest: The Structure and Development of an Expansionist System* (Ann Arbor: University of Michigan Press, 1985), p. 1.
10. Sahlins, "The Segmentary Lineage," p. 345.
11. Neville Dyson-Hudson, *Karimojong Politics* (Oxford: Clarendon Press, 1966), chapters 5 and 6.
12. Ibid.

13. Marshall Sahlins, *Moala: Culture and Nature on a Fijian Island* (Ann Arbor: University of Michigan Press, 1962), pp. 293–94.

14. Marshall D. Sahlins, "Poor Man, Rich Man, Big-Man, Chief: Political Types in Melanesia and Polynesia," *Comparative Studies in Society and History,* 5 (1963): 295.

15. Marshall Sahlins, "Other Times, Other Customs: The Anthropology of History," *American Anthropologist,* 85 (1983): 519.

16. Sahlins, "Poor Man, Rich Man, Big-Man, Chief," p. 297.

17. Robert L. Carneiro, "A Theory of the Origin of the State," *Science,* August 21, 1970, p. 733.

18. See Max Weber, *The Theory of Social and Economic Organization,* trans. A. M. Henderson and Talcott Parsons (New York: Oxford University Press, 1947), p. 154.

19. Hakan Wiberg, "Self-Determination as an International Issue," in I. M. Lewis, ed., *Nationalism and Self-Determination in the Horn of Africa* (London: Ithaca Press, 1983), pp. 43–65.

20. For an extensive review of the various theories about legitimacy, see Ronald Cohen, "Introduction," in Ronald Cohen and Judith D. Toland, eds., *State Formation and Political Legitimacy,* vol. 1, *Political Anthropology* (New Brunswick, NJ: Transaction Books, 1988), pp. 1–3.

21. M. I. Finley, *Politics in the Ancient World* (Cambridge: Cambridge University Press, 1983).

22. Jerome Carcopino, *Daily Life in Ancient Rome: The People and the City at the Height of the Empire,* edited with bibliography and notes by Henry T. Rowell, translated from the French by E. O. Lorimer (New Haven, CT: Yale University Press, 1940), pp. 18–20.

23. Our discussion of Nupe is based on S. F. Nadel, "Nupe State and Community," *Africa,* 8 (1935): 257–303.

24. Melvin Ember, "The Relationship between Economic and Political Development in Nonindustrialized Societies," *Ethnology,* 2 (1963): 228–48.

25. Data from Robert B. Textor, comp., *A Cross-Cultural Summary* (New Haven, CT: HRAF Press, 1967).

26. Ember, "Relationship between Economic and Political Development in Nonindustrialized Societies."

27. Data from Textor, comp., *A Cross-Cultural Summary.*

28. Raoul Naroll, "Two Solutions to Galton's Problem," *Philosophy of Science,* 28 (January 1961): 15–39. See also Marc H. Ross, "Socioeconomic Complexity, Socialization, and Political Differentiation: A Cross-Cultural Study," *Ethos,* 9 (1981): 217–47.

29. Ember, "Relationship between Economic and Political Development in Nonindustrialized Societies," pp. 244–46.

30. Service, *Primitive Social Organization*; see also David P. Braun and Stephen Plog, "Evolution of 'Tribal' Social Networks: Theory and Prehistoric North American Evidence," *American Antiquity,* 47 (1982): 504–25; Jonathan Haas, "Warfare and the Evolution of Tribal Polities in the Prehistoric Southwest," in Jonathan Haas, ed., *The Anthropology of War* (New York: Cambridge University Press, 1990), pp. 171–89.

31. Allen Johnson and Timothy Earle, *The Evolution of Human Societies: From Foraging Group to Agrarian State* (Stanford, CA: Stanford University Press, 1987), p. 158; Robert L. Carneiro, "Chiefdom-Level Warfare as Exemplified in Fiji and the Cauca Valley," in Haas, ed., *The Anthropology of War,* pp. 190–211.

32. Service, *Primitive Social Organization,* pp. 112, 145.

33. Gary Feinman and Jill Nietzel, "Too Many Types: An Overview of Sedentary Prestate Societies in the Americas," in Michael B. Schiffer, ed., *Advances in Archaeological Method and Theory,* vol. 7 (Orlando, FL: Academic Press, 1984), pp. 39–102.

34. See earlier discussion in the chapter on origins of cities and states. See also Ronald Cohen and Elman R. Service, eds., *Origins of the State: The Anthropology of Political Evolution* (Philadelphia: Institute for the Study of Human Issues, 1978).

35. William H. McNeill, *Plagues and Peoples* (Garden City, NY: Doubleday/Anchor, 1976).

36. Robert L. Carneiro, "Political Expansion as an Expression of the Principle of Competitive Exclusion," in Ronald Cohen and Elman R. Service, eds., *Origins of the State: The Anthropology of Political Evolution* (Philadelphia: Institute for the Study of Human Issues, 1978), p. 215.

37. Data from Textor, comp., *A Cross-Cultural Summary.*

38. Carneiro, "Political Expansion as an Expression of the Principle of Competitive Exclusion." See also Hornell Hart, "The Logistic Growth of Political Areas," *Social Forces,* 26 (1948): 396–408; Raoul Naroll, "Imperial Cycles and World Order," *Peace Research Society: Papers,* No. 7, Chicago Conference (1967): 83–101; and Louis A. Marano, "A Macrohistoric Trend toward World Government," *Behavior Science Notes,* 8 (1973): 35–40.

39. For a review of the descriptive literature until the late 1970s, see Joan Vincent, "Political Anthropology: Manipulative Strategies," *Annual Review of Anthropology,* 7 (1978): 175–94.

40. Dennis Werner, "Chiefs and Presidents: A Comparison of Leadership Traits in the United States and among the Mekranoti-Kayapo of Central Brazil," *Ethos,* 10 (1982): 136–48.

41. Waud H. Kracke, *Force and Persuasion: Leadership in an Amazonian Society* (Chicago: University of Chicago Press, 1979), p. 232.

42. Werner, "Chiefs and Presidents."

43. Sahlins, "Poor Man, Rich Man, Big-Man, Chief," pp. 285–303.

44. Kracke, *Force and Persuasion,* p. 41.

45. Rena Lederman, "Big Men, Large and Small? Towards a Comparative Perspective," *Ethnology,* 29 (1990): 3–15.

46. Ernest Brandewie, "The Place of the Big Man in Traditional Hagen Society in the Central Highlands of New Guinea," in Frank McGlynn and Arthur Tuden, eds., *Anthropological Approaches to Political Behavior* (Pittsburgh: University of Pittsburgh Press, 1991), pp. 62–82.

47. Maria Lepowsky, "Big Men, Big Women and Cultural Autonomy," *Ethnology,* 29 (1990): 35–50.

48. Marc Howard Ross, "Political Organization and Political Participation: Exit, Voice, and Loyalty in Preindustrial Societies," *Comparative Politics,* 21 (1988): 73. The discussion in this section draws mostly from ibid., pp. 73–89, and from Marc Howard Ross, "Political Participation," in Carol R. Ember and Melvin Ember, eds., *Cross-Cultural Research for Social Science,* in Carol R. Ember and Melvin Ember, eds., *New Directions in Anthropology* (Upper Saddle River, NJ: Prentice Hall, CD-ROM, 2003).

49. Dmitri Bondarenko and Andrey Korotayev, "Family Size and Community Organization: A Cross-Cultural Comparison," *Cross-Cultural Research,* 34 (2000): 152–89; Andrey Korotayev and Dmitri Bondarenko, "Polygyny and Democracy: A Cross-Cultural Comparison," *Cross-Cultural Research,* 34 (2000): 190–208.

50. For studies of international relations that support these conclusions, see footnotes 2 and 3 in Carol R. Ember, Melvin Ember, and Bruce Russett, "Peace between Participatory Polities: A Cross-Cultural Test of the 'Democracies Rarely Fight Each Other' Hypothesis," *World Politics,* 44 (1992): 573–99; see also chapter 3 in Bruce Russett and John R. Oneal, *Triangulating Peace: Democracy, Interdependence, and International Organizations* (New York: Norton, 2001).

51. Ember, Ember, and Russett, "Peace between Participatory Polities."

52. R. J. Rummel, "Democracies Are Less Warlike Than Other Regimes." At **http://www.hawaii.edu/powerkills/DP95.HTM**, August 2002.

53. Richard Scaglion, "Law and Society," in Ember and Ember, eds., *Cross-Cultural Research for Social Science.*

54. E. Adamson Hoebel, *The Law of Primitive Man* (New York: Atheneum, 1968 [originally published 1954]), p. 4, quoting S. P. Simpson and Ruth Field, "Law and the Social Sciences," *Virginia Law Review,* 32 (1946): 858.

55. Douglas Fry and Kaj Björkqvist, *Cultural Variation in Conflict Resolution: Alternatives to Violence* (Mahwah, NJ: Lawrence Erlbaum Associates, 1997).

56. Donald Black, *The Social Structure of Right and Wrong* (San Diego: Academic Press, 1993), pp. 79–83.

57. Ross, "Political Organization and Political Participation."

58. Franz Boas, *Central Eskimos.* Bureau of American Ethnology Annual Report No. 6 (Washington, DC, 1888), p. 668.

59. Keith F. Otterbein, *The Ultimate Coercive Sanction: A Cross-Cultural Study of Capital Punishment* (New Haven, CT: HRAF Press, 1986), p. 107.

60. Dane Archer and Rosemary Gartner, *Violence and Crime in Cross-National Perspective* (New Haven, CT: Yale University Press, 1984), pp. 118–39.

61. Scaglion, "Law and Society"; Black, *The Social Structure of Right and Wrong,* pp. 83–86.

62. Ibid.

63. E. E. Evans-Pritchard, "The Nuer of the Southern Sudan," in M. Fortes and E. E. Evans-Pritchard, eds., *African Political Systems* (New York: Oxford University Press, 1940), p. 291. The discussion of the Nuer follows this source.

64. Letitia Hickson, "The Social Contexts of Apology in Dispute Settlement: A Cross-Cultural Study," *Ethnology,* 25 (1986): 283–94.

65. Ibid.; and Klaus-Friedrich Koch, Soraya Altorki, Andrew Arno, and Letitia Hickson, "Ritual Reconciliation and the Obviation of Grievances: A Comparative Study in the Ethnography of Law," *Ethnology,* 16 (1977): 279.

66. John M. Roberts, "Oaths, Autonomic Ordeals, and Power," in Clellan S. Ford, ed., *Cross-Cultural Approaches: Readings in Comparative Research* (New Haven, CT: HRAF Press, 1967), p. 169.

67. Alois Musil, *The Manners and Customs of the Rwala Bedouins.* American Geographical Society Oriental Exploration Studies No. 6 (New York, 1928), p. 430, as cited in Roberts, "Oaths, Autonomic Ordeals, and Power," pp. 169–70.

68. Roberts, "Oaths, Autonomic Ordeals, and Power," p. 192.

69. Hoebel, *The Law of Primitive Man,* chapter 9.

70. Richard D. Schwartz, "Social Factors in the Development of Legal Control: A Case Study of Two Israeli Settlements," *Yale Law Journal,* 63 (February 1954): 475.

71. Textor, comp., *A Cross-Cultural Summary.*

72. Wilfred T. Masumura, "Law and Violence: A Cross-Cultural Study," *Journal of Anthropological Research,* 33 (1977): 388–99.

73. Scaglion, "Law and Society"; Black, *The Social Structure of Right and Wrong,* pp. 83–86; Katherine S. Newman, *Law and Economic Organization: A Comparative Study of Preindustrial Societies* (Cambridge, MA: Cambridge University Press, 1983), p. 131.

74. Carol R. Ember and Melvin Ember, "War, Socialization, and Interpersonal Violence: A Cross-Cultural Study," *Journal of Conflict Resolution,* 38 (1994): 620–46.

75. Newman, *Law and Economic Organization,* p. 131.

76. Nicholas J. Gubser, *The Nunamiut Eskimos: Hunters of Caribou* (New Haven, CT: Yale University Press, 1965), p. 151.

77. Keith F. Otterbein and Charlotte Swanson Otterbein, "An Eye for an Eye, a Tooth for a Tooth: A Cross-Cultural Study of Feuding," *American Anthropologist,* 67 (1965): 1476.

78. Douglas R. White, "Rethinking Polygyny: Co-Wives, Codes, and Cultural Systems," *Current Anthropology* (1988): 529–58.

79. Orlando Patterson, *Slavery and Social Death: A Comparative Study* (Cambridge, MA: Harvard University Press, 1982), pp. 345–52.

80. Karl Heider, *The Dugum Dani* (Chicago: Aldine, 1970), pp. 105–11. See also Karl Heider, *Grand Valley Dani: Peaceful Warriors* (New York: Holt, Rinehart & Winston, 1979), pp. 88–99.

81. Melvin Ember and Carol R. Ember, "Cross-Cultural Studies of War and Peace: Recent Achievements and Future Possibilities," in S. P. Reyna and R. E. Downs, eds., *Studying War: Anthropological Perspectives* (New York: Gordon & Breach, 1992), pp. 188–89.

82. Carol R. Ember and Melvin Ember, "Resource Unpredictability, Mistrust, and War: A Cross-Cultural Study," *Journal of Conflict Resolution,* 36 (1992): 242–62. See also Melvin Ember, "Statistical Evidence for an Ecological Explanation of Warfare," *American Anthropologist,* 84 (1982): 645–49. For a discussion of how Dani warfare seems to be motivated mainly by economic considerations, see Paul Shankman, "Culture Contact, Cultural Ecology, and Dani Warfare," *Man,* 26 (1991): 299–321. Bang W. Kang, "A Reconsideration of Population Pressure and Warfare: A Protohistoric Korean Case," *Current Anthropology,* 41 (2000): 878–79, finds a strong correlation between environmental stress and warfare frequency in Korean history.

83. Keith Otterbein, *The Evolution of War* (New Haven, CT: HRAF Press, 1970).

84. Ember and Ember, "Resource Unpredictability, Mistrust, and War." See also Otterbein, *The Evolution of War*; and Colin K. Loftin, "Warfare and Societal Complexity: A Cross-Cultural Study of Organized Fighting in Preindustrial Societies," Ph.D. dissertation, University of North Carolina, Chapel Hill, 1971.

85. Carol R. Ember, "An Evaluation of Alternative Theories of Matrilocal versus Patrilocal Residence," *Behavior Science Research,* 9 (1974): 135–49.

86. Keith F. Otterbein, "Internal War: A Cross-Cultural Study," *American Anthropologist,* 70 (1968): 283. See also Marc H. Ross, "Internal and External Conflict and Violence," *Journal of Conflict Resolution,* 29 (1985): 547–79.

87. William T. Divale and Marvin Harris, "Population, Warfare, and the Male Supremacist Complex," *American Anthropologist,* 78 (1976): 521–38; see also Ann Gibbons, "Warring over Women," *Science,* August 20, 1993, pp. 987–88.

88. Ember and Ember, "Resource Unpredictability, Mistrust, and War," pp. 251–52.

89. Russett and Oneal, *Triangulating Peace,* p. 89.

90. Russett and Oneal, *Triangulating Peace,* pp. 145–48.

91. J. David Singer, "Accounting for International War: The State of the Discipline," *Annual Review of Sociology,* 6 (1980): 349–67.

CHAPTER 25

1. Edward B. Tylor, "Animism" (originally published 1871), in William A. Lessa and Evon Z. Vogt, eds., *Reader in Comparative Religion: An Anthropological Approach,* 4th ed. (New York: Harper & Row, 1979), pp. 9–18.

2. R. R. Marett, *The Threshold of Religion* (London: Methuen, 1909).

3. Stewart Elliott Guthrie, *Faces in the Clouds: A New Theory of Religion* (New York: Oxford University Press, 1993).

4. Sigmund Freud, *Moses and Monotheism,* trans. Katherine Jones (New York: Vintage Books, 1967 [originally published 1939]); Christopher Badcock, *Essential Freud* (Oxford: Blackwell, 1988), pp. 126–27, 133–36.

5. Bronislaw Malinowski, "The Group and the Individual in Functional Analysis," *American Journal of Sociology,* 44 (1939): 959; Bronislaw Malinowski, "Magic, Science, and Reli-

gion," in *Magic, Science, and Religion and Other Essays* (Garden City, NY: Doubleday, 1948), pp. 50–51.

6. William James, *The Varieties of Religious Experience: A Study in Human Nature* (New York: Modern Library, 1902).

7. Carl G. Jung, *Psychology and Religion* (New Haven, CT: Yale University Press, 1938).

8. Erich Fromm, *Psychoanalysis and Religion* (New Haven, CT: Yale University Press, 1950).

9. Abraham H. Maslow, *Religions, Values, and Peak-Experiences* (Columbus: Ohio State University Press, 1964).

10. Émile Durkheim, *The Elementary Forms of the Religious Life*, trans. Joseph W. Swain (New York: Collier Books, 1961 [originally published 1912]).

11. Guy E. Swanson, *The Birth of the Gods: The Origin of Primitive Beliefs* (Ann Arbor: University of Michigan Press, 1969), pp. 1–31.

12. Anthony Wallace, *Religion: An Anthropological View* (New York: Random House, 1966), pp. 60–61.

13. Annemarie De Waal Malefijt, *Religion and Culture: An Introduction to Anthropology of Religion* (New York: Macmillan, 1968), p. 153.

14. Verne F. Ray, *The Sanpoil and Nespelem: Salishan Peoples of Northeastern Washington* (New Haven, CT: HRAF Press, 1954), pp. 172–89.

15. Paul C. Rosenblatt, R. Patricia Walsh, and Douglas A. Jackson, *Grief and Mourning in Cross-Cultural Perspective* (New Haven, CT: HRAF Press, 1976), p. 51.

16. Ibid., p. 55.

17. Swanson, *The Birth of the Gods*, pp. 97–108; see also Dean Sheils, "Toward a Unified Theory of Ancestor Worship: A Cross-Cultural Study," *Social Forces*, 54 (1975): 427–40.

18. John Middleton, "The Cult of the Dead: Ancestors and Ghosts," in William A. Lessa and Evon Z. Vogt, eds., *Reader in Comparative Religion: An Anthropological Approach*, 3rd ed. (New York: Harper & Row, 1971), p. 488.

19. Melford E. Spiro and Roy G. D'Andrade, "A Cross-Cultural Study of Some Supernatural Beliefs," *American Anthropologist*, 60 (1958): 456–66.

20. William W. Lambert, Leigh Minturn Triandis, and Margery Wolf, "Some Correlates of Beliefs in the Malevolence and Benevolence of Supernatural Beings: A Cross-Societal Study," *Journal of Abnormal and Social Psychology*, 58 (1959): 162–69. See also Ronald P. Rohner, *They Love Me, They Love Me Not: A Worldwide Study of the Effects of Parental Acceptance and Rejection* (New Haven, CT: HRAF Press, 1975), p. 108.

21. H. G. Barnett, *Being a Palauan* (New York: Holt, Rinehart & Winston, 1960), pp. 79–85.

22. Swanson, *The Birth of the Gods*, p. 56.

23. Ibid., pp. 55–81; see also William D. Davis, "Societal Complexity and the Nature of Primitive Man's Conception of the Supernatural," Ph.D. dissertation, University of North Carolina, Chapel Hill, 1971. Peter Peregrine, "The Birth of the Gods Revisited: A Partial Replication of Guy Swanson's (1960) Cross-Cultural Study of Religion," *Cross-Cultural Research*, 30 (1996): 84–112, replicated Swanson's finding for North American societies.

24. Robert B. Textor, comp., *A Cross-Cultural Summary* (New Haven, CT: HRAF Press, 1967); see also Ralph Underhill, "Economic and Political Antecedents of Monotheism: A Cross-Cultural Study," *American Journal of Sociology*, 80 (1975): 841–61.

25. Clifford Geertz, "Religion as a Cultural System," in Michael Banton, ed., *Anthropological Approaches to the Study of Religion*. Association of Social Anthropologists of the Commonwealth Monograph No. 3 (New York: Praeger, 1966), pp. 1–46.

26. Swanson, *The Birth of the Gods*, pp. 153–74.

27. Ruth Bunzel, "The Nature of Katcinas," in Lessa and Vogt, eds., *Reader in Comparative Religion*, 3rd ed., pp. 493–95.

28. Gary H. Gossen, "Temporal and Spiritual Equivalents in Chamula Ritual Symbolism," in Lessa and Vogt, eds., *Reader in Comparative Religion*, 4th ed., pp. 116–28.

29. Wallace, *Religion: An Anthropological View*, pp. 52–67.

30. Michael Winkelman, "Trance States: A Theoretical Model and Cross-Cultural Analysis," *Ethos*, 14 (1986): 178–83.

31. Erika Bourguignon, "Introduction: A Framework for the Comparative Study of Altered States of Consciousness," in Erika Bourguignon, *Religion, Altered States of Consciousness, and Social Change* (Columbus: Ohio State University Press, 1973), pp. 3–35.

32. Erika Bourguignon and Thomas L. Evascu, "Altered States of Consciousness within a General Evolutionary Perspective: A Holocultural Analysis," *Behavior Science Research*, 12 (1977): 197–216. See also Winkelman, "Trance States," pp. 196–98.

33. Alice B. Kehoe and Dody H. Giletti, "Women's Preponderance in Possession Cults: The Calcium-Deficiency Hypothesis Extended," *American Anthropologist*, 83 (1981): 549–61.

34. Douglas Raybeck, "Toward More Holistic Explanations: Cross-Cultural Research, and Cross-Level Analysis," *Cross-Cultural Research*, 32 (1998): 123–42, referring to Douglas Raybeck, J. Shoobe, and J. Grauberger, "Women, Stress and Participation in Possession Cults: A Reexamination of the Calcium Deficiency Hypothesis," *Medical Anthropology Quarterly*, 3 (1989): 139–61.

35. Omar Khayyam Moore, "Divination: A New Perspective," *American Anthropologist*, 59 (1957): 69–74.

36. Dean Sheils, "A Comparative Study of Human Sacrifice," *Behavior Science Research*, 15 (1980): 245–62.

37. M. Adler, *Drawing Down the Moon* (Boston: Beacon Press, 1986), p. 418, as referred to in T. M. Luhrmann, *Persuasions of the Witch's Craft: Ritual Magic and Witchcraft in Present-Day England* (Oxford: Blackwell, 1989), pp. 4–5.

38. E. E. Evans-Pritchard, "Witchcraft Explains Unfortunate Events," in Lessa and Vogt, eds., *Reader in Comparative Religion*, 4th ed., pp. 362–66.

39. Swanson, *The Birth of the Gods*, p. 150. See also H. R. Trevor-Roper, "The European Witch-Craze of the Sixteenth and Seventeenth Centuries," in Lessa and Vogt, eds., *Reader in Comparative Religion*, 3rd ed., pp. 444–49.

40. Swanson, *The Birth of the Gods*, pp. 150–51.

41. Linnda R. Caporael, "Ergotism: The Satan Loosed in Salem?" *Science*, April 2, 1976, pp. 21–26; Mary K. Matossian, "Ergot and the Salem Witchcraft Affair," *American Scientist*, 70 (1982): 355–57; and Mary K. Matossian, *Poisons of the Past: Molds, Epidemics, and History* (New Haven, CT: Yale University Press, 1989), pp. 70–80. For possible reasons to dismiss the ergot theory, see Nicholas P. Spanos, "Ergotism and the Salem Witch Panic: A Critical Analysis and an Alternative Conceptualization," *Journal of the History of the Behavioral Sciences*, 19 (1983): 358–69.

42. Michael Harner, "The Role of Hallucinogenic Plants in European Witchcraft," in Michael Harner, ed., *Hallucinogens and Shamanism* (New York: Oxford University Press, 1972), pp. 127–50.

43. Beatrice B. Whiting, *Paiute Sorcery*. Viking Fund Publications in Anthropology No. 15 (New York: Wenner-Gren Foundation, 1950), pp. 36–37. See also Swanson, *The Birth of the Gods*, pp. 137–52, 240–41.

44. Michael James Winkelman, "Magico-Religious Practitioner Types and Socioeconomic Conditions," *Behavior Science Research*, 20 (1986): 17–46.

45. Ibid., pp. 28–29.

46. Michael Harner and Gary Doore, "The Ancient Wisdom in Shamanic Cultures," in Shirley Nicolson, comp., *Shamanism: An Expanded View of Reality* (Wheaton, IL: Theosophical Publishing House, 1987), pp. 3, 8–9; Richard Noll, "The Presence of Spirits in Magic and Madness," in Nicolson, comp.,

Shamanism, p. 49; Stanley Krippner, "Dreams and Shamanism," in Nicolson, comp., *Shamanism*, p. 128.

47. Frederica de Laguna, *Under Mount Saint Elias: The History and Culture of the Yakutat Tlingit* (Washington, DC: Smithsonian Institution Press, 1972), p. 701C, as appearing in the HRAF Collection of Ethnography on the Web, 2000.

48. See Krippner and Noll in Nicolson, comp., *Shamanism*, pp. 126–27 and 49–50, respectively.

49. Winkelman, "Magico-Religious Practitioner Types and Socioeconomic Conditions," pp. 27–28.

50. Ibid., p. 27.

51. Ibid., pp. 35–37.

52. Marvin Harris, "The Cultural Ecology of India's Sacred Cattle," *Current Anthropology*, 7 (1966): 51–63.

53. Wallace, *Religion*, p. 30.

54. Anthony Wallace, *The Death and Rebirth of the Seneca* (New York: Knopf, 1970), p. 239.

55. The Quakers, long-time neighbors and trusted advisers of the Seneca, took pains not to interfere with Seneca religion, principles, and attitudes.

56. Peter Worsley, *The Trumpet Shall Sound: A Study of "Cargo" Cults in Melanesia* (London: MacGibbon & Kee, 1957), p. 12.

57. Ibid., pp. 11, 115.

58. Ibid., p. 122.

59. David Aberle, "A Note on Relative Deprivation Theory as Applied to Millenarian and Other Cult Movements," in Lessa and Vogt, eds., *Reader in Comparative Religion*, 3rd ed., pp. 528–31.

60. Bruce M. Knauft, "Cargo Cults and Relational Separation," *Behavior Science Research*, 13 (1978): 185–240.

CHAPTER 27

1. Ralph Linton, *The Study of Man* (New York: Appleton-Century-Crofts, 1936), p. 306.

2. Ibid., pp. 310–11.

3. Harry R. Silver, "Calculating Risks: The Socioeconomic Foundations of Aesthetic Innovation in an Ashanti Carving Community," *Ethnology*, 20 (1981): 101–14.

4. Patricia M. Greenfield, Ashley E. Maynard, and Carla P. Childs, "History, Culture, Learning, and Development," *Cross-Cultural Research*, 34 (2000): 351–74.

5. Everett M. Rogers, *Diffusion of Innovations*, 3rd ed. (New York: Free Press, 1983), pp. 263–69.

6. Frank Cancian, "Risk and Uncertainty in Agricultural Decision Making," in Peggy F. Barlett, ed., *Agricultural Decision Making: Anthropological Contributions to Rural Development* (New York: Academic Press, 1980), pp. 161–202.

7. Barry S. Hewlett and L. L. Cavalli-Sforza, "Cultural Transmission among Aka Pygmies," *American Anthropologist*, 88 (1986): 922–34; L. L. Cavalli-Sforza and M. W. Feldman, *Cultural Transmission and Evolution: A Quantitative Approach* (Princeton, NJ: Princeton University Press, 1981).

8. Thomas W. Valente, *Network Models of the Diffusion of Innovations* (Cresskill, NJ: Hampton Press, 1995), p. 21.

9. Wesley Cohen, "Empirical Studies of Innovative Activity," in Paul Stoneman, ed., *Handbook of the Economics of Innovation and Technological Change* (Oxford: Blackwell, 1995), pp. 182–264.

10. Linton, *The Study of Man*, pp. 326–27. © 1936, renewed 1964; reprinted by permission of Prentice Hall, Inc.

11. "Printing, Typography, and Photoengraving: History of Prints: Origins in China: Transmission of Paper to Europe (12th Century)," *Britannica Online*, February 1998; "Paper," *Academic American Encyclopedia* (Princeton, NJ: Areté, 1980).

12. Linton, *The Study of Man*, pp. 338–39.

13. George M. Foster, *Traditional Cultures and the Impact of Technological Change* (New York: Harper & Row, 1962), p. 26.

14. John H. Bodley, *Victims of Progress*, 3rd ed. (Mountain View, CA: Mayfield, 1990), p. 7.

15. Pertti J. Pelto and Ludger Müller-Wille, "Snowmobiles: Technological Revolution in the Arctic," in H. Russell Bernard and Pertti J. Pelto, eds., *Technology and Social Change*, 2nd ed. (Prospect Heights, IL: Waveland Press, 1987), pp. 207–43.

16. Bodley, *Victims of Progress*, pp. 38–41.

17. Theodora Kroeber, *Ishi in Two Worlds* (Berkeley: University of California Press, 1967), pp. 45–47.

18. Robert W. Schrauf, "Mother Tongue Maintenance among North American Ethnic Groups," *Cross-Cultural Research*, 33 (1999): 175–92.

19. The historical information we refer to comes from a book by Allan Nevins, *The American States during and after the Revolution* (New York: Macmillan, 1927). For how radical the American Revolution was, see Gordon S. Wood, *The Radicalism of the American Revolution* (New York: Knopf, 1992).

20. Crane Brinton, *The Anatomy of Revolution* (Upper Saddle River, NJ: Prentice Hall, 1938).

21. Jeffrey M. Paige, *Agrarian Revolution: Social Movements and Export Agriculture in the Underdeveloped World* (New York: Free Press, 1975).

22. Eric Abella Roth, "Demise of the Sepaade Tradition: Cultural and Biological Explanations," *American Anthropologist*, 103 (2001): 1014–23.

23. Robert Boyd and Peter J. Richerson, *Culture and the Evolutionary Process* (Chicago: University of Chicago Press, 1985), p. 106.

24. Ibid., p. 135.

25. Donald T. Campbell, "Variation and Selective Retention in Socio-Cultural Evolution," in Herbert Barringer, George Blankstein, and Raymond Mack, eds., *Social Change in Developing Areas: A Re-Interpretation of Evolutionary Theory* (Cambridge, MA: Schenkman, 1965), pp. 19–49. See also Boyd and Richerson, *Culture and the Evolutionary Process*; and William H. Durham, *Coevolution: Genes, Culture and Human Diversity* (Stanford, CA: Stanford University Press, 1991).

26. William H. McNeill, *A World History* (New York: Oxford University Press, 1967), pp. 283–87.

27. See, for example, Daniel R. Gross, George Eiten, Nancy M. Flowers, Francisca M. Leoi, Madeline Lattman Ritter, and Dennis W. Werner, "Ecology and Acculturation among Native Peoples of Central Brazil," *Science*, November 30, 1979, 1043–50.

28. The description of Tikopia is based on Raymond Firth, *Social Change in Tikopia* (New York: Macmillan, 1959), chapters 5, 6, 7, and 9, passim.

29. Most of this discussion is based on Robert F. Murphy and Julian H. Steward, "Tappers and Trappers: Parallel Process in Acculturation," *Economic Development and Cultural Change*, 4 (July 1956): 335–55.

30. S. Brian Burkhalter and Robert F. Murphy, "Tappers and Sappers: Rubber, Gold and Money among the Mundurucú," *American Ethnologist*, 16 (1989): 100–16.

31. Eric Wolf, *Peasants* (Upper Saddle River, NJ: Prentice Hall, 1966), pp. 3–4.

32. E. J. Hobsbawm, *Age of Revolution* (New York: Praeger, 1970).

33. Daniel R. Gross and Barbara A. Underwood, "Technological Change and Caloric Costs: Sisal Agriculture in Northeastern Brazil," *American Anthropologist*, 73 (1971): 725–40.

34. Daniel O. Larson, John R. Johnson, and Joel C. Michaelsen, "Missionization among the Coastal Chumash of Central California: A Study of Risk Minimization Strategies," *American Anthropologist*, 96 (1994): 263–99.

35. Discussion is based on Raymond Firth, *Rank and Religion in Tikopia* (Boston: Beacon Press, 1970).

36. Ibid., p. 387.

37. Ibid., p. 418.

38. Phillip Mason, Prospero's Magic (London: Oxford University Press, 1962).

39. Bruce Russett, with the collaboration of William Antholis, Carol R. Ember, Melvin Ember, and Zeev Maoz, *Grasping the Democratic Peace: Principles for a Post–Cold War World* (Princeton, NJ: Princeton University Press, 1993), pp. 10–11, 14, 138.

40. H. Russell Bernard and Pertti J. Pelto, "Technology and Anthropological Theory: Conclusions," in Bernard and Pelto, eds., *Technology and Social Change*, p. 367.

41. Pelto and Müller-Wille, "Snowmobiles," p. 237.

42. Theodore C. Bestor, "Supply-Side Sushi: Commodity, Market, and the Global City," *American Anthropologist,* 103 (2001): 76.

43. Michel-Rolph Trouillot, "The Anthropology of the State in the Age of Globalization: Close Encounters of the Deceptive Kind," *Current Anthropology,* 42 (2001): 128.

44. E. Paul Durrenberger, "Anthropology and Globalization," *American Anthropologist,* 103 (2001): 531–35; see also Ulf Hannerz, *Transnational Connections: Culture, People, Places* (London: Routledge, 1996).

45. Trouillot, "The Anthropology of the State in the Age of Globalization," p. 128.

46. Keith Bradsher, "Pakistanis Fume as Clothing Sales to U.S. Tumble," *New York Times,* June 23, 2002, p. 3.

47. Daniel Yergin, "Giving Aid to World Trade," *New York Times,* June 27, 2002, p. A29.

48. Ginger Thompson, "Mexico Is Attracting a Better Class of Factory in Its South," *New York Times,* June 29, 2002, p. A3.

49. Somini Sengupta, "Money from Kin Abroad Helps Bengalis Get By," *New York Times,* June 24, 2002, p. A3.

50. Jonathan Hill, "Introduction: Ethnogenesis in the Americas. 1492-1992," in Jonathan D. Hill, ed., *Ethnogenesis in the Americas,* 1492–1992 (Iowa City: University of Iowa Press, 1996), p. 1.

51. Kenneth Bilby, "Ethnogenesis in the Guianas and Jamaica: Two Maroon Cases," in Jonathan D. Hill, ed., *Ethnogenesis in the Americas,* pp. 127–28, referring to the work of Wim Hoogbergen, *The Boni Maroon Wars in Suriname* (Leiden: E. J. Brill), pp. 23–51.

52. Bilby, "Ethnogenesis in the Guianas and Jamaica," pp. 128–37.

53. Richard A. Sattler, "Remnants, Renegades, and Runaways: Seminole Ethnogenesis Reconsidered," in Hill, *Ethnogenesis in the Americas,* p. 42.

54. Ibid., pp. 50–51.

55. Ibid., p. 54.

56. Ibid., pp. 58–59.

57. Conrad Phillip Kottak, "The Media, Development, and Social Change," in Emilio F. Moran, *Transforming Societies, Transforming Anthropology* (Ann Arbor: University of Michigan Press, 1996), pp. 136, 153.

58. Eugeen E. Roosens, *Creating Ethnicity: The Process of Ethnogenesis* (Newbury Park, CA: Sage, 1989), p. 9.

59. Elizabeth Cashdan, "Ethnic Diversity and Its Environmental Determinants: Effects of Climate, Pathogens, and Habitat Diversity," *American Anthropologist,* 103 (2001): 968–91.

60. Carol R. Ember and David Levinson, "The Substantive Contributions of Worldwide Cross-Cultural Studies Using Secondary Data," *Behavior Science Research,* special issue, "Cross-Cultural and Comparative Research: Theory and Method," 25 (1991): 79–140.

BIBLIOGRAPHY

'ABD ALLAH, MAHMUD M. "Siwan Customs." *Harvard African Studies,* 1 (1917): 1–28.

ABERLE, DAVID. "A Note on Relative Deprivation Theory as Applied to Millenarian and Other Cult Movements." In Lessa and Vogt, eds., *Reader in Comparative Religion,* 3rd ed.

ABLER, THOMAS S. "Iroquois: The Tree of Peace and the War Kettle." In M. Ember and Ember, eds., *Portraits of Culture.*

ADAMS, DAVID B. "Why There Are So Few Women Warriors." *Behavior Science Research,* 18 (1983): 196–212.

ADAMS, ROBERT M. "The Origin of Cities." *Scientific American,* September 1960, 153–68.

ADAMS, ROBERT McC. *Heartland of Cities: Surveys of Ancient Settlement and Land Use on the Central Floodplain of the Euphrates.* Chicago: University of Chicago Press, 1981.

ADLER, MORTIMER. *Drawing Down the Moon.* Boston: Beacon, 1986.

ADOVASIO, J. AND PAGE, J. *The First Americans: In Pursuit of Archaeology's Greatest Mystery.* New York: Random House, 2002.

AHERN, EMILY M. "Sacred and Secular Medicine in a Taiwan Village: A Study of Cosmological Disorders." In Arthur Kleinman et al., eds., *Medicine in Chinese Cultures: Comparative Studies of Health Care in Chinese and Other Societies.* Washington, DC: U.S. Department of Health, Education, and Welfare, National Institutes of Health, 1975, as seen in the eHRAF Collection of Ethnography on the Web, 2000.

AIELLO, L. C. "Body Size and Energy Requirements." In Jones, Martin, and Pilbeam, eds., *The Cambridge Encyclopedia of Human Evolution.*

AIELLO, LESLIE. "The Origin of the New World Monkeys." In W. George and R. Lavocat, eds., *The Africa-South America Connection.* Oxford: Clarendon Press, 1993, pp. 100–18.

AIELLO, LESLIE AND MARK COLLARD, "Our Newest Oldest Ancestor?" *Nature* 410 (29 Nov. 2001), pp. 526–527.

AIELLO, LESLIE, AND CHRISTOPHER DEAN. *An Introduction to Human Evolutionary Anatomy.* London: Academic Press, 1990, pp. 268–74.

AITKEN, M. J. *Thermoluminescence Dating.* London: Academic Press, 1985.

AKMAJIAN, ADRIAN, RICHARD A. DEMERS, AND ROBERT M. HARNISH. *Linguistics: An Introduction to Language and Communication.* 2nd ed. Cambridge, MA: MIT Press, 1984.

AKMAJIAN, ADRIAN, RICHARD A. DEMERS, AND ROBERT M. HARNISH. *Linguistics: An Introduction to Language and Communication.* 4th ed. Cambridge, MA: MIT Press, 1995.

AKMAJIAN, ADRIAN, RICHARD A. DEMERS, AND ROBERT M. HARNISH. *Linguistics: An Introduction to Language and Communication,* 5th ed. Cambridge, MA: MIT Press, 2001.

ALBERT, STEVEN M., AND MARIA G. CATTELL. *Old Age in Global Perspective: Cross-Cultural and Cross-National Views.* New York: G. K. Hall/Macmillan, 1994.

ALBERTS, BRUCE, president of the National Academy of Sciences, November 9, 2000, "Setting the Record Straight Regarding Darkness in El Dorado," which can be found at the Web address: http://www4.nationalacademies. org/nas/nashome.nsf

ALBERTS, BRUCE, DENNIS BRAY, JULIAN LEWIS, MARTIN RAFF, KEITH ROBERTS, AND JAMES D. WATSON. *Molecular Biology of the Cell.* New York: Garland, 1983.

ALEXANDER, JOHN P. "Alas, Poor Notharctus." *Natural History,* August 1992, 55–59.

ALGAZE, GUILLERMO. *The Uruk World System: The Dynamics of Expansion of Early Mesopotamian Civilization.* Chicago: University of Chicago Press, 1993.

ALLEN, JOHN S., A. J. LAMBERT, F. Y. ATTAH JOHNSON, K. SCHMIDT, AND K. L. NERO. "Antisaccadic Eye Movements and Attentional Asymmetry in Schizophrenia in Three Pacific Populations." *Acta Psychiatrica Scandinavia,* 94 (1996): 258–65.

ALLEN, JOHN S., AND SUSAN M. CHEER. "The Non-Thrifty Genotype." *Current Anthropology,* 37 (1996): 831–42.

ALROY, JOHN. "A Multispecies Overkill Simulation of the End-Pleistocene Megafaunal Mass Extinction," *Science* 292 (8 Jun 2001): 1893–1896.

ANDERSON, CONNIE M. "The Persistence of Polygyny as an Adaptive Response to Poverty and Oppression in Apartheid South Africa," *Cross-Cultural Research* 34 (2000): 99–112.

ANDERSON, RICHARD L. "Do Other Cultures Have 'Art'?" *American Anthropologist,* 94 (1992): 926–29.

ANDERSON, RICHARD L. *Art in Small-Scale Societies.* 2nd ed. Englewood Cliffs, NJ: Prentice Hall, 1989.

ANDERSON, RICHARD L. *Calliope's Sisters: A Comparative Study of Philosophies of Art.* Englewood Cliffs, NJ: Prentice Hall, 1990.

ANDERSON, SEAN K. and STEPHEN SLOAN. *Historical Dictionary of Terrorism.* 2nd edition. Lanham, Maryland: The Scarecrow Press, 2002.

ANDERSON, WILLIAM L. "Cherokee: The European Impact on the Cherokee Culture," in M. Ember and Ember, eds. *Portraits of Culture: Ethnographic Originals,* in Carol R. Ember and Melvin Ember, eds., *New Directions in Anthropology.*

ANDREWS, ELIZABETH. "Territoriality and Land Use among the Akulmiut of Western Alaska." In Burch and Ellanna, *Key Issues in Hunter-Gatherer Research.*

ANDREWS, PETER, AND CHRISTOPHER STRINGER. *Human Evolution: An Illustrated Guide.* London: British Museum, 1989.

ANDREWS, PETER. "Proconsul." In Tattersall, Delson, and van Couvering, eds., *Encyclopedia of Human Evolution and Prehistory.*

ANDREWS, PETER. "Propliopithecidae." In Tattersall, Delson, and van Couvering, eds., *Encyclopedia of Human Evolution and Prehistory.*

ANGIER, NATALIE. "Why We're So Nice: We're Wired to Cooperate," Science Times in the *New York Times,* Tuesday, July 23, 2002, p. F1 and F8.

ANTHONY, DAVID, DIMITRI Y. TELEGIN, AND DORCAS BROWN. "The Origin of Horseback Riding." *Scientific American,* December 1991, 94–100.

ANYON, ROGER, AND T. J. FERGUSON. "Cultural Resources Management at the Pueblo of Zuni, New Mexico, USA." *Antiquity,* 69 (1995): 913–30.

"Appendix A: Report of the Committee on Ethics, Society for Applied Anthropology." In Fluehr-Lobban, ed., *Ethics and the Profession of Anthropology.*

"Appendix C: Statements on Ethics: Principles of Professional Responsibility, Adopted by the Council of the American Anthropological Association, May 1971." In Fluehr-Lobban, ed., *Ethics and the Profession of Anthropology.*

"Appendix F: Professional and Ethical Responsibilities, SfAA." In Fluehr-Lobban, ed., *Ethics and the Profession of Anthropology.*

"Appendix H: National Association of Practicing Anthropologists' Ethical Guidelines for Practitioners, 1988." In Fluehr-Lobban, ed., *Ethics and the Profession of Anthropology.*

"Appendix I: Revised Principles of Professional Responsibility, 1990." In Fluehr-Lobban, ed., *Ethics and the Profession of Anthropology.*

APTEKAR, LEWIS. "Are Colombian Street Children Neglected? The Contributions of Ethnographic and Ethnohistorical Approaches to the Study of Children." *Anthropology and Education Quarterly,* 22 (1991): 326–49.

APTEKAR, LEWIS. *Environmental Disasters in Global Perspective.* New York: G. K. Hall/Macmillan, 1994.

APTEKAR, LEWIS. *Street Children of Cali.* Durham, NC: Duke University Press, 1988.

ARCHER, DANE, and ROSEMARY GARTNER. *Violence and Crime in Cross-National Perspective.* New Haven, CT: Yale University Press, 1984.

ARDENER, SHIRLEY. "The Comparative Study of Rotating Credit Associations." In Ardener and Burman, *Money-Go-Rounds.*

ARDENER, SHIRLEY. "Women Making Money Go Round: ROSCAs Revisited." In Ardener and Burman, *Money-Go-Rounds.*

ARDENER, SHIRLEY, AND SANDRA BURMAN. *Money-Go-Rounds: The Importance of Rotating Savings and Credit Associations for Women.* Oxford/Washington, DC: Berg, 1995.

ARGYLE, MICHAEL. *The Psychology of Social Class.* New York: Routledge, 1994.

ARMELAGOS, GEORGE J., AND ALAN H. GOODMAN. "Race, Racism, and Anthropology." In Goodman and Leatherman, eds., *Building a New Biocultural Synthesis: Political-Economic Perspectives on Human Biology.*

ARMSTRONG, ROBERT P. *The Powers of Presence.* Philadelphia: University of Pennsylvania Press, 1981.

ARONOFF, JOEL, ANDREW M. BARCLAY, AND LINDA A. STEVENSON. "The Recognition of Threatening Facial Stimuli." *Journal of Personality and Social Psychology,* 54 (1988): 647–55.

ARONOFF, JOEL, BARBARA A. WOIKE, AND LESTER M. HYMAN. "Which Are the Stimuli in Facial Displays of Anger and Happiness? Configurational Bases of Emotion Recognition." *Journal of Personality and Social Psychology,* 62 (1992): 1050–66.

ASCH, NANCY B., AND DAVID L. ASCH. "The Economic Potential of *Iva annua* and Its Prehistoric Importance in the Lower Illinois Valley." In Ford, ed., *The Nature and Status of Ethno-botany.*

ASCH, SOLOMON. "Studies of Independence and Conformity: A Minority of One against a Unanimous Majority." *Psychological Monographs,* 70 (1956): 1–70.

ASCHER, ROBERT. "Analogy in Archaeological Interpretation." *Southwestern Journal of Anthropology,* 17 (1961): 317–25.

ASFAW, BERHANE, TIM WHITE, OWEN LOVEJOY, BRUCE LATIMER, SCOTT SIMPSON, AND GLEN SUWA. "*Australopithecus garhi:* A New Species of Early Hominid from Ethiopia." *Science,* 284 (1999): 629–36.

ASHTON, HUGH. *The Basuto.* 2nd ed. London: Oxford University Press, 1967.

"Association Business: Clyde Snow, Forensic Anthropologist, Works for Justice." *Anthropology News,* October 2000, 12.

AUSTIN, LEWIS. "Visual Symbols, Political Ideology, and Culture." *Ethos,* 5 (1977): 306–25.

AYALA, FRANCISCO J. "The Myth of Eve: Molecular Biology and Human Origins." *Science,* December 22, 1995, 1930–936.

AYALA, FRANCISCO J. Communication in *Science,* November 29, 1996, 1354.

AYRES, BARBARA C. "Effects of Infant Carrying Practices on Rhythm in Music." *Ethos,* 1 (1973): 387–404.

AYRES, BARBARA C. "Effects of Infantile Stimulation on Musical Behavior." In Lomax, ed., *Folk Song Style and Culture.*

BACHNIK, JANE M. "The Two 'Faces' of Self and Society in Japan." *Ethos* (1992): 3–32.

BACON, MARGARET, IRVIN L. CHILD, AND HERBERT BARRY III. "A Cross-Cultural Study of Correlates of Crime." *Journal of Abnormal and Social Psychology,* 66 (1963): 291–300.

BADCOCK, C. R. *Evolutionary Psychology: A Critical Introduction.* (Cambridge: Blackwell, 2000).

BADCOCK, CHRISTOPHER. *Essential Freud.* Oxford: Blackwell, 1988.

BAER, HANS A., MERRILL SINGER, AND IDA SUSSER. *Medical Anthropology and the World System: A Critical Perspective.* Westport, CT: Bergin & Garvey, 1997.

BAHN, PAUL. "Neanderthals Emancipated." *Nature,* 394 (1998): 719–20.

BAHN, PAUL. *Archaeology: A Very Short Introduction.* New York: Oxford University Press, 1996.

BAHN, PAUL, AND J. VERTUT. *Images of the Ice Age.* New York: Facts on File, 1988.

BAILEY, ROBERT C., GENEVIEVE HEAD, MARK JENIKE, BRUCE OWEN, ROBERT RECTMAN, AND ELZBIETA ZECHENTER. "Hunting and Gathering in Tropical Rain Forest: Is It Possible?" *American Anthropologist,* 91 (1989): 59–82.

BALDI, PHILIP. *An Introduction to the Indo-European Languages.* Carbondale: Southern Illinois University Press, 1983.

BALIKCI, ASEN. *The Netsilik Eskimo.* Garden City, NY: Natural History Press, 1970.

BALTER, MICHAEL, AND ANN GIBBONS. "A Glimpse of Humans' First Journey Out of Africa." *Science,* 288 (2000): 948–50.

BALTER, MICHAEL. "In Search of the First Europeans," *Science,* 291 (2001): 1722–25.

BANTON, MICHAEL, ED. *Anthropological Approaches to the Study of Religion.* Association of Social Anthropologists of the Commonwealth, Monograph No. 3. New York: Praeger, 1966.

BARAK, GREGG. *Gimme Shelter: A Social History of Homelessness in Contemporary America.* New York: Praeger, 1991.

BARASH, DAVID P. *Sociobiology and Behavior.* New York: Elsevier, 1977.

BARBER, NIGEL. "The Sex Ratio as a Predictor of Cross-National Variation in Violent Crime," *Cross-Cultural Research,* 34 (2000): 264–282.

BARINAGA, MARIA. "Priming the Brain's Language Pump." *Science,* January 31, 1992, 535.

BARLETT, PEGGY F. "Industrial Agriculture." In Plattner, ed., *Economic Anthropology.*

BARLETT, PEGGY F., ED. *Agricultural Decision Making: Anthropological Contributions to Rural Development.* New York: Academic Press, 1980.

BARNARD, ALAN. *History and Theory in Anthropology.* Cambridge, UK: Cambridge University Press, 2000.

BARNETT, H. G. *Being a Palauan.* New York: Holt, Rinehart & Winston, 1960.

BARNOUW, VICTOR. *Culture and Personality.* 4th ed. Homewood, IL: Dorsey Press, 1985.

BARRETT, D. E. "Malnutrition and Child Behavior: Conceptualization, Assessment and an Empirical Study of Social-Emotional Functioning." In J. Brozek and B. Schürch, eds., *Malnutrition and Behavior: Critical Assessment of Key Issues.* Lausanne, Switzerland: Nestlé Foundation, 1984, pp. 280–306.

BARRETT, STANLEY R. *Paradise: Class, Commuters, and Ethnicity in Rural Ontario.* Toronto: University of Toronto Press, 1994.

BARRINGER, HERBERT, GEORGE BLANKSTEIN, AND RAYMOND MACK, EDS. *Social Change in Developing Areas: A Re-Interpretation of Evolutionary Theory.* Cambridge, MA: Schenkman, 1965.

BARRY, HERBERT III, IRVIN L. CHILD, AND MARGARET K. BACON. "Relation of Child Training to Subsistence Economy." *American Anthropologist,* 61 (1959): 51–63.

BARTH, FREDRIK. "Enduring and Emerging Issues in the Analysis of Ethnicity." In Vermeulen and Govers, eds., *The Anthropology of Ethnicity.*

BARTH, FREDRIK. *Normads of South Persia.* Oslo: Universitetsforlaget 1964; Boston: Little, Brown, 1968.

BATES, DANIEL G., AND SUSAN H. LEES, EDS. *Case Studies in Human Ecology.* New York: Plenum, 1996.

BATES, E. and V. A. MARCHMAN, "What Is and Is Not Universal in Language Acquisition." In F. Plum, ed. *Language, Communication, and the Brain.* New York: Raven Press, 1988, pp. 19–38.

BAUMAN, RICHARD, ED. *Folklore, Cultural Performances, and Popular Entertainments: A Communications-Centered Handbook.* New York: Oxford University Press, 1992.

BAUMAN, RICHARD. "Folklore." In Bauman, ed., *Folklore, Cultural Performances, and Popular Entertainments.*

BAUMAN, RICHARD, AND JOEL SHERZER. *Explorations in the Ethnography of Speaking.* 2nd ed. New York: Cambridge University Press, 1989.

BAXTER, ELLEN, AND KIM HOPPER. *Private Lives/Public Spaces: Homeless Adults on the Streets of New York City.* New York: Community Service Society of New York, 1981.

BEADLE, GEORGE, AND MURIEL BEADLE. *The Language of Life.* Garden City, NY: Doubleday, 1966.

BEARDER, SIMON K. "Lorises, Bushbabies, and Tarsiers: Diverse Societies in Solitary Foragers." In Smuts et al., eds., *Primate Societies.*

BEATTIE, JOHN. *Bunyoro: An African Kingdom.* New York: Holt, Rinehart & Winston, 1960.

BEGLER, ELSIE B. "Sex, Status, and Authority in Egalitarian Society." *American Anthropologist,* 80 (1978): 571–88.

BEGUN, DAVID. "Miocene Apes." In Peregrine, Ember, and Ember, eds., *Physical Anthropology.*

BELLMAN, BERYL L. *The Language of Secrecy: Symbols and Metaphors in Poro Ritual.* New Brunswick, NJ: Rutgers University Press, 1984.

BENEDICT, RUTH. *Patterns of Culture.* New York: Mentor, 1959. (Originally published 1934).

BENJAMIN, LOIS. *The Black Elite: Facing the Color Line in the Twilight of the Twentieth Century.* Chicago: Nelson-Hall, 1991.

BERG, PAUL, AND MAXINE SINGER. *Dealing with Genes: The Language of Heredity.* Mill Valley, CA: University Science Books, 1992.

BERGGREN, WILLIAM A., DENNIS V. KENT, JOHN D. OBRADOVICH, AND CARL C. SWISHER III. "Toward a Revised Paleogene Geochronology." In Prothero and Berggren, eds., *Eocene-Oliocene Climatic and Biotic Evolution.*

BERLIN, BRENT. *Ethnobiological Classification: Principles of Categorization of Plants and Animals in Traditional Societies.* Princeton, NJ: Princeton University Press, 1992.

BERLIN, BRENT, AND PAUL KAY. *Basic Color Terms: Their Universality and Evolution.* Berkeley: University of California Press, 1969.

BERLIN, E. A. "General Overview of Maya Ethnomedicine." In Berlin and Berlin, *Medical Ethnobiology of the Highland Maya of Chiapas,* Mexico, pp. 52–53.

BERLIN, ELOIS ANN, AND BRENT BERLIN. *Medical Ethnobiology of the Highland Maya of Chiapas, Mexico: The Gastrointestinal Diseases.* Princeton, NJ: Princeton University Press, 1996.

BERNARD, H. RUSSELL. *Research Methods in Cultural Anthropology: Qualitative and Quantitative Approaches.* 3rd ed. Walnut Creek, CA: AltaMira Press, 2002.

BERNARD, H. RUSSELL. *Research Methods in Cultural Anthropology: Qualitative and Quantitative Approaches,* 2nd ed. Walnut Creek, CA: AltaMira Press, 2001.

BERNARD, H. RUSSELL, AND PERTTI J. PELTO, EDS. *Technology and Social Change.* 2nd ed. Prospect Heights, IL: Waveland, 1987.

BERNARD, H. RUSSELL, AND PERTTI J. PELTO. "Technology and Anthropological Theory: Conclusions." In Bernard and Pelto, eds., *Technology and Social Change,* 2nd ed.

BERNARDI, B. "The Age-System of the Nilo-Hamitic Peoples." *Africa,* 22 (1952): 316–32.

BERREMAN, GERALD D. "Caste in India and the United States." *American Journal of Sociology,* 66 (1960): 120–27.

BERREMAN, GERALD D. "Race, Caste and Other Invidious Distinctions in Social Stratification." *Race,* 13 (1972): 403–14.

BERREMAN, GERALD D. *Caste in the Modern World.* Morristown, NJ: General Learning Press, 1973.

BERRY, JOHN W. "Ecological and Cultural Factors in Spatial Perceptual Development." *Canadian Journal of Behavioural Science,* 3 (1971): 324–36.

BERRY, JOHN W. *Human Ecology and Cognitive Style.* New York: Wiley, 1976.

BERRY, JOHN W., AND J. BENNETT. "Syllabic Literacy and Cognitive Performance among the Cree." *International Journal of Psychology,* 24 (1989): 429–50.

BERRY, JOHN W., YPE H. POORTINGA, MARSHALL H. SEGALL, AND PIERRE R. DASEN. *Cross-Cultural Psychology: Research and Applications.* New York: Cambridge University Press, 1992.

BESTOR, THEODORE C. "Supply-Side Sushi: Commodity, Market, and the Global City," *American Anthropologist,* 103 (2001): 76–95.

BETZIG, LAURA. "Redistribution: Equity or Exploitation?" In Laura Betzig, Monique Borgerhoff Multer, and Paul Turke, eds., *Human Reproductive Behavior.* Cambridge: Cambridge University Press, 1988, pp. 49–63.

BICKERTON, DEREK. "Creole Languages." *Scientific American,* July 1983, 116–22.

BILBY, KENNETH. "Ethnogenesis in the Guianas and Jamaica: Two Maroon Cases." In Hill, ed., *Ethnogenesis in the Americas,* pp. 119–41.

BILSBOROUGH, ALAN. *Human Evolution.* New York: Blackie Academic & Professional, 1992.

BINDON, JAMES R., AMY KNIGHT, WILLIAM W. DRESSLER, AND DOUGLAS E. CREWS. "Social Context and Psychosocial Influences on Blood Pressure among American Samoans." *American Journal of Physical Anthropology,* 103 (1997): 7–18.

BINDON, JAMES R., AND DOUGLAS E. CREWS. "Changes in Some Health Status Characteristics of American Samoan Men: Preliminary Observations from a 12-Year Follow-up Study." *American Journal of Human Biology,* 5 (1993): 31–37.

BINFORD, LEWIS R. "Interassemblage Variability: The Mousterian and the 'Functional' Argument." In Renfrew, ed., *The Explanation of Culture Change.*

BINFORD, LEWIS R. "Mobility, Housing, and Environment: A Comparative Study." *Journal of Anthropological Research,* 46 (1990): 119–52.

BINFORD, LEWIS R. "Post-Pleistocene Adaptations." In Struever, ed., *Prehistoric Agriculture.*

BINFORD, LEWIS R. "Were There Elephant Hunters at Torralba?" In Nitecki and Nitecki, eds., *The Evolution of Human Hunting.*

BINFORD, LEWIS R. *Faunal Remains from Klasies River Mouth.* Orlando, FL: Academic Press, 1984.

BINFORD, LEWIS R., AND CHUAN KUN HO. "Taphonomy at a Distance: Zhoukoudian, 'The Cave Home of Beijing Man'?" *Current Anthropology,* 26 (1985): 413–42.

BINFORD, SALLY R., AND LEWIS R. BINFORD. "Stone Tools and Human Behavior." *Scientific American,* April 1969, 70–84.

BISHOP, W. A., AND J. A. MILLER, EDS. *Calibration of Hominid Evolution.* Toronto: University of Toronto Press, 1972.

BLACK, DONALD. *The Social Structure of Right and Wrong.* San Diego: Academic Press, 1993.

BLACK, FRANCIS L. "Why Did They Die?" *Science,* December 11, 1992, 1739–40.

BLALOCK, HUBERT M., JR. *Social Statistics.* 2nd ed. New York: McGraw-Hill, 1972.

BLANTON, RICHARD E. "The Rise of Cities." In Sabloff, ed., *Supplement to the Handbook of Middle American Indians,* Vol. 1.

BLANTON, RICHARD E. "Variation in Economy." In C. R. Ember and Ember, eds., *Cross-Cultural Research for Social Science.*

BLANTON, RICHARD. "The Origins of Monte Albán." In Cleland, ed., *Cultural Continuity and Change.*

BLANTON, RICHARD. *Monte Albán: Settlement Patterns at the Ancient Zapotec Capital.* New York: Academic Press, 1978.

BLANTON, RICHARD E., PETER N. PEREGRINE, DEBORAH WINSLOW, AND THOMAS D. HALL, EDS. *Economic Analysis beyond the Local System.* Lanham, MD: University Press of America, 1997.

BLANTON, RICHARD E., STEPHEN A. KOWALEWSKI, GARY FEINMAN, AND JILL APPEL. *Ancient Mesoamerica: A Comparison of Change in Three Regions.* New York: Cambridge University Press, 1981.

BLANTON, RICHARD E., STEPHEN A. KOWALEWSKI, GARY M. FEINMAN, AND LAURA M. FINSTEN. *Ancient Mesoamerica: A Comparison of Change in Three Regions.* 2nd ed. Cambridge: Cambridge University Press, 1993.

BLEDSOE, CAROLINE H. *Women and Marriage in Kpelle Society.* Stanford, CA: Stanford University Press, 1980.

BLOCK, JEAN L. "Help! They've All Moved Back Home!" *Woman's Day,* April 26, 1983, 72–76.

BLOCK, JONATHAN I. AND DOUG M. BOYER, "Grasping Primate Origins," *Science* 298 (22 Nov. 2002), pp. 1606– 1610.

BLOUNT, BEN G. "The Development of Language in Children." In Munroe, Munroe, and Whiting, eds., *Handbook of Cross-Cultural Human Development.*

BLOUNT, BEN G., ED. *Language, Culture, and Society; A Book of Readings.* 2nd ed. Prospect Heights, IL: Waveland, 1995.

BLUMENSCHINE, ROBERT J. et al., "Late Pliocene Homo and Hominid Land use from Western Olduvai Gorge, Tanzania," *Science* 299 (21 Feb. 2003), pp. 1217–1221.

BLUMLER, MARK A., AND ROGER BYRNE. "The Ecological Genetics of Domestication and the Origins of Agriculture." *Current Anthropology,* 32 (1991): 23–35.

BOAS, FRANZ. "On Grammatical Categories." In Hymes, ed., *Language in Culture and Society.* (Originally published 1911.)

BOAS, FRANZ. "The Religion of the Kwakiutl." *Columbia University Contributions to Anthropology,* Vol. 10, pt. 2. New York: Columbia University, 1930.

BOAS, FRANZ. *Central Eskimos.* Bureau of American Ethnology Annual Report No. 6. Washington, DC, 1888.

BOAZ, N. T., AND A. J. ALMQUIST. *Biological Anthropology: A Synthetic Approach to Human Evolution.* Upper Saddle River, NJ: Prentice Hall, 1997.

BOAZ, NOEL T., AND ALAN J. ALMQUIST. *Essentials of Biological Anthropology.* Upper Saddle River, NJ: Prentice Hall, 1999.

BOAZ, NOEL. T., and ALAN J. ALMQUIST. *Biological Anthropology: A Synthetic Approach to Human Evolution.* 2nd ed. Upper Saddle River, NJ: Prentice Hall, 2001.

BODINE, JOHN J. "Taos Pueblo: Maintaining Tradition," in M. Ember and Ember, *Portraits of Culture: Ethnographic Originals,* in C. R. Ember and Melvin Ember, eds., *New Directions in Anthropology.*

BODLEY, J. H. *Victims of Progress.* 4th ed. Mountain View, CA: Mayfield, 1998.

BODLEY, JOHN H. *Anthropology and Contemporary Human Problems,* 4th ed. New York: McGraw Hill, 2000.

BODLEY, JOHN H. *Victims of Progress.* 3rd ed. Mountain View, CA: Mayfield, 1990.

BOEHM, CHRISTOPHER. "Egalitarian Behavior and Reverse Dominance Hierarchy." *Current Anthropology,* 34 (1993): 230–31.

BOEHM, CHRISTOPHER. *Hierarchy in the Forest: The Evolution of Egalitarian Behavior.* Cambridge, MA: Harvard University Press, 1999.

BOESCHE, C, et al., "Is Nut Cracking in Wild Chimpanzees a Cultural Behavior?" *Journal of Human Evolution* 26 (1994): 325–338.

BOGIN, BARRY. *Patterns of Human Growth.* Cambridge: Cambridge University Press, 1988.

BOGORAS, WALDEMAR. "The Chukchee." Pt. 3. *Memoirs of the American Museum of Natural History,* 2 (1909).

BOHANNAN, LAURA, AND PAUL BOHANNAN. *The Tiv of Central Nigeria.* London: International African Institute, 1953.

BOHANNAN, PAUL. "The Migration and Expansion of the Tiv." *Africa,* 24 (1954): 2–16.

BOHANNAN, PAUL, AND JOHN MIDDLETON, EDS. *Marriage, Family and Residence.* Garden City, NY: Natural History Press, 1968.

BOLLEN, KENNETH A. "Liberal Democracy: Validity and Method Factors in Cross-National Measures." *American Journal of Political Science,* 37 (1993): 1207–30.

BOLTON, RALPH. "Aggression and Hypoglycemia among the Qolla: A Study in Psychobiological Anthropology." *Ethnology,* 12 (1973): 227–57.

BOLTON, RALPH. "AIDS AND Promiscuity: Muddled in the Models of HIV Prevention." *Medical Anthropology,* 14 (1992): 145–223.

BOLTON, RALPH. "Introduction: The AIDS Pandemic, a Global Emergency." *Medical Anthropology,* 10 (1989): 93–104.

BONDARENKO, DMITRI AND ANDREY KOROTAYEV, "Family Size and Community Organization: A Cross-Cultural Comparison." *Cross-Cultural Research,* 34 (2000): 152–189.

BORCHERT, CATHERINE, AND ADRIENNE ZIHLMAN. "The Ontogeny and Phylogeny of Symbolizing." In M. LeC. Foster and L. J. Botsharow. *The Life of Symbols.* Boulder, CO: Westview, 1990, pp. 15–44.

BORDAZ, JACQUES. *Tools of the Old and New Stone Age.* Garden City, NY: Natural History Press, 1970.

BORDES, FRANÇOIS. "Mousterian Cultures in France." *Science,* September 22, 1961, 803–10.

BORDES, FRANÇOIS. *The Old Stone Age.* New York: McGraw-Hill, 1968, pp. 51–97.

BORGERHOFF MULDER, MONIQUE, MARGARET GEORGE-CRAMER, JASON ESHLEMAN, AND ALESSIA ORTOLANI, "A Study of East African Kinship and Marriage Using a Phylogenetically Based Comparative Method," *American Anthropologist* 103 (2001): 1059–1082.

BORNSTEIN, MARC H. "The Psychophysiological Component of Cultural Difference in Color Naming and Illusion Susceptibility." *Behavior Science Notes,* 8 (1973): 41–101.

BORTEI-DOKU, ELLEN, AND ERNEST ARYEETEY. "Mobilizing Cash for Business: Women in Rotating Susu Clubs in Ghana." In Ardener and Burman, *Money-Go-Rounds.*

BOSERUP, ESTER. *The Conditions of Agricultural Growth: The Economics of Agrarian Change under Population Pressure.* Toronto: Earthscan Publishers, 1993 (orig. 1965).

BOSERUP, ESTER. *Woman's Role in Economic Development.* New York: St. Martin's, 1970.

BOURGUIGNON, ERIKA. *Religion, Altered States of Consciousness, and Social Change.* Columbus: Ohio State University Press, 1973.

BOURGUIGNON, ERIKA. "Introduction: A Framework for the Comparative Study of Altered States of Consciousness." In Bourguignon, *Religion, Altered States of Consciousness, and Social Change.*

BOURGUIGNON, ERIKA, AND THOMAS L. EVASCU. "Altered States of Consciousness within a General Evolutionary Perspective: A Holocultural Analysis." *Behavior Science Research,* 12 (1977): 197–216.

BOWEN, GABRIEL J. et al., "Mammalian Dispersal at the Paleocene/Eocene Boundary," *Science* 295 (15 Mar 2002), pp. 2062–2064.

BOYD, ROBERT, AND JOAN SILK. *How Humans Evolved.* 2nd ed. New York: Norton, 2000.

BOYD, ROBERT, AND PETER J. RICHERSON. "Group Selection among Alternative Evolutionarily Stable Strategies." *Journal of Theoretical Biology,* 145 (1990): 331–42.

BOYD, ROBERT, AND PETER J. RICHERSON. *Culture and the Evolutionary Process.* Chicago: University of Chicago Press, 1996. Originally published 1985.

BRACE, C. LORING. "A Four-Letter Word Called Race." In Larry T. Reynolds and Leonard Leiberman, eds., *Race and Other Misadventures: Essays in Honor of Ashley Montague in His Ninetieth Year.* New York: General Hall, 1996.

BRACE, C. LORING, DAVID P. TRACER, LUCIA ALLEN YAROCH, JOHN ROBB, KARI BRANDT, AND A. RUSSELL NELSON. "Clines and Clusters versus 'Race': A Test in Ancient Egypt and the Case of a Death on the Nile." *Yearbook of Physical Anthropology,* 36 (1993): 1–31.

BRADLEY, CANDICE. "Keeping the Soil in Good Heart: Weeding, Women and Ecofeminism." In Warren, ed., *Ecofeminism.*

BRADLEY, CANDICE. "The Sexual Division of Labor and the Value of Children." *Behavior Science Research,* 19 (1984–1985): 159–85.

BRADSHER, KEITH, "Pakistanis Fume as Clothing Sales to U.S. Tumble," *New York Times,* June 23, 2002, p. 3.

BRAIDWOOD, ROBERT J. "The Agricultural Revolution." *Scientific American,* September 1960, 130–48.

BRAIDWOOD, ROBERT J., AND GORDON R. WILLEY, EDS. *Courses toward Urban Life: Archaeological Considerations of Some Cultural Alternatives.* Viking Fund Publications in Anthropology No. 32. Chicago: Aldine, 1962.

BRAIDWOOD, ROBERT J., AND GORDON R. WILLEY. "Conclusions and Afterthoughts." In Braidwood and Willey, eds., *Courses Toward Urban Life.*

BRAIN, C. K., AND A. SILLEN. "Evidence from the Swartkrans Cave for the Earliest Use of Fire." *Nature,* December 1, 1988, 464–66.

BRANDA, RICHARD F., AND JOHN W. EATON. "Skin Color and Nutrient Photolysis: An Evolutionary Hypothesis." *Science,* August 18, 1978, 625–26.

BRANDEWIE, ERNEST. "The Place of the Big Man in Traditional Hagen Society in the Central Highlands of New Guinea." In McGlynn and Tuden, eds., *Anthropological Approaches to Political Behavior.*

BRANDON, GEORGE. "African-Americans: Getting into the Spirit." In M. Ember and Ember, eds., *Portraits of Culture.*

BRANDON, ROBERT N. *Adaptation and Environment.* Princeton, NJ: Princeton University Press, 1990.

BRÄUER, GÜNTER. "A Craniological Approach to the Origin of Anatomically Modern Homo sapiens in Africa and Implications for the Appearance of Modern Europeans." In F. Smith and Spencer, eds., *The Origins of Modern Humans.*

BRAUN, DAVID P., AND STEPHEN PLOG. "Evolution of 'Tribal' Social Networks: Theory and Prehistoric North American Evidence." *American Antiquity,* 47 (1982): 504–25.

BRETTELL, CAROLINE B., AND CAROLYN F. SARGENT, eds. *Gender in Cross-Cultural Perspective,* 3rd edition. Upper Saddle River, NJ: Prentice Hall, 2000.

BRIGGS, JEAN L. "Eskimo Women: Makers of Men." In Matthiasson, *Many Sisters: Women in Cross-Cultural Perspective.*

BRINGA, TONE. *Being Muslim the Bosnian Way: Identity and Community in a Central Bosnian Village.* Princeton, NJ: Princeton University Press, 1995, as examined in the eHRAF Collection of Ethnography on the Web.

BRINTON, CRANE. *The Anatomy of Revolution.* Englewood Cliffs, NJ: Prentice Hall, 1938.

BRITTAIN, JOHN A. *Inheritance and the Inequality of Material Wealth.* Washington, DC: Brookings Institution, 1978.

BRODY, JANE E. "Effects of Milk on Blacks Noted." *New York Times,* October 15, 1971, p. 15.

BROMAGE, TIMOTHY G. "Paleoanthropology and Life History, and Life History of a Paleoanthropologist." In Peregrine, Ember, and Ember eds., *Physical Anthropology.*

BROMAGE, TIMOTHY G., AND M. CHRISTOPHER DEAN. "Reevaluation of the Age at Death of Immature Fossil Hominids." *Nature,* October 10, 1985, 525–27.

BROOKS, ALISON S., FATIMAH LINDA COLLIER JACKSON, AND R. RICHARD GRINKER. "Race and Ethnicity in America." *Anthro Notes* (National Museum of Natural History Bulletin for Teachers), 15, no. 3 (Fall 1993): 1–3, 11–15.

BROOM, ROBERT. *Finding the Missing Link.* London: Watts, 1950.

BROTHWELL, DON, AND ERIC HIGGS, EDS. *Science in Archaeology.* New York: Basic Books, 1963.

BROUDE, GWEN J. "Cross-Cultural Patterning of Some Sexual Attitudes and Practices." *Behavior Science Research,* 11 (1976): 227–62.

BROUDE, GWEN J. "Extramarital Sex Norms in Cross-Cultural Perspective." *Behavior Science Research,* 15 (1980): 181–218.

BROUDE, GWEN J. "Variations in Sexual Attitudes, Norms, and Practices." In C. R. Ember and Ember, eds., *Cross-Cultural Research for Social Science.*

BROUDE, GWEN J., AND SARAH J. GREENE. "Cross-Cultural Codes on Twenty Sexual Attitudes and Practices." *Ethnology,* 15 (1976): 409–29.

BROWN, CECIL H. "Folk Botanical Life-Forms: Their Universality and Growth." *American Anthropologist,* 79 (1977): 317–42.

BROWN, CECIL H. "Folk Zoological Life-Forms: Their Universality and Growth." *American Anthropologist,* 81 (1979): 791–817.

BROWN, CECIL H. "World View and Lexical Uniformities." *Reviews in Anthropology,* 11 (1984): 99–112.

BROWN, CECIL H., AND STANLEY R. WITKOWSKI. "Language Universals." Appendix B in Levinson and Malone, eds., *Toward Explaining Human Culture.*

BROWN, DONALD E. *Human Universals.* Philadelphia: Temple University Press, 1991.

BROWN, FRANK H. "Geochronometry." In Tattersall, Delson, and van Couvering, eds., *Encyclopedia of Human Evolution and Prehistory.*

BROWN, FRANK H. "Methods of Dating." In Jones, Martin, and Pilbeam, eds., *The Cambridge Encyclopedia of Human Evolution.*

BROWN, JAMES A. "Long-Term Trends to Sedentism and the Emergence of Complexity in the American Midwest." In Price and Brown, eds., *Prehistoric Hunter-Gatherers,* pp. 201–31.

BROWN, JAMES A. "Summary." In J. L. Phillips and J. A. Brown, eds., *Archaic Hunters and Gatherers in the American Midwest.* New York: Academic Press, 1983, pp. 5–10.

BROWN, JAMES A., AND T. DOUGLAS PRICE. "Complex Hunter-Gatherers: Retrospect and Prospect." In Price and Brown, *Prehistoric Hunter-Gatherers.*

BROWN, JUDITH K. "A Note on the Division of Labor by Sex." *American Anthropologist,* 72 (1970): 1073–78.

BROWN, JUDITH K. "Economic Organization and the Position of Women among the Iroquois." *Ethnohistory,* 17 (1970): 151–67.

BROWN, PETER J. "Culture and the Evolution of Obesity." In Podolefsky and Brown, eds., *Applying Cultural Anthropology.*

BROWN, ROGER. "The First Sentence of Child and Chimpanzee." In Sebeok and Umiker-Sebeok, eds., *Speaking of Apes.*

BROWN, ROGER. *Social Psychology.* New York: Free Press, 1965.

BROWN, ROGER, AND MARGUERITE FORD. "Address in American English." *Journal of Abnormal and Social Psychology,* 62 (1961): 375–85.

BROWNER, C. H. "Criteria for Selecting Herbal Remedies." *Ethnology,* 24 (1985): 13–32.

BRUMFIEL, ELIZABETH M. "Distinguished Lecture in Archeology: Breaking and Entering the Ecosystem—Gender, Class, and

Faction Steal the Show." *American Anthropologist,* 94 (1992): 551–67.

BRUMFIEL, ELIZABETH M. "Origins of Social Inequality," in C. R. Ember, Ember, and Peregrine, eds., *Research Frontiers in Anthropology,* in C. R. Ember and Ember, eds., *New Directions in Anthropology.*

BRUMFIEL, ELIZABETH M. "Origins of Social Inequality." In C. R. Ember, Ember, and Peregrine, *Research Frontiers in Anthropology,* reprinted in Peregrine, Ember, and Ember, eds., *Archaeology.*

BRUMFIEL, ELIZABETH M. "Regional Growth in the Eastern Valley of Mexico: A Test of the 'Population Pressure' Hypothesis." In Flannery, ed., *The Early Mesoamerican Village.*

BRUMFIEL, ELIZABETH M., ED. *The Economic Anthropology of the State.* Lanham, MD: University Press of America, 1994.

BRUMFIEL, ELIZABETH. "Aztec State Making: Ecology, Structure, and the Origin of the State." *American Anthropologist,* 85 (1983): 261–84.

BRUNET, MICHEL, et al., "A New Hominid from the Upper Miocene of Chad, Central Africa," *Nature* 418 (11 Jul 2002), pp. 145–151.

BRUNVAND, JAN HAROLD. *The Baby Train: And Other Lusty Urban Legends.* New York: Norton, 1993.

BRYANT, CAROL A., AND DORAINE F. C. BAILEY. "The Use of Focus Group Research in Program Development." In van Willigen and Finan, eds., *Soundings.*

BRYNE, RICHARD, AND ANDREW WHITEN, EDS. *Machiavellian Intelligence: Social Expertise and the Evolution of Intellect in Monkeys, Apes, and Humans.* Oxford: Clarendon Press, 1988.

BUDIANSKY, STEPHEN. *The Covenant of the Wild: Why Animals Chose Domestication.* New York: Morrow, 1992.

BUETTNER-JANUSCH, JOHN. *Physical Anthropology: A Perspective.* New York: Wiley, 1973.

BUNZEL, RUTH. "The Nature of Katcinas." In Lessa and Vogt, eds., *Reader in Comparative Religion,* 3rd ed.

BURBANK, VICTORIA K. "Adolescent Socialization and Initiation Ceremonies." In C. R. Ember and Ember, eds., *Cross-Cultural Research for Social Science.*

BURBANK, VICTORIA K. "Australian Aborigines: An Adolescent Mother and Her Family." In M. Ember, Ember, and Levinson, eds., *Portraits of Culture.*

BURBANK, VICTORIA K. *Fighting Women: Anger and Aggression in Aboriginal Australia.* Berkeley: University of California Press, 1994.

BURCH, ERNEST S., JR. "North Alaskan Eskimos: A Changing Way of Life." In M. Ember and Ember, eds., *Portraits of Culture.*

BURCH, ERNEST S., JR. *The Eskimos.* Norman: University of Oklahoma Press, 1988.

BURCH, ERNEST S., JR., AND LINDA J. ELLANNA. *Key Issues in Hunter-Gatherer Research.* Oxford: Berg, 1994.

BURENHULT, G., ED. *Old World Civilizations: The Rise of Cities and States.* St. Lucia, Queensland, Australia: University of Queensland Press, 1994.

BURKHALTER, S. BRIAN, AND ROBERT F. MURPHY. "Tappers and Sappers: Rubber, Gold and Money among the Mundurucú." *American Ethnologist,* 16 (1989): 100–16.

BURLING, ROBBINS. "Motivation, Conventionalization, and Arbitrariness in the Origin of Language," in King, ed. The Origins of Language, pp. 307–350.

BURNS, ALISA, AND CATH SCOTT. *Mother-Headed Families and Why They Have Increased.* Hillsdale, NJ: Lawrence Erlbaum Associates, 1994.

BURTON, ROGER V., AND JOHN W. M. WHITING. "The Absent Father and Cross-Sex Identity." *Merrill-Palmer Quarterly of Behavior and Development,* 7, no. 2 (1961): 85–95.

BUSBY, ANNETTE. "Kurds: A Culture Straddling National Borders." In M. Ember and Ember, eds., *Portraits of Culture.*

BUTZER, KARL W. "Geomorphology and Sediment Stratigraphy." In Singer and Wymer, *The Middle Stone Age at Klasies River Mouth in South Africa.*

BYRNE, BRYAN. "Access to Subsistence Resources and the Sexual Division of Labor among Potters." *Cross-Cultural Research,* 28 (1994): 225–50.

BYRNE, ROGER. "Climatic Change and the Origins of Agriculture." In Manzanilla, ed., *Studies in the Neolithic and Urban Revolutions.*

CALVIN, WILLIAM H. *The Throwing Madonna: Essays on the Brain.* New York: McGraw-Hill, 1983.

CAMPBELL, ALLAN M. "Microbes: The Laboratory and the Field." In Davis, ed., *The Genetic Revolution.*

CAMPBELL, BERNARD G. *Humankind Emerging.* 4th ed. Boston: Little, Brown, 1985.

CAMPBELL, DONALD T. "Variation and Selective Retention in Socio-Cultural Evolution." In Barringer, Blankstein, and Mack, eds., *Social Change in Developing Areas.*

CAMPBELL, JOSEPH. *The Hero with a Thousand Faces.* New York: Pantheon, 1949.

CANCIAN, FRANK. "Risk and Uncertainty in Agricultural Decision Making." In Barlett, ed., *Agricultural Decision Making.*

CANN, REBECCA. "DNA and Human Origins." *Annual Review of Anthropology,* 17 (1988): 127–43.

CANN, REBECCA, M. STONEKING, AND A. C. WILSON. "Mitochondrial DNA and Human Evolution." *Nature,* 325 (1987): 31–36.

CAPORAEL, LINNDA R. "Ergotism: The Satan Loosed in Salem?" *Science,* April 2, 1976, 21–26.

CARCOPINO, JEROME. *Daily Life in Ancient Rome: The People and the City at the Height of the Empire.* Edited with bibliography and notes by Henry T. Rowell. Translated from the French by E. O. Lorimer. New Haven, CT: Yale University Press, 1940.

CARNEIRO, ROBERT L. "A Theory of the Origin of the State." *Science,* August 21, 1970, 733–38.

CARNEIRO, ROBERT L. "Chiefdom-Level Warfare as Exemplified in Fiji and the Cauca Valley." In Haas, ed., *The Anthropology of War.*

CARNEIRO, ROBERT L. "Political Expansion as an Expression of the Principle of Competitive Exclusion." In R. Cohen and Service, eds., *Origins of the State.*

CARNEIRO, ROBERT L. "Slash-and-Burn Cultivation among the Kuikuru and Its Implications for Settlement Patterns." In Y. Cohen, ed., *Man in Adaptation.*

CARNEIRO, ROBERT L. "The Circumscription Theory: Challenge and Response." *American Behavioral Scientist,* 31 (1988): 497–511.

CARPENTER, C. R. "A Field Study in Siam of the Behavior and Social Relations of the Gibbon (Hylobates lar)." *Comparative Psychology Monographs,* 16, no. 5 (1940): 1–212.

CARPENTER, SANDRA. "Effects of Cultural Tightness and Collectivism on Self-Concept and Causal Attributions," *Cross-Cultural Research,* 34 (2000): 38–56.

CARRASCO, PEDRO. "The Civil-Religious Hierarchy in Mesoamerican Communities: Pre-Spanish Background and Colonial Development." *American Anthropologist,* 63 (1961): 483–97.

CARRIER, JAMES G. "Marine Tenure and Conservation in Papua New Guinea." In McCay and Acheson, eds., *The Question of the Commons.*

CARRIER, JOSEPH, AND RALPH BOLTON. "Anthropological Perspectives on Sexuality and HIV Prevention." *Annual Review of Sex Research,* 2 (1991): 49–75.

CARROLL, JOHN B., ED. *Language, Thought, and Reality: Selected Writings of Benjamin Lee Whorf.* New York: Wiley, 1956.

CARROLL, MICHAEL. "A New Look at Freud on Myth." *Ethos*, 7 (1979): 189–205.

CARTMILL, MATT. "Explaining Primate Origins." In Peregrine, Ember, and Ember, eds., *Physical Anthropology*.

CARTMILL, MATT. "New Views on Primate Origins." *Evolutionary Anthropology*, 1 (1992): 105–11.

CARTMILL, MATT. "Non-Human Primates." In Jones, Martin, and Pilbeam, eds., *The Cambridge Encyclopedia of Human Evolution*.

CARTMILL, MATT. "Rethinking Primate Origins," *Science*, April 26, 1974, 436–37.

CASHDAN, ELIZABETH A. "Egalitarianism among Hunters and Gatherers." *American Anthropologist*, 82 (1980): 116–20.

CASHDAN, ELIZABETH, ED. *Risk and Uncertainty in Tribal and Peasant Economies*. Boulder, CO: Westview, 1990.

CASHDAN, ELIZABETH. "Ethnic Diversity and Its Environmental Determinants: Effects of Climate, Pathogens, and Habitat Diversity." *American Anthropologist*, 103: 968–991.

CATTELL, MARIA G., AND STEVEN M. ALBERT. "Caring for the Elderly." In C. R. Ember, Ember, and Peregrine, *Research Frontiers in Anthropology*.

CAULKINS, D. DOUGLAS. "Norwegians: Cooperative Individualists." In M. Ember and Ember, eds., *Portraits of Culture*.

CAVALLI-SFORZA, L. L., AND M. W. FELDMAN. *Cultural Transmission and Evolution: A Quantitative Approach*. Princeton, NJ: Princeton University Press, 1981.

CAVALLI-SFORZA, L. LUCA AND MARCUS W. FELDMAN, "The Application of Molecular Genetic Approaches to the Study of Human Evolution." *Nature Genetics Supplement 33* (2003): 266–275.

CAWS, PETER. "The Structure of Discovery." *Science*, December 12, 1969, 1375–80.

CERNEA, MICHAEL M., ED. *Putting People First: Sociological Variables in Development*. 2nd ed. New York: Oxford University Press, 1991.

CHAFETZ, JANET SALTZMAN. *Gender Equity: An Integrated Theory of Stability and Change*. Sage Library of Social Research No. 176. Newbury Park, CA: Sage, 1990.

CHAGNON, NAPOLEON, AND WILLIAM IRONS, EDS. *Evolutionary Biology and Human Social Behavior: An Anthropological Perspective*. North Scituate, MA: Duxbury, 1979.

CHAGNON, NAPOLEON. *Yanomamö: The Fierce People*. 3rd ed. New York: CBS College Publishing, 1983.

CHAMBERS, ERVE. *Applied Anthropology: A Practical Guide*. Rev. ed. Prospect Heights, IL: Waveland, 1989.

CHANG, K. C. "In Search of China's Beginnings: New Light on an Old Civilization." *American Scientist*, 69 (1981): 148–60.

CHANG, KWANG-CHIH. "The Beginnings of Agriculture in the Far East." *Antiquity*, 44, no. 175 (September 1970): 175–85.

CHANG, KWANG-CHIH. *Archaeology of Ancient China*. 4th ed. New Haven, CT: Yale University Press, 1986, pp. 234–94.

CHANG, KWANG-CHIH. *The Archaeology of Ancient China*. New Haven, CT: Yale University Press, 1968.

CHAPMAN, JEFFERSON. *Tellico Archaeology*. Knoxville: Tennessee Valley Authority, 1985.

CHARD, CHESTER S. *Man in Prehistory*. New York: McGraw-Hill, 1969.

CHARLES-DOMINIQUE, PIERRE. *Ecology and Behaviour of Nocturnal Primates*. Trans. R. D. Martin. New York: Columbia University Press, 1977.

CHARNAIS, PETER. "Economic Factors in the Decline of the Roman Empire." *Journal of Economic History*, 13 (1953): 412–24.

CHASE, PHILIP AND HAROLD DIBBLE, "Middle Paleolithic Symbolism: A Review of Current Evidence and Interpretations," *Journal of Anthropological Archaeology* 6 (1987): 263–269.

CHATTERJEE, SANKAR, *The Rise of Birds: 225 Million Years of Evolution*. (Baltimore, Johns Hopkins, 1997)

CHATTY, DAWN. *Mobile Pastoralists: Development Planning and Social Change in Oman*. New York: Columbia University Press, 1996.

CHAUCER, GEOFFREY. *The Prologue to the Canterbury Tales, the Knights Tale, the Nonnes Prestes Tale*. Ed. Mark H. Liddell. New York: Macmillan, 1926.

CHAYANOV, ALEXANDER V. *The Theory of Peasant Economy*, eds. Daniel Thorner, Basile Kerblay, and R. E. F. Smith. Homewood, IL: Richard D. Irwin, 1966.

CHEN, F. C., AND W. H. LI. "Genomic Divergences between Humans and Other Hominoids and the Effective Population Size of the Common Ancestor of Humans and Chimpanzees." *American Journal of Human Genetics*, 68 (2001): 445–56.

CHENEY, DOROTHY, AND ROBERT SEYFARTH. *How Monkeys See the World*. Chicago: University of Chicago Press, 1990.

CHENEY, DOROTHY, L., AND RICHARD W. WRANGHAM. "Predation." In Smuts et al., eds., *Primate Societies*.

CHIA, L. *The Story of Peking Man: From Archaeology to Mystery*. Oxford: Oxford University Press, 1990.

CHIBNIK, MICHAEL. "The Economic Effects of Household Demography: A Cross-Cultural Assessment of Chayanov's Theory." In MacLachlan, ed., *Household Economies and Their Transformations*.

CHIBNIK, MICHAEL. "The Evolution of Cultural Rules." *Journal of Anthropological Research*, 37 (1981): 256–68.

CHIBNIK, MICHAEL. "The Statistical Behavior Approach: The Choice between Wage Labor and Cash Cropping in Rural Belize." In Barlett, ed., *Agricultural Decision Making*.

CHICK, GARRY. "Games in Culture Revisited: A Replication and Extension of Roberts, Arth, and Bush (1959)," *Cross-Cultural Research*, 32 (1998): 185–206.

CHILD, ALICE B., AND IRVIN L. CHILD. *Religion and Magic in the Life of Traditional Peoples*. Englewood Cliffs, NJ: Prentice Hall, 1993.

CHILDE, V. GORDON. "The Urban Revolution." *Town Planning Review*, 21 (1950): 3–17.

"Children as Victims." *Juvenile Justice Bulletin*. 1999 National Report Series. Washington, DC: U.S. Department of Justice, May 2000.

CHIRAS, D. D. *Human Biology: Health, Homeostasis, and the Environment*, 4th ed. Boston: Jones and Bartlett, 2002.

CHIVERS, DAVID J., ED. *Malayan Forest Primates: Ten Years' Study in Tropical Rain Forest*. New York: Plenum, 1980.

CHIVERS, DAVID JOHN. *The Siamang in Malaya*. Basel, Switzerland: Karger, 1974.

CHIVERS, DAVID J., BERNARD A. WOOD, AND ALAN BILSBOROUGH, EDS. *Food Acquisition and Processing in Primates*. New York: Plenum, 1984.

CHOMSKY, NOAM. *Reflections on Language*. New York: Pantheon, 1975.

CHRISTENSEN, PIA, JENNY HOCKEY, and ALLISON JAMES, "Talk, Silence and the Material World: Patterns of Indirect Communication among Agricultural Farmers in Northern England," in Joy Hendry and C. W. Watson, eds. *An Anthropology of Indirect Communication* (London: Routledge, 2001), pp. 68–82.

CIOCHON, RUSSELL, JOHN OLSEN, AND JAMIE JAMES. *Other Origins: The Search for the Giant Ape in Human Prehistory*. New York: Bantam, 1990.

CIOCHON, RUSSELL L., AND DENNIS A. ETLER. "Reinterpreting Past Primate Diversity." In Corruccini and Ciochon, eds., *Integrative Paths to the Past*.

CIOCHON, RUSSELL L., AND JOHN G. FLEAGLE, EDS. *The Human Evolution Source Book*. Englewood Cliffs, NJ: Prentice Hall, 1993.

CIOCHON, RUSSELL L., AND ROBERT S. CORRUCCINI, EDS. *New Interpretations of Ape and Human Ancestry*. New York: Plenum, 1983.

CLAASSEN, CHERYL. "Gender and Archaeology." In Peregrine, Ember, and Ember, eds., *Archaeology*.

CLAASSEN, CHERYL. "Gender, Shellfishing, and the Shell Mound Archaic." In Gero and Conkey, eds., *Engendering Archaeology.*

CLARK, GEOFFREY A., ED. *Perspectives on the Past: Theoretical Biases in Mediterranean Hunter-Gatherer Research.* Philadelphia: University of Pennsylvania Press, 1991.

CLARK, GRAHAME. *The Earlier Stone Age Settlement of Scandinavia.* Cambridge: Cambridge University Press, 1975.

CLARK, GRAHAME, AND STUART PIGGOTT. *Prehistoric Societies.* New York: Knopf, 1965.

CLARK, J. DESMOND. "Interpretations of Prehistoric Technology from Ancient Egyptian and Other Sources. Pt. II: Prehistoric Arrow Forms in Africa as Shown by Surviving Examples of the Traditional Arrows of the San Bushmen." *Paleorient,* 3 (1977): 127–50.

CLARK, J. DESMOND. *The Prehistory of Africa.* New York: Praeger, 1970.

CLARK, W. E. LEGROS. *The Fossil Evidence for Human Evolution.* Chicago: University of Chicago Press, 1964, p. 184.

CLARKE, RONALD J., AND P. V. TOBIAS. "Sterkfontein Member 2 Foot Bones of the Oldest South African Hominid." *Science,* 269 (1995): 521–24.

CLAYMAN, CHARLES B., ED. *American Medical Association Encyclopedia of Medicine.* New York: Random House, 1989, pp. 857–58.

CLELAND, C., ED. *Cultural Continuity and Change.* New York: Academic Press, 1976.

CLIFFORD, JAMES. "Introduction: Partial Truths." In James Clifford and George E. Marcus, eds. *Writing Culture: The Poetics and Politics of Ethnography.* Berkeley: University of California Press, 1986.

CLIFTON, JAMES H., ED. *Introduction to Cultural Anthropology.* Boston: Houghton Mifflin, 1968.

CLUTTON-BROCK, JULIET. "Dog." In Mason, *Evolution of Domesticated Animals.*

CLUTTON-BROCK, JULIET. "Domestication of Animals." In Jones, Martin, and Pilbeam, eds., *The Cambridge Encyclopedia of Human Evolution.*

CLUTTON-BROCK, JULIET. "Origins of the Dog: Domestication and Early History." In James Serpell, ed., *The Domestic Dog: Its Evolution, Behaviour, and Interactions with People.* Cambridge: Cambridge University Press, 1995, pp. 8–20.

CLUTTON-BROCK, T. H., AND PAUL H. HARVEY. "Primate Ecology and Social Organization." *Journal of Zoology,* London, 183 (1977): 1–39.

CLUTTON-BROCK, T. H., AND PAUL H. HARVEY. "Primates, Brains and Ecology." *Journal of Zoology,* London, 190 (1980): 309–23.

COALE, ANSLEY J. "The History of the Human Population." *Scientific American,* 1974.

COE, MICHAEL D. *The Maya.* New York: Praeger, 1966.

COHEN, ALEX. "A Cross-Cultural Study of the Effects of Environmental Unpredictability on Aggression in Folktales." *American Anthropologist,* 92 (1990): 474–79.

COHEN, ALEX. *The Mental Health of Indigenous Peoples: An International Overview.* Geneva: Department of Mental Health, World Health Organization, 1999.

COHEN, ALEX, AND PAUL KOEGEL. "Homelessness." In C. R. Ember, Ember, and Peregrine, eds., *Research Frontiers in Anthropology.*

COHEN, MARK N. "Population Pressure and the Origins of Agriculture." In Reed, ed., *Origins of Agriculture.*

COHEN, MARK N. "The Significance of Long-Term Changes in Human Diet and Food Economy." In Harris and Ross, eds., *Food and Evolution.*

COHEN, MARK N. "Were Early Agriculturalists Less Healthy Than Food Collectors?" In Peregrine, Ember, and Ember, eds., *Archaeology.*

COHEN, MARK N. *The Food Crisis in Prehistory: Overpopulation and the Origins of Agriculture.* New Haven, CT: Yale University Press, 1977.

COHEN, MARK NATHAN. *Culture of Intolerance: Chauvinism, Class, and Racism in the United States.* New Haven, CT: Yale University Press, 1998.

COHEN, MARK NATHAN. *Health and the Rise of Civilization.* New Haven, CT: Yale University Press, 1989.

COHEN, MARK NATHAN, AND GEORGE J. ARMELAGOS, EDS. *Paleopathology at the Origins of Agriculture.* Orlando, FL: Academic Press, 1984.

COHEN, MARK NATHAN, AND GEORGE J. ARMELAGOS. "Paleopathology at the Origins of Agriculture: Editors' Summation." In M. N. Cohen and Armelagos, eds., *Paleopathology at the Origins of Agriculture.*

COHEN, MYRON L. *House United, House Divided: The Chinese Family in Taiwan.* New York: Columbia University Press, 1976.

COHEN, MYRON. "Developmental Process in the Chinese Domestic Group." In Maurice Freedman, ed., *Family and Kinship in Chinese Society.* Stanford, CA: Stanford University Press, 1970.

COHEN, RONALD. "Introduction." In R. Cohen and Toland, eds., *State Formation and Political Legitimacy.* Vol. 6.

COHEN, RONALD, AND ELMAN R. SERVICE, EDS. *Origins of the State: The Anthropology of Political Evolution.* Philadelphia: Institute for the Study of Human Issues, 1978.

COHEN, RONALD, AND JUDITH D. TOLAND, EDS. *State Formation and Political Legitimacy.* Vol. 1: *Political Anthropology.* New Brunswick, NJ: Transaction Books, 1988.

COHEN, RONALD, AND JUDITH D. TOLAND, EDS. *State Formation and Political Legitimacy.* Vol. 6: *Political Anthropology.* New Brunswick, NJ: Transaction Books, 1988.

COHEN, WESLEY. "Empirical Studies of Innovative Activity." In Paul Stoneman, ed., *Handbook of the Economics of Innovation and Technological Change.* Oxford: Blackwell, 1995.

COHEN, YEHUDI, ED. *Man in Adaptation: The Cultural Present.* Chicago: Aldine, 1968.

COHMAP PERSONNEL. "Climatic Changes of the Last 18,000 Years." *Science,* 241 (1988): 1043–52.

COLLIER, STEPHEN, AND J. PETER WHITE. "Get Them Young? Age and Sex Inferences on Animal Domestication in Archaeology." *American Antiquity,* 41 (1976): 96–102.

COLLINS, DESMOND. "Later Hunters in Europe," in Desmond Collins, ed., *The Origins of Europe* (New York: Thomas Y. Crowell, 1976).

COLLINS, DESMOND. "Later Hunters in Europe." In Collins, ed., *The Origins of Europe.*

CONNAH, GRAHAM. *African Civilizations: Precolonial Cities and States in Tropical Africa, an Archaeological Perspective.* Cambridge: Cambridge University Press, 1987.

CONROY, GLENN C. *Primate Evolution.* New York: Norton, 1990.

CONROY, GLENN C. *Reconstructing Human Origins: A Modern Synthesis.* New York: W. W. Norton, 1997.

COOPER, RICHARD S., CHARLES N. ROTIMI, AND RYK WARD. "The Puzzle of Hypertension in African-Americans." *Scientific American,* February 1999, 56–63.

COREIL, JEANNINE. "Lessons from a Community Study of Oral Rehydration Therapy in Haiti." In van Willigen, Rylko-Bauer, and McElroy, eds., *Making Our Research Useful.*

CORRUCCINI, ROBERT S., AND RUSSELL L. CIOCHON, EDS. *Integrative Paths to the Past: Paleoanthropological Advances in Honor of F. Clark Howell.* Englewood Cliffs, NJ: Prentice Hall, 1994.

COSTIN, CATHY LYNNE. "Cloth Production and Gender Relations in the Inka Empire." In Peregrine, Ember, and Ember, eds., *Archaeology.*

COULT, ALLAN D., AND ROBERT W. HABENSTEIN. *Cross Tabulations of Murdock's World Ethnographic Sample.* Columbia: University of Missouri Press, 1965.

COWAN, C. WESLEY, AND PATTY JO WATSON, EDS. *The Origins of Agriculture*. Washington, DC: Smithsonian Institution Press, 1992.

CRAWFORD, GARY W. "Prehistoric Plant Domestication in East Asia." In Cowan and Watson, eds., *The Origins of Agriculture*.

CRAWFORD, R. D. "Turkey." In Mason, ed., *Evolution of Domesticated Animals*.

CREED, GERALD W. "Bulgaria: Anthropological Corrections to Cold War Stereotypes." In M. Ember and Ember, eds., *Portraits of Culture*.

CROCKETT, CAROLYN, AND JOHN F. EISENBERG. "Howlers: Variations in Group Size and Demography." In Smuts et al., eds., *Primate Societies*.

"Cross-Cultural and Comparative Research: Theory and Method." *Behavior Science Research*, 25 (1991): 1–270.

CRYSTAL, DAVID. *Linguistics*. Middlesex, England: Penguin, 1971.

CULOTTA, ELIZABETH. "New Hominid Crowds the Field." *Science*, August 18, 1995.

CURTIN, PHILIP D. *Cross-Cultural Trade in World History*. Cambridge: Cambridge University Press, 1984.

CUTRIGHT, PHILLIPS. "Inequality: A Cross-National Analysis." *American Sociological Review*, 32 (1967): 562–78.

DAHLBERG, FRANCES, ED. *Woman the Gatherer*. New Haven, CT: Yale University Press, 1981.

DALTON, GEORGE, ED. *Tribal and Peasant Economies: Readings in Economic Anthropology*. Garden City, NY: Natural History Press, 1967.

DALY, MARTIN, AND MARGO WILSON. *Homicide*. New York: Aldine, 1988.

DAMON, ALBERT, ED. *Physiological Anthropology*. New York: Oxford University Press, 1975.

DANIEL, I. RANDOLPH. "Early Eastern Archaic." In P. N. Peregrine and M. Ember, eds., *Encyclopedia of Prehistory*. Vol. 6: North America (Kluwer Academic/Plenum, 2001).

DART, RAYMOND. "*Australopithecus africanus*: The Man-Ape of South Africa." *Nature*, 115 (1925): 195.

DARWIN, CHARLES. "The Origin of Species." (Originally published 1859.) In Young, ed., *Evolution of Man*.

DASEN, PIERRE R., AND ALASTAIR HERON. "Cross-Cultural Tests of Piaget's Theory." In Triandis and Heron, eds., *Handbook of Cross-Cultural Psychology*. Vol. 4: *Developmental Psychology*.

DASEN, PIERRE R., JOHN W. BERRY, AND N. SARTORIUS, EDS. *Health and Cross-Cultural Psychology: Toward Applications*. Newbury Park, CA: Sage, 1988.

DAVENPORT, WILLIAM. "Nonunilinear Descent and Descent Groups." *American Anthropologist*, 61 (1959): 557–72.

DAVIS, BERNARD D. "Summary and Comments: The Scientific Chapters." In Davis, ed., *The Genetic Revolution*.

DAVIS, BERNARD D. "The Issues: Prospects versus Perceptions." In Davis, ed., *The Genetic Revolution*.

DAVIS, BERNARD D., ED. *The Genetic Revolution: Scientific Prospects and Public Perceptions*. Baltimore: Johns Hopkins University Press, 1991.

DAVIS, DEBORAH, AND STEVAN HARRELL, EDS. *Chinese Families in the Post-Mao Era*. Berkeley: University of California Press, 1993.

DAVIS, SUSAN SCHAEFER. "Morocco: Adolescents in a Small Town." In M. Ember, Ember, and Levinson, eds., *Portraits of Culture*.

DAVIS, SUSAN SCHAEFER. "Rebellious Teens? A Moroccan Instance." Paper presented at MESA, November 1993.

DAVIS, WILLIAM D. "Societal Complexity and the Nature of Primitive Man's Conception of the Supernatural." Ph.D. dissertation. University of North Carolina, Chapel Hill, 1971.

DAWSON, ALISTAIR. *Ice Age Earth*. London: Routledge, 1992, pp. 24–71.

DAWSON, J. L. M. "Cultural and Physiological Influences upon Spatial-Perceptual Processes in West Africa." *International Journal of Psychology*, 2 (1967): 115–28, 171–85.

DAY, MICHAEL. *Guide to Fossil Man*. 4th ed. Chicago: University of Chicago Press, 1986.

DE LAGUNA, FREDERICA. *Under Mount Saint Elias: The History and Culture of the Yakutat Tlingit*. Washington, DC: Smithsonian Institution Press, 1972, as seen in the eHRAF Collection of Ethnography on the Web, 2000.

DE LUMLEY, HENRY. "A Paleolithic Camp at Nice." *Scientific American*, May 1969, 42–50.

DE MUNCK, VICTOR C. and ANDREY KOROTAYEV, "Sexual Equality and Romantic Love: A Reanalysis of Rosenblatt's Study on the Function of Romantic Love," *Cross-Cultural Research*, 33 (1999): 265–273.

DE MUNCK, VICTOR C., and ELISA J. SOBO, eds. *Using Methods in the Field: A Practical Introduction and Casebook*. Walnut Creek, CA: AltaMira Press, 1998.

DE VILLIERS, PETER A., AND JILL G. DE VILLIERS. *Early Language*. Cambridge, MA: Harvard University Press, 1979.

DE VITA, PHILIP, AND JAMES D. ARMSTRONG. *Distant Mirrors: America as a Foreign Culture*, 3rd ed. Belmont, CA: Wadsworth, 2001.

DE WAAL, FRANS, AND FRANS LANTING. *Bonobo: The Forgotten Ape*. Berkeley: University of California Press, 1997.

DE WAAL, FRANS. *The Ape and the Sushi Master: Cultural Reflections of a Primatologist*. New York: Basic Books, 2001.

DEACON, TERRENCE. "Primate Brains and Senses." In Jones, Martin, and Pilbeam, eds., *The Cambridge Encyclopedia of Human Evolution*.

DEACON, TERRENCE. *The Symbolic Species: The Co-Evolution of Language and the Brain*. New York: Norton, 1997.

DELSON, ERIC, ED. *Ancestors: The Hard Evidence*. New York: Alan R. Liss, 1985.

DENNY, J. PETER. "The 'Extendedness' Variable in Classifier Semantics: Universal Features and Cultural Variation." In Mathiot, ed., *Ethnolinguistics*.

DENTAN, ROBERT K. *The Semai: A Nonviolent People of Malaya*. New York: Holt, Rinehart & Winston, 1968.

DEUTSCH, A., ED. *Sex Habits of American Men*. Englewood Cliffs, NJ: Prentice Hall, 1948.

DEVILLERS, CHARLES, AND JEAN CHALINE. *Evolution: An Evolving Theory*. New York: Springer Verlag, 1993.

DEVORE, IRVEN, AND MELVIN J. KONNER. "Infancy in Hunter-Gatherer Life: An Ethological Perspective." In N. F. White, ed., *Ethology and Psychiatry*.

DIAMOND, JARED. "Location, Location, Location: The First Farmers." *Science*, November 14, 1997, 1243–244.

DIAMOND, JARED. "The Accidental Conqueror." *Discover*, December 1989, 71–76.

DIAMOND, JARED. "The Saltshaker's Curse—Physiological Adaptations That Helped American Blacks Survive Slavery May Now Be Predisposing Their Descendants to Hypertension." *Natural History*, October 1991.

DIAMOND, JARED. "Who Are the Jews?" *Natural History*, November 1993, 12–19.

DIAMOND, JARED. *Guns, Germs, and Steel*. New York: Norton, 1997, pp. 205–207.

DIAMOND, NORMA. "Collectivization, Kinship, and the Status of Women in Rural China." In Reiter, *Toward an Anthropology of Women*.

DIAMOND, STANLEY. *In Search of the Primitive: A Critique of Civilization*. New Brunswick, NJ: Transaction Books, 1974.

DIBBLE, H. L., AND P. MELLARS, EDS. *The Middle Paleolithic: Adaptation, Behavior, and Variability*. Philadelphia: University Museum, 1992.

DIBBLE, HAROLD P. CHASE, S. MCPHERRON, AND A. TUFFREAU. "Testing the Reality of a 'Living Floor' with Archaeological Data." *American Antiquity*, 62 (1997): 629–51.

Dickson, D. Bruce. *The Dawn of Belief.* Tucson: University of Arizona Press, 1990, pp. 42–44.

Dillehay, Thomas. *The Settlement of the Americas.* New York: Basic Books, 2000.

Dirks, Robert. "Hunger and Famine." In C. R. Ember, Ember, and Peregrine, eds., *Research Frontiers in Anthropology.* Vol. 3.

Dirks, Robert. "Starvation and Famine." *Cross-Cultural Research,* 27 (1993): 28–69.

Divale, William T. "Migration, External Warfare, and Matrilocal Residence." *Behavior Science Research,* 9 (1974): 75–133.

Divale, William T., and Marvin Harris. "Population, Warfare, and the Male Supremacist Complex." *American Anthropologist,* 78 (1976): 521–38.

Divale, William, and Clifford Zipin. "Hunting and the Development of Sign Language: A Cross-Cultural Test." *Journal of Anthropological Research,* 33 (1977): 185–201.

Dobres, Marcia-Anne. "Venus Figurines." In B. Fagan, ed., *Oxford Companion to Archaeology.* Oxford: Oxford University Press, 1998, pp. 740–41.

Dobzhansky, Theodosius. *Mankind Evolving: The Evolution of the Human Species.* New Haven, CT: Yale University Press, 1962.

Dohlinow, Phyllis Jay, ed., *Primate Patterns* (New York: Holt, Rinehart & Winston, 1972).

Dohlinow, Phyllis Jay, and Naomi Bishop. "The Development of Motor Skills and Social Relationships among Primates through Play." In Phyllis Jay Dohlinow, ed., *Primate Patterns.* New York: Holt, Rinehart & Winston, 1972.

Donaldson, Peter. *Worlds Apart: The Economic Gulf between Nations.* London: British Broadcasting Corporation, 1971.

Dow, James W. "Sierra Otomí: People of the Mexican Mountains." In M. Ember and Ember, eds., *Portraits of Culture.*

Dow, James. *The Shaman's Touch: Otomi Indian Symbolic Healing.* Salt Lake City: University of Utah Press, 1986.

Dowling, John H. "Property Relations and Productive Strategies in Pastoral Societies." *American Ethnologist,* 2 (1975): 419–26.

Doyle, G. A., and R. D. Martin, eds. *The Study of Prosimian Behavior.* New York: Academic Press, 1979.

Draper, Patricia. "!Kung Women: Contrasts in Sexual Egalitarianism in Foraging and Sedentary Contexts." In Reiter, ed., *Toward an Anthropology of Women.*

Draper, Patricia, and Elizabeth Cashdan. "Technological Change and Child Behavior among the !Kung." *Ethnology,* 27 (1988): 339–65.

Dressler, William W. "Health in the African American Community: Accounting for Health Inequalities." *Medical Anthropology Quarterly,* 7 (1993): 325–45.

Dressler, William W. *Stress and Adaptation in the Context of Culture.* Albany: State University of New York Press, 1991.

Dressler, William W., and Michael C. Robbins. "Art Styles, Social Stratification, and Cognition: An Analysis of Greek Vase Painting." *American Ethnologist,* 2 (1975): 427–34.

Drucker, Philip. "The Potlatch." In Dalton, ed., *Tribal and Peasant Economies.*

Drucker, Philip. *Cultures of the North Pacific Coast.* San Francisco: Chandler, 1965.

Du Bois, Cora. *The People of Alor: A Social-Psychological Study of an East Indian Island.* Minneapolis: University of Minnesota Press, 1944.

Duarte, Cidalia, J. Mauricio, P. B. Pettitt, P. Souto, E. Trinkaus, H. van der Plicht, and J. Zilhao. "The Early Upper Paleolithic Human Skeleton from the Abrigo do Lagar Velho (Portugal) and Modern Human Emergence in Iberia." *Proceedings of the National Academy of Sciences of the United States,* 96 (1999): 7604–609.

Duhard, Jean-Pierre. "Upper Paleolithic Figures as a Reflection of Human Morphology and Social Organization." *Antiquity,* 67 (1993): 83–91.

Dunbar, Robin. *Primate Social Systems.* Ithaca, NY: Comstock, 1988, pp. 107–10.

Dundes, Alan, ed. *The Study of Folklore.* Englewood Cliffs, NJ: Prentice Hall, 1965.

Dundes, Alan. "Structural Typology in North American Indian Folktales." In Dundes, ed., *The Study of Folklore.*

Dundes, Alan. *Folklore Matters.* Knoxville: University of Tennessee Press, 1989.

Durham, William H. *Coevolution: Genes, Culture and Human Diversity.* Stanford, CA: Stanford University Press, 1991.

Durkheim, Émile. *The Elementary Forms of the Religious Life.* Trans. Joseph W. Swain. New York: Collier Books, 1961. (Originally published 1912.)

Durkheim, Émile. *The Rules of Sociological Method.* 8th ed. Trans. Sarah A. Soloway and John H. Mueller. Ed. George E. Catlin. New York: Free Press, 1938. (Originally published 1895.)

Durrenberger, E. Paul. "Anthropology and Globalization," *American Anthropologist* 103 (2001): 531–535.

Durrenberger, E. Paul. "Chayanov's Economic Analysis in Anthropology." *Journal of Anthropological Research,* 36 (1980): 133–48.

Dyson-Hudson, Neville. *Karimojong Politics.* Oxford: Clarendon Press, 1966.

Dyson-Hudson, Rada, and Eric Alden Smith. "Human Territoriality: An Ecological Reassessment." *American Anthropologist,* 80 (1978): 21–41.

Eckhardt, William. "Primitive Militarism." *Journal of Peace Research,* 12 (1975): 55–62.

Eddy, Elizabeth M., and William L. Partridge, eds. *Applied Anthropology in America.* New York: Columbia University Press, 1978.

Eddy, Elizabeth M., and William L. Partridge, eds. *Applied Anthropology in America.* 2nd ed. New York: Columbia University Press, 1987.

Edgerton, Robert B. "Conceptions of Psychosis in Four East African Societies." *American Anthropologist,* 68 (1966): 408–25.

Edgerton, Robert B. *Sick Societies: Challenging the Myth of Primitive Harmony.* New York: Free Press, 1992.

Edgerton, Robert B. *The Individual in Cultural Adaptation: A Study of Four East African Peoples.* Berkeley: University of California Press, 1971.

Eiseley, Loren C. "The Dawn of Evolutionary Theory." In Loren C. Eiseley, *Darwin's Century: Evolution and the Men Who Discovered It.* Garden City, NY: Doubleday, 1958.

Eisenberg, John F. "Comparative Ecology and Reproduction of New World Monkeys." In Devra Kleinman, ed., The Biology and Conservation of the Callitrichidae. Washington, DC: Smithsonian Institution, 1977.

Eisenstadt, S. N. "African Age Groups." *Africa,* 24 (1954): 100–111.

Eisenstadt, S. N. *From Generation to Generation: Age Groups and Social Structure.* New York: Free Press, 1956.

Ekman, Paul, and Dachner Keltner. "Universal Facial Expressions of Emotion: An Old Controversy and New Findings." In Ullica Segerstrale, and Peter Molnar, eds., *Nonverbal Communication: Where Nature Meets Culture.* Mahwah, NJ: Lawrence Erlbaum, 1997.

Eldredge, Niles, and Ian Tattersall. *The Myths of Human Evolution.* New York: Columbia University Press, 1982.

Eliot, T. S. "The Love Song of J. Alfred Prufrock." In *Collected Poems, 1909–1962.* New York: Harcourt, Brace & World, 1963.

Ellis, Lee. "Evidence of Neuroandrogenic Etiology of Sex Roles from a Combined Analysis of Human, Nonhuman Primate and Nonprimate Mammalian Studies." *Personality and Individual Differences,* 7 (1986): 519–52.

ELLISON, P. *On Fertile Ground: A Natural History of Human Reproduction.* Cambridge, MA: Harvard, 2001.

ELLISON, PETER T. "Natural Variation in Human Fecundity." In Peregrine, Ember, and Ember, eds., *Physical Anthropology.*

ELWIN, VERRIER. *The Religion of an Indian Tribe.* London: Oxford University Press, 1955.

EMBER, CAROL R. "A Cross-Cultural Perspective on Sex Differences." In Munroe, Munroe, and Whiting, eds., *Handbook of Cross-Cultural Human Development.*

EMBER, CAROL R. "An Evaluation of Alternative Theories of Matrilocal versus Patrilocal Residence." *Behavior Science Research,* 9 (1974): 135–49.

EMBER, CAROL R. "Cross-Cultural Cognitive Studies." *Annual Review of Anthropology,* 6 (1977): 33–56.

EMBER, CAROL R. "Feminine Task Assignment and the Social Behavior of Boys." *Ethos,* 1 (1973): 424–39.

EMBER, CAROL R. "Men's Fear of Sex with Women: A Cross-Cultural Study." *Sex Roles,* 4 (1978): 657–78.

EMBER, CAROL R. "Myths about Hunter-Gatherers." *Ethnology,* 17 (1978): 439–48.

EMBER, CAROL R. "Residential Variation among Hunter-Gatherers." *Behavior Science Research,* 9 (1975): 135–49.

EMBER, CAROL R. "The Relative Decline in Women's Contribution to Agriculture with Intensification." *American Anthropologist,* 85 (1983): 285–304.

EMBER, CAROL R. "Universal and Variable Patterns of Gender Difference." In C. R. Ember and Ember, eds. *Cross-Cultural Research for Social Science* in Carol R. Ember and Melvin Ember, eds. *New Directions in Anthropology.*

EMBER, CAROL R. AND MELVIN EMBER, EDS. *Cross-Cultural Research for Social Science,* in Carol R. Ember and Melvin Ember, eds., *New Directions in Anthropology.* Upper Saddle River, NJ: Prentice Hall, CD-ROM, 2003.

EMBER, CAROL R. AND MELVIN EMBER, EDS., *New Directions in Anthropology.* Upper Saddle River, NJ: Prentice Hall, CD-ROM, 2003.

EMBER, CAROL R., AND DAVID LEVINSON. "The Substantive Contributions of Worldwide Cross-Cultural Studies Using Secondary Data." *Behavior Science Research* (special issue, "Cross-Cultural and Comparative Research: Theory and Method"), 25 (1991): 79–140.

EMBER, CAROL R., AND MELVIN EMBER, EDS. *Cross-Cultural Research for Social Science,* in Carol R. Ember and Melvin Ember, eds., *New Directions in Anthropology.* Upper Saddle River, NJ: Prentice Hall, CD-ROM, 2003.

EMBER, CAROL R., AND MELVIN EMBER. "Issues in Cross-Cultural Studies of Interpersonal Violence." *Violence and Victims,* 8 (1993): 217–33.

EMBER, CAROL R., AND MELVIN EMBER. "On Cross-Cultural Research." In C. R. Ember and Ember, eds., *Cross-Cultural Research for Social Science.*

EMBER, CAROL R., AND MELVIN EMBER. "Resource Unpredictability, Mistrust, and War: A Cross-Cultural Study." *Journal of Conflict Resolution,* 36 (1992): 242–62.

EMBER, CAROL R., AND MELVIN EMBER. "The Conditions Favoring Multilocal Residence." *Southwestern Journal of Anthropology,* 28 (1972): 382–400.

EMBER, CAROL R., AND MELVIN EMBER. "The Evolution of Human Female Sexuality: A Cross-Species Perspective." *Journal of Anthropological Research,* 40 (1984): 202–10.

EMBER, CAROL R., AND MELVIN EMBER. "Violence in the Ethnographic Record: Results of Cross-Cultural Research on War and Aggression." In Frayer and Martin, eds., *Troubled Times.*

EMBER, CAROL R., AND MELVIN EMBER. "War, Socialization, and Interpersonal Violence: A Cross-Cultural Study." *Journal of Conflict Resolution,* 38 (1994): 620–46.

EMBER, CAROL R., AND MELVIN EMBER. *Cross-Cultural Research Methods.* Walnut Creek, CA: AltaMira Press, 2001.

EMBER, CAROL R., MELVIN EMBER, AND BRUCE RUSSETT. "Peace between Participatory Polities: A Cross-Cultural Test of the 'Democracies Rarely Fight Each Other' Hypothesis." *World Politics,* 44 (1992): 573–99.

EMBER, CAROL R., MELVIN EMBER, AND BURTON PASTERNAK. "On the Development of Unilineal Descent." *Journal of Anthropological Research,* 30 (1974): 69–94.

EMBER, CAROL R., MELVIN EMBER, AND PETER N. PEREGRINE, EDS. *Research Frontiers in Anthropology,* in Carol R. Ember and Melvin Ember, eds., *New Directions in Anthropology.* Upper Saddle River, NJ: Prentice Hall, CD-ROM, 2003.

EMBER, MELVIN. "Alternative Predictors of Polygyny." *Behavior Science Research,* 19 (1984–1985): 1–23.

EMBER, MELVIN. "Evidence and Science in Ethnography: Reflections on the Freeman-Mead Controversy." *American Anthropologist,* 87 (1985): 906–909.

EMBER, MELVIN. "On the Origin and Extension of the Incest Taboo." *Behavior Science Research,* 10 (1975): 249–81.

EMBER, MELVIN. "Size of Color Lexicon: Interaction of Cultural and Biological Factors." *American Anthropologist,* 80 (1978): 364–67.

EMBER, MELVIN. "Statistical Evidence for an Ecological Explanation of Warfare." *American Anthropologist,* 84 (1982): 645–49.

EMBER, MELVIN. "Taxonomy in Comparative Studies." In Naroll and Cohen, eds., *A Handbook of Method in Cultural Anthropology.*

EMBER, MELVIN. "The Conditions That May Favor Avunculocal Residence." *Behavior Science Research,* 9 (1974): 203–209.

EMBER, MELVIN. "The Emergence of Neolocal Residence." *Transactions of the New York Academy of Sciences,* 30 (1967): 291–302.

EMBER, MELVIN. "The Nonunilinear Descent Groups of Samoa." *American Anthropologist,* 61 (1959): 573–77.

EMBER, MELVIN. "The Relationship between Economic and Political Development in Nonindustrialized Societies." *Ethnology,* 2 (1963): 228–48.

EMBER, MELVIN. "Warfare, Sex Ratio, and Polygyny." *Ethnology,* 13 (1974): 197–206.

EMBER, MELVIN, AND CAROL R. EMBER. "Cross-Cultural Studies of War and Peace: Recent Achievements and Future Possibilities." In Reyna and Downs, eds., *Studying War.*

EMBER, MELVIN, AND CAROL R. EMBER. "Cross-Language Predictors of Consonant-Vowel Syllables." *American Anthropologist,* 101 (1999): 730–42.

EMBER, MELVIN, AND CAROL R. EMBER. "Male-Female Bonding: A Cross-Species Study of Mammals and Birds." *Behavior Science Research,* 14 (1979): 37–56.

EMBER, MELVIN, AND CAROL R. EMBER. "The Conditions Favoring Matrilocal versus Patrilocal Residence." *American Anthropologist,* 73 (1971): 571–94.

EMBER, MELVIN, AND CAROL R. EMBER. *Marriage, Family, and Kinship: Comparative Studies of Social Organization.* New Haven, CT: HRAF Press, 1983.

EMBER, MELVIN AND CAROL R. EMBER, EDS. *Portraits of Culture: Ethnographic Originals,* in Carol R. Ember and Melvin Ember, eds., *New Directions in Anthropology.* Upper Saddle River, NJ: Prentice Hall, CD-ROM, 2003.

EMBER, MELVIN, AND CAROL R. EMBER, EDS. *Portraits of Culture: Ethnographic Originals,* in Carol R. Ember and Melvin Ember, eds., *New Directions in Anthropology.* Upper Saddle River, NJ: Prentice Hall, CD-ROM, 2003.

EMBER, MELVIN, CAROL R. EMBER, AND BRUCE RUSSETT. "Inequality and Democracy in the Anthropological Record." In Manus I. Midlarsky, ed., *Inequality, Democracy, and Economic Development.* Cambridge: Cambridge University Press, 1997.

EMENER, WILLIAM G., AND MARGARET DARROW, EDS. *Career Explorations in Human Services.* Springfield, IL: Charles C Thomas, 1991.

"Energy: Investing for a New Century," *New York Times,* October 30, 2000, pp. EN1–EN8, 2002.

ENSMINGER, JEAN, ED. *Theory in Economic Anthropology.* Lanham, MD: AltaMira Press, 2002.

EPSTEIN, CYNTHIA FUCHS. *Deceptive Distinctions: Sex, Gender, and the Social Order.* New York: Russell Sage Foundation, 1988.

ERCHAK, GERALD M. "Family Violence." In C. R. Ember, Ember, and Peregrine, eds., *Research Frontiers in Anthropology.*

ERICKSEN, KAREN PAIGE. "Male and Female Age Organizations and Secret Societies in Africa." *Behavior Science Research,* 23 (1989): 234–64.

ERICKSON, EDWIN. "Self-Assertion, Sex Role, and Vocal Rasp." In Lomax, ed., *Folk Song Style and Culture.*

ERRINGTON, J. JOSEPH. "On the Nature of the Sociolinguistic Sign: Describing the Javanese Speech Levels." In Mertz and Parmentier, eds., *Semiotic Mediation.*

ERVIN, ALEXANDER M. "Styles and Strategies of Leadership during the Alaskan Native Land Claims Movement: 1959–71." *Anthropologica,* 29 (1987): 21–38.

ESWARAN, VINAYAK. "A Diffusion Wave Out of Africa," *Current Anthropology* 43 (2002): 749–774.

ETIENNE, MONA, AND ELEANOR LEACOCK, EDS. *Women and Colonization: Anthropological Perspectives.* New York: Praeger, 1980.

ETIENNE, ROBERT. *Pompeii: The Day a City Died.* New York: Abrams, 1992.

ETKIN, NINA L., AND PAUL J. ROSS. "Malaria, Medicine, and Meals: A Biobehavioral Perspective." In Romanucci-Ross, Moerman, and Tancredi, eds., *The Anthropology of Medicine,* pp. 169–209.

EURIPIDES. "The Trojan Women." In Edith Hamilton, trans., *Three Greek Plays.* New York: Norton, 1937, p. 52.

EVANS-PRITCHARD, E. E. "Sexual Inversion among the Azande." *American Anthropologist,* 72 (1970): 1428–34.

EVANS-PRITCHARD, E. E. "The Nuer of the Southern Sudan." In Fortes and Evans-Pritchard, eds., *African Political Systems.*

EVANS-PRITCHARD, E. E. "Witchcraft Explains Unfortunate Events." In Lessa and Vogt, eds., *Reader in Comparative Religion,* 4th ed.

EVELETH, PHYLLIS B., AND JAMES M. TANNER. *Worldwide Variation in Human Growth.* 2nd ed. Cambridge: Cambridge University Press, 1990.

EZZELL, CAROL. "Hope in a Vial: Will There Be An AIDS Vaccine Anytime Soon? *Scientific American,* June 2002, pp. 36–45.

FAGAN, B. M. *People of the Earth: An Introduction to World Prehistory.* 9th ed. New York: HarperCollins, 1997.

FAGAN, BRIAN M. *Ancient North America: The Archaeology of a Continent.* London: Thames and Hudson, 1991.

FAGAN, BRIAN M. *In the Beginning.* Boston: Little, Brown, 1972.

FAGAN, BRIAN M. *People of the Earth: An Introduction to World Prehistory.* 7th ed. New York: HarperCollins, 1992.

FAGAN, BRIAN M. *People of the Earth: An Introduction to World Prehistory,* 6th ed. (Glenview, IL: Scott, Foresman, 1989).

FAGAN, BRIAN. M. *People of the Earth: An Introduction to World Prehistory,* 10th ed. Upper Saddle River: Prentice Hall, 2001.

FALK, D. "Enlarged Occipital/Marginal Sinuses and Emissary Foramina: Their Significance in Hominid Evolution." In Grine, ed., *Evolutionary History of the "Robust" Australopithecines.*

FALK, DEAN. "A Good Brain Is Hard to Cool." *Natural History,* 102 (August 1993): 65–66.

FALK, DEAN. "Cerebral Cortices of East African Early Hominids." *Science,* 221 (1983): 1072–74.

FALK, DEAN. "Hominid Paleoneurology." *Annual Review of Anthropology,* 16 (1987): 13–30.

FALK, DEAN. *Brain Dance.* New York: Henry Holt, 1992.

FARLEY, REYNOLDS. *The New American Reality: Who We Are, How We Got Here, Where We Are Going.* New York: Russell Sage Foundation, 1996.

FARMER, PAUL. "Ethnography, Social Analysis, and the Prevention of Sexually Transmitted HIV Infection among Poor Women in Haiti." In Inhorn and Brown, *The Anthropology of Infectious Disease,* pp. 413–38.

FEATHERMAN, DAVID L., AND ROBERT M. HAUSER. *Opportunity and Change.* New York: Academic Press, 1978.

FEDER, K. *Past in Perspective.* Mountain View, CA: Mayfield, 1996.

FEDER, K. *Past in Perspective.* Mountain View, CA: Mayfield Publishing Company, 2000.

FEDIGAN, LINDA MARIE. *Primate Paradigms: Sex Roles and Social Bonds.* Montreal: Eden Press, 1982.

FEIBEL, CRAIG S., AND FRANCIS H. BROWN. "Microstratigraphy and Paleoenvironments." In Walker and Leakey, eds., *The Nariokotome* Homo erectus *Skeleton.*

FEINMAN, GARY M., AND J. MARCUS, EDS. *Archaic States.* Santa Fe, NM: School of American Research Press, 1998.

FEINMAN, GARY M., STEPHEN A. KOWALEWSKI, LAURA FINSTEN, RICHARD E. BLANTON, AND LINDA NICHOLAS. "Long-Term Demographic Change: A Perspective from the Valley of Oaxaca, Mexico." *Journal of Field Archaeology,* 12 (1985): 333–62.

FEINMAN, GARY, AND JILL NEITZEL. "Too Many Types: An Overview of Sedentary Prestate Societies in the Americas." In Schiffer, ed., *Advances in Archaeological Methods and Theory.* Vol. 7.

FELDMAN, DOUGLAS A., AND JULIA W. MILLER. *The AIDS Crisis: A Documentary History.* Westport, CT: Greenwood Press, 1998.

FELDMAN, DOUGLAS A., AND THOMAS M. JOHNSON, EDS. *The Social Dimensions of AIDS: Method and Theory.* New York: Praeger, 1986.

FELDMAN, DOUGLAS A., AND THOMAS M. JOHNSON. "Introduction." In Feldman and Johnson, eds., *The Social Dimensions of AIDS.*

FERGUSON, R. BRIAN., ED. *Warfare, Culture, and Environment.* Orlando, FL: Academic Press, 1984.

FERGUSON, R. BRIAN, AND NEIL L. WHITEHEAD. "The Violent Edge of Empire." In R. B. Ferguson and N. Whitehead, eds., *War in the Tribal Zone.* Santa Fe: School of American Research Press, 1992, pp. 1–30.

FERNEA, ELIZABETH, AND ROBERT FERNEA, as reported in M. Kay Martin and Barbara Voorhies, *Female of the Species.* New York: Columbia University Press, 1975.

FERRARO, GARY P. *The Cultural Dimension of International Business.* 4th ed. Englewood Cliffs, NJ: Prentice Hall, 2002.

FINERMAN, RUTHBETH. "Saraguro: Medical Choices, Medical Changes," in M. Ember and Ember, eds., *Portraits of Culture: Ethnographic Originals,* in Carol R. Ember and Melvin Ember, eds., *New Directions in Anthropology.*

FINLEY, M. I. *Politics in the Ancient World.* Cambridge: Cambridge University Press, 1983.

"The First Dentist." *Newsweek,* March 5, 1973, 73.

"The First Tool Kit." *Science,* January 31, 1997, 623.

FIRTH, RAYMOND. *Rank and Religion in Tikopia.* Boston: Beacon Press, 1970.

FIRTH, RAYMOND. *Social Change in Tikopia.* New York: Macmillan, 1959.

FIRTH, RAYMOND. *We, the Tikopia.* Boston: Beacon Press, 1957.

FISCHER, JOHN L. "Social Influences on the Choice of a Linguistic Variant." *Word,* 14 (1958): 47–56.

FISCHER, JOHN. "Art Styles as Cultural Cognitive Maps." *American Anthropologist,* 63 (1961): 80–83.

FISH, PAUL R. "Beyond Tools: Middle Paleolithic Debitage Analysis and Cultural Inference." *Journal of Anthropological Research,* 37 (1981): 374–86.

FISHER, JULIE. "Grassroots Organizations and Grassroots Support Organizations: Patterns of Interaction." In Moran, Transforming Societies, *Transforming Anthropology.*

FISHER, WILLIAM H. "Megadevelopment, Environmentalism, and Resistance: The Institutional Context of Kayapo Indigenous Politics in Central Brazil." *Human Organization,* 53 (1994): 220–32.

FLANNERY, KENT V. "Adaptation, Evolution, and Archaeological Phases: Some Implications of Reynolds' Simulation." In Flannery, ed., *Guila Naquitz,* p. 502.

FLANNERY, KENT V. "Guila Naquitz in Spatial, Temporal, and Cultural Context." In Flannery, ed., *Guila Naquitz,* pp. 31–42.

FLANNERY, KENT V. "The Cultural Evolution of Civilizations." *Annual Review of Ecology and Systematics,* 3 (1972): 399–426.

FLANNERY, KENT V. "The Ecology of Early Food Production in Mesopotamia." *Science,* March 12, 1965, 1247–56.

FLANNERY, KENT V. "The Origins and Ecological Effects of Early Domestication in Iran and the Near East." In Struever, ed., *Prehistoric Agriculture.*

FLANNERY, KENT V. "The Origins of Agriculture." *Annual Review of Anthropology,* 2 (1973): 271–310.

FLANNERY, KENT V. "The Origins of the Village as a Settlement Type in Mesoamerica and the Near East: A Comparative Study." In Tringham, ed., *Territoriality and Proxemics.*

FLANNERY, KENT V. "The Research Problem." In Flannery, ed., *Guila Naquitz.*

FLANNERY, KENT V., ED. *Guila Naquitz: Archaic Foraging and Early Agriculture in Oaxaca, Mexico.* Orlando, FL: Academic Press, 1986.

FLANNERY, KENT V., ED. *The Early Mesoamerican Village.* New York: Academic Press, 1976.

FLEAGLE, JOHN G. "Anthropoid Origins." In Corruccini and Ciochon, eds., *Integrative Paths to the Past.*

FLEAGLE, JOHN G. *Primate Adaptation and Evolution,* 2nd ed. San Diego: Academic Press, 1999.

FLEAGLE, JOHN G. *Primate Adaptation and Evolution.* San Diego: Academic Press, 1988.

FLEAGLE, JOHN G., AND R. F. KAY, EDS. *Anthropoid Origins.* New York: Plenum, 1994.

FLEAGLE, JOHN G., AND R. F. KAY. "The Phyletic Position of the *Parapithecidae.*" *Journal of Human Evolution,* 16 (1987): 483–531.

FLEAGLE, JOHN G., AND RICHARD F. KAY. "New Interpretations of the Phyletic Position of Oligocene Hominoids." In Ciochon and Corruccini, eds., *New Interpretations of Ape and Human Ancestry.*

FLEAGLE, JOHN G., AND RICHARD F. KAY. "The Paleobiology of Catarrhines." In Delson, ed., *Ancestors.*

FLEAGLE, JOHN G., CHARLES H. JANSON, AND KAYE E. REED, EDS. *Primate Communities.* Cambridge: Cambridge University Press, 1999.

FLEISCHER, ROBERT L., AND HOWARD R. HART, JR. "Fission-Track Dating: Techniques and Problems." In Bishop and Miller, eds., *Calibration of Hominid Evolution.*

FLEISCHER, ROBERT L., P. B. PRICE, R. M. WALKER, AND L. S. B. LEAKEY. "Fission-Track Dating of Bed I, Olduvai Gorge." *Science,* April 2, 1965, 72–74.

FLUEHR-LOBBAN, C., ED. *Ethics and the Profession of Anthropology: Dialogue for a New Era.* 2nd edition. Philadelphia: University of Pennsylvania Press, 2002.

FLUEHR-LOBBAN, CAROLYN, ED. *Ethics and the Profession of Anthropology: Dialogue for a New Era.* Philadelphia: University of Pennsylvania Press, 1991.

FOLEY, W. A. *Anthropological Linguistics: An Introduction.* Malden, MA: Blackwell, 1997.

FORD, CLELLAN S. *Smoke from Their Fires.* New Haven, CT: Yale University Press, 1941.

FORD, CLELLAN S., ED. *Cross-Cultural Approaches: Readings in Comparative Research.* New Haven, CT: HRAF Press, 1967.

FORD, CLELLAN S., AND FRANK A. BEACH. *Patterns of Sexual Behavior.* New York: Harper, 1951.

FORD, RICHARD I., ED. *The Nature and Status of Ethnobotany.* Anthropological Papers No. 67, Museum of Anthropology. Ann Arbor: University of Michigan, 1978.

FORTES, MEYER. *The Web of Kinship among the Tallensi.* New York: Oxford University Press, 1949.

FORTES, MEYER, AND E. E. EVANS-PRITCHARD, EDS. *African Political Systems.* New York: Oxford University Press, 1940.

FOSSEY, DIAN. *Gorillas in the Mist.* Boston: Houghton Mifflin, 1983.

FOSTER, BRIAN L. "Ethnicity and Commerce." *American Ethnologist,* 1 (1974): 437–47.

FOSTER, GEORGE M. *Applied Anthropology.* Boston: Little, Brown, 1969.

FOSTER, GEORGE M. *Hippocrates' Latin American Legacy: Humoral Medicine in the New World.* Amsterdam: Gordon and Breach, 1994.

FOSTER, GEORGE M. *Traditional Cultures and the Impact of Technological Change.* New York: Harper & Row, 1962.

FOSTER, PHILIPS. *The World Food Problem: Tackling the Causes of Undernutrition in the Third World.* Boulder, CO: Lynne Rienner, 1992.

FOWLER, BRENDA. *Iceman: Uncovering the Life and Times of a Prehistoric Man Found in an Alpine Glacier.* New York: Random House, 2000.

FOWLER, MELVIN L. "A Pre-Columbian Urban Center on the Mississippi." *Scientific American,* August 1975, 92–101.

FRAKE, CHARLES O. "The Eastern Subanun of Mindanao." In Murdock, ed., *Social Structure in Southeast Asia.*

FRANCISCUS, ROBERT G., AND ERIK TRINKAUS. "Nasal Morphology and the Emergence of Homo erectus." *American Journal of Physical Anthropology,* 75 (1988): 517–27.

FRANK, ANDRÉ GUNDER. *Capitalism and Underdevelopment in Latin America: Historical Studies of Chile and Brazil.* New York: Monthly Review Press, 1967.

FRANKEL, BARBARA, AND M. G. TREND. "Principles, Pressures and Paychecks: The Anthropologist as Employee." In Fluehr-Lobban, ed., *Ethics and the Profession of Anthropology.*

FRAYER, DAVID W. "Body Size, Weapon Use, and Natural Selection in the European Upper Paleolithic and Mesolithic." *American Anthropologist,* 83 (1981): 57–73.

FRAYER, DAVID W. "Testing Theories and Hypotheses about Human Origins." In Peregrine, Ember, and Ember, eds., *Physical Anthropology.*

FRAYER, DAVID W., AND MILFORD H. WOLPOFF. "Sexual Dimorphism." *Annual Review of Anthropology,* 14 (1985): 429–73.

FRAYER, DAVID, AND DEBRA MARTIN, EDS. *Troubled Times: Osteological and Archaeological Evidence of Violence.* Langhorne, PA: Gordon and Breach, 1997.

FRAYER, DAVID, M. WOLPOFF, A. THORNE, F. SMITH, AND G. POPE. "Theories of Modern Human Origins: The Paleontological Test." *American Anthropologist,* 95 (1993): 24–27.

FRAYSER, SUZANNE G. *Varieties of Sexual Experience.* New Haven, CT: HRAF Press, 1985.

FREEDMAN, DANIEL G. "Ethnic Differences in Babies." *Human Nature,* January 1979, 36–43.

FREEMAN, DEREK. *Margaret Mead and Samoa: The Making and Unmaking of an Anthropological Myth.* Cambridge, MA: Harvard University Press, 1983.

FREEMAN, J. D. "On the Concept of the Kindred." *Journal of the Royal Anthropological Institute,* 91 (1961): 192–220.

FREEMAN, LESLIE G. "Torralba and Ambrona: A Review of Discoveries." In Corruccini and Ciochon, eds., *Integrative Paths to the Past.*

FREUD, SIGMUND. *A General Introduction to Psychoanalysis.* Garden City, NY: Garden City Publishing, 1943. (Originally published in German, 1917.)

FREUD, SIGMUND. *Moses and Monotheism.* Katherine Jones, trans. New York: Vintage Books, 1967. (Originally published 1939.)

FREYMAN, R. "The First Technology" in *Scientific American.*

FRIED, MORTON H. *The Evolution of Political Society: An Essay in Political Anthropology.* New York: Random House, 1967.

FRIED, MORTON H., ED. *Readings in Anthropology.* 2nd ed., Vol. 1. New York: Thomas Y. Crowell, 1968.

FRIEDL, ERNESTINE. *Vasilika: A Village in Modern Greece.* New York: Holt, Rinehart & Winston, 1962.

FRIEDMAN, J., AND M. J. ROWLANDS, EDS. *The Evolution of Social Systems.* London: Duckworth, 1977.

FRIEDMAN, SAUL S. "Holocaust." In *Academic American* [now Grolier] *Encyclopedia.* Vol. 10. Princeton, NJ: Arete, 1980.

FRIEDRICH, PAUL. *Proto-Indo-European Trees: The Arboreal System of a Prehistoric People.* Chicago: University of Chicago Press, 1970.

FRIEDRICH, PAUL. *The Language Parallax.* Austin: University of Texas Press, 1986.

FRISANCHO, A. ROBERTO, AND LAWRENCE P. GREKSA. "Development Responses in the Acquisition of Functional Adaptation to High Altitude." In Little and Haas, eds., *Human Population Biology.*

FRISCH, JOHN. "Individual Behavior and Intergroup Variability in Japanese Macaques." In P. C. Jay, ed., *Primates: Studies in Adaptation and Variability.* New York: Holt, Rinehart & Winston, 1968, pp. 243–52.

FRISCH, ROSE E. "Fatness, Puberty, and Fertility." *Natural History,* October 1980, 16–27.

FROMM, ERICH. *Psychoanalysis and Religion.* New Haven, CT: Yale University Press, 1950.

FRUNET, MICHEL, ALAIN BEAUVILAIN, YVES COPPENS, ELILE HEINTZ, ALADJI H. E. MOUTAYE, AND DAVID PILBEAM. "The First Australopithecine 2500 Kilometers West of the Rift Valley (Chad)." *Nature,* 378 (1995): 273–75.

FRY, DOUGLAS P., AND KAJ BJÖRKQVIST, EDS. *Cultural Variation in Conflict Resolution: Alternatives to Violence.* Mahwah, NJ: Lawrence Erlbaum Associates, 1997.

FUTUYMA, DOUGLAS. *Science on Trial.* New York: Pantheon, 1982.

GABUNIA, LEO, A. VEKUA, D. LORDKIPANIDZE, ET AL. "Earliest Pleistocene Hominid Cranial Remains from Dmanisi, Republic of Georgia: Taxonomy, Geological Setting, and Age." *Science,* 288 (2000): 1019–25.

GAL, SUSAN. "The Political Economy of Code Choice." In Heller, ed., *Codeswitching.*

GALDIKAS, BIRUTÉ M. F. "Orangutan Adaptation at Tanjung Puting Reserve: Mating and Ecology." In Hamburg and McCown, eds., *The Great Apes.*

GARB, PAULA. "Abkhazians: Growing in Age and Wisdom," in M. Ember and Ember, eds. *Portraits of Culture: Ethnographic Originals,* in Carol R. Ember and Melvin Ember, eds., *New Directions in Anthropology.*

GARDNER, BEATRICE T., AND R. ALLEN GARDNER. "Two Comparative Psychologists Look at Language Acquisition." In Nelson, ed., *Children's Language,* Vol. 2.

GARDNER, R. ALLEN, AND BEATRICE T. GARDNER. "Teaching Sign Language to a Chimpanzee." *Science,* August 15, 1969, 664–72.

GARFIELD, VIOLA E., ED. *Symposium: Patterns of Land Utilization, and Other Papers.* Proceedings of the Annual Spring Meeting of American Ethnological Society, 1961. Seattle: University of Washington Press, 1962.

GARN, STANLEY M. *Human Races.* 3rd ed. Springfield, IL: Charles C Thomas, 1971.

GARTNER, ROSEMARY. "Crime Variations across Cultures and Nations." In C. R. Ember and Ember, eds., *Cross-Cultural Research for Social Science.*

GAT, AZAR. "The Pattern of Fighting in Simple, Small-Scale, Prestate Societies." *Journal of Anthropological Research,* 55 (1999): 563–583.

GAULIN, STEVEN J. C., AND JAMES S. BOSTER. "Dowry as Female Competition." *American Anthropologist,* 92 (1990): 994–1005.

GEERTZ, CLIFFORD. "'From the Native's Point of View': On the Nature of Anthropological Understanding." In Shweder and LeVine, eds., *Culture Theory.*

GEERTZ, CLIFFORD. "Deep Play: Notes on the Balinese Cockfight." In Geertz, *The Interpretation of Cultures.*

GEERTZ, CLIFFORD. "Religion as a Cultural System." In Banton, ed., *Anthropological Approaches to the Study of Religion.*

GEERTZ, CLIFFORD. "Thick Description: Toward an Interpretative Theory of Culture." In Geertz, *The Interpretation of Cultures.*

GEERTZ, CLIFFORD. *The Interpretation of Cultures: Selected Essays.* New York: Basic Books, 1973.

GEERTZ, CLIFFORD. *The Religion of Java.* New York: Free Press, 1960.

GELLES, RICHARD J., AND MURRAY A. STRAUS. *Intimate Violence.* New York: Simon & Schuster, 1988.

GENTNER, W., AND H. J. LIPPOLT. "The Potassium-Argon Dating of Upper Tertiary and Pleistocene Deposits." In Brothwell and Higgs, eds., *Science in Archaeology.*

GERO, JOAN M., AND MARGARET W. CONKEY, EDS. *Engendering Archaeology: An Introduction to Women and Prehistory.* Oxford: Blackwell, 1991.

GESLER, W. *The Cultural Geography of Health Care.* Pittsburgh: University of Pittsburgh Press, 1991.

GIBBON, G. *Anthropological Archaeology.* New York: Columbia University Press, 1984.

GIBBONS, ANN, "One Scientist's Quest for the Origin of Our Species," *Science* 298 (29 Nov 2002), pp. 1708–1711.

GIBBONS, ANN. "First Americans: Not Mammoth Hunters, but Forest Dwellers?" *Science,* April 19, 1995, 346–47.

GIBBONS, ANN. "The Riddle of Co-Existence," *Science,* 291 (2001): 1725–29.

GIBBONS, ANN. "Warring over Women." *Science,* August 20, 1993, 987–88.

GIBBS, JAMES L., JR. "The Kpelle of Liberia." In Gibbs, ed., *Peoples of Africa.*

GIBBS, JAMES L., JR., ED. *Peoples of Africa.* New York: Holt, Rinehart & Winston, 1965.

GIBSON, KATHLEEN R. AND STEPHEN JESSEE. "Language Evolution and Expansions of Multiple Neurological Processing Areas," In King, ed. *The Origins of Language,* pp. 189–227.

GILLIGAN, CAROL. *In a Different Voice: Psychological Theory and Women's Development.* Cambridge, MA: Harvard University Press, 1982.

GILLIGAN, CAROL, AND JANE ATTANUCCI. "Two Moral Orientations." In Gilligan, Ward, and Taylor, eds., *Mapping the Moral Domain.*

GILLIGAN, CAROL, JANIE VICTORIA WARD, AND JILL MCLEAN TAYLOR, EDS. *Mapping the Moral Domain: A Contribution of Women's Thinking to Psychological Theory and Education.* Cambridge, MA: Harvard University Press, 1988.

GILLILAND, MARY KAY. "Nationalism and Ethnogenesis in the Former Yugoslavia." In Romanucci-Ross and De Vos, eds., *Ethnic Identity,* pp. 197–221.

GILMAN, ANTONIO. "The Development of Social Stratification in Bronze Age Europe." *Current Anthropology,* 22 (1990): 1–23.

GIMBUTAS, MARIJA. "An Archaeologist's View of PIE* in 1975." *Journal of Indo-European Studies,* 2 (1974): 289–307.

GINGERICH, P. D. "Pleisiadipis and the Delineation of the Order Primates." In B. Wood, L. Martin, and P. Andrews, eds., *Major Topics in Primate Evolution.* Cambridge: Cambridge University Press, 1986, pp. 32–46.

GLADWIN, CHRISTINA H. "A Theory of Real-Life Choice: Applications to Agricultural Decisions." In Barlett, ed., *Agricultural Decision Making.*

GLADWIN, THOMAS, AND SEYMOUR B. SARASON. *Truk: Man in Paradise.* New York: Wenner-Gren Foundation for Anthropological Research, 1953, as seen in eHRAF Collection of Ethnography on the Web, 2000.

GLASS, H. BENTLEY. "The Genetics of the Dunkers." *Scientific American,* August 1953, 76–81.

GLASSER, IRENE. *Homelessness in Cross-Cultural Perspective.* New York: G. K. Hall/Macmillan, 1994.

GLEITMAN, LILA R., AND ERIC WANNER. "Language Acquisition: The State of the State of the Art." In Wanner and Gleitman, eds., *Language Acquisition.*

GOLDEN, FREDERIC, MICHAEL LEMONICK, AND DICK THOMPSON. "The Race Is Over." *Time,* July 3, 2000, 18–23.

GOLDIZEN, ANNE WILSON. "Tamarins and Marmosets: Communal Care of Offspring." In Smuts et al., eds., *Primate Societies.*

GOLDSTEIN, JOSHUA S. *War and Gender: How Gender Shapes the War System and Vice Versa.* New York: Cambridge University Press, 2001.

GOLDSTEIN, MELVYN C. "Stratification, Polyandry, and Family Structure in Central Tibet." *Southwestern Journal of Anthropology,* 27 (1971): 65–74.

GOLDSTEIN, MELVYN C. "When Brothers Share a Wife." *Natural History,* March 1987, 39–48.

GOLDSTONE, J. A. "The Comparative and Historical Study of Revolutions." *Annual Review of Sociology,* 8 (1982): 187–207.

GOODALL, JANE. "My Life among Wild Chimpanzees." *National Geographic,* August 1963, 272–308.

GOODALL, JANE. *Through a Window.* Boston: Houghton Mifflin, 1990.

GOODE, WILLIAM J. *The Family.* 2nd ed. Englewood Cliffs, NJ: Prentice Hall, 1982.

GOODE, WILLIAM J. *World Revolution and Family Patterns.* New York: Free Press, 1970.

GOODENOUGH, WARD H. *Cooperation in Change.* New York: Russell Sage Foundation, 1963.

GOODENOUGH, WARD H. *Property, Kin, and Community on Truk.* New Haven, CT: Yale University Press, 1951.

GOODENOUGH, WARD H., ED. *Explorations in Cultural Anthropology.* New York: McGraw-Hill, 1964.

GOODMAN, ALAN H., AND GEORGE J. ARMELAGOS. "Disease and Death at Dr. Dickson's Mounds." *Natural History,* September 1985, 12–19.

GOODMAN, ALAN H., AND THOMAS L. LEATHERMAN, EDS. *Building a New Biocultural Synthesis: Political-Economic Perspectives on Human Biology.* Ann Arbor: University of Michigan Press, 1998.

GOODMAN, ALAN H., JOHN LALLO, GEORGE J. ARMELAGOS, AND JEROME C. ROSE. "Health Changes at Dickson Mounds, Illinois (A.D. 950–1300)." In M. N. Cohen and Armelagos, eds., *Paleopathology at the Origins of Agriculture.*

GOODMAN, MADELEINE J., P. BION GRIFFIN, AGNES A. ESTIOKO-GRIFFIN, AND JOHN S. GROVE. "The Compatability of Hunting and Mothering among the Agta Hunter-Gatherers of the Philippines." *Sex Roles,* 12 (1985): 1199–209.

GOODMAN, MORRIS. "Reconstructing Human Evolution from Proteins." In Jones, Martin, and Pilbeam, eds., *The Cambridge Encyclopedia of Human Evolution.*

GOODRICH, L. CARRINGTON. *A Short History of the Chinese People.* 3rd ed. New York: Harper & Row, 1959.

GOODY, JACK. "Bridewealth and Dowry in Africa and Eurasia." In Good and Tambiah, eds., *Bridewealth and Dowry.*

GOODY, JACK. "Cousin Terms." *Southwestern Journal of Anthropology,* 26 (1970): 125–42.

GOODY, JACK, AND S. H. TAMBIAH, EDS. *Bridewealth and Dowry.* Cambridge: Cambridge University Press, 1973.

GORE, RICK, "The First Pioneer?," *National Geographic* (Aug. 2002).

GORMAN, CHESTER. "The Hoabinhian and After: Subsistence Patterns in Southeast Asia during the Late Pleistocene and Early Recent Periods." *World Archaeology,* 2 (1970): 315–19.

GOSSEN, GARY H. "Temporal and Spatial Equivalents in Chamula Ritual Symbolism." In Lessa and Vogt, eds., *Reader in Comparative Religion,* 4th ed.

GOUGH, KATHLEEN. "The Nayars and the Definition of Marriage." *Journal of the Royal Anthropological Institute,* 89 (1959): 23–34.

GOULD, RICHARD A. *Yiwara: Foragers of the Australian Desert.* New York: Scribner's, 1969.

GOULD, S. J. *The Mismeasure of Man.* New York: W. W. Norton, 1996.

GRABURN, NELSON H. *Eskimos without Igloos.* Boston: Little, Brown, 1969.

GRAHAM, SUSAN BRANDT. "Biology and Human Social Behavior: A Response to van den Berghe and Barash." *American Anthropologist,* 81 (1979): 357–60.

GRANT, BRUCE S., "Sour Grapes of Wrath," *Science* 297 (9 Aug. 2002), 940–941.

GRANT, PETER R. "Natural Selection and Darwin's Finches." *Scientific American,* October 1991, 82–87.

GRAY, J. PATRICK, *Primate Sociobiology.* New Haven, CT: HRAF Press, 1985.

GRAY, J. PATRICK, AND LINDA D. WOLFE. "Height and Sexual Dimorphism of Stature among Human Societies." *American Journal of Physical Anthropology,* 53 (1980): 446–52.

GRAY, J. PATRICK, AND LINDA WOLFE. "What Accounts for Population Variation in Height?" In Peregrine, Ember, and Ember, eds., *Physical Anthropology.*

GRAYSON, DONALD K. "Explaining Pleistocene Extinctions: Thoughts on the Structure of a Debate." In P. S. Martin and Klein, eds., *Quaternary Extinctions.*

GRAYSON, DONALD K. "Pleistocene Avifaunas and the Overkill Hypothesis." *Science,* February 18, 1977, pp. 691–92.

GREENBERG, JOSEPH H. "Linguistic Evidence Regarding Bantu Origins." *Journal of African History,* 13 (1972): 189–216.

GREENBERG, JOSEPH H., AND MERRITT RUHLEN. "Linguistic Origins of Native Americans." *Scientific American,* November 1992, 94–99.

GREENE, L., AND F. E. JOHNSTON, EDS. *Social and Biological Predictors of Nutritional Status, Physical Growth, and Neurological Development.* New York: Academic Press, 1980.

GREENFIELD, PATRICIA M., ASHLEY E. MAYNARD, AND CARLA P. CHILDS. "History, Culture, Learning, and Development." *Cross-Cultural Research,* 34 (2000): 351–374.

GREENFIELD, PATRICIA MARKS, AND E. SUE SAVAGE-RUMBAUGH. "Grammatical Combination in *Pan paniscus:* Processes of Learning and Invention in the Evolution and Development of Language." In Parker and Gibson, eds., *"Language" and Intelligence in Monkeys and Apes.*

GREGORY, C. A. *Gifts and Commodities.* New York: Academic Press, 1982.

GREKSA, LAWRENCE P., AND CYNTHIA M. BEALL. "Development of Chest Size and Lung Function at High Altitude." In Little and Haas, eds., *Human Population Biology.*

GRINE, FREDERICK E. "Australopithecine Taxonomy and Phylogeny: Historical Background and Recent Interpretation." In Ciochon and Fleagle, eds., *The Human Evolution Source Book.*

GRINE, FREDERICK E. "Dental Evidence for Dietary Differences in *Australopithecus* and *Paranthropus:* A Quantitative Analysis of

Permanent Molar Microwear." *Journal of Human Evolution,* 15 (1986): 783–822.

GRINE, FREDERICK E. "Evolutionary History of the 'Robust' Australopithecines: A Summary and Historical Perspective." In Grine, ed., *Evolutionary History of the "Robust" Australopithecines.*

GRINE, FREDERICK E., ED. *Evolutionary History of the "Robust" Australopithecines.* New York: Aldine, 1988.

GRÖGER, B. LISA. "Of Men and Machines: Cooperation among French Family Farmers." *Ethnology,* 20 (1981): 163–75.

GROSS, DANIEL R., AND BARBARA A. UNDERWOOD. "Technological Change and Caloric Costs: Sisal Agriculture in Northeastern Brazil." *American Anthropologist,* 73 (1971): 725–40.

GROSS, DANIEL R., GEORGE EITEN, NANCY M. FLOWERS, FRANCISCA M. LEOI, MADELINE LATTMAN RITTER, AND DENNIS W. WERNER. "Ecology and Acculturation among Native Peoples of Central Brazil." *Science,* November 30, 1979, 1043–50.

GROSSMAN, DANIEL, "Parched Turf Battle," *Scientific American* (Dec. 2002).

GRUBB, HENRY J. "Intelligence at the Low End of the Curve: Where Are the Racial Differences?" *Journal of Black Psychology,* 14 (1987): 25–34.

GRUBB, HENRY J., AND ANDREA G. BARTHWELL. "Superior Intelligence and Racial Equivalence: A Look at Mensa." Paper presented at the 1996 annual meeting of the Society for Cross-Cultural Research.

GUBSER, NICHOLAS J. *The Nunamiut Eskimos: Hunters of Caribou.* New Haven, CT: Yale University Press, 1965.

GUIORA, ALEXANDER Z., BENJAMIN BEIT-HALLAHMI, RISTO FRIED, AND CECELIA YODER. "Language Environment and Gender Identity Attainment." *Language Learning,* 32 (1982): 289–304.

GUMPERZ, JOHN J. "Dialect Differences and Social Stratification in a North Indian Village." In *Language in Social Groups: Essays by John J. Gumperz,* selected and introduced by Anwar S. Dil. Stanford, CA: Stanford University Press, 1971.

GUMPERZ, JOHN J. "Speech Variation and the Study of Indian Civilization." *American Anthropologist,* 63 (1961): 976–88.

GUNDERS, S., AND J. W. M. WHITING. "Mother-Infant Separation and Physical Growth." *Ethnology,* 7 (1968): 196–206.

GURR, TED ROBERT, ED. *Violence in America.* Vol. 1: The History of Crime. Newbury Park, CA: Sage, 1989.

GURR, TED ROBERT. "Historical Trends in Violent Crime: Europe and the United States." In Gurr, ed., *Violence in America.* Vol. 1.

GURR, TED ROBERT. "The History of Violent Crime in America: An Overview." In Gurr, ed., *Violence in America.* Vol. 1.

GURVEN, MICHAEL, KIM HILL, AND HILLARD KAPLAN, "From Forest to Reservation: Transitions in Food-sharing Behavior Among the Ache of Paraguay." *Journal of Anthropological Research* 58 (2002): 93–120.

GUTHRIE, DALE R. "Mosaics, Allelochemics, and Nutrients: An Ecological Theory of Late Pleistocene Megafaunal Extinctions." In P.S. Martin and Klein, eds., *Quaternary Extinctions.*

GUTHRIE, STEWART ELLIOTT. *Faces in the Clouds: A New Theory of Religion.* New York: Oxford University Press, 1993.

HAAS, JONATHAN, ED. *The Anthropology of War.* New York: Cambridge University Press, 1990.

HAAS, JONATHAN. "Warfare and the Evolution of Tribal Polities in the Prehistoric Southwest." In Haas, ed., *The Anthropology of War.*

HAAS, MARY R. "Men's and Women's Speech in Koasati." *Language,* 20 (1944): 142–49.

HABICHT, J.K. A. *Paleoclimate, Paleomagnetism, and Continental Drift.* Tulsa, OK: American Association of Petroleum Geologists, 1979.

HACKENBERG, ROBERT A. "Scientists or Survivors? The Future of Applied Anthropology under Maximum Uncertainty." In Trotter, ed., *Anthropology for Tomorrow.*

HAGE, JERALD, AND CHARLES H. POWERS. *Post-Industrial Lives: Roles and Relationships in the 21st Century.* Newbury Park, CA: Sage, 1992.

HAHN, ROBERT A. *Sickness and Healing: An Anthropological Perspective.* New Haven, CT: Yale University Press, 1995.

HAILIE-SELASSIE, YOHANNES, "Late Miocene Hominids from the Middle Awash, Ethiopia," *Nature* 412 (12 Jul 2001), pp. 178–181.

HALDANE, J. B. S. "Human Evolution: Past and Future." In Jepsen, Mayr, and Simpson, eds., *Genetics, Paleontology, and Evolution.*

HALL, EDWARD T. *The Hidden Dimension.* Garden City, NY: Doubleday, 1966.

HALL, EDWARD T., AND M. R. HALL. *Hidden Differences: Doing Business with the Japanese.* New York: Doubleday, 1990.

HALL, K. L. R. "Social Learning in Monkeys." In P. C. Jay, ed., *Primates: Studies in Adaptation and Variability.* New York: Holt, Rinehart & Winston, 1968, pp. 383–97.

HALLOWELL, A. IRVING. "Ojibwa World View and Disease." In *Contributions to Anthropology: Selected Papers of A. Irving Hallowell.* Chicago: University of Chicago Press, 1976, pp. 410–13.

HAMBURG, DAVID A., AND ELIZABETH R. MCCOWN, EDS. *The Great Apes.* Menlo Park, CA: Benjamin/Cummings, 1979.

HAMES, RAYMOND. "Sharing among the Yanomamö. Pt. I. The Effects of Risk." In Cashdan, ed., *Risk and Uncertainty in Tribal and Peasant Economies.*

HAMES, RAYMOND. "Yanomamö: Varying Adaptations of Foraging Horticulturalists." In M. Ember and Ember, eds., *Portraits of Culture.*

HAMILTON, EDITH, TRANS. *Three Greek Plays.* New York: Norton, 1937.

HAMMER, MICHAEL F. AND STEPHEN L. ZEGURA, "The Human Y Chromosome Haplogroup Tree," *Annual Review of Anthropology* 31 (2002): 303–321.

HAMMER, MICHAEL F. AND STEPHEN L. ZEGURA, "The Role of the Y Chromosome in Human Evolutionary Studies." *Evolutionary Anthropology* 5 (1996): 116–134.

HANDWERKER, W. PENN, AND PAUL V. CROSBIE. "Sex and Dominance." *American Anthropologist,* 84 (1982): 97–104.

HANNA, JOEL M., MICHAEL A. LITTLE, AND DONALD M. AUSTIN. "Climatic Physiology." In Little and Haas, eds., *Human Population Biology.*

HANNAH, ALISON C., AND W. C. MCGREW. "Chimpanzees Using Stones to Crack Open Oil Palm Nuts in Liberia." *Primates,* 28 (1987): 31–46.

HANNERZ, ULF. *Transnational Connections: Culture, People, Places.* London: Routledge, 1996.

HANOTTE, OLIVIER ET AL., "African Pastoralism: Genetic Imprints of Origins and Migrations," *Science* 296 (12 Apr 2002): 336–343; Clutton-Brock, "Domestication of Animals," p. 384.

HANSON, JEFFERY R. "Age-Set Theory and Plains Indian Age-Grading: A Critical Review and Revision," *American Ethnologist,* 15 (1988): 349–64.

HARCOURT, A. H. "The Social Relations and Group Structure of Wild Mountain Gorillas." In Hamburg and McCown, eds., *The Great Apes.*

HARDIN, GARRETT. "The Tragedy of the Commons." *Science,* 162 (1968): 1243–48.

HARDOY, JORGE, AND DAVID SATTERTHWAITE. "The Legal and the Illegal City." In Rodwin, ed., *Shelter, Settlement, and Development.*

HARE, BRIAN, MICHELLE BROWN, CHRISTINA WILLIAMSON, AND MICHAEL TOMASELLO, "The Domestication of Social Cognition in Dogs," *Science* 298 (22 Nov. 2002), 1634– 1636.

HARKNESS, SARA AND CHARLES M. SUPER, "An Infant's Three Rs." A box in Small, "Our Babies, Ourselves," p. 45.

HARKNESS, SARA, AND CHARLES. M SUPER, EDS. *Parents' Cultural Belief Systems: Their Origins, Expressions, and Consequences.* New York: Guilford, 1996.

HARLAN, JACK R. "A Wild Wheat Harvest in Turkey." *Archaeology,* 20, no. 3 (June 1967): 197–201.

HARLOW, HARRY F., ET AL. "Maternal Behavior of Rhesus Monkeys Deprived of Mothering and Peer Association in Infancy." *Proceedings of the American Philosophical Society,* 110 (1966): 58–66.

HARNER, MICHAEL J. "Scarcity, the Factors of Production, and Social Evolution." In Polgar, ed., *Population, Ecology, and Social Evolution.*

HARNER, MICHAEL, ED. *Hallucinogens and Shamanism.* New York: Oxford University Press, 1972.

HARNER, MICHAEL. "The Role of Hallucinogenic Plants in European Witchcraft." In Harner, ed., *Hallucinogens and Shamanism.*

HARNER, MICHAEL, AND GARY DOORE. "The Ancient Wisdom in Shamanic Cultures." In Nicholson, comp., Shamanism, pp. 3–16.

HARRIS, DAVID R. "Settling Down: An Evolutionary Model for the Transformation of Mobile Bands into Sedentary Communities." In Friedman and Rowlands, eds., *The Evolution of Social Systems.* London: Duckworth, 1977.

HARRIS, MARVIN. "The Cultural Ecology of India's Sacred Cattle." *Current Anthropology,* 7 (1966): 51–63.

HARRIS, MARVIN. *Cows, Pigs, Wars and Witches: The Riddles of Culture.* New York: Random House, Vintage, 1975.

HARRIS, MARVIN. *Cultural Materialism: The Struggle for a Science of Culture.* New York: Random House, 1979.

HARRIS, MARVIN. Patterns of Race in the Americas. New York: Walker, 1964.

HARRIS, MARVIN, AND ERIC B. ROSS. *Food and Evolution: Toward a Theory of Human Food Habits.* Philadelphia: Temple University Press, 1987.

HARRISON, G. A., JAMES M. TANNER, DAVID R. PILBEAM, AND P. T. BAKER. *Human Biology: An Introduction to Human Evolution, Variation, Growth, and Adaptability.* 3rd ed. Oxford: Oxford University Press, 1988.

HARRISON, GAIL G. "Primary Adult Lactase Deficiency: A Problem in Anthropological Genetics." *American Anthropologist,* 77 (1975): 812–35.

HARRISON, PETER D., AND B. L. TURNER II, EDS. *Pre-Hispanic Maya Agriculture.* Albuquerque: University of New Mexico Press, 1978.

HARRISON, T. "A Reassessment of the Phylogenetic Relationships of Oreopithecus bamboli." *Journal of Human Evolution,* 15 (1986): 541–84.

HARRISON, T., AND L. ROOK. "Enigmatic Anthropoid or Misunderstood Ape? The Phylogenetic Status of *Oreopithecus bamboli* Reconsidered." In D. R. Begun, C. V. Ward, and M. D. Rose, eds., *Function, Phylogeny and Fossils: Miocene Hominoid Evolution and Adaptation.* New York: Plenum, 1997, pp. 327–62.

HART, HORNELL. "The Logistic Growth of Political Areas." *Social Forces,* 26 (1948): 396–408.

HARTWIG, W. C. "Pattern, Puzzles and Perspectives on Platyrrhine Origins." In Corruccini and Ciochon, eds., *Integrative Paths to the Past,* pp. 69–93.

HARTWIG, W.C., ED. The Primate Fossil Record. Cambridge: Cambridge University Press, 2002. *Human Development Report 2001,* published for the United Nations Development Programme (New York: Oxford University Press, 2001), pp. 9–25.

HARVEY, PHILIP W., AND PETER F. HEYWOOD. "Twenty-five Years of Dietary Change in Simbu Province, Papua New Guinea." *Ecology of Food and Nutrition,* 13 (1983): 27–35.

HASSAN, FEKRI A. *Demographic Archaeology.* New York: Academic Press, 1981.

HASTORF, CHRISTINE. "Gender, Space, and Food Prehistory." In Gero and Conkey, eds., *Engendering Archaeology.*

HATCH, ELVIN. "The Good Side of Relativism." *Journal of Anthropological Research,* 53 (1997): 371–81.

HAUG, GERALD ET AL., "Climate and the Collapse of Maya Civilization," *Science* 299 (14 Mar. 2003): 1731–1735.

HAUSFATER, GLENN, JEANNE ALTMANN, AND STUART ALTMANN. "Long-Term Consistency of Dominance Relations among Female Baboons." *Science,* August 20, 1982, 752–54.

HAWKINS, ALICIA, AND M. KLEINDIENST. "Aterian." In P. N. Peregrine and M. Ember, eds., *Encyclopedia of Prehistory.* Vol. 1: Africa. New York: Kluwer Academic/ Plenum, 2001, pp. 23–45.

HAYDEN, THOMAS. "A Genome Milestone." *Newsweek,* July 3, 2000, 51–52.

HAYNES, VANCE. "The Calico Site: Artifacts or Geofacts?" *Science,* 181 (1973): 305–10.

HAYS, TERENCE E. "From Ethnographer to Comparativist and Back Again." In C. R. Ember, Ember, and Peregrine, eds., *Research Frontiers in Anthropology.*

HAYS, TERENCE E. "Sound Symbolism, Onomatopoeia, and New Guinea Frog Names." *Journal of Linguistic Anthropology,* 4 (1994): 153–74.

HEATH, DWIGHT B., AND RICHARD N. ADAMS, EDS. *Contemporary Cultures and Societies of Latin America.* New York: Random House, 1965.

HEIDER, KARL. *Grand Valley Dani: Peaceful Warriors.* New York: Holt, Rinehart & Winston, 1979.

HEIDER, KARL. *The Dugum Dani.* Chicago: Aldine, 1970.

HEISE, DAVID R. "Cultural Patterning of Sexual Socialization." *American Sociological Review,* 32 (1967): 726–39.

HELLER, MONICA, ED. *Codeswitching: Anthropological and Sociolinguistic Perspectives.* Berlin: Mouton de Gruyter, 1988.

HELMS, MARY W. "Miskito: Adaptations to Colonial Empires, Past and Present." In M. Ember and Ember, eds., *Portraits of Culture.*

HELMS, MARY W. *Middle America.* Englewood Cliffs, NJ: Prentice Hall, 1975.

HEMPEL, CARL G. *Aspects of Scientific Explanation.* New York: Free Press, 1965.

HENDERSON, A. M., AND TALCOTT PARSONS, TRANS. *The Theory of Social and Economic Organization.* New York: Oxford University Press, 1947.

HENDERSON, HARRY. *Global Terrorism: The Complete Reference Guide.* New York: Checkmark Books, 2001.

HENDRIX, LLEWELLYN. "Economy and Child Training Reexamined." *Ethos,* 13 (1985): 246–61.

HENDRIX, LLEWELLYN. "Varieties of Marital Relationships." In C. R. Ember and Ember, eds., *Cross-Cultural Research for Social Science.*

HENDRY, JOY AND C. W. WATSON, EDS. *An Anthropology of Indirect Communication.* London: Routledge, 2001.

HENNIG, WILLI. *Phylogenetic Systematics.* Urbana: University of Illinois Press, 1966.

HENRY, DONALD O. "Foraging, Sedentism, and Adaptive Vigor in the Natufian: Rethinking the Linkages." In G. A. Clark, ed., *Perspectives on the Past.*

HENRY, DONALD O. *From Foraging to Agriculture: The Levant at the End of the Ice Age.* Philadelphia: University of Pennsylvania Press, 1989.

HENRY, EDWARD O. "The Variety of Music in a North Indian Village: Reassessing Cantometrics." *Ethnomusicology,* 20 (1976): 49–66.

HENSHILWOOD, CHRISTOPHER, et al., "Emergence of Modern Human Behavior: Middle Stone Age Engravings from South Africa," *Science* 295 (15 Feb 2002): 1278–1280.

HERBIG, PAUL A. *The Innovation Matrix: Culture and Structure Prerequisites to Innovation.* Westport, CT: Quorum Books, 1994.

HERDT, GILBERT. "Sexual Cultures and Population Movement: Implications for AIDS/STDs." In Gilbert Herdt, ed., *Sexual Cultures and Migration in the Era of AIDS: Anthropological and Demographic Perspectives.* Oxford: Oxford University Press, 1997, pp. 3–22.

HERRMAN, HELEN. "A Survey of Homeless Mentally Ill People in Melbourne, Australia." *Hospital and Community Psychiatry,* 41 (1990): 1291–92.

HERRNSTEIN, RICHARD J., AND CHARLES MURRAY. *The Bell Curve: Intelligence and Class Structure in American Life.* New York: Free Press, 1994.

HEWES, GORDON W. "Food Transport and the Origin of Hominid Bipedalism." *American Anthropologist,* 63 (1961): 687–710.

HEWLETT, BARRY. "Diverse Contexts of Human Infancy." In C. R. Ember and Ember, eds., *Cross-Cultural Research for Social Science.*

HEWLETT, BARRY S., AND L. L. CAVALLI-SFORZA. "Cultural Transmission among Aka Pygmies." *American Anthropologist,* 88 (1986): 922–34.

HIATT, L. R. "Polyandry in Sri Lanka: A Test Case for Parental Investment Theory," *Man,* 15 (1980): 583–98.

HICKEY, GERALD CANNON. *Village in Vietnam.* New Haven, CT: Yale University Press, 1964.

HICKSON, LETITIA. "The Social Contexts of Apology in Dispute Settlement: A Cross-Cultural Study." *Ethnology,* 25 (1986): 283–94.

HIGGINS, PATRICIA J. AND ANTHONY PAREDES, EDS. *Classics of Practicing Anthropology: 1978–1998.* Society for Applied Anthropology, 2000.

HIGGINS, PATRICIA J., AND J. ANTHONY PAREDES, EDS. *Classics of Practicing Anthropology: 1978–1998.* Oklahoma City, OK: Society for Applied Anthropology, 2000.

HIGLEY, STEPHEN RICHARD. *Privilege, Power, and Place: The Geography of the American Upper Class* (Lanham, MD: Rowman & Littlefield, 1995), pp. 1–47.

HILL, JANE H. "Apes and Language." *Annual Review of Anthropology,* 7 (1978): 89–112.

HILL, JANE H. "Do Apes Have Language?" In C. R. Ember, Ember, and Peregrine, eds., *Research Frontiers in Anthropology.* Vol. 3.

HILL, JONATHAN D. "Introduction: Ethnogenesis in the Americas. 1492–1992." In Hill, ed., *Ethnogenesis in the Americas,* pp. 1–19.

HILL, JONATHAN D., ED. *Ethnogenesis in the Americas, 1492–1992.* Iowa City: University of Iowa Press, 1996.

HILL, KIM, HILLARD KAPLAN, KRISTEN HAWKES, AND A. MAGDALENA HURTADO. "Foraging Decisions among Aché Hunter-Gatherers: New Data and Implications for Optimal Foraging Models." *Ethology and Sociobiology,* 8 (1987): 1–36.

HOBSBAWM, E. J. *Age of Revolution.* New York: Praeger, 1970.

HOCKETT, C. F., AND R. ASCHER. "The Human Revolution." *Current Anthropology,* 5 (1964): 135–68.

HODDER, I. *The Domestication of Europe: Structure and Contingency in Neolithic Societies.* Oxford: Blackwell, 1990.

HOEBEL, E. ADAMSON. *The Cheyennes: Indians of the Great Plains.* New York: Holt, Rinehart & Winston, 1960.

HOEBEL, E. ADAMSON. *The Law of Primitive Man.* New York: Atheneum, 1968. (Originally published 1954.)

HOFFECKER, JOHN F., W. ROGER POWERS, AND TED GOEBEL. "The Colonization of Beringia and the Peopling of the New World." *Science,* January 1, 1993, 46–53.

HOFFMAN, LOIS WLADIS. "Cross-Cultural Differences in Child-Rearing Goals." In LeVine, Miller, and West, eds., *Parental Behavior in Diverse Societies.*

HOIJER, HARRY. "Cultural Implications of Some Navaho Linguistic Categories." In Hymes, ed., *Language in Culture and Society.*

HOLDAWAY, R. N., AND C. JACOMB. "Rapid Extinction of the Moas (Aves: Dinornithiformes): Model, Test, and Implications." *Science,* 287 (2000): 2250–57.

HOLDEN, CONSTANCE. "Selective Power of UV." *Science,* 289 (2000): 1461.

HOLE, FRANK, ED. *Archaeology of Western Iran.* Washington, DC: Smithsonian Institution Press, 1987.

HOLE, FRANK. "Environmental Shock and Urban Origins." In Stein and Rothman, eds., *Chiefdoms and Early States in the Near East.*

HOLE, FRANK. "Origins of Agriculture." In Jones, Martin, and Pilbeam, eds., *The Cambridge Encyclopedia of Human Evolution.*

HOLE, FRANK, AND ROBERT F. HEIZER. *An Introduction to Prehistoric Archeology.* 3rd ed. New York: Holt, Rinehart & Winston, 1973.

HOLE, FRANK, KENT V. FLANNERY, AND JAMES A. NEELY. *Prehistory and Human Ecology of the Deh Luran Plain.* Memoirs of the Museum of Anthropology No. 1. Ann Arbor: University of Michigan, 1969.

HOLLAN, DOUGLAS. "Cross-Cultural Differences in the Self." *Journal of Anthropological Research,* 48 (1992): 289–90.

HOLLAND, DOROTHY, AND NAOMI QUINN, EDS. *Cultural Models in Language and Thought.* Cambridge: Cambridge University Press, 1987.

HOLLOWAY, MARGUERITE. "Sustaining the Amazon." *Scientific American,* July 1993, 91–99.

HOLLOWAY, RALPH L. "The Casts of Fossil Hominid Brains." *Scientific American,* July 1974, 106–15.

HOLMES, JANET. *An Introduction to Sociolinguistics.* 2nd ed. London: Longman, 2001.

HOLMES, JANET. *An Introduction to Sociolinguistics.* London: Longman, 2001.

HONIGMANN, JOHN J. *Personality in Culture.* New York: Harper & Row, 1967.

HOOGBERGEN, WIM. *The Boni Maroon Wars in Suriname.* Leiden: E. J. Brill, 1990.

HOOPER, JUDITH, *Of Moths and Men: The Untold Story of Science and the Peppered Moth* (New York: W.W. Norton, 2002)

HOPKINS, K. "Brother-Sister Marriage in Roman Egypt." *Comparative Studies in Society and History,* 22 (1980): 303–54.

HOROWITZ, MICHAEL M. "Donors and Deserts: The Political Ecology of Destructive Development in the Sahel." In Huss-Ashmore and Katz, eds., *African Food Systems in Crisis,* Part Two.

HOUSTON, STEPHEN D. "The Phonetic Decipherment of Mayan Glyphs." *Antiquity,* 62 (1988): 126–35.

HOWARD, ALAN, AND JAN RENSEL. "Rotuma: Interpreting a Wedding." In M. Ember and Ember, eds., *Portraits of Culture.*

HOWELL, F. CLARK. "Observations on the Earlier Phases of the European Lower Paleolithic." In *Recent Studies in Paleoanthropology. American Anthropologist,* special publication, April 1966, pp. 88–200.

HOWELL, NANCY. *Demography of the Dobe !Kung.* New York: Academic Press, 1979.

HOWELLS, W. *Getting Here: The Story of Human Evolution.* 2nd ed. Washington, DC: Compass Press, 1997.

HRDY, SARAH BLAFFER. *The Langurs of Abu: Female and Male Strategies of Reproduction.* Cambridge, MA: Harvard University Press, 1977.

HSU, FRANCIS L. K., ED. *Psychological Anthropology.* 2nd ed. Cambridge, MA: Schenkman, 1972.

HUANG, H.T., "Hypolactasia and the Chinese Diet," *Current Anthropology* 43 (Dec. 2002), 809–819.

HUMPHREY, CAROLINE, AND STEPHEN HUGH-JONES, EDS. *Barter, Exchange and Value: An Anthropological Approach.* New York: Cambridge University Press, 1992.

HUMPHREY, CAROLINE, AND STEPHEN HUGH-JONES. "Introduction: Barter, Exchange and Value." In Humphrey and Hugh-Jones, eds., *Barter, Exchange and Value.*

HUNT, MORTON. *Sexual Behavior in the 1970s.* Chicago: Playboy Press, 1974.

HUNT, ROBERT C. "Labor Productivity and Agricultural Development: Boserup Revisited." *Human Ecology,* 28 (2000): 251–277.

HUNT, ROBERT C., AND GILMAN, ANTONIO, EDS. *Property in Economic Context.* Lanham, MD: University Press of America, 1998.

HURTADO, ANA M., KRISTEN HAWKES, KIM HILL, AND HILLARD KAPLAN. "Female Subsistence Strategies among the Aché Hunter-Gatherers of Eastern Paraguay." *Human Ecology,* 13 (1985): 1–28.

HUSS-ASHMORE, REBECCA, AND FRANCIS E. JOHNSTON. "Bioanthropological Research in Developing Countries." *Annual Review of Anthropology,* 14 (1985): 475–527.

HUSS-ASHMORE, REBECCA, AND SOLOMON H. KATZ, EDS. *African Food Systems in Crisis.* Part Two: *Contending with Change.* New York: Gordon and Breach, 1990.

HUXLEY, THOMAS H. "Man's Place in Nature." In Young, ed., *Evolution of Man.*

HYMES, DELL, ED. *Language in Culture and Society: A Reader in Linguistics and Anthropology.* New York: Harper & Row, 1964.

HYMES, DELL. *Foundations in Sociolinguistics: An Ethnographic Approach.* Philadelphia: University of Pennsylvania Press, 1974.

INGOLD, TIM, DAVID RICHES, AND JAMES WOODBURN, EDS. *Hunters and Gatherers.* 1: History, Evolution and Social Change. New York: St. Martin's, 1988.

INHORN, M. C., AND BROWN, P. J., EDS. *The Anthropology of Infectious Disease.* Amsterdam: Gordon and Breach, 1997.

INHORN, MARCIA C., AND PETER J. BROWN. *The Anthropology of Infectious Disease: International Health Perspectives.* Amsterdam: Gordon and Breach, 1997.

IRONS, WILLIAM. "Natural Selection, Adaptation, and Human Social Behavior." In Chagnon and Irons, eds., *Evolutionary Biology and Human Social Behavior.*

IRWIN, MARC H., GARY N. SCHAFER, AND CYNTHIA P. FEIDEN. "Emic and Unfamiliar Category Sorting of Mano Farmers and U.S. Undergraduates." *Journal of Cross-Cultural Psychology,* 5 (1974): 407–23.

ISAAC, GLYNN, ED., assisted by Barbara Isaac. *Plio-Pleistocene Archaeology.* Oxford: Clarendon Press, 1997.

ISAAC, GLYNN. "The Archaeology of Human Origins: Studies of the Lower Pleistocene in East Africa, 1971–1981." In Wendorf and Close, eds., *Advances in World Archaeology.*

ISAAC, GLYNN. "The Diet of Early Man: Aspects of Archaeological Evidence from Lower and Middle Pleistocene Sites in Africa." *World Archaeology,* 2 (1971): 277–99.

ITKONEN, T. I. "The Lapps of Finland." *Southwestern Journal of Anthropology,* 7 (1951): 32–68.

ITOIGAWA, NAOSUKE, YUKIMARU SUGIYAMA, GENE P. SACKETT, AND ROGER K. R. THOMPSON, EDS. *Topics in Primatology.* Vol. 2. Tokyo: University of Tokyo Press, 1992.

JABLONSKI, NINA, AND GEORGE CHAPLIN. "The Evolution of Human Skin Color." *Journal of Human Evolution,* 39 (2000): 57–106.

JABLONSKY, NINA G. AND GEORGE CHAPLIN, "Skin Deep," *Scientific American* (Oct. 2002), 74–81.

JACOBS, SUE-ELLEN, AND CHRISTINE ROBERTS. "Sex, Sexuality, Gender and Gender Variance." In Morgen, ed., *Gender and Anthropology.*

JAEGER, J., T. THEIN, M. BENAMMI, Y. CHAIMANEE, A. N. SOE, T. LWIN, T. TUN, S. WAI, AND S. DUCROCQ. "A New Primate from the Middle Eocene of Myanmar and the Asian Early Origins of Anthropoids." *Science,* 286 (1999): 528–30.

JAMES, WILLIAM. *The Varieties of Religious Experience: A Study in Human Nature.* New York: Modern Library, 1902.

JANKOWIAK, WILLIAM R. "Urban Mongols: Ethnicity in Communist China." In M. Ember and Ember, eds., *Portraits of Culture.*

JANKOWIAK, WILLIAM R., AND EDWARD F. FISCHER. "A Cross-Cultural Perspective on Romantic Love." *Ethnology,* 31 (1992): 149–55.

JANZEN, DANIEL H. "Tropical Agroecosystems." *Science,* December 21, 1973, 1212–19.

JAYASWAL, VIDULA. "South Asian Upper Paleolithic." In P. N. Peregrine and M. Ember, eds., *Encyclopedia of Prehistory.* Vol. 8: South and Southwest Asia. New York: Kluwer Academic/ Plenum, 2002.

JELLIFFE, DERRICK B., AND E. F. PATRICE JELLIFFE. "Human Milk, Nutrition, and the World Resource Crisis." *Science,* May 9, 1975, 557–61.

JENNINGS, J. D. *Prehistory of North America.* New York: McGraw-Hill, 1968.

JENSEN, ARTHUR. "How Much Can We Boost IQ and Scholastic Achievement?" *Harvard Educational Review,* 29 (1969): 1–123.

JEPSEN, GLENN L., ERNST MAYR, AND GEORGE GAYLORD SIMPSON, EDS. *Genetics, Paleontology, and Evolution.* New York: Atheneum, 1963.

JOACHIM, MICHAEL. "Hunting and Gathering Societies." In Levinson and Ember, eds., *Encyclopedia of Cultural Anthropology.*

JOANS, BARBARA. "Problems in Pocatello: A Study in Linguistic Misunderstanding," *Practicing Anthropology* 6 (1984); reprinted in Aaron Podolefsky and Peter J. Brown, eds., *Applying Cultural Anthropology: An Introductory Reader,* 3rd edition. (Mountain View: CA: Mayfield, 1997), pp. 51–54.

JOHANNES, R. E. *Words of the Lagoon: Fishing and Marine Lore in the Palau District of Micronesia.* Berkeley: University of California Press, 1981.

JOHANSON, DONALD C., AND MAITLAND EDEY. *Lucy: The Beginnings of Humankind.* New York: Simon & Schuster, 1981.

JOHANSON, DONALD C., AND TIM D. WHITE. "A Systematic Assessment of Early African Hominids." *Science,* January 26, 1979, 321–30.

JOHNSON, ALLEN, AND TIMOTHY EARLE. *The Evolution of Human Societies: From Foraging Group to Agrarian State.* Stanford, CA: Stanford University Press, 1987.

JOHNSON, AMBER LYNN. "Cross-Cultural Analysis of Pastoral Adaptations and Organizational States: A Preliminary Study." *Cross-Cultural Research,* 36 (2002): 151–180.

JOHNSON, GREGORY A. "Aspects of Regional Analysis in Archaeology." *Annual Review of Anthropology,* 6 (1977): 479–508.

JOHNSON, GREGORY. "The Changing Organization of Uruk Administration on the Susiana Plain." In Hole, ed., *Archaeology of Western Iran.*

JOHNSON, THOMAS M., AND CAROLYN F. SARGENT, EDS. *Medical Anthropology: Contemporary Theory and Method.* Westport, CT: Praeger, 1990.

JOHNSTON, DAVID CAY. "Gap Between Rich and Poor Found Substantially Wider," *New York Times National,* Sunday, September 5, 1999, p. 16.

JOLLY, ALISON. *The Evolution of Primate Behavior.* 2nd ed. New York: Macmillan, 1985.

JOLLY, CLIFFORD. "The Seed-Eaters: A New Model of Hominid Differentiation Based on a Baboon Analogy." *Man,* 5 (1970): 5–28.

JONES, NICHOLAS BLURTON, KRISTEN HAWKES, AND JAMES F. O'CONNELL. "The Global Process and Local Ecology: How Should We Explain Differences between the Hadza and the !Kung?" In Kent, *Cultural Diversity among Twentieth-Century Foragers.*

JONES, STEVE, ROBERT MARTIN, AND DAVID PILBEAM, EDS. *The Cambridge Encyclopedia of Human Evolution.* New York: Cambridge University Press, 1992.

JORDAN, ANN T., ED. *Practicing Anthropology in Corporate America: Consulting on Organizational Culture.* NAPA Bulletin No. 14. Arlington, VA: American Anthropological Association, 1994.

JUDGE, W. JAMES, AND JERRY DAWSON. "Paleo-Indian Settlement Technology in New Mexico." *Science,* June 16, 1972, 1210–16.

JUNG, CARL G. *Psychology and Religion.* New Haven, CT: Yale University Press, 1938.

JUNGERS, WILLIAM L. "New Estimates of Body Size in Australopithecines." In Grine, ed., *Evolutionary History of the "Robust" Australopithecines.*

JUNGERS, WILLIAM L. "Relative Joint Size and Hominoid Locomotor Adaptations with Implications for the Evolution of Hominid Bipedalism." *Journal of Human Evolution,* 17 (1988): 247–65.

KAMIN, LEON J. "Behind the Curve." *Scientific American,* February 1995, 99–103.

KANG, BONG W. "A Reconsideration of Population Pressure and Warfare: A Protohistoric Korean Case," *Current Anthropology,* 41 (2000): 873–881.

KANG, GAY ELIZABETH. "Exogamy and Peace Relations of Social Units: A Cross-Cultural Test." *Ethnology,* 18 (1979): 85–99.

KAPLAN, HILLARD, AND KIM HILL. "Food Sharing among Aché Foragers: Tests of Explanatory Hypotheses." *Current Anthropology,* 26 (1985): 223–46.

KAPLAN, HILLARD, KIM HILL, AND A. MAGDALENA HURTADO. "Risk, Foraging and Food Sharing among the Aché." In Cashdan, ed., *Risk and Uncertainty in Tribal and Peasant Economies.*

KAPPELMAN, JOHN. "The Attraction of Paleomagnetism." *Evolutionary Anthropology,* 2, no. 3 (1993): 89–99.

KARDINER, ABRAM, with Ralph Linton. *The Individual and His Society.* New York: Golden Press, 1946. (Originally published 1939 by Columbia University Press.)

KASARDA, JOHN D. "Economic Structure and Fertility: A Comparative Analysis." *Demography,* 8, no. 3 (August 1971): 307–18.

KAY, RICHARD F. "*Parapithecidae.*" In Tattersall, Delson, and van Couvering, eds., *Encyclopedia of Human Evolution and Prehistory.*

KAY, RICHARD F. "Teeth." In Tattersall, Delson, and van Couvering, eds., *Encyclopedia of Human Evolution and Prehistory.*

KAY, RICHARD F., C. ROSS, AND B. A. WILLIAMS. "Anthropoid Origins." *Science,* 275 (1997): 797–804.

KEELEY, LAWRENCE H. *Experimental Determination of Stone Tool Uses: A Microwear Analysis.* Chicago: University of Chicago Press, 1980.

KEELEY, LAWRENCE. "The Functions of Paleolithic Flint Tools." *Scientific American,* 237 (1977): 108–26.

KEENAN, ELINOR. "Norm-Makers, Norm-Breakers: Uses of Speech by Men and Women in a Malagasy Community." In Bauman and Sherzer, *Explorations in the Ethnography of Speaking,* 2nd ed.

KEHOE, ALICE B. AND DODY H. GILETTI, "Women's Preponderance in Possession Cults: The Calcium-Deficiency Hypothesis Extended." *American Anthropologist,* 83 (1981): 549–561.

KELLER, HELEN. *The Story of My Life.* New York: Dell, 1974. (Originally published 1902.)

KELLEY, JAY. "The Evolution of Apes." In Jones, Martin, and Pilbeam, eds., *The Cambridge Encyclopedia of Human Evolution.*

KELLY, RAYMOND C. "Witchcraft and Sexual Relations: An Exploration in the Social and Semantic Implications of the Structure of Belief." Paper presented at the annual meeting of the American Anthropological Association, Mexico City, 1974.

KELLY, RAYMOND C. *The Nuer Conquest: The Structure and Development of an Expansionist System.* Ann Arbor: University of Michigan Press, 1985.

KELLY, ROBERT L. "Lithic Analysis: Chipped Stone Tools and Waste Flakes in Archaeology," in Peter N. Peregrine, Carol R. Ember, and Melvin Ember, *Archaeology: Original Readings in Method and Practice* (Upper Saddle River, NJ: Prentice Hall, 2002).

KELLY, ROBERT L. *The Foraging Spectrum: Diversity in Hunter-Gatherer Lifeways.* Washington, DC: Smithsonian Institution Press, 1995.

KENT, SUSAN, ED. *Cultural Diversity among Twentieth-Century Foragers: An African Perspective.* Cambridge: Cambridge University Press, 1996.

KERR, RICHARD A. "Sea-Floor Dust shows Drought Felled Akkadian Empire." *Science,* January 16, 1998, 325–26.

KHOSROSHASHI, FATEMEH. "Penguins Don't Care, but Women Do: A Social Identity Analysis of a Whorfian Problem." *Language in Society,* 18 (1989): 505–25.

KILBRIDE, PHILIP L., AND JANET C. KILBRIDE. "Polygyny: A Modern Contradiction?" In Kilbride and Kilbride, *Changing Family Life in East Africa.*

KILBRIDE, PHILIP L., AND JANET C. KILBRIDE. *Changing Family Life in East Africa: Women and Children at Risk.* University Park: Pennsylvania State University Press, 1990.

KIMBEL, WILLIAM H., T. D. WHITE, AND D. C. JOHANSEN. "Cranial Morphology of *Australopithecus afarensis:* A Comparative Study Based on Composite Reconstruction of the Adult Skull." *American Journal of Physical Anthropology,* 64 (1984): 337–88.

KING, BARBARA J. "Introduction," In King, ed. *The Origins of Language,* pp. 3–19.

KING, BARBARA. *The Origins of Language: What Nonhuman Primates Can Tell Us.* Santa Fe, New Mexico, 1999.

KING, J. C. H. "Tradition in Native American Art." In Wade, ed., *The Arts of the North American Indian.*

KING, MARIE-CLAIRE AND ARNO MOTULSKY, "Mapping Human History," *Science* 298 (20 Dec. 2002), 2342– 2343.

KING, SETH S. "Some Farm Machinery Seems Less Than Human." *New York Times,* April 8, 1979, p. E9.

KINGSTON, JOHN D., BRUNO D. MARINO, AND ANDREW HILL. "Isotopic Evidence for Neogene Hominid Paleoenvironments in the Kenya Rift Valley." *Science,* May 13, 1994, 955–59.

KLASS, MORTON. "Is There 'Caste' Outside of India?" In C.R. Ember and Ember, eds., *Cross-Cultural Research for Social Science.*

KLEIN, J, AND TAKAHATA, N. *Where Do We Come From?: The Molecular Evidence for Human Descent.* New York: Springer Verlag, 2002.

KLEIN, RICHARD G. "Ice-Age Hunters of the Ukraine." *Scientific American,* June 1974, 96–105.

KLEIN, RICHARD G. "Reconstructing How Early People Exploited Animals: Problems and Prospects." In Nitecki and Nitecki, eds., *The Evolution of Human Hunting.*

KLEIN, RICHARD G. "Southern Africa before the Ice Age." In Corruccini and Ciochon, eds., *Integrative Paths to the Past.*

KLEIN, RICHARD G. "The Ecology of Early Man in Southern Africa." *Science,* July 8, 1977, 115–26.

KLEIN, RICHARD G. "The Stone Age Prehistory of Southern Africa." *Annual Review of Anthropology,* 12 (1983): 25–48.

KLEIN, RICHARD G. *The Human Career: Human Biological and Cultural Origins.* Chicago: University of Chicago Press, 1989.

KLEINBERG, JILL. "Practical Implications of Organizational Culture Where Americans and Japanese Work Together." In Jordan, ed., *Practicing Anthropology in Corporate America.*

KLEINMAN, ARTHUR. *Rethinking Psychiatry: From Cultural Category to Personal Experience.* New York: Macmillan, 1988.

KLEINMAN, ARTHUR, AND BYRON GOOD, EDS. *Culture and Depression: Studies in the Anthropology and Cross-Cultural Psychiatry of Affect and Disorder.* Berkeley: University of California Press, 1985.

KLEINMAN, ARTHUR, VEENA DAS, AND MARGARET LOCK, EDS. *Social Suffering.* Berkeley: University of California Press, 1997.

KLEINMAN, DEVRA, ED., *The Biology and Conservation of the Callitrichidae* (Washington, DC: Smithsonian Institution, 1977).

KLIMA, BOHUSLAV. "The First Ground-Plan of an Upper Paleolithic Loess Settlement in Middle Europe and Its Meaning." In Braidwood and Willey, eds., *Courses Toward Urban Life.*

KLINEBERG, OTTO, ED. *Characteristics of the American Negro.* New York: Harper & Brothers, 1944.

KLINEBERG, OTTO. "Foreword." In Segall, *Cross-Cultural Psychology.*

KLINEBERG, OTTO. *Negro Intelligence and Selective Migration.* New York: Columbia University Press, 1935.

KLUCKHOHN, CLYDE. "As an Anthropologist Views It." In Deutsch, ed., *Sex Habits of American Men.*

KLUCKHOHN, CLYDE. "Recurrent Themes in Myths and Mythmaking." In Dundes, ed., *The Study of Folklore.*

KNAUFT, BRUCE M. "Cargo Cults and Relational Separation." *Behavior Science Research,* 13 (1978): 185–240.

KNUDSEN, DEAN D., AND JoANN L. MILLER, EDS. *Abused and Battered: Social and Legal Responses to Family Violence.* New York: Aldine, 1991.

KOCH, KLAUS-FRIEDRICH, SORAYA ALTORKI, ANDREW ARNO, AND LETITIA HICKSON. "Ritual Reconciliation and the Obviation of Grievances: A Comparative Study in the Ethnography of Law." *Ethnology,* 16 (1977): 269–84.

KONNER, MELVIN, AND CAROL WORTHMAN. "Nursing Frequency, Gonadal Function, and Birth Spacing among !Kung Hunter-Gatherers." *Science,* February 15, 1980, 788–91.

KORBIN, JILL E. "Introduction." In Korbin, ed., *Child Abuse and Neglect.*

KORBIN, JILL E., ED. *Child Abuse and Neglect: Cross-Cultural Perspectives.* Berkeley: University of California, 1981.

KOROTAYEV, ANDREY AND DMITRI BONDARENKO. "Polygyny and Democracy: A Cross-Cultural Comparison." *Cross-Cultural Research,* 34 (2000): 190–208.

KOTTAK, CONRAD P. "The New Ecological Anthropology." *Current Anthropology,* 101 (1999): 23–35.

KOTTAK, CONRAD P. *Assault on Paradise: Social Change in a Brazilian Village.* New York: Random House, 1983.

KOTTAK, CONRAD PHILLIP. "The Media, Development, and Social Change." In Moran, *Transforming Societies, Transforming Anthropology.*

KOZLOWSKI, S. K., ED. *The Mesolithic in Europe.* Warsaw: Warsaw University Press, 1973.

KRACKE, WAUD H. *Force and Persuasion: Leadership in an Amazonian Society.* Chicago: University of Chicago Press, 1979.

KRAHN, H., T. F. HARTNAGEL, AND J. W. GARTRELL. "Income Inequality and Homicide Rates: Cross-National Data and Criminological Theories." *Criminology,* 24 (1986): 269–95.

KRAMER, ANDREW. "The Natural History and Evolutionary Fate of *Homo erectus.*" In Peregrine, Ember, and Ember, eds., *Physical Anthropology.*

KRAMER, SAMUEL NOEL. *The Sumerians: Their History, Culture, and Character.* Chicago: University of Chicago Press, 1963.

KREBS, J. R., AND N. B. DAVIES, EDS. *Behavioural Ecology: An Evolutionary Approach.* 2nd ed. Sunderland, MA: Sinauer, 1984.

KREBS, J. R., AND N. B. DAVIES. *An Introduction to Behavioural Ecology.* 2nd ed. Sunderland, MA: Sinauer, 1987.

KRINGS, MATTHIAS, A. STONE, R. W. SCHMITZ, H. KRAINITZKI, M. STONEKING, AND S. PAABO. "Neandertal DNA Sequences and the Origin of Modern Humans." *Cell,* 90 (1997): 19–30.

KRIPPNER, STANLEY. "Dreams and Shamanism." In Nicholson, *Shamanism,* pp. 125–32.

KRISTOF, NICHOLAS D. "Japan's Invisible Minority: Better Off Than in Past, but Still Outcasts." *New York Times International,* November 30, 1995, p. A18.

KROEBER, ALFRED L. *The Nature of Culture.* Chicago: University of Chicago Press, 1952.

KROEBER, THEODORA. *Ishi in Two Worlds.* Berkeley: University of California Press, 1967.

KUEHN, STEVEN. "New Evidence for Late Paleoindian–Early Archaic Subsistence Behavior in the Western Great Lakes." *American Antiquity,* 63 (1998): 457–76.

KUSHNER, GILBERT. "Applied Anthropology." In Emener and Darrow, eds., *Career Explorations in Human Services.*

KUZNAR, LAWRENCE A. *Reclaiming a Scientific Anthropology.* Walnut Creek, CA: AltaMira Press, 2002.

LAKOFF, ROBIN. "Language and Woman's Place." *Language in Society,* 2 (1973): 45–80.

LAKOFF, ROBIN. "Why Can't a Woman Be Less Like a Man?" In Lakoff, *Talking Power.*

LAKOFF, ROBIN. *Talking Power: The Politics of Language in Our Lives.* New York: Basic Books, 1990.

LAMBERT, HELEN. "Not Talking About Sex in India: Indirection and the Communication of Bodily Intention." In Hendry and Watson, eds. *An Anthropology of Indirect Communication,* pp. 51–67.

LAMBERT, WILLIAM W., LEIGH MINTURN TRIANDIS, AND MARGERY WOLF. "Some Correlates of Beliefs in the Malevolence and Benevolence of Supernatural Beings: A Cross-Societal Study." *Journal of Abnormal and Social Psychology,* 58 (1959): 162–69.

LANDAUER, THOMAS K. "Infantile Vaccination and the Secular Trend in Stature." *Ethos,* 1 (1973): 499–503.

LANDAUER, THOMAS K., AND JOHN W. M. WHITING. "Correlates and Consequences of Stress in Infancy." In Munroe, Munroe, and Whiting, eds., *Handbook of Cross-Cultural Human Development.*

LANDAUER, THOMAS K., AND JOHN W. M. WHITING. "Infantile Stimulation and Adult Stature of Human Males." *American Anthropologist,* 66 (1964): 1007–28.

LANGNESS, LEWIS L. *The Study of Culture.* San Francisco: Chandler and Sharp, 1974.

LARSEN, CLARK SPENSER. "Bare Bones Anthropology: The Bioarchaeology of Human Remains." In Peregrine, Ember, and Ember, eds., *Archaeology.*

LARSON, DANIEL O., JOHN R. JOHNSON, AND JOEL C. MICHAELSEN. "Missionization among the Coastal Chumash of Central California: A Study of Risk Minimization Strategies." *American Anthropologist,* 96 (1994): 263–99.

LASSWELL, HAROLD. *Politics: Who Gets What, When, How.* New York: McGraw-Hill, 1936.

"The Last of the Cahokians." *Science,* April 19, 1996, 351.

LAWLESS, ROBERT. "Haitians: From Political Repression to Chaos," in M. Ember and Ember, eds. *Portraits of Culture: Ethnographic Originals,* in Carol R. Ember and Melvin Ember, eds., *New Directions in Anthropology.*

LAWLESS, ROBERT, VINSON H. SUTLIVE, JR., AND MARIO D. ZAMORA, EDS. *Fieldwork: The Human Experience.* New York: Gordon and Breach, 1983.

LAYTON, ROBERT. *Australian Rock Art: A New Synthesis.* Cambridge: Cambridge University Press, 1992.

LEACH, JERRY W. "Introduction." In Leach and Leach, eds., *The Kula.*

LEACH, JERRY W., AND EDMUND LEACH, EDS. *The Kula: New Perspectives on Massim Exchange.* Cambridge: Cambridge University Press, 1983.

LEACOCK, ELEANOR. "The Montagnais 'Hunting Territory' and the Fur Trade." *American Anthropological Association Memoir* 78 (1954): 1–59.

LEACOCK, ELEANOR, AND RICHARD LEE, EDS. *Politics and History in Band Societies.* Cambridge: Cambridge University Press, 1982.

LEACOCK, ELEANOR, AND RICHARD LEE. "Introduction." In Leacock and Lee, eds., *Politics and History in Band Societies.*

LEAKEY, L. S. B. "Finding the World's Earliest Man." *National Geographic,* September 1960, 420–35.

LEAKEY, L. S. B. *Olduvai Gorge, 1951–1961,* Volume I: Preliminary Report on the Geology and Fauna. (Cambridge: Cambridge University Press, 1965).

LEAKEY, LOUIS. *Olduvai Gorge.* Vol. 1: *A Preliminary Report on the Geology and Fauna.* Cambridge: Cambridge University Press, 1965.

LEAKEY, MAEVE, C. S. FEIBEL, I. MCDOUGALL, AND A. WALKER. "New Four-Million-Year-Old Hominid Species from Kanapoi and Allia Bay, Kenya." *Nature,* 376 (1995): 565–71.

LEAKEY, MAEVE, IAN TATTERSALL, *The Fossil Trail.* Adapted from *New York Times,* September 5, 1995, p. C9.

LEAKEY, MEAVE, FRED SPOOR, FRANK BROWN, PATRICK GATHOGO, CHRISTOPHER KIARIE, LOUISE LEAKEY, IAN MCDOUGALL, "New Hominin Genus from Eastern Africa Shows Diverse Middle Pliocene Lineages," Nature, 410 (2001): 433–451.

LEAKEY, MARY. *Olduvai Gorge: Excavations in Beds I and II.* Cambridge: Cambridge University Press, 1971.

LEAKEY, MARY. *Olduvai Gorge: My Search for Early Man.* London: Collins, 1979.

LEAKEY, RICHARD E. *The Making of Mankind.* New York: Dutton, 1981.

LEDERMAN, RENA. "Big Men, Large and Small? Towards a Comparative Perspective." *Ethnology,* 29 (1990): 3–15.

LEE, PHYLLIS C. "Home Range, Territory and Intergroup Encounters." In Robert A. Hinde, ed., *Primate Social Relationship: An Integrated Approach.* Sunderland, MA: Sinauer, 1983.

LEE, PHYLLIS C. *Comparative Primate Socioecology.* New York: Cambridge University Press, 1999.

LEE, RICHARD B. "Population Growth and the Beginnings of Sedentary Life among the !Kung Bushmen." In Spooner, ed., *Population Growth.*

LEE, RICHARD B. "What Hunters Do for a Living, or, How to Make Out on Scarce Resources." In Lee and DeVore, eds., *Man the Hunter.*

LEE, RICHARD B. *The !Kung San: Men, Women, and Work in a Foraging Society.* Cambridge: Cambridge University Press, 1979.

LEE, RICHARD B., AND IRVEN DEVORE, EDS. *Man the Hunter.* Chicago: Aldine, 1968.

LEES, SUSAN H., AND DANIEL G. BATES. "The Origins of Specialized Nomadic Pastoralism: A Systemic Model." *American Antiquity,* 39 (1974): 187–93.

LEIBOWITZ, LILA. *Females, Males, Families: A Biosocial Approach.* North Scituate, MA: Duxbury, 1978.

LEIS, NANCY B. "Women in Groups: Ijaw Women's Associations." In Rosaldo and Lamphere, eds., *Woman, Culture, and Society.*

LENSKI, GERHARD. *Power and Privilege: A Theory of Social Stratification.* Chapel Hill: University of North Carolina Press, 1984. (First published 1966.)

LEONARD, WILLIAM R., "Food for Thought: Dietary Change Was a Driving Force in Human Evolution," *Scientific American* (Dec. 2002), pp. 108–115.

LEPOWSKY, MARIA. "Big Men, Big Women and Cultural Autonomy." *Ethnology,* 29 (1990): 35–50.

LESLIE, C. "Introduction." In C. Leslie, ed., *Asian Medical Systems: A Comparative Study.* Los Angeles: University of California Press, 1976.

LESSA, WILLIAM A., AND EVON Z. VOGT, EDS. *Reader in Comparative Religion: An Anthropological Approach.* 3rd ed. New York: Harper & Row, 1971.

LESSA, WILLIAM A., AND EVON Z. VOGT, EDS. *Reader in Comparative Religion: An Anthropological Approach.* 4th ed. New York: Harper & Row, 1979.

LETT, J. *Science, Reason, and Anthropology: The Principles of Rational Inquiry.* Lanham, MD: Rowman & Littlefield, 1997.

LETT, JAMES. "Scientific Anthropology." In Levinson and Ember, eds., *Encyclopedia of Cultural Anthropology.*

LEVINE, JAMES A., ROBERT WEISELL, SIMON CHEVASSUS, CLAUDIO D. MARTINEZ, AND BARBARA BURLINGAME. "The Distribution of Work Tasks for Male and Female Children and Adults Separated by Gender" in "Looking at Child Labor," *Science* 296 (10 May 2002): 1025.

LEVINE, NANCY E. "Women's Work and Infant Feeding: A Case from Rural Nepal." *Ethnology,* 27 (1988): 231–51.

LEVINE, ROBERT A. "Human Parental Care: Universal Goals, Cultural Strategies, Individual Behavior." In LeVine, Miller, and West, eds., *Parental Behavior in Diverse Societies.*

LEVINE, ROBERT A. *Dreams and Deeds: Achievement Motivation in Nigeria.* Chicago: University of Chicago Press, 1966.

LEVINE, ROBERT A., AND BARBARA B. LEVINE. "Nyansongo: A Gusii Community in Kenya." In Whiting, ed., *Six Cultures.*

LEVINE, ROBERT A., PATRICE M. MILLER, AND MARY MAXWELL WEST, EDS. *Parental Behavior in Diverse Societies.* San Francisco: Jossey-Bass, 1988.

LEVINSON, DAVID. *Family Violence in Cross-Cultural Perspective.* Newbury Park, CA: Sage, 1989.

LEVINSON, DAVID, AND MARTIN J. MALONE, EDS. *Toward Explaining Human Culture: A Critical Review of the Findings of Worldwide Cross-Cultural Research.* New Haven, CT: HRAF Press, 1980.

LEVINSON, DAVID, AND MELVIN EMBER, EDS. *Encyclopedia of Cultural Anthropology.* 4 vols. New York: Henry Holt, 1996.

LÉVI-STRAUSS, CLAUDE. "The Sorcerer and His Magic." In Lévi-Strauss, *Structural Anthropology.*

LÉVI-STRAUSS, CLAUDE. *Structural Anthropology.* Trans. Claire Jacobson and Brooke Grundfest Schoepf. New York: Basic Books, 1963.

LEVY, JERROLD E. "Hopi Shamanism: A Reappraisal." In Raymond J. DeMallie and Alfonzo Ortiz, eds., *North American Indian Anthropology: Essays on Society and Culture.* Norman: University of Oklahoma Press, 1994, pp. 307–27, as seen in eHRAF Collection of Ethnography on the Web, 2000.

LEV-YADUN, SIMCHA, AVI GOPHER, AND SHAHAL ABBO, "The Cradle of Agriculture," *Science* 288 (2 Jun 2000): 1602–1603.

LEWIN, ROGER. "Fossil Lucy Grows Younger, Again." *Science,* January 7, 1983, 43–44.

LEWIN, ROGER. "Is the Orangutan a Living Fossil?" *Science,* December 16, 1983, 1222–23.

LEWIN, TAMAR. "Sex in America: Faithfulness in Marriage Is Overwhelming." *New York Times* (National), October 7, 1994, pp. A1, A18.

LEWIS, I. M., ED. *Nationalism and Self-Determination in the Horn of Africa.* London: Ithaca Press, 1983.

LEWIS, OSCAR (with the assistance of Victor Barnouw). *Village Life in Northern India.* Urbana: University of Illinois Press, 1958.

LEWIS, OSCAR. *Life in a Mexican Village: Tepoztlan Revisited.* Urbana: University of Illinois Press, 1951.

LICHTER, DANIEL T., DIANE K. MCLAUGHLIN, GEORGE KEPHART, AND DAVID J. LANDRY. "Race and the Retreat from Marriage: A Shortage of Marriageable Men?" *American Sociological Review,* 57 (1992): 781–99.

LIEBERMAN, DANIEL E. "Testing Hypotheses about Recent Human Evolution from Skulls: Integrating Morphology, Function, Development, and Phylogeny." *Current Anthropology,* 36 (1995): 159–97.

LIEBERMAN, LEONARD. "Scientific Insignificance." *Anthropology Newsletter,* 40, no. 8 (1999): 11–12.

LIEBERMAN, PHILIP. *Uniquely Human: The Evolution of Speech, Thought, and Selfless Behavior.* Cambridge, MA: Harvard University Press, 1991.

LIGHT, IVAN, AND ZHONG DENG. "Gender Differences in ROSCA Participation within Korean Business Households in Los Angeles." In Ardener and Burman, *Money-Go-Rounds: The Importance of Rotating Savings and Credit Associations for Women.*

LINGENFELTER, SHERWOOD G. "Yap: Changing Roles of Men and Women." In M. Ember and Ember, eds., *Portraits of Culture.*

LINTON, RALPH. *The Cultural Background of Personality.* New York: Appleton-Century-Crofts, 1945.

LINTON, RALPH. *The Study of Man.* New York: Appleton-Century-Crofts, 1936.

LITTLE, KENNETH. "The Political Function of the Poro." *Africa,* 35 (1965): 349–65; 36 (1966): 62–71.

LITTLE, KENNETH. "The Role of Voluntary Associations in West African Urbanization." *American Anthropologist,* 59 (1957): 582–93.

LITTLE, KENNETH. *West African Urbanization.* New York: Cambridge University Press, 1965.

LITTLE, M. A. "Growth and Development of Turkana Pastoralists." In Peregrine, Ember, and Ember, *Physical Anthropology.*

LITTLE, MICHAEL A., AND JERE D. HAAS, EDS. *Human Population Biology: A Transdisciplinary Science.* New York: Oxford University Press, 1989.

LOCK, MARGARET. "Japan: Glimpses of Everyday Life." In M. Ember and Ember, eds., *Portraits of Culture.*

LOFTIN, COLIN K. "Warfare and Societal Complexity: A Cross-Cultural Study of Organized Fighting in Preindustrial Societies." Ph.D. dissertation, University of North Carolina at Chapel Hill, 1971.

LOFTIN, COLIN, DAVID MCDOWALL, AND JAMES BOUDOURIS. "Economic Change and Homicide in Detroit, 1926–1979." In Gurr, ed., *Violence in America.* Vol. 1.

LOMAX, ALAN, ED. *Folk Song Style and Culture.* American Association for the Advancement of Science Publication No. 88. Washington, DC, 1968.

LOOMIS, W. FARNSWORTH. "Skin-Pigment Regulation of Vitamin-D Biosynthesis in Man." *Science,* August 4, 1967, 501–506.

LOUSTAUNAU, MARTHA O., AND ELISA J. SOBO. *The Cultural Context of Health, Illness, and Medicine.* Westport, CT: Bergin & Garvey, 1997.

LOVEJOY, ARTHUR O. *The Great Chain of Being: A Study of the History of an Idea.* Cambridge, MA: Harvard University Press, 1964.

LOVEJOY, C. OWEN. "Evolution of Human Walking." *Scientific American,* November 1988, 118–25.

LOVEJOY, C. OWEN. "The Origin of Man." *Science,* January 23, 1981, 341–50.

LOVEJOY, OWEN, KINGSBURY HEIPLE, AND ALBERT BERNSTEIN. "The Gait of *Australopithecus.*" *American Journal of Physical Anthropology,* 38 (1973): 757–79.

LOW, BOBBI. "Human Responses to Environmental Extremeness and Uncertainty." In Cashdan, ed., *Risk and Uncertainty in Tribal and Peasant Economies.*

LOW, BOBBI S. "Behavioral Ecology, 'Sociobiology' and Human Behavior." In C. R. Ember, Ember, and Peregrine, eds., *Research Frontiers in Anthropology.* Vol. 3.

LOW, BOBBI. "Marriage Systems and Pathogen Stress in Human Societies." *American Zoologist,* 30 (1990): 325–39.

LUCY, JOHN A. *Grammatical Categories and Cognition: A Case Study of the Linguistic Relativity Hypothesis.* Cambridge: Cambridge University Press, 1992.

LUHRMANN, TANYA M. *Persuasions of the Witch's Craft: Ritual Magic and Witchcraft in Present-Day England.* Oxford: Blackwell, 1989.

LUMBRERAS, LUIS. *The Peoples and Cultures of Ancient Peru.* Washington, DC: Smithsonian Institution Press, 1974.

LURIA, A. R. *Cognitive Development: Its Cultural and Social Foundations.* Cambridge, MA: Harvard University Press, 1976.

LUTZ, CATHERINE. "Depression and the Translations of Emotional Worlds." In Kleinman and Good, eds., *Culture and Depression.*

LYND, ROBERT S., AND HELEN MERRELL LYND. *Middletown in Transition.* New York: Harcourt, Brace, 1937.

LYND, ROBERT S., AND HELEN MERRELL LYND. *Middletown.* New York: Harcourt, Brace, 1929.

LYON, PATRICIA J., ED. *Native South Americans: Ethnology of the Least Known Continent.* Boston: Little, Brown, 1974.

LYONS, NONA PLESSNER. "Two Perspectives: On Self, Relationships, and Morality." In Gilligan, Ward, and Taylor, eds., *Mapping the Moral Domain.*

LYTTLETON, CHRIS. *Endangered Relations: Negotiating Sex and AIDS in Thailand.* Bangkok: White Lotus Press, 2000.

MACARTHUR, R. H., AND E. O. WILSON. *Theory of Island Biogeography.* Princeton, NJ: Princeton University Press, 1967.

MACCOBY, ELEANOR E. *The Two Sexes: Growing Up Apart, Coming Together.* Cambridge, MA: Belknap Press of Harvard University Press, 1998.

MACCOBY, ELEANOR E., AND CAROL N. JACKLIN. *The Psychology of Sex Differences.* Stanford, CA: Stanford University Press, 1974.

MACDONALD, DOUGLAS H. AND BARRY S. HEWLETT. "Reproductive Interests and Forager Mobility." *Current Anthropology,* 40 (1999): 501–523.

MACIONIS, JOHN J. *Sociology.* 4th ed. Englewood Cliffs. NJ: Prentice Hall, 1993.

MACKINNON, JOHN, AND KATHY MACKINNON. "The Behavior of Wild Spectral Tarsiers." *International Journal of Primatology,* 1 (1980): 361–79.

MACKINTOSH, N. J. *IQ and Human Intelligence.* Oxford: Oxford University Press, 1998.

MACLACHLAN, MORGAN D., ED. *Household Economies and Their Transformations.* Monographs in Economic Anthropology No. 3. Lanham, MD: University Press of America, 1987.

MACNEISH, RICHARD S. "The Evaluation of Community Patterns in the Tehuacán Valley of Mexico and Speculations about the Cultural Processes." In Tringham, ed., *Ecology and Agricultural Settlements.*

MACNEISH, RICHARD S. *The Origins of Agriculture and Settled Life.* Norman: University of Oklahoma Press, 1991.

MADIGRAL, LORENA. "Hemoglobin Genotype, Fertility, and the Malaria Hypothesis." *Human Biology,* 61 (1989): 311–25.

MAGNER, L. *A History of Medicine.* New York: Marcel Dekker, 1992.

MAHONY, FRANK JOSEPH. *A Trukese Theory of Medicine.* Ann Arbor, MI: University Microfilms, 1070 [1971], as seen in the eHRAF Collection of Ethnography on the Web, 2000.

MALEFIJT, ANNEMARIE DE WAAL. *Religion and Culture: An Introduction to Anthropology of Religion.* New York: Macmillan, 1968.

MALIN, EDWARD. *Totem Poles of the Pacific Northwest Coast.* Portland, OR: Timber Press, 1986.

MALINOWSKI, BRONISLAW. "Kula: The Circulating Exchange of Valuables in the Archipelagoes of Eastern New Guinea." *Man,* 51, no. 2 (1920): 97–105.

MALINOWSKI, BRONISLAW. "Magic, Science, and Religion." In Malinowski, *Magic, Science, and Religion and Other Essays.*

MALINOWSKI, BRONISLAW. "The Group and the Individual in Functional Analysis." *American Journal of Sociology,* 44 (1939): 938–64.

MALINOWSKI, BRONISLAW. *Magic, Science and Religion and Other Essays.* Garden City, NY: Doubleday, 1954.

MALINOWSKI, BRONISLAW. *Sex and Repression in Savage Society.* London: Kegan Paul, Trench, Trubner, 1927.

MALINOWSKI, BRONISLAW. *The Sexual Life of Savages in Northwestern Melanesia.* New York: Halcyon House, 1932.

MANGIN, WILLIAM P. "The Role of Regional Associations in the Adaptation of Rural Migrants to Cities in Peru." In Health and Adams, eds., *Contemporary Cultures and Societies of Latin America.*

MANGIN, WILLIAM. "Latin American Squatter Settlements: A Problem and a Solution." *Latin American Research Review,* 2 (1967): 65–98.

MANHEIN, MARY H. *The Bone Lady: Life as a Forensic Anthropologist.* Baton Rouge: Louisiana State University Press, 1999.

MANZANILLA, LINDA, ED. *Studies in the Neolithic and Urban Revolutions.* British Archaeological Reports International Series 349. Oxford, 1987.

MANZANILLA, LINDA, ED., Studies in the Neolithic and Urban Revolutions. British Archaeological Reports International Series 349 (Oxford, 1987).

MAQUET, JACQUES. *The Aesthetic Experience: An Anthropologist Looks at the Visual Arts.* New Haven, CT: Yale University Press, 1986.

MARANO, LOUIS A. "A Macrohistoric Trend toward World Government." *Behavior Science Notes,* 8 (1973): 35–40.

MARCUS, GEORGE E., AND MICHAEL M. J. FISCHER. *Anthropology as Cultural Critique: An Experimental Moment in the Human Sciences.* Chicago: University of Chicago Press, 1986.

MARCUS, JOYCE. "Maya Hieroglyphs: History or Propaganda?" In Peregrine, Ember, and Ember, eds., *Archaeology.*

MARCUS, JOYCE. "On the Nature of the Mesoamerican City." In Vogt and Leventhal, eds., *Prehistoric Settlement Patterns.*

MARCUS, JOYCE, AND KENT V. FLANNERY. *Zapotec Civilization.* London: Thames and Hudson, 1996, pp. 49–50.

MARETT, R. R. *The Thresholds of Religion.* London: Methuen, 1909.

MARKS, JONATHAN. "Black, White, Other: Racial Categories Are Cultural Constructs Masquerading as Biology." *Natural History,* December 1994, 32–35.

MARKS, JONATHAN. "Genes, Bodies, and Species," in Peregrine, Ember, and Ember, eds., *Physical Anthropology: Original Reading in Method and Practice.* Upper Saddle River, NJ: Prentice Hall, 2002.

MARSHACK, ALEXANDER. *The Roots of Civilization.* New York: McGraw-Hill, 1972.

MARSHALL, ELIOT. "Pre-Clovis Sites Fight for Acceptance," *Science,* 291 (2001): 1730–32.

MARSHALL, ELIOT. "Rival Genome Sequencers Celebrate a Milestone Together." *Science,* June 30, 2000, 2294–295.

MARSHALL, LARRY G. "Who Killed Cock Robin? An Investigation of the Extinction Controversy." In Martin and Klein, eds., *Quaternary Extinctions.*

MARSHALL, LORNA. "Sharing, Talking and Giving: Relief of Social Tensions among !Kung Bushmen." *Africa,* 31 (1961): 239–42.

MARTIN, M. KAY, AND BARBARA VOORHIES. *Female of the Species.* New York: Columbia University Press, 1975.

MARTIN, PAUL S. "The Discovery of America." *Science,* March 9, 1973, 969–74.

MARTIN, PAUL S., AND H. E. WRIGHT, EDS. *Pleistocene Extinctions: The Search for a Cause.* New Haven, CT: Yale University Press, 1967.

MARTIN, PAUL S., AND RICHARD KLEIN, EDS. *Quaternary Extinctions: A Prehistoric Revolution.* Tucson: University of Arizona Press, 1984.

MARTIN, ROBERT. "Classification and Evolutionary Relationships." In Jones, Martin, and Pilbeam, eds., *The Cambridge Encyclopedia of Human Evolution.*

MARTIN, ROBERT D. "Strategies of Reproduction." *Natural History,* November 1975, 48–57.

MARTIN, ROBERT D. *Primate Origins and Evolution: A Phylogenetic Reconstruction.* Princeton, NJ: Princeton University Press, 1990.

MARTIN, ROBERT D., AND SIMON K. BEARDER. "Radio Bush Baby." *Natural History,* October 1979, 77–81.

MARTORELL, REYNALDO. "Interrelationships between Diet, Infectious Disease and Nutritional Status." In Greene and Johnston, eds., *Social and Biological Predictors of Nutritional Status, Physical Growth and Neurological Development.*

MARTORELL, REYNALDO, JUAN RIVERA, HALEY KAPLOWITZ, AND ERNESTO POLLITT. "Long-Term Consequences of Growth Retardation during Early Childhood." Paper presented at the Sixth International Congress of Auxology, September 15–19, 1991, Madrid.

MASCIE-TAYLOR, AND C. G. NICHOLAS. "The Biology of Social Class," in C. G. Nicholas. Mascie-Taylor, ed., *Biosocial Aspects of Social Class* (Oxford: Oxford University Press, 1990), pp. 118–21.

MASCIE-TAYLOR, C. G. N., AND G. W. LASKER. *Applications of Biological Anthropology to Human Affairs.* New York: Cambridge University Press, 1991.

MASCIE-TAYLOR, C. G. NICHOLAS. "The Biology of Social Class." In C. G. Nicholas Mascie-Taylor, ed., *Biosocial Aspects of Social Class.* Oxford: Oxford University Press, 1990, pp. 117–42.

MASLOW, ABRAHAM H. *Religions, Values, and Peak-Experiences.* Columbus: Ohio State University Press, 1964.

MASON, IAN L. *Evolution of Domesticated Animals.* New York: Longman, 1984.

MASON, PHILIP. *Prospero's Magic.* London: Oxford University Press, 1962.

MASUMURA, WILFRED T. "Law and Violence: A Cross-Cultural Study." *Journal of Anthropological Research,* 33 (1977): 388–99.

MATEJCEK, ZDENEK. "Perceived Parental Acceptance-Rejection and Personality Organization among Czech Elementary School Children." *Behavior Science Research,* 18 (1983): 259–68.

MATHIASSEN, THERKEL. *Material Culture of Iglulik Eskimos.* Copenhagen: Glydendalske, 1928.

MATHIOT, MADELEINE, ED. *Ethnolinguistics: Boas, Sapir and Whorf Revisited.* The Hague: Mouton, 1979.

MATLOCK, JAMES G. "Universals and Variation in Religious Belief and Practice." In C. R. Ember and Ember, eds., *Cross-Cultural Research for Social Science.*

MATOSSIAN, MARY K. "Ergot and the Salem Witchcraft Affair." *American Scientist,* 70 (1982): 355–57.

MATOSSIAN, MARY K. *Poisons of the Past: Molds, Epidemics, and History.* New Haven, CT: Yale University Press, 1989.

MATTHIASSON, CAROLYN J. *Many Sisters: Women in Cross-Cultural Perspective.* New York: Free Press, 1974.

MAYBURY-LEWIS, DAVID. *Akwe-Shavante Society.* Oxford: Clarendon Press, 1967.

MAYR, E. *What Evolution Is.* New York: Basic Books, 2002.

MAYR, ERNST. "The Nature of the Darwinian Revolution." *Science,* June 2, 1972, 981–89.

MAYR, ERNST. *One Long Argument: Charles Darwin and the Genesis of Modern Evolutionary Thought.* Cambridge, MA: Harvard University Press, 1993.

MAYR, ERNST. *The Growth of Biological Thought: Diversity, Evolution, and Inheritance.* Cambridge, MA: Belknap Press of Harvard University Press, 1982.

MAZESS, RICHARD B. "Human Adaptation to High Altitude." In Damon, ed., *Physiological Anthropology.*

MCCLELLAND, DAVID C. *The Achieving Society.* New York: Van Nostrand, 1961.

MCANANY, PATRICIA. "Ancestor Veneration in Lowland Maya Society: A Case Study from K'axob, Belize." In Peregrine, Ember, and Ember, eds., *Archaeology: Original Readings in Method and Practice.*

MCCAIN, GARVIN, AND ERWIN M. SEGAL. *The Game of Science.* 5th ed. Monterey, CA: Brooks/Cole, 1988.

MCCARTHY, FREDERICK D., AND MARGARET MCARTHUR. "The Food Quest and the Time Factor in Aboriginal Economic Life." In Mountford, ed., *Records of the Australian-American Scientific Expedition to Arnhem Land.* Vol. 2.

MCCAY, BONNIE M, AND JAMES M. ACHESON, EDS. *The Question of the Commons: The Culture and Ecology of Communal Resources.* Tucson: University of Arizona Press, 1987.

MCCAY, BONNIE M, AND JAMES M. ACHESON. "Introduction." In McCay and Acheson, eds., *The Question of the Commons.*

McCorriston, Joy, and Frank Hole. "The Ecology of Seasonal Stress and the Origins of Agriculture in the Near East." *American Anthropologist,* 93 (1991): 46–69.

McCracken, Robert D. "Lactase Deficiency: An Example of Dietary Evolution." *Current Anthropology,* 12 (1971): 479–500.

McDermott, LeRoy. "Self-Representation in Female Figurines." *Current Anthropology,* 37 (1996): 227–75.

McDonald, Kim A. "New Evidence Challenges Traditional Model of How the New World Was Settled." *Chronicle of Higher Education,* March 13, 1998, A22.

McDowell, Nancy. "Mundugumor: Sex and Temperament Revisited." In M. Ember and Ember, eds., *Portraits of Culture.*

McElroy, A. and P. R. Townsend, *Medical Anthropology* (North Scituate, MA: Duxbury Press, 1979).

McElroy, A., and P. K. Townsend *Medical Anthropology in Ecological Perspective,* 3rd ed. Boulder, CO: Westview, 2002.

McElroy, Ann, and Patricia Townsend. *Medical Anthropology in Ecological Perspective.* 3rd ed. Boulder, CO: Westview, 2002.

McGarvey, Stephen T. "The Thrifty Gene Concept and Adiposity Studies in Biological Anthropology." *Journal of the Polynesian Society,* 103 (1994): 29–42.

McGlynn, Frank, and Arthur Tuden, eds. *Anthropological Approaches to Political Behavior.* Pittsburgh: University of Pittsburgh Press, 1991.

McGrew, W. *Chimpanzee Material Culture: Implications for Human Evolution.* Cambridge: Cambridge University Press, 1992.

McHenry, Henry M. "'Robust' Australopithecines, Our Family Tree, and Homoplasy." In Peregrine, Ember, and Ember, eds., *Physical Anthropology.*

McHenry, Henry M. "New Estimates of Body Weight in Early Hominids and Their Significance to Encephalization and Megadontia in 'Robust' Australopithecines." In Grine, ed., *Evolutionary History of the "Robust" Australopithecines.*

McHenry, Henry M. "The Pattern of Human Evolution: Studies on Bipedalism, Mastication, and Encephalization." *Annual Review of Anthropology,* 11 (1982): 151–73.

McKee, Lauris A. "Andean Mestizos: Growing Up Female and Male," in M. Ember and Ember, eds. *Portraits of Culture: Ethnographic Originals,* in Carol R. Ember and Melvin Ember, eds., *New Directions in Anthropology.*

McKee, Lauris. "Sex Differentials in Survivorship and the Customary Treatment of Infants and Children." *Medical Anthropology,* 8 (1984): 91–108.

McNeill, W. H. *Plagues and Peoples.* Magnolia, MA: Peter Smith Publisher, 1992.

McNeill, W. H. *Plagues and Peoples.* New York: Anchor Books/Doubleday, 1998.

McNeill, William H. *A World History.* New York: Oxford University Press, 1967.

McNeill, William H. *Plagues and Peoples.* Garden City, NY: Doubleday/Anchor, 1976.

McNeill, William H. *Plagues and Peoples.* New York: Anchor Books/Doubleday, 1998.

Mead, Margaret. "Applied Anthropology: The State of the Art." In Wallace et al., eds., *Perspectives on Anthropology* 1976.

Mead, Margaret. "The Evolving Ethics of Applied Anthropology." In Eddy and Partridge, eds., *Applied Anthropology in America.*

Mead, Margaret. *Coming of Age in Samoa.* 3rd ed. New York: Morrow, 1961. (Originally published 1928.)

Mead, Margaret. *Growing Up in New Guinea.* London: Routledge & Kegan Paul, 1931.

Mead, Margaret. *Sex and Temperament in Three Primitive Societies.* New York: Mentor, 1950. (Originally published 1935.)

Meek, C. K. *Land Law and Custom in the Colonies.* London: Oxford University Press, 1940.

Meggers, Betty J., ed. *Anthropological Archaeology in the Americas.* Washington, DC: Anthropological Society of Washington, 1968.

Meggitt, Mervyn J. "Male-Female Relationships in the Highlands of Australian New Guinea." *American Anthropologist,* 66 (special issue, 1964): 204–24.

Meggitt, Mervyn. *Blood Is Their Argument: Warfare among the Mae Enga Tribesmen of the New Guinea Highlands.* Palo Alto, CA: Mayfield, 1977.

Meillassoux, Claude. *Urbanization of an African Community.* Seattle: University of Washington Press, 1968.

Mellaart, James. "A Neolithic City in Turkey." *Scientific American,* April 1964, 94–104.

Mellaart, James. "Roots in the Soil." In Piggott, ed., *The Dawn of Civilization.*

Mellars, Paul. "The Fate of the Neanderthals." *Nature,* 395 (1998): 539–40.

Mellars, Paul. "The Upper Paleolithic Revolution." In B. Cunliffe, ed., *The Oxford Illustrated Prehistory of Europe.* Oxford: Oxford University Press, 1994, pp. 42–78.

Mellars, Paul. *The Neanderthal Legacy.* Princeton, NJ: Princeton University Press, 1996, pp. 405–19.

Mellor, John W., and Sarah Gavian. "Famine: Causes, Prevention, and Relief." *Science,* January 30, 1987, 539–44.

Meltzer, David J. "Pleistocene Peopling of the Americas." *Evolutionary Anthropology,* Vol. 1, 1993.

Meltzer, David J. *Search for the First Americans.* Washington, DC: Smithsonian Institution, 1993.

Meltzer, David J., Don D. Fowler, and Jeremy A. Sabloff, eds. *American Archaeology Past and Future.* Washington, DC: Smithsonian Institution Press, 1986.

Merbs, Charles F. "A New World of Infectious Disease." *Yearbook of Physical Anthropology,* 35 (1992): 3–42.

Merrill, Elizabeth Bryant. "Art Styles as Reflections of Sociopolitical Complexity." *Ethnology,* 26 (1987): 221–30.

Mertz, Elizabeth, and Richard J. Parmentier, eds. *Semiotic Mediation: Sociocultural and Psychological Perspectives.* Orlando, FL: Academic Press, 1985.

Messer, Ellen. "Hunger Vulnerability from an Anthropologist's Food System Perspective." In Moran, ed., *Transforming Societies, Transforming Anthropology.*

Michel, R. H., McGovern, P. E., and Badler, V. R. "The First Wine and Beer: Chemical Detection of Ancient Fermented Beverages." *Analytical Chemistry,* 65 (1993): 408A–13A.

Middleton, John. "The Cult of the Dead: Ancestors and Ghosts." In Lessa and Vogt, eds., *Reader in Comparative Religion,* 3rd ed.

Middleton, Russell. "Brother-Sister and Father-Daughter Marriage in Ancient Egypt." *American Sociological Review,* 27 (1962): 603–11.

Midlarsky, Manus I., ed., *Inequality, Democracy, and Economic Development* (Cambridge: Cambridge University Press, 1997.)

Milanovic, Branko. "True World Income Distribution, 1988 and 1993: First Calculation Based on Household Surveys Alone." *The Economic Journal,* 112 (2002): 51–92.

Milanovic, Branko. *The Economic Journal,* 112 (2002): 51–92; "State of the World 1994: A Worldwatch Institute Report on Progress toward a Sustainable Society" (New York: Norton, 1994).

Miller, Bruce G. "Women and Politics: Comparative Evidence from the Northwest Coast." *Ethnology,* 31 (1992): 367–82.

Miller, Henry I. "Regulation." In Davis, ed., *The Genetic Revolution.*

Miller, Joan G. "Cultural Diversity in the Morality of Caring: Individually Oriented versus Duty-Based Interpersonal Moral Codes." *Cross-Cultural Research,* 28 (1994): 3–39.

MILLER, NAOMI F. "The Origins of Plant Cultivation in the Near East." In Cowan and Watson, eds., *The Origins of Agriculture.*

MILLON, RENÉ. "Social Relations in Ancient Teotihuacán." In Wolf, ed., *The Valley of Mexico.*

MILLON, RENÉ. "Teotihuacán." *Scientific American*, June 1967, 38–48.

MILTON, KATHARINE. "Distribution Patterns of Tropical Plant Foods as an Evolutionary Stimulus to Primate Mental Development." *American Anthropologist*, 83 (1981): 534–48.

MILTON, KATHARINE. "Foraging Behaviour and the Evolution of Primate Intelligence." In Byrne and Whiten, eds., *Machiavellian Intelligence.*

MILTON, KATHARINE. "The Evolution of a Physical Anthropologist." In Peregrine, Ember, and Ember, eds., *Physical Anthropology.*

MINER, HORACE. "Body Rituals among the Nacirema." *American Anthropologist*, 58 (1956): 504–505.

MINTURN, LEIGH. *Sita's Daughters: Coming Out of Purdah: The Rajput Women of Khalapur Revisited.* New York: Oxford University Press, 1993.

MINTURN, LEIGH, AND JERRY STASHAK. "Infanticide as a Terminal Abortion Procedure." *Behavior Science Research*, 17 (1982): 70–85.

MINTURN, LEIGH, AND WILLIAM W. LAMBERT. *Mothers of Six Cultures: Antecedents of Child Rearing.* New York: Wiley, 1964.

MINTZ, SIDNEY W. "Canamelar: The Subculture of a Rural Sugar Plantation Proletariat." In Steward et al., *The People of Puerto Rico.*

MINUGH-PURVIS, NANCY. "Neandertal Growth: Examining Developmental Adaptations in Earlier *Homo sapiens.*" In Peregrine, Ember, and Ember, eds., *Physical Anthropology.*

MIRACLE, ANDREW W. "A Shaman to Organizations." In C. R. Ember, and Peregrine, eds., *Research Frontiers in Anthropology.*

MITCHELL, DONALD. "Nimpkish: Complex Foragers on the Northwest Coast of North America." In M. Ember and Ember, eds., *Portraits of Culture.*

MITTERMEIER, RUSSELL A., AND ELEANOR J. STERLING. "Conservation of Primates." In Jones, Martin, and Pilbeam, eds., *The Cambridge Encyclopedia of Human Evolution.*

MOERMAN, DANIEL E. "Physiology and Symbols: The Anthropological Implications of the Placebo Effect." In Romanucci-Ross, Moerman, and Tancredi, eds., *The Anthropology of Medicine*, pp. 240–53.

MOLNAR, STEPHEN. *Human Variation: Races, Types, and Ethnic Groups.* 4th ed. Upper Saddle River, NJ: Prentice Hall, 1998.

MONTAGU, A. *A Man's Most Dangerous Myth: The Fallacy of Race.* 6th ed. Walnut Creek, CA: AltaMira, 1997.

MOONEY, KATHLEEN A. "The Effects of Rank and Wealth on Exchange among the Coast Salish." *Ethnology*, 17 (1978): 391–406.

MOORE, CARMELLA C. "Is Love Always Love?" *Anthropology Newsletter*, November 1997, 8–9.

MOORE, CARMELLA C., A. KIMBALL ROMNEY, TI-LIEN HSIA, CRAIG D. RUSCH. "The Universality of the Semantic Structure of Emotion Terms: Methods for the Study of Inter- and Intra-Cultural Variability." *American Anthropologist* 101 (1999): 529–546.

MOORE, CARMELLA CARACCI. "An Optimal Scaling of Murdock's Theories of Illness Data—An Approach to the Problem of Interdependence." *Behavior Science Research*, 22 (1988): 161–79.

MOORE, OMAR KHAYYAM. "Divination: A New Perspective." *American Anthropologist*, 59 (1957): 69–74.

MORAN, EMILIO F. *Human Adaptability: An Introduction to Ecological Anthropology.* 2nd ed. Boulder, CO: Westview, 2000.

MORAN, EMILIO F. *Through Amazon Eyes: The Human Ecology of Amazonian Populations.* Iowa City: University of Iowa Press, 1993.

MORAN, EMILIO F., ED. *Transforming Societies, Transforming Anthropology.* Ann Arbor: University of Michigan Press, 1996.

MORELL, VIRGINIA. "The Earliest Art Becomes Older—And More Common." *Science*, March 31, 1995, 1908–1909.

MORGEN, SANDRA, ED. *Gender and Anthropology: Critical Reviews for Research and Teaching.* Washington, DC: American Anthropological Association, 1989.

MORRIS, B. *Anthropological Studies of Religion: An Introductory Text.* Cambridge: Cambridge University Press, 1987.

MORRIS, JOHN. *Living with Lepchas: A Book about the Sikkim Himalayas.* London: Heinemann, 1938.

MORRIS, LAURA NEWELL, ED. *Human Populations, Genetic Variation, and Evolution.* San Francisco: Chandler, 1971.

MOSER, STEPHANIE. *Ancestral Images: The Iconography of Human Origins.* Ithaca, NY: Cornell University Press, 1998.

MOTULSKY, ARNO. "Metabolic Polymorphisms and the Role of Infectious Diseases in Human Evolution." In Morris, ed., *Human Populations, Genetic Variation, and Evolution.*

MOUNTFORD, C. P., ED. *Records of the Australian-American Scientific Expedition to Arnhem Land.* Vol. 2: Anthropology and Nutrition. Melbourne: Melbourne University Press, 1960.

MUKERJEE, MADHUSREE. "Field Notes: Interview with a Parrot." *Scientific American*, April 1996.

MUKHOPADHYAY, CAROL C., AND PATRICIA J. HIGGINS. "Anthropological Studies of Women's Status Revisited: 1977–1987." *Annual Review of Anthropology*, 17 (1988): 461–95.

MULLER, EDWARD N. "Economic Determinants of Democracy." Paper presented at a conference on Inequality and Democracy, organized by Manus I. Midlarsky at Rutgers University, February 1994.

MÜLLER-HAYE, B. "Guinea Pig or Cuy." In Mason, *Evolution of Domesticated Animals.*

MUNROE, ROBERT L., ROBERT HULEFELD, JAMES M. RODGERS, DAMON L. TOMEO, STEVEN K. YAMAZAKI. "Aggression Among Children in Four Cultures." *Cross-Cultural Research*, 34 (2000): 3–25.

MUNROE, ROBERT L., AND RUTH H. MUNROE. "A Cross-Cultural Study of Sex, Gender, and Social Structure." *Ethnology*, 8 (1969): 206–11.

MUNROE, ROBERT L., RUTH H. MUNROE, AND JOHN W.M. WHITING. "Male Sex-Role Resolutions." In Munroe, Munroe, and Whiting, eds., *Handbook of Cross-Cultural Human Development.*

MUNROE, ROBERT L., RUTH H. MUNROE, AND STEPHEN WINTERS. "Cross-Cultural Correlates of the Consonant-Vowel (CV) Syllable." *Cross-Cultural Research*, 30 (1996): 60–83.

MUNROE, RUTH H., AND ROBERT L. MUNROE. "Household Structure and Socialization Practices." *Journal of Social Psychology*, 111 (1980): 293–94.

MUNROE, RUTH H., AND ROBERT L. MUNROE. "Infant Experience and Childhood Affect among the Logoli: A Longitudinal Study." *Ethos*, 8 (1980): 295–315.

MUNROE, RUTH H., ROBERT L. MUNROE, AND BEATRICE B. WHITING, EDS. *Handbook of Cross-Cultural Human Development.* New York: Garland, 1981.

MUNROE, RUTH H., ROBERT L. MUNROE, AND HAROLD S. SHIMMIN. "Children's Work in Four Cultures: Determinants and Consequences." *American Anthropologist*, 86 (1984): 369–79.

MURDOCK, GEORGE P. "Ethnographic Atlas: A Summary." *Ethnology*, 6 (1967): 109–236.

MURDOCK, GEORGE P. "World Ethnographic Sample." *American Anthropologist*, 59 (1957): 664–87.

MURDOCK, GEORGE P. *Social Structure.* New York: Macmillan, 1949.

MURDOCK, GEORGE P., ED. *Social Structure in Southeast Asia.* Viking Fund Publications in Anthropology No. 29. Chicago: Quadrangle, 1960.

MURDOCK, GEORGE PETER. *Theories of Illness: A World Survey.* Pittsburgh: University of Pittsburgh Press, 1980.

MURDOCK, GEORGE P., AND CATERINA PROVOST. "Factors in the Division of Labor by Sex: A Cross-Cultural Analysis." *Ethnology,* 12 (1973): 203–25.

MURDOCK, GEORGE P., AND DOUGLAS R. WHITE. "Standard Cross-Cultural Sample." *Ethnology,* 8 (1969): 329–69.

MURPHY, JANE. "Abnormal Behavior in Traditional Societies: Labels, Explanations, and Social Reactions." In Munroe, Munroe, and Whiting, eds., *Handbook of Cross-Cultural Human Development.*

MURPHY, ROBERT F. *Headhunter's Heritage: Social and Economic Change among the Mundurucú.* Berkeley: University of California Press, 1960.

MURPHY, ROBERT F., AND JULIAN H. STEWARD. "Tappers and Trappers: Parallel Process in Acculturation." *Economic Development and Cultural Change,* 4 (July 1956): 335–55.

MURRAY, GERALD F. "The Domestication of Wood in Haiti: A Case Study in Applied Evolution." In Podolefsky and Brown, eds., *Applying Cultural Anthropology.*

MUSIL, ALOIS. *The Manners and Customs of the Rwala Bedouins.* American Geographical Society, Oriental Exploration Studies No. 6. New York, 1928.

MUSSEN, PAUL, ED. *Carmichael's Manual of Child Psychology.* 3rd ed. Vol. 1. New York: Wiley, 1970.

MYERS, FRED R. "Critical Trends in the Study of Hunter-Gatherers." *Annual Review of Anthropology,* 17 (1988): 261–82.

NADEL, S. F. "Nupe State and Community." *Africa,* 8 (1935): 257–303.

NADEL, S. F. *A Black Byzantium: The Kingdom of Nupe in Nigeria.* London: Oxford University Press, 1942.

NAG, MONI, BENJAMIN N. F. WHITE, AND R. CREIGHTON PEET. "An Anthropological Approach to the Study of the Economic Value of Children in Java and Nepal." *Current Anthropology,* 19 (1978): 293–301.

NAGEL, ERNEST. *The Structure of Science: Problems in the Logic of Scientific Explanation.* New York: Harcourt, Brace & World, 1961.

NAPIER, J. R. "Paleoecology and Catarrhine Evolution." In J. R. Napier and P. H. Napier, eds., *Old World Monkeys: Evolution, Systematics, and Behavior.* New York: Academic Press, 1970.

NAPIER, J. R., AND P. H. NAPIER. *A Handbook of Living Primates.* New York: Academic Press, 1967.

NAROLL, RAOUL. "Imperial Cycles and World Order." *Peace Research Society: Papers,* 7, Chicago Conference (1967): 83–101.

NAROLL, RAOUL. "Two Solutions to Galton's Problem." *Philosophy of Science,* 28 (January 1961): 15–39.

NAROLL, RAOUL. *The Moral Order: An Introduction to the Human Situation.* Beverly Hills, CA: Sage, 1983.

NAROLL, RAOUL, AND RONALD COHEN, EDS. *A Handbook of Method in Cultural Anthropology.* Garden City, NY: Natural History Press, 1970.

NASH, MANNING. *The Cauldron of Ethnicity in the Modern World.* Chicago: University of Chicago Press, 1989.

NEEL, JAMES V., WILLARD R. CENTERWALL, NAPOLEON A. CHAGNON, AND HELEN L. CASEY. "Notes on the Effect of Measles and Measles Vaccine in a Virgin-Soil Population of South American Indians." *American Journal of Epidemiology,* 91 (1970): 418–29.

NELSON, K. E., ED. *Children's Language.* Vol. 2. New York: Halsted Press, 1980.

NELSON, NICI. "The Kiambu Group: A Successful Women's ROSCA in Mathare Valley, Nairobi (1971 to 1990)." In Ardener and Burman, *Money-Go-Rounds: The Importance of Rotating Savings and Credit Associations for Women.*

NERLOVE, SARA B. "Women's Workload and Infant Feeding Practices: A Relationship with Demographic Implications." *Ethnology,* 13 (1974): 207–14.

NEVINS, ALLAN. *The American States during and after the Revolution.* New York: Macmillan, 1927.

New York Times International, Tuesday, September 30, 1997, p. A26.

NEWMAN, KATHERINE S. *Law and Economic Organization: A Comparative Study of Preindustrial Societies.* Cambridge, MA: Cambridge University Press, 1983.

NICHOLSON, SHIRLEY, COMP. *Shamanism: An Expanded View of Reality.* Wheaton, IL: Theosophical Publishing House, 1987.

NICOLSON, NANCY A. "Infants, Mothers, and Other Females." In Smuts et al., eds., *Primate Societies.*

NIEDERBERGER, CHRISTINE. "Early Sedentary Economy in the Basin of Mexico." *Science,* January 12, 1979, 131–42.

NIEHOFF, ARTHUR H. *A Casebook of Social Change.* Chicago: Aldine, 1966.

NIMKOFF, M. F., AND RUSSELL MIDDLETON. "Types of Family and Types of Economy." *American Journal of Sociology,* 66 (1960): 215–25.

NISHIDA, TOSHISADA. "Introduction to the Conservation Symposium." In Naosuke Itoigawa, Yukimaru Sugiyama, Gene P. Sackett, and Roger K. R. Thompson, *Topics in Primatology.* Vol. 2. Tokyo: University of Tokyo Press, 1992.

NISHIDA, TOSHISADA, WILLIAM C. MCGREW, PETER MARLER, MARTIN PICKFORD, AND FRANS B. M. DE WAAL, EDS. *Topics in Primatology.* Vol. 1: Human Origins. Tokyo: University of Tokyo Press, 1992.

NISSEN, HENRY W. "Axes of Behavioral Comparison." In Anne Roe and George Gaylord Simpson, eds., *Behavior and Evolution.* New Haven, CT: Yale University Press, 1958.

NITECKI, MATTHEW H., AND DORIS V. NITECKI, EDS. *The Evolution of Human Hunting.* New York: Plenum, 1987.

NOBLE, WILLIAM, AND IAN DAVIDSON, *Human Evolution, Language, and Mind.* Cambridge: Cambridge University Press, 1996, pp. 162–214.

NOLL, RICHARD. "The Presence of Spirits in Magic and Madness." In Nicholson, *Shamanism,* pp. 47–61.

NORMILE, DENNIS. "Habitat Seen Playing Larger Role in Shaping Behavior," *Science,* March 6, 1998, 1454–455.

NOSS, ANDREW J., AND BARRY S. HEWLETT. "The Contexts of Female Hunting in Central Africa." *American Anthropologist,* 103 (2001): 1024–1040.

NUSSBAUM, MARTHA C. "Introduction." In Martha C. Nussbaum and Jonathan Glover, *Women, Culture, and Development: A Study of Human Capabilities.* Oxford: Clarendon Press, 1995.

O'BRIEN, DENISE. "Female Husbands in Southern Bantu Societies." In Schlegel, ed., *Sexual Stratification.*

O'BRIEN, ROBIN. "Who Weaves and Why? Weaving, Loom Complexity, and Trade." *Cross-Cultural Research,* 33 (1999): 30–42.

OAKLEY, KENNETH P. "Analytical Methods of Dating Bones." In Brothwell and Higgs, eds., *Science in Archaeology.*

OAKLEY, KENNETH. "On Man's Use of Fire, with Comments on Tool-Making and Hunting." In Washburn, ed., *Social Life of Early Man.*

OBOLER, REGINA SMITH. "Is the Female Husband a Man? Woman/Woman Marriage among the Nandi of Kenya." *Ethnology,* 19 (1980): 69–88.

OBOLER, REGINA SMITH. "Nandi: From Cattle-Keepers to Cash-Crop Farmers." In M. Ember and Ember, eds., *Portraits of Culture.*

OGBURN, WILLIAM F. *Social Change.* New York: Huebsch, 1922.

OKAMURA, JONATHAN Y. "Filipino Hometown Associations in Hawaii." *Ethnology,* 22 (1983): 341–53.

OLIVER, DOUGLAS L. *A Solomon Island Society*. Cambridge, MA: Harvard University Press, 1955.

OLIVER, DOUGLAS L. *Ancient Tahitian Society*. Vol. 1: *Ethnography*. Honolulu: University of Hawaii Press, 1974.

OLSEN, STEVE, "Seeking the Signs of Selection," *Science* 298 (15 Nov. 2002), 1324–1325.

OLSZEWSKI, DEBORAH I. "Social Complexity in the Natufian? Assessing the Relationship of Ideas and Data." In Clark, ed., *Perspectives on the Past*.

ORTIZ DE MONTELLANO, B. R., AND C. H. BROWNER. "Chemical Bases for Medicinal Plant Use in Oaxaca, Mexico." *Journal of Ethnopharmacology*, 13 (1985): 57–88.

ORTNER, SHERRY B. "Theory in Anthropology since the Sixties." *Comparative Studies in Society and History*, 26 (1984): 126–66.

OSTI, ROBERTO. "The Eloquent Bones of Abu Hureyras." *Scientific American*, Aug. 1994.

OSTROM, ELINOR, JOANNA BURGER, CHRISTOPHER B. FIELD, RICHARD B. NORGAARD, AND DAVID POLICANSKY. "Revisiting the Commons: Local Lessons, Global Challenges." *Science*, April 9, 1999, 278–82.

OTTERBEIN, KEITH. "Internal War: A Cross-Cultural Study." *American Anthropologist*, 70 (1968): 277–89.

OTTERBEIN, KEITH. *The Evolution of War*. New Haven, CT: HRAF Press, 1970.

OTTERBEIN, KEITH. *The Ultimate Coercive Sanction: A Cross-Cultural Study of Capital Punishment*. New Haven, CT: HRAF Press, 1986.

OTTERBEIN, KEITH, AND CHARLOTTE SWANSON OTTERBEIN. "An Eye for an Eye, a Tooth for a Tooth: A Cross-Cultural Study of Feuding." *American Anthropologist*, 67 (1965): 1470–82.

OVCHINNIKOV, IGOR V. ET AL., "Molecular Analysis of Neanderthal DNA from the Northern Caucasus," *Nature* 404 (30 Mar. 2000): 490–494.

OXBY, CLARE. "Farmer Groups in Rural Areas of the Third World." *Community Development Journal*, 18 (1983): 50–59.

PAIGE, JEFFERY M. *Agrarian Revolution: Social Movements and Export Agriculture in the Underdeveloped World*. New York: Free Press, 1975.

PAINE, ROBERT. *Herds of the Tundra*. Washington, DC: Smithsonian Institution Press, 1994.

PALSSON, GISLI. "Hunters and Gatherers of the Sea." In Ingold, Riches, and Woodburn, eds., *Hunters and Gatherers*. 1.

PANTER-BRICK, CATHERINE, DEBORAH S. LOTSTEIN, AND PETER T. ELLISON. "Seasonality of Reproductive Function and Weight Loss in Rural Nepali Women." *Human Reproduction*, 8 (1993): 684–90.

"Paper," Academic American Encyclopedia (Princeton, NJ: Areté, 1980).

PARFIT, MICHAEL. "Who Were the First Americans?" *National Geographic*, December 2000, pp. 41–67.

PARKER, HILDA, AND SEYMOUR PARKER. "Father-Daughter Sexual Abuse: An Emerging Perspective." *American Journal of Orthopsychiatry*, 56 (1986): 531–49.

PARKER, SEYMOUR. "Cultural Rules, Rituals, and Behavior Regulation." *American Anthropologist*, 86 (1984): 584–600.

PARKER, SEYMOUR. "The Precultural Basis of the Incest Taboo: Toward a Biosocial Theory." *American Anthropologist*, 78 (1976): 285–305.

PARKER, SUE TAYLOR. "Why Big Brains Are So Rare." In Parker and Gibson, eds., *"Language" and Intelligence in Monkeys and Apes*.

PARKER, SUE TAYLOR, AND KATHLEEN RITA GIBSON, EDS. *"Language" and Intelligence in Monkeys and Apes: Comparative Developmental Perspectives*. New York: Cambridge University Press, 1990.

PARRY, WILLIAM J. "When and How Did Humans Populate the New World?" In Peregrine, Ember, and Ember, eds., *Archaeology*.

PARTRIDGE, WILLIAM L., AND ELIZABETH M. EDDY. "The Development of Applied Anthropology in America." In Eddy and Partridge, eds., *Applied Anthropology in America*, 2nd ed.

PASTERNAK, BURTON. "Family and Household: Who Lives Where, Why Does It Vary, and Why Is It Important?" In C. R. Ember and Ember, eds., *Cross-Cultural Research for Social Science*.

PASTERNAK, BURTON. "Han: Pastoralists and Farmers on a Chinese Frontier." In M. Ember and Ember, eds., *Portraits of Culture*.

PASTERNAK, BURTON. *Introduction to Kinship and Social Organization*. Englewood Cliffs, NJ: Prentice Hall, 1976.

PASTERNAK, BURTON, CAROL R. EMBER, AND MELVIN EMBER. "On the Conditions Favoring Extended Family Households." *Journal of Anthropological Research*, 32 (1976): 109–23.

PASTERNAK, BURTON, CAROL R. EMBER, AND MELVIN EMBER. *Sex, Gender, and Kinship: A Cross-Cultural Perspective*. Upper Saddle River, NJ: Prentice Hall, 1997.

PATTERSON, LELAND. "Criteria for Determining the Attributes of Man-Made Lithics." *Journal of Field Archaeology*, 10 (1983): 297–307.

PATTERSON, ORLANDO. Review of *One Drop of Blood: The American Misadventure of Race* by Scott L. Malcomson. *New York Times Book Review*, October 22, 2000, pp. 15–16.

PATTERSON, ORLANDO. *Slavery and Social Death: A Comparative Study*. Cambridge, MA: Harvard University Press, 1982.

PATTERSON, THOMAS C. "Central Peru: Its Population and Economy." *Archaeology*, 24 (1971): 316–21.

PATTERSON, THOMAS C. *The Evolution of Ancient Societies: A World Archaeology*. Englewood Cliffs, NJ: Prentice Hall, 1981.

PEACOCK, JAMES L. *The Anthropological Lens: Harsh Light, Soft Focus*. Cambridge: Cambridge University Press, 1986.

PEACOCK, NADINE, AND ROBERT BAILEY. "Efe: Investigating Food and Fertility in the Ituri Rain Forest." In M. Ember and Ember, eds., *Portraits of Culture*.

PEAK, LOIS. *Learning to Go to School in Japan: The Transition from Home to Preschool*. Berkeley: University of California Press, 1991.

PEARSALL, DEBORAH. "The Origins of Plant Cultivation in South America." In Cowan and Watson, eds., *The Origins of Agriculture*.

PEARSON, J. D., GARY D. JAMES, AND DANIEL E. BROWN. "Stress and Changing Lifestyles in the Pacific: Physiological Stress Responses of Samoans in Rural and Urban Settings." *American Journal of Human Biology*, 5 (1993): 49–60.

PELTO, PERTTI J., AND GRETEL H. PELTO. "Intra-Cultural Diversity: Some Theoretical Issues." *American Ethnologist*, 2 (1975): 1–18.

PELTO, PERTTI J., AND LUDGER MÜLLER-WILLE. "Snowmobiles: Technological Revolution in the Arctic." In Bernard and Pelto, eds., *Technology and Social Change*, 2nd ed.

PENNISI, E., "Genetic Change Wards Off Malaria." *Science* 294 (16 Nov. 2001), 1439.

PENNISI, E., "Malaria's Beginnings: On the Heels of Hoes?" *Science* 293 (20 July 2001), 416–417. The malarial parasite may have emerged much earlier—see Deirdre Joy.

PENNISI, ELIZABETH. "Finally, the Book of Life and Instructions for Navigating It." *Science*, June 30, 2000, 2304– 307.

PEPPERBERG, IRENE MAXINE. *The Alex Studies: Cognitive and Communicative Abilities of Grey Parrots*. Cambridge, MA: Harvard University Press, 1999.

PEREGRINE, PETER N. "Cross-Cultural Approaches in Archaeology." *Annual Review of Anthropology*, 30 (2001).

PEREGRINE, PETER N. "Social Change in the Woodland-Mississippian Transition: A Study of Household and Community Patterns in the American Bottom." *North American Archaeologist,* 13 (1992): 131–47.

PEREGRINE, PETER N. "Southern and Eastern Africa Later Stone Age." In Peregrine and Ember, *Encyclopedia of Prehistory.* Vol. 1, *Africa,* pp. 272–73.

PEREGRINE, PETER N. "Variation in Stratification." In C. R. Ember and Ember, eds., *Cross-Cultural Research for Social Science.*

PEREGRINE, PETER N. *Outline of Archaeological Traditions.* New Haven, CT: HRAF, 2001.

PEREGRINE, PETER N. *World Prehistory: Two Million Years of Human Life.* Upper Saddle River: Prentice Hall. 2002.

PEREGRINE, PETER. "The Birth of the Gods Revisited: A Partial Replication of Guy Swanson's (1960) Cross-Cultural Study of Religion." *Cross-Cultural Research,* 30 (1996): 84–112.

PEREGRINE, PETER. *Archaeological Research: A Brief Introduction.* Upper Saddle River, NJ: Prentice Hall, 2001.

PEREGRINE, PETER N., AND MELVIN EMBER, EDS. *Encyclopedia of Prehistory.* Vol. 1: *Africa.* New York: Kluwer Academic/Plenum, 2001.

PEREGRINE, PETER N., AND PETER BELLWOOD. "Southeast Asia Upper Paleolithic." In P. N. Peregrine and M. Ember, eds., *Encyclopedia of Prehistory.* Vol. 3: *East Asia and Oceania.* New York: Kluwer Academic/Plenum, 2001, pp. 307–309.

PEREGRINE, PETER N., C. R. EMBER, AND M. EMBER. "Teaching Critical Evaluation of Rushton." *Anthropology Newsletter,* 41, no. 2 (2000): 29–30.

PEREGRINE, PETER N., CAROL R. EMBER, AND MELVIN EMBER, EDS. *Archaeology: Original Readings in Method and Practice.* Upper Saddle River, NJ: Prentice Hall, 2002.

PEREGRINE, PETER N., CAROL R. EMBER, AND MELVIN EMBER, EDS. *Physical Anthropology: Original Readings in Method and Practice.* Upper Saddle River, NJ: Prentice Hall, 2002.

PEREGRINE, PETER N., CAROL R. EMBER, AND MELVIN EMBER. "Cross-Cultural Evaluation of Predicted Associations between Race and Behavior," *Evolution and Human Behavior* 24 (2003): 357–364.

PEREGRINE, PETER. N. AND M. EMBER, EDS., *Encyclopedia of Prehistory* Vol. 8: *South and Southwest Asia* (New York: Kluwer Academic/Plenum, 2002).

PEREGRINE, PETER. N. AND M. EMBER, EDS., *Encyclopedia of Prehistory,* Vol. 3: *East Asia and Oceania* (New York: Kluwer Academic/Plenum, 2001).

PETERSEN, ERIK B. "A Survey of the Late Paleolithic and the Mesolithic of Denmark." In Kozlowski, ed., *The Mesolithic in Europe.*

PETERSEN, L. R., G. R. LEE, AND G. J. ELLIS. "Social Structure, Socialization Values, and Disciplinary Techniques: A Cross-Cultural Analysis." *Journal of Marriage and the Family,* 44 (1982): 131–42.

PFAFF, C. "Constraints on Language Mixing." Language, 55 (1979): 291–318, as cited in Wardhaugh, *An Introduction to Sociolinguistics,* 2nd ed.

PFEIFFER, JOHN E. *The Emergence of Man.* 3rd ed. New York: Harper & Row, 1978.

PHILIPS, SUSAN U., SUSAN STEELE, AND CHRISTINE TANZ, EDS. *Language, Gender, and Sex in Comparative Perspective.* Cambridge: Cambridge University Press, 1987.

PHILLIPS, KEVIN. *The Politics of Rich and Poor: Wealth and the American Electorate in the Reagan Aftermath.* New York: Random House, 1990.

PHILLIPSON, D. W. "Archaeology and Bantu Linguistics." *World Archaeology,* 8 (1976): 65–82.

PHILLIPSON, DAVID W. *African Archaeology.* 2nd ed. New York: Cambridge University Press, 1993.

PIAGET, JEAN. "Piaget's Theory." In Mussen, ed., Carmichael's *Manual of Child Psychology.*

PICCHI, DEBRA. "Bakairí: The Death of an Indian." In M. Ember and Ember, eds., *Portraits of Culture.*

PICCHI, DEBRA. "The Impact of an Industrial Agricultural Project on the Bakairí Indians of Central Brazil." *Human Organization,* 50 (1991): 26–38.

PICKFORD, MARTIN, BRIGETTE SENUT, DOMINIQUE GOMMERCY AND JACQUES TREIL, "Bipedalism in Orrorin tugenensis Revealed by its Femora," *Comptes Rendu de l'Académie des Science des Paris: Palevol* 1 (2002), pp. 1–13.

PIGGOT, STUART, ED. *The Dawn of Civilization.* London: Thames & Hudson, 1961.

PILBEAM, DAVID. *The Ascent of Man.* New York: Macmillan, 1972.

PILBEAM, DAVID, AND STEPHEN JAY GOULD. "Size and Scaling in Human Evolution." *Science,* December 6, 1974, 892–900.

PIPERNO, DOLORES AND KAREN STOTHERT, "Phytolith Evidence for Early Holocene Cucurbita Domestication in Southwest Ecuador," *Science* 299 (14 Feb 2003): 1054–1057.

PLATTNER, STUART, ED. *Economic Anthropology.* Stanford, CA: Stanford University Press, 1989.

PLATTNER, STUART, ED. *Markets and Marketing.* Monographs in Economic Anthropology No. 4. Lanham, MD: University Press of America, 1985.

PLATTNER, STUART. "Marxism." In Plattner, ed., *Economic Anthropology.*

"Plundering Earth Is Nothing New." *Los Angeles Times* News Service, as reported in the New Haven Register, June 12, 1994, A18–A19.

PODOLEFSKY, AARON, AND PETER J. BROWN. *Applying Cultural Anthropology: An Introductory Reader.* Mountain View, CA: Mayfield, 1997.

PODOLEFSKY, AARON., AND BROWN, PETER J. *Applying Cultural Anthropology: An Introductory Reader.* 4th edition. Mountain View, CA: Mayfield, 1999.

POGGIE, JOHN J., JR., AND RICHARD B. POLLNAC. "Danger and Rituals of Avoidance among New England Fishermen." *MAST: Maritime Anthropological Studies,* 1 (1988): 66–78.

POGGIE, JOHN J., JR., BILLIE R. DEWALT, AND WILLIAM W. DRESSLER, EDS. *Anthropological Research: Process and Application.* Albany: State University of New York Press, 1992.

POGGIE, JOHN J., JR., RICHARD B. POLLNAC, AND CARL GERSUNY. "Risk as a Basis for Taboos among Fishermen in Southern New England." *Journal for the Scientific Study of Religion,* 15 (1976): 257–62.

POLANYI, KARL. "The Economy as Instituted Process." In Polanyi, Arensberg, and Pearson, eds., *Trade and Market in the Early Empires.*

POLANYI, KARL, CONRAD M. ARENSBERG, AND HARRY W. PEARSON, EDS. *Trade and Market in the Early Empires.* New York: Free Press, 1957.

POLEDNAK, ANTHONY P. "Connective Tissue Responses in Negroes in Relation to Disease." *American Journal of Physical Anthropology,* 41 (1974): 49–57.

POLGAR, STEVEN, ED. *Population, Ecology, and Social Evolution.* The Hague: Mouton, 1975.

POPE, GEOFFREY G. "Bamboo and Human Evolution." *Natural History,* October 1989, 49–57.

POPENOE, DAVID. *Disturbing the Nest: Family Change and Decline in Modern Societies.* New York: Aldine, 1988.

POSPISIL, LEOPOLD. *The Kapauku Papuans of West New Guinea.* New York: Holt, Rinehart & Winston, 1963.

POST, PETER W., FARRINGTON DANIELS, JR., AND ROBERT T. BINFORD, JR. "Cold Injury and the Evolution of 'White' Skin." *Human Biology,* 47 (1975): 65–80.

POTTS, RICHARD. "Home Bases and Early Hominids." *American Scientist,* 72 (1984): 338–47.

POTTS, RICHARD. *Early Hominid Activities at Olduvai.* New York: Aldine, 1988.

POWERS, WILLIAM K., AND MARLA N. POWERS. "Lakota: A Study in Cultural Continuity." In M. Ember and Ember, eds., *Portraits of Culture.*

PRAG, JOHN, AND RICHARD NEAVE. *Making Faces: Using Forensic and Archaeological Evidence.* College Station: Texas A&M University Press, 1997.

PREUSCHOFT, HOLGER, DAVID J. CHIVERS, WARREN Y. BROCKELMAN, AND NORMAN CREEL, EDS. *The Lesser Apes: Evolutionary and Behavioural Biology.* Edinburgh: Edinburgh University Press, 1984.

"Prevalence, Incidence, and Consequences of Violence against Women: Findings from the National Violence against Women Survey." Washington, DC: U.S. Department of Justice, November 1998.

PRICE, SALLY. *Primitive Art in Civilized Places.* Chicago: University of Chicago Press, 1989.

PRICE, T. DOUGLAS, AND A. B. GEBAUER, EDS. *Last Hunters, First Farmers: New Perspectives on the Prehistoric Transition to Agriculture.* Santa Fe, NM: School of American Research Press, 1995.

PRICE, T. DOUGLAS, AND JAMES A. BROWN. *Prehistoric Hunter-Gatherers: The Emergence of Cultural Complexity.* Orlando, FL: Academic Press, 1985.

PRICE-WILLIAMS, DOUGLASS. "A Study Concerning Concepts of Conservation of Quantities among Primitive Children." *Acta Psychologica,* 18 (1961): 297–305.

PRINGLE, HEATHER. "The Slow Birth of Agriculture." *Science,* 282 (1998): 1446–50.

PROTHERO, DONALD R., AND WILLIAM A. BERGGREN, EDS. *Eocene-Oliocene Climatic and Biotic Evolution.* Princeton, NJ: Princeton University Press, 1992.

PRYOR, FREDERIC L. *The Origins of the Economy: A Comparative Study of Distribution in Primitive and Peasant Economies.* New York: Academic Press, 1977.

PUNTENNEY, PAMELA J. ED., *Global Ecosystems: Creating Options through Anthropological Perspectives, NAPA Bulletin 15* (1995): 60–70.

PURDY, B. *How to Do Archaeology the Right Way.* Gainesville: University Press of Florida, 1996.

QUANDT, SARA A. "Nutrition in Anthropology." In Sargent and Johnson, eds., *Handbook of Medical Anthropology,* pp. 272–89.

QUINN, NAOMI. "Anthropological Studies on Women's Status." *Annual Review of Anthropology,* 6 (1977): 181–225.

RADCLIFFE-BROWN, A. R. *The Andaman Islanders: A Study in Social Anthropology.* Cambridge: Cambridge University Press, 1922.

RADIN, PAUL, ED. *African Folktales and Sculpture.* New York: Pantheon, 1952.

RADINSKY, LEONARD. "The Oldest Primate Endocast." *American Journal of Physical Anthropology,* 27 (1967): 358–88.

RAPPAPORT, ROY A. "Ritual Regulation of Environmental Relations among a New Guinea People." *Ethnology,* 6 (1967): 17–30.

RASMUSSEN, D. TAB. "Primate Origins: Lessons from a Neotropical Marsupial." *American Journal of Primatology,* 22 (1990): 263–77.

RASMUSSEN, T., ED. *The Origin and Evolution of Humans and Humanness.* Boston: Jones and Bartlett, 1993.

RATHJE, WILLIAM L. "The Origin and Development of Lowland Classic Maya Civilization." *American Antiquity,* 36 (1971): 275–85.

RAVESLOOT, JOHN. "Changing Native American Perceptions of Archaeology and Archaeologists." In N. Swidler et al., eds., *Native Americans and Archaeologists.* Walnut Creek, CA: AltaMira Press.

RAY, VERNE F. *The Sanpoil and Nespelem: Salishan Peoples of Northeastern Washington.* New Haven, CT: Human Relations Area Files, 1954, pp. 172–89.

RAYBECK, DOUGLAS. "Toward More Holistic Explanations: Cross-Cultural Research and Cross-Level Analysis." *Cross-Cultural Research,* 32 (1998): 123–142.

RAYBECK, DOUGLAS, J. SHOOBE, AND J. GRAUBERGER, "Women, Stress and Participation in Possession Cults: A Reexamination of the Calcium Deficiency Hypothesis." *Medical Anthropology Quarterly,* 3 (1989): 139–161.

REDMAN, CHARLES L. *The Rise of Civilization: From Early Farmers to Urban Society in the Ancient Near East.* San Francisco: W. H. Freeman, 1978.

REED, CHARLES A., ED. *Origins of Agriculture.* The Hague: Mouton, 1977.

REISNER, MARC. *Cadillac Desert: The American West and Its Disappearing Water.* Rev. ed. New York: Penguin, 1993.

REITER, RAYNA R., ED. *Toward an Anthropology of Women.* New York: Monthly Review Press, 1975.

RELETHFORD, JOHN. *The Human Species: An Introduction to Biological Anthropology.* Mountain View, CA: Mayfield, 1990.

RENFREW, COLIN, ED. *The Explanation of Culture Change: Models in Prehistory.* Pittsburgh: University of Pittsburgh Press, 1973.

RENFREW, COLIN. "Trade and Culture Process in European History." *Current Anthropology,* 10 (April–June 1969): 156–69.

RENFREW, COLIN. "World Linguistic Diversity." *Scientific American,* January 1994, 116–23.

RENFREW, COLIN. *Archaeology and Language: The Puzzle of Indo-European Origins.* London: Jonathan Cape, 1987.

RENFREW, COLIN, AND P. BAHN. *Archaeology; Theories, Methods, and Practice.* New York: Thames and Hudson, 1996.

RENNIE, JOHN, "15 Answers to Creationist Nonsense," *Scientific American* (July 2002), 83.

REYNA, S. P., AND R. E. DOWNS, EDS. *Studying War: Anthropological Perspectives.* New York: Gordon and Breach, 1992.

RHINE, STANLEY. *Bone Voyage: A Journey in Forensic Anthropology.* Albuquerque: University of New Mexico Press, 1998.

RICE, PATRICIA. "Prehistoric Venuses: Symbols of Motherhood or Womanhood?" *Journal of Anthropological Research,* 37 (1981): 402–14.

RICE, PATRICIA C., AND ANN L. PATERSON. "Cave Art and Bones: Exploring the Interrelationships." *American Anthropologist,* 87 (1985): 94–100.

RICE, PATRICIA C., AND ANN L. PATERSON. "Validating the Cave Art—Archeofaunal Relationship in Cantabrian Spain." *American Anthropologist,* 88 (1986): 658–67.

RICHARD, ALISON F. "Malagasy Prosimians: Female Dominance." In Smuts et al., eds., *Primate Societies.*

RICHARD, ALISON F. *Primates in Nature.* New York: W. H. Freeman, 1985.

RIESENFELD, ALPHONSE. "The Effect of Extreme Temperatures and Starvation on the Body Proportions of the Rat." *American Journal of Physical Anthropology,* 39 (1973): 427–59.

RIGHTMIRE, G. PHILIP. "*Homo erectus.*" In Tattersall, Delson, and van Couvering, eds., *Encyclopedia of Human Evolution and Prehistory.*

RIGHTMIRE, G. PHILIP. "*Homo sapiens* in Sub-Saharan Africa." In F. H. Smith and Spencer, eds., *The Origins of Modern Humans.*

RIGHTMIRE, G. PHILIP. "Human Evolution in the Middle Pleistocene: The Role of *Homo heidelbergensis.*" *Evolutionary Anthropology,* 6 (1997): 281–27.

RIGHTMIRE, G. PHILIP. "The Tempo of Change in the Evolution of Mid-Pleistocene *Homo.*" In Delson, ed., *Ancestors.*

RIGHTMIRE, G. PHILIP. *The Evolution of* Homo erectus: *Comparative Anatomical Studies of an Extinct Human Species.* Cambridge: Cambridge University Press, 1990.

RIJKSEN, H. D. *A Fieldstudy on Sumatran Orang Utans (Pongo Pygmaeus Abelii Lesson 1827): Ecology, Behaviour and Conservation.* Wageningen, The Netherlands: H. Veenman and Zonen, 1978.

RITTER, MADELINE LATTMAN. "The Conditions Favoring Age-Set Organization." *Journal of Anthropological Research,* 36 (1980): 87–104.

RIVERS, W. H. R. *The Todas.* Oosterhout, N.B., The Netherlands: Anthropological Publications, 1967. (Originally published 1906.)

ROBERTS, D. F. "Body Weight, Race, and Climate." *American Journal of Physical Anthropology* (1953): 533–58.

ROBERTS, D. F. *Climate and Human Variability.* 2nd ed. Menlo Park, CA: Cummings, 1978.

ROBERTS, JOHN M. "Oaths, Autonomic Ordeals, and Power." In Ford, ed., *Cross-Cultural Approaches.*

ROBERTS, JOHN M., AND BRIAN SUTTON-SMITH. "Child Training and Game Involvement." *Ethnology,* 1 (1962): 166–85.

ROBERTS, JOHN M., MALCOLM J. ARTH, AND ROBERT R. BUSH. "Games in Culture." *American Anthropologist,* 61 (1959): 597–605.

ROBINS, ASHLEY H. *Biological Perspectives on Human Pigmentation.* Cambridge University Press.

ROBINSON, JOHN G., AND CHARLES H. JANSON. "Capuchins, Squirrel Monkeys, and Atelines: Socioecological Convergence with Old World Primates." In Smuts et al., eds., *Primate Societies.*

ROBINSON, JOHN G., PATRICIA C. WRIGHT, AND WARREN G. KINZEY. "Monogamous Cebids and Their Relatives: Intergroup Calls and Spacing." In Smuts et al., eds., *Primate Societies.*

ROBINSON, ROY. "Cat." In Mason, *Evolution of Domesticated Animals.*

RODWIN, LLOYD, ED. *Shelter, Settlement, and Development.* Boston: Allen & Unwin, 1987.

RODWIN, LLOYD, AND BISHWAPRIYA SANYAL. "Shelter, Settlement, and Development: An Overview." In Rodwin, ed., *Shelter, Settlement, and Development.*

ROGERS, E. M. *Diffusion of Innovations,* 5th ed. New York: Simon & Schuster, 2003.

ROGERS, EVERETT M. *Diffusion of Innovations,* 5th ed. New York: Simon & Schuster, 2003.

ROGERS, EVERETT M. *Diffusion of Innovations.* 3rd ed. New York: Free Press, 1983.

ROGOFF, B. *The Cultural Nature of Human Development.* New York: Oxford University Press.

ROGOFF, BARBARA. "Schooling and the Development of Cognitive Skills." In Triandis and Heron, eds., *Handbook of Cross-Cultural Psychology,* Vol. 4.

ROGOFF, BARBARA. *Apprenticeship in Thinking: Cognitive Development in Social Context.* New York: Oxford University Press, 1990.

ROGOFF, BARBARA. *The Cultural Nature of Human Development.* New York: Oxford University Press, 2002.

ROHNER, RONALD P. "Sex Differences in Aggression: Phylogenetic and Enculturation Perspectives." *Ethos,* 4 (1976): 57–72.

ROHNER, RONALD P. *The Warmth Dimension.* Beverly Hills, CA: Sage, 1986.

ROHNER, RONALD P. *They Love Me, They Love Me Not: A Worldwide Study of the Effects of Parental Acceptance and Rejection.* New Haven, CT: HRAF Press, 1975.

ROHNER, RONALD P., AND EVELYN ROHNER, EDS. "Special Issue on Worldwide Tests of Parental Acceptance-Rejection Theory: An Overview." *Behavior Science Research,* 15 (1980): v–88.

ROHNER, RONALD P., and PRESTON A. BRITNER. "Worldwide Mental Health Correlates of Parental Acceptance-Rejection: Review of Cross-Cultural Research and Intracultural Evidence." *Cross-Cultural Research,* 36 (2002): 16–47.

ROMAINE, SUZANNE. *Language in Society: An Introduction to Sociolinguistics.* Oxford: Oxford University Press, 1994.

ROMANUCCI-ROSS, LOLA, AND GEORGE A. DE VOS, EDS. *Ethnic Identity: Creation, Conflict, and Accommodation.* 3rd ed. Walnut Creek, CA: AltaMira Press, 1995.

ROMANUCCI-ROSS, LOLA, DANIEL E. MOERMAN, AND LAURENCE R. TANCREDI, EDS. *The Anthropology of Medicine: From Culture to Method.* 3rd ed. Westport, CT: Bergin & Garvey, 1997.

ROMNEY, A. KIMBALL, CARMELLA C. MOORE, AND CRAIG D. RUSCH. "Cultural Universals: Measuring the Semantic Structure of Emotion Terms in English and Japanese." *Proceedings of the National Academy of Sciences,* U.S.A., 94 (1997): 5489–494.

ROMNEY, A. KIMBALL, SUSAN C. WELLER, AND WILLIAM H. BATCHELDER. "Culture as Consensus: A Theory of Culture and Informant Accuracy." *American Anthropologist,* 88 (1986): 313–38.

ROOSENS, EUGEEN E. *Creating Ethnicity: The Process of Ethnogenesis.* Newbury Park, CA: Sage, 1989.

ROOSEVELT, ANNA CURTENIUS. "Population, Health, and the Evolution of Subsistence: Conclusions from the Conference." In Cohen and Armelagos, eds., *Paleopathology at the Origins of Agriculture.*

ROOSEVELT, ANNA CURTENIUS, ET AL. "Paleoindian Cave Dwellers in the Amazon: The Peopling of the Americas." *Science,* April 19, 1996, 373–84.

ROSALDO, MICHELLE Z., AND LOUISE LAMPHERE, EDS. *Woman, Culture, and Society.* Stanford, CA: Stanford University Press, 1974.

ROSCOE, PAUL. "The Hunters and Gatherers of New Guinea." *Current Anthropology,* 43 (2002): 153–162.

ROSE, M. D. "Food Acquisition and the Evolution of Positional Behaviour: The Case of Bipedalism." In Chivers, Wood, and Bilsborough, eds., *Food Acquisition and Processing in Primates.*

ROSEBERRY, WILLIAM. "Political Economy." *Annual Review of Anthropology,* 17 (1988): 161–259.

ROSENBERG, JOHN D., ED. *The Genius of John Ruskin: Selection from His Writings.* New York: Braziller, 1963.

ROSENBERGER, A. L. "Cranial Anatomy and Implications of Dolichocebus, a Late Oligocene Ceboid Primate." *Nature,* 279 (1979): 416–18.

ROSENBLATT, PAUL C. "Human Rights Violations." In C. R. Ember, Ember, and Peregrine, eds., *Research Frontiers in Anthropology.*

ROSENBLATT, PAUL C., R. PATRICIA WALSH, AND DOUGLAS A. JACKSON. *Grief and Mourning in Cross-Cultural Perspective.* New Haven, CT: HRAF Press, 1976.

ROSENBLUM, L. A., ED. *Primate Behavior.* Vol. 1. New York: Academic Press, 1970.

ROSS, MARC HOWARD. "Ethnocentrism and Ethnic Conflict." In C. R. Ember, Ember, and Peregrine, eds., *Research Frontiers in Anthropology.* Vol. 3.

ROSS, MARC HOWARD. "Female Political Participation: A Cross-Cultural Explanation." *American Anthropologist,* 88 (1986): 843–58.

ROSS, MARC HOWARD. "Internal and External Conflict and Violence." *Journal of Conflict Resolution,* 29 (1985): 547–79.

ROSS, MARC HOWARD. "Political Organization and Political Participation: Exit, Voice, and Loyalty in Preindustrial Societies." *Comparative Politics,* 21 (1988): 73–89.

ROSS, MARC HOWARD. "Political Participation." In C. R. Ember and Ember, eds., *Cross-Cultural Research for Social Science.*

ROSS, MARC HOWARD. "Socioeconomic Complexity, Socialization, and Political Differentiation: A Cross-Cultural Study." *Ethos,* 9 (1981): 217–47.

ROTH, ERIC ABELLA. "Demise of the Sepaade Tradition: Cultural and Biological Explanations." *American Anthropologist,* 103 (2001): 1014–1023.

ROWE, N. *The Pictorial Guide to the Living Primates.* East Hampton, NY: Pogonias Press, 1996.

RUBEL, ARTHUR J. AND MICHAEL R. HASS, in Thomas M. Johnson and Carolyn F. Sargent, *Medical Anthropology: Contemporary Theory and Method* (Westport, CT: Praeger, 1990), p. 120, rev. ed. 1996.

RUBEL, ARTHUR J., AND MICHAEL R. HASS. "Ethnomedicine." In Johnson and Sargent, Medical Anthropology, pp. 115–31; reprinted in Sargent and Johnson, *Handbook of Medical Anthropology.*

RUBEL, ARTHUR J., CARL O. NELL, AND ROLANDO COLLADO-ARDÓN (with the assistance of John Krejci and Jean Krejci). *Susto: A Folk Illness.* Berkeley: University of California Press, 1984.

RUBIN, J. Z., F. J. PROVENZANO, AND R. F. HASKETT. "The Eye of the Beholder: Parents' Views on the Sex of New Borns." *American Journal of Orthopsychiatry,* 44 (1974): 512–19.

RUDMIN, FLOYD WEBSTER. "Dominance, Social Control, and Ownership: A History and a Cross-Cultural Study of Motivations for Private Property." *Behavior Science Research,* 22 (1988): 130–60.

RUFF, CHRISTOPHER B., AND ALAN WALKER. "Body Size and Body Shape." In Walker and Leakey, eds., *The Nariokotome* Homo erectus *Skeleton.* Cambridge, MA: Harvard University Press, 1993.

RUMBAUGH, DUANE M. "Learning Skills of Anthropoids." In Rosenblum, ed., *Primate Behavior,* Vol. 1.

RUMMEL, R. J. "Death by Government." Chapter 1. Published on the Web, August 2002, at http://www.hawaii.edu/powerkills/DBG.CHAP1.HTM21.

RUMMEL, R. J. "Democracies are Less Warlike than Other Regimes." At http://www.hawaii.edu/powerkills/DP95.HTM, August 2002.

RUMMEL, R. J. "Statistics of Democide." Chapter 17. Published on the Web, August 2002, at http://www.hawaii.edu/powerkills/SOD.CHAP17.HTM.

RUMMEL, R. J. "Statistics of Democide." Chapter 21. Published on the Web, August 2002, at http://www. hawaii.edu/powerkills/SOD.CHAP21.HTM.

RUSKIN, JOHN. "Of King's Treasures." In Rosenberg, ed., *The Genius of John Ruskin.*

RUSSELL, ELBERT W. "Factors of Human Aggression." *Behavior Science Notes,* 7 (1972): 275–312.

RUSSETT, BRUCE (with the collaboration of William Antholis, Carol R. Ember, Melvin Ember, and Zeev Maoz). *Grasping the Democratic Peace: Principles for a Post-Cold War World.* Princeton, NJ: Princeton University Press, 1993.

RUSSETT, BRUCE AND JOHN R. ONEAL. *Triangulating Peace: Democracy, Interdependence, and International Organizations.* New York: Norton, 2001.

RUSSON, ANNE E. "The Development of Peer Social Interaction in Infant Chimpanzees: Comparative Social, Piagetian, and Brain Perspectives." In Parker and Gibson, eds., *"Language" and Intelligence in Monkeys and Apes.*

SABLOFF, JEREMY A., ED. *Supplement to the Handbook of Middle American Indians.* Vol. 1. Austin: University of Texas Press, 1981.

SADE, D. S. "Some Aspects of Parent-Offspring and Sibling Relationships in a Group of Rhesus Monkeys, with a Discussion of Grooming." *American Journal of Physical Anthropology,* 23 (1965): 1–17.

SAGAN, CARL. "A Cosmic Calendar." *Natural History,* December 1975, 70–73.

SAHLINS, MARSHALL D. "Poor Man, Rich Man, Big-Man, Chief: Political Types in Melanesia and Polynesia." *Comparative Studies in Society and History,* 5 (1963): 285–303.

SAHLINS, MARSHALL D. "The Segmentary Lineage: An Organization of Predatory Expansion." *American Anthropologist,* 63 (1961): 332–45.

SAHLINS, MARSHALL D. *Moala: Culture and Nature on a Fijian Island.* Ann Arbor: University of Michigan Press, 1962.

SAHLINS, MARSHALL D. *Social Stratification in Polynesia.* Seattle: University of Washington Press, 1958.

SAHLINS, MARSHALL D. *Stone Age Economics.* Chicago: Aldine, 1972.

SAHLINS, MARSHALL. "Other Times, Other Customs: The Anthropology of History." *American Anthropologist,* 85 (1983): 517–44.

SALZMAN, PHILIP CARL. "Is Inequality Universal?" Current Anthropology, 40 (1999): 31–61.

SALZMAN, PHILIP CARL. "Pastoralism." In David Levinson and Melvin Ember, eds., *Encyclopedia of Cultural Anthropology,* Vol. 3. New York: Henry Holt, 1996, pp. 899–905.

SANDAY, PEGGY R. "Female Status in the Public Domain." In Rosaldo and Lamphere, eds., *Woman, Culture, and Society.*

SANDAY, PEGGY R. "Toward a Theory of the Status of Women." *American Anthropologist,* 75 (1973): 1682– 700.

SANDERS, WILLIAM T. "Hydraulic Agriculture, Economic Symbiosis, and the Evolution of States in Central Mexico." In Meggers, ed., *Anthropological Archaeology in the Americas.*

SANDERS, WILLIAM T., AND BARBARA J. PRICE. *Mesoamerica.* New York: Random House, 1968.

SANDERS, WILLIAM T., JEFFREY R. PARSONS, AND ROBERT S. SANTLEY. *The Basin of Mexico: Ecological Processes in the Evolution of a Civilization.* New York: Academic Press, 1979.

SANDERSON, STEPHEN K. "Expanding World Commercialization: The Link between World-Systems and Civilizations." In Stephen K. Sanderson, ed., *Civilizations and World Systems: Studying World-Historical Change.* Walnut Creek, CA: Alta Mira Press, 1995.

SAPIR, EDWARD. "Conceptual Categories in Primitive Languages." Paper presented at the autumn meeting of the National Academy of Sciences, New Haven, CT, 1931. Published in *Science,* 74 (1931).

SAPIR, EDWARD. "Why Cultural Anthropology Needs the Psychiatrist." *Psychiatry,* 1 (1938): 7–12.

SAPIR, EDWARD. *Language: An Introduction to the Study of Speech.* New York: Harcourt Brace Jovanovich, 1949. (Originally published 1921.)

SAPIR, EDWARD, AND M. SWADESH. "American Indian Grammatical Categories." In Hymes, ed., *Language in Culture and Society.*

SARGENT, CAROLYN F., AND THOMAS M. JOHNSON, EDS. *Handbook of Medical Anthropology: Contemporary Theory and Method.* Rev. ed. Westport, CT: Greenwood Press, 1996, pp. 272–89.

SARICH, VINCENT M. "The Origin of Hominids: An Immunological Approach." In Washburn and Jay, eds., *Perspectives on Human Evolution,* Vol. 1.

SARICH, VINCENT M., AND ALLAN C. WILSON. "Quantitative Immunochemistry and the Evolution of Primate Albumins: Micro-Component Fixations." *Science,* December 23, 1966, 1563–66.

SASSAMAN, KENNETH. "Early Archaic Settlement in the South Carolina Coastal Plain." In D. G. Anderson and K. E. Sassaman, eds., *The Paleoindian and Early Archaic Southeast.* Tuscaloosa: University of Alabama Press, 1996, pp. 58–83.

SATTLER, RICHARD A. "Remnants, Renegades, and Runaways: Seminole Ethnogenesis Reconsidered." In J. D. Hill, *Ethnogenesis in the Americas,* pp. 36–69.

SAUL, MAHIR. "Work Parties, Wages, and Accumulation in a Voltaic Village." *American Ethnologist,* 10 (1983): 77–96.

SAVAGE-RUMBAUGH, E. S. "Hominid Evolution: Looking to Modern Apes for Clues." In Duane Quiatt and Junichiro Itani, eds., *Hominid Culture in Primate Perspective.* Niwot: University Press of Colorado, 1994.

SAVAGE-RUMBAUGH, E. S. "Language Training of Apes." In Jones, Martin, and Pilbeam, eds., *The Cambridge Encyclopedia of Human Evolution.*

SCAGLION, RICHARD. "Abelam: Giant Yams and Cycles of Sex, Warfare and Ritual." In M. Ember and Ember, eds., *Portraits of Culture.*

SCAGLION, RICHARD. "Law and Society." In C. R. Ember and Ember, eds., *Cross-Cultural Research for Social Science.*

SCAGLION, RICHARD. "Legal Adaptation in a Papua New Guinea Village Court." *Ethnology,* 29 (1990): 17–33.

SCAGLION, RICHARD, AND ROSE WHITTINGHAM. "Female Plaintiffs and Sex-Related Disputes in Rural Papua New Guinea." In Toft, ed., *Domestic Violence in Papua New Guinea.*

SCARR, SANDRA, AND KATHLEEN MCCARTNEY. "How People Make Their Own Environments: A Theory of Genotype—Environment Effects." *Child Development,* 54 (1983): 424–35.

SCHAEFER, STACY B. "Huichol: Becoming a Godmother." In M. Ember and Ember, eds., *Portraits of Culture.*

SCHALLER, GEORGE B. *The Serengeti Lion: A Study of Predator-Prey Relations.* Chicago: University of Chicago Press, 1972.

SCHALLER, GEORGE. *The Mountain Gorilla: Ecology and Behavior.* Chicago: University of Chicago Press, 1963.

SCHALLER, GEORGE. *The Year of the Gorilla.* Chicago: University of Chicago Press, 1964.

SCHICK, KATHY D., AND NICHOLAS TOTH. *Making Silent Stones Speak.* New York: Simon & Schuster, 1993.

SCHIFFER, MICHAEL B. *Formation Processes of the Archaeological Record.* Albuquerque: University of New Mexico Press, 1987.

SCHIFFER, MICHAEL B., ED. *Advances in Archaeological Method and Theory.* Vol. 7. Orlando, FL: Academic Press, 1984.

SCHLEGEL, ALICE, ED. *Sexual Stratification: A Cross-Cultural View.* New York: Columbia University Press, 1977.

SCHLEGEL, ALICE. "Gender Issues and Cross-Cultural Research." *Behavior Science Research,* 23 (1989): 265–80.

SCHLEGEL, ALICE. "Status, Property, and the Value on Virginity." *American Ethnologist,* 18 (1991): 719–34.

SCHLEGEL, ALICE. "The Status of Women." In C. R. Ember and Ember, eds., *Cross-Cultural Research for Social Science.*

SCHLEGEL, ALICE. *Male Dominance and Female Autonomy.* New Haven, CT: HRAF Press, 1972.

SCHLEGEL, ALICE, AND HERBERT BARRY III. "The Cultural Consequences of Female Contribution to Subsistence." *American Anthropologist,* 88 (1986): 142–50.

SCHLEGEL, ALICE, AND HERBERT BARRY III. *Adolescence: An Anthropological Inquiry.* New York: Free Press, 1991.

SCHLEGEL, ALICE, AND ROHN ELOUL. "A New Coding of Marriage Transactions." *Behavior Science Research,* 21 (1987): 118–40.

SCHLEGEL, ALICE, AND ROHN ELOUL. "Marriage Transactions: Labor, Property, and Status." *American Anthropologist,* 90 (1988): 291–309.

SCHNEIDER, DAVID M. "The Distinctive Features of Matrilineal Descent Groups." In Schneider and Gough, eds., *Matrilineal Kinship.*

SCHNEIDER, DAVID M. "Truk." In Schneider and Gough, eds., *Matrilineal Kinship.*

SCHNEIDER, DAVID M., AND KATHLEEN GOUGH, EDS. *Matrilineal Kinship.* Berkeley: University of California Press, 1961.

SCHOEPF, B. "Women, AIDS and Economic Crisis in Central Africa." *Canadian Journal of African Studies,* 22 (1988): 625–44.

SCHRAUF, ROBERT W. "Mother Tongue Maintenance Among North American Ethnic Groups." *Cross-Cultural Research,* 33 (1999): 175–192.

SCHRIRE, CARMEL, ED. *Past and Present in Hunter-Gatherer Studies.* Orlando, FL: Academic Press, 1984.

SCHRIRE, CARMEL. "An Inquiry into the Evolutionary Status and Apparent Identity of San Hunter-Gatherers." *Human Ecology,* 8 (1980): 9–32.

SCHRIRE, CARMEL. "Wild Surmises on Savage Thoughts." In Schrire, ed., *Past and Present in Hunter-Gatherer Studies.*

SCHWARCZ, HENRY P. "Uranium-Series Dating and the Origin of Modern Man." In Schwarcz, *The Origin of Modern Humans and the Impact of Chronometric Dating.*

SCHWARCZ, HENRY P. *The Origin of Modern Humans and the Impact of Chronometric Dating.* Princeton, NJ: Princeton University Press, 1993.

SCHWARTZ, J. *Sudden Origins: Fossils, Genes, and the Emergence of Species.* New York: John Wiley, 1999.

SCHWARTZ, RICHARD D. "Social Factors in the Development of Legal Control: A Case Study of Two Israeli Settlements." *Yale Law Journal,* 63 (February 1954): 471–91.

SCOLLON, RON, AND SUSAN WONG SCOLLON. *Intercultural Communication: A Discourse Approach.* 2nd edition. Malden, Mass.: Blackwell Publishers, 2001.

SCOLLON, RON, AND SUZANNE B. K. SCOLLON. *Narrative, Literacy and Face in Interethnic Communication.* Norwood, NJ: ABLEX, 1981.

SCRIBNER, SYLVIA, AND MICHAEL COLE. *The Psychology of Literacy.* Cambridge, MA: Harvard University Press, 1981.

SCUDDER, THAYER. "Opportunities, Issues and Achievements in Development Anthropology since the Mid-1960s: A Personal View." In Eddy and Partridge, eds., *Applied Anthropology in America,* 2nd ed.

SEBEOK, THOMAS A., AND JEAN UMIKER-SEBEOK, EDS. *Speaking of Apes: A Critical Anthology of Two-Way Communication with Man.* New York: Plenum, 1980.

SEEMANOVÁ, EVA. "A Study of Children of Incestuous Matings." *Human Heredity,* 21 (1971): 108–28.

SEGAL, ROBERT A. *Joseph Campbell: An Introduction.* New York: Garland, 1977.

SEGALL, MARSHALL H. *Cross-Cultural Psychology: Human Behavior in Global Perspective.* Monterey, CA: Brooks/Cole, 1979.

SEGALL, MARSHALL, PIERRE R. DASEN, JOHN W. BERRY, AND YPE H. POORTINGA. *Human Behavior in Global Perspective: An Introduction to Cross-Cultural Psychology.* New York: Pergamon, 1990.

SEGERSTRÅLE, ULLICA, AND PETER MOLNAR, EDS. *Nonverbal Communication: Where Nature Meets Culture.* Mahwah, NJ: Lawrence Erlbaum, 1997.

SELIG, RUTH OSTERWEIS, AND MARILYN R. LONDON, EDS. *Anthropology Explored: The Best of Smithsonian AnthroNotes.* Washington, DC: Smithsonian Institution Press, 1998. Also in E-book format. 2000.

SEMENOV, S. A. *Prehistoric Technology.* Trans. M. W. Thompson. Bath, England: Adams & Dart, 1970.

SENGUPTA, SOMINI. "Money From Kin Abroad Helps Bengalis Get By." *New York Times,* June 24, 2002, p. A3.

SENNER, WAYNE M. "Theories and Myths on the Origins of Writing: A Historical Overview." In Senner, ed., *The Origins of Writing.*

SENNER, WAYNE M., ED. *The Origins of Writing.* Lincoln: University of Nebraska Press, 1989.

SERED, SUSAN S. *Priestess, Mother, Sacred Sister.* New York: Oxford University Press, 1994.

SERVICE, ELMAN R. *Origins of the State and Civilization: The Process of Cultural Evolution.* New York: Norton, 1975.

SERVICE, ELMAN R. *Primitive Social Organization: An Evolutionary Perspective.* New York: Random House, 1962.

SERVICE, ELMAN R. *Profiles in Ethnology*. 3rd ed. New York: Harper & Row, 1978.

SERVICE, ELMAN R. *The Hunters*. 2nd ed. Englewood Cliffs, NJ: Prentice Hall, 1979.

SEYFARTH, ROBERT M., AND DOROTHY L. CHENEY. "How Monkeys See the World: A Review of Recent Research on East African Vervet Monkeys." In Snowdon, Brown, and Petersen, eds., *Primate Communication*.

SEYFARTH, ROBERT M., DOROTHY L. CHENEY, AND PETER MARLER. "Monkey Response to Three Different Alarm Calls: Evidence of Predator Classification and Semantic Communication." *Science*, November 14, 1980, 801–803.

SHANKLIN, EUGENIA. *Anthropology and Race*. Belmont, CA: Wadsworth, 1994.

SHANKMAN, PAUL. "Culture Contact, Cultural Ecology, and Dani Warfare." *Man*, 26 (1991): 299–321.

SHANKMAN, PAUL. "Sex, Lies, and Anthropologists: Margaret Mead, Derek Freeman, and Samoa." In C.R. Ember, Ember, and Peregrine, eds., *Research Frontiers in Anthropology*. Vol. 3.

SHEILS, DEAN. "A Comparative Study of Human Sacrifice." *Behavior Science Research*, 15 (1980): 245–62.

SHEILS, DEAN. "Toward a Unified Theory of Ancestor Worship: A Cross-Cultural Study." *Social Forces*, 54 (1975): 427–40.

SHEN, XUEFEI, AND ROBERT F. SILICIANO. "Preventing AIDS but Not HIV-1 Infection with a DNA Vaccine." *Science*, October 20, 2000, 463–65.

SHIBAMOTO, JANET S. "The Womanly Woman: Japanese Female Speech." In Philips, Steele, and Tanz, eds., *Language, Gender, and Sex in Comparative Perspective*.

SHIPMAN, PAT. "Scavenging or Hunting in Early Hominids: Theoretical Framework and Tests." *American Anthropologist*, 88 (1986): 27–43.

SHIPMAN, PAT. *The Evolution of Racism: Human Differences and the Use and Abuse of Science*. New York: Simon & Schuster, 1994.

SHIPMAN, PAT. *The Man Who Found the Missing Link: Eugene Dubois and His Lifelong Quest to Prove Darwin Right*. New York: Simon & Schuster, 2001.

SHULMAN, SETH. "Nurturing Native Tongues." *Technology Review*, May/June 1993, 16.

SHWEDER, RICHARD A., AND ROBERT A. LeVINE, EDS. *Culture Theory: Essays on Mind, Self, and Emotion*. New York: Cambridge University Press, 1984.

SIH, ANDREW, AND KATHARINE A. MILTON. "Optimal Diet Theory: Should the !Kung Eat Mongongos?" *American Anthropologist*, 87 (1985): 395–401.

SILK, JOAN B. AND ROBERT BOYD, "Why Are Primates So Smart?" in Peter N. Peregrine, Carol R. Ember, and Melvin Ember, eds., Physical Anthropology: Original Readings in Method and Practice (Upper Saddle River, NJ: Prentice Hall, 2002), pp. 53–67. Also in Carol R. Ember and Melvin Ember, eds., *New Directions in Anthropology* (Upper Saddle River, NJ: Prentice Hall, CD-ROM, 2003).

SILVER, HARRY R. "Calculating Risks: The Socioeconomic Foundations of Aesthetic Innovation in an Ashanti Carving Community." *Ethnology*, 20 (1981): 101–14.

SIMMONS, ALAN H., ILSE KÖHLER-ROLLEFSON, GARY O. ROLLEFSON, ROLFE MANDEL, AND ZEIDAN KAFAFI. "'Ain Ghazal: A Major Neolithic Settlement in Central Jordan." *Science*, April 1, 1988, 35–39.

SIMMONS, JANIE, PAUL FARMER, AND BROOKE G. SCHOEPF, "A Global Perspective," in Paul Farmer, Margaret Connors, and Janie Simmons, eds., *Women, Poverty, and AIDS: Sex, Drugs, and Structural Violence* (Monroe, ME: Common Courage Press, 1996), pp. 44–45.

SIMMONS, JANIE, PAUL FARMER, AND BROOKE G. SCHOEPF. "A Global Perspective." In Paul Farmer, Margaret Connors, and Janie Simmons, eds., *Women, Poverty, and AIDS: Sex, Drugs, and Structural Violence*. Monroe, ME: Common Courage Press, 1996, pp. 39–90.

SIMONS, ELWYN L. "Skulls and Anterior Teeth of Catopithecus (Primates: Anthropoidea) from the Eocene Shed Light on Anthropoidean Origins." *Science*, 268 (1995): 1885–88.

SIMONS, ELWYN. "The Primate Fossil Record." In Jones, Martin, and Pilbeam, eds., *The Cambridge Encyclopedia of Human Evolution*.

SIMONS, ELWYN L., AND D. T. RASSMUSSEN. "Skull of Catopithecus browni, an Early Tertiary Catarrhine." *American Journal of Physical Anthropology*, 100 (1996): 261–92.

SIMPSON, GEORGE GAYLORD. *The Meaning of Evolution*. New York: Bantam, 1971.

SIMPSON, S. P., AND RUTH FIELD. "Law and the Social Sciences." *Virginia Law Review*, 32 (1946): 858.

SIMPSON, SCOTT W. "Australopithecus afarensis and Human Evolution." In Peregrine, Ember, and Ember, eds., *Physical Anthropology*.

SINGER, J. DAVID. "Accounting for International War: The State of the Discipline." *Annual Review of Sociology*, 6 (1980): 349–67.

SINGER, RONALD, AND JOHN WYMER. *The Middle Stone Age at Klasies River Mouth in South Africa*. Chicago: University of Chicago Press, 1982.

SINOPOLI, CARLA. "Learning about the Past through Archaeological Ceramics: An Example from Yijayanagara, India." In Peregrine, Ember, and Ember, eds., *Archaeology*.

SIPES, RICHARD G. "War, Sports, and Aggression: An Empirical Test of Two Rival Theories." *American Anthropologist*, 75 (1973): 64–86.

SIVARD, RUTH LEGER. *World Military and Social Expenditures 1993*. 15th ed. Washington, DC: World Priorities, 1993.

SKOMAL, SUSAN N., AND EDGAR C. POLOMÉ, EDS. *Proto-Indo-European: The Archaeology of a Linguistic Problem*. Washington, DC: Washington Institute for the Study of Man, 1987.

SMALL, DAVID B. AND NICOLA B. TANNENBAUM, EDS. *At the Interface: The Household and Beyond*. Lanham, MD, University Press of America, 1999.

SMALL, MEREDITH. "Our Babies, Ourselves." *Natural History*, October 1997, pp. 42–51.

SMITH, B. HOLLY. "Dental Development in Australopithecus and Early Homo." *Nature*, September 25, 1986, 327–30.

SMITH, BRUCE D. "Prehistoric Plant Husbandry in Eastern North America." In Cowan and Watson, eds., *The Origins of Agriculture*.

SMITH, BRUCE D. *Rivers of Change*. Washington, DC: Smithsonian Institution Press, 1992.

SMITH, BRUCE D. *The Emergence of Agriculture*. New York: Scientific American Library, 1995.

SMITH, ERIC A. "Anthropological Applications of Optimal Foraging Theory: A Critical Review." *Current Anthropology*, 24 (1983): 625–40.

SMITH, FRED H. "Fossil Hominids from the Upper Pleistocene of Central Europe and the Origin of Modern Humans." In F. H. Smith and Spencer, eds., *The Origins of Modern Humans*.

SMITH, FRED H., AND FRANK SPENCER, EDS. *The Origins of Modern Humans: A World Survey of the Fossil Evidence*. New York: Alan R. Liss, 1984.

SMITH, JOHN MAYNARD. *Evolutionary Genetics*. New York: Oxford University Press, 1989.

SMITH, M. W. "Alfred Binet's Remarkable Questions: A Cross-National and Cross-Temporal Analysis of the Cultural Biases Built into the Stanford-Binet Intelligence Scale and Other Binet Tests." *Genetic Psychology Monographs*, 89 (1974): 307–34.

SMITH, MICHAEL G. "Pre-Industrial Stratification Systems." In Neil J. Smelser and Seymour Martin Lipset, eds., *Social Structure and Mobility in Economic Development.* Chicago: Aldine, 1966.

SMITH, WALDEMAR R. *The Fiesta System and Economic Change.* New York: Columbia University Press, 1977.

SMUTS, BARBARA B., DOROTHY L. CHENEY, ROBERT M. SEYFARTH, RICHARD W. WRANGHAM, AND THOMAS T. STRUHSAKER, EDS. *Primate Societies.* Chicago: University of Chicago Press, 1987.

SNOWDON, CHARLES T. "An Empiricist View of Language Evolution and Development." In King, *The Origins of Language,* pp. 79–114.

SNOWDON, CHARLES T., CHARLES H. BROWN, AND MICHAEL R. PETERSEN, EDS. *Primate Communication.* New York: Cambridge University Press, 1982.

SOFFER, O. *The Upper Paleolithic of the Central Russian Plain.* Orlando, FL: Academic Press, 1985.

SOFFER, OLGA. "Upper Paleolithic Adaptations in Central and Eastern Europe and Man-Mammoth Interactions." In Soffer and Praslov, eds., *From Kostenki to Clovis.*

SOFFER, OLGA, AND N. D. PRASLOV, EDS. *From Kostenki to Clovis: Upper Paleolithic–Paleo-Indian Adaptations.* New York: Plenum, 1993.

SOFFER, OLGA, J. M. ADOVASIO, AND D. C. HYLAND. "The 'Venus' Figurines: Textiles, Basketry, Gender, and Status in the Upper Paleolithic." *Current Anthropology,* 41 (2000): 511–37.

SOSA, JOHN R. "Maya: The Sacred in Everyday Life." In M. Ember and Ember, eds., *Portraits of Culture.*

SOUTHWORTH, FRANKLIN C., AND CHANDLER J. DASWANI. *Foundations of Linguistics.* New York: Free Press, 1974.

SPANOS, NICHOLAS P. "Ergotism and the Salem Witch Panic: A Critical Analysis and an Alternative Conceptualization." *Journal of the History of the Behavioral Sciences,* 19 (1983): 358–69.

SPENCER, FRANK. "The Neandertals and Their Evolutionary Significance: A Brief Historical Survey." In F. H. Smith and Spencer, eds., *The Origins of Modern Humans.*

SPENCER, ROBERT F. "Spouse-Exchange among the North Alaskan Eskimo." In Bohannan and Middleton, eds., *Marriage, Family and Residence.*

SPERBER, DAN. *On Anthropological Knowledge: Three Essays.* Cambridge: Cambridge University Press, 1985.

SPETH, JOHN D. "Were Our Ancestors Hunters or Scavengers?" In Peregrine, Ember, and Ember, eds., *Physical Anthropology.*

SPETH, JOHN D., AND DAVE D. DAVIS. "Seasonal Variability in Early Hominid Predation." *Science,* April 30, 1976, 441–45.

SPETH, JOHN D., AND KATHERINE A. SPIELMANN. "Energy Source, Protein Metabolism, and Hunter-Gatherer Subsistence Strategies." *Journal of Anthropological Archaeology,* 2 (1983): 1–31.

SPIRO, MELFORD E. *Oedipus in the Trobriands.* Chicago: University of Chicago Press, 1982.

SPIRO, MELFORD. "On the Strange and the Familiar in Recent Anthropological Thought." In C. R. Ember, Ember, and Peregrine, eds., *Research Frontiers in Anthropology.*

SPIRO, MELFORD. "Is the Western Conception of the Self 'Peculiar' within the Context of the World Cultures?" *Ethos,* 21 (1993): 107–53.

SPIRO, MELFORD E., AND ROY G. D'ANDRADE. "A Cross-Cultural Study of Some Supernatural Beliefs." *American Anthropologist,* 60 (1958): 456–66.

SPOONER, BRIAN, ED. *Population Growth: Anthropological Implications.* Cambridge, MA: MIT Press, 1972.

SPRING, ANITA. *Agricultural Development and Gender Issues in Malawi.* Lanham, MD: University Press of America, 1995.

STAIRS, ARLENE. "Self-Image, World-Image: Speculations on Identity from Experiences with Inuit." *Ethos,* 20 (1992): 116–26.

STANFORD, CRAIG. "Chimpanzee Hunting Behavior and Human Evolution." In Peregrine, Ember, and Ember, eds., *Physical Anthropology.*

STANFORD, CRAIG B. "The Social Behavior of Chimpanzees and Bonobos: Empirical Evidence and Shifting Assumptions." *Current Anthropology,* 39 (1998): 399–420.

STANFORD, CRAIG B., JANETTE WALLIS, HILALI MATAMA, AND JANE GOODALL. "Patterns of Predation by Chimpanzees on Red Colobus Monkeys in Gombe National Park, Tanzania, 1982–1991." *American Journal of Physical Anthropology,* 94 (1994): 213–29.

STARK, RODNEY. *The Future of Religion: Secularization, Revival and Cult Formation.* Berkeley: University of California Press, 1985.

State of the World 1994: A Worldwatch Institute Report on Progress toward a Sustainable Society. New York: Norton, 1994.

STEEGMAN, A. T., JR. "Human Adaptation to Cold." In Damon, ed., *Physiological Anthropology.*

STEIN, GIL, AND MITCHELL ROTHMAN, EDS. *Chiefdoms and Early States in the Near East: The Organizational Dynamics of Complexity.* Madison, WI: Prehistory Press, 1994.

STEIN, P., AND B. ROWE. *Physical Anthropology.* 7th ed. Boston: McGraw Hill, 2000.

STEINER, CHRISTOPHER B. "Body Personal and Body Politic: Adornment and Leadership in Cross-Cultural Perspective." *Anthropos,* 85 (1990): 431–45.

STEPHENS, WILLIAM N. "A Cross-Cultural Study of Modesty." *Behavior Science Research,* 7 (1972): 1–28.

STEPHENS, WILLIAM N. *The Family in Cross-Cultural Perspective.* New York: Holt, Rinehart & Winston, 1963.

STERN, CURT. *Principles of Human Genetics.* 3rd ed. San Francisco: W. H. Freeman, 1973.

STEWARD, JULIAN H. "The Concept and Method of Cultural Ecology." In Steward, *Theory of Culture Change.*

STEWARD, JULIAN H. *Theory of Culture Change.* Urbana: University of Illinois Press, 1955.

STEWARD, JULIAN H., AND LOUIS C. FARON. *Native Peoples of South America.* New York: McGraw-Hill, 1959.

STEWARD, JULIAN H., ROBERT A. MANNERS, ERIC R. WOLF, ELENA PADILLA SEDA, SIDNEY W. MINTZ, AND RAYMOND L. SCHEELE. *The People of Puerto Rico.* Urbana: University of Illinois Press, 1956.

STEWART, T. D. "Deformity, Trephanating, and Mutilation in South American Indian Skeletal Remains." In J. A. STEWARD, ed., *Handbook of South American Indians.* Vol. 6: *Physical Anthropology, Linguistics, and Cultural Geography.* Bureau of American Ethnology Bulletin 143. Washington, DC: Smithsonian Institution.

STILLE, ALEXANDER. "Grounded by an Income Gap," *New York Times,* Arts & Ideas, Saturday, December 15, 2001.

STIMPSON, DAVID, LARRY JENSEN, AND WAYNE NEFF. "Cross-Cultural Gender Differences in Preference for a Caring Morality." *Journal of Social Psychology,* 132 (1992): 317–22.

STINI, WILLIAM A. "Evolutionary Implications of Changing Nutritional Patterns in Human Populations." *American Anthropologist,* 73 (1971): 1019–30.

STINI, WILLIAM A. *Ecology and Human Adaptation.* Dubuque, IA: Wm. C. Brown, 1975.

STOCKING, GEORGE W., JR., ED. *History of Anthropology.* Vols. 1–6. Madison: University of Wisconsin Press, 1983–1989.

STODDER, JAMES, "The Evolution of Complexity in Primitive Exchange." *Journal of Comparative Economics,* 20 (1995): 205.

STOGDILL, RALPH M. *Handbook of Leadership: A Survey of Theory and Research.* New York: Macmillan, 1974.

STONEKING, MARK, "Recent African Origin of Human Mitochondrial DNA," in P. Donnelly and S. Tavaré, eds., *Progress in Population Genetics and Human Evolution* (New York: Springer), pp. 1–13.

STRAUS, MURRAY A. "Physical Aggression in the Family: Prevalence Rates: Links to Non-Family Violence, and Implications for Primary Prevention of Societal Violence." In Manuela Martinez, ed. *Prevention and Control of Aggression and the Impact on Its Victims.* New York: Kluwer Academic/Plenum, 2001, pp. 181–200.

STRAUS, MURRAY A. "Physical Violence in American Families: Incidence Rates, Causes, and Trends." In Knudsen and Miller, eds., *Abused and Battered.*

STRAUS, MURRAY A. "Trends in Cultural Norms and Rates of Partner Violence: An Update to 1992." In Sandra M. Stith and Murray A. Straus, eds. *Understanding Partner Violence: Prevalence, Causes, Consequences, and Solutions.* Minneapolis, MN: National Council on Family Relations, 1995, pp. 30–33, as seen at http://pubpages.unh.edu/~mas2/v56.pdf/, August 2002.

STRAUS, MURRAY A. AND CARRIE L. YODANIS, "Corporal Punishment in Adolescence and Physical Assaults on Spouses in Later Life: What Accounts for the Link?" *Journal of Marriage and the Family,* 58 (1996): 825–841.

STRAUS, MURRAY A. AND GLENDA KAUFMAN KANTOR, "Trends in Physical Abuse by Parents From 1975 to 1992: A Comparison of Three National Surveys." Paper presented at the annual meeting of the American Society of Criminology, Boston, November 18, 1995, as seen at http://pubpages.unh.edu/~mas2/V57.pdf/, August 2002.

STRAUS, MURRAY A. AND GLENDA KAUFMAN KANTOR. "Change in Spouse Assault Rates from 1975 to 1992: A Comparison of Three National Surveys in the United States." Paper presented at the 13th World Congress of Sociology, Bielefeld, Germany, July 1994. Found at http://pubpages.unh.edu/~mas2/v55.pdf/, August 2002.

STRAUSS, LAWRENCE GUY. "Comment on White." *Current Anthropology,* 23 (1982): 185–86.

STRAUSS, LAWRENCE GUY. "On Early Hominid Use of Fire." *Current Anthropology,* 30 (1989): 488–91.

STRAUSS, LAWRENCE GUY. "Solutrean Settlement of North America? A View of Reality." *American Antiquity,* 65 (2000): 219–26.

STRINGER, CHRISTOPHER B. "Neandertals." In Tattersall, Delson, and van Couvering, eds., *Encyclopedia of Human Evolution and Prehistory.*

STRINGER, CHRISTOPHER. "Evolution of a Species." *Geographical Magazine,* 57 (1985): 601–607.

STRINGER, C. B., J. J. HUBLIN, AND B. VANDERMEERSCH. "The Origin of Anatomically Modern Humans in Western Europe." In F. H. Smith and Spencer, eds., *The Origins of Modern Humans.*

STRINGER, CHRISTOPHER, AND CLIVE GAMBLE. *In Search of the Neandertals.* New York: Thames and Hudson, 1993.

STROUTHES, DANIEL P. *Law and Politics: A Cross-Cultural Encyclopedia.* Santa Barbara, CA: ABC-CLIO, 1995.

STRUEVER, STUART, ED. *Prehistoric Agriculture.* Garden City, NY: Natural History Press, 1971.

SUÁREZ-OROZCO, MARCELO. "A Grammar of Terror: Psychocultural Responses to State Terrorism in Dirty War and Post-Dirty War Argentina." In Carolyn Nordstrom and JoAnn Martin, eds. *The Paths to Domination, Resistance, and Terror.* Berkeley, CA: University of California Press, 1992, pp. 219–259.

SUPER, CHARLES M., AND SARA HARKNESS, "The Cultural Structuring of Child Development," in John W. Berry, Pierre R. Dasen, and T. S. Saraswathi, eds. *Handbook of Cross-Cultural Psychology,* Vol. 2. 2nd edition. Boston: Allyn and Bacon, 1997, pp. 1–39.

SUSMAN, RANDALL L. "Fossil Evidence for Early Hominid Tool Use." *Science,* September 9, 1994, 1570–73.

SUSMAN, RANDALL L., ED. *The Pygmy Chimpanzee: Evolutionary Biology and Behavior.* New York: Plenum, 1984.

SUSMAN, RANDALL L., JACK T. STERN, JR., AND WILLIAM L. JUNGERS. "Locomotor Adaptations in the Hadar Hominids." In Delson, ed., *Ancestors.*

SUSMAN, RANDALL L., JACK T. STERN, JR., AND WILLIAM L. JUNGERS, "Locomotor Adaptations in the Hadar Hominids," in Eric Delson, ed., *Ancestors: The Hard Evidence* (New York: Alan R. Liss, 1985), pp. 184–92.

SUSSMAN, ROBERT W. *Primate Ecology and Social Structure.* Needham Heights, MA: Pearson Custom Publishing, 1999.

SUSSMAN, ROBERT W., AND PETER H. RAVEN. "Pollination by Lemurs and Marsupials: An Archaic Coevolutionary System." *Science,* May 19, 1978, 734–35.

SUSSMAN, ROBERT. "Child Transport, Family Size, and the Increase in Human Population Size during the Neolithic." *Current Anthropology,* 13 (April 1972): 258–67.

SUSSMAN, ROBERT. "Primate Origins and the Evolution of Angiosperms." *American Journal of Primatology,* 23 (1991): 209–23.

SUSSMAN, ROBERT W., AND W. G. KINZEY. "The Ecological Role of the Callitrichidae: A Review." *American Journal of Physical Anthropology,* 64 (1984): 419–49.

SWANSON, GUY E. *The Birth of the Gods: The Origin of Primitive Beliefs.* Ann Arbor: University of Michigan Press, 1969.

SWEENEY, JAMES J. "African Negro Culture." In Radin, ed., *African Folktales and Sculpture.*

SWISHER, C. C., III, G. H. CURTIS, T. JACOB, A. G. GETTY, A. SUPRIJO, AND WIDIASMORO. "Age of the Earliest Known Hominids in Java, Indonesia." *Science,* February 25, 1994, 1118–21.

SZALAY, FREDERICK S. "Hunting-Scavenging Protohominids: A Model for Hominid Origins." *Man,* 10 (1975): 420–29.

SZALAY, FREDERICK S. "Paleobiology of the Earliest Primates." In R. Tuttle, ed., *The Functional and Evolutionary Biology of the Primates.* Chicago: University of Chicago Press, 1972, pp. 3–35.

SZALAY, FREDERICK S., AND ERIC DELSON. *Evolutionary History of the Primates.* New York: Academic Press, 1979.

SZALAY, FREDERICK S., I. TATTERSALL, AND R. DECKER. "Phylogenetic Relationships of *Plesiadipis*—Postcranial Evidence." *Contributions to Primatology,* 5 (1975): 136–66.

SZATHMARY, EMÖKE J. E. "Genetics of Aboriginal North Americans." *Evolutionary Anthropology,* 1 (1993): 202–20.

TAINTER, JOSEPH. *The Collapse of Complex Societies.* Cambridge: Cambridge University Press, 1988, pp. 128–52.

TALMON, YONINA. "Mate Selection in Collective Settlements." *American Sociological Review,* 29 (1964): 491–508.

TANNENBAUM, NICOLA. "The Misuse of Chayanov: 'Chayanov's Rule' and Empiricist Bias in Anthropology." *American Anthropologist,* 86 (1984): 927–42.

TATTERSALL, IAN. "Paleoanthropology and Evolutionary Theory." In Peregrine, Ember, and Ember, eds., *Physical Anthropology.*

TATTERSALL, IAN. *The Fossil Trail: How We Know What We Think We Know about Human Evolution.* New York: Oxford University Press, 1995.

TATTERSALL, IAN. *The Human Odyssey.* Englewood Cliffs, NJ: Prentice Hall, 1993.

TATTERSALL, IAN. *The Last Neanderthal.* Boulder, CO: Westview, 1999, pp. 115–16.

TATTERSALL, IAN. *The Primates of Madagascar.* New York: Columbia University Press, 1982.

TATTERSALL, IAN, AND JEFFREY SCHWARTZ. *Extinct Humans.* Boulder, CO: Westview, 2000, p. 93.

TATTERSALL, IAN, ERIC DELSON, AND JOHN VAN COUVERING, EDS. *Encyclopedia of Human Evolution and Prehistory.* New York: Garland, 1988.

TAYLOR, R. E., AND M. J. AITKEN, EDS. *Chronometric Dating in Archaeology.* New York: Plenum, 1997.

TELEKI, GEZA. "The Omnivorous Chimpanzee." *Scientific American*, January 1973, 32–42.

TEMPLETON, ALAN R. "Gene Lineages and Human Evolution." *Science*, May 31, 1996, 1363.

TEMPLETON, ALAN R. "The 'Eve' Hypotheses: A Genetic Critique and Reanalysis." *American Anthropologist*, 95 (1993): 51–72.

TERBORGH, JOHN. *Five New World Primates: A Study in Comparative Ecology*. Princeton, NJ: Princeton University Press, 1983.

TEXTOR, ROBERT B., COMP. *A Cross-Cultural Summary*. New Haven, CT: HRAF Press, 1967.

THOMAS, DAVID H. *Refiguring Anthropology: First Principles of Probability and Statistics*. Prospect Heights, IL: Waveland, 1986.

THOMAS, ELIZABETH MARSHALL. *The Harmless People*. New York: Knopf, 1959.

THOMASON, SARAH GREY, AND TERRENCE KAUFMAN. *Language Contact, Creolization, and Genetic Linguistics*. Berkeley: University of California Press, 1988.

THOMPSON, ELIZABETH BARTLETT. *Africa, Past and Present*. Boston: Houghton Mifflin, 1966.

THOMPSON, GINGER. "Mexico Is Attracting a Better Class of Factory in Its South." *New York Times*, June 29, 2002, p. A3.

THOMPSON, RICHARD H. "Chinatowns: Immigrant Communities in Transition." In M. Ember and Ember, eds., *Portraits of Culture*.

THOMPSON, STITH. "Star Husband Tale." In Dundes, ed., *The Study of Folklore*.

THOMPSON-HANDLER, NANCY, RICHARD K. MALENKY, AND NOEL BADRIAN. "Sexual Behavior of *Pan paniscus* under Natural Conditions in the Lomako Forest, Equateur, Zaire." In Susman, ed., *The Pygmy Chimpanzee*.

THORNE, ALAN G. AND MILFORD H. WOLPOFF. "The Multiregional Evolution of Humans." *Scientific American*, April 1992, 76–83.

THURNWALD, R. C. "Pigs and Currency in Buin: Observations about Primitive Standards of Value and Economics." *Oceania*, 5 (1934): 119–41.

TIERNEY, PATRICK. *Darkness in El Dorado*. New York: Norton, 2000.

TIMPANE, JOHN. "Essay: The Poetry of Science." *Scientific American*, July 1991, 128.

TOBIAS, PHILIP V. "The Craniocerebral Interface in Early Hominids: Cerebral Impressions, Cranial Thickening, Paleoneurobiology, and a New Hypothesis on Encephalization." In Corruccini and Ciochon, eds., *Integrative Paths to the Past*.

TOBIAS, PHILIP. "The Brain of *Homo habilis*: A New Level of Organization in Cerebral Evolution." *Journal of Human Evolution*, 16 (1987): 741–61.

TOBIN, JOSEPH J., DAVID Y. H. WU, AND DANA H. DAVIDSON. *Preschool in Three Cultures: Japan, China, and the United States*. New Haven, CT: Yale University Press, 1989.

TOFT, S., ED. *Domestic Violence in Papua New Guinea*. Monograph No. 3. Port Moresby, Papua New Guinea: Law Reform Commission, 1985.

TOLLEFSON, KENNETH D. "Tlingit: Chiefs Past and Present." In M. Ember and Ember, eds., *Portraits of Culture*.

TOMASELLO, MICHAEL. "Cultural Transmission in the Tool Use and Communicatory Signaling of Chimpanzees." In Parker and Gibson, eds., *"Language" and Intelligence in Monkeys and Apes*.

TORREY, E. FULLER. *The Mind Game: Witchdoctors and Psychiatrists*. New York: Emerson Hall, n.d.

TORRY, WILLIAM I. "Morality and Harm: Hindu Peasant Adjustments to Famines." *Social Science Information*, 25 (1986): 125–60.

TRAVIS, JOHN. "Human Genome Work Reaches Milestone." *Science News*, July 1, 2000, 4–5.

TREIMAN, DONALD J., AND HARRY B. G. GANZEBOOM. "Cross-National Comparative Status-Attainment Research." *Research in Social Stratification and Mobility*, 9 (1990): 117.

TREVOR-ROPER, H. R. "The European Witch-Craze of the Sixteenth and Seventeenth Centuries." In Lessa and Vogt, eds., *Reader in Comparative Religion*, 3rd ed.

TRIANDIS, HARRY C. *Individualism and Collectivism*. Boulder, CO: Westview, 1995.

TRIANDIS, HARRY C., AND ALASTAIR HERON, EDS. *Handbook of Cross-Cultural Psychology*. Vol. 4: Developmental Psychology. Boston: Allyn & Bacon, 1981.

TRIGGER, B. G. *Understanding Early Civilizations: A Comparative Study*. Cambridge: Cambridge University Press, 2003.

TRIGGER, BRUCE G. *A History of Archaeological Thought*. Cambridge: Cambridge University Press, 1989.

TRINGHAM, RUTH, ED. *Ecology and Agricultural Settlements*. R2. Andover, MA: Warner Modular, 1973.

TRINGHAM, RUTH, ED. *Territoriality and Proxemics*. R1. Andover, MA: Warner Modular, 1973.

TRINKAUS, E., ED. *The Emergence of Modern Humans: Biocultural Adaptations in the Later Pleistocene*. Cambridge: Cambridge University Press, 1989.

TRINKAUS, ERIC, *The Shanidar Neandertals*. (New York: Academic, 1983).

TRINKAUS, ERIK. "Bodies, Brawn, Brains and Noses: Human Ancestors and Human Predation." In Nitecki and Nitecki, eds., *The Evolution of Human Hunting*.

TRINKAUS, ERIK. "Pathology and the Posture of the La Chapelle-aux-Saints Neandertal." *American Journal of Physical Anthropology*, 67 (1985): 19–41.

TRINKAUS, ERIK. "The Neandertal Face: Evolutionary and Functional Perspectives on a Recent Hominid Face." *Journal of Human Evolution*, 16 (1987): 429–43.

TRINKAUS, ERIK. "The Neandertals and Modern Human Origins." *Annual Review of Anthropology*, 15 (1986): 193–218.

TRINKAUS, ERIK. "Western Asia." In F. H. Smith and Spencer, eds., *The Origins of Modern Humans*.

TRINKAUS, ERIK, AND PAT SHIPMAN. "Neandertals: Images of Ourselves." *Evolutionary Anthropology*, 1, no. 6 (1993): 194–201.

TRINKAUS, ERIK, AND PAT SHIPMAN. *The Neandertals: Changing the Image of Mankind*. New York: Knopf, 1993.

TRINKAUS, ERIK, AND WILLIAM W. HOWELLS. "The Neanderthals." *Scientific American*, December 1979, 118–33.

TROMPF, G. W., ED. *Cargo Cults and Millenarian Movements: Transoceanic Comparisons of New Religious Movements*. Berlin: Mouton de Gruyter, 1990.

TROTTER, ROBERT T., II, ED. *Anthropology for Tomorrow: Creating Practitioner-Oriented Applied Anthropology Programs*. Washington, DC: American Anthropological Association, 1988.

TROUILLOT, MICHEL-ROLPH. "The Anthropology of the State in the Age of Globalization: Close Encounters of the Deceptive Kind." *Current Anthropology*, 42: 125–138.

TRUDGILL, PETER. *Sociolinguistics: An Introduction to Language and Society*. Rev. ed. New York: Penguin, 1983.

TURNER, B. L. "Population Density in the Classic Maya Lowlands: New Evidence for Old Approaches." *Geographical Review*, 66, no. 1 (January 1970): 72–82.

TURNER, B. L., AND STEVEN B. BRUSH. *Comparative Farming Systems*. New York: Guilford, 1987.

TURNER, CHRISTY G., II. "Teeth and Prehistory in Asia." *Scientific American*, February 1989.

TURNER, CHRISTY G., II. "Telltale Teeth." *Natural History*, January 1987.

TURNER, TERENCE, AND CAROLE NAGENGAST, EDS. "Universal Human Rights versus Cultural Relativity." *Journal of Anthropological Research*, 53, no. 3 (1997): 267–381.

TUTIN, CAROLINE, AND L. WHITE. "The Recent Evolutionary Past of Primate Communities: Likely Environmental Impacts during the Past Three Millennia." In J. G. Fleagle, C. Janson, and K. E.

Reed, eds., *Primate Communities*. Cambridge: Cambridge University Press, 1999, pp. 230–31.

TUTTLE, RUSSELL H. *Apes of the World: Their Social Behavior, Communication, Mentality, and Ecology*. Park Ridge, NJ: Noyes, 1986.

TYLOR, EDWARD B. "Animism." In Lessa and Vogt, eds., *Reader in Comparative Religion*, 4th ed.

U.S. BUREAU OF THE CENSUS. *Statistical Abstract of the United States: 1993*. 113th ed. Washington, DC: U.S. Government Printing Office, 1993.

UBEROI, J. P. SINGH. *The Politics of the Kula Ring: An Analysis of the Findings of Bronislaw Malinowski*. Manchester, England: University of Manchester Press, 1962.

UCKO, PETER J., AND ANDRÉE ROSENFELD. *Paleolithic Cave Art*. New York: McGraw-Hill, 1967.

UCKO, PETER J., AND G. W. DIMBLEBY, EDS. *The Domestication and Exploitation of Plants and Animals*. Chicago: Aldine, 1969.

UCKO, PETER J., RUTH TRINGHAM, AND G. W. DIMBLEBY, EDS. *Man, Settlement, and Urbanism*. Cambridge, MA: Schenkman, 1972.

UDY, STANLEY H., JR. *Work in Traditional and Modern Society*. Englewood Cliffs, NJ: Prentice Hall, 1970.

UNDERHILL, ANNE. "Investigating Craft Specialization during the Longshan Period of China." In Peregrine, Ember, and Ember, eds., *Archaeology*.

UNDERHILL, RALPH. "Economic and Political Antecedents of Monotheism: A Cross-Cultural Study." *American Journal of Sociology*, 80 (1975): 841–61.

UNDERHILL, RUTH M. *Social Organization of the Papago Indians*. New York: Columbia University Press, 1938.

UNITED NATIONS DEVELOPMENT PROGRAMME. *Human Development Report 2001*. New York: Oxford University Press, 2001.

UNNITHAN, N. PRABHA. "Nayars: Tradition and Change in Marriage and Family." In M. Ember and Ember, eds., *Portraits of Culture*.

UPHAM, STEADMAN, ED. *The Evolution of Political Systems: Sociopolitics in Small-Scale Sedentary Societies*. Cambridge: Cambridge University Press, 1990.

URBAN INSTITUTE. "America's Homeless II: Populations and Services." Washington, DC: Urban Institute, February 1, 2000. Published on the Web at http://www.urban.org/housing/homeless/numbers/index.htm.

VALENTE, THOMAS W. *Network Models of the Diffusion of Innovations*. Cresskill, NJ: Hampton Press, 1995.

VALLADAS, H., J. L. JORON, G. VALLADAS, O. BAR-YOSEF, AND B. VANDERMEERSCH. "Thermoluminescence Dating of Mousterian 'Proto-Cro-Magnon' Remains from Israel and the Origin of Modern Man." *Nature*, February 18, 1988, 614–16.

VAN DER MERWE, N. J. "Reconstructing Prehistoric Diet." In Jones, Martin, and Pilbeam, eds., *The Cambridge Encyclopedia of Human Evolution*.

VAN LAWICK-GOODALL, JANE. *In the Shadow of Man*. Boston: Houghton Mifflin, 1971.

VAN SCHAIK, C.P. et al., "Orangutan Cultures and the Evolution of Material Culture." *Science* 299 (3 Jan 2003), pp. 102–105.

VAN WILLIGEN, J. *Applied Anthropology: An Introduction*. Rev. ed. Westport, CT: Bergin & Garvey, 1993.

VAN WILLIGEN, JOHN. *Applied Anthropology: An Introduction*, 3rd ed. Westport, CT: Bergin and Garvey, 2002.

VAN WILLIGEN, JOHN, AND TIMOTHY L. FINAN, EDS. *Soundings: Rapid and Reliable Research Methods for Practicing Anthropologists*. NAPA Bulletin No. 10. Washington, DC: American Anthropological Association, 1990.

VAN WILLIGEN, JOHN, BARBARA RYLKO-BAUER, AND ANN McELROY. *Making Our Research Useful: Case Studies in the Utilization of Anthropological Knowledge*. Boulder, CO: Westview, 1989.

VANNEMAN, REEVE, AND LYNN WEBER CANNON. *The American Perception of Class*. Philadelphia: Temple University Press, 1987.

VAYDA, ANDREW P. "Pomo Trade Feasts." In Dalton, ed., *Tribal and Peasant Economies*.

VAYDA, ANDREW P., AND ROY A. RAPPAPORT. "Ecology: Cultural and Noncultural." In Clifton, ed., *Introduction to Cultural Anthropology*.

VAYDA, ANDREW P., ANTHONY LEEDS, AND DAVID B. SMITH. "The Place of Pigs in Melanesian Subsistence." In Garfield, ed., *Symposium*.

VEKUA, ABESALOM, et al., "A New Skull of Early Homo from Dmanisi, Georgia," *Science* 297 (5 Jul. 2002), pp. 85–89.

VERMEULEN, HANS, AND GOVERS, CORA, EDS. *The Anthropology of Ethnicity*. Amsterdam: Het Spinhuis, 1994.

VIGIL, JAMES DIEGO. "Group Processes and Street Identity: Adolescent Chicano Gang Members." *Ethos*, 16 (1988): 421–45.

VIGIL, JAMES DIEGO. "Mexican Americans: Growing Up on the Streets of Los Angeles." In M. Ember and Ember, eds., *Portraits of Culture*.

VIGILANT, LINDA, MARK STONEKING, HENRY HARPENDING, KRISTEN HAWKES, AND ALLAN C. WILSON. "African Populations and the Evolution of Human Mitochrondrial DNA." *Science*, September 27, 1991, 1503–507.

VINCENT, JOAN. "Political Anthropology: Manipulative Strategies." *Annual Review of Anthropology*, 7 (1978): 175–94.

"Violent Crime." NCJ-147486. Washington, DC: U.S. Department of Justice, April 1994.

VISABERGHI, ELISABETTA, AND DOROTHY MUNKENBECK FRAGASZY. "Do Monkeys Ape?" In Parker and Gibson, eds., *"Language" and Intelligence in Monkeys and Apes*.

VOGEL, GRETCHEN. "Chimps in the Wild Show Stirrings of Culture." *Science*, 284 (1999): 2070–73.

VOGEL, JOSEPH O. "De-Mystifying the Past: Great Zimbabwe, King Solomon's Mines, and Other Tales of Old Africa." In Peregrine, Ember, and Ember, eds., *Archaeology*.

VOGT, EVON Z., AND RICHARD M. LEVANTHAL, EDS. *Prehistoric Settlement Patterns: Essays in Honor of Gordon R. Willey*. Albuquerque: University of New Mexico Press, 1983.

VON FRISCH, KARL. "Dialects in the Language of the Bees." *Scientific American*, August 1962, 78–87.

VRBA, ELIZABETH S. "On the Connection between Paleoclimate and Evolution." In E. S. Vrba, G. H. Denton, T. C. Partridge, and L. H. Burckle, eds., Paleoclimate and Evolution. New Haven, CT: Yale University Press, 1995, pp. 24–45.

WADE, EDWIN L., ED. *The Arts of the North American Indian: Native Traditions in Evolution*. New York: Hudson Hills Press, 1986.

WAGLEY, CHARLES. "Cultural Influences on Population: A Comparison of Two Tupi Tribes." In Lyon, ed., *Native South Americans*.

WALD, MATTHEW L. "Hybrid Cars Show Up in M.I.T.'s Crystal Ball." *New York Times*, November 3, 2000, Fl; and the special advertisement produced by energy companies, "Energy: Investing for a New Century," *New York Times*, October 30, 2000, EN1–EN8.

WALKER, ALAN, AND M. PICKFORD. "New Postcranial Fossils of *Proconsul Africanus* and *Proconsul Nyananzae*." In Ciochon and Corruccini, eds., *New Interpretation of Ape and Human Ancestry*.

WALKER, ALAN, AND PAT SHIPMAN. *The Wisdom of the Bones: In Search of Human Origins*. New York: Knopf, 1996.

WALKER, ALAN, AND R. LEAKEY. "The Evolution of *Australopithecus boisei*," in Grine, ed., *Evolutionary History of the "Robust" Australopithecines*, pp. 247–58.

WALKER, ALAN, AND RICHARD LEAKEY, EDS. *The Nariokotome* Homo erectus *Skeleton*. Cambridge, MA: Harvard University Press, 1993.

WALLACE, ALFRED RUSSELL. "On the Tendency of Varieties to Depart Indefinitely from the Original Type." *Journal of the Proceedings of the Linnaean Society,* August 1858. In Young, ed., *Evolution of Man.*

WALLACE, ANTHONY. "Mental Illness, Biology and Culture." In Hsu, ed., *Psychological Anthropology.*

WALLACE, ANTHONY. *Religion: An Anthropological View.* New York: Random House, 1966.

WALLACE, ANTHONY. *The Death and Rebirth of the Seneca.* New York: Knopf, 1970.

WALLACE, ANTHONY, J. LAWRENCE ANGEL, RICHARD FOX, SALLY MCLENDON, RACHEL SADY, AND ROBERT SHARER, EDS. *Perspectives on Anthropology 1976.* American Anthropological Association Special Publication No. 10. Washington, DC: American Anthropological Association, 1977.

WALLERSTEIN, IMMANUEL. *The Modern World-System.* New York: Academic Press, 1974.

WANNER, ERIC, AND LILA R. GLEITMAN, EDS. *Language Acquisition: The State of the Art.* Cambridge: Cambridge University Press, 1982.

WARD, PETER M. "Introduction and Purpose." In Ward, ed., *Self-Help Housing.*

WARD, PETER M., ED. *Self-Help Housing: A Critique.* London: Mansell, 1982.

WARD, S. "The Taxonomy and Phylogenetic Relationships of Sivapithecus Revisited." In D. R. Begun, C. V. Ward, and M. D. Rose, eds. *Function, Phylogeny and Fossils: Miocene Hominoid Evolution and Adaptation.* New York: Plenum, 1997, pp. 269–90.

WARD, STEVE, B. BROWN, A. HILL, J. KELLEY, AND W. DOWNS. "Equatorius; A New Hominoid Genus from the Middle Miocene of Kenya." *Science,* 285 (1999): 1382–86.

WARDHAUGH, RICHARD. *An Introduction to Sociolinguistics,* 4th ed. Oxford: Blackwell, 2002.

WARDHAUGH, RICHARD. *An Introduction to Sociolinguistics.* 2nd ed. Oxford: Blackwell, 1992.

WARDHAUGH, RICHARD. *An Introduction to Sociolinguistics.* 3rd ed. Oxford: Blackwell, 1997.

WARNER, JOHN ANSON. "The Individual in Native American Art: A Sociological View." In Wade, ed., *The Arts of the North American Indian.*

WARNER, W. LLOYD. *A Black Civilization: A Social Study of an Australian Tribe.* New York: Harper, 1937.

WARREN, DENNIS M. "Utilizing Indigenous Healers in National Health Delivery Systems: The Ghanaian Experiment." In van Willigen, Rylko-Bauer, and McElroy, eds., *Making Our Research Useful.*

WARREN, KAREN, ED. *Ecofeminism: Multidisciplinary Perspectives.* Bloomington: Indiana University Press, 1995.

WARRY, WAYNE. "Doing unto Others: Applied Anthropology, Collaborative Research and Native Self-Determination." *Culture,* 10 (1990): 61–62.

WARRY, WAYNE. "Kafaina: Female Wealth and Power in Chuave, Papua New Guinea." *Oceania,* 57 (1986): 4–21.

WASHBURN, DOROTHY K., ED. *Structure and Cognition in Art.* Cambridge: Cambridge University Press, 1983.

WASHBURN, S. L., ED. *Social Life of Early Man.* Chicago: Aldine, 1964.

WASHBURN, SHERWOOD. "Tools and Human Evolution." *Scientific American,* September 1960, 62–75.

WASHBURN, S. L., AND PHYLLIS C. JAY, EDS. *Perspectives on Human Evolution.* Vol. 1. New York: Holt, Rinehart & Winston, 1968.

WEAVER, MURIEL PORTER. *The Aztecs, Maya, and Their Predecessors.* 3rd ed. San Diego: Academic Press, 1993.

WEBB, KAREN E. "An Evolutionary Aspect of Social Structure and a Verb 'Have.'" *American Anthropologist,* 79 (1977): 42–49.

WEBER, MAX. *The Theory of Social and Economic Organization.* Trans. A. M. Henderson and Talcott Parsons. New York: Oxford University Press, 1947.

Webster's New World Dictionary, Third College Edition (New York: Webster's New World, 1988).

WEINER, ANNETTE B. *Women of Value, Men of Renown: New Perspectives in Trobriand Exchange.* Austin: University of Texas Press, 1976.

WEINER, J. S. "Nose Shape and Climate." *Journal of Physical Anthropology,* 4 (1954): 615–18.

WEINER, JONATHAN. *Beak of the Finch.* New York: Vintage, 1994.

WEINREICH, URIEL. *Languages in Contact.* The Hague: Mouton, 1968.

WEISNER, THOMAS S., AND RONALD GALLIMORE. "My Brother's Keeper: Child and Sibling Caretaking." *Current Anthropology,* 18 (1977): 169–90.

WEISNER, THOMAS S., MARY BAUSANO, AND MADELEINE KORNFEIN. "Putting Family Ideals into Practice: Pronaturalism in Conventional and Nonconventional California Families." *Ethos,* 11 (1983): 278–304.

WEISS, HARVEY AND RAYMOND S. Bradley. "What Drives Societal Collapse?" *Science,* January 26, 2001, pp. 609–610.

WEISS, HARVEY, M. A. COURTY, W. WETTERSTROM, F. GUICHARD, L. SENIOR, R. MEADOW, AND A. CURNOW. "The Genesis and Collapse of Third Millennium North Mesopotamian Civilization." *Science,* 261 (1993): 995–1004.

WELLER, SUSAN C. "The Research Process." In C. R. Ember, Ember, and Peregrine, eds., *Research Frontiers in Anthropology.*

WELLS, S. *The Journey of Man: A Genetic Odyssey.* Princeton, NJ: Princeton University Press.

WENDORF, FRED, AND ANGELA E. CLOSE, EDS. *Advances in World Archaeology.* Vol. 3. Orlando, FL: Academic Press, 1984.

WENKE, ROBERT J. *Patterns in Prehistory: Humankind's First Three Million Years.* 2nd ed. New York: Oxford University Press, 1984.

WENKE, ROBERT. *Patterns in Prehistory: Humankind's First Three Million Years.* 3rd ed. New York: Oxford University Press, 1990.

WERNER, DENNIS. "A Cross-Cultural Perspective on Theory and Research on Male Homosexuality." *Journal of Homosexuality,* 4 (1979): 345–62.

WERNER, DENNIS. "Chiefs and Presidents: A Comparison of Leadership Traits in the United States and among the Mekranoti-Kayapo of Central Brazil." *Ethos,* 10 (1982): 136–48.

WERNER, DENNIS. "Child Care and Influence among the Mekranoti of Central Brazil." *Sex Roles,* 10 (1984): 395–404.

WERNER, DENNIS. "On the Societal Acceptance or Rejection of Male Homosexuality." M.A. thesis, Hunter College of the City University of New York, 1975.

WERNER, DENNIS. "Trekking in the Amazon Forest." *Natural History,* November 1978, 42–54.

WERNER, OSWALD, AND G. MARK SCHOEPFLE. *Systematic Fieldwork.* Vol. 1: Foundations of Ethnography and Interviewing. Newbury Park, CA: Sage, 1987.

WESTERMARCK, EDWARD. *The History of Human Marriage.* London: Macmillan, 1894.

WEYER, E. M. *The Eskimos: Their Environment and Folkways.* New Haven, CT: Yale University Press, 1932.

WHEAT, JOE B. "A Paleo-Indian Bison Kill." *Scientific American,* January 1967, 44–52.

WHEATLEY, PAUL. *The Pivot of the Four Quarters.* Chicago: Aldine, 1971.

WHEELER, PETER. "The Evolution of Bipedality and Loss of Functional Body Hair in Hominids." *Journal of Human Evolution,* 13 (1984): 91–98.

WHEELER, PETER. "The Influence of Bipedalism in the Energy and Water Budgets of Early Hominids." *Journal of Human Evolution,* 23 (1991): 379–88.

WHITAKER, IAN. *Social Relations in a Nomadic Lappish Community.* Oslo: Utgitt av Norsk Folksmuseum, 1955.

WHITE, BENJAMIN. "Demand for Labor and Population Growth in Colonial Java." *Human Ecology,* 1, no. 3 (March 1973): 217–36.

WHITE, DOUGLAS R. "Rethinking Polygyny: Co-Wives, Codes, and Cultural Systems." *Current Anthropology* (1988): 529–88.

WHITE, DOUGLAS R., AND MICHAEL L. BURTON. "Causes of Polygyny: Ecology, Economy, Kinship, and Warfare." *American Anthropologist,* 90 (1988): 871–87.

WHITE, DOUGLAS R., MICHAEL L. BURTON, AND LILYAN A. BRUDNER. "Entailment Theory and Method: A Cross-Cultural Analysis of the Sexual Division of Labor." *Behavior Science Research,* 12 (1977): 1–24.

WHITE, F. J. "*Pan paniscus* 1973 to 1996: Twenty-three Years of Field Research." *Evolutionary Anthropology,* 5 (1996): 11–17.

WHITE, LESLIE A. "A Problem in Kinship Terminology." *American Anthropologist,* 41 (1939): 569–70.

WHITE, LESLIE A. "The Expansion of the Scope of Science." In Morton H. Fried, ed., *Readings in Anthropology.* 2nd ed. Vol. 1. New York: Thomas Y. Crowell, 1968.

WHITE, LESLIE A. *The Science of Culture: A Study of Man and Civilization.* New York: Farrar, Straus & Cudahy, 1949.

WHITE, N. F., ED. *Ethology and Psychiatry.* Toronto: Ontario Mental Health Foundation and University of Toronto Press, 1974.

WHITE, RANDALL. "Rethinking the Middle/Upper Paleolithic Transition." *Current Anthropology,* 23 (1982): 169–75.

WHITE, TIM, "Early Hominids—Diversity or Distortion?", *Science* 299 (28 Mar 2003), pp. 1994–1997.

WHITE, TIM D., DONALD C. JOHANSON, AND WILLIAM H. KIMBEL. "*Australopithecus africanus:* Its Phyletic Position Reconsidered." *South African Journal of Science,* 77 (1981): 445–70.

WHITE, TIMOTHY D., G. SUWA, AND B. ASFAW. "*Australopithecus ramidus,* a New Species of Early Hominid from Aramis, Ethiopia." *Nature,* 371 (1994): 306–33.

WHITE, TIMOTHY D., G. SUWA, AND B. ASFAW. "Corrigendum: *Australopithecus ramidus,* a New Species of Early Hominid from Aramis, Ethiopia." *Nature,* 375 (1995): 88.

WHITEN, A, et al., "Cultures in Chimpanzees," *Nature* 399 (17 June 1999), pp. 682–685.

WHITING, BEATRICE B. "Sex Identity Conflict and Physical Violence." *American Anthropologist,* 67 (1965): 123–40.

WHITING, BEATRICE B. *Paiute Sorcery.* Viking Fund Publications in Anthropology No. 15. New York: Wenner-Gren Foundation, 1950.

WHITING, BEATRICE B., ED. *Six Cultures.* New York: Wiley, 1963.

WHITING, BEATRICE BLYTH. "Culture and Social Behavior: A Model for the Development of Social Behavior." *Ethos,* 8 (1980): 95–116.

WHITING, BEATRICE B., AND CAROLYN POPE EDWARDS (in collaboration with Carol R. Ember, Gerald M. Erchak, Sara Harkness, Robert L. Munroe, Ruth H. Munroe, Sara B. Nerlove, Susan Seymour, Charles M. Super, Thomas S. Weisner, and Martha Wenger). *Children of Different Worlds: The Formation of Social Behavior.* Cambridge, MA: Harvard University Press, 1988.

WHITING, BEATRICE B., AND CAROLYN POPE EDWARDS. "A Cross-Cultural Analysis of Sex Differences in the Behavior of Children Aged Three through Eleven." *Journal of Social Psychology,* 91 (1973): 171–88.

WHITING, BEATRICE B., AND JOHN W.M. WHITING (in collaboration with Richard Longabaugh). *Children of Six Cultures: A Psycho-Cultural Analysis.* Cambridge, MA: Harvard University Press, 1975.

WHITING, JOHN W.M. "Cultural and Sociological Influences on Development." In *Maryland Child Growth and Development Institute: Growth and Development of the Child in His Setting.* Baltimore: Maryland State Department of Health, 1959.

WHITING, JOHN W.M. "Effects of Climate on Certain Cultural Practices." In Goodenough, ed., *Explorations in Cultural Anthropology.*

WHITING, JOHN W.M. *Becoming a Kwoma.* New Haven, CT: Yale University Press, 1941.

WHITING, JOHN W.M., AND IRVIN L. CHILD. *Child Training and Personality: A Cross-Cultural Study.* New Haven, CT: Yale University Press, 1953.

WHITTAKER, JOHN C. *Flintknapping: Making and Understanding Stone Tools.* Austin: University of Texas Press, 1994.

WHYTE, MARTIN K. "Cross-Cultural Codes Dealing with the Relative Status of Women." *Ethnology,* 17 (1978): 211–37.

WHYTE, MARTIN K. *The Status of Women in Preindustrial Societies.* Princeton, NJ: Princeton University Press, 1978.

WIBERG, HAKAN. "Self-Determination as an International Issue." In Lewis, ed., *Nationalism and Self-Determination in the Horn of Africa.*

WIENER, STEVE, Q. XI, P. GOLDBERG, J. LIU, AND O. BAR-YOUSEF. "Evidence for the Use of Fire at Zhoukoudian, China." *Science,* 281 (1998): 251–53.

WILCOX, SHERMAN. "The Invention and Ritualization of Language." In King, ed. The Origins of Language, pp. 351–384.

WILDEN, ANTHONY. *The Rules are No Game: The Strategy of Communication.* London: Routledge and Kegan Paul, 1987.

WILFORD, JOHN NOBLE. "Ancient German Spears Tell of Mighty Hunters of Stone Age." *New York Times,* March 4, 1997, p. C6.

WILFORD, JOHN NOBLE. "The Transforming Leap, from 4 Legs to 2." *New York Times,* September 5, 1995, p. C1ff.

WILKINSON, ROBERT L. "Yellow Fever: Ecology, Epidemiology, and Role in the Collapse of the Classic Lowland Maya Civilization." *Medical Anthropology,* 16 (1995): 269–94.

WILLIAMS, GEORGE C. *Natural Selection: Domains, Levels, and Challenges.* New York: Oxford University Press, 1992.

WILLIAMS, MELVIN D. "Racism: The Production, Reproduction, and Obsolescence of Social Inferiority." In C.R. Ember, Ember, and Peregrine, eds., *Research Frontiers in Anthropology.* Vol. 3.

WILMSEN, EDWIN N., ED. *We Are Here: Politics of Aboriginal Land Tenure.* Berkeley: University of California Press, 1989.

WILSON, ALLAN C., AND REBECCA L. CANN. "The Recent African Genesis of Humans." *Scientific American,* April 1992, 68–73.

WILSON, EDWARD O. *Sociobiology: The New Synthesis.* Cambridge, MA: Belknap Press of Harvard University Press, 1975.

WILSON, MONICA. *Good Company: A Study of Nyakyusa Age Villages.* Boston: Beacon Press, 1963. (Originally published 1951.)

WINKELMAN, MICHAEL JAMES. "Magico-Religious Practitioner Types and Socioeconomic Conditions." *Behavior Science Research,* 20 (1986): 17–46.

WINKELMAN, MICHAEL. "Trance States: A Theoretical Model and Cross-Cultural Analysis." *Ethos,* 14 (1986): 174–203.

WINTERBOTTOM, ROBERT. "The Tropical Forestry Plan: Is It Working?" In Pamela J. Puntenney, ed., *Global Ecosystems: Creating Options through Anthropological Perspectives, NAPA Bulletin 15* (1995).

WINTERHALDER, BRUCE. "Open Field, Common Pot: Harvest Variability and Risk Avoidance in Agricultural and Foraging Societies." In Cashdan, ed., *Risk and Uncertainty in Tribal and Peasant Economies.*

WITKIN, HERMAN A. "A Cognitive Style Approach to Cross-Cultural Research." *International Journal of Psychology,* 2 (1967): 233–50.

WITKOWSKI, STANLEY R. "Polygyny, Age of Marriage, and Female Status." Paper presented at the annual meeting of the American Anthropological Association, San Francisco, 1975.

WITKOWSKI, STANLEY R., AND CECIL H. BROWN. "Lexical Universals." *Annual Review of Anthropology,* 7 (1978): 427–51.

WITKOWSKI, STANLEY R., AND HAROLD W. BURRIS. "Societal Complexity and Lexical Growth." *Behavior Science Research,* 16 (1981): 143–59.

WITTFOGEL, KARL. *Oriental Despotism: A Comparative Study of Total Power.* New Haven, CT: Yale University Press, 1957.

WOLF, ARTHUR. "Adopt a Daughter-in-Law, Marry a Sister: A Chinese Solution to the Problem of the Incest Taboo." *American Anthropologist,* 70 (1968): 864–74.

WOLF, ARTHUR P., AND CHIEH-SHAN HUANG. *Marriage and Adoption in China, 1845–1945.* Stanford, CA: Stanford University Press, 1980.

WOLF, ERIC R. "San José: Subcultures of a 'Traditional' Coffee Municipality." In Steward et al., *The People of Puerto Rico.*

WOLF, ERIC R., ED. *The Valley of Mexico: Studies in Pre-Hispanic Ecology and Society.* Albuquerque: University of New Mexico Press, 1976.

WOLF, ERIC. "Culture: Panacea or Problem." *American Antiquity,* 49 (1984): 393–400.

WOLF, ERIC. "Types of Latin American Peasantry: A Preliminary Discussion." *American Anthropologist,* 57 (1955): 452–71.

WOLF, ERIC. *Peasants.* Englewood Cliffs, NJ: Prentice Hall, 1966.

WOLF, NAOMI. *The Beauty Myth: How Images of Beauty Are Used against Women.* New York: Morrow, 1991.

WOLFF, RONALD G. *Functional Chordate Anatomy.* Lexington, MA: D. C. Heath, 1991.

WOLPOFF, MILFORD H. "Competitive Exclusion among Lower Pleistocene Hominids: The Single Species Hypothesis." *Man,* 6 (1971): 601–13.

WOLPOFF, MILFORD H. "*Ramapithecus* and Human Origins: An Anthropologist's Perspective of Changing Interpretations." In Ciochon and Corruccini, eds., *New Interpretations of Ape and Human Ancestry.*

WOLPOFF, MILFORD. *Paleoanthropology.* 2nd ed. Boston: McGraw-Hill, 1999, pp. 501–504, 727–31.

WOLPOFF, MILFORD H., AND ABEL NIKINI. "Early and Early Middle Pleistocene Hominids from Asia and Africa." In Delson, ed., *Ancestors.*

WOLPOFF, MILFORD, A. G. THORNE, J. JELINEK, AND ZHANG YINYUN. "The Case for Sinking *Homo erectus:* 100 years of *Pithecanthropus* Is Enough!" In J. L. Franzen, ed., *100 Years of Pithecanthropus: The* Homo Erectus *Problem. Courier Forshungsinstitut Senckenberg,* 171 (1993): 341–61.

WOMACK, MARI, AND JUDITH MARTI. *The Other Fifty Percent: Multicultural Perspectives on Gender Relations.* Prospect Heights, IL: Waveland, 1993.

"Women in Science '93: Gender and the Culture of Science." *Science,* April 16, 1993, 383–430.

WONG, KATE, "An Ancestor to Call Our Own," *Scientific American* (Jan 2003), pp. 54–63.

WOOD, BERNARD A. "Evolution of Australopithecines." In Jones, Martin, and Pilbeam, eds., *The Cambridge Encyclopedia of Human Evolution.*

WOOD, BERNARD. "Hominid Paleobiology: Recent Achievements and Challenges." In Corruccini and Ciochon, eds., *Integrative Paths to the Past.*

WOOD, GORDON S. *The Radicalism of the American Revolution.* New York: Knopf, 1992.

WOODBURN, JAMES. "An Introduction to Hadza Ecology." In Lee and DeVore, eds., *Man the Hunter.*

WORLD BANK. *World Development Report 1995. Workers in an Integrating World.* Oxford: Oxford University Press, 1995.

Worldwatch Institute. "State of the World 1994: A Worldwatch Institute Report on Progress toward a Sustainable Society." New York: Norton, 1994.

WORSLEY, PETER. *The Trumpet Shall Sound: A Study of "Cargo" Cults in Melanesia.* London: MacGibbon & Kee, 1957.

WRANGHAM, RICHARD W. "An Ecological Model of Female-Bonded Primate Groups." *Behaviour,* 75 (1980): 262–300.

WRIGHT, GARY A. "Origins of Food Production in Southwestern Asia: A Survey of Ideas." *Current Anthropology,* 12 (1971): 447–78.

WRIGHT, GEORGE O. "Projection and Displacement: A Cross-Cultural Study of Folktale Aggression." *Journal of Abnormal and Social Psychology,* 49 (1954): 523–28.

WRIGHT, HENRY T. "The Evolution of Civilizations." In Meltzer, Fowler, and Sabloff, eds., *American Archaeology Past and Future.*

WRIGHT, HENRY T., AND GREGORY A. JOHNSON. "Population, Exchange, and Early State Formation in Southwestern Iran." *American Anthropologist,* 77 (1975): 267–77.

WULFF, ROBERT and SHIRLEY FISTE. "The Domestication of Wood in Haiti" in Robert Wulff and Shirley Fiste, *Anthropological Praxis,* 1987.

WYNN, THOMAS. "The Intelligence of Later Acheulean Hominids." *Man,* 14 (1979): 371–91.

YAMEI, HOU, R. POTTS, Y. BAOYIN, ET AL. "Mid-Pleistocene Acheulean-like Stone Technology of the Bose Basin, South China." *Science,* 287 (2000): 1622–26.

YERGIN, DANIEL. "Giving Aid to World Trade," *New York Times,* June 27, 2002, p. A29.

YINGER, J. MILTON. "*Ethnicity: Source of Strength? Source of Conflict?*" Albany: State University Press, 1994.

YOUNG, FRANK W. "A Fifth Analysis of the Star Husband Tale." *Ethnology,* 9 (1970): 389–413.

YOUNG, LOUISE B., ED. *Evolution of Man.* New York: Oxford University Press, 1970.

YOUNG, T. CUYLER, JR. "Population Densities and Early Mesopotamian Urbanism." In Ucko, Tringham, and Dimbleby, eds., *Man, Settlement and Urbanism.*

ZECHENTER, ELIZABETH M. "In the Name of Culture: Cultural Relativism and the Abuse of the Individual." *Journal of Anthropological Research,* 53 (1997): 319–47.

ZEDER, MELINDA A. "After the Revolution: Post-Neolithic Subsistence in Northern Mesopotamia." *American Anthropologist,* 96 (1994): 97–126.

ZEDER, MELINDA. *Feeding Cities: Specialized Animal Economy in the Ancient Near East.* Washington, DC: Smithsonian Institution Press, 1991.

ZEDER, MELINDA. *The American Archaeologist: A Profile.* Walnut Creek, CA: AltaMira, 1997.

ZENNER, WALTER P. AND GEORGE GMELCH, "Urbanism and Urbanization," in Carol R. Ember and Melvin Ember, eds., *New Directions in Anthropology* (Upper Saddle River, NJ: Prentice Hall, 2003).

ZIHLMAN, ADRIENNE L. "The Emergence of Human Locomotion: The Evolutionary Background and Environmental Context." In Nishida et al., eds., *Topics in Primatology,* Vol. 1.

ZIHLMAN, ADRIENNE. "Women's Bodies, Women's Lives: An Evolutionary Perspective." In M.E. Morbeck, A. Galloway, and A. Zihlman, eds., *The Evolving Female: A Life-History Perspective.* Princeton, NJ: Princeton University Press, 1997, pp. 185–97.

ZIMMER, CARL. "Kenyan Skeleton Shakes Ape Family Tree." *Science,* 285 (1999): 1335–337.

ZOHARY, DANIEL. "The Progenitors of Wheat and Barley in Relation to Domestication and Agriculture Dispersal in the Old World." In Ucko and Dimbleby, eds., *The Domestication and Exploitation of Plants and Animals.*